THE LETTERS OF
FREDERIC WILLIAM MAITLAND

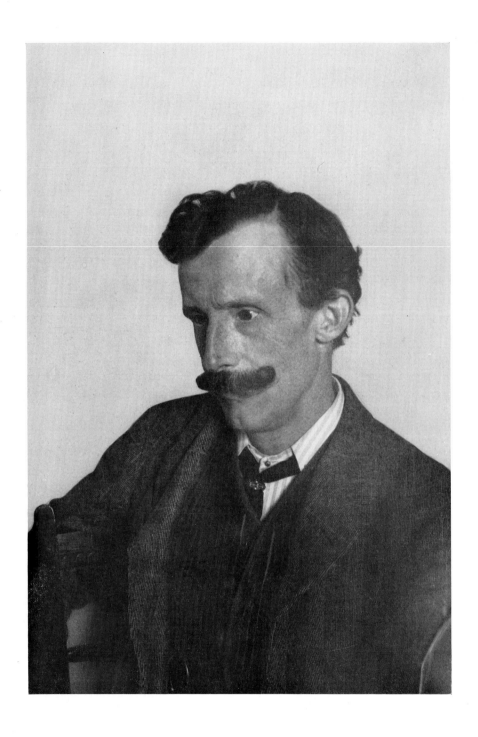

THE LETTERS OF FREDERIC WILLIAM MAITLAND

EDITED BY

C. H. S. FIFOOT, M.A., F.B.A.

HARVARD UNIVERSITY PRESS

PUBLISHED IN ASSOCIATION WITH
THE SELDEN SOCIETY

CAMBRIDGE, MASSACHUSETTS

1965

Published by the Selden Society, 25 Russell Square, London, W.C.1 as Volume I in its Supplementary Series.

Published in the United Kingdom and the British Commonwealth, excluding Canada, by the Syndics of the Cambridge University Press, Bentley House, 200 Euston Road, London, N.W.1.

Published in the United States of America, Canada, and elsewhere throughout the world except as noted above, by Harvard University Press, Cambridge, Massachusetts.

Printed in Great Britain by
Spottiswoode, Ballantyne and Co. Ltd.
London and Colchester

FOREWORD

In this edition I have sought to include all the letters of Maitland which I know to exist, save those which—conspicuously in the Selden Society correspondence—are mere notes of business engagements or agenda. Some letters undoubtedly written by Maitland I have failed to recover. Thus Mrs. Reynell and Professor Buckland quoted in their memoirs isolated sentences from letters which no longer survive and cannot be identified. So, too, all efforts, public and private, have proved unavailing to trace letters written to such Continental scholars as Gierke, Liebermann and Redlich.

In adding three short introductions to different periods of Maitland's life, I have tried to set the stage for the letters and to introduce the chief correspondents without intruding between writer and reader. I have also made notes wherever these seemed necessary or desirable; and if they appear either inadequate or superfluous I must take refuge behind the ample shade of Dr. Johnson. In the Preface to his edition of Shakespeare he wrote, 'It is impossible for an expositor not to write too little for some and too much for others. He can only judge what is necessary by his own experience; and how long soever he may deliberate, will at last explain many lines which the learned will think impossible to be mistaken and omit many for which the ignorant will want his help. These are censures merely relative and must be quietly endured.'

I have many debts of gratitude to pay. First and most warmly I must thank Miss Ermengard Maitland, in whose eager mind, shrewd judgment and trenchant phrase her father lives again; Miss Elizabeth Reynell who ungrudgingly shared her family memories; Mrs. John Bennett who made me free of the letters of her father, H. A. L. Fisher. General Sir Henry Jackson, whose father was, at least in later years, Maitland's most intimate friend, has placed all his letters at my disposal and shown the liveliest interest in the progress of the book.

To individual members of the Council of the Selden Society I owe much. Sir Cecil Carr, who was President when this task was entrusted to me, has supported me with constant encouragement and detailed help; and, while he has enriched my sense of the contemporary scene with personal recollections of Maitland, Professor Hollond has spared no efforts to portray and explain the many Cambridge men and matters with which the letters abound. Professor Helen Cam, Lady Stenton and Professor Bailey have not only suffered but, with infinite patience, have professed to welcome my importunate ignorance and have saved me from egregious error. In the United States Professors Samuel E. Thorne and Mark DeWolfe Howe have found time, amid their heavy preoccupations, to trace letters and impart knowledge. Mr. Derek Hall and Mr. D. E. C. Yale have been kind enough to read the proofs, and for the same office I am indebted to Mr. R. A. Storey, Assistant Registrar, the

National Register of Archives. Nor must I fail to acknowledge my debt to Mr. K. Howard Drake, whose energy and experience have been placed unremittingly at my disposal.

To many others I owe gratitude, the bare recital of whose names is a poor return for their help: Professor Warren O. Ault, Rev. T. N. Benson, M.C., M.A., H. S. Cox, Esq., Professor J. A. Coutts, Professor Seaborne Davies, Professor P. W. Duff, Miss A. G. Foster and the Yorkshire Archaeological Society, Sir Keith Hancock, Mrs. Heigham, Professor E. F. Jacob, Professor F. H. Lawson, Lord McNair, Dr. Clive Parry, Miss P. McPeake and the Alpine Club, B. S. Pell, Esq., H. L. Pink, Esq., M.A., R. L. Rickard, Esq., C. W. Ringrose, Esq., Professor P. G. Stein, W. A. F. P. Steiner, Esq., LL.M., Professor Sheldon Tefft, Ernest Thorp, Esq., M.A.

I have to thank all who have so courteously made letters available for publication: Mrs. John Bennett, Sir Cecil Carr, Q.C., K.C.B., Henry N. Ess, Esq., III, Professor M. DeWolfe Howe, General Sir Henry Jackson, K.C.B., Miss Ermengard Maitland, Judge Paul I. Myers, Professor T. F. T. Plucknett, the late Sir John Pollock, Sir Maurice Powicke, Miss Elizabeth Reynell, Sir Frank Stenton, Professor Samuel E. Thorne, E. M. Wise, Esq.: The Bodleian Library, Oxford, Boston University Archives and Boston University Law Review, Cambridge Historical Journal, Cambridge Law Journal, Cambridge University Library, Girton College, Cambridge, Harvard University, Houghton Library, and Harvard Law School Library, Law Quarterly Review, Public Record Office (whence any unpublished Crown Copyright material has been reproduced by permission of the Controller of H.M. Stationery Office), Trinity College, Cambridge, Trustees of the Smuts Archives, Jagger Library, University of Cape Town, University of London Library, Yale University Library.

Further, I should indeed be churlish if I were not to make two intimate acknowledgments—to my friend Eric Ronald Guest, who allowed me to inflict upon him all my tentative annotations, joined in the pursuit of the obscure and, at once firm and tactful, pruned excess and curbed irrelevance; and to my wife, who read with me every letter from the first transcript to the last proof.

The frontispiece has been reproduced from a small photograph owned by Miss Maitland, and the two facsimiles in the text from letters in the possession respectively of Sir Cecil Carr and the Selden Society. I wish to offer my compliments on the skill with which this work has been done, and indeed to thank the printers comprehensively for the care and understanding with which they have met exigent demands.

C. H. S. FIFOOT

CONTENTS

		PAGE
Foreword		v
Abbreviations		viii
List of Letters		ix
List of Correspondents		xx
1850–1888		1
1889–1898		53
1899–1906		189
Index		391

ILLUSTRATIONS

Frontispiece	*Facing title page*
Facsimile Letters Nos. 360 and 384 . .	*Between pp* 280 *and* 281

ABBREVIATIONS

M.	Frederic William Maitland.
A.A.L.H.	Select Essays in Anglo-American Legal History.
B.N.B.	Maitland, *Bracton's Note Book* (1887).
Bodley	Bodleian Library, Oxford.
C. Hist. J.	Cambridge Historical Journal.
C.L.J.	Cambridge Law Journal.
C.P.	*The Collected Papers of Frederic William Maitland*, 3 vols. (1911).
C.U.L.	Cambridge University Library.
D.B. and Beyond.	Maitland, *Domesday Book and Beyond* (1897).
E.H.R.	English Historical Review.
Fisher, Memoir	*Frederick William Maitland: A Biographical Sketch*, by H. A. L. Fisher (1910).
Gierke	Gierke, *Political Theories of the Middle Age*, translated with an Introduction by F. W. Maitland (1900).
Harv. L. Sch. Lib.	Harvard Law School Library.
Harv. L. Rev.	Harvard Law Review.
Hollond, F.W.M.	*Frederic William Maitland*, by H. A. Hollond (Selden Society Lecture, 1953).
Life of L.S.	Maitland, *Life and Letters of Leslie Stephen* (1906).
L.Q.R.	Law Quarterly Review.
L.U.L.	London University Library.
P. and M.	Pollock and Maitland, *The History of English Law before the time of Edward I*, 1st ed. 1895, 2nd ed. 1898 (references, unless otherwise stated, are to the 2nd ed.).
P.R.O.	Public Record Office.
R.S.	Rolls Series.
S.S.	Selden Society.
Selected Hist. Essays.	Helen M. Cam, *Selected Historical Essays of F. W. Maitland* (1957).

LIST OF LETTERS

No. of Letter	Date [If uncertain, in square brackets]	Place from which written [If different from superscribed address, in square brackets]	Correspondent	Source from which now printed. Original: O. Printed: P. Transcript: T.
	1868			
1	10 May	Eton	Selina Maitland	O: C.U.L.
	1869			
2	30 June	Eton	Selina Maitland	O: C.U.L.
	1877			
3	11 Feb.	Cambridge	Henry Sidgwick	O: C.U.L.
	1880			
4	26 Jan.	London	Henry Sidgwick	O: C.U.L.
5	4 Oct.	London	Henry Sidgwick	O: C.U.L.
6	7 Oct.	London	Henry Sidgwick	O: C.U.L.
	1881			
7	Jan.	?	Frederick Pollock	P: Fisher, *Memoir*
8	**[1882]** ?	London	Henry Sidgwick	O: C.U.L.
	1883			
9	[March]	?	Frederick Pollock	P: Sir John Pollock, *Time's Chariot*
10	[June]	London	Selina Maitland (Mrs. Reynell)	O: C.U.L.
11	21 Aug.	Windisch Matrei	Selina Maitland (Mrs. Reynell)	O: C.U.L.
	1884			
12	28 April	London	Paul Vinogradoff	T: C.U.L.
12A	28 Aug.	London	Paul Vinogradoff	O: Mr. Henry N. Ess, III
	1885			
13	13 March	Cambridge	Alfred Marshall	O: Prof. T. F. T. Plucknett
14	31 Oct.	Cambridge	M. M. Bigelow	P: Boston Univ. Law Rev.
15	?	London	Frederick Pollock	O: Harv. L. Sch. Lib.
	1886			
16	20 April	London	Selina Maitland (Mrs. Reynell)	O: C.U.L.
17	24 April	London	Maxwell Lyte	O: P.R.O.
18	17 July	London	Selina Maitland (Mrs. Reynell)	O: C.U.L.
19	25 July	Lustleigh	Selina Maitland (Mrs. Reynell)	O: C.U.L.
20	3 Oct.	Cambridge	J. B. Thayer	O: Harv. L. Sch. Lib.
21	7 Oct.	Cambridge	M. M. Bigelow	P: Boston Univ. Law Rev.
22	12 Dec.	Cambridge	J. B. Thayer	O: Harv. L. Sch. Lib.
23	20 Dec.	Cambridge	F. J. H. Jenkinson	O: C.U.L.
	1887			
24	27 Feb.	Cambridge	J. B. Thayer	O: Harv. L. Sch. Lib.
25	20 April	Cambridge	J. B. Thayer	O: Harv. L. Sch. Lib.
26	27 April	Cambridge	P. E. Dove	O: S.S.
27	13 May	Cambridge	M. M. Bigelow	P: Boston Univ. Law Rev.
28	12 June	Cambridge	Paul Vinogradoff	T: C.U.L.

ix

List of Letters

No. of Letter	Date [If uncertain, in square brackets]	Place from which written [If different from superscribed address, in square brackets]	Correspondent	Source from which now printed. Original: O. Printed: P. Transcript: T.
	1887			
29	23 June	Cambridge	M. M. Bigelow	P: Boston Univ. Law Rev.
30	26 July	Horrabridge	Frederick Pollock	P: Fisher, *Memoir*
31	29 July	Horrabridge	J. B. Thayer	O: Harv. L. Sch. Lib.
32	11 Aug.	Cambridge	M. M. Bigelow	P: Boston Univ. Law Rev.
33	12 Nov.	Cambridge	Frederick Pollock	P: Fisher, *Memoir*
	1888			
34	1 Jan.	Cambridge	M. M. Bigelow	P: Boston Univ. Law Rev.
35	30 Jan.	Cambridge	J. B. Ames	P: C.L.J.
36	7 April	Cambridge	Frederick Pollock	P: Fisher, *Memoir*
37	3 May	Cambridge	P. E. Dove	O: S.S.
38	5 May	Cambridge	Henry Sidgwick	O: Trin. Coll. Camb.
39	6 May	Cambridge	J. B. Ames	P: C.L.J.
40	9 May	?	Frederick Pollock	P: Fisher, *Memoir*
41	15 May	Cambridge	P. E. Dove	O: S.S.
42	[31 May]	Cambridge	J. B. Thayer	O: Harv. L. Sch. Lib.
43	25 July	St. Ives	Paul Vinogradoff	P: Fisher, *Memoir*
44	31 July	[St. Ives]	M. M. Bigelow	P: Boston Univ. Law Rev.
45	5 Aug.	St. Ives	Frederick Pollock	P: Fisher, *Memoir*
46	6 Aug.	St. Ives	Frederick Pollock	P: Fisher, *Memoir*
47	17 Aug.	St. Ives	J. H. Round	O: L.U.L.
48	15 Sept.	London	J. B. Thayer	O: Harv. L. Sch. Lib.
49	[Sept.]	London	Paul Vinogradoff	T: C.U.L.
50	Sept.	London	Paul Vinogradoff	P: Fisher, *Memoir*
51	14 Oct.	Cambridge	Paul Vinogradoff	P: Fisher, *Memoir*
52	14 Oct.	Cambridge	J. B. Ames	P: C.L.J.
53	11 Dec.	Cambridge	Henry Sidgwick	O: Trin. Coll. Camb.
54	16 Dec.	Cambridge	J. B. Thayer	O: Harv. L. Sch. Lib.
	1889			
55	6 Jan.	Brighton	Maxwell Lyte	T.: P.R.O.
56	20 Jan.	Cambridge	M. M. Bigelow	P.: Boston Univ. Law Rev.
57	20 Jan.	Cambridge	J. B. Thayer	O: Harv. L. Sch. Lib.
58	16 Feb.	Cambridge	J. B. Thayer	O: Harv. L. Sch. Lib.
59	20 Feb.	[Cambridge]	Paul Vinogradoff	P: Fisher, *Memoir*
60	24 Feb.	Cambridge	M. M. Bigelow	P: Boston Univ. Law Rev.
61	9 March	Cambridge	Maxwell Lyte	O: P.R.O.
62	12 March	Cambridge	Paul Vinogradoff	T: C.U.L.
63	21 April	Cambridge	J. B. Thayer	O: Harv. L. Sch. Lib.
64	28 April	Cambridge	O. C. Pell	O: C.U.L.
65	29 April	Cambridge	P. E. Dove	O: S.S.
66	3 May	Cambridge	O. C. Pell	O: C.U.L.
67	3 May	Cambridge	J. B. Ames	P: C.L.J.
68	5 June	Cambridge	M. M. Bigelow	P: Boston Univ. Law Rev.
69	15 June	Cambridge	O. C. Pell	O: C.U.L.
70	27 June	Cambridge	Maxwell Lyte	T: P.R.O.
71	7 Aug.	Malvern	Maxwell Lyte	T: P.R.O.
72	27 Aug.	Cambridge	Paul Vinogradoff	T: C.U.L.
73	1 Oct.	Cambridge	Maxwell Lyte	T: P.R.O.
74	5 Oct.	Cambridge	M. M. Bigelow	P: Boston Univ. Law Rev.
75	27 Oct.	Cambridge	J. C. Gray	O: Harv. L. Sch. Lib.
76	31 Oct.	Cambridge	J. B. Thayer	O: Harv. L. Sch. Lib.

List of Letters

No. of Letter	Date [If uncertain, in square brackets]	Place from which written [If different from superscribed address, in square brackets]	Correspondent	Source from which now printed. Original: O. Printed: P. Transcript: T.
	1889			
77	24 Nov.	Cambridge	Maxwell Lyte	T: P.R.O.
78	24 Nov.	Cambridge	M. M. Bigelow	P: Boston Univ. Law Rev.
	1890			
79	26 Jan.	Cambridge	H. A. L. Fisher	O: Bodley
80	16 Feb.	Cambridge	M. M. Bigelow	P: Boston Univ. Law Rev.
81	11 March	Cambridge	H. A. L. Fisher	O: Bodley
82	[16 March]	Cambridge	J. B. Ames	P: C.L.J.
83	23 March	Cambridge	J. B. Ames	P: C.L.J.
84	13 June	Cambridge	P. E. Dove	O: S.S.
85	21 Sept.	Cambridge	H. A. L. Fisher	O: Bodley
86	21 Sept.	Cambridge	J. B. Thayer	O: Harv. L. Sch. Lib.
87	18 Oct.	Cambridge	Frederick Pollock	O: C.U.L.
88	10 Nov.	Cambridge	F. J. H. Jenkinson	O: C.U.L.
	1891			
89	1 Feb.	Cambridge	M. M. Bigelow	P: Boston Univ. Law Rev.
90	8 Feb.	Cambridge	M. M. Bigelow	P: Boston Univ. Law Rev.
91	17 Feb.	Cambridge	H. A. L. Fisher	O: Bodley
92	3 March	Cambridge	H. A. L. Fisher	O: Bodley
93	19 April	Cambridge	M. M. Bigelow	P: Boston Univ. Law Rev.
94	24 May	Cambridge	P. E. Dove	O: S.S.
95	10 Oct.	Cambridge	Frederick Pollock	O: C.U.L.
96	1 Nov.	Cambridge	Frederick Pollock	O: Harv. L. Sch. Lib.
97	15 Nov.	Cambridge	Paul Vindgradoff	P: Fisher, *Memoir*
98	22 Nov.	Cambridge	Selina Maitland (Mrs. Reynell)	O: C.U.L.
99	29 Nov.	Cambridge	H. A. L. Fisher	O: Bodley
100	29 Nov.	Cambridge	Maxwell Lyte	O: P.R.O.
	1892			
101	28 Feb.	Cambridge	Maxwell Lyte	O: P.R.O.
102	6 March	Cambridge	Maxwell Lyte	O: P.R.O.
103	20 March	Cambridge	Maxwell Lyte	O: P.R.O.
104	24 March	Cambridge	H. A. L. Fisher	O: Bodley
105	4 April	Cambridge	Maxwell Lyte	O: P.R.O.
106	10 April	Cambridge	J. H. Round	O: L.U.L.
107	15 April	Cambridge	Maxwell Lyte	O: P.R.O.
108	7 May	Cambridge	Maxwell Lyte	O: P.R.O.
109	29 May	Cambridge	Paul Vinogradoff	T: C.U.L.
110	5 June	Cambridge	Maxwell Lyte	O: P.R.O.
111	25 July	Horsepools	J. H. Round	O: L.U.L.
112	4 Sept.	Cambridge	Paul Vinogradoff	T: C.U.L.
113	6 Sept.	Horsepools	J. H. Round	O: L.U.L.
	1893			
114	?	Cambridge	Henry Sidgwick	O: Trin. Coll. Camb.
115	14 Jan.	Cambridge	Maxwell Lyte	O: P.R.O.
116	16 Jan.	Cambridge	Charles Gross	O: Harv. L. Sch. Lib.
117	5 March	Cambridge	Maxwell Lyte	O: P.R.O.
118	21 May	Cambridge	Charles Gross	O: Harv. L. Sch. Lib.
119	30 May	Cambridge	Maxwell Lyte	O: P.R.O.
120	11 June	Cambridge	Maxwell Lyte	O: P.R.O.
121	5 July	Horsepools	Charles Gross	O: Harv. L. Sch. Lib.
122	[7 July]	Horsepools	Charles Gross	O: Harv. L. Sch. Lib.
123	7 July	Horsepools	H. A. L. Fisher	O: Bodley

xi

List of Letters

No. of Letter	Date [If uncertain, in square brackets]	Place from which written [If different from superscribed address, in square brackets]	Correspondent	Source from which now printed. Original: O. Printed: P. Transcript: T.
	1893			
124	14 Aug.	Horsepools	Charles Gross	O: Harv. L. Sch. Lib.
125	30 Aug.	Horsepools	Charles Gross	O: Harv. L. Sch. Lib.
126	22 Oct.	Cambridge	R. Lane Poole	P: C. Hist. J.
127	30 Oct.	Cambridge	J. H. Round	O: L.U.L.
128	10 Nov.	Cambridge	Charles Gross	O: Harv. L. Sch. Lib.
129	12 Nov.	Cambridge	J. B. Thayer	O: Harv. L. Sch. Lib.
130	26 Nov.	Cambridge	Charles Gross	O: Harv. L. Sch. Lib.
	1894			
131	8 March	Cambridge	Henry Sidgwick	O: C.U.L.
132	22 April	Cambridge	J. B. Thayer	O: Harv. L. Sch. Lib.
133	17 May	Cambridge	H. A. L. Fisher	O: Bodley
134	8 June	Cambridge	J. H. Round	O: Girton College, Camb.
135	15 June	Cambridge	J. C. Smuts	{ O: Jagger Lib. Univ. of Cape Town
136	6 July	Horsepools	H. A. L. Fisher	O: Bodley
137	15 July	Horsepools	J. H. Round	O: L.U.L.
138	27 July	Horsepools	Leslie Stephen	T: C.U.L.
139	20 Oct.	Cambridge	Charles Gross	O: Harv. L. Sch. Lib.
140	25 Nov.	Cambridge	M. M. Bigelow	P: Boston Univ. Law Rev.
141	25 Nov.	Cambridge	J. B. Thayer	O: Harv. L. Sch. Lib.
142	26 Nov.	Cambridge	H. A. L. Fisher	O: Bodley
143	2 Dec.	Cambridge	J. B. Thayer	O: Harv. L. Sch. Lib.
144	13 Dec.	Horsepools	R. Lane Poole	P: C. Hist. J.
145	13 Dec.	Horsepools	H. A. L. Fisher	O: Bodley
146	16 Dec.	Horsepools	H. A. L. Fisher	O: Bodley
147	[Dec.]	Horsepools	J. H. Round	O: L.U.L.
	1895			
148	1 Feb.	Cambridge	Sidney Lee	O: Bodley
149	3 Feb.	Cambridge	H. A. L. Fisher	O: Bodley
150	3 March	Cambridge	R. Lane Poole	P: C. Hist. J.
151	22 March	Horsepools	B. Fossett Lock	O: S.S.
152	25 March	Horsepools	B. Fossett Lock	O: S.S.
153	30 March	Horsepools	M. M. Bigelow	P: Boston Univ. Law Rev.
154	30 March	Horsepools	J. H. Round	O: L.U.L.
155	16 April	Horsepools	B. Fossett Lock	O: S.S.
156	21 April	Cambridge	Charles Gross	O: Harv. L. Sch. Lib.
157	9 May	Cambridge	Leslie Stephen	T: C.U.L.
158	26 May	Cambridge	B. Fossett Lock	O: S.S.
159	6 June	Cambridge	B. Fossett Lock	O: S.S.
160	7 June	Cambridge	R. Lane Poole	P: C. Hist. J.
161	16 June	Cambridge	B. Fossett Lock	O: S.S.
162	22 June	Horsepools	Charles Gross	O: Harv. L. Sch. Lib.
163	15 July	Horsepools	B. Fossett Lock	O: S.S.
164	15 July	Horsepools	R. Lane Poole	P: C. Hist. J.
165	29 July	Horsepools	J. B. Thayer	O: Harv. L. Sch. Lib.
166	29 July	Horsepools	M. M. Bigelow	P: Boston Univ. Law Rev.
167	6 Aug.	Horsepools	B. Fossett Lock	O: S.S.
168	15 Aug.	Horsepools	R. Lane Poole	P: C. Hist. J.
169	30 Aug.	Horsepools	Charles Gross	O: Harv. L. Sch. Lib.
170	23 Sept.	Horsepools	R. Lane Poole	P: C. Hist. J.
171	[Sept.]	Horsepools	R. Lane Poole	P: C. Hist. J.
172	5 Oct.	Horsepools	B. Fossett Lock	O: S.S.
173	3 Nov.	Cambridge	M. M. Bigelow	P: Boston Univ. Law Rev.

No. of Letter	Date [If uncertain, in square brackets]	Place from which written [If different from superscribed address, in square brackets]	Correspondent	Source from which now printed. Original: O. Printed: P. Transcript: T.
	1896			
174	8 Feb.	Cambridge	B. Fossett Lock	O: S.S.
175	28 Feb.	Cambridge	Henry Sidgwick	O: C.U.L.
176	17 May	Cambridge	H. A. L. Fisher	O: Bodley
177	20 June	Cambridge	R. Lane Poole	P: C. Hist. J.
178	26 July	Horsepools	J. B. Thayer	O: Harv. L. Sch. Lib.
179	7 Sept.	Horsepools	J. H. Round	O: L.U.L.
180	29 Sept.	Horsepools	J. H. Round	O: L.U.L.
181	25 Oct.	Cambridge	B. Fossett Lock	O: S.S.
182	8 Nov.	Cambridge	B. Fossett Lock	O: S.S.
183	6 Dec.	Cambridge	B. Fossett Lock	O: S.S.
184	17 Dec.	Horsepools	J. H. Round	O: L.U.L.
	1897			
185	24 Jan.	Cambridge	B. Fossett Lock	O: S.S.
186	15 Feb.	Cambridge	Maxwell Lyte	O: P.R.O.
187	20 Feb.	Cambridge	Maxwell Lyte	O: P.R.O.
188	21 Feb.	Cambridge	H. A. L. Fisher	O: Bodley
189	23 Feb.	Cambridge	J. H. Round	O: L.U.L.
190	23 Feb.	Cambridge	R. Lane Poole	P: C. Hist. J.
191	23 Feb.	Cambridge	Henry Sidgwick	O: C.U.L.
192	28 Feb.	Cambridge	B. Fossett Lock	O: S.S.
193	14 March	Cambridge	B. Fossett Lock	O: S.S.
194	24 March	Horsepools	Henry Sidgwick	O: C.U.L.
195	17 April	Horsepools	Alfred Marshall	O: T. F. T. Plucknett
196	5 May	Cambridge	B. Fossett Lock	O: S.S.
197	3 June	Cambridge	Henry Sidgwick	O: C.U.L.
198	6 June	Cambridge	M. M. Bigelow	P: Boston Univ. Law Rev.
199	9 July	Horsepools	B. Fossett Lock	O: S.S.
200	20 Oct.	Cambridge	James Tait	P: Powicke, *Modern Historians*
201	3 Dec.	Cambridge	H. A. L. Fisher	O: Bodley
202	[8 Dec.]	Cambridge	Henry Sidgwick	O: C.U.L.
203	27 Dec.	Horsepools	J. H. Round	O: Girton College, Camb.
	1898			
204	3 Jan.	Horsepools	B. Fossett Lock	O: S.S.
205	8 Jan.	Horsepools	B. Fossett Lock	O: S.S.
206	16 Jan.	Cambridge	B. Fossett Lock	O: S.S.
207	19 Jan.	Cambridge	B. Fossett Lock	O: S.S.
208	29 Jan.	Cambridge	B. Fossett Lock	O: S.S.
209	20 Feb.	Cambridge	J. H. Round	O: Girton College, Camb.
210	4 March	Cambridge	J. H. Round	O: L.U.L.
211	22 March	Horsepools	J. H. Round	O: L.U.L.
212	23 April	Cambridge	B. Fossett Lock	O: S.S.
213	6 July	Horsepools	F. J. H. Jenkinson	O: C.U.L.
214	26 July	Horsepools	E. J. Watson	O: Judge Paul I. Myers
215	[Aug.]	Horsepools	Charles Gross	O: Harv. L. Sch. Lib.
216	7 Aug.	Horsepools	Charles Gross	O: Harv. L. Sch. Lib.
217	15 Aug.	Horsepools	F. J. H. Jenkinson	O: C.U.L.
218	17 Aug.	Horsepools	Charles Gross	O: Harv. L. Sch. Lib.
219	19 Aug.	Horsepools	R. Lane Poole	P: C. Hist. J.
220	29 Aug.	Horsepools	R. Lane Poole	P: C. Hist. J.
221	31 Aug.	Horsepools	J. H. Round	O: L.U.L.
222	2 Sept.	Horsepools	Charles Gross	O: Harv. L. Sch. Lib.
223	6 Sept.	Horsepools	F. J. H. Jenkinson	O: C.U.L.
224	7 Sept.	Horsepools	R. Lane Poole	P: C. Hist. J.

No. of Letter	Date [If uncertain, in square brackets]	Place from which written [If different from superscribed address, in square brackets]	Correspondent	Source from which now printed. Original: O. Printed: P. Transcript: T.
	1898			
225	12 Sept.	Horsepools	R. Lane Poole	P: C. Hist. J.
226	4 Oct.	Horsepools	Charles Gross	O: Harv. L. Sch. Lib.
227	7 Oct.	Horsepools	Henry Sidgwick	O: C.U.L.
228	17 Oct.	Horsepools	F. J. H. Jenkinson	O: C.U.L.
229	18 Oct.	Horsepools	Henry Sidgwick	O: C.U.L.
230	31 Oct.	Canaries	Henry Sidgwick	O: C.U.L.
231	5 Nov.	Canaries	Leslie Stephen	P: Fisher, *Memoir*
232	22 Dec.	Canaries	H. A. L. Fisher	O: Bodley
233	29 Dec.	Canaries	J. H. Round	O: L.U.L.
	1899			
234	8 Jan.	Canaries	H. A. L. Fisher	O: Bodley
235	9 Jan.	Canaries	Leslie Stephen	P: Fisher, *Memoir*
236	22 Jan.	Canaries	M. M. Bigelow	P: Boston Univ. Law Rev.
237	23 Jan.	Canaries	Leslie Stephen	P: Fisher, *Memoir*
238	29 Jan.	Canaries	R. Lane Poole	P: C. Hist. J.
239	25 Feb.	Canaries	Henry Sidgwick	O: C.U.L.
240	16 March	Canaries	H. A. L. Fisher	O: Bodley
241	6 April	Cambridge	J. H. Round	O: L.U.L.
242	9 April	Cambridge	J. B. Thayer	O: Harv. L. Sch. Lib
243	7 July	Cambridge	J. H. Round	O: L.U.L.
244	3 Aug.	Shelford	R. Lane Poole	P: C. Hist. J.
245	25 Aug.	Stapleford	Charles Gross	O: Harv. L. Sch. Lib.
246	28 Sept.	Stapleford	B. Fossett Lock	O: S.S.
247	1 Oct.	Stapleford	Charles Gross	O: Harv. L. Sch. Lib.
248	8 Oct.	Stapleford	R. Lane Poole	P: C. Hist. J.
249	10 Oct.	Stapleford	R. Lane Poole	P: C. Hist. J.
250	13 Oct.	Cambridge	Charles Gross	O: Harv. L. Sch. Lib.
251	25 Oct.	Cambridge	Henry Jackson	O: C.U.L.
252	26 Nov.	Canaries	R. Lane Poole	P: C. Hist. J.
253	4 Dec.	Canaries	Frederick Pollock	P: Fisher, *Memoir*
254	4 Dec.	Canaries	Henry Sidgwick	O: C.U.L.
255	12 Dec.	Canaries	F. J. H. Jenkinson	O: C.U.L.
	1900			
256	5 Jan.	Canaries	B. Fossett Lock	O: S.S.
257	5 Jan.	Canaries	Frederick Pollock	T: C.U.L.
258	22 Jan.	Canaries	Leslie Stephen	P: Fisher, *Memoir*
259	22 Jan.	Canaries	Henry Sidgwick	O: C.U.L.
260	5 Feb.	Canaries	Frederick Pollock	T: C.U.L.
261	18 Feb.	Canaries	Henry Jackson	O: C.U.L.
262	11 March	Canaries	B. Fossett Lock	O: S.S.
263	28 April	Cambridge	Henry Jackson	O: C.U.L.
264	6 May	Cambridge	R. Lane Poole	P: C. Hist. J.
265	20 May	Cambridge	R. Lane Poole	P: C. Hist. J.
266	25 June	Brookthorpe	Charles Gross	O: Harv. L. Sch. Lib.
267	1 July	Cambridge	B. Fossett Lock	O: S.S.
268	4 July	Cambridge	B. Fossett Lock	O: S.S.
269	18 July	Cambridge	B. Fossett Lock	O: S.S.
270	25 July	Cambridge	B. Fossett Lock	O: S.S.
271	26 Aug.	Cambridge	R. Lane Poole	P: C. Hist. J.
272	11 Oct.	Cambridge	Mrs. Sidgwick	O: Trin. Coll. Camb.
273	14 Oct.	Cambridge	B. Fossett Lock	O: S.S.
274	17 Oct.	Cambridge	R. Lane Poole	P: C. Hist. J.
275	28 Oct.	Cambridge	B. Fossett Lock	O: S.S.
276	30 Oct.	Cambridge	R. Lane Poole	P: C. Hist. J.
277	12 Nov.	Cambridge	Edwin Ashworth	O: Yale Univ. Lib.

No. of Letter	Date [If uncertain, in square brackets]	Place from which written [If different from superscribed address, in square brackets]	Correspondent	Source from which now printed. Original: O. Printed: P. Transcript: T.
1901				
278	12 Jan.	Canaries	Henry Jackson	O: C.U.L.
279	21 Jan.	Canaries	Frederick Pollock	O: C.U.L.
280	11 Feb.	Canaries	B. Fossett Lock	O: S.S.
281	23 Feb.	Canaries	H. A. L. Fisher	O: Bodley
282	21 April	Cambridge	J. C. Gray	P: Fisher, *Memoir*
283	29 April	Cambridge	R. Lane Poole	P: C. Hist. J.
284	6 May	Cambridge	R. Lane Poole	P: C. Hist. J.
285	19 May	Cambridge	R. Lane Poole	P: C. Hist. J.
286	2 June	Cambridge	R. Lane Poole	P: C. Hist. J.
287	9 June	Cambridge	R. Lane Poole	P: C. Hist. J.
288	16 June	Cambridge	B. Fossett Lock	O: S.S.
289	1 July	Taynton	B. Fossett Lock	O: S.S.
290	30 July	Cambridge	R. Lane Poole	P: C. Hist. J.
291	18 Aug.	Cambridge	M. M. Bigelow	P: Boston Univ. Law Rev.
292	6 Oct.	Cambridge	B. Fossett Lock	O: S.S.
293	20 Oct.	Cambridge	Henry Jackson	O: C.U.L.
294	22 Oct.	Cambridge	Henry Jackson	O: C.U.L.
295	25 Oct.	Cambridge	Henry Jackson	O: C.U.L.
296	10 Nov.	Cambridge	B. Fossett Lock	O: S.S.
297	12 Nov.	Cambridge	B. Fossett Lock	O: S.S.
298	14 Nov.	Cambridge	R. Lane Poole	P: C. Hist. J.
299	18 Nov.	Cambridge	Mr. Justice Holmes	O: Harv. L. Sch. Lib.
300	30 Dec.	Canaries	Henry Jackson	O: C.U.L.
301	[30 Dec.]	Canaries	Leslie Stephen	P: Fisher, *Memoir*
1902				
302	5 Jan.	Canaries	B. Fossett Lock	O: S.S.
303	20 Jan.	Canaries	Leslie Stephen	P: Fisher, *Memoir*
304	1 Feb.	Canaries	Henry Jackson	O: C.U.L.
305	23 Feb.	Canaries	G. B. Adams	O: Yale Univ. Lib.
306	2 March	Canaries	F. J. H. Jenkinson	O: C.U.L.
307	17 March	Canaries	M. M. Bigelow	P: Boston Univ. Law Rev.
308	17 April	Cambridge	B. Fossett Lock	O: S.S.
309	17 April	Cambridge	G. B. Adams	O: Yale Univ. Lib.
310	[19 April]	Cambridge	J. C. Gray	P: Fisher, *Memoir*
311	22 April	Cambridge	R. Lane Poole	P: C. Hist. J.
312	24 April	Cambridge	H. D. Hazeltine	O: Harv. L. Sch. Lib.
313	5 May	Cambridge	Henry Jackson	O: C.U.L.
314	6 May	Cambridge	H. A. L. Fisher	O: Bodley
315	18 May	Cambridge	B. Fossett Lock	O: S.S.
316	25 May	Cambridge	B. Fossett Lock	O: S.S.
317	22 June	Cambridge	R. Lane Poole	P: C. Hist. J.
318	26 June	Cambridge	Henry Jackson	O. C.U.L.
319	26 June	Cambridge	Leslie Stephen	T: C.U.L.
320	27 June	Cambridge	R. Lane Poole	P: C. Hist. J.
321	[early July]	?	R. Lane Poole	P: C. Hist. J.
322	6 July	Cambridge	Henry Jackson	O: C.U.L.
323	13 July	Cambridge	Henry Jackson	O: C.U.L.
324	13 July	Cambridge	B. Fossett Lock	O: S.S.
325	1 Aug.	Cambridge	Henry Jackson	O: C.U.L.
326	3 Aug.	Cambridge	B. Fossett Lock	O: S.S.
327	11 Aug.	Cambridge	B. Fossett Lock	O: S.S.
328	12 Aug.	Cambridge	Mrs. Jenkinson	O: C.U.L.
329	13 Aug.	Cambridge	B. Fossett Lock	O: S.S.
330	15 Aug.	Cambridge	B. Fossett Lock	O: S.S.
331	[Mid-Aug.]	?	Sir W. Markby	O: C.U.L.
332	30 Aug.	Cambridge	R. Lane Poole	P: C. Hist. J.

List of Letters

No. of Letter	Date [If uncertain, in square brackets]	Place from which written [If different from superscribed address, in square brackets]	Correspondent	Source from which now printed. Original: O. Printed: P. Transcript: T.
	1902			
333	15 Sept.	Hove	B. Fossett Lock	O: S.S.
334	24 Sept.	Hove	R. Lane Poole	P: C. Hist. J.
335	27 Sept.	Cambridge	Henry Jackson	O: C.U.L.
336	28 Sept.	Cambridge	R. Lane Poole	P: C. Hist. J.
337	28 Sept.	Cambridge	B. Fossett Lock	O: S.S.
338	30 Sept.	Cambridge	Henry Jackson	O: C.U.L.
339	5 Oct.	Cambridge	B. Fossett Lock	O: S.S.
340	6 Oct.	Cambridge	Henry Jackson	O: C.U.L.
341	14 Oct.	Cambridge	R. Lane Poole	P: C. Hist. J.
342	19 Oct.	Cambridge	R. Lane Poole	P: C. Hist. J.
343	26 Oct.	Cambridge	A. J. Balfour	O: C.U.L.
344	25 Nov.	Cambridge	F. J. H. Jenkinson	O: C.U.L.
345	20 Dec.	Canaries	Henry Jackson	O: C.U.L.
	1903			
346	17 Jan.	Canaries	Frederick Pollock	T: C.U.L.
347	17 Jan.	Canaries	Leslie Stephen	P: Fisher, *Memoir*
348	14 Feb.	Canaries	A. W. Verrall	P: Fisher, *Memoir*
349	14 Feb.	Canaries	W. W. Buckland	O: C.U.L.
350	14 Feb.	Canaries	Henry Jackson	O: C.U.L.
351	1 March	Canaries	C. C. Soule	O: C.U.L.
352	14 March	Canaries	Frederick Pollock	T: C.U.L.
353	5 April	Canaries	Henry Jackson	O: C.U.L.
354	1 May	Cambridge	Leslie Stephen	T: C.U.L.
355	12 June	Cambridge	B. Fossett Lock	O: S.S.
356	14 June	Cambridge	B. Fossett Lock	O: S.S.
357	20 June	Cambridge	R. Lane Poole	P: C. Hist. J.
358	2 July	Cambridge	R. Lane Poole	P: C. Hist. J.
359	7 July	Cambridge	R. Lane Poole	P: C. Hist. J.
360	12 July	Cambridge	B. Fossett Lock	O: S.S.
361	19 July	Cambridge	B. Fossett Lock	O: S.S.
362	9 Aug.	Cambridge	M. M. Bigelow	P: Boston Univ. Law Rev.
363	13 Sept.	Cambridge	B. Fossett Lock	O: S.S.
364	4 Oct.	Cambridge	J. C. Gray	P: Fisher, *Memoir*
365	17 Oct.	Cambridge	H. A. L. Fisher	O: Bodley
366	15 Nov.	Cambridge	J. C. Gray	P: Fisher, *Memoir*
367	16 Nov.	Cambridge	H. A. L. Fisher	O: Bodley
368	6 Dec.	Canaries	Leslie Stephen	P: Fisher, *Memoir*
369	13 Dec.	Canaries	W. W. Buckland	O: C.U.L.
370	13 Dec.	Canaries	Henry Jackson	O: C.U.L.
371	20 Dec.	Canaries	B. Fossett Lock	O: S.S.
	1904			
372	10 Jan.	Canaries	H. A. L. Fisher	O: Bodley
373	10 Jan.	Canaries	Henry Jackson	O: C.U.L.
374	[Jan.]	Canaries	Paul Vinogradoff	P: Fisher, *Memoir*
375	20 Jan.	Canaries	B. Fossett Lock	O: S.S.
376	23 Jan.	Canaries	Charles Sweet	P: L.Q.R.
377	14 Feb.	Canaries	Henry Jackson	O: C.U.L.
378	25 Feb.	Canaries	Henry Jackson	O: C.U.L.
379	5 March	Canaries	Henry Jackson	O: C.U.L.
380	5 March	Canaries	H. A. L. Fisher	O: Bodley
381	18 March	Canaries	H. A. L. Fisher	O: Bodley
382	18 March	Canaries	R. Lane Poole	P: C. Hist. J.
383	28 March	Canaries	Henry Jackson	O: Trin. Coll. Camb.
384	27 April	Cambridge	Henry Jackson	O: Sir Cecil Carr
385	1 May	Cambridge	H. A. L. Fisher	O: Bodley

List of Letters

No. of Letter	Date [If uncertain, in square brackets]	Place from which written [If different from superscribed address, in square brackets]	Correspondent	Source from which now printed. Original: O. Printed: P. Transcript: T.
1904				
386	19 May	Cambridge	R. Lane Poole	P: C. Hist. J.
387	22 May	Cambridge	R. Lane Poole	P: C. Hist. J.
388	22 May	Cambridge	H. A. L. Fisher	O: Bodley
389	14 June	Cambridge	H. A. L. Fisher	O: Bodley
390	26 June	Cambridge	B. Fossett Lock	O: S.S.
391	26 June	Cambridge	Sidney Lee	O: Bodley
392	3 July	Cambridge	Sidney Lee	O: Bodley
393	6 July	Cambridge	Sidney Lee	O: Bodley
394	6 July	Cambridge	R. Lane Poole	P: C. Hist. J.
395	8 July	Cambridge	R. Lane Poole	P: C. Hist. J.
396	11 July	Cambridge	B. Fossett Lock	O: S.S.
397	17 July	Cambridge	B. Fossett Lock	O: S.S.
398	17 July	Cambridge	James Bryce	O: Bodley
399	19 July	Cambridge	James Bryce	O: Bodley
400	7 Aug.	Cambridge	Henry Jackson	O: C.U.L.
401	28 Sept.	Kensington	H. A. L. Fisher	O: Bodley
402	9 Oct.	Cambridge	Henry Jackson	O: C.U.L.
403	27 Oct.	Cambridge	Sidney Lee	O: Bodley
404	30 Oct.	Cambridge	C. E. Norton	O: Harv. Univ. Houghton Lib.
405	30 Oct.	Cambridge	Mr. Justice Holmes	O: Harv. L. Sch. Lib.
406	6 Nov.	Cambridge	Alfred Marshall	O: C.U.L.
407	7 Nov.	Cambridge	Alfred Marshall	O: C.U.L.
408	20 Nov.	Cambridge	H. A. L. Fisher	O: Bodley
409	23 Nov.	Cambridge	B. Fossett Lock	O: S.S.
410	27 Nov.	Cambridge	Mr. Justice Holmes	O: Harv. L. Sch. Lib.
411	18 Dec.	Funchal	W. W. Buckland	O: C.U.L.
412	18 Dec.	Funchal	Henry Jackson	O: C.U.L.
1905				
413	2 Jan.	Funchal	W. W. Buckland	O: C.U.L.
414	9 Jan.	Funchal	Henry Jackson	O: C.U.L.
415	15 Jan.	Funchal	A. W. Verrall	P: Fisher, *Memoir*
416	15 Jan.	Funchal	H. A. L. Fisher	O: Bodley
417	24 Jan.	Funchal	Henry Jackson	O: C.U.L.
418	6 Feb.	Funchal	H. A. L. Fisher	O: Bodley
419	6 Feb.	Funchal	C. E. Norton	O: Harv. Univ. Houghton Lib.
420	13 Feb.	Funchal	W. W. Buckland	O: C.U.L.
421	20 Feb.	Funchal	Henry Jackson	O: C.U.L.
422	25 Feb.	Funchal	W. W. Buckland	O: C.U.L.
423	5 March	Funchal	W. W. Buckland	O: C.U.L.
424	5 March	Funchal	H. A. L. Fisher	O: Bodley
425	12 March	Funchal	C. E. Norton	O: Harv. Univ. Houghton Lib.
426	25 March	Funchal	Henry Jackson	O: C.U.L.
427	26 March	Funchal	W. W. Buckland	O: C.U.L.
428	10 April	Funchal	H. A. L. Fisher	O: C.U.L.
429	30 April	Cambridge	C. E. Norton	O: Harv. Univ. Houghton Lib.
430	30 April	Cambridge	James Bryce	O: Bodley
431	29 May	Cambridge	Henry Jackson	O: C.U.L.
432	6 June	Cambridge	Henry Jackson	O: C.U.L.
433	9 June	Cambridge	A. T. Carter	O: E. M. Wise
434	10 June	Cambridge	Henry Jackson	O: C.U.L.
435	12 June	Cambridge	Henry Jackson	O: C.U.L.
436	22 June	Cambridge	H. D. Hazeltine	O: Harv. L. Sch. Lib.
437	26 June	Cambridge	Henry Jackson	O: C.U.L.

No. of Letter	Date [If uncertain, in square brackets]	Place from which written [If different from superscribed address, in square brackets]	Correspondent	Source from which now printed. Original: O. Printed: P. Transcript: T.
	1905			
438	27 June	Cambridge	Henry Jackson	O: C.U.L.
439	13 July	Cambridge	A. T. Carter	O: E. M. Wise
440	16 July	Cambridge	Henry Jackson	O: C.U.L.
441	23 July	Cambridge	Henry Jackson	O: C.U.L.
442	23 July	Cambridge	R. Lane Poole	P: C. Hist. J.
443	30 July	Cambridge	Mrs. Sidgwick	O: Trin. Coll. Camb.
444	30 July	Cambridge	Henry Jackson	O: C.U.L.
445	[Aug.]	Cambridge	Henry Jackson	O: C.U.L.
446	1 Sept.	Cambridge	Henry Jackson	O: C.U.L.
447	4 Sept.	Cambridge	Henry Jackson	O: C.U.L.
448	26 Sept.	Cambridge	Mrs. Sidgwick	O: Trin. Coll. Camb.
449	22 Oct.	Cambridge	B. Fossett Lock	O: S.S.
450	25 Oct.	Cambridge	Henry Jackson	O: C.U.L.
451	1 Nov.	Cambridge	C. H. Firth	O: Sir Frank Stenton
452	8 Nov.	Cambridge	Henry Jackson	O: C.U.L.
453	9 Nov.	Cambridge	Henry Jackson	O: C.U.L.
454	10 Nov.	Cambridge	R. Lane Poole	P: C. Hist. J.
455	17 Nov.	Cambridge	H. A. L. Fisher	O: Bodley
456	19 Nov.	Cambridge	R. Lane Poole	P: C. Hist. J.
457	30 Nov.	Cambridge	Mr. Justice Holmes	O: Harv. L. Sch. Lib.
458	1 Dec.	Cambridge	Sidney Lee	O: Bodley
459	2 Dec.	Cambridge	Henry Jackson	O: C.U.L.
460	2 Dec.	Cambridge	B. Fossett Lock	O: S.S.
461	5 Dec.	Cambridge	F. J. H. Jenkinson	O: C.U.L.
462	25 Dec.	Canaries	Henry Jackson	O: C.U.L.
	1906			
463	15 Jan.	Canaries	Henry Jackson	O: C.U.L. and Trin. Coll. Camb.
464	[17 Jan.]	Canaries	H. A. L. Fisher	O: Bodley
465	17 Jan.	Canaries	B. Fossett Lock	O: S.S.
466	12 Feb.	Canaries	Henry Jackson	O: C.U.L.
467	18 Feb.	Canaries	J. C. Gray	O: Harv. L. Sch. Lib.
468	25 Feb.	Canaries	Henry Jackson	O: C.U.L.
469	11 March	Canaries	H. A. L. Fisher	O: Bodley
470	26 March	Canaries	Henry Jackson	O: Trin. Coll. Camb.
471	10 April	Canaries	B. Fossett Lock	O: S.S.
472	19 April	Canaries	M. M. Bigelow	P: Boston Univ. Law Rev.
473	1 May	Cambridge	Mrs. Sidgwick	O: Trin Coll. Camb.
474	6 May	Cambridge	Henry Jackson	O: C.U.L.
475	13 May	Cambridge	C. T. Carr	O: Sir Cecil Carr
476	1 June	Cambridge	C. T. Carr	O: Sir Cecil Carr
477	3 June	Cambridge	Selina Maitland (Mrs. Reynell)	O: C.U.L.
478	[30 June]	Cambridge	Henry Jackson	O: C.U.L.
479	15 July	Cambridge	B. Fossett Lock	O: S.S.
480	9 Sept.	Cambridge	H. A. L. Fisher	O: Bodley
481	21 Sept.	Cambridge	Frederick Pollock	O: Prof. S. E. Thorne
482	21 Sept.	Cambridge	H. A. L. Fisher	O: Bodley
483	22 Sept.	Cambridge	H. A. L. Fisher	O: Bodley
484	14 Oct.	Cambridge	J. C. Gray	O: Harv. L. Sch. Lib.
485	14 Oct.	Cambridge	C. E. Norton	O: Harv. Univ. Houghton Lib.
486	14 Oct.	Cambridge	Mr. Justice Holmes	O: Harv. L. Sch. Lib.
487	26 Oct.	Cambridge	R. Lane Poole	P: C. Hist. J.
488	9 Nov.	Cambridge	F. J. H. Jenkinson	O: C.U.L.
489	12 Nov.	Cambridge	H. A. L. Fisher	O: Bodley
490	13 Nov.	Cambridge	B. Fossett Lock	O: S.S.

List of Letters

No. of Letter	Date [If uncertain, in square brackets]	Place from which written [If different from superscribed address, in square brackets]	Correspondent	Source from which now printed. Original: O. Printed: P. Transcript: T.
	1906			
491	16 Nov.	Cambridge	Florence Maitland	O: C.U.L.
492	25 Nov.	Cambridge	W. W. Buckland	O: C.U.L.
493	27 Nov.	Cambridge	James Bryce	O: Bodley
494	27 Nov.	Cambridge	Florence Maitland	O: C.U.L.
495	28 Nov.	Cambridge	W. W. Buckland	O: C.U.L.
496	28 Nov.	Cambridge	Mrs. Sidgwick	O: Trin. Coll. Camb.
497	2 Dec.	Cambridge	Henry Jackson	O: C.U.L.
498	3 Dec.	Cambridge	F. J. H. Jenkinson	O: C.U.L.
499	3 Dec.	Cambridge	Henry Jackson	O: C.U.L.
500	5 Dec.	Cambridge	R. Lane Poole	P: C. Hist. J.

LIST OF CORRESPONDENTS

ADAMS, GEORGE BURTON (1851–1925). Professor of History, Yale University, 1886–1925. Published *Civilisation during the Middle Ages* (1894), *History of England from 1066 to 1216* (1905), *Constitutional History of England* (1920), *Council and Courts in Anglo-Norman England* (posth. 1926).

AMES, JAMES BARR (1846–1910). Bussey Professor of Law, Harvard University, 1879–1903; Dane Professor of Law, Harvard University, 1903–9; Dean of the Harvard Law School, 1895–1909. His collected *Lectures on Legal History* were published in 1913.

ASHWORTH, THOMAS EDWYN (1861–1907), of Todmorden, Yorkshire. Archaeologist and book collector.

BALFOUR, ARTHUR JAMES, later Earl of Balfour (1848–1930). Ed. Eton and Trinity College, Cambridge. Chief Secretary for Ireland, 1887–91; First Lord of the Treasury, 1891–2 and 1895–1902; Prime Minister, 1902–5; First Lord of the Admiralty, 1915–16; Foreign Secretary, 1916–19.

BIGELOW, MELVILLE MADISON (1846–1921). Professor of Law, Boston University, 1873–1921. Published *Law of Estoppel* (1872), *Leading Cases on the Law of Torts* (1875), *Elements of the Law of Torts* (1878), *Placita Anglo-Normannica* (1879), *History of Procedure in England, 1066–1204* (1880), *Law of Fraud on its Civil Side* (1888–90), *Elements of the Law of Bills, Notes and Cheques* (1893), etc.

BRYCE, JAMES, later Viscount Bryce (1838–1922). Regius Professor of Civil Law, Oxford, 1870–93; Chief Secretary for Ireland, 1905–7; Ambassador to the United States, 1907–13. Published *The Holy Roman Empire* (1864), *The American Commonwealth* (1888), *Studies in History and Jurisprudence* (1901), etc.

BUCKLAND, WILLIAM WARWICK (1859–1946). Fellow of Gonville and Caius College, Cambridge, 1889; Regius Professor of Civil Law, Cambridge, 1914–45. Published *The Roman Law of Slavery* (1908), *Elementary Principles of the Roman Private Law* (1912), *A Text Book of Roman Law* (1921), *A Manual of Roman Private Law* (1925), *The Main Institutions of Roman Private Law* (1931), etc.

CARR, SIR CECIL THOMAS (b. 1878), Q.C., K.C.B. Scholar of Trinity College, Cambridge; of the Inner Temple, Barrister-at-law; Counsel to the Speaker, 1943–55; President, Selden Society, 1958–60. Published *The Law of Corporations* (1905), *Select Charters of Trading Companies*, S.S. Vol. 28 (1913), *Delegated Legislation* (1921), *Concerning English Administrative Law* (1941).

CARTER, ALBERT THOMAS (1861–1946), K.C. Student of Christ Church, Oxford; Reader in Constitutional Law and Legal History to the Inns of Court, 1898–1910. Published *History of English Legal Institutions* (1902).

DOVE, P. EDWARD (1854–94). Of Lincoln's Inn, Barrister-at-law; Hon. Secretary and Treasurer, Selden Society, 1887–94. Edited *Domesday Studies*, 2 vols. (1888–91).

FIRTH, SIR CHARLES HARDING (1857–1936). Regius Professor of Modern History, Oxford, 1904–25. Published *Cromwell's Army* (1902), *The Last Years of the Protectorate* (1909), *The House of Lords during the Civil War* (1910).

FISHER, HERBERT ALBERT LAURENS (1865–1940), O.M. Fellow of New College, Oxford, 1888–1912; Vice-Chancellor of Sheffield University, 1912–16; President of the Board of Education, 1916–22; Warden of New College, Oxford, 1925–40. Published *The Medieval Empire* (1898) *Napoleonic Statesmanship, Germany* (1903), *Frederick William Maitland: A Biographical Sketch* (1910), *History of Europe* (1935), etc.

GRAY, JOHN CHIPMAN (1839–1915). Story Professor of Law, Harvard University, 1875; Royall Professor of Law, Harvard University, 1893–1913. Published *Restraints on the Alienation of Property* (1883), *The Rule against Perpetuities* (1886), *Select Cases and other Authorities on the Law of Property*, 6 vols. (1888–92), *The Nature and Sources of the Law* (1909), etc.

GROSS, CHARLES (1857–1909). Professor of History, Harvard University. Published *The Gild Merchant*, 2 vols. (1890), *Select Cases from the Coroners' Rolls*, A.D. *1265–1413*, S.S. Vol. 9 (1896), *A Bibliography of British Municipal History* (1897), *Sources and Literature of English History from the earliest times to about 1485* (1900), *Select Cases concerning the Law Merchant*, A.D. 1270–1638, Vol. 1, S.S. Vol. 23 (1908), etc.

HAZELTINE, HAROLD DEXTER (1871–1960). Studied at Harvard Law School, 1895–8, and in Berlin, Paris and London, 1898–1906; Fellow of Emmanuel College, Cambridge, and Reader in English Law, Cambridge University, 1907–19; Downing Professor of the Laws of England, 1919–42. Published many articles on English legal history, was general editor of *Cambridge Studies in English Legal History* and joint editor of *Maitland: Selected Essays* (1936).

HOLMES, OLIVER WENDELL (1841–1935). Professor of Law, Harvard University, 1882–3; Associate Justice of the Supreme Judicial Court of Massachusetts, 1882–99, and Chief Justice, 1899–1902; Justice of the Supreme Court of the United States, 1902–32. Published *The Common Law* (1881) and *Collected Legal Papers* (1920).

JACKSON, HENRY (1839–1921), O.M. Fellow of Trinity College, Cambridge, 1864–1921, Vice-Master, 1914–19; Regius Professor of Greek, Cambridge, 1906–21. Published an edition of *The Fifth Book of the Nicomachean Ethics* (1899), *Texts to illustrate a course of Elementary Lectures on the history of Greek Philosophy* (1901) and many papers on Greek Philosophy.

JENKINSON, FRANCIS JOHN HENRY (1853–1923). Fellow of Trinity College, Cambridge, 1878, and Lecturer in Classics, 1881. University Librarian, Cambridge, 1889–1923.

List of Correspondents

JENKINSON, MARGARET. Married Francis John Henry Jenkinson, as his second wife, in 1902.

LEE, SIR SIDNEY (1859–1926). Assistant editor, Dictionary of National Biography, 1883–9, Joint editor with Leslie Stephen, 1889–91, Sole editor, 1891–1912. Published *A Life of William Shakespeare* (1898), *Queen Victoria, A Biography* (1902), *Life of Edward VII* (Vol. I, 1905; Vol. II, posth. 1927).

LOCK, BENJAMIN FOSSETT (1847–1922). Ed. Eton and King's College, Cambridge; of Lincoln's Inn, Barrister-at-law; Hon. Secretary, Selden Society, 1895–1913; County Court Judge, 1913–22.

LYTE, SIR HENRY CHURCHILL MAXWELL (1848–1940). Deputy Keeper of the Public Records, 1886–1926. Instituted the series of Calendars of the Chancery Rolls and the series of Lists and Indexes. Published the *Book of Fees* (Part I, 1920; Part II, 1923), and *Historical Notes on the Great Seal* (1926).

MAITLAND, FLORENCE HENRIETTA (1864–1920). The eldest daugher of Herbert Fisher and sister of H. A. L. Fisher, she married Frederic William Maitland in 1886. In 1913 she married Sir Francis Darwin.

MAITLAND, SELINA CAROLINE (1849–1928). The elder sister of Frederic William Maitland, she married Rev. Vincent Reynell in 1883.

MARKBY, SIR WILLIAM (1829–1914). Judge of the High Court of Calcutta, 1866–78; Reader in Indian Law, Oxford, 1878–1900; Fellow of All Souls College, Oxford. Published *Elements of Law* (1871).

MARSHALL, ALFRED (1842–1924). Lecturer in Moral Science, St. John's College, Cambridge, 1868–77; Professor of Political Economy, Bristol, 1877–83; Professor of Political Economy, Cambridge, 1884–1908. Published *Principles of Economics* (1890), *Elements of Economics of Industry* (1892), *Industry and Trade* (1919), *Money, Credit and Commerce* (1923).

NORTON, CHARLES ELIOT (1827–1908). Professor of Fine Arts at Harvard University 1873–97. Published *Church Building in the Middle Ages* (1876), a prose translation of Dante, *Vita Nuova* (1867) and *Divina Commedia* (1891–2), *Carlyle's Letters and Reminiscences* (1887), etc.

PELL, OLIVER CLAUDE (1825–1891), of Wilburton Manor, Ely, Cambridgeshire. Ed. Rugby School and Trinity College, Cambridge. Played cricket for Cambridge and the Gentlemen, and member of All England shooting eight. Barrister-at-law and antiquarian. Contributed to *Domesday Studies*, vol. I (1888), and to the proceedings of the Cambridge Antiquarian Society.

POLLOCK, FREDERICK (1845–1937), succeeded his father as third baronet, 1888. Fellow of Trinity College, Cambridge, 1868; called to the Bar, Lincoln's Inn, 1871; Corpus Professor of Jurisprudence, Oxford, 1883–1903; editor of *Law Quarterly Review*, 1885–1919, and of the Law Reports, 1895–1935. Published *Principles of Contract* (1876), *Spinoza, his life and philosophy* (1880), *The Law of Torts* (1887), *Possession in the Common Law, Parts I and II* (1888), *A First Book of Jurisprudence* (1896), etc.

POOLE, REGINALD LANE (1857–1939). Fellow of Magdalen College, Oxford; Keeper of the University Archives, 1909–27; Assistant editor of the *English Historical Review* on its foundation in 1885 and later editor until 1920. Published *Illustrations of the History of Medieval Thought* (1884), *The Exchequer in the 12th century* (1912), *Lectures on the History of the Papal Chancery* (1915), etc. Edited (with William Hunt) *The Political History of England*, 12 vols. (1905–10).

ROUND, JOHN HORACE (1854–1928). Ed. Balliol College, Oxford, he pursued historical studies without accepting an academic post. He wrote many introductions to the volumes of the Pipe Roll Society and to the Domesday surveys of twelve counties for the Victoria History of the Counties of England. Published *Geoffrey de Mandeville* (1892), *Feudal England* (1895), *The Commune of London* (1899), *Studies in Peerage and Family History* (1901), *Peerage and Pedigree* (1910), etc.

SIDGWICK, HENRY (1838–1900). Fellow of Trinity College, Cambridge, 1859–1900; Knightbridge Professor of Moral Philosophy, Cambridge, 1883–1900. Published *The Methods of Ethics* (1874), *The Principles of Political Economy* (1883), *Outlines of the History of Ethics for English Readers* (1886), *The Elements of Politics* (1891), *Practical Ethics* (1898), etc.

SIDGWICK, ELEANOR MILDRED (1845–1936). The sister of Arthur James Balfour, she married Henry Sidgwick in 1876. Vice-Principal of Newnham College, Cambridge, 1880–92; Principal, 1892–1910.

SMUTS, JAN CHRISTIAN (1870–1950). Christ's College, Cambridge; admitted to the Cape Bar, 1895. A member of General Botha's Cabinet in the Union of South Africa, 1910–19, and of the Imperial War Cabinet, 1917–19; succeeded Botha as Prime Minister of the Union, 1919–24, and again Prime Minister, 1939–48.

SOULE, CHARLES CARROLL (1842–1913). Publisher and President of the Boston Book Co., 1889–1913. Published *Year-Book Bibliography* (1901).

STEPHEN, SIR LESLIE (1832–1904), K.C.B. Fellow of Trinity Hall, Cambridge, 1854–67; took holy orders in 1855 and renounced them in 1875. After leaving Cambridge he devoted himself to literature. He edited the *Cornhill Magazine* from 1871 to 1882 and the *Dictionary of National Biography* from 1882 to 1891. His large literary output included *The Playground of Europe* (1871), *Hours in a Library*, 3 vols. (1874, 1876 and 1879), *History of English Thought in the Eighteenth Century*, 2 vols. (1876), *The Life of Sir James Fitz James Stephen* (1895), *Studies of a Biographer*, 4 vols. (1899, 1902), *The English Utilitarians*, 3 vols. (1900).

SWEET, CHARLES (1849–1919), Barrister-at-law and Conveyancing Counsel to the Court. Published *A Dictionary of English Law* (1882), and edited the third edition of Challis, *Real Property* (1911).

TAIT, JAMES (1863–1944). Assistant Lecturer in History, The Owens College, Manchester, 1887, Lecturer, 1896, Professor, 1902; Professor of History, Manchester University, 1904–19. Published *Mediaeval Manchester and the beginnings of Lancashire* (1904), *The Medieval English Borough* (1936), etc., and edited a number of volumes for the Chetham Society.

THAYER, JAMES BRADLEY (1831–1902). Royall Professor of Law in Harvard University, 1873–93, Weld Professor of Law, 1893–1902. Published *Cases on Evidence* (1892), *Cases on Constitutional Law* (1894–5), *A Preliminary Treatise on Evidence at the Common Law* (1898).

VERRALL, ARTHUR WOOLLGAR (1851–1912). Fellow of Trinity College, Cambridge, 1874–1911; King Edward VII Professor of English Literature, Cambridge, 1911–12. Published *Studies in the Odes of Horace* (1884), *Euripides, the rationalist,* (1895), *Essays on four plays of Euripides* (1905), *The Bacchants of Euripides and other essays* (1910).

VINOGRADOFF, SIR PAUL GAVRILOVITCH (1854–1925). Professor of History at Moscow University, 1884–1901; Corpus Professor of Jurisprudence, Oxford, 1903–25. Published *Villainage in England* (1892), *The Growth of the Manor* (1905), *English Society in the Eleventh Century* (1908), *Outlines of Historical Jurisprudence* (Vol. I, 1920, Vol. II, 1922), etc. Edited eight vols. of *Oxford Studies in Social and Legal History*. Literary Director, Selden Society (with Sir Frederick Pollock), 1907–19.

WATSON, EDWARD JAMES (1865–1934). Solicitor, Bristol, and Fellow of the Royal Historical Society. Published *Pleas of the Crown for the Hundred of Swineshead and the Township of Bristol in A.D. 1221* (1902).

1850–1888

Frederic William Maitland was born on 28 May 1850, the only son of John Gorham Maitland and Emma Daniell. He had two sisters, Selina Caroline, born in 1849, and Emma Katherine, born in 1851. His father had been a Fellow of Trinity College, Cambridge, and had been called to the Bar, but had left it to become a Civil Servant and ultimately Secretary to the Civil Service Commissioners. His paternal grandfather was Samuel Roffey Maitland, at one time Librarian at Lambeth and a historian of originality and power. His maternal grandfather was John Frederic Daniell, a Fellow of the Royal Society and Professor of Chemistry at King's College, London. His mother died in December 1851 and her place was affectionately filled by her sister Charlotte Louisa Daniell. His father died in 1863 and his paternal grandfather in 1866, and through the latter he inherited a small estate in Gloucestershire.

From 1863 to 1869 Maitland was at school at Eton and in 1869 he entered Trinity College, Cambridge. At school, though he was enthralled by music and intrigued by Chaucer, he had little relish for the classics upon which the teaching still essentially depended. In his first year as an undergraduate, while he rowed with sufficient skill and won his 'Blue' as a runner, he made no special mark upon the intellectual life of the University. His individual gifts were not yet plain for all to see nor had he found for himself the fitting means to harness or direct them. But at the beginning of his second year 'the idle whim of an idle undergraduate'[1] led him to the lectures of Henry Sidgwick, Fellow of Trinity College and later Professor of Moral Philosophy. Sidgwick's influence and example aroused and disciplined Maitland's intellectual interests. He abandoned the desultory pursuit of mathematics for philosophy, and in the Moral Science Tripos of 1872 he was bracketed senior with his friend William Cunningham, the future economic historian. His contemporaries no less than his examiners discovered him. A brilliant speaker in the Union Society, he became successively its Secretary and President, and he received the rarer or more precious honour of election to the 'Cambridge Conversazione Society', profanely called the 'Apostles'. This Society, which had been formed some fifty years previously and had numbered Tennyson among its early members, met in Cambridge to hear and discuss essays and tasted from time to time the less austere delights of a dinner at the 'Star and Garter' at Richmond.

'The meetings were held every Saturday at 8.30 in the rooms of the "Moderator", that is to say, the man who was to read the essay. The business began with tea, to which anchovy toast was an indispensable, and perhaps, symbolic adjunct; and then the essay was read, the "brethren" sitting round the fire, the reader usually at the table. Next came the discussion. Everyone

---

[1] Maitland's words, spoken on 26 Nov. 1900 at a meeting to promote a memorial to Sidgwick: *Henry Sidgwick*, 305.

1

who was there stood up in turn before the fire and gave his views on the subject or on the essay or on the arguments used by previous speakers or, indeed, on anything which he was pleased to consider relevant to any one of these.'[1]

In 1875 Maitland tried and failed to obtain a Fellowship at Trinity and left Cambridge for London, where he lived with his sisters and 'Aunt Louisa' until 1880 when the latter died, with both his sisters until 1883 when Selina married, and for one more year with Kate. He had become a student of Lincoln's Inn in 1872 and was called to the Bar in 1876. He was a pupil of Benjamin Bickley Rogers, distinguished both as counsel and as classical scholar; and in 1879 Rogers, whose health was uncertain, asked him to come to his help.

'Maitland', wrote Rogers,[2] 'gave up his own chambers and took a seat in mine, ... superintended the whole of my business, managed my pupils, saw my clients and in case of necessity held my briefs in Court. I doubt if he would have succeeded as a barrister; all the time that I knew him he was the most retiring and diffident man I ever knew; not the least shy or awk-ward—his manners were always easy and self-possessed; but he was the last man to put himself forward in any way. But his opinions, had he sud-denly been made a judge, would have been an honour to the Bench.'

For three years Maitland remained in Rogers' chambers, and for two more years he continued to practise in Lincoln's Inn. Yet, though congenitally in-capable of working without applying his full mind to his task, whatever it might be, and though in later years he put the art or craft of conveyancing to the study of more congenial documents, his heart was not in the work of the Bar. He was a scholar rather than a practitioner—indeed a historian rather than a lawyer, even if he was able happily to reconcile divergent aims in a supreme and unique achievement.

What awoke in him the sense of the past and showed him his vocation it is idle to conjecture—perhaps the chance reading in his club of Stubbs's *Constitutional History*, as apparently casual as his earlier venture into Sidgwick's lecture room.[3] But as early as 1881, while he was still busy in Rogers' cham-bers, he published a paper on *The Laws of Wales*; and a common interest in legal history brought him into closer contact with Frederick Pollock with whom he already had links, not only through Trinity and Lincoln's Inn but also through the Apostles. Moreover in 1880 he had been enrolled in the 'goodly company, fellowship or brotherhood of the Sunday Tramps', formed in the previous year by Leslie Stephen with Pollock as lieutenant, and whose 'rule was to walk on every other Sunday for about eight months in the year.'[4]

---

1 *Henry Sidgwick*, 29–30. See also Pollock, *For my Grandson*, 30–8, and *Walter Leaf, Some Chapters of Autobiography* (1932), 85–91.
2 Fisher, *Memoir*, 16.
3 Maitland's obituary of William Stubbs, C.P. III. 495–511.
4 Maitland, *Life of Leslie Stephen*, 357–62.

Still more significant was his meeting in 1884 with Paul Vinogradoff, whose ubiquitous learning and impetuous mind confirmed or sanctioned the pursuit of legal history.

The way was opened for him by the generosity of Henry Sidgwick who financed a new Readership in English Law at Cambridge. To this he was elected in November 1884, and in the same year he published his *Pleas of the Crown for the County of Gloucester*. The next four years were fruitful. He published in 1887 the three volumes of *Bracton's Note-Book*. He began to correspond with the American scholars who were already exploring the origins of the Common Law: Bigelow, Ames and Thayer. He was the prime begetter of the Selden Society and prepared its first volume; and in August 1888 he was elected Downing Professor of the Laws of England. Academic success was enriched by private happiness. Through the Sunday Tramps he had become the friend of Leslie Stephen, and through Stephen, whose niece she was, he met and married Florence Fisher.

1. To Selina Maitland
[Date from the body of the letter, 10 May, 1868.]

Eton Coll:

4th Sunday after Easter

MY DEAR SELA,

I was so glad to hear that your two hops were so pleasant; they must have been very jolly.

To-morrow morning I shall arise a reformed Etonian—'My! ain't it terrible, what shall we du'[1]—We are going to learn all manner of abominations, have all manner of extra schools and be turned wholesale into radicals. To-day the 10th of May 1868—the fourth Sunday after Easter, the festival of the blessed Antoninus bishop and confessor—is our last day of unreformed bliss. The old masters are furious (bless their dear old conservative souls), the young ones jubilant (like a lot of nasty radicals that they are). I have got my choice of five subjects—French, German, Italian, Logic or Political Economy. The choice lies between German and Johnson[2] on Political Economy.

Bathing is allowed and I got up early this morning and had my first bathe while tutor[3] was in bed: we being allowed to bathe very early on Sundays.

I was tried for an oar in the 'Dreadnaught' but of course I did not get in, which was no disappointment. I have still just the chance of being in the 'Thetis'.[4]

Tell aunt Louisa that I am getting stronger though my voice goes in the evening and has made tutor exclaim several times: it is better though and will I hope return very soon. Oh! tutor's exam hangs over me like a great bugbear. By the bye, why cannot tutor be a radical though he wishes to reform us? Give it up? Because he is only a curly W(h)ig. Eugh! After that I had better go to chapel, don't you think?

So good bye, and, thanking Aunt L. for her letter and sending much love to all of you, I remain your very affect. brother

FRED. W. MAITLAND

2. To Selina Maitland

Eton College

June 30th, 1869

MY DEAR SELA,

I suppose from what you said that Kate is at Gilmorton,[5] if so just send me her direction and I will drop her a line. I have lots of things to tell you of and

[1] Lowell, *The Biglow Papers*, 1st Series, No. III.
[2] William Johnson, afterwards Cory, (1823–92), Eton master and poet. He was Sir Frederick Pollock's tutor: Pollock, *For My Grandson*, 21–3. On the 'reforms' at Eton, see Wortham, *Victorian Eton and Cambridge*, chaps. 3–5.
[3] E. D. Stone.
[4] 'Dreadnought' and 'Thetis' are the two Upper Boats, containing the best oars, in the Fourth of June procession of boats at Eton.
[5] A maternal uncle of the Maitlands was the Rector of Gilmorton in Leicestershire.

scarce know where to begin but will take a plunge into the middle. Last week Browning[1] took me and some other fellows by train to Goring, the station on this side and next to Didcot, and thence we rowed down in a 'gig'—the whole distance was 42 miles, we took from 11.30 a.m. to midnight getting over it, including stoppages for dinner etcetera. I was dreadfully 'beat' after it but it was a right jolly expedition—we passed Pangbourne, with its lovely woods, and Reading which is not particularly picturesque, on to Henley by the Fuller-Maitlands'[2] place (which is about the prettiest spot I ever saw), over the regatta course, past the celebrated Medmenham Abbey, to Marlow, where we dined at the inn famous for the bargees' feast off the 'puppy-pie'[3]— past Cookham, Cliefden and Maidenhead in the moonlight to our couches, right sore as you may guess. I fell asleep in every school the next day but was not sorry that I went as the scenery was perfect—besides Browning, though he does make you do all the rowing, gave us lots to drink —not to mention ducks and peas such as the banks of the Thames alone produce.

Then again on Saturday I had a splendid sight of the review of the Guards, as there were places reserved for us close to the Queen—it was a glorious spectacle—all the lot of the Royal Family were there and the marching of the Coldstreams was perfect. On Sunday I went up to the camp in the evening and there I beheld Her most gracious Majesty Victoria walking about among the tents—she did look a guy! She wore a huge white mushroom hat coming right over her eyes—just fancy it—and on a Sunday too. The Princesses were on the other hand prettily dressed and looked nice.

Who do you suppose is coming to tea with me to-night? Why, the Piggy-wiggy![4] He said that he was coming down to try a boat for a friend, so I proposed that he should grace my board. These last two days were sacred to the Winchester match which we won very easily—would that we could repeat our success next week.

William Rogers was down here and has asked me to attend an Eton dinner at S. Botolphs on the Friday, so I hope that you will come to Lords on the first day or else I shall see but little of you. We can easily arrange a meeting place. I shall write to Aunt Louisa to tell her about my leave.[5]

I have heard nothing from Trinity, so it must be alright and I feel that I can accept your congratulations by this time.[6]

[1] Oscar Browning (1837–1923), Eton master and later Fellow of King's College, Cambridge: see Wortham, *Victorian Eton and Cambridge*, a study of 'O.B.'
[2] Distant cousins of the Maitlands. J. A. Fuller-Maitland (1856–1936) was the musical critic of *The Times*.
[3] The landlady of the inn found that bargees were pillaging her larder. Having drowned a litter of puppies, she baked them in a large pie. The bargees stole it, and, after watching them eat it near Marlow bridge, she took her revenge by telling them the recipe.
[4] Allusion unknown.
[5] 'Leave' to watch the Eton and Harrow match at Lord's. William Rogers (1819–96), a cousin of the Maitlands and himself an Etonian, became Rector of St. Botolph's Bishopsgate, in 1863. He devoted himself to the relief and education of the poor. See his *Reminiscences* (London, 1888) and article in Encycl. Brit.
[6] M. had been sitting an entrance examination at Trinity College, Cambridge.

Love to Kate, if she be at home, to Aunt Louisa and to yourself. I remain your most affectionate brother,

FRED. W. MAITLAND

P.S. The envelopes I took were too small for the paper.

3. To Henry Sidgwick

15 Brookside
Cambridge
11 Feb. 1877

MY DEAR SIDGWICK,[1]

The main authorities as to void statutes are

Calvin's Case, Coke, Reports, Part 7. f. 12b (i.e. in the modern edition vol. 4, p. 21)

Bonham's Case, Coke, Reports, Part 8. f. 118a (vol. 4, p. 375)

City of London v. Wood, 12 Modern Reports, 669.

I have been looking at Coke's mediaeval authorities and I do not think that they bear him out. In one case the judges say that a statute is 'void' because, according to the meaning they put on it, it is simply non-sensical. In another the contest is between statute and dispensing power, and this of course is a different matter. I can not find any distinct claim to hold statutes void as being contrary to a higher law, law of nature or the like. But the judges of Coke's day did not make this claim very plainly. *Calvin's case* was decided with more than usual solemnity and deliberation, and Coke is professedly stating the judgment of a very full court upon a case which was considered of the gravest importance.

Yours very truly
F. W. MAITLAND

4. To Henry Sidgwick

19 Southwell Gardens
S.W.
26th Jan 1880.

MY DEAR SIDGWICK

With regard to a certain MS of mine which you were kind enough to read, I hope that if you have not already destroyed the same you will do so. You were also kind enough to say that you would read certain other chapters of a projected explanation of Property Law, but these I will not send you for I have found it practically impossible to continue the work except by making it a

[1] This letter may reflect Sidgwick's current interest in the 'Elements of Politics' for which he was preparing lectures and 'reading Law books': *Henry Sidgwick*, 322. On the subject-matter of the letter see Prof. S. E. Thorne, Introduction to *A Discourse upon the Statutes* (1942).

prolonged attack on the distinction between real and personal property. I was therefore beginning afresh, but now it is said that the government is going to abolish the law of inheritance, and though I fear that they will not cut deep enough to do all the good that might be done, it becomes necessary to wait and see whether they are in earnest.

I do not regard the time which I have spent in writing as lost for I have come to some definite opinions about law reforms and I am grateful to you for having set me on the inquiry.[1] If we can once abolish all that is distinctive of real property the most important reform will be concerned with the law of marital property and to this I am giving my attention. I do not wish to trespass on your time, but should you be able to spare me a few lines I should be glad to know whether you think the following a reasonable scheme.—

(1) Marriage (apart from any contract made on marriage) has no effect as a transfer of property or debts. The husband keeps his property, the wife hers; the husband is liable on his ante-nuptial debts, the wife on hers.

(2) The wife remains capable of disposing of and acquiring property and needs no protection against the influence of her husband save (perhaps) such as is afforded by the requirement that she shall only be able to convey away landed or other permanent property by a deed the effect of which is explained to her by an official in her husband's absence.

(3) Husband and wife respectively can make contracts; but the one cannot bind the other except when authorized so to do, or represented to third persons as so authorized.

(4) On dissolution of the marriage by death, the two properties must be divided. The husband's consists of what belonged to him at marriage and what he has subsequently acquired:— so the wife's. As to the debts actually outstanding at the dissolution and on which both parties would be liable (the one having contracted both personally and as agent for the other), these, as between the two estates, are to be equally divided,—or (perhaps) the husband's estate should pay two thirds.

(5) Except as regards debts so outstanding at the dissolution of the marriage, no account will ever be taken or contribution enforced between husband and wife unless there has been coercion or deception.

(6) During the marriage husband and wife are capable of making gifts to each other, but not so as to defeat creditors.

It seems to me that this 'separation of goods' is what we shall come to—for all the foreign systems of 'community' with which I have been trying to make myself acquainted, are I think very alien to our law—and the Common Law, the law which operates in default of settlement, should be as simple as possible. Practically the plan above stated is the French system of separation, under which people can marry, but not the common law of France, which establishes a community or quasi partnership. It makes no provision for the children, but

1 Presumably the MS referred to in the first sentence of this letter was part of the 'projected explanation of Property Law'. Under Sidgwick's stimulus M. had published anonymously in the *Westminster Review* in 1879 an attack upon primogeniture and upon the distinction between real and personal property: reprinted, C.P. I. 162.

I do not see how such provision can be made by common law and independently of special contract. At the same time everything should be done to induce those about to marry to make some settlement such as that usually made by well-to-do persons of personalty, giving life interests to husband and wife and preserving the capital for the children. There might be short statutory forms of such settlements.

Pray forgive this long statement and do not answer my question unless it be convenient—but I should greatly value your opinion, for the law of Husband and Wife is in an awful mess (I don't think that a layman would readily believe how bad it is), and I would willingly write something which should be useful.— I have been reading my Bentham.

I hope we may soon see your Political Economy, and then shall we not have some Methods of Metaphysics?[1]

> Believe me
> Yours very truly
> F. W. MAITLAND

5. To Henry Sidgwick

[Written on two post-cards. Postmark London, W., and addressed to H. Sidgwick, Esq., Hill Side, Chesterton Road, Cambridge. Date stamped Oct. 4, 1880. M. is presumably answering three questions from Sidgwick, who was working on *The Principles of Political Economy*, pub. 1883.]

(1) As I understand, private letter carrying is unlawful except within *very* narrow limits. You may send a letter by 'a private friend' ... 'in his way, journey or travel' ... if the letter is to be delivered by him to the person to whom it is addressed. But apparently it is not lawful to *collect* letters from your friends for the purpose of carrying them, even though you do it not for gain but 'for love'; and if you do so you are liable to a fine of £5, and if you make a practice of so doing a fine of £100 for every week during which such practice is continued. [The whole law seems to be in two sections, viz. Stat. 7 Gul. IV and 1 Vic. c. 33, sec. 2; c. 36, sec. 2].

(2) There is no 'legal rate of interest' in the sense of a rate which is the maximum for which you can stipulate. The phrase must I think refer to the rate which must be given by a Court of Justice in the absence of special provision between the parties. The law starts with the rule that debts do not carry interest unless this is expressly provided; but this is overgrown by exceptions. When a debt carries interest and no rate is named, 5% is I believe generally allowed—but when the matter comes before a jury, it is left to the jury to give more or less.

(3) 'No piece of gold, silver, copper or bronze or of any metal or mixed metal, of any value whatever, shall be made or issued, except by the Mint, as

---

[1] Sidgwick's *The Principles of Political Economy* was published in 1883. He did not publish any book on the 'Methods of Metaphysics'. M. possibly hoped for a companion to the *Methods of Ethics* (1874).

a coin or token for money, or as purporting that the holder thereof is entitled to demand any value denoted thereon. Every person who acts in contravention of this section shall be liable on summary conviction to a penalty not exceeding £20' (Stat. 33 Vic. c. 10. s. 5). This is quite distinct from the heavy punishment for making or uttering *counterfeit* coin.

F. W. MAITLAND

6. To Henry Sidgwick

[Written on two post-cards. Postmark London, E.C., and addressed to H. Sidgwick, Esq., Trinity College, Cambridge. Date stamped Oct. 7, 1880.]

I do not think that there is any legal definition of a coin nor do I know that *much* light is thrown on the section[1] by any other authority. At first I was inclined to think that it could not be intended as a prohibition of making anything that could be mistaken for a current coin, because the penalty is so small and of course the making of counterfeit money is a very grave crime. But looking at the history of the Act I think that this section may not be intended as a prohibition of marking with a mark denoting quantity and quality pieces of metal which could not conceivably be taken as current coin. The Act was a consolidation Act passed in 1870, and the section in question apparently comes from an Act of 1812 (52 Geo. iii. c. 107, sec. 1). This old Act, as appears from a recital, was against a certain practice (of which I was not aware) of issuing pieces of metal as 'tokens', which tokens, as I understand, purported to be of a certain value of the current money—a value (it is said) much greater than that of the actual metal. It would, I take it, clearly be illegal to mark a piece of gold as 'one sovereign' or 'equal in value to one sovereign' or 'entitling the bearer to one sovereign from Jones & Co.', but, reading the modern Act in the light of the old Act, I imagine that it would not be illegal to mark a piece of gold (such that it could not be possibly mistaken for current coin) with such words as 'one oz. fine'.

F. W. M.

Please address 2 New Sq. Linc. Inn and answers shall come with less delay. I have no books of the legal sort at Southwell Gardens.[2]

7. To Frederick Pollock

[Post-card. No original: printed Fisher, *Memoir*, 38: no beginning or ending.]

Jan. 1881.

Et Fredericus de Cantebrigia essoniavit se de malo lecti, et essoniator dixit quod habuit languorem. Set quia essonium non jacet in brevi de trampagio consideratum est quod summoneatur et quod sit in misericordia pro falso

---

[1] Stat. 33 Vic. c. 10, s. 5: see Letter 5, *supra*.
[2] M. was living at 19 Southwell Gardens with Aunt Louisa, Selina and Kate.

essonio suo. Postea venit et defendit omnem defaltam et sursisam et dicit quod non debet ad hoc breve respondere quia non tenetur ire in trampagio nisi tantum quando dominus capitalis suus[1] eat in persona sua propria nec vult nec debet ire cum ballivo vel preposito, et ipse et omnes antecessores sui semper a conquestu Anglie usque nunc habuerunt et habent talem libertatem et de hoc ponit se super patriam, etc.

Revera predictus F. seisitus fuit de uno frigore valde damnando. Judicium— Recuperet se ipsum.

8. To Henry Sidgwick

[No date. Sidgwick's letter, here answered, is not extant; but the subject is one in which Sidgwick would have been interested in preparing his *Principles of Political Economy*, pub. 1883. The annual Law Lists give 3 Stone Buildings as M.'s professional address from 1882–4. All that can be suggested is that the letter was written some time in 1882.]

> 3 Stone Buildings
> Lincoln's Inn.

DEAR SIDGWICK,

I am afraid that I cannot give a very precise answer to your question. The regulations concerning railway companies are contained in a large number of statutes with which I am not very familiar. Many of these are certainly only applicable to *companies*, and to companies having statutory powers of purchasing land and the like. But there are others which I think would apply to any railway in case the proprietors of it offered to carry for hire. I am not aware that any question has ever arisen concerning a railway made without statutory powers. It is almost impossible to construct such a railway because, even if the owners of the land agreed to make it, some statutory powers would be required for the obstruction of highways and the like. Most of the Railway Acts are apparently drawn on the assumption that the railways to which they relate are railways made and worked by companies under statutory powers, but some of them by means of an interpretation clause would I think apply to any railway the proprietors of which offered to carry for hire. I think that before such a railway can be opened it must be inspected and approved by the Board of Trade, and with more doubt I think that it might be inspected from time to time, that accidents must be reported and that official inquiries into accidents on it might be held. Apparently the provision for communication between guard and passengers would apply to such a railway, as also the provision as to smoking carriages. On the other hand the regulations as to 'parliamentary trains', as to purchase by Government, and generally as to fares and tolls would not apply—no more would the regulations against 'undue preference'.

In each case the question would turn on the words of the particular Act, but I think in case of doubt, looking at the general scheme of the Acts, a court of law would be inclined to hold that regulations devised for the *safety* of passengers or others apply to all railways, while regulations devised for having

[1] Leslie Stephen, the 'chief lord' of the Sunday Tramps.

cheap, convenient and equitable* traffic are the price paid for monopoly and apply only to railway companies to whom statutory powers have been granted.

Yours truly

F. W. MAITLAND

* I refer to regulations which forbid a company to show 'undue preference' to a particular trader in taking his goods at a lower rate than usual.

9. To Frederick Pollock

[No original: printed by Sir John Pollock, *Time's Chariot* (1950), 59. No date; but presumably in March 1883 and before March 25, when Holmes wrote to congratulate Pollock: *Pollock-Holmes Letters*, I. 19.]

To F. Pollock, Professor of All Laws in all Universes and Universities and reputed Universities.

May it please your Enormity to accept the congratulations of your sincere votary and humble brother over the fact brought to his notice by the *Times* that you have become more vested than ever and having had the animus to profess the law in Oxford have now the Corpus also.[1]

Ave verum Corpus Juris!

F. W. MAITLAND

10. To Selina Maitland (Mrs. Reynell)

[No date; but Selina was married to the Rev. Vincent Charles Reynell Reynell, M.A., at St. Mary Abbots Church, Kensington, on 19 June, 1883, and the letter must have been written almost immediately afterwards.]

19 Southwell Gardens

Sunday.

MY DEAR SELA,

When or whether this letter will be posted I do not know, for it can not be posted until we know whither to send it and you are now enjoying the delight, not unknown to me, of having no address—but Sundays being tolerably rare I will not wait until I know where you are to be found, and all I have to say will keep for an indefinite time. Everybody says that your wedding 'went off very well', so I suppose that this is true, though its not exactly the form of words that I should have chosen—so much depends upon one's point of view—however it is thought by competent judges that all was as it ought to have been. I can assure you that it was not my fault that a young lady secreted an absurd white shoe about her person or covered the sacred person of your uncle with a shower of rice. The household has been slowly recovering itself—and the flowers are fading.

On Thursday I dined at Richmond with the Apostles. We were not a very cheerful party—(interruption caused by Mr. Willcocks who calls to return

[1] The chair to which Pollock had just been elected was that of Corpus Professor of Jurisprudence at Oxford.

thanks)—and—(interruption caused by Dent who calls to inquire generally)—this sentence must go unfinished. To-night I am to dine with the Rabelais Club[1] at the Grosvenor Gallery—they are going to feast Henry Irving. On Monday Kate and I are going to the Richter[2] concert, and since Kate will be away on the next Monday I have engaged your uncle Frederic—you I suppose are making the best of the bagpipe while we listen to 'Am stillen Herd'[3]—well, after all, London has its consolations.

I wonder whether you have visited Loch Awe and shall be curious to follow your route on the map—for the maps, all maps, are now permanently on the drawing-room table. I shall tell you nothing of Kate's movements for I doubt not that she will keep you fully informed—and as to myself I am working at my Liverpool lectures[4] and deep in the difference between larceny and embezzlement—but you may be sure that you often come between me and my book. I won't say that I hope you are happy for of course you are—but farewell.

Your affectionate brother

F. W. MAITLAND

11. To Selina Maitland (Mrs. Reynell)

Windisch Matrei

21 Aug. 1883.

MY VERY DEAR SELA,

I have been on my legs for very many hours and began my day's walk by bright moonlight, but before I go to bed (only a straw shake-down in a hut last night) must thank you for your letter and the note therein enclosed. If you will kindly send a cheque for £10 to 5, Offord Road, Barnsbury, N., saying that you send it on my behalf I shall be grateful to you and will repay you as soon as I reach England. The boy will expect the cheque, for I am writing to him. Whether he is a proper 'object of charity' I have great doubts—but I think that on this occasion I must help him. I am telling him to acknowledge the receipt to you and he knows that you are my sister. If you will send it as soon as may be, this will be all the kinder of you.

And now as to Kate and myself. Everything has gone well. She most pluckily undertook a night journey from Munich and found the Butlers here (it seems that a postcard of hers to you has miscarried) while I met Gurney and Myers

---

[1] 'That most delectable of dining clubs': Saintsbury, *A Last Scrap Book*, 203, where he gives a list of the members, including—beside M.—Frederick Pollock, Thomas Hardy, O. W. Holmes, Henry Irving, Henry James, George Meredith.

[2] Hans Richter, the conductor who acclimatised Wagner in England. His London concerts date from 1876.

[3] From *Die Meistersinger*.

[4] M. gave twelve lectures at the then University College, Liverpool, in the session 1883–4 on 'The Ownership and Possession of Goods'. In the session 1884–5 he gave another twelve lectures on 'The Courts of Law and Equity and their Jurisdiction' and took a class with Snell's *Equity* as text-book.

13. To Alfred Marshall

22 King's Parade

13 March 1885

MY DEAR MARSHALL,

I am very grateful to you for a copy of your inaugural lecture.[1] I have read it with delight and I hope with profit. I still find myself too much your pupil to be your critic. Sometimes I wish that I could give up lecturing about law and once more prepare myself for the Moral Science Tripos at your feet and Sidgwick's.

Yours very truly

F. W. MAITLAND

14. To Melville M. Bigelow

[This and the subsequent letters to Bigelow are in the Boston University Archives and were first printed in Boston Univ. Law Review, Vol. XXXVII, No. 3, Summer 1957, by Professor Warren O. Ault. In the present edition notes by Professor Ault are given in square brackets.]

Trinity College

Cambridge

31 Oct. 1885

MY DEAR SIR,

I have to thank you for a very kind letter.[2] I am what is called a reader of English law in the University of Cambridge and as such it is my duty to attempt to teach the law of torts. You therefore are no stranger to me for your books are constantly in my hands and your name in my mouth. It is therefore very pleasant to me to find you taking an interest in what I am doing for I know that you are intimately acquainted with Bracton's text and will be one of the best judges of my edition of what perhaps is Bracton's own note-book. You will I think get a better idea of that book from the few sheets that I send you than from any description that I can give. The honour of having unearthed it belongs altogether to a Moscow professor, Paul Vinogradoff. Its existence was known to a few antiquarians but it was our Russian visitor who first saw its importance as material for legal history and connected it with Bracton's name. He described his discovery in the Athenaeum for 19 July 1884. The book is large; when in print it will make two thick volumes and I fear that it will not all be printed for a long time yet.[3] I am obliged to reside here during term time and consequently can only carry on my copying by fits and starts; also I am trying to verify the extracts from the plea rolls by collating them with such of the said rolls as are still to be found, and this is a rather long job. You will understand that the mass of the book consists of cases extracted from the

[1] Alfred Marshall had been elected Professor of Political Economy at Cambridge on 13 Dec. 1884.

[2] Not extant.

[3] *Bracton's Note-Book* was published in 3 vols. in 1887. Vinogradoff's letter to the *Athenaeum* is reproduced in the Preface to Vol. 1 at pp. xvii–xxiii.

rolls; they were transcribed by divers clerks who obviously did their work in a mechanical and sometimes stupid fashion. Then there are marginal notes written by another hand and these notes I think may come from Bracton himself. I do not yet know that I shall be able to prove this to be their origin, but at present this seems their probable origin.

The connection between the note book and Bracton's text is of this kind.

(1) The note book has cases from just those rolls which Bracton cites. And Bracton's selection of authorities was not, as we should think, a 'natural selection', that is to say, he did not cite the latest rolls but picked out the decisions of two judges both of whom were already dead.[1] The note book shows the same picking and choosing.

(2) Only a small part of any one roll is transcribed into the note book, but the part so transcribed comprises most (not however all) of the cases that Bracton cites. My labour here is of course increased by the fact that many of his citations have become incorrect owing to the stupidity of copyists and the culpable negligence of an editor.[2]

(3) Some of the marginal notes are very similar to passages in Bracton. Vinogradoff's article will give you some of the more striking coincidences.

(4) The annotator has 'noted up' some decisions. I suppose that you in America 'note up' your text books and reports much as we do here. Some of these noted decisions are, I believe, Bracton's own. But I shall not be able to work up this matter until I have the whole book in print.

And you will understand that I have not yet said in public that the note book was made by Bracton. I am endeavouring to keep an open mind until the whole is legible in type and shall be quite ready to say that Bracton can not have been the annotator, for whoever may have made the collection and adorned it with notes the book is still valuable, a collection of leading cases made in the middle of the thirteenth century by a lawyer or judge, a collection containing many of the authorities cited by our great text writer.

I should like to go on chattering to you over this note book and still better should I like to show it to you in the British Museum—but the 19th century calls; so I must take your leading cases to the law school and explain to the studious youth what[3] only are actionable *per se*.

Believe me
Yours faithfully and gratefully
F. W. MAITLAND

I live in constant fear that some German or Russian or even Turk will edit Bracton and shame the nation which produced certain six volumes of rubbish[4] (innuendo, etc). Sicut scriptum est, 'Vocabo super eos gentem robustam et longinquam et ignotam cujus linguam ignorabunt', etc. See Br. f. 34.

---

1 Martin Pateshall and William Rayleigh.
2 Sir Travers Twiss: see Vinogradoff, *The Text of Bracton*, 1 L.Q.R., 189, reprinted Vinogradoff, C.P. I. 77.
3 Semble 'what torts'. Bigelow's *Leading Cases on the Law of Torts* was first pub. in 1875.
4 The edition by Sir Travers Twiss, 1878–83: see note 2, *supra*.

15. To Frederick Pollock

[No date on letter as written by M., but [1885] added by unknown hand.
This year seems justified by the reference in the letter to *Justice and Police*.]

Common Room
Lincoln's Inn, W.C.

MY DEAR POLLOCK,

I hope that you and your learned friend[1] will forgive my rude silence on the occasion of our meeting this morning, but when suddenly called on to utter French sounds I feel that to fly would be comparatively easy—this I hope was as obvious to him and to you as it was painful to me.

Herewith a copy of Justice and Police.[2] I had at one time a thought of dedicating it to you. This I have not done because I don't like it well enough. I began writing on much too large a scale and at the end had to sacrifice whatever interested me most. This I hope is a wholesome lesson. I am glad to see the third[3] edition of your Contract.

I go back to my workhouse this afternoon.

Yours very truly

F. W. MAITLAND

I feel half sorry that you have brought to light my lord Coke's pretty phrase about the gladsome light of jurisprudence.[4] I have had my eye upon it for some time past and was thinking of it this very morning just before your book came to my hands. I must allow however that you have put it to the best of uses—and one should sometimes be public spirited.

16. To Selina Maitland (Mrs. Reynell)

[No year given, but clearly 1886, when M. became engaged to Florence Henrietta Fisher.]

18 Campden Hill Gardens

20 April.

MY DEAREST SELA,

I must send you a few lines of thanks for your kind letter which added greatly to my happiness. One has, as you yourself must know, strange mixed feelings on occasions such as this, and the good wishes of sisters and friends are pleasant and seem to help one. I am sorry indeed that times and seasons have so fallen out that you will hardly know Florence Fisher as such. Still you will

---

[1] No clue to his identity.

[2] M. published this book in 1885 as one of the series *The English Citizen*.

[3] 'Third' underlined and [4th] put against it by unknown hand. The 4th is the relevant edition.

[4] *Coke upon Littleton*, Epilogus: 'And for a farewell to our jurisprudent, I wish unto him the gladsome light of jurisprudence, the loveliness of temperance, the stabilitie of fortitude and the soliditie of justice'. M. used the 'pretty phrase' in *B.N.B.*, Introduction, at p. 5.

know her when she has changed her name and I make no doubt that you will like her. I shall not attempt a description, for naturally Kate will be more impartial than I can be and will tell you how *she* appears (bother! my grammar has broken down! 'she' ought to mean Kate but it doesn't) to one of her future sisters-in-law. I feel inclined to leave 'in law' out of the term, for I think that you will some day come to regard Florence as a sister, be the law what it may. To tell truth, for a fortnight past I have not thought very much of the law, for Florence and I have been singularly well treated. We have been allowed to go about together without a keeper and I have spent whole days in her company. I am very glad of this—not merely because 'courting' is far from disagreeable, but because we have been learning to know each other very well, and I hope and trust that we are going to be not only good husband and good wife but also good friends, sharing thoughts about all things as well as joys and sorrows. But I must not rhapsodize before you!

We went last night to the last of the Pops.[1] and heard some of the good old tunes that you and I have so often heard together—Schumann's quintet, Brahms' sextet, Hungarian dances, etc. It is a great pleasure to me to find that Florence, though a splendid player,[2] has really not heard very much music—there is much for her to hear for the first time along with me.

In about ten days I must be in Cambridge and shall see you, but I shall have to work like a galley slave. Florence I hope will pay me one visit in the middle of term accompanied by Mrs. Stephen. I hope that you may be well enough to see her—but you must risk nothing—see her in good time you will. And now, my dear, take my best wishes and may you soon be well and strong enough to dance at my wedding if need be.

Your most affectionate brother
F. W. Maitland

17. To Maxwell Lyte

18 Campden Hill
Gardens, W.
24th April 1886

Dear Sir,

Since we met last Wednesday I have thought over some of the points in the scheme for editing the Year Books about which you did me the honour of asking my opinion.

Both the rapidity with which the work can be done and the remuneration of those who do it must in part depend on the decision of certain questions which, as I understand, are still open. What I suppose to be wanted is a

[1] The Monday Popular Concerts had been instituted by Chappell & Co., the music publishers, for the performance of chamber music by the best living instrumentalists: admission one shilling. They were so successful that from 1865 additional concerts were given on Saturdays.
[2] On the violin, viola and piano.

thoroughly good text, based on a comparison of the black-letter books with all available MSS, and an English translation. I take it that the editor will be bound to supply in foot-notes all various readings which in any way affect the sense, but that on the other hand mere differences of spelling and phrasing should go unnoticed. If account is to be taken of all such differences the expense and bulk of the work may be very greatly increased, for when there are many MSS these immaterial variations will probably be very numerous. No annotations will I suppose be required or permitted save such as explain the state of the text, but the cases might be traced into the Abridgments of Brooke and Fitzherbert and, when possible, reference to the record might be supplied. Whether an abstract of the record should be given in order to clear up the meaning of obscure discussions seems a question very worthy of consideration. Probably nothing in the shape of an Introduction would be required beyond a full account of the MSS, their relation to each other and the like. As the completion of the series will take a long time, each volume should have a good index, but a more elaborate index or digest might be made at the end of every reign or of every period of twenty years. To put a glossary in each volume would be to do the same work many times over. Perhaps when the whole edition is finished a glossary should be made, but meanwhile the translation should suffice.

As regards mode of printing:— The use of 'record type'[1] seems undesirable; it deters readers and purchasers and saves but few mistakes. An editor who can not be trusted to expound the stenographic signs can hardly be trusted to copy correctly, for he will not copy correctly what he does not understand. Another plan would be to use roman and italic type so as to distinguish letters actually written from letters represented by dashes and similar marks. This would I believe be costly; certainly it would be laborious, and I do not think it would prevent many blunders or convey much valuable information. Would it not be enough that the editor should be required to note the occurrence of any signs which seemed to him at all dubious or ambiguous?

Supposing that I have rightly foreseen what will be demanded, then it seems to me that at least for some time to come the work must be mainly done by one man. It would indeed be well were there some small committee keeping a careful eye on his proceedings and directing him as to essential matters, but I do not think that a committee can make a text or a translation. Nor do I think that at present it would be advisable to set different men to work on different books. This may some day be done, but not until a definite plan has been generally accepted as quite the best. So very little is now known about the Year Books and their history that the first volumes of a new edition must necessarily be an experiment. The assistance most useful to the editor would in my opinion be that of some one thoroughly competent to correct the proof-sheets with a full understanding of the text, for it is most desirable that the

---

[1] 'In the Record Edition of Domesday Book, volumes I and II (1783) . . . it was attempted by a special record type to reproduce the original abbreviations of the manuscript': Galbraith, *The Making of Domesday Book*, xi. See also Galbraith, *The Public Records*, 77.

sheets should be examined by at least two pairs of eyes. Also some help in the
heavy work of transcribing MS may be needed, for it can not be foreseen that
the old printed books will in all cases provide even raw material for a tolerable
text. Perhaps also in the search for the records of cases some assistance might
be given by the staff of the Public Record Office; the search may sometimes
be a lengthy business.

It is difficult to say how fast an editor with such help as I have just mentioned
would be able to produce his volumes. This must depend of course on the
amount of time that he gives to his task. Were rapidity the only object it would
be well to secure his whole time; but almost certainly it will be more economical,
and I believe that it will be safer also, to obtain but part of the time of some
one who has other work to do and who will not be tempted to press forward
the work at a dangerously rapid pace. It seems to me that when the editor has
settled to his work three volumes a year (each volume of about 600 pages)
might possibly be published and also that a higher rate of speed would be
perilous. The mere correcting of proof-sheets will, if thoroughly done, take a
long time, for the text of this old French must be examined letter by letter.
Again, it should be known that many months may elapse before a line can
be sent to press. The editor may at the outset have to determine the pedigree
of several intricately related MSS and for this purpose to carefully read the
whole or a large part of them. This he may have to do before he begins making
his text. If it be not done, something will be overlooked and the edition will
be third rate. For my own part I can not even guess how much labour of this
preparatory kind will have to be done and I doubt whether there is any one
who would venture a confident opinion, for I believe that the MSS of the Year
Books have long gone utterly unread. I am inclined to think that for some time
to come an average output of two volumes a year is all that should be expected. If the work is to be done once for all, there must be no hurry.

How the editor should be paid is, for the same reasons, another difficult
question. It is hard to foretell what his task will really be. The only suggestion
that I can make is this:— the work will, one may hope, be somewhat lighter
per sheet than that done by the best editors of books in the Rolls series, for
one may hope that the old printed books may save some labour and half of
every volume will consist of a translation, the making of which should not
be very arduous. I think then by way of experiment six guineas per sheet
might be considered sufficient by a competent editor, or even five guineas. A
good deal of expense and time will of course be saved if the owners of the
various MSS can be induced to allow their being deposited in some one
library for the editor's use.

I know not whether it is too late to suggest that the tentative and experimental
character of the first volumes should be explicitly recognized. An editor might
be engaged to publish some one book, e.g. the *Liber Assisarum*[1] which stands
somewhat apart from the regular series of Year Books. It seems to me that so
very much will have to be learned both by the editor and by those who super-

[1] See Winfield, *Chief Sources of Legal History*, 175, and Bolland, C.L.J. II. 192–211.

vise him—so much that can only be learned by experience—that the first steps in this important undertaking should be taken very cautiously and that, whatever plan be formed at the outset, it should be a plan which can be easily modified.

When we met you were good enough to say that conceivably I might be asked to take a part in the work. This I should regard as a very high honour and therefore you may permit me to say what I have to offer. I consider that the readership I hold at Cambridge ought to require of me about half my working time. The other half I would very willingly devote to work on the Year Books; but I could hardly begin the task before next Christmas. For a year and a half I have been transcribing and getting into print a collection of some two thousand cases from a period earlier than the earliest Year Book (it is the collection which has been called 'Bracton's note-book', MS Brit. Add. 12269). I should be sorry to break off this work and hope that by the end of the year the really laborious part of it will be accomplished. Until this is done I would rather not begin any more editing; but this autumn I might learn a great deal about the Year Book MSS. The tenure of my readership obliges me to make Cambridge my home, but some very good MSS are in Cambridge and during the last two years I have found it possible to spend a great deal of time in the British Museum and the Record Office.

Believe me

Yours very sincerely

F. W. MAITLAND

18. To Selina Maitland (Mrs. Reynell)

18, Campden Hill Gardens

17th July 1886

MY OWN VERY DEAR SELA,

I know that your thoughts will be with me on Tuesday and that Florence and I will have your kindest wishes. Would that you could be there! I should like to see your dear old face at the great moment of my life. I dare say that you think that I am rushing into marriage in a rather haphazard way. I don't think it is so but can not quite explain it all; so believe the best—at least believe what is good, for I think it is good. Very likely I shall not be a very gay bridegroom or Florence a very gay bride—but we have thought it over, we love each other and are neither of us very sanguine of getting nothing but happiness. I believe that there is no illusion on her part—I have said all I could to dispel any; I am sure that there is none on mine. So if not gay I am not gloomy but very hopeful of the life before us. I am going to give you a framed photograph of her, it seems to me the best thing I have to give you. It may not come to you for some little time as I shall be away and not able to see to the framing of it. But it makes me happy to think that she and I will be near you and Vincent[1]

---

[1] Selina and Vincent Reynell lived from 1883 to 1887 in Cambridge, where Reynell was headmaster of King's College Choir School.

and that we need not rely on photographs—my own good sister. I too think of the days that we three had together when Aunt Louisa was with us[1]—and I fear that Kate will be lonely now.

Good bye my dearest

F. W. M.

19. To Selina Maitland (Mrs. Reynell)

Lustleigh
S. Devon
25th July 1886

My dearest Sela,

Many thanks for your kind letter. Kate will probably have told you of the wedding ceremony. On the whole we were very well treated; there was very little fuss or delay and the whole proceeding was not so intensely disagreeable as I had imagined it. On Wednesday we came here. I think that you have seen Lustleigh and if so you know that it is very beautiful. Our house here is close to the famous Cleave[2] and is very comfortable and pleasant. It belongs to a Revd. Wilfred Fisher, uncle of Florence. From the front we have a lovely view towards the Teign valley, Dartmoor lies behind us. The weather is the only thing that needs improvement: to-day we have a heavy steady downpour. Do you mean to stay at Cambridge all the summer? Ought not you to have a change for a while? Can you tell me, by the way, whether it is safe to leave the house at Brookside[3] with no one to look after it? At present I have not hired any one. My dear, I am quite certain that Florence will love both her sisters in law. Kate's kindness during the past month has been overwhelming; I hope that she will now get a good holiday.

Your loving brother

F. W. Maitland

20. To James Bradley Thayer

15 Brookside
Cambridge
England.
3 Oct. 1886

Dear Sir,

Dr. Markby of Oxford has drawn my attention to two passages in the Year Book of 9 Henry 6 (f. 11.33) and has asked me to write to you if I have any explanation to give of them. But I am afraid that I have nothing to say. Unfortunately I know but little of the manner in which pleas were recorded at so

---

[1] She had died on 30 April, 1880.
[2] See Cecil Torr, *Small Talk at Wreyland.*
[3] On his marriage M. had taken a house at 15, Brookside, Cambridge, where he lived until his election to the Downing Professorship.

late a time. I have some acquaintance with the looser practices of the thirteenth century and in rolls of that period it is not uncommon to find an assertion followed by another assertion which tends to prove the former: thus, in the case of the Abbot of Fountains which is reported on p. 33, were it a case of Henry the Third's reign I should not be surprised to find a plea 'quod predictus F non fuit Abbas, et hoc bene patet quia'—and then a statement about the double election. This formula 'et hoc bene patet quia' is quite common on these old rolls; but then the rigorous system of pleading to one single issue was yet in its infancy and there is much argumentation on the record. But what would have been the effect temp. Henry VI of getting a piece of evidence on to the record I do not know.[1]

As I know that you take a very deep interest in the history of the common law I venture to send you a few proof sheets, part of a transcript that I am making of a collection of cases preserved in the British Museum. It is possible that you have heard of the MS which Vinogradoff of Moscow declared to be 'Bracton's note book'. I will not yet use this title though I have not much doubt that when my investigations are at an end I shall be entitled to do so. The work is a long one—there are some 2000 cases; but I hope that the result may be interesting and I know that if I find any readers at all at least half of them will live on your side of the Atlantic.

Believe me
Yours very sincerely
F. W. MAITLAND

21. To Melville M. Bigelow

15 Brookside
Cambridge
7th Oct. 1886

DEAR MR. BIGELOW,

I am indeed very much obliged to you for sending me the third edition of your book on Torts,[2] more especially as I hope that in a very short while it will be a text book in our law school. There is still a faint prejudice against American books among those who do not know how closely the courts on your side of the water have kept to "the common law"; but this is fading and I have, I hope, insisted successfully that there is no book for beginners so good as yours.

The Note-Book has been a heavy task. I have now more than three quarters of the text in print; but there is still much to be done, an introduction to be written and indexes made. There will be three stout volumes and I fear that the look of them will frighten readers. I send you two stray sheets which may interest you. May I particularly draw your notice to Case 1290? I can not rely

---

[1] See Thayer, *Preliminary Treatise on Evidence at the Common Law*, 114–20.
[2] [AULT. Pub. Boston, 1886].

on this before a tribunal of general readers, but I think that one so familiar with Bracton as you are will say that the discussion of the rights of the *firmarius*[1] is very much in Bracton's manner. Case 1291 is very like a piece of Bracton's text. I have not very much doubt who it was who had the book made. I believe too that I can prove past doubt that all the cases which Fitzherbert in his Abridgement gives from the reign of Hen. 3, he took from this book.

Believe me
Yours very truly
F. W. MAITLAND

I have left Trinity for a house in the town of Cambridge in which I hope that some day you will be my guest.

22. To James Bradley Thayer

15 Brookside
Cambridge.

12 Decr. 1886

DEAR SIR,

Many thanks for your kind letter.[2] I shall look forward with great interest to the outcome of your investigations. There is I am sure a great deal to be said about our ancient modes of trial which will be new and valuable. However I do not suppose that I have as yet found much that would be of great use to you. What has most struck me has been the prominent part played in my period 1216–1240 by the *secta*. Plaintiffs are constantly failing because they produce no suit or a suit which is *minus sufficiens*. I have found it required of the suitors that they shall have seen the facts to which they speak. My annotator remarks that it will not suffice that they speak *de auditu*, they must speak *de visu*. Sometimes, though not as a general rule, their names appear upon the roll. I have one case of a very 'distinguished' *secta*[3]: the Bishop of Winchester alleges that a certain Katerina of Montacute was not a supposititious child but is heir apparent to John of Montacute and Lucy his wife; *producit sectam scilicet* Savary of Bohun, Peter of Maulay, the Earl of Chester, the Earl Marshall *et multos alios* who in various ways were connected with the family. Again I find it objected in one case that one of the suitors is the plaintiff's attorney. Altogether it looks as if a rational witness procedure were being developed out of the *secta*, and I can not well understand why the production of suitors became first a mere formality and then a fiction.

As regards witnesses who give evidence before the jurors, the nearest approach to anything of the sort that I have found is Case 1187, which I send

[1] See Simpson, *Introduction to the History of the Land Law*, 73–4, and Lennard, *Rural England*, chap. V.
[2] Not extant.
[3] *B.N.B.*, Case 247.

you, where, as it seems, the freeholders of the manor are to come before the jurors and inform them whether homage was done. Case 1189 is a very good example of a trial by jurors and charter-witnesses; but there is nothing new in it. As regards criminal procedure, I think that I wrote too hastily, not understanding the wide scope given to the idea of capture with the mainour; of course the capture has to be proved by witnesses. I doubt whether, apart from this, any evidence is taken save that of the jurors and think that Stephen may have misled me.[1]

I am glad that Wakelin of Stoke is an old friend of yours and am thankful for the reference to Fortescue. When I copied the case I thought that it was not quite new to me, but I had forgotten all about Fortescue.[2]

Yesterday I finished copying the Note Book and hope that it may be published in the year that is coming.

Believe me
Yours very faithfully

F. W. MAITLAND.

23. To F. J. H. Jenkinson

15, Brookside
Cambridge
20th Dec. 1886

MY DEAR JENKINSON,

I am very grateful indeed to you for the Birds and am looking forward to hearing some of the music.[3] Your kind gift cheered my eyes last night when I returned from a cold expedition to the Bodleian. Are you going to be in Cambridge next week? If so, do dine here in the least solemn manner—e.g. on Tuesday or some other day that suits you better—that is, if you can put up with very homely entertainment—7.30 is a good lawful hour. I have come back from Oxford full of envy and jealousy: one may be very comfortable in the Library there.

Yours very truly

F. W. MAITLAND

---

[1] See Thayer, *Preliminary Treatise*, 13, esp. n. 1. The reference to Stephen is to *Hist. Crim. Law*, i. 259. See also M., *Pleas of the Crown for the County of Gloucester*, pleas 174 and 394 and pp. 145, 150.

[2] See *B.N.B.*, Case 1115 and Thayer, *Preliminary Treatise*, 15, n. 7, and 21–2. The reference to Fortescue is to Selden's Note 8 to Fortescue, *De Laudibus Legum Angliae*, c. xxi.

[3] The music composed by Sir Hubert Parry for a performance in Cambridge of *The Birds* of Aristophanes.

24. To James Bradley Thayer

15 Brookside
Cambridge

27 Feb. 1887.

MY DEAR SIR,

I hope that I have executed your commission aright. When I got to Deighton's[1] I found that T. J. Lawrence had published two books, a set of Essays which were known to me and a small manual of which I knew nothing. I conjectured that you meant the Essays and hope that they will have come to your hands before you get this note. If in this I was mistaken I will gladly take the wrong book off your hands and procure you the right. Our chair of International Law is at this moment empty: Westlake, Hall and Lawrence are the candidates of whom most is said.[2]

I have to thank you for a very interesting letter.[3] I make no doubt that you are right about the *secta*. It belongs to the preliminary procedure. It could not I think be developed into witnesses before a jury: but it seems to me that in the 13th century there was some danger that it would grow at the expense of the jury. I observe, for example, that in actions for dower such questions as whether the husband is dead, whether he endowed the wife in this way or that, never get to a jury but are decided by the court after hearing the *sectatores*. This left a trace in our later law, for, as you will remember, if the tenant pleaded that the would-be widow's husband were not dead, this question was 'tried by witnesses', not 'tried by jury' (Blackstone, vol. 3, p. 336), and possibly the procedure in actions for dower was made unusually summary as a favour to widows. Still it seems to me that in my note book trial by witnesses threatens the further development of trial by jury. I have seen a few other cases besides that which I sent you[4] in which 'transaction witnesses' are joined to the jurors; they are cases in which there is dispute about a partition previously made and the persons who made the extent are summoned along with other jurors; so when there is question as to how much land the demandant put in view the bailiff and other viewers are summoned along with other jurors. Such cases, as you say, are analogous to those in which 'deed witnesses' are joined to the jury. I have also been struck by the frequency of questions put by the Court to the parties; question and answer often appear on the roll and not uncommonly the result is a fatal admission and an immediate judgment. Coke notices this (Co. Lit. 304a) and I can not but think that this practice must have had good results. Also I have been struck by the frequency with

---

[1] The well-known Cambridge bookseller. The two books then published by the Rev. T. J. Lawrence (Deputy Professor of International Law, 1883–5) were *Essays on some disputed questions of International Law* and *A Handbook of International Law*.

[2] John Westlake (1828–1913) was elected in 1888 to succeed Sir Henry Maine as Whewell Professor of International Law.

[3] Not extant. On the question of 'trial by witnesses' raised by M. in the second paragraph of his letter, see Thayer, *Preliminary Treatise*, 17–24, 97–104.

[4] See Letter 22, *supra*.

which third parties are brought before the Court by a *Quid juris clamat*. The procedure in this respect seems to me surprisingly free and reasonable.

Will you, if you have an opportunity, give my best thanks to Professor Ames for the references that he has kindly sent me? I am reserving the pleasure of looking them out in the books for my next holiday.

Believe me

Yours very sincerely

F. W. MAITLAND.

25. To James Bradley Thayer

15 Brookside

Cambridge.

20 April 1887

MY DEAR SIR,

I have I hope performed your commission aright and am sorry that at first I sent you the wrong book.[1] And now I shall venture to trouble you with a question, namely, whether there is not some good American book on the real actions.[2] I have a vague reminiscence of having read or heard of such a book, but not knowing the author's name I have not been able to find it. If such a book there is I will go so far as to ask you to have it sent to me and I will then at once send the price. I fancy that in some of the states the real action flourished after it had become extinct in England, and if a good book was written about it this would be of great value to me. If, as seems possible, there was such a book but it has now become obsolete, a second hand copy would serve my turn very well.

I was glad to see your name on a draft prospectus of the nascent Selden Society.

Very truly yours

F. W. MAITLAND

26. To P. E. Dove

15 Brookside

Cambridge

27th April 1887

To P. E. DOVE, ESQ.
Secretary of the Selden Society.

I venture to suggest that the Society might well begin its labours by publishing a few volumes of select Pleas of the Crown illustrating the development of the criminal law throughout the middle ages. Of course, were it certain that the

---

[1] See Letter 24, *supra.*   [2] See Letter 27, *infra.*

Society's books would find many purchasers, there would be much to be said for working through the plea rolls in their chronological order and taking thence all cases of interest no matter what their subject matter. I doubt however whether at the present time the first volumes of a series made on this principle would prove attractive. The extracts in any volume would be very miscellaneous and some years would elapse before there would be a sufficient mass of matter about any one topic to make any inductions safe or profitable. Subscribers will naturally demand results of which they can at once take advantage. Besides it must be confessed that records of real actions would be found dull by many who would gladly read of matters for the understanding of which no great amount of obsolete technical knowledge is required. What is more, the selection of the records best worth copying will in the case of the real actions demand such a thorough knowledge of mediaeval procedure as is (to say the very least) extremely rare at the present day; it may come in time as editors are trained by lighter tasks, but it is hardly to be had at a moment's notice.

If then some one topic should be chosen, 'pleas of the crown' seem entitled to the first place—and this for several reasons. The subject is well defined; the boundary will be no arbitrary line of the editor's drawing. In the second place many of these criminal cases are very interesting and even entertaining and, at least when translated, would be found readable by many who would not care to study the effects of warranty, discontinuance and so forth. They bring one at once to the great rules of right and wrong. Again, they are very intelligible, both because criminal procedure always was a much simpler affair than civil procedure and because our criminal procedure retained many or most of its antiquities until a very recent time. The indictment we still have with us: the assize of novel disseisin is a thing of the past. Lastly, there must be a great deal to be learned about the history of the criminal law. The number of criminal cases in the Year Books is by no means large and yet it has to fill the long interval between Bracton and Staunford.[1] To name one matter which should be of great interest—the whole history of the petty jury is still but very vaguely known; we ought to be able to trace the precise process by which the twelve hundredors and four townships of Bracton[2] become, or are supplanted by, the two juries of a later time.

As an alternative I may mention cases illustrating villein status and villein tenure. At the present time these might be found very attractive, for much is being written about villeinage and the want of authentic materials is widely felt. However the understanding of such cases will often demand a great deal of technical knowledge of civil procedure in general and the real actions in particular. Also if the Society wishes to have a book published without delay villeinage seems to me a subject to be avoided, for cases about it are particularly difficult for a transcriber because of the many unusual words which occur in them.

[1] Staunford, *Plees del Coron* (1557): Winfield, *Chief Sources*, 324–5.
[2] *P. and M.* ii. 647–8.

My notion is that by some four or five volumes of no very great size the criminal law of the middle ages would be amply illustrated and that this would be a very valuable work. I should doubt the advisability of promising beforehand any particular number of volumes. Unless the Society can command the services of some one very familiar with the plea rolls, to discover how much is worth printing must be a matter of time. I feel certain however that at least one interesting volume could be made from the rolls of the thirteenth century; I am inclined to think that there should be two. Also it seems to me that the editor should be instructed to collect not merely the cases which for any reason are of special value but also a sufficient number of cases which illustrate just the ordinary procedure and the common crimes; in particular, the proceedings before justices in eyre will be best understood if occasionally all the entries relating to some one hundred be printed, even though many of these entries are 'common form'.

There are several points about which the Society will have to make up its mind and as to a few of these I will take the opportunity of saying a word. I take it that at first it will be well that the extracts from the records should be accompanied by translations. Of course if translations were not required the Society could at the same cost publish twice as many records; but probably there are many persons who will only begin to believe that records are interesting when they see them in English. By publishing translations the Society will be able to issue its volumes the more speedily, because the work of turning Latin into English can be done by the editor at his own place and time and will be much lighter than the work of finding and copying cases at the Record Office.

The Society will have to decide the question how records are best printed; it will certainly be well that some one plan should be adopted. I refer particularly to the expansion of contractions. There seem to be three courses open, namely, (i) to use what is called 'record type,'[1] (ii) to represent by italic type those letters which in the original are represented by stenographic signs, (iii) to expand all contractions and to print the whole in ordinary type. It is fairly certain that, whichever course be adopted, some persons will be dissatisfied. I do not myself believe that many readers have been found or will be found for documents printed in record type, and in my opinion the number of mistakes which can be saved by its use is extremely small. Again as to the use of italics—this tells the reader very little, while it must add to the cost of printing and must add very largely to the labour of transcribing documents and correcting proofs. The vocabulary of our law Latin is really very small, the grammatical structure of the records is in general very simple and I much doubt whether an editor will transcribe correctly stenographic signs the meaning of which he does not understand.

It seems to me that at present the main object of the Society should be to print records and not to print essays. An editor should of course be required to give a precise description of the documents that he has been using, to compare

1 See Letter 17, *supra*.

duplicate records when this is possible, to supply dates and so forth, but not to write dissertations about the law. What is wanted above all things is as much first-hand evidence as can be obtained.

If the services of a better editor are not to be had, I am willing to undertake the preparation of a volume, and I think that if I were set to work at once a volume might be finished by the end of the year; but as it is not possible for me to work continuously at the Record Office during the University terms, much would depend upon my being able to begin the task early in the summer. The subject that I would suggest is Select Pleas of the Crown from the Thirteenth Century. It would I think be a mistake to fix as the starting point so late a date as the accession of Edward I, because the preceding half-century is of great importance in the history of trial by jury. It seems to me that if the book is to cover the whole century it should have some five or six hundred pages—half of which will be filled with translation. If the Society will not be rich enough to pay for so large a book, then I think that the extracts should not go beyond Edward's accession—I mean that there should be no later extracts. Its value will very much depend upon its giving a complete picture of the criminal law.[1]

I very much wish that I could offer to do the work for nothing. This however I can not do, and that of course is a reason why the Society should if possible find another editor. I have very little idea what it would be fair to ask or what the Society will be able to give. I have lately been engaged in copying and getting printed a large collection of pleas (very few of these are criminal) of the reign of Henry III. I send a sheet of this book[2] as a specimen (there is no need to return it) of what I mean when I say that I should be ready to make such sheets at the rate of four guineas a sheet. If the Society is going to be very small and another editor is not forthcoming, I will try to make a better offer.

Believe me,

Yours very truly

F. W. MAITLAND.

27. To Melville M. Bigelow

15 Brookside
Cambridge

13 May 1887

MY DEAR MR. BIGELOW,

I send you a list of the Law Lectures delivered in this University. I am sorry to say that at present we have a great deal of Roman Law and of what is called General Jurisprudence in our scheme—but I hope that a projected alteration

---

[1] S.S. Vol. 1 was in fact confined to Pleas of the Crown, A.D. 1200–1225.
[2] *Bracton's Note-Book.*

may give English law a fairer chance. I send you a copy of the project[1]—at present it is no more than a project—but you may perhaps care to see it. I hope that my 'note book' will be published this autumn; I have done all my work except the heavy task of correcting proofs. I have lately had occasion to use your Placita Anglo-Normannica and your History of Procedure and see that when writing the Appendix for Pollock's Torts I ought to have referred to what you have said about the check put to the invention of writs by the Provisions of Oxford.[2] No doubt I had seen this, but I did not remember it at the time. I think it important that this point should be made. We here are too much given to thinking of the original writs as having existed from all eternity.

Your little book on Torts is now definitely established at the head of the books on that subject which we recommend to law students. I was glad to see a lot of copies of it at Macmillans[3] the other day. A friend of mine—R. T. Wright, a barrister and one of our lecturers[4]—wants me to ask you whether you would publish an edition of it in England, in which edition a little further prominence might be given to some of the specifically English doctrines. I hardly like making this request because I do not think it a bad thing that even beginners should know both that a great deal of 'common law' is common to you and to us and that in some cases your courts have come to different conclusions from those which obtain here. Still I believe that the book would have a great sale; so perhaps you will give the matter a thought. There would be no competition between your book and Pollock's, for the two are laid out on different lines and his is a decidedly hard book for undergraduates who were yesterday schoolboys.

I have just acquired Stearns on Real Actions and Jackson on Real Actions[5]— I find both of them very interesting. The old learning was so much better kept up on your side of the water than on ours. When you next write—and I hope this is not the end of our correspondence—will you tell me, if you can do so without trouble, whether in America the doctrine that an entry is tolled by a descent cast[6] has flourished within quite recent times; it seems to have been active in 1830. But do not be at any pains about this.

Believe me

Yours very truly

F. W. Maitland

---

[1] Not extant.

[2] Bigelow's *Placita Anglo-Normannica*, a collection of cases from William I to Richard I, was pub. in 1879, and his *History of Procedure in England from the Norman Conquest, 1066–1204*, in 1880. M. wrote as an appendix to Pollock's *The Law of Torts* (1887) a 'Historical note on the classification of the forms of personal action'.

[3] Alexander and Daniel Macmillan started as publishers in Cambridge in 1843. They moved to London in 1863 but kept a shop in Cambridge in partnership with Robert Bowes, later to become Bowes and Bowes: Charles Morgan, *The House of Macmillan, 1843–1943*.

[4] Fellow of Christ's College, Cambridge, and editor (with W. W. Buckland) of the 2nd edition of Finch's *Cases on Contract* (1896).

[5] *Stearns on Real Actions*, pub. Boston in 1824, and *Jackson on Real Actions*, pub. Boston in 1828.

[6] M. *Forms of Action*, 60: Blackstone, *Comm.* III, 176–7.

28. To Paul Vinogradoff

[No original. Transcript by Fisher in Camb. Univ. MSS: no ending.]

15 Brookside
Cambridge

12 June 1887

MY DEAR VINOGRADOFF,

'Cuius linguam ignorabant'—I feel now the full force of these words—I am *in tenebris exterioribus* and there is *stridor dencium*; but I heartily congratulate you upon having finished your book[1] and thank you warmly for the copy of it that you sent me and for the kind words that you wrote upon the outside. Also I can just make out my name in the Preface and am very proud to see it there. Also I have read the footnotes and they are enough to show me that this is a great book, destined in course of time to turn the current of English and German learning.

My book[2] also is finished, but the printers are slow. I hope to send you a copy in the autumn. I have been able to add a few links to the chain of argument that you forged. My happiest discovery was about a note that you may remember 'Ermeiard et herede de Hokesham'. I found (1) that the heir of Huxham was in ward to William of Punchardon, (2) that William's wife was Ermengard, (3) that Ermengard brought an action for her dower against Henry of Bratton. I have also had some success with Whitchurch, Gorges, Corner and Winscot.

29. To Melville M. Bigelow

15 Brookside
Cambridge

23rd June 1887

MY DEAR MR. BIGELOW,

I have to thank [*sic*] for your letter, for the photograph and for the proof sheets of your book.[3] I am glad that you are meditating an English edition of it. For my own part I am by no means sorry that our students even at the very beginning of their career should learn that in some instances 'the common law' has arrived at different conclusions in different courts. This may prevent their regarding every rule as obvious and matter of course. Still you will understand that a book published by English publishers is likely to make its way better than one which we must import from America. I have handed over

[1] *Investigations into the Social History of Medieval England*, pub. St. Petersburg, 1887. It was written in Russian and in 1892 published in English as *Villainage in England*. The copy sent to M. was inscribed 'To my dear friend F. W. Maitland'.
[2] *Bracton's Note-Book*. For the allusions in the ensuing paragraph see Introduction, pp. 93, 98, 100–1, and Case 1843.
[3] Bigelow's letter is not extant. The book seems to have been a new edition of *Elements of the Law of Torts*, first published in 1878: see Letter 32, *infra*.

one set of sheets to Wright. He has been teaching 'Torts' for some time past and I hope that he will have some remarks to make within the next fortnight. I will myself try to make a few suggestions. The most difficult matters are, as it seems to me, copyright, patent right, trade mark, etc. I am not at all certain that it is prudent to teach these topics at all in an elementary text book on 'Tort'—they are so much the creatures of statute. But I will think this over. I must not forget to thank you for the information about descents cast.[1] I am now leaving Cambridge for a very brief holiday. When that is over I will write to you again.

Yours very truly

F. W. MAITLAND

30. To Frederick Pollock

[No original. Printed Fisher, *Memoir*, 41–2: no beginning or ending.]

Jubilee Teapot Tor,

Horrabridge.

26 July 1887.

Horrabridge seems to be as much our post town as any other place; but I have not fully fathomed our postal relations. The legend is that the old gentleman who squatted here—and if ever I saw an untitled squatment I see one now —held that the post was 'a new found holiday'[2] and charged the postman never to come near him; and the postman, holding this to be an acquittance for all time, refused and still refuses to visit Pu Tor, but leaves our letters somewhere, I know not where, whence they are fetched by Samuel the son of the house—which Samuel learned the first half of the alphabet in the school 'to' Sumpford Spiney Church-town when as yet there was a school, but the school scattered and beyond N Samuel does not go—howbeit there will be a school again some day if ever Mr. Collier[3] can catch A. J. Butler at the Education Office, which is hardly to be expected. But if I begin to tell the acts of the Putorians I shall never cease, for they are a race with a history and a language and (it may be) a religion of their own. Villani de Tawystock fecerunt cariagium[4]—but the ignorant beggars did not know Pu Tor cottage and it seemed that we should wander about all night. This is a right good spot and we are grateful to you for discovering it. We have a sitting-room and two bedrooms and we could find place for a visitor if his stomach were not high. Have you seen the new ordnance map of the moor? Mr. Collier showed it me. *Pew* Tor is the spelling that it adopts.

[1] See Letter 27, *supra.*
[2] *Malpas' Case* (1455), Y.B. 33 Hen. 6, Trin. f. 26, pl. 12.
[3] William Collier, a friend of Pollock, who lived on Dartmoor and was 'a famous wine merchant in the West Country': Sir John Pollock, *Time's Chariot*, 56. For A. J. Butler's connection with the Education Office, see Letter 11, *supra.*
[4] Carrying-service or toll for carriage.

31. To James Bradley Thayer

15 Brookside
Cambridge
29 July 1887

DEAR SIR,

I write this on Dartmoor and am sorry to say that my absence from Cambridge has lost me the pleasure of making Mr. Soule's acquaintance. He tells me by letter that he is leaving the country in a few days. I trust that I may be fortunate enough to see Mr. Williams.[1] After I have got a little fresh air here I shall be in London for a time, copying some records for the Selden Society. Before long I hope to send you a copy of Bracton's Note Book which please accept.

Believe me
Yours very truly
F. W. MAITLAND

32. To Melville M. Bigelow

15 Brookside
Cambridge[2]
11 Aug. 1887

MY DEAR SIR,

I hoped to have studied your Elements of the Law of Torts along with some of our recent English Reports with a view to making some modest suggestions for your English edition; but I have been invalided and write this in a Devonshire village where I have been living an animal or vegetable life for some weeks past without law books. I am able however to send you a letter in which my colleague Wright makes some suggestions. I think that what we really want most is what I fear you will not be able to let us have in the next edition, namely references to English cases. We want if possible to induce our students to look beyond the text books to the reports. This is at best a difficult task, for our students are I believe much younger and much less instructed than those whom you have to teach. But difficult as it is to persuade them to study English reports, it is more difficult to send them to American cases. For one thing, the only library at their command, our University Library, is—I regret to say it—by no means wealthy in American Reports. In the second place, it is of course desirable that the few cases which they master and remember should be cases which are of the very highest authority in our own courts.

What therefore we should like would be an edition of your book which when possible referred to English rather than to American cases. But the

---

[1] Possibly C. F. Williams, one of the editors of *The American and English Encyclopaedia of Law* (1887–96).
[2] Though headed as from Cambridge, this letter was in fact written from Horrabridge.

making of such an edition would I suppose be impossible so long as you retain your stereotyped plates. At present we are using your American edition and I believe that we shall continue to use it, for I believe that all those who have used it in teaching think it the best book for beginners that we have. If, as I understand you purpose doing, you publish this in England, the sale of it will be increased, and we shall be glad that it is no longer necessary to send for copies to America. Perhaps when that edition is running out—and I wish you a rapid sale—you will consider the suggestion that Wright and I have ventured to make, of a more purely English edition, i.e. an edition in which, for choice, English rather than American authorities are cited. Probably this suggestion comes too late to influence your first English edition, and I hope you will understand that even a reprint of the stereotyped plates will be valuable here and valued. What Wright says about our University Press will not escape your notice—I should be glad to think that it would be useful to you—as yet it has done nothing for the study of law, but I think that very likely it would publish your book. I return one of the sets of sheets that you were kind enough to send me—with many thanks but (I am sorry to say it) without any notes—I did not like to keep it longer.

In a few weeks time I hope to send you a copy of 'Bracton's Note Book', which please accept from

Yours very faithfully

F. W. MAITLAND

33. To Frederick Pollock

[No original. Printed Fisher, *Memoir*, 39: no beginning.]

15, Brookside,
Cambridge.

12 Nov. 1887.

Very many thanks to you for a copy of your book on 'Torts'[1]—I am already deep in it and am reading it with delight. You will believe that coming from me this is not an empty phrase, for you will do me the justice of believing that I can find a good book of law very delightful. I hope that it may be as great a success as 'Contracts'—I can hardly wish you better. I now see some prospect of getting the Law of Torts pretty well studied by the best of the undergraduates. For weeks I have been in horrible bondage to my lectures. Stephen's chapters about the Royal Prerogatives and so forth—I speak of the Stephen of the Commentaries—are a terrible struggle; when one is set to lecture on them three days a week one practically has to write a book on constitutional law against time.[2]

[1] See Letter 27, *supra*.
[2] M.'s lectures on Constitutional Law, delivered in 1887-8, were published posthumously in 1908.

I cannot, alas, be at the Selden meeting on Monday, for I have undertaken to audit some accounts.

With many more thanks I rest

Sectator tuus set minus sufficiens

F. W. MAITLAND

34. To Melville M. Bigelow

15 Brookside

Cambridge

1 Jan. 1888

DEAR MR. BIGELOW,[1]

I am afraid that I am to blame. I did not understand from your letter written in the summer that you wished to set to work at once on an English edition of your 'Torts'. But I will now take care that a proposal shall be laid before our Press Syndicate so soon as it meets, which will be very shortly. Wright will make the proposal and I have little doubt that it will be accepted. At present however I am not authorized by you to mention any terms—so the only question that I can raise will be—Will the Syndics publish your book and, if so, on what terms? I hope and trust that no pirate will appear on the scene. I shall never forgive myself if owing to my misunderstanding the black flag floats over your barque.[2]

Many thanks for what you have said about my 'Note Book' and for the promise of 'Fraud'.

A happy new year to you and all who further the study of legal history.

Yours very truly

F. W. MAITLAND

35. To James Barr Ames

[Printed C.L.J., Vol. II (1924), pp. 4–5.]

15 Brookside,

Cambridge,

30th Jan. 1888.

DEAR SIR,

Professor Thayer has been kind enough to forward to me some notes which you were kind enough to make upon my edition of *Bracton's Note Book*.[3]

[1] M. is answering a letter of 19 Dec. 1887 (Camb. Univ. MSS) in which Bigelow (a) awaits a decision of the Cambridge University Press on the publication of an English edition of his *Torts*, (b) thanks M. for *Bracton's Note-Book*, (c) promises to send his own *Law of Fraud on its Civil Side*, Vol. I, then on the eve of publication.

[2] In 1888 a foreigner could obtain copyright in the United Kingdom only by first or simultaneous publication here.

[3] The letter from Thayer to M. (30 Dec. 1887) is in Camb. Univ. MSS, but the 'notes' are not with it.

I am very grateful to you for them, and perhaps I can best show my gratitude by sending a few notes in return, premising, however, that I do not mean them as a reply to your criticisms, which are very just.

Like you I have been struck by the sudden popularity of actions of trespass, especially of trespass *quare clausum fregit*. There are some rolls from the end of Henry III's reign which are *covered* with actions of this class. The passage in Bracton of which you speak you will, I think, find on f. 413, and a very curious passage it is:— one must not bring the *quare vi et armis* for a disseisin, seemingly because this puts in issue the *modus et qualitas facti*, i.e., the violence, when the *factum* itself, i.e. the disseisin, is the real matter in dispute. This seems to us, at least it seems to me, a rather artificial and scholastic objection and one likely to give way in course of time. What I know of the rolls certainly bears out the impression given by the *Placitorum Abbrev.*,[1] namely, that trespass *q.cl.fr.* suddenly became a common form of action. I should not be much surprised if this turned out to be the result of an ordinance. All that I meant about outlawry was that the possibility of outlawry made trespass preferable to other civil actions.[2] Where the wrong was a breach of a close an appeal was inappropriate. I have got in a volume of *Pleas of the Crown* that I am editing for the Selden Society a case from John's reign of an appeal founded on breach of a close, and this is quashed on the ground that *appellum de pratis pastis non pertinet ad coronam domini regis*.[3] The writ of trespass seems a modification of the appeal of felony; the *verba de felonia* are omitted, while the *vi et armis* and the *contra pacem* are retained. Doubtless you are right, however, in saying that the fact that the plaintiff in trespass could get a jury had much to do with the popularity of that form of action; this is well brought out by the description of trespass in the *Statutum Walliae: 'vix in placito transgressionis evadere poterit reus quin defendat se per patriam'*.

As to uses, I did not mean to imply that they were enforceable, but there seems to me some evidence that already in the thirteenth century the idea had occurred to men that it was sometimes convenient to have as owner one who was bound by good faith to let another enjoy the land. I send you a passage which I copied the other day from a very early manorial roll, in which an attempt is made to evade a rule of the manor that villein tenements are to be holden only by such as are personally the lord's villeins. Possibly you may care to see it. I know no rolls more interesting than the earliest manorial rolls; they are covered with litigation; I hope that the Selden Society will soon make a selection from them.[4]

With renewed thanks,

Believe me,

Yours very truly

F. W. MAITLAND

[1] On *Placitorum Abbreviatio* see Prof. G. O. Sayles, Introduction to S.S. Vol. 57.
[2] See *P. and M.* ii. 467 and *B.N.B.*, Cases 85 and 1232.
[3] S.S. Vol. 1, plea 35.
[4] S.S. Vol. 2, and esp. pp. 105–6.

36. To Frederick Pollock

[No original. Printed Fisher, *Memoir*, 42–3, with no beginning or ending and with omissions.]

15, Brookside,
Cambridge.

7 April, 1888.

I have returned from a brief incursion of Devonshire. Verrall and I made a descent upon Lynton which is still beautiful and at this time of year unbe-touristed. Bank Holiday was tolerable. I suppose that you spent it upon your freehold and are now returning to the law. You have got an excellent number of the L.Q.R. this quarter; really it ought to sell and if it doesn't the consti-tution of the universe wants reforming . . .

If P.[1] objects to 'ville' as a termination for names in America what does he say to 'wick' as a termination for names in England? I have been puzzling over the use of 'villa' in Kemble's *Codex*.[2] It seems to be used now for a village or township and now for a single messuage, and thus seems similarly elastic. One never can be quite certain what is meant when a villa is conveyed.

I have had some thoughts about a plan of campaign for the history of the manor. The graver question is whether the story should be told forwards or backwards. I am not at all certain whether it would not be well to begin by describing the situation as it was at the end of cent. XIII. and then to go back to earlier times. But we can talk of this when 'possession' is off your mind.[3] Remember that you have to stay here as an examiner. Meanwhile I hope to form a provisional scheme for your consideration.

I have got hold of a German, one Inama Sternegg,[4] who seems to be the modern authority as to the growth of the manorial system on the continent.

37. To P. E. Dove

15, Brookside
Cambridge

3 May 1888

MY DEAR DOVE,

I cannot be at the forthcoming meeting of the Selden Society. I hope that any members of the Council who have criticisms to make on volume 1 will make them and that you will tell me of them for they will be very useful to me in preparing vol. 2. I am not quite satisfied with our printers. They set up the type very accurately but in striking off the copies they have allowed letters to

---

[1] Possibly Charles Plummer (1851–1927), Fellow of Corpus Christi College, Oxford: editor of Bede, *Historia Ecclesiastica* (1896) and of *Two Saxon Chronicles*, 2 vols. (1892, 1899).
[2] J. H. Kemble, *Codex Diplomaticus aevi Saxonici*, 6 vols. (1839–48).
[3] Pollock was engaged, with R. S. Wright, on *Possession in the Common Law*, pub. 1888.
[4] Karl Theodor von Inama-Sternegg, *Deutsche Wirtschaftsgeschichte*, 3 vols.

slip from their places. I think that they must have done the actual printing somewhat roughly.

You will not forget what I said to you about a letter to the Athenaeum appealing for information about early manorial rolls. I hope to use those which are at the Record Office during the summer. I have already copied a number of extracts from rolls now at King's College which formerly belonged to the Abbey of Bec.[1]

I am extremely anxious that the Society should flourish and also that it should not be dependent upon a single editor. It would be an extremely good thing if for the second year you could announce some other work besides mine. There are for example some very early manorial custumals, 'extenta', which cry aloud for publication.[2]

I do not know what is the state of your budget, but I wish to say that I will not take more than ten guineas *at most* for volume 1; this will very handsomely cover all expense to which it put me. I had originally dreams of a large and rich society and they may yet be fulfilled—but at present we must give the subscribers as much as possible for as little as possible:— so let it be as I say.

I shall hope to hear from you that the Council has seen its way to get a second editor to work. Would not, for example, Mr. Round do something, or is he too busy with his charters?

Yours very truly

F. W. MAITLAND

38. To Henry Sidgwick

[M. gives no year at the head of his letter; but from the calendar reference in the body of the letter it should be 1888. Sidgwick was then engaged upon his *Elements of Politics*, ultimately pub. 1891.]

Trinity

5 May

MY DEAR SIDGWICK,

I very gladly accept your invitation for Wednesday the 13th. Your dealings with Austin are very delightful to me, for the formal jurisprudent sits heavy upon us and you will deprive him of his terrors. Since your youths won't ask you questions I dare to send you one—about the meaning of a 'right', by which of course I mean a legal right. I don't well know how to answer it myself: the language of 'our books' is not so precise as it might be.[3]

A father will get himself punished if (having means) he omits to supply a child of tender years with food to the damage of the child's health, but the

---

[1] S.S. Vol. 2, pp. 3–47.

[2] *Ibid*, Introduction xi–xii.

[3] Sidgwick complained of the reluctance of pupils to ask questions: *Henry Sidgwick*, 322. M.'s question accompanied his letter and is here reproduced as an *addendum* to the letter. The original is in print and seems to be taken from an examination paper. M. discusses it in the rest of his letter.

child has no civil action—has the child a right? If we say 'Yes', does this follow merely from the fact that in this country the private person can begin criminal proceedings? Suppose that a rule of this kind is only sanctioned by penal process and that none can prosecute but a government officer, does the rule give a right? I do not think that to the question about the use of words our legal orthodoxy has any certain answer, but there is a strong tendency to make 'No right without a (civil) remedy' an analytical proposition. On the other hand this tag is used as a constructive (? synthetic) proposition to mean something of this kind:— 'If a statute imposes a duty on A which apparently is imposed for the benefit of B but specifies no means of enforcing the duty, then B if damaged by non-performance has a civil action.' On the whole I should like to make the said tag a truism, because to do so would I think give a 'right' its most usual meaning.

The point about the Statute of Limitations is that the creditor loses his direct remedy by action but, if the debtor pays, can keep the money: we usually say the right remains, the remedy is gone.

I am trying to avoid 'right' as much as possible and to speak always of 'duty'.

Yours very truly

F. W. MAITLAND.

(ADDENDUM)

1. 'Indeed it is a vain thing to imagine a right without a remedy: for want of right and want of remedy are reciprocal'. HOLT, C.J.

Do you think this (a) true, (b) a truism?

A wealthy father omits to supply a child of tender years with sufficient food and the child falls ill: has any right been infringed?

It is sometimes said that the Statute of Limitations does not take away the creditor's right, but merely bars his remedy; what do you think of this?

Do you know how the maxim "There is no right without a remedy" has been applied in English courts?

39. To James Barr Ames

[Printed C.L.J., Vol. II (1924), pp. 5–8.]

15, Brookside,
Cambridge.

6th May, 1888.

DEAR SIR,

I have to thank you for a letter[1] full of interesting remarks, and first let me answer as best I can your question as to the possibility of tracing cases from the Year Books to the Rolls. I shall always be happy to make the attempt

---

[1] Dated 24 March 1888: in Camb. Univ. MSS.

to find any case that you may want. I hope always to make some leisure for study at the Record Office, and I enjoy a good hunt. I fear, however, that I know of nobody who takes to such work as to a profession: there is not sufficient demand for this. Now if, for example, you wished to discover a pedigree or prove your title to an English peerage, it would be easy to put you into good hands, for there are many professional searchers who are in the habit of going through the rolls in quest of names; but they are not in the habit of serving those who merely want cases of a certain legal class. It is a misfortune that the Year Books so seldom mention names, for this makes it difficult to find the cases on the rolls or to be quite certain that one has found them. Still, in a little time one's eye gets accustomed to looking for cases of a particular kind; *e.g.* the $\overline{Ass}$ $\overline{ven}$ $\overline{rec}$ will tell one that it is an assize. I shall always be happy to look for anything that you may want, but I cannot promise to find it. You will see that Mr. Pike in his edition of the Year Books has often been successful in finding the record. Whenever the happy day comes when the Year Books are reprinted the records will have to be used. I think that the Selden Society might do worse than publish a specimen Year Book, in which the record of every important case should be given in full or in abstract. I very much wish that I could train up a few Cambridge men to use the Record Office; but they all believe that they are going to succeed at the Bar.

I did not mean to imply in my essay on Seisin that a termor ever had the assize. I do not think that he ever had it, though the *Mirror* says that he ought to have it. (I cannot at this moment find that queer book, but I spoke of this in L.Q.R. i. 337.)[1] But as to 'the bare possessor'—meaning thereby one who has no title—surely he had the assize. Suppose that A is the true owner and that B without a shadow of right disseises him—then A has a brief interval allowed him for re-ejectment—but from the very moment of the disseisin B is seised as regards all others, and if X turns him out, then B will have the assize against X. I cannot read Bracton to mean anything else than this—*e.g.* on f. 209 b, line 25: 'Et unde cum tenens disseisitor vel intrusor.' Even against A, B will be protected so soon as a brief interval has elapsed. The end of my discourse will appear some day in the L.Q.R.; it was written last year.[2] I try to show how the courts gradually lost their grasp of the notion that possession as such is to be protected, and allowed defendants in an assize to plead title. But surely to the very last a bare possessor could have recovered in an assize against one who pretended no title. Put it that A is the owner, that B without any title turns him out, and that then C without any title turns B out—could not B recover from C? I did not know that this had been disputed, though I must confess that in the eighteenth century when 'the feudal system' was in its prime some of our judges had a notion that 'seisin' implied title. The question did not get raised in modern times, because men had ceased to eject each other without shadow of right, but I should have thought that had it been raised the decision must have been in favour of B against C.

---

[1] *The Seisin of Chattels*, C.P. I. 329: see also S.S. Vol. 7, p. 67.
[2] *Possession for Year and Day*, 5 L.Q.R. (1889), 253: C.P. II. 61.

As regards trespass, I know too little to speak of it in a letter to you—but the impression that I got some years ago from reading the cases was not quite that which they have evidently made upon you. My notion (which very likely may be wrong) was this, that possession, bare possession, had been quite enough for the plaintiff in trespass, but that when under a cloud of fictions trespass (in the form of ejectment) was made to do the duty of a proprietary action, the old principle was for a while confused by the maxim (appropriate only to proprietary actions) that a plaintiff must recover on the strength of his own title and not on the weakness of the defendant's; but then that further reflection set the old principle free again in the form that 'title' is a relative term, and that in the case stated above B has good title *as against* C. However, I submit this to you very diffidently.

I do not think that the cases of the bare possessor and of the termor can be spoken of in the same sentence. The bare possessor of the thirteenth century has, I think, the assize; the termor has not, because the termor has hitherto been regarded as the freeholder's bailiff, and to eject him is to disseise the freeholder.

I have just been reading with very great interest your article upon Assumpsit; it is most valuable, and will go far towards settling the question.[1]

For the references to seisin and disseisin of chattels I am very grateful. I have now a large number of instances beyond those that I originally quoted.

I am getting on with selections from the early manor rolls. At King's College they have a beautiful set beginning in 1246 which once belonged to the Norman Abbey of Bec.[2] I hope that the book will be interesting. The forms of pleading in the manorial courts are closely similar to the forms which prevailed in the King's courts—except that *secundum consuetudinem manerii* is constantly inserted. Before the end of the thirteenth century, the chief outlines of what, by anticipation, one may call 'copyhold conveyancing' seem to have been drawn.

I hope that you will not think this letter too long: it is pleasant to me to gossip about legal history.

Believe me

Yours very truly

F. W. MAITLAND

40. To Frederick Pollock

[Post card. No original: printed Fisher, *Memoir*, 43.]

9 May, 1888.

Predicti sokemanni habebunt remedium per tale breve de Monstraverunt.[3]
R tali duci salutem. Monstraverunt nobis N N homines de trampagio

---

[1] Harv. L. Rev. II. p. 1; *Lectures on Legal History*, 128.
[2] S.S. Vol. 2, pp. 3–48.
[3] See S.S. Vol. 2, pp. 99–100 and *P. and M*. i. 385–94.

vestro quod exigis ab eis alia servicia et alias consuetudines quam facere debent et solent videlicet in operibus et ambulationibus, et ideo vobis precipimus quod predictis hominibus plenum rectum teneas in curia tua ne amplius inde clamorem audiamus, quod nisi feceris vicecomes noster faciat.

Teste Meipso apud Cantebrigiam die Ascen. Dñi.

41. To P. E. Dove

15, Brookside
Cambridge
15 May 1888

MY DEAR DOVE

I feel very grateful to the Council of the Selden Society for the handsome cheque that you have sent me, painfully grateful, for I can only accept it in the hope that I may do a lot more without any more pay. I hope and trust that I am not crippling the Society.

Do not send me another copy of the book for I have still the proofs, and so soon as I can get a few minutes to spare I will mark on them the passages which require correction. You shall have them in a few days.

At this moment I am somewhat overwhelmed by things to do. A series of unfortunate accidents has left our law school very short-handed and I hardly like to think how many examinations lie before me in the next month. If however I can string together some remarks about the trials of the thirteenth century I will do so.[1] I have already engagements for several days in the first fortnight of June. What would come easiest to me would be some observations as to the procedure of the manorial courts, because I have recently been thinking over this matter with a view to volume ii. In a few days I will let you know whether I shall have anything to read.

Yours very truly

F. W. MAITLAND

42. To James Bradley Thayer

[M.'s date at the head of this letter—31 June—should probably be 31 May. On and about this date he was seeking testimonials for his candidature.]

15 Brookside
Cambridge
31 June 1888

DEAR PROFESSOR THAYER,

I have a request to make of you. A professorship of English law is vacant in this University and I mean to stand for it. Shall you mind my telling the electors

[1] Mr. Justice Wills, a member of the Council of the Selden Society, had suggested to M. the possibility of a lecture to the Society 'on the scene presented by a trial in the early days of the 13th century' (Letter of 9 May 1888: Camb. Univ. MSS). M. does not seem to have given any such lecture.

that the review of the Note Book in the 'Nation' was your work? I want to send them the review in any case, because it explains the way in which I have been using my time since I was appointed reader, and I can not expect all of them to know anything at all about Bracton. But I should very much like to be able to add that you wrote it; it is so much more than favourable that I may be suspected of having written it myself. However I can well understand that you may have a dozen reasons for not wishing me to mention your name and of course I shall not mention it without your permission. I hope that at any rate you will not treat this request as a trespass. All the answer that I want is Yes or No on a post-card.

Mr. Maunde Thompson of the British Museum has been attempting to trace the recent histury of the Note Book, but has not I believe been able to discover how it came to the hands of Holmes of East Retford.[1]

Believe me

Yours very truly

F. W. MAITLAND

43. To Paul Vinogradoff

[No original. Printed Fisher, *Memoir*, 43–4: no beginning or ending.]

3 Albany Terrace

St. Ives

Cornwall

25 July 1888

I ought before now to have sent you my address to meet the case of your having any MS to send me. I have been going over and over again in my mind many parts of the pleasant talk that we had at Cambridge during two of the most delightful days of my life. I hope that you were not weary of instructing me.[2] Let me say that the more I think of your theory of folk land the better I like it. Of course it is a theory that must be tested and I know that you will test it thoroughly; but it seems to me a true inspiration, capable of explaining so very much, and I think that it will be for English readers one of the most striking things in your book.[3] Should you care for notes on any of the following matters I can send them to you out of my Selden materials—(1) persons with surname of 'le Freman' paying merchet, (2) free men refuse to serve on manorial jury, (3) the lord makes an exchange with the Communa Villanorum, (4) persons who pay merchet on an ancient demesne manor use the little writ of right.[4]

---

[1] See *B.N.B.*, Intro. p. 61, n. 1: 'John Holmes of East Retford published at intervals between 1828 and 1840 a catalogue of his large collection of printed books; but this does not comprise manuscripts. His library was, as I gather from his Preface, the outcome of purchases made by him'.

[2] See S.S. Vol. 2, Preface and p. 99.

[3] *Villainage in England*, pub. 1892. See also Vinogradoff's paper on *Folkland*, E.H.R. Jan. 1893: Vinogradoff, *Coll. Pap.* I. 91. See also Letters 49 and 50, *infra*.

[4] S.S. Vol. 2, pp. 94, 99, 172.

44. To Melville M. Bigelow

[This letter, though headed as from Cambridge, was in fact written from St. Ives, Cornwall.]

15 Brookside
Cambridge
31 July 1888

DEAR MR. BIGELOW,

I am away in Cornwall making holiday, but if any question occurs in the publication of your book on Torts about which I can give any advice I will very willingly give it. I am glad that the work is so far advanced and I shall indeed be proud if you do me the honour of dedicating it to me and Wright. I think that it has a successful career before it. Several writers on this side of the ocean have of late been turning their attention to torts; but none of them have supplied just what is wanted as an elementary text book. Pollock is a little too philosophical for beginners.

I have already got together a great deal of material for the Selden Society's volume II. It interests me very much and will I hope interest you and others. We are very dependent on our American subscribers. I can't tell why it is, but certainly you seem to care a deal more for legal history on your bank of the Atlantic than we do here. It is a malarrangement of the universe which puts the records in one continent and those who would care to read them in another.

Believe me
Yours very truly
F. W. MAITLAND

45. To Frederick Pollock

[No original. Printed Fisher, *Memoir*, 44–5: no beginning or ending and with omissions.]

3, Albany Terrace,
St. Ives,
Cornwall.
5 Aug. 1888.

Many thanks for your telegram: it was kind of you to send so prompt a message.[1] I feel it a little absurd that I should be thanking you for the telegram and no more—but I must be decorous. However, let us put the case that in a public capacity you regret the result, still it is allowed me to think that in the capacity of friend you rejoice with me, and of course I am very happy. I wonder whether you dined in Downing. I hope that my essoin was taken in good part; but really I thought that there would be an insolent confidence apparent in my journeying from St. Ives to Cambridge in order to be present at a dinner. It might, I think, have been reasonably said that I did not come all that way to grace the triumph of another man. . . . Well, I am glad that I have ceased to regard you as my judge and can resume unrestrained conversation.

[1] That M. had been elected Downing Professor. Pollock was an elector.

46. To Frederick Pollock

[No original. Printed Fisher, *Memoir*, 45: no beginning or ending.]

3, Albany Terrace,

St. Ives,

Cornwall.

6 Aug. 1888.

Your letter from Downing tells me what I expected, namely, that the struggle was severe. I can very well understand that there was much to be said against me—some part of it at all events I have said to myself day by day for the last month. My own belief to the last moment was that some Q.C. who was losing health or practice would ask for the place and get it. As it is, I am reflecting that in spite of all complaints the bar at large must still be doing a pretty profitable trade, otherwise this post would not have gone begging.

47. To J. H. Round

[No year, but clearly 1888, as M. was then in St. Ives: see Letters 43–6, *supra*. This and all the subsequent letters written to Round by M., save Letters 134, 203 and 209, are in the University of London Library, ref. I.H.R. M.S. 653.]

3 Albany Terrace

St. Ives

Cornwall

17 Augt.

DEAR MR. ROUND,

I have been at Cambridge; hence my delay in answering your letter. I now return your proof sheets.[1] I have very little doubt that you are right in thinking that this elaborate mortgage is a device for evading the law against usury. My only doubt is as to whether the words 'reddo eidem Ricardo medietatem predicti debiti' can refer to the discharge of half the debt by the retention of the annual mark; still I can not see any other explanation. I can not quite see how you arrive at the term of $49\frac{1}{2}$ years. I suppose that you have some reason for changing 45 into $49\frac{1}{2}$, but I do not understand it.

Any notes that you have collected about the phrase 'manum in manu' are likely to be of the very greatest value to legal historians—for the whole subject is very obscure and of great importance—I mean the existence of a contract binding because of its form. The 'affidatio' of these times sadly needs explanation: you will be familiar with such phrases as 'A affidavit in manu B'—anything that throws light on this ceremony would be most valuable.[2]

As to 'group common' I should say that it is *not* 'recognized that several vills might have joint rights of pasture etc. over a common waste' except this

[1] Probably of *Ancient Charters*, Pipe Roll Society (1888).
[2] See *P. and M*. ii. 188–90.

were *pur cause de vicinage*.[1] It has long seemed to me however that the ortho-dox doctrine about *common pur cause de vicinage*, namely that it is no more than an excusable trespass, is comparatively modern. I do not know exactly what it is that you have found, but I should guess from what you say that it is certainly something that is not 'already familiar', something that e.g. Coke would have condemned as impossible.

I am extremely sorry that I should have been the cause, though the innocent cause, of any row in the P. R. Socy.[2] I have no doubt that you are equally innocent.

Yours very truly

F. W. MAITLAND

I did not see the Athenaeum for 28 July,[3] but shall look it up when I return, as soon I must, to the world in which newspapers circulate.

48. To James Bradley Thayer

22 Hyde Park Gate
London, S.W.

15 Sept. 1888

DEAR MR. THAYER,

I am very grateful to you for your kind exertions on my behalf. I made use of your article though merely as that of an anonymous critic, and I was suc-cessful[4]; so henceforth my address will be 'Downing College, Cambridge', for the professorship carries with it a home in Downing, where I hope you will be someday my guest. And now I have something to add to the odd chapter of accidents into which our correspondence has run. When I was making holiday at St. Ives in Cornwall, I received a telegram stating that I might make use of your name. It was an English telegram and on its face purported to have been sent from 'Newnham, Cambridge'! This led me to believe and to hope that you were in England and had been to our Cambridge of which Newnham is a suburb. I made inquiries but could hear nothing of you. I even wrote to you at Newnham in the hope that if you were anywhere about a postman might have heard of you. My letter came back to me through the Dead Letter Office. Then arrived your postcard about Keilway[5] and this looked as if you were in America. The explanation of the telegram that I received turns out to be that your message was opened at Cambridge by a cousin of mine and that he telegraphed its substance to St. Ives using your name. I was sorry that the prospect of meeting you vanished.

I am very much obliged to you for drawing my attention to Keilway. He

---

[1] See *P. and M.* i. 608 and M. *D.B. and Beyond*, Essay II, s. 6.
[2] Pipe Roll Society.
[3] Containing a review of *B.N.B.*
[4] See Letter 42, *supra.*
[5] See Winfield, *Chief Sources*, 189–90, and Veeder, *Anglo-American Legal History*, II. 135.

has several cases which will be of great value to me and I hope to make good use of him.[1]

The most interesting set of rolls that I have come across records the doings of the court of the fair of St. Ives (1275)—the St. Ives in Huntingdonshire. There are numerous cases of actions for goods sold, etc., references to 'lex mercatoria' and so forth. It gives one a little shock to read in so early a document of a 'scriptum obligatorium' made payable to bearer (*portatori*). As this court had a lord—it belonged to the Abbot of Ramsey—I think that it may be possible for me to include some selections from its rolls in my next volume.[2]

> Renewing my thanks to you,
> I am
> Yours very truly
> F. W. MAITLAND

49. To Paul Vinogradoff

[No original. Transcript by Fisher in Camb. Univ. MSS: no beginning, ending or date. But this letter, like Letter 50, must be dated September, 1888, since each was written from Leslie Stephen's house, Hyde Park Gate, where, as is clear from Letter 48, M. was then staying. It would also seem that Letter 49 was written before Letter 50. In Letter 49 M. is reading the first pages of the English manuscript of *Villainage in England:* in Letter 50 he has reached Chapter IV: in Letter 51 he is ready to see proofs.

> 22 Hyde Park Gate
> S.W.

'I' say it? 'I' is a little severe. This is as it should be—*res severa est verum gaudium*—but the generality of Englishmen, even of learned Englishmen, will only grapple with the exposition of medieval law if you first persuade them that important conclusions are to be gained thereby. I feel certain that you can do what is needful and, without abandoning your high standard of work, can let folk see in the two first pages of your book that the work is worth doing.

And now what say you to manorial rolls of 6 *John*? Lord Justice Fry assures me there are such in the custody of the solicitors to the Ecclesiastical Commissioners—but they are the most pedantically cautious of human beings, and I fear that it will be a long time before I get sight of these documents. I must make friends in high quarters first—but possibly a foreigner would succeed where an Englishman would fail.[3]

I have become enormously interested in certain rolls, temp. Ed. I, of the fair of St. Ives, which belonged to Ramsey Abbey.[4] They are, I think, of the

---

[1] S.S. Vol. 2, Introduction, xxiii, xxiv, xxxv, xli.
[2] *Ibid.*, esp. pp. 130–7, 152.
[3] See S.S. Vol. 2, Introduction, xiii, note.
[4] S.S. Vol. 2, pp. 130–60.

utmost importance in the history of the *lex mercatoria*—law of contract, sale of goods, etc. I wish that I were allowed to make *three* Selden books this year.

50. To Paul Vinogradoff

[No original. Printed Fisher, *Memoir*, 46: no beginning or ending.]

22 Hyde Park Gate

S.W.

Sept. 1888

Has this occurred to you?—how extremely different the whole fate of English land law would have been if the King's court had not opened its doors to the under-vassals, to the lowest freeholders. But this was a startling interference with feudal justice and only compassed by degrees, in particular by remedies which in theory were but possessory, etc. Now, if the lower freehold tenants had not had the assizes, the line between them and the villein tenants would have been far less sharp. You hint at all this in chap. IV,[1] but might it not be worth a few more words—for there will be a tendency among your readers to say *of course* freeholders had remedies in the King's courts while really there is no of course in the matter. The point that I should like emphasized—but perhaps you are coming to this—is that not having remedies in the King's own court is not equivalent to not having rights.

51. To Paul Vinogradoff

[No original. Printed Fisher, *Memoir*, 46–7: no beginning or ending and with omissions.]

Downing,

14 Oct. 1888

I have been picking up my strength and am doing a little work. Yesterday I got through my inaugural lecture; possibly I may print it and in that case I will ask you to accept a copy; but it was meant to be heard and not read and so I allowed myself some exaggerations.[2]

. . . I am now quite ready to see proofs of your book[3] . . . My Introduction for the manorial rolls is taking shape; it will deal only with the courts, their powers and procedure. You can I think trust me not to take an unfair advantage of our correspondence and your kindness—but if you had rather that I did not see the sheets of your book which deal with the courts, please say so. I hope to have got this Introduction written in a month or six weeks.[4]

[1] In Vinogradoff's manuscript of *Villainage in England*. From the last sentence of this letter it is clear that it was coming to M. piece by piece.
[2] *Why the history of English law is not written*. It was published separately and reprinted C.P. I. 480. See Plucknett, *Early English Legal Literature*, 11–13.
[3] See Letters 58 and 97, *infra*.
[4] See Preface and Introduction to S.S. Vol. 2.

52. To James Barr Ames

[Printed C.L.J., Vol. II (1924), p. 8.]

> Downing College,
> Cambridge.
> *14 Oct. 1888.*

DEAR SIR,

Your letter of last August[1] has gone too long without an answer; but a change of house consequent on an appointment to the Downing Professorship has kept me busy, and I have had many manorial rolls in my hands. You say that you have written an essay on the disseisin of chattels. I take in your Harvard Law Review, but no number has come for some time past; I must interrogate my publisher about this. I hope that the essay is in print and that I may soon see it, for it will be most interesting to me.[2] I have never been through the cases diligently, but I know the way that the judges of the Y.B. period have of ascribing 'property' to an unlawful taker and even to a thief—and I cannot understand it. It is, of course, easy to say that they confound 'property' with 'possession'—but is such a confusion conceivable? In what sense can a thief have property? I have long been desirous of getting some answer to such questions and am happy to think that when I have leisure to search the YBB. I shall be able to do so under your guidance.

I have found some interesting rolls of the Court of the Fair of St. Ives (Hunts), temp. Edward I. It professed to administer *lex mercatoria*; many of the cases deal with the sale of goods, and I have even found a case about an obligation payable to bearer (*portatori*). I did not expect such luck as this; I feared that the *lex mercatoria* of the middle ages would always be for us a mere name. I mean to drag in some extracts from these rolls in the next Selden volume[3]—pleading that, though the court was not 'manorial', still it was 'seignorial', for it belonged to the Abbot of Ramsey.

> Believe me,
> Yours very truly,
> F. W. MAITLAND

53. To Henry Sidgwick

[Printed Fisher, *Memoir*, 47–8, with some omissions: now printed from the original at Trinity College, Cambridge.]

> The West Lodge
> Downing College
> Cambridge
> *11th Dec. 1888*

DEAR SIDGWICK,

I have been reading your proof sheets[4] with great interest and delight, and really as regards the parts which most concern me I have little to suggest. I

---

[1] Not extant. [2] Harv. L. Rev. III. 23: *Lectures on Legal History*, 172.
[3] S.S. Vol. 2, pp. 130–60.
[4] *The Elements of Politics*. Though not published until 1891, Sidgwick was getting it into print from the beginning of 1888: see *Henry Sidgwick*, 487 and 499.

think the chapter on law and morality particularly good. Were I writing the book I should in my present stage of ignorance 'hedge' a little about continental notions of law. Since I had some talk with you I have been reading several German law books and my view of the duties of a German judge is all the more hazy. I find that a jurist, even when he is writing about elementary legal ideas, e.g. possession, will cite 'Entscheidungen der oberste Gerichte von Celle, Darmstadt, Rostock', etc., *if he thinks them sound*—but how far he would think himself bound as judge by decisions which made against his theory I cannot tell. All seems rendered so vague by the notion of a 'heutige römische Recht'. But I think that you have just hit off the English idea of a good judge—he does *justice* when he sees an opportunity of doing it. I do not think that a man could be a judge of quite the highest order without a strong feeling for positive morality. On p. 92, (ch. XII) you might add, if you cared to do so, that our highest courts of appeal, House of Lords and Judicial Committee, hold themselves bound by their own decisions in earlier cases.

As regards the existence of different laws in different parts of a country, you might reckon among the advantages the gain in experience. I have no doubt that Scotch experience has improved English law and English experience Scotch law. Thus some use of an experimental method is made possible; e.g. take 'Sunday closing',[1] we can experiment on Wales and Cornwall. On the whole I have been surprised to find how little harm is done by the differences between Scotch and English law. I have read but very few cases that were caused by such differences.

I admire the chapter on International Law and Morality; it is the best thing that I have read about the subject. In my view the great difficulty in obtaining a body of international rules deserving the name of law lies in the extreme fewness of the 'persons' subject to that law and the infrequency and restricted range of the arguable questions which arise between them. The 'code' of actually observed rules is thus all shreds and patches. In short International Law is so incoherent.

Yours very truly

F. W. MAITLAND

54. To James Bradley Thayer

The West Lodge
Downing College
Cambridge.

16 Decr. 1888.

DEAR MR. THAYER,

I was surprised to hear that 'copy' of mine had gone by mistake to you; I hoped this meant that you also were sending MS. to Spottiswoode.[2] Many

---

1 See Sunday Closing (Wales) Act, 1881.
2 Printer to the Selden Society. The 'copy' was presumably that of S.S. Vol. 2.

thanks to you for so promptly setting the mistake right and for kind words about the proof sheets that you have seen. Dove evidently is afraid that the book will be very dull and writes me many letters adjuring me to be lively. I do not see my way to satisfying him and yet I must own that I am giving our subscribers an unpalatable morsel. I have written a long introduction but this may only make matters worse.

I quite agree with you about that unlucky prospectus, and Pike's criticisms are but too just. I hope that Dove will no longer flourish it before the public.[1]

Also I quite agree with you about Pike's merits. I had the last Year Book for review from the L.Q.R. and did not like the job, just because Pike had been so very civil to me. I did not want just to pay back a compliment or to seem to be doing so; but his work is so flawless that I had to look about for anything to say, and now I may seem to him captious.[2]

I wonder whether either you or Prof. Ames would give me an opinion as to the suggestion which I make on the enclosed paper and which I designed for my glossary. In my extracts from the fair of St. Ives I have many cases in which a defendant comes to grief because he fails to defend the 'verba curiae'. The phrase puzzles me and I should very much like to have your opinion about it. In my etymological scrapes I generally apply for relief to Prof. Skeat, but in this case a student of the Year Books may help me better than a philologist.[3]

Believe me

Yours very truly

F. W. MAITLAND

[1] Dove's prospectus, in which he aired his views on a variety of subjects, was 'flourished' for some little while longer: it appears at the end of S.S. Vol. 4 (1891).
On Luke Owen Pike see Winfield, *Chief Sources*, 179, and Bolland, *Manual of Year Book Studies*, 80–2. He was responsible for the majority of the Year Books published in the Rolls Series and was the author of *A History of Crime in England* (1873).
[2] M.'s review is in 5 L.Q.R., 82–3.
[3] The 'enclosed paper' is not extant. But its contents are clearly indicated in M.'s glossary to S.S. Vol. 2 at pp. 186–7, where M. suggests that *verba curiae*, 'words of court', are a corruption of *verba de cursu*, 'words of course'. See, however, Letter 76, *infra*.
Professor W. W. Skeat (1835–1912), philologist and Early English scholar, author of *An Etymological Dictionary of the English Language*, and editor of Chaucer and Langland, was thanked by M. for help in the Preface to S.S. Vol. 2.

1889–1898

In these years, while he continued to explore the borderland of law and history, Maitland advanced ever more boldly into the province of the medieval historian. He became a frequent contributor to the English Historical Review and a friend of its guiding spirit, Reginald Lane Poole, with whom for the rest of his life he exchanged letters at once learned and intimate. These wider historical interests provoked as well an active correspondence with John Horace Round, equally learned and, in the beginning at least, a testimony of mutual respect. But with Round's devotion to scholarship was mingled a sensitive vanity which marred his personal relations, and not even Maitland's magnanimity could do more than delay the almost inevitable breach. When Maitland felt constrained to dilute praise with criticism, the friendship and the letters ended. In a happier environment the touch of history coloured his letters to Herbert Fisher whom he welcomed with sympathetic encouragement as a scholar and with affection as his wife's brother.

In the prolific output of this, his middle age, he was quick to mark, digest and value the work of his contemporaries not only in England but in America, where he added Charles Gross to his correspondents, and on the continent of Europe, where the masters of his craft were at least as ready as his compatriots to recognize genius.[1] To comment upon the range of learning revealed by essays, lectures and reviews would be inappropriate and presumptuous. Three major works may be noted. In 1893 the Rolls Series produced his edition of the Parliament Roll of 1305, the germ and development of which may be traced in the letters to Maxwell Lyte, the Deputy Keeper of the Public Records. In 1895 he published the History of English Law before the time of Edward I, to be known thenceforth, with doubtful propriety, as *Pollock and Maitland*. Following the History in 1897, and indeed its offshoot, came the rich and suggestive *Domesday Book and Beyond*. Throughout these preoccupations his time and his mind were at the call of the Selden Society, to set its standards and to foster its growth. Between 1889 and 1898 he was solely responsible for two volumes, jointly responsible for a third and closely associated with a fourth. These direct contributions were but a fraction of the debt owed to him by the Society. His letters to the Honorary Secretaries, first to P. E. Dove and still more vividly, after Dove's death, to Fossett Lock, show him not only ready but able, and not only able but eager, to master every detail of the office of Literary Director which he held *de facto* from the beginning and *de jure* from 1894. Income and expense, the minutiae of printing, the style of binding, even the compilation of indexes for other contributors (a task that he professed to relish)—nothing was too small to escape his eyes or exhaust his patience.

[1] It is to be regretted that none of Maitland's letters to such scholars as Gierke and Liebermann seem to have survived.

These achievements must be set against the background of the years. Maitland never shunned the obligations of his Chair, not only as teacher and lecturer but in the intricacies and intrigues of University and College business. On Board and Syndicate his quick perception and power of decision were conspicuous; but the discharge of duties, as tiresome as they were demanding, taxed energies that could have been better spared for less ephemeral needs and for work that he alone could have done. The dissipation of effort he could ill afford. Even on his appointment as Downing Professor his health was precarious, and he grew relentlessly worse until in 1898 'a chorus of doctors bade him go abroad for the winter'.[1] Henceforth he could no longer retreat to Gloucestershire where, with his family, he usually stayed in Little Horsepools House, owned by his sister Selina, and where, tempered by walks through the woods and along the common, there was still 'the sense of urgent work'.[2] Each winter the price of life was exile and each summer conscience surrendered his vacation to Cambridge.

[1] Letter 236.
[2] Ermengard Maitland, *F. W. Maitland, A Child's-Eye View*, p. 13.

55. To Maxwell Lyte

[No original. Transcript in Public Record Office: P.R.O. 37, 16.]

c/o Herbert Fisher, Esq.[1]

19, Second Avenue,

Brighton

6 Jan. 1889.

DEAR MR. MAXWELL LYTE,

After weighing your kind proposal relating to the Petitions to Parliament, I think that I can accept it.[2] I can not, however, hope to begin work in London very seriously before the summer, and if, before the summer comes, I see any reason to fear that I shall be condemned to idleness, I will at once let you know of this. My first business must be to make myself familiar with the already printed Petitions of Edward I's reign. At Easter I may be ready to borrow the first of the MS volumes that you showed me, and I could do a great deal of the work of settling dates at Cambridge. Supposing that this volume of transcripts was found to contain the earliest extant petitions, I might then be able to get a volume ready in the course of this year.

I hope that my delay in answering your proposal has not put you to any inconvenience.

Believe me, etc.

F. W. MAITLAND

56. To Melville M. Bigelow

The West Lodge

Downing College

Cambridge

20 Jan. 1889

DEAR MR. BIGELOW,

The English 'Torts' is to hand and looks charming. Many congratulations on your exploit and many thanks for the dedication which is very gratifying to me.[3] I sincerely hope that the book will sell well.

I am glad to hear that you think of visiting England. Here at Downing I am provided with an official residence and I hope that I need not say either that its doors yearn to receive you or that its possessor will be grievously disappointed if you do not enter them. After so much correspondence we ought to meet.

Yours very truly

F. W. MAITLAND

[1] Herbert Fisher, the father of H. A. L. Fisher and of Mrs. Maitland, had been Secretary to the Prince of Wales (afterwards Edward VII) and Vice-Warden of the Stannaries, an office of the Duchy of Cornwall.

[2] On this proposal, resulting in M.'s edition of the Parliament Roll of 1305, see Cam, Introduction to *Selected Hist. Essays of F. W. Maitland*, xv–xx.

[3] The English edition of *Elements of the Law of Torts* was published by the Cambridge University Press in 1889 and dedicated to 'my friends F. W. Maitland and R. T. Wright'.

57. To James Bradley Thayer

The West Lodge
Downing College
Cambridge.

20 Jan. 1889

DEAR PROFESSOR THAYER,

I have been making holiday and have let my debts to you accumulate. So first let me thank you for your words in the Nation and then for the delightful commentary on them—

'Wal! its a mussy we've someun to tell us
The rights and the wrongs of these cases I vow'—

as a poet of your side sings.[1] Then I must tell you that I had not the good luck to meet your kinsman at St. Ives; and let me express my regret that you have been obliged to watch at a sick-bed.

Then again I must thank for two kind suggestions for my Placita. That about the proper translation of 'serviens' I should have taken had it come a little sooner. As to the jurors, the reason for my doing what I did was 'to affect the conscience of the reader with notice' of a question that is not easily solved from these early rolls, viz. as to whether the court had a standing jury, i.e. a jury sworn in at the opening of the sitting to make all presentments and find all issues, or whether, when issue was taken, a jury was sworn in just for that issue.[2]

I have had a pleasant offer of work for the Rolls Series, an edition of some of the many thousand Petitions in Parliament not yet printed; but I am a little uncertain as to whether I have time and strength for the work.[3]

I hope that you will like the fair of St. Ives when it comes to you; it has cheered the soul of the apprehensive Dove.[4]

With good wishes for the year,
Yours very truly
F. W. MAITLAND

58. To James Bradley Thayer

The West Lodge
Downing College
Cambridge.

16 Feb. 1889

DEAR MR. THAYER,

Many thanks for your letter and the papers enclosed with it. Bigelow's remarks will force me to an 'erratum'. How wonderfully keen he is. I can not however find room in the forthcoming volume for anything about forms of

[1] James Russell Lowell, *The Biglow Papers*, 1st Series, No. III.
[2] On this paragraph see S.S. Vol. 1, Case 3, and Introduction, xxii–xxiii.
[3] See Letter 55, *supra*.   [4] See Letter 54, *supra*.

action. That must stand over.[1] So again I have had to shirk the great problem of customary tenure. I have avoided that partly because I am having the advantage of reading in MS and proof a volume in which Vinogradoff is going deeply into the matter. I think that his book will let in a great deal of light on the manor.[2]

I am indeed proud to see the list of names that you have collected—proud but a little frightened, for I do not want to make your great lawyers sponsors for poor work and I have by no means done all that I wanted to do. I am glad to say that the Society has found another editor for its next volume. It is I think very important that we should not rely upon one man only, and I am not sorry to get a little time without proof sheets during which I can look around me.[3]

Have you any views about the 'Mirror'? I am inclined to think that when properly read it is a very instructive book and that the Society might do far worse than edit it. It is a protest by a conservative full of strange opinions about law and history. I believe that there is but one MS. of it and that in Cambridge.[4]

We are just going to make an attempt to reestablish 'the moot' in our law school.

By the way I have also to thank both you and Mr. Ames for your trouble over 'the words of court'. I have looked for the phrase in 'Wort und Form' without finding it—what a beautiful essay that is! I think that hardly anyone in England has read it.[5]

Believe me

Yours very truly

F. W. MAITLAND

59. To Paul Vinogradoff

[No original. Printed Fisher, *Memoir*, 49: no address heading, beginning or ending.]

20 Feb. 1889

You ask me about the Preface[6]—well, I think it grand work and on the whole I think it will attract readers because of its very strangeness; but you will let me say that it will seem strange to English readers, this attempt to connect the development of historical study with the course of politics; and it leads you into what will be thought paradoxes—e.g. it so happens that our leading 'village communists', Stubbs and Maine, are men of the most conservative type, while Seebohm, who is to mark conservative reaction, is a

---

[1] See Letter 60, *infra*.
[2] See Letters 49 to 51, *supra*.
[3] The 'list of names' is that of the Hon. Secretaries for the S.S. in the United States: see prospectus at end of S.S. Vol. 3, at p. 26. The editor of Vol. 3 was William Paley Baildon, Barrister-at-law, one of the original members of the Selden Society.
[4] See S.S. Vol. 7.
[5] See Letter 54, *supra*. M. refers to Brunner, *Wort und Form im altfranzösischen Process* in S.S. Vol. 2, p. 187.
[6] To the English edition of *Villainage in England*, still in preparation.

thorough liberal.[1] I am not speaking of votes at the polling booth but of radical and essential habits of mind. I think that you hardly allow enough for a queer twist of the English mind which would make me guess that the English believer in 'free village communities' would very probably be a conservative— I don't mean a Tory or an aristocrat, but a conservative. On the other hand with us the man who has the most splendid hopes for the masses is very likely to see in the past nothing but the domination of the classes. Of course this is no universal truth—but it comes in as a disturbing element.

60. To Melville M. Bigelow

The West Lodge
Downing College
Cambridge

24 Feb. 1889

DEAR MR. BIGELOW,

There have come to my hands some notes of yours upon the book that I am doing for the Selden Society.[2] I need hardly say that I have read them with much interest. On the present occasion I shall not be able to turn them to profit because I have already written and seen through the press an over long Introduction which I have devoted to matters other than 'the forms of action'. If however I again find myself dealing with manorial rolls I may have to speak about these forms and then I shall not forget what you wrote. Some of your notes came to me from Thayer, some from Dove; all of them are now with Dove and you may bring detinue against him.

You have found me out in a mistranslation of 'alia enormia ei intulit'; I am trying to put this right by means of a corrigendum. I hope that I have yet time to do this; anyway I am grateful to you for exposing the blunder.[3]

It is quite clear that 'defamation' was a cause of action in the manorial courts. Instances are beyond number, and oddly enough the words complained of are often such as, according to our notion, are not 'actionable per se'— 'meretrix' is quite cause enough and a common cause too.

If you read my Introduction you will see that I have adopted your opinion about distress for rent in arrear.[4] I feel pretty certain that you are right though it runs counter to a belief that is common enough in England.

[1] William Stubbs (1825–1901), Regius Professor of History, Oxford, 1866–84, then successively Bishop of Chester and of Oxford. Edited 19 vols. of the Rolls Series and *Select Charters*, first pub. 1870. His major original work was *Constitutional History of England*, 3 vols. (1873–8).
Sir Henry Sumner Maine (1822–88), Corpus Professor of Jurisprudence, Oxford, 1869–77, Master of Trinity Hall, Cambridge, 1877–88. Published *Ancient Law* (1861), *Village Communities* (1871), *Early History of Institutions* (1875), etc.
Frederick Seebohm (1833–1912), banker and historian. Published *The English Village Community* (1883), *The Tribal System in Wales* (1895), *Tribal Custom in Anglo-Saxon Law* (1902).
[2] See Letter 58, *supra*.
[3] See S.S. Vol. 2, p. 109, where M. corrects in a footnote and refers to Bigelow.
[4] S.S. Vol. 2, Introduction, lvii–lviii.

We have just tried a moot by way of experiment and on the whole it was a success.

I hope that your Torts is selling here. I have been reading it with pleasure, but the subject is one that I have not got to teach at present.

I look forward to seeing you at Cambridge this summer.

Yours very truly
F. W. MAITLAND

61. To Maxwell Lyte

The West Lodge
Downing College
Cambridge
9 March 1889

DEAR MR. MAXWELL LYTE,

I have no right to trespass upon your time, but if you can spare me a few words about some matters within your knowledge I shall be extremely grateful to you. My questions arise out of some work that I have got to do for an American journal; and I hope that you will not be offended at my asking them.[1]

When we met at Christmas you showed me the proof sheets of a book containing a calendar of early Chancery proceedings. Am I right in supposing that there are large quantities of such proceedings still unprinted?

Did you not also tell me that there are Books of the Privy Council extant later than those published by the Record Commissioners?

My third and last question relates to the Star Chamber. Our historians at present seem to have stopped very far short of a complete investigation of the development of this court. I want to know whether this is due to a dearth of materials. Did not the proceedings before the court get recorded at all?

I have got to speak of these things and do not wish to display gross ignorance, so I shall be very much obliged to you if at your leisure you can give me or put me in the way of an answer.

Believe me,
Yours very truly
F. W. MAITLAND.

62. To Paul Vinogradoff

[No original. Transcript by Fisher in Camb. Univ. MSS, and printed by him in *Memoir*, the bulk at pp. 50–1 and most of the penultimate paragraph at p. 111: the last two lines not printed. No beginning or ending.]

The West Lodge
12 March 1889

Your long letter[2] was very welcome. When I wrote I must have been in a bad temper and after I had written I wished to recall my letter. But now I no

---

[1] *The Materials for English legal history*, Pol. Science Quart., 1889, pp. 496–518, 628–47, New York: reprinted C.P. II. 1, and A–A.L.H. II. 53.
[2] Not extant: but from the contents of the present letter Vinogradoff would seem to have replied to Letter 59, *supra*.

longer regret what has brought from you so pleasant an answer. Really I
have no fear at all about the success of your book; if I had I would expatriate
myself. But it stands thus:— Introductions are of 'crucial importance', by
which I mean that they are of importance to critics, being often the only parts
of a book which casual reviewers care to read. As a matter of prudence therefore I put into an Introduction a passage about the book which I mean critics
to copy, and they catch the bait—it saves them trouble and mistakes. But your
'philosophy of history', I mean philosophy of historiography, will not lend
itself to such ready treatment and may give occasion to remarks as obvious
and as foolish as mine were. But I hope for better things. All that you say
about Stubbs and Seebohm and Maine is, I dare say, very true if you regard
them as European, not merely English, phenomena and attribute to them a
widespread significance—and doubtless it is very well that Englishmen should
see this. Still, looking at England only and our insular ways of thinking, I see
Stubbs and Maine as two pillars of conservatism, while as to Seebohm I
think that his book[1] is as utterly devoid of political importance as, shall I
say, Madox's *History of the Exchequer*. But you are cosmopolitan and I doubt
not that you are right. You are putting things in a new light—that is all. If
'the darkness comprehendeth it not', that is the darkness's fault.

And now as to Essay I I have nothing to withdraw or to qualify. I think it
superb, by far the greatest thing done for English legal history. I am looking
forward with the utmost anxiety to Essay II.

Pollock tells me that you are not coming to England this year. I hope that
this is not true. I very much want to see you again and I don't know that I
can wait for another year: this I say rather seriously and *only to you*. Many
things are telling me that I have not got unlimited time at my command and I
have to take things very easily.

Miss Maitland No. 2 is named Fredegond. After that, don't I belong to the
Germanistic school?

63. To James Bradley Thayer

The West Lodge
Downing College
Cambridge.

21 April 1889.

DEAR MR. THAYER,

I am on the point of sending you a MS. which contains some remarks on the
history of the Register of Original Writs and am going to ask you to be kind
enough to lay it before the editors of the Harvard Law Review. If they will
accept it, it is at their service; but I shall be quite prepared to hear that it is
too antiquarian for admission. I ought not to trouble you with this matter,
but I fear that I have already taxed Pollock's patience and driven away his

[1] *English Village Community* (1883).

readers, so with the instinct of a true bore I look out for other victims. Perhaps however I may say in self-defence that I do not think the contents of the ancient Registers have ever yet been described.[1]

I know that you are interested in the history of Evidence, and I hope some day to read a great book by you on that subject[2]; so at the risk of bearing stale news I will say that there are some curious passages in the complicated little literature which one may cover by the title 'Modus tenendi Curiam Baronis'. This literature consists of a number of little books of the 16th century, some of which contain more, some less—e.g. there are two Pynsons, 1516 (?) and 1520, a Redman, 1539, a Berthelet, 1544, an Elisabeth Pickering, a Robert Toye, 1546—the later the book the more it contains. In some of these one finds good matter about the 'secta' and wager of law, e.g. the rule that if the defendant insists on having the 'secta' examined, he does so at his peril— he can not after that wage his law. 'If plaintiff bring in 2 or 3 that will sweare that they were prevy to the contracte and give evydence as the plaintiff hath declaryd, in that case the plaintiff shall recover his demaunde with his damages'. Also this verse (if verse it may be called)—

> Qui legem vadiat, nisi lex in tempore fiat,
> Mox condemnetur, taxatio non sibi detur.

i.e. *semble* that he has to pay the damages as laid without taxation.

I have not got these books; some of them are precious; but I had a morning with them in Brit. Mus. and of course shall be happy to search them for anything that you want.[3]

Is there no hope of your being here this summer? I should be happy to welcome you to Cambridge the elder. I shall hardly get so far as St. Ives this year.

Yours very truly

F. W. MAITLAND

64. To O. C. Pell

The West Lodge
Downing College
Cambridge
28th April 1889

MY DEAR SIR,

I have been thoroughly enjoying your kind loan. In a very few days I will restore the chest and the key. If you have any special instructions as to how the case should be sent I will obey them.

I think that you said that the Littleport rolls were not your own. Do you think that I could obtain permission to make use of them in one of the Selden

[1] *The History of the Register of Original Writs* appeared in Harv. L. Rev. Vol. III, pp. 97–115, 167–79, 212–25, and was reprinted in C.P. II, 110–73 and in A-A.L.H. II. 549–96.
[2] Thayer published his *Preliminary Treatise on Evidence at the Common Law* in 1898.
[3] On these books see Introductory Note to S.S. Vol. 4. The verses appear on p. 17.

Society's volumes?[1] In the hope of obtaining such a permission I have been making abstracts from them, but of course I will at once destroy my copies if the owner objects to my keeping them and of course I shall be very willing to submit the transcripts to him before he licenses their publication. These Littleport rolls are of great interest to me because they record so many actions of debt, covenant and trespass. Either the men of Littleport were singularly litigious or the steward of Edward II's time was singularly careful. I have learnt a great deal from your fine set of Wilburton rolls also. Certainly your manor has a very continuous history.[2]

What you say about the sale of services at Wilburton is very interesting. I see at Littleport the bishop has begun to commute the *opera* for money rents in Edward I's time.

When I next see Skeat I will ask him about 'wara',[3] but I fear that etymology can seldom do much to help in the solution of those problems upon which you are engaged; words so easily acquire secondary and technical meanings. Your theory about the 'wara' is certainly valuable and seems to me to fit the Wilburton case beautifully.

I trust that when the rolls return to you they will be none the worse for my use of them.

> Believe me
> Yours very truly
> F. W. MAITLAND

65. To P. E. Dove

> The West Lodge
> Downing College
> Cambridge
> *29 April 1889*

MY DEAR DOVE,

I send herewith my subscription to the Selden Society for this year, also a second guinea in consideration of which I hope that you will allow a copy of vol. 2 to be sent to 'Paul Vinogradoff, The University, Moscow'. I don't know whether you ever send copies to foreign periodicals, but I think that a notice in the Zeitschrift der Savigny Stiftung might do us some good. The editor is Dr. Heinrich Brunner, Luther Strasse, Berlin. If he would say a few words some German libraries might subscribe.

When I was last in London I saw Baildon. I think that we have got a very good man in him and am looking forward eagerly to his volume.[4]

---

[1] S.S. Vol. 4, Preface and pp. 107–47.
[2] See *The History of a Cambridgeshire Manor*, E.H.R., July 1894: C.P. II. 366–406: Cam, *Selected Hist. Essays of F. W. Maitland*, 16–40.
[3] See S.S. Vol. 4, pp. 108–9: *D.B. and Beyond*, 123: Vinogradoff, *Villainage in England*, 243.
[4] S.S. Vol. 3.

I have no wish to force on the society a second manorial volume and of course it will be for you to ascertain the wishes of the members; but should you want such a volume I think that I could make it better than No. 1, for I should not again deluge the book with common forms but could take a knowledge of these for granted. I have now in my possession a beautiful set of rolls of one of the Ely manors and am making extracts in the hope that at some time or another they will be useful.[1]

Believe me
Yours very truly
F. W. MAITLAND

66. To O. C. Pell

The West Lodge
Downing College
Cambridge
3 May 1889

MY DEAR SIR,

I am once more in your debt—this time for permission to make use of the Wilburton and Littleport rolls[2] and for your paper on weights. I regret to say that your interesting conclusions are quite beyond my criticism. Nor do I know of any one here who would be able to say much to the point, though I think that Dr. Cunningham of Trinity[3] would be interested in the discussion. As to 'wara', though I have little right to speak of such a matter, I suspect that, be the root of it what it may, the word came to England from France. Ducange[4] has some French instances—though not very many—such as 'une piece de terre estart en waret'. The inability of Frenchmen to pronounce a *w* seems to have led to such forms as 'jachere', 'gachere' and so forth. I don't think that it meant waste; it seems primarily to have meant fallow, and I think that this is quite consistent with your theory as to what so much 'wara' really was. I should doubt it having any reference to inhabitants or community. Is it not the case that 'ware' for inhabitants, folk, only occurs as a termination?

Believe me
Yours very truly
F. W. MAITLAND

[1] See Letter 64, *supra.*
[2] See Letter 64, *supra.*
[3] William Cunningham (1849–1919), economic historian. Fellow of Trinity College, Cambridge; Professor at King's College, London, 1891–7; Archdeacon of Ely, 1907. His major work was *The Growth of English Industry and Commerce* (1882).
[4] C. Dufresne Du Cange, *Glossarium mediae et infimae Latinitatis* (1840–50). On 'wara see Letter 64, *supra.*

67. To James Barr Ames

[Printed C.L.J., Vol. II (1924), pp. 9–11.]

The West Lodge,
Downing College,
Cambridge,
3 May, 1889.

MY DEAR SIR,

I should like to tell you, but hardly can, how much real pleasure I have got out of your Disseisin of Chattels.[1] For a long time past my mind has been flickering round that subject; but I have not had the courage to write about it. Thus some, though by no means all, of your authorities were familiar to me, but I never hoped to see them arrayed in so solid a phalanx. A great deal of what you say I at once accept. In the first place I think it certain that, when once the owner of a chattel had his property reduced to a mere right of action, that right, like all other rights of action, was inalienable. In the second place I think it highly probable that if he bailed the chattel all that was left to him was a right of action, though this rule was modified at a remote time, modified by allowing him in many cases an action against the trespasser who took the chattel from the bailee. In the third place it seems fairly clear that the owner whose chattel was taken from him by a thief or other trespasser had no alienable right.

But there are two conclusions towards which the Year Books seem to lead us and from which I shrink. The first of these is that the owner who lost a chattel had no action against the finder for its recovery. The second is that the owner whose chattel was taken from him by trespass had no action for recovering it from any bailee or vendee claiming under the trespasser, or from the second trespasser who took it from the first. Now it may be that this was so, and I must confess that the evidence known to me is in your favour. Still I cannot bring myself to believe that all this is the natural outcome of the English substantive law, that it truly expresses the notion that our ancestors had of the ownership of goods. The typical action, one may say, of early English law is the action for the recovery of stolen cattle which have already passed into the second, third or fourth hand. Positive legislation is necessary to prevent the voucher of an infinite number of warrantors. Glanville (x. 15) still knows this action, and so does Bracton (f. 150 b), the action for *bona adirata*. Why do we not hear more of it?[2] The answer that occurs to me is—because it goes on in the local courts. And similarly, when goods have been lost, it is in some court baron that the man of the thirteenth century will sue for them. To deny the owner a recuperatory action against (1) his bailee's vendee or bailee, (2) the trespasser who takes from the bailee, is, as I understand, quite in accordance with the old French and old German law; but I have in vain been reading

---

[1] Harv. L. Rev. III. 23: *Lectures on Legal History*, 172.
[2] See Ames, *Lectures on Legal History*, 80–3.

through books in number for the purpose of finding some refusal of an action against (1) a thief's or trespasser's vendee or bailee [there being no question of market overt], (2) a second thief or second trespasser, (3) a finder or one who claims under a finder. I can't help thinking that the law of the King's courts is only a part of the law, and that the lawyers in those courts, having to do only with the remedies there given, get into a way of speaking about 'property' which really is misleading. I cannot otherwise bring the rule about market overt into harmony with what they say. As to the fact that there was the greatest difficulty in preventing the stolen goods becoming forfeited to the King, I am inclined to regard this rather as a fruit of the King's power than as justified by any of the ordinary rules of law—it was ill arguing with a King.

Perhaps I ought not to burden you with these loose remarks, especially as I have to confess over and over again that you have the books, at all events the later books, at your back; but I am so interested by your excellent paper that I should much like to know your opinion as to the early history of the very curious state of things that you have expounded:—Is it the natural outcome of very ancient ideas of 'property,' or is it due to the fact that our King's courts begin by administering only a part of the law, which part, however, is in course of time regarded, and indeed actually becomes, the whole, owing to the decadence of the local tribunals. In the former case we have much to teach the Germans that they don't know. So I am asking for more, and have to hope that you will not think me impertinent for so doing.[1]

A book that has taught me a great deal is *Jobbé-Duval* on *Revendication des Meubles*, Paris, 1880. If you have not yet seen it, you will, I think, enjoy it.

With regard to what you say about trespass, I can add this—that the writ of trespass does not appear in MS. *Registra Brevium* of Henry III's reign, nor even in all the *Registra* of Edward I's. I have little doubt that you are right in thinking that it became a writ of course late in the former reign. I have sent some tidings of these early Registers to Professor Thayer, thinking it just possible that your Harvard magazine would print my notes; but I don't want to blight its promise or check its circulation.[2]

I am delighted in particular by the part of your paper that deals with 're-plevin'[3]; much of it is new to me, but it accords well with the little that I knew.

Is it altogether useless to express a hope that you may think the old Cambridge worth a visit?

Believe me,

Yours very truly,

F. W. MAITLAND.

[1] On all the questions thus raised by M. see letter from Ames to M. printed C.L.J., Vol. II (1924), pp. 11–14, though for the date of this letter see Letter 83, *infra*. See also *P. and M.* ii, Book II, Chap. IV, s. 7.
[2] See Letter 63, *supra*.
[3] Ames, *Lectures on Legal History*, 181–5.

68. To Melville M. Bigelow

[Post-card: date from post mark.]

Downing
June 5, 1889.

MY DEAR BIGELOW,

One line to tell you that a post card from F. Pollock has been sent to the Randolph[1]; another to assure you that to have had you and Mrs. Bigelow as my guests has been one of the greatest pleasures of my life.

Yours very truly
F. W. MAITLAND

69. To O. C. Pell

Downing College
Cambridge
15 June 1889

MY DEAR SIR,

I am sending herewith the key of your deed box and when I hear that you have received it I will send the box itself. Have you any instructions as to the way in which it should be sent?

I trust that the rolls are none the worse for having been in my hands, but must confess that the small label that was on the key got broken and that I have put a new one in its stead. I hope that you will not think this accident serious.

And now I must thank you once more very heartily for what has been to me a great treat. I have made extracts from the Littleport rolls and notes on the Wilburton rolls. The special point of interest in the latter is to my mind that they prove that the labour services, week work as well as boon work, were largely done in kind so late as Henry IV, a full century after the time when, according to Thorold Rogers,[2] such services were generally commuted. Also it is very interesting to see the old 'full lands' and 'cottaries' existing in Henry VII's day.[3] As to your theory about 'wara', there can I think be no doubt whatever that 12 acres of 'wara' were really 24 acres; this seems amply proved.[4]

As some small return for your very great kindness may I ask you to accept a copy of 'Bracton's Note Book'? I hardly dare think that it will interest you but it is all that I have to send.

Believe me
Yours very truly
F. W. MAITLAND

[1] Hotel, Oxford.
[2] James Edwin Thorold Rogers (1823–90), Drummond Professor of Political Economy, Oxford. His main published work was *History of Agriculture and Prices*, 6 vols., 1866–87.
[3] See *History of a Cambridgeshire Manor*, C.P. II. 368–70.
[4] See Letter 64, *supra*.

70. To Maxwell Lyte

[No original. Transcript in Public Record Office, ref. P.R.O., 37, 16.]

Downing College
Cambridge

27 June 1889

Dear Mr. Maxwell Lyte,

After thinking carefully and anxiously about the work that has to be done upon the Petitions to Parliament, I am persuaded that I ought to give you an opportunity of reconsidering the step that you have taken in committing that work to me.[1] If it turns out that there is no evidence of the date of the petitions except the character of the handwriting and the names of the persons mentioned in them, there is really but one course open for the editor if he is to produce a really satisfactory result, namely, to date to the best of his ability all the petitions before he sends any of them to the printer. Some of course he might for a while put on one side as being obviously of recent date, but many thousand he would have to examine very carefully, hunting in many indexes for the names of the persons mentioned. I very much doubt whether he would be able to do all that he ought to do for more than five or six petitions per diem. I think that to date 1000 petitions would be a good year's work. Now really I cannot hope to give more than two months a year to work in the Record Office. It seems therefore that, if the course that I have indicated is to be pursued, I should have nothing for the printer for the next five or six years. Of this you and the public would justly complain, and I should not be able to say anything in defence, for indubitably there are plenty of men who would give you ten months in the year, whereas I can give but two, and men better qualified for the task than I am. If, therefore, I find that there is really nothing for it but to go through all the petitions, I shall be obliged to ask you to give me my dismissal.

I still hope for better things. The assignment of dates by the light of internal evidence only can not possibly lead to a very satisfactory result. In many cases the editor, however skilled, would be obliged to leave a margin of twenty or thirty years. I still hope therefore to find that the dates which have been put upon the transcripts were due to external evidence. If that be so, these dates are of the utmost importance, and I think that the right course would then be to publish, in the first instance, the petitions concerning which we have this external evidence, leaving the other petitions alone for the present. If what I call the external evidence be trustworthy, then we may be able to assign several thousand petitions to particular years, while if we must trust only to internal evidence we may think ourselves lucky if we can pin down a petition to a particular decade.

The first question, therefore, that has to be decided is this (so it seems to me)—Is any, and what degree of credence to be given to the dates placed in the transcripts? It is to this question that I propose to address myself. If I

---

[1] See Letters 55, *supra*, and 73, *infra*.

become persuaded that Sir Francis Palgrave[1] (or some one else) took the dates from labels attached to the files or similar external sources, and if you agree with me that in that case it will be best to print, in the first place, the petitions to which dates have been thus assigned, then I see no reason why I should not get a few volumes printed within a reasonable time; but if it falls out otherwise (and I must be careful not to argue myself into a pleasant belief) then I fear that I shall have to ask you to fill my place with some one who can work at his task continuously.

I shall be sorry to do this, both because it may cause you some trouble and vexation and because I should like the work, while I regard the pay as more than handsome; but I should not like to have before me the alternative of publishing nothing for six years or of being hurried into producing some slovenly work. So I shall regard my work in August as experimental. I will try to record the results of it in such a way that they might be used by a successor. This, of course, must be by your leave. If, after what I have said, you think it better to have done with me at once, I shall most certainly have no cause to say that you are not in the right.

Do you think that there is any inhabitant of the Record Office who can remember the petitions being taken off their files? If so, his testimony would be valuable.

If I call at the Record Office next Tuesday, may I be allowed to carry away the second volume (No. 93) of the Transcripts of Petitions?

I regret that I have to trouble you with so long a letter.

Yours very truly

F. W. MAITLAND

71. To Maxwell Lyte

[No original. Transcript in Public Record Office, ref. P.R.O., 37, 16.]

St. Olave's
West Malvern
7th Augt. 1889

DEAR MR. MAXWELL LYTE,

I have stayed away from London longer than I had intended, but chiefly in order that I might begin my campaign against the Petitions in Parliament with greater vigour. I mean to begin next week and now write, in the expectation that you may be taking a holiday, to ask for certain privileges at the Record Office.

I want, in the first place, to be allowed to borrow the volumes of transcripts; I will never keep away any more than two at any one time. I hope also that the

---

[1] (1788–1861), Deputy Keeper of the Public Records from 1838–61. Edited *Parliamentary Writs* (1827–34), *Rotuli Curiae Regis*, covering period 6 Rich. I to John (1836), etc., and published *Calendar to the Patent Rolls of Edward V and Richard III* (1848), etc. On his transcripts of the petitions see M. *Memoranda de Parliamento*, Intro. xxvi–xxviii, lv–lvi, lxii–lxv.

'three documents rule' may be relaxed in my favour. I will not abuse the concession, but a strict observance of the rule sometimes occasions a loss of time. I fear that it is useless to ask for the use of ink and will do my best with pencil.

I have gone through the volumes of transcripts that I took away with the Calendarium Genealogicum, and am persuaded that the dates assigned in red ink were assigned for good reason. Also I have lighted on proof—in an old Quarterly Review—that Palgrave found the petitions in dated bundles. My present plan is to print first the petitions of Edward I's reign which are thus assigned to particular years, and then all petitions which appear from internal evidence to belong to that reign. I think that there can be no harm in printing *all* the petitions that belong to this early period. As regards later times, I am inclined to think that what is most wanted is a full and well arranged calendar giving the substance of every petition and the very words of every petition that is of public importance. Very many of these petitions have no interest whatever save for genealogists, and I am afraid if we began passing them out in full the Treasury might stop the work and so, for a second time, prevent the publication of really valuable documents. But of this I can speak to you hereafter; at present I intend to get together all that seems to belong to Edward I, and, as I have hopes of securing Baildon as an assistant, I look to get something done within a reasonable time.

Believe me, etc.

F. W. MAITLAND.

72. To Paul Vinogradoff

[This fragment is a transcript by Fisher in Camb. Univ. MSS, but not printed in the *Memoir*. It is printed by Professor Cam in her Introduction to *Selected Hist. Essays of F. W. Maitland*, at p. xv.]

Downing

27 Aug. 1889

I have had a good holiday and now am going to try to do a little work in the Record Office. I want just to start the edition of the 10,000 odd petitions to King and Council, but when it is well started I hope to get out of it.

73. To Maxwell Lyte

[No original. Transcript in Public Record Office, ref. P.R.O., 37, 16.]

Downing College

Cambridge

1 Oct. 1889

DEAR MR. MAXWELL LYTE,

I fear that before this letter is finished it will have grown to a formidable size, but at your leisure perhaps you will read it; for I am obliged to suggest to you another change of plan and must ask your opinion about it.

As yet I have found it impossible to make a very serious attack upon the mass of petitions, for the new set was not ready for me and divers other classes of documents that I wanted, in particular the Privy Seals and the Chancery Miscellaneous Portfolios were 'under arrangement'. However, I do not think that I have lost time.

There is one very early Roll of Parliament that has not yet been printed, that namely for the Lenten Parliament of 33 Edward I (Feb. 1305) and it is a very interesting roll. The reason why it was not printed was, I take it, this:— such other Parliament Rolls of Edward I as are extant were at the Chapter House; they are now contained in one of the Chapter House Boxes and I have examined them; on the other hand, the roll of which I speak was among the Q.R. Anc. Miscell.[1] I believe that even Palgrave when he printed the Parliamentary Writs was not aware of the existence of this roll, for he has transcribed from a secondary source, the Vetus Codex,[2] a document for which this roll is the primary source. However, the roll was discovered and is fully described in one of the MS. Indexes of the Q.R. Miscellanies. I say that it has not been printed and this is true of the roll as a whole; but selections from it have been printed. The maker of the Vetus Codex picked cases out of the roll. I think that his mark is still apparent in the margin, for the cases that appear in the V.C. have a mark against them (∴) which looks ancient. Ryley[3] (p. 240) printed what he found in the V.C. and the Editor of the Rolls of Parliament printed what he found in Ryley (p. 159); he does not even profess to have gone back as far as the V.C. The selection of cases thus printed is but small, and the many Irish and Scottish petitions were utterly neglected.

Now it seems to me that an opportunity is thus given for the publication of one of the very oldest Rolls of Parliament in an instructive form; for I should propose to illustrate the enrolments of the petitions and responses (1) by the petitions themselves which in many cases are extant, (2) by the writs whereby effect was given to the responses.

(1) The petition, as enrolled, is but a Latin abstract of the petition itself, which is usually in French. By comparing the two we can get a curious insight into the manner in which the business was conducted. And I think that some important points will be brought out; e.g. that, although these petitions are said to be heard at or in a Parliament, they are addressed to the King or to the King and Council.[4]

(2) The response to the petition seldom, if ever, does all that the petitioner wants. It becomes the authority for some writ or some charter, and the Patent, Close, Liberate and Charter Rolls, the Exchequer Memoranda and even the Coram Rege Rolls are full of entries which are the result of responses to petitions—such entries generally bear the words 'per petitionem de consilio.'

[1] Queen's Remembrancer Ancient Miscellanea.
[2] Alternatively called *Liber Irrotulamentorum de Parliamentis*: see M. *Memoranda de Parliamento*, Intro. App. IV.
[3] For William Ryley see M. *Memoranda de Parliamento*, Intro. I, and Cooper, *Public Records*, Chap. XX.
[4] See Cam, *Selected Hist. Essays of F. W. Maitland*, Intro. xviii.

I have been through most of the rolls of 33 Edward I and can say that the relation between the response and the consequent writ throws a great deal of light on the meaning of the response and the connection between the different parts of the governmental machinery.

It seems to me that one Parliament Roll, edited with the original petitions and the consequent writs, would be an excellent forerunner for a calendar of petitions. My notion is that the entries on the Roll should be printed in large type and that after each entry the petition and the writ, if discoverable, should be given in smaller type. If the petition as stated on the Roll was just a translation of the real petition, I should simply say so in English, and I should only give references to the writs that were of an interesting kind; in the case of charters or lengthy writs an abstract of them might be enough.

As I have said, a selection of the entries on this Roll has been printed, first by Ryley and then in the 'Rolls of Parliament'. This of course raises a difficulty. I did not want to print anything that had been printed before. On the other hand another imperfect representation of the Roll seemed unsatisfactory. The plan which I adopted was that of printing in full what had not been printed and giving a brief English statement of the entries that were in print. But having pursued this plan for a while I find that the result does not look well. In many cases the original petition which forms the basis for one of the printed entries is extant, and I feel that the work is mutilated if I give the petition and send the reader to another book for the inrolment. The amount of the matter in question fills 25 pages in Ryley, 12 pages in the Rolls of Parliament. If you accept my proposal, I shall have to ask you whether you would object to the reproduction of this already printed matter.

I have said that in many cases the original petitions are extant, but I must ask for some help in finding them. I found transcripts of them in Vol. 151 of the Record Commissioners Transcripts. No date is there given to them, but this volume proves that the petitions belonging to the parliament with which I am dealing were still lying together when the transcripts were made and were not then in the mass of Parliamentary Petitions. At the beginning of the volume is a pencil note:—'Only two or three of these transcripts have been identified; the originals are not with the set J.R.A.[1] 6/3/69.' I have some hope that this batch of petitions may yet be found existing as a batch. Bain[2] seems to have found some of them which relate to Scotland in 'Chancery Miscellaneous Portfolios, No. 41'; but on asking for this set of documents I was told that they were 'under re-arrangement.' If the contents of this portfolio are not already dispersed, I should much like to see them, for I think that the volume of transcripts affords strong evidence that until lately the petitions belonging to this parliament were in a bundle by themselves. Of course, when the new set of petitions is ready, I will look through it, though I shall not be able to do this

[1] Note by unknown hand in margin of letter—'John R. Atkins': see Letter 108, *infra*.
[2] Joseph Bain edited *Calendar of Documents relating to Scotland, preserved in Her Majesty's Record Office, London, A.D. 1108–1509*, 4 vols. Edinburgh (1881–8). In his Introduction to *Memoranda de Parliamento* M. thanks him 'for valuable assistance in Scottish affairs'.

until the Christmas vacation; but I cannot help hoping that in some way or another the source of the volume of transcripts may be traced.

With the work of copying the parliament roll I am far advanced, and Baildon will be able to copy the rest of it. In any case this work will not be thrown away. But I should like at your leisure to have your decision on the proposal that I have made. I have not estimated accurately the amount of matter that I should have if I illustrated the entries in the roll by the corresponding petitions and writs, but I think that it would fill a volume of the Rolls Series, though not a very large one. I have also seen so much of the various rolls and other documents of this 33rd year of Edward I—the 'privy seals' which may be important I could not see—that I could get the book ready without any great delay.[1]

I cannot help thinking that this proposal is worthy of your consideration and that one roll of parliament properly illustrated by petitions and writs would be of much greater historical value than a mere collection of petitions conjecturally dated. Also I am coming to see more and more clearly that the work of publishing and calendaring the petitions will hardly be done unless some one will give the whole of his time to it; indeed it will hardly be done except by some one in your office. There are petitions lying about in many quarters; for instance I came across a bundle of petitions of 30 Edw. I among the Q.R. Miscellanies, a bundle which certainly ought not to be broken up. Without continuous labour and free access to all classes of documents little can be done. Besides all this, I feel sure that in most cases the date of a petition might be accurately fixed if one had the leisure to begin by indexing all the entries on the Patent, Close and other Rolls which have the formula 'per petitionem de consilio', while I can scarcely hope to do much towards so long an operation which, after all, would be but a preliminary occupation; and yet it seems so useless to be speculating about dates which might be accurately fixed.

However, all this I submit to your judgment, and if you wish me to go on with the calendar I will do my best.

Our term is now beginning; but I am often able to spend some hours in London and, should you wish to speak to me about this matter, I shall find no difficulty in waiting on you and shall be glad to do so.

Believe me, etc.

F. W. MAITLAND

74. To Melville M. Bigelow

The West Lodge
Downing College
Cambridge
5th Oct. 1889

MY DEAR BIGELOW,

I ought to have written to you before now, for I am in your debt. We have had a pleasant summer, first in Gloucestershire, then at Malvern, and then I

---

[1] It was published in the Rolls Series in 1893.

got a little work done in London while my wife and children were near at hand in the parts of Surrey; and now, as a friend of mine says, the term cometh when no man can work. I am however going to try a little Americanism with Finch's Cases on Contract,[1] but whether I shall be able to induce our shy undergraduates to talk is a doubtful question. I had hoped to see Holmes while he was in England for I am among his worshippers, but owing to one thing and another I could not manage it. This morning I have received a letter from H. W. Fuller asking me to contribute to the Green Bag,[2] and I must try to find something for him, especially as he promises me the back numbers which I shall much like to have. Wright tells me, and I am truly glad of the news, that you are meditating a small book on Fraud to be published by our Press; I much hope that this scheme will not fall through. Is it possible for me to acquire the 'Am. Law Rev.'? In your leading cases you cite thence an article by N. St. John Green on the history of defamation.[3] I should very much like to see this; for I can not find that any Englishman has dealt with the early history of the subject, and investigations among the manorial rolls have persuaded me that there is an interesting story to be told.[4] If then you could without much trouble find me a copy of this number I shall be very glad; though probably I could see it at the Museum.

I trust that you and Mrs. Bigelow were refreshed by your visit and that the rough passage home was but a temporary evil. My wife sends her love to Mrs. Bigelow.

I am just now feeling wondrous well and quite hope to get through term without any break down.

Believe me
Yours very truly
F. W. MAITLAND

75. To John Chipman Gray

Downing College
Cambridge
27 Oct. 1889

MY DEAR SIR,

I have put off until now my answer to your kind note[5]; because I did not want to say that I had nothing fit for the Green Bag and, as you were kind enough not only to ask for a contribution but also to send the said receptacle to my great enjoyment, I felt bound to make some effort before saying that I could do nothing for you. Perhaps I had better have sent an immediate but polite refusal. As it is I have strung together some notes which you may or

---

[1] *A Selection of Cases on the English Law of Contract* (1886), by Gerard Brown Finch, Fellow of Queens' College, Cambridge. See also Letter 78, *infra.*
[2] [AULT. Published monthly in Boston from 1889 to 1914.] See Letter 78, *infra.*
[3] (1872) 6 Am. Law. Rev. 593.
[4] See *P. and M.* ii. 536–8.
[5] Not extant. On the letter as a whole see Letters 74, *supra*, and 78, *infra.*

may not think too ponderous or too stale or too inaccurate for your magazine. But it is term time and I have not much leisure. At any rate you can regard my paper as a testimony of my gratefulness to you and my respect for the G.B. and its contents.

Yours very truly

F. W. MAITLAND

76. To James Bradley Thayer
[Post-card.]

Downing Coll.
Cambridge
31 Oct. 1889

I am exceedingly glad of your post-card even though it brings to naught my speculation about the words of court—as I must confess that it does.[1]

As regards the little manorial treatises of which I spoke and about which you asked, I am putting their titles, dates and publishers' names into an article which will I believe appear in the next number of the Political Science Quarterly.[2]

Yours very truly

F. W. MAITLAND

77. To Maxwell Lyte

[No original. Transcript in Public Record Office, ref. P.R.O. 37, 16.]

The West Lodge
Downing College
Cambridge
24 Nov. 1889

DEAR MR. MAXWELL LYTE,

I am much obliged to you for your letter and extremely glad of the news that it contains.[3] I hope before Christmas to have a week in the Record Office and to find a good many of the petitions that I want. What will at present give me the best help will be a sight of the 'new set' of petitions, and I hope that you will be able to trust me with such of them as are already bound. I want to go through them rapidly, taking note of those that belong to my parliament but leaving the work of copying until I can form some estimate of their number. The transcription of the Parliament Roll is nearly finished and, as I am making

---

[1] Thayer's card is not extant: but see Letter 54, *supra*, and *P. and M.* ii. 608, note 3.
[2] See Letter 63, *supra*, and *The Materials for English legal History*, Pol. Sci. Quart. (1889) and C. P. II, at pp. 49–50.
[3] Letter not extant; but it presumably approved M.'s proposals as set out in Letter 73, *supra*.

an alphabetical index of the petitions that I want, I hope to be able to work rapidly so soon as I can examine the new set.

Yours very truly

F. W. MAITLAND

78. To Melville M. Bigelow

The West Lodge
Downing College
Cambridge

24 Nov. 1889

MY DEAR BIGELOW,

I am extremely obliged to you for the number of the American Law Review. I fear that I must return it as my prospect of seeing America seems remote enough. I have enjoyed the article on Slander and Libel which is an able performance[1]; but as you know I don't think that it contains the whole truth. Under pleasant pressure on the part of the editor of the Green Bag, I have put together some remarks on Slander in the Local Courts, which he will I believe print in January[2]—I had to put them together hurriedly for this term I have been busy.

We have just been 'Americanizing our institutions', i.e. holding a moot. The theme was—offer of contract—acceptance posted—attempt to revoke acceptance by anticipatory telegram. I was solicitor for the party who said 'Contract', Kenny for the party who said 'Revocation'. E. C. Clark presided— to my surprise and delight—Wright, Finch, Mayley were among the judges; the advocates were bachelors and undergraduates—the Court was equally divided. Altogether it was a pretty exercise and we must have more like it.[3]

Yes, Pollock and I have mapped out a big work, too big I fear for the residue of our joint lives and the life of the survivor. Vol. I is to bring things down to the end of Henry III.[4] I am already struggling with a chapter on tenure but can not make progress for the ground is full of unsuspected pitfalls. Also I am seeing to an edition of a roll of parliament for 1305 which has hitherto lain unprinted. But I have been keeping wondrous well this autumn and am not without hopes of getting a few things done.

I hear from Wright that our Press is to have a little book on Fraud from your pen—I hope that this is true. I suppose you know that Wright has a daughter; if not, then my wife bids me tell you to tell your wife that this is so. She also

---

[1] See Letter 74, *supra*.

[2] [AULT. *Slander in the Middle Ages*, Green Bag, Vol. II.]

[3] Edwin Charles Clark, Regius Professor of Civil Law, Cambridge, 1872–1914, Fellow of Trinity College and later of St. John's College, Cambridge. Published *Cambridge Legal Studies* (1888), *History of Roman Private Law* (1906), etc.

Courtney Stanhope Kenny (1847–1930), Fellow of Downing College, Cambridge. Succeeded M. as University Reader in English Law, 1888, and as Downing Professor, 1907–18. Published *Cases on Criminal Law* (1901), *Outlines of Criminal Law* (1902), *Cases on the Law of Tort* (1904), etc.

Mayley has not been identified.

[4] *P. and M. Hist. of Eng. Law* was ultimately confined to the end of Henry III's reign.

sends her love to Mrs. Bigelow and we trust that you are finding your new home pleasant.

Good bye.

Yours very truly

F. W. MAITLAND

79. To H. A. L. Fisher

The West Lodge
Downing College
Cambridge

26 Jan. 1890

MY DEAR HERBERT,

I must write a few lines to congratulate you on your article in the English Historical Review and am very glad that the editor has given it the place of honour and feel sure that it must deserve its place; at all events it has given me a great deal of pleasure. Your stay in Paris has enabled you to write about Fustel in a way that very few Englishmen could have done, for the reader is made to feel that you are 'in the swim' and can judge the work from the proper point of view. It was news and good news to me that there are three more volumes to come, for I feel that the success of Fustel's method must depend on his power of explaining the feudal period without recourse to any of those elements of 'Teutonic freedom' which he has rejected.[1]

I have been making use of the list of French books which we compiled at Brighton, endeavouring to secure them for the University Library, but have myself had little time for reading, for I have had many lectures to prepare and the college accounts to audit. The sudden death of my uncle[2] will give me many things to do during the next weeks.

If in the course of your studies you come across any French information about the limitation of the feudal military service to forty days in the year and the acceptance of money (*auxilium exercitus*) in lieu of such service, will you kindly make a note of it for me?[3] These matters are giving me a good deal of trouble. I think that you told me that Delisle's essay on the state of the Norman peasantry is hard to get.[4] I should much like to have a copy of it,

---

[1] Fisher, after election to a Prize Fellowship at New College, Oxford, in 1888, went to Paris in October 1889 to sit at the feet of French historians, esp. of the medievalist Fustel de Coulanges who, in contrast to the 'Germanists', found the origin of medieval society in Western Europe in Roman influences. Fustel's *Histoire des Institutions de la France* in 6 vols. included *Les Origines du Système féodal*. Fisher's essay on Fustel appeared in E.H.R., Jan. 1890.

[2] Frederic William Daniell (1829–90), M.'s maternal uncle.

[3] See *P. and M.* i. 254 and 267.

[4] Léopold Delisle, palaeographist and medievalist, was appointed in 1852 to the manuscript dept. of the then Imperial Library, became its head in 1874 and remained there until 1905. The 'essay on the state of the Norman peasantry' was originally published in 1851. See Powicke, *Modern Historians and the Study of History*, Chap. VII.

and should one fall in your way will you secure it for me? But please do not put yourself to any pains about this.

I understand that you have preferred history to philosophy. I do not think that you will regret the choice, though certainly there was much to be said on each side of the question.

F. Pollock is very full of Fustel's last book. I hope that he will not rush from one extreme to another.[1]

> Florence sends you her love.
> Believe me
> Yours affectionately
>
> F. W. MAITLAND

80. To Melville M. Bigelow

> The West Lodge
> Downing College
> Cambridge
> *16 Feb. 1890*

MY DEAR BIGELOW,

Many thanks for the last proof for the time being of your amazing industry, the fifth edition of your Estoppel.[2] I am very glad indeed to have it and think that I now have all your books.

This abominable influenza has been giving us trouble; first it seized all our servants at one and the same time; then it attacked my wife, lastly our eldest child. I am glad to say that they are all on the way to recovery, but recovery from this pest seems a long process. Hitherto I have escaped. I am now in the middle of our busiest term and lecturing daily; but the middle is past and I am beginning to look forward to Easter and pleasanter occupations.

Our lads are being diligently taught out of your little book on Torts and I make no doubt are enjoying it. We are to have a moot this week, but the subject is not a very interesting one; about a gift to husband, wife and a third person. I myself wanted to raise a question of 'privileged occasion'.

I wish that we could have you again here this next summer term. My wife sends her love to Mrs. Bigelow and will send daisies so soon as there are any that are in bloom.[3]

> Yours always most truly
>
> F. W. MAITLAND

[1] From 'Germanist' to 'Romanist'.
[2] [AULT. *The Law of Estoppel and its Application in Practice* (5th ed. Boston, 1890).]
[3] In a later letter to Mrs. Bigelow Mrs. Maitland refers to 'the little daisy that does not grow with you': Boston Univ. Law Rev. xxxvii. 308.

81. To H. A. L. Fisher

The West Lodge
Downing College
Cambridge

11 March 1890

MY DEAR HERBERT,

I have left your pleasant note unanswered for two days because one puts off evil moments, and I feel the moment an evil one when I have to say 'no' to this delightful project; but the truth is that daily lectures have left me weary and I feel that a week of rapid movement might do me a good deal of harm. I am obliged to be careful of all sorts of details of which it is impossible to be careful in hotels and railway trains. So I fear that my holiday must be spent in a less pleasant and less exciting fashion. I regret this extremely and shall regret it still more if your plans have been dependent on mine.

I have been reading Luchaire[1] with great delight. He seems to me a really great man.

You speak as though Delisle had been despatched. He has not arrived, but I hope is safe.[2]

On the subject of the forty days I have a reference to Guérard's edition of Irminon, tome ii, 2e partie, p. 665, note 21.[3] I cannot look this up for I cannot find the book in our Library! Shall I be asking too much of you if I ask you to look at this passage and tell me of its contents? Please do not put yourself to any trouble about this; but if the book is under your hands you may be able to send me a note on the back of a post-card.

I hear that you are going to speak of Viollet in the English Historical and am delighted. A reviewer in the Law Quarterly hardly saw the importance of the book, or at all events hardly said enough about it.[4]

I must dine in Oxford one Saturday early in next term. I am trying to persuade Florence to accompany me. If you are to be there, this will be another reason why she should go. I suppose that a sojourn in Paris runs away with money; but I wish that I were you.

Yours very truly

F. W. MAITLAND.

---

[1] Denis Jean Achille Luchaire (1846–1908), Professor of Medieval History, Sorbonne. M. may have been reading his *Histoire des institutions monarchiques de la France sous les premières Capétiens* (1883).
[2] See Letter 79, *supra.*
[3] *Ibid.* Guérard was Director of the École des Chartes. 'His life-work was to edit the Chartularies of the great Abbeys, and the Polyptique of the Abbot Irminon won him European fame' (Gooch, *History and Historians of the Nineteenth Century*, 197–8).
[4] Fisher's review of Viollet, *Histoire des Institutions politiques et administratives de la France*, is in E.H.R. VI (1891), 165. See also 6 L.Q.R. 100.

82. To James Barr Ames

[Printed C.L.J. Vol. II (1924), pp. 14–15.]

The West Lodge,
Downing College,
Cambridge.
22 March, 1890.[1]

DEAR PROFESSOR AMES,

I am exceedingly grateful to you for a copy of the number of the *Harvard Law Review* which contains 'Disseisin of Chattels, No. 2'; for though I take in the Review, yet I shall be particularly glad of a second copy of this number to lend about.[2] Already I have been strongly recommending your earlier article to the best of our students. I am deeply interested in your speculations, especially in those which relate to the action of the Statute of Limitations in complex cases. I am delighted to read what you say of *Doe v. Barnard*.[3] I thought that Pollock's attempt to save some part of that unfortunate case was desperate.

I am still ruminating over your first article, I mean the first on Disseisin. There are some things in it which perplex me—not that your opinions are ever obscure—far from it!—but because I cannot fit them in with some of my own beliefs.[4] So much the worse for my beliefs, I dare say. But some day I may ask your Review to let me have a word about the matter; it will be written with great humility.

I am getting a good deal of evidence together which tends to show that throughout the fourteenth century the local courts were busy in enforcing unwritten, and therefore unsealed, agreements.[5] They are called *convenciones*, but they are of so trivial a kind that I cannot believe them to have been clothed with Latin and parchment and wax. Would this shock you very much? It seems to me that the deed must have been an aristocratic institution quite unsuited to the needs of *villani* and that, as older 'forms' became obsolete, the local courts may have given up form altogether and required no more than suit. The action on a *convencio* is apparently kept quite distinct from the action of debt.

With one more word of thanks,
Believe me,
Yours very truly

F. W. MAITLAND

---

[1] From the first sentence of Letter 83, *infra*, it seems that the real date of Letter 82 is 16 March, 1890.
[2] Harv. L. Rev. III. 313: *Lectures on Legal History*, 192.
[3] (1849) 13 Q.B. 945: see Pollock and Wright, *Possession in the Common Law*, 97, 99.
[4] See Letter 67, *supra*, and *P. and M.* ii. 168, n. 2.
[5] S.S. Vol. 4, esp. pp. 115–18.

83. To James Barr Ames

[Printed C.L.J., Vol. II (1924), pp. 15–18.]

The West Lodge
Downing College
Cambridge

23 March 1890

DEAR MR. AMES,

You will, I hope, understand that a letter which I wrote a week ago—I have some confused notion that under the influence of a newly-acquired almanac I misdated it—was not an answer to your delightful letter of 6th March, 1890.[1] I call it delightful, for not only has it taught me a great deal, but also it has removed the only cause of quarrel that I had with you. I had got it into my head that you were carrying your denial of ownership to the point of holding that within historic times if B stole, or otherwise by trespass took, A's horse and sold it to C, then A had no means of getting the horse from C, but could merely appeal B of larceny or sue him in trespass. This doubtless was my stupidity, and I ought not even in thought to have charged you with neglect of the vast mass of authority that we have as to the voucher of warrantors. I now see that you have carefully considered this subject, and I am inclined to agree with your conclusions. Probably in cent. XII, and even in cent. XIII, the advice that one ought to give to A is—'Bring what is generally known as an *actio furti* against C. You can begin without words of felony, and possibly C will give in. If he does not, then you will have to add words of felony and may be obliged to fight C or C's vouchee.' I have just read through once more Bracton's account of the *actio furti*, and I think that you have put the right interpretation on it, *i.e.* that if C sets up title then A must *agere criminaliter* against him.[2]

It seems to me that the critical question is, What will happen if A, instead of going to law against C, disseises C of the horse? C, let us say, will thereupon appeal A of larceny. Can A plead his title, or will jurors be justified in swearing that A did not in felony take C's horse? This is the question upon which I cannot find authority. The law about retaking is unfortunately much obscured by the law about waif. I think it very possible that the sphere of self-help was gradually enlarged as time went on—this certainly was the case as regards land—but I should like to be able to trace the different stages.[3]

The laws, English and foreign, which set limits to the voucher of warrantors are very interesting. I dare say you know that in the passage in which Glanvill speaks of this matter (x. 15) there is very possibly a misreading: 'Sed nunquid warrantus poterit warrantum in curia vocare? Quod si sic est ad *quotum* warrantum erit standum.' Some MS. have *quartum* instead of *quotum*, so that the rule looks like a repetition of that which occurs in Canute, II, 24, § 2

---

[1] Ames' letter to M. is in Camb. Univ. MSS and dated by Ames 6 March 1890. It is in fact the letter printed in C.L.J. Vol. II (1924) at pp. 11–14 and there dated 27 November 1889.
[2] Bracton, f. 150b and Ames's letter in C.L.J. at p. 12. See also Letter 67, *supra*.
[3] See *P. and M.* ii. 164–70.

(Schmid): 'tunc licet[1] inde ter advocari et quarta vice proprietur aut reddatur ei cujus erit.' I am now looking to this quarter as the hopeful quarter for the solution of a problem which has much vexed me, viz. the limitation (before Stat. Marlbridge) of the writs of entry to 'the degrees' of *per* and *per* and *cui*.[2] In the Norman *Custumal*, c. ci (de Gruchy, p. 242), I find a limitation of warranty in an action for land 'tertius autem vocatus ad garantum non potest quartum vocare, quia sic contingeret ultra quartam in defensione personam querelam protendere.' I have some hope that here also land law and chattel law may help to explain each other. Meanwhile I watch anxiously for every word you say. I have been plunged for some months past in a big job. Pollock and I had a hope of turning out a historical book, but I am not sure now that he will be able to give his time, and if that be so I shall hardly get very much done in my lifetime. However, I have set to work on the more public side of the law of cent. XII and XIII, and am struggling with tenures and scutages and such like. Leaving the constitutional importance of these matters to Stubbs and others, I still find that there is much of legal interest to be discovered about them. Some day I hope to get free of tenures and villainage and so on, and to tackle the pure private law of ownership, possession, &c., and then I shall value every word of the Disseisin of Chattels. I hope that this time may come; but have my doubts—for the topic of 'Jurisdiction' stares me in the face, and looks even more threatening than 'Land Tenure'. However, I am very glad to find that I was stupid enough to misunderstand your view, and that I can make my submission.

I have just made acquaintance with a book that will, I think, interest you, viz. vol. 1 of *Records of the Borough of Nottingham*, published by the municipal corporation (Quaritch, 1882). It has some actions of 'covenant' from cent. XIV, which suggest to me that in the Court of Nottingham *conventio* did not imply writing, *e.g.* (p. 150) in 1352 there is a very curious action on a wager—in form 'debt'. J. D. complains that H. D. detains 20s. for that, whereas it was agreed (*conventum*) between them that they should ride together from N. to C. and back, so that the one who came in last should pay the other 20s.; nevertheless H. D. refused to fulfil the said *conventio*, and of this J. D produces suit. H. D says 'nullam talem conventionem fecit', and waged his law. So, p. 159 (1355), breach of a *conventio* to carry water for a year; p. 161, breach of a *conventio* to make a pyx. I think that you will find several things in this book to your purpose; for the present I must leave it alone, and go back to the cartularies. I wish that they would give me more mortgages and fewer miracles, but one must take the bad with the good.

With many thanks for your kind explanations and an assurance that your letter goes into my most sacred drawer to be read hereafter from time to time,

Believe me,

Yours very truly,

F. W. MAITLAND

[1] [Note by Hazeltine in C.L.J. at p. 16: *Liceat* in the text. So, too, Liebermann, *Gesetze der Angelsachsen*, i. 327.]
[2] See *P. and M.* ii. 70–1.

84. To P. E. Dove

Downing College
Cambridge

13th June 1890

DEAR DOVE,

I very much regret that the necessity I am under of sitting in the Schools at Oxford on Tuesday the 17th will prevent my attending the meeting of the Council of the Selden Society called for that day, for as editor of the last volume that has appeared I ought to report myself. Possibly also you may be in want of suggestions for future volumes. At any rate I will allow myself to make a few. I have seen some of the sheets of Baildon's forthcoming volume.[1] He seems to me to be doing his work extremely well and I think that the book will be very interesting. I very much doubt whether you could do better than to ask him to go on with his task for another year, for the rolls of John's reign are extremely important.

An alternative would be another volume of manorial pleas. I must not offer to edit it for I have many tasks already in hand, but I would join Baildon in the work if he wished it. We have worked together before now for the Master of the Rolls[2] and get on well together. I could contribute a collection of French precedents for proceedings in manorial courts—rather I should say precedents in French—which has not yet seen the light. It seems to me very interesting; I have already copied and translated it; perhaps it would fill a third of a volume. Its date is very doubtful, but not later than the middle of the fourteenth century. The rest of the volume might be filled with actual cases from court rolls; but in this case I should recommend not a series of disconnected excerpts but a continuous abstract in English, the important entries being given in full and both in Latin and English. Much space would thus be saved and the volume might cover a good deal of ground. I would, e.g., say, 'Court holden on such a day. Seven essoins. Twenty presentments of trespasses and nuisances including the following—Four surrenders, the form of which is as follows', and so forth.

If the Society would like to attack a text book, it seems to me that the one to begin with is the Mirror of Justices.[3] It is extremely curious and has never been properly edited. I believe that the only MS of it is in Cambridge at Corpus, and I think that I could find a good editor for it. Perhaps there is more than a year's work in it and the Society would like to look ahead beyond next year.

But probably you will have many other proposals.

Yours very truly

F. W. MAITLAND

---

[1] S.S. Vol. 3.   [2] See Letter 71, *supra.*
                 [3] S.S. Vol. 7.

85. To H. A. L. Fisher

The West Lodge
Downing College
Cambridge
21 Sept. 1890

DEAR HERBERT,

I hear that you are to be in Oxford very soon and, as an Oxford man might do me a great service, I shall make bold to ask it of you. There is a MS. in the Bodleian that I shall probably have to see, but before I face the journey via Bletchley, a thing not lightly to be undertaken, I should like to know (1) whether Bodley is now open, and (2) whether the MS. is really what I want. The first question you will be able to answer. I must not press for an answer to the second as you must be busy. Nevertheless if you will be at pains to look for two or three minutes at the book in question, you will make me very grateful. For convenience sake I put the question on another sheet of paper.[1]

I have had the great pleasure of reading some of your letters from Switzerland. I have not enjoyed any letters so much this long while, for they brought back to me many happy days. But you are a great climber and have actually been out with Hans Grass with whose heroisms I was once familiar.[2]

I had a vision of you heading the revolt at Bellinzona—red flag in one hand, Baedeker in the other. That is studying politics.[3]

Believe me
Yours affectionately
F. W. MAITLAND

86. To James Bradley Thayer

The West Lodge
Downing College
Cambridge
21 Sept. 1890

DEAR PROFESSOR THAYER,

I have to thank you—I sincerely do so—for two post-cards,[4] one about words of court, the other about Holmes of Retford. From what I can learn of Holmes's collection I fear that it was not ancestral, but still I must see what can be done for his pedigree.

---

[1] Not extant. It is not known to what MS M. is referring.
[2] Hans Grass (1828–1902), 'by far the most famous Engadine guide of his day', *Alpine Journal, Feb.* 1914, pp. 129–30.
[3] 'In September 1890 I happened upon civil war in what most people believe to be the quietest land in Europe—Switzerland. . . . The Liberal faction in Canton Ticino rose against the dominant Catholic faction, stormed the cantonal palace at Bellinzona with some little bloodshed and established a revolutionary government which lasted precisely three days before it was crushed by Federal troops': Oman, *Memories of Victorian Oxford*, 190.
[4] Not extant. See Letters 42, 54, 58 and 76, *supra.*

A while ago you asked me about the early printed books on 'court keeping'. I hope that the Selden Society's Vol. 4 will contain a list of them.[1] I believe that there were two by Pynson (no date), one by J. Rastell (n.d. ?1530), one by W. Rastell (?1534), one by Berthelet (1543), one by Elizabeth Pykeringe, one by W. Middleton—all older than 1550. Into Vol. 4 I am going to put four little books of precedents for courts, three of which belong as I think to cent. xiii, while the fourth is but little later. I constantly find things that ought to be printed, e.g. three different sets of conveyancing precedents all older than 1300[2]—I wish I were three men with three Selden Societies at my back.

It was much to my regret that I did not see Prof. Gray. Pollock asked me to meet him, Challis and Elphinstone, but it could not be. I guess they settled the *scintilla juris* for good and all.[3]

I will take this occasion to ask a queer question of you, but a post-card will carry answer enough. Did the existence of slavery in the southern states give rise to any considerable jurisprudence—to any good text-book for example? I have been writing about villeinage and have been puzzled by our law's way of treating the villein as 'free against all men but his lord'. I should like to know how the lawyers of the south treated cases of damage done (1) by a slave to one not his master, (2) to a slave by one not his master. Did people write books about these things, or did the law work so smoothly that there was no need for scientific exposition?

The monk also troubles me; but I must not go to America for him.[4]

Let us have more about Evidence.

Yours very truly

F. W. MAITLAND

87. To Frederick Pollock

Downing Coll. Camb.

18th Oct. 1890

MY DEAR POLLOCK,

I have sundry things to say which may fill a waste of paper, so I take a large sheet.

As to Roman law in the A-S time you have probably flung a foot note to the well known passages; they prove extremely little but we ought not to seem to have neglected them.

The first is Beda, Hist. Ecclesiast. lib. 2 cap. 5 about Ethelbert of Kent putting

---

[1] S.S. Vol. 4, pp. 3–5. See Letters 63 and 76, *supra*.

[2] See M., *A Conveyancer in the Thirteenth Century*, L.Q.R. Jan. 1891, reprinted C.P. II. 190.

[3] Henry William Challis (1841–98), of the Inner Temple, Barrister-at-law, author of *Law of Real Property* (1885). Sir H. W. Elphinstone (1830–1917), Conveyancing Counsel to the Court, Professor of Real Property to the Inns of Court, author of *Introduction to Conveyancing*, etc.

[4] See *P. and M.* i. 433–8.

laws into writing *juxta exempla Romanorum*. For my own part I think this only means that the notion of written law was new and introduced by the Roman missionaries.

The second is in a letter ascribed to S. Aldhelm (of whom a good life in Dict. Nat. Biog.). This may be found in Savigny, Geschichte des R.R.[1] vol. 1, p. 467 (kap. VI, sec. 135). And there also may be found a little bit of Alcuin about a school at York. In the Dictionary Hunt[2] (a careful man) ascribes to Aldhelm a study of 'Roman jurisprudence.' I guess that there may be something about this in the life of Aldhelm by Faritius (Abbot of Malmesbury circ. 1100), which is in Gale's *Patres*, a book that I have not by me. I think that all that this comes to at the utmost is a little, a very little dabbling in Roman law of an academic kind.[3]

I gather from what you said of Maine in the Sat. Rev. article lately sent to me that you are disposed to separate the question of Roman law from that of Roman civilization. While prepared to go any length in denying that A-S law is Roman, I am not prepared to deny that all modern civilization is Roman, or if you please Catholic. Our first written 'doom' mentions churches, bishops, priests, deacons, clerics and ministers—in short is full of foreign words. Therefore I think that a great general influence must be ascribed to Catholicism, besides the specific influence apparent in the landbook, the testament and so forth. As to agriculture I leave this to your judgment, but I can not help thinking that the German invaders must have learnt a good deal about tillage from the Britons, however slightly romanized the latter may have been.

As to the Celt, I repudiate him as an ancestor in the law. Still I should say some cautious words about the possible survival of Celtic customs in the lowest courses of the social structure. Thus several good scholars have a strong suspicion that *merchet*, name and thing, is Celtic—Waitz[4] for example. And then there are *two* channels for Celtic influence, for undoubtedly there seems to be a Celtic strain in French, and therefore in Norman, law—*vassal* and *felony* are both said to be Celtic.

See too Reg. of Worcester Priory (Camden Soc.) p. xl, a charter of Margaret Say touching a place in Worcestershire—'relaxavi etiam *douereth* servientium' —a Welsh word and a Welsh thing.

But that Welsh Law was well marked off from English is shown e.g. by Domesday for Herefordshire, in particular D.B. i. 185b, 'iij Walenses lege Walensi viventes'—a curious trace of a 'system of personal laws' or better 'racial laws'.

[1] *Geschichte des römischen Rechts im Mittelalter.*
[2] William Hunt (1842–1931), historian. Pub. *The English Church from its foundation to the Norman Conquest* (1899), *History of England, 1760–1801* (Vol. X of *Political History of England*, of which he was joint editor with R. L. Poole), etc. He contributed many biographies to D.N.B.
[3] In the above paragraph M. seems to be commenting on Pollock's draft chapter on Anglo-Saxon Law for *P. and M.* In *P. and M.* i. pp. 11–13 are cited Beda, St. Aldhelm (D.N.B., Hunt), Life of Aldhelm by Faritius and Gale's *Patres*. On Thomas Gale (?1636–1702), see Douglas, *English Scholars*, 69–72.
[4] Georg Waitz (1813–66), German historian and disciple of Ranke; principal editor of *Monumenta Germaniae Historica*. For 'merchet' see *P. and M.* i. 368–73.

By all means print the Introductory Chapter in L.Q.R. if you think fit.[1] But it will be all your work and should bear your name.

And now I want to speak about the size of our book. I go on writing and writing, for I have so arranged my lectures that I have little else to do. Thus matter accumulates at a great rate. I know that some of it deals with rather minute points; but the more I see of cents. XII and XIII the more convinced am I that their legal history must be written afresh with full proof of every point. Well, I think that when we have done our 'chronological' chapters and added to these our chapters on public law, we shall have a good large volume and that the private law will want another volume. Under the 'public law' we shall have to speak of tenure, status, jurisdiction, criminal law and (I think) prerogative or administrative law (uniting under this last head and other heads such matter as is usually considered 'constitutional'), and then will come our say about the genesis of feudalism. This means a great pile of stuff. For example, for six weeks past I have had 'juristic persons' on my mind, have been grubbing for the English evidence and reading the Germans, in particular Gierke's great book (it is a splendid thing though G. is too metaphysical).[2] Now I don't think that any good would come of speaking of such a matter in a few brief paragraphs—if I am to write about it I can not but write at length. So you see the person that you have to deal with, and if you decide to dissolve partnership I shall not be in a position to complain of the decision. I quite see that a brief history of English law is much wanted and might be written, but I also see that I can not write it. Every day my admiration for Stubbs grows and you know what this form of worship condemns one to. I hardly hope to bring the history beyond Edward I because there seems to me to be matter for two good volumes in the earlier time. But I feel that I may be hampering you and preventing you from writing a famous book. No one living could deal with the YBB. as you could—do you like the notion of having to lay down pen just when they are coming into sight? There—I have delivered my soul of its burden. In time— there is no hurry—you will tell me what you think.

The actual state of my work is this. Tenure is practically finished. A large part of Jurisdiction is written but requires re-arrangement. In Status I have done the baron, the knight, the unfree. I am prepared to deal with the monks and the clergy and have opinions about corporations. Aliens will not take me long but of Jews I have hardly yet thought.

To leave personal affairs—Do you know the great case about the nature of corporations discussed four times in Y.B. 21 Edw. IV, beginning at f. 7? It is a splendid example of Year Book style and would interest you.[3] By the way I learn from Gierke that the dictum about the bottomless and soulless nature of corporations which we ascribe to Lord Westbury is a coarsened version of a

1 Pollock did not do so.
2 Otto Gierke (1844–1921), *Das deutsche Genossenschaftsrecht*, 3 vols., pub. 1868, 1873 and 1881.
3 P. and M. i. 491–2.

maxim laid down by Johannes Andreae,[1] a mighty canonist, also that the canonists raised the question whether a corporation can be a godmother!

If you look at Engl. Hist. Rev. for this month you will see some remarks on drengage and thegnage cast forth from my chapter on tenures. Just too late I discovered that Ellenborough on two occasions referred the peculiarities of the 'customary freeholds' of Northumbria to the burden of military service.[2]

But this is a long epistle.

Yrs. ever

F. W. MAITLAND

88. To F. J. H. Jenkinson

The West Lodge
Downing College
Cambridge

10 Novr. 1890

MY DEAR JENKINSON,

I have looked at the Red Book of Thorney. I can make no guess whatever about its selling price; but undoubtedly it is a cartulary of first-rate importance. It was used by Dugdale, being then in the possession of the Earl of Westmoreland; Dugdale's editors seem not to have had access to it, nor I think had Kemble access to it when he published the Codex Diplomaticus. Cambridge is of course the place where it ought to be and I hope that we may have an offer of it at what experts will consider a reasonable price—but I must again say that I can form no opinion at all as to what price would be reasonable. But I have no doubt at all that to any historian of the eastern counties the Thorney Cartulary would be invaluable.[3]

As to Beaudoin's[4] article, I can hardly recommend the Library to take in a magazine on the strength of one paper; perhaps some one else will know more about it. But I want to read the article, and if the Library does not take the number which contains it I shall be happy to relieve you of it.

Yours very truly

F. W. MAITLAND

---

[1] Joh. Andreae Mugellanus (1270–1348). See *Political Theories of the Middle Age*, IV (M's translation), and Gierke's notes thereto.
[2] *Northumbrian Tenures*, E.H.R. V (1890), 625, reprinted C.P. II. 96.
[3] The Camb. Univ. Library bought the Red Book of Thorney from Quaritch on 22 Nov. 1890 (Add. 3020, 3021). See also G. R. C. Davis, *Medieval Cartularies of Great Britain*, no. 964. For William Dugdale, *Monasticon Anglicanum*, see Douglas, *English Scholars*, chap. 2. For J. H. Kemble, *Codex Diplomaticus aevi Saxonici*, see *P. and M*. i. 28.
[4] Beaudoin, *Étude sur les origines du régime féodal* (Annales de l'enseignement supérieur de Grenoble, vol. 1, p. 43): cited M. *D.B. and Beyond*, 279.

89. To Melville M. Bigelow

Downing Coll.
Cambridge
England

1 Feb. 1891

MY DEAR BIGELOW,

I have again been slow in writing. I was on the point of writing you my thanks for your note about the liability of townships,[1] when the smaller of my two babes was taken very ill with pneumonia. My wife and I have had a bad fortnight and many times we thought that the child was leaving us. However by dint of very careful nursing the worst has been avoided and this morning we are beginning to be cheerful once more. My wife and her mother, who is with us, send their joint and several loves to Mrs. Bigelow.

And now I can, must and hereby do thank for your valuable contribution of which I shall forthwith make use. The matter is, I think, a very interesting one. I believe that the old English rule certainly was that the members of a 'communitas' are liable for the debts of the communitas: very often the communitas—county, hundred, township—has no property of its own. But before the last of the Year Books this rule has undergone a change, at least so far as it concerns the debts of a 'communitas' which has been brought within the new idea of a 'corporation' or 'body politic'—the corporators are not liable, and their property is not liable, for the debts of the corporation.[2] It comes to be regarded as an anomaly that this (new) rule does not apply to debts due to the crown—the property of the burgesses can still be attached if the 'firma burgi' be not paid (Lord Eldon remembered this), and if the borough be fined the goods of the townsfolk can be seized.[3] In England, as you know, the rural township never succeeds in becoming a 'juristic person'.

As to the American rule I should, in my ignorance, have some scruple in supposing it to be a genuine 'survival' of the old English law, because I think that our old rule as to the debts of corporate bodies had got altered (save in the king's case) before America was colonised. I should rather imagine that there was a sort of 'atavism', a 'throw back' to ancient law brought about by your recognition of the corporate character of the rural township. Thus, as I take it, you came by corporations which often had no property of their own. But the whole thing is wonderfully interesting.

Believe me
Yours very truly

F. W. MAITLAND

[1] Bigelow's note is not extant, but its contents appear from the present letter.
[2] See Y.B. Trin. 12 Hen. VII. f. 27. pl. 7 (A.D. 1497): cited by M. *Gierke*, Intro. xxxv, note 1.
[3] *P. and M.* i. 679–88.

90. To Melville M. Bigelow

Downing Coll.
Cambridge
8th Feb. 1891

MY DEAR BIGELOW,

A horrible suspicion, nay, conviction! That I sent my last letter to you out to the post with other letters and that it was insufficiently stamped. I fear that you are having to pay for rubbish shot upon you. However I thus get an opportunity, after some apologies, of saying that our little girl is rapidly recovering, also of thanking Mrs. Bigelow for her kind letter to my wife, who will send her own thanks so soon as she resumes her correspondence—at present she still has much nursing to do.

Now I resolve to stamp this letter adequately, and grovel once more.

Yours very truly

F. W. MAITLAND

91. To H. A. L. Fisher

The West Lodge
Downing College
Cambridge
17 Feb. 1891

MY DEAR HERBERT,

Perhaps I may be in time before you slip away to tell you how good I thought your criticism of Paul Viollet.[1] I have been wanting these weeks to say that it is excellent and taught me a lot of things—but as you know we have been in trouble. All is going well now, and Florence, wonderful to say, is not worn out by her prolonged anxiety.

I wish that I were going to Munich; the opera is—words fail me!

Yours affectionately

F. W. MAITLAND

92. To H. A. L. Fisher

The West Lodge
Downing College
Cambridge
3rd March 1891

MY DEAR HERBERT,

I am going to ask you whether your kindness will go the length of attempting to get some German books for me either at first or at second hand.

[1] See Letter 81, *supra*.

89

Sohm, Fränkische Reichs-und-Gerichtsverfassung—Weimar 1872.

Sohm, Recht der Eheschliessung—Weimar 1875.

Roth, Beneficialwesen—Erlangen 1850.

Roth, Feudalität und Unterthanenverband—Weimar 1863.

Heusler, Ursprung der deutschen stadtverfassung.[1]

If you can lay your hand on any of these I shall be grateful and will send its price. I fear that Sohm's books are out of print.

I hope that you are having good times. The two F's[2] are doing well; I hope that they may get to the sea-side at Easter. I suppose that our 'Spinning House Case'[3] has hardly got into the German papers—someday I shall have a story to tell you about it.

Yours truly

F. W. MAITLAND

I hope that I am not asking too much.

93. To Melville M. Bigelow

The West Lodge

Downing College

Cambridge

19 April 1891

MY DEAR BIGELOW,

You will be glad to hear that all has gone well with us. Our little girl after a very bad time is growing strong and well. I was able to get a short holiday at Malvern, but my wife would not leave the child.

Your last letter about the liability of corporates[4] was very interesting and I took the liberty of reading it at a lecture. The truth seems to me to be that if you have corporations which have no property or none that can be taken into execution or but little property, you must hold the corporators liable, at all events subsidiarily liable, for the acts of the corporation. So the case of your American townships seems to me rather a reproduction than a continuation of old English law—a reproduction all the more interesting because I dare say that the colonists knew little of legal antiquities.

I am very glad that you like Selden Vol. IV and am grateful for the kind notes that you inserted in the Harvard Law Review.[5] When the Littleport rolls come before you, you will see that I am making a somewhat revolutionary suggestion about the enforceability of parol agreements—but I do not think that you will be shocked at it though some folk may be.[6]

---

[1] Weimar, 1872.

[2] Florence and Fredegond: see Letters 89–91, *supra*.

[3] See Winstanley, *Later Victorian Cambridge*, chap. IV. The 'case' concerned the powers of the University Proctors to arrest and of the University to punish women suspected of being prostitutes. Such cases were tried by the Vice-Chancellor sitting in the Spinning House. See Letter 114, *infra*.

[4] *Sic.* Bigelow's 'last letter' is not extant, but it clearly pursued the subject of Letter 89, *supra*.

[5] 4 Harv. L. Rev. 282.   [6] S.S. Vol. 4, pp. 115–18.

At present I am up to my eyes in Domesday and I hope to get some theory out of it that will enable me to attack the A-S land books.[1] But studying Domesday involves a great deal of drudgery.

I suppose you know Gross of the Gild Merchant.[2] I admire his book immensely. What do they think of it and of him at Harvard?

And what are you doing? Doubtless you have two or three tomes in the press?

Yours very truly and with a grateful memory of your kind letter which came when I was in trouble

F. W. MAITLAND

94. To P. E. Dove

Downing College
Cambridge
24 May 1891

MY DEAR DOVE,

It will soon be time for the Selden Society's Council to make arrangements for the volume due in 1893. I dare say that many suggestions will occur to you; but I will venture to make a few.

1. Another volume of Manorial Pleas. Baildon and I have a good deal of material left over from Vol. iv and I think that we could make an interesting book.

2. More Civil Pleas in the King's Court. But you say that these are dull.

3. *Brevia Placitata*. This book of precedents for pleadings—French XIIIth cent.—has never been printed. I have said something of it in my Introduction to Vol. iv.[3] It resembles the first tract that I have there printed, but the precedents are for pleadings in the King's Courts. Some time or another this ought to be printed.[4]

4. Conveyancing Precedents. There are several interesting sets belonging to cent. xiii: the mercantile transactions are very curious.

5. The History of the Register of Original Writs. One might print a register of Henry III's reign, another of Edw. I, another of Edw. III, another of cent. XV—or at any rate give an account of these books. The materials for such a history are very ample.[5]

6. Fleta—but I do not recommend this, for I think that, after Miss Lamond's Walter of Henley, nothing remains in Fleta but a poor epitome of Bracton.[6]

7. Bracton's Roman Law. A good text of those portions of Bracton's work in which he was following Azo printed in parallel columns with Azo—the

---

[1] *P. and M.* ii. 251–3: *D.B. and Beyond*, Essay II, s. 1.
[2] Gross's two vols. on The Gild Merchant were reviewed by M. in the *Economic Journal*, June 1891, and reprinted C.P. II, 223.
[3] At p. 11.
[4] It was ultimately printed in 1951 in S.S. Vol. 66.
[5] See Letters 63 and 67, *supra*.
[6] M. reviewed Miss Lamond's book in *Economic Journal*, 1891, pp. 225–6.

texts cited from Code and Digest being printed in foot notes. This should be a good book. It wants a good man.[1]

May I also suggest that at the next meeting of the Council the thanks of the Society should be given to Mr. O. C. Pell for having allowed me to copy and print extracts from the rolls of the manor of Littleport?[2]

I ought to add that there are early Chancery Proceedings claiming our notice, but I am not familiar with them.[3]

Yours very truly

F. W. MAITLAND

95. To Frederick Pollock

Downing Coll. Cambridge

10th Oct. 1891

MY DEAR POLLOCK,

Et in octabis S. Michaelis tenuit Dñs Latimerus de Nova Villa concilium sive capitulum suum in Gildhalla burgensium de Grantebrigge cum caucidicis [sic] suis et cum omnibus bovibus taurensibus [sic]—but this MS. is really a hopeless one! I went and found myself in strange company: if anything could have made me a Home Ruler!—but then nothing will. The objection that R. C. J. was astrict to residence was urged by R. T. Wright (L.U.) but was not received with any favour. My chief cause for grief was that the friends of Sir J. G. made, as it were, a favour of postponing him and not indistinctly stipulated that something should be done for him next year.[4]

'Pre-Aryan here! Pre-Aryan there! I mind the bigging o't'.[5] You seem to have spoken a word in season to these eager folk-lorists. I have written at length about the Malmesbury case and about the Aston case. All the talk about chiefs and tribesmen is I feel sure pure bosh. The Malmesbury constitution has all the marks of the Tudor, and of no earlier, age. If you think that any good would come of this, I would furbish up what I have written and send it to the L.Q.R.[6]

As to the A-S 'immunities'—to-morrow I will send you what I have written and if you care to read it you can keep it by you for some weeks, but I may want it before the end of term for lectures. Of course it is very rough. I don't

[1] S.S. Vol. 8: by M.
[2] Preface to S.S. Vol. 4: see Letters 64, 66 and 69, *supra*.
[3] S.S. Vol. 10.
[4] In the above paragraph M. describes a meeting to choose a candidate to succeed H. C. Raikes as M.P. for Cambridge University. R. C. Jebb was chosen despite Wright's objection that, as Regius Professor of Greek, he was *quasi adscriptus glebae*. 'Sir J. G.' was Sir John Eldon Gorst (1835–1916), who joined Professor Jebb as second member for Cambridge University in 1892. M., unlike Wright and other friends, including Henry Sidgwick, never became a Liberal Unionist (L.U.) and remained a Liberal; but the paragraph shows the disturbance of mind among Liberals caused by the Home Rule controversy.
[5] 'Praetorian here, Praetorian there, I mind the bigging o't': *The Antiquary*, chap. 4. See M., C.P. II. 314.
[6] *The Survival of Archaic Communities*, L.Q.R. Jan. 1893: C.P. II. 313.

think we can dissociate the English from the Frankish question. Adams's essay represents the school of Roth. Against this there has been a marked reaction both in France and in Germany, and for once Fustel is in agreement with what seems to be the 'herrschende Meinung' among orthodox Germanists.[1]

And now a question. Is it utterly impossible that a Roman lawyer, of the time let us say of Theodosius, should have used the term *jus commune* in such a sense that we should be right in rendering it by *common law*? In the Theodosian Code there is a constitution in which the Emperor is dealing with a certain heretical sect—Eunomians I think.[2] He says that by a previous law he had decreed that they should neither make testaments nor receive anything by testament. This law he now revokes and then he adds—'Vivant jure communi; scribant et scribantur haeredes'. It is Sunday and I have not the book with me, but of these words I am sure. I was brought to this question by observing that the canonists habitually use *jus commune* almost precisely in our sense of common law—the instances that I have seen in the Corpus Juris and in Joh. Andreae,[3] also in very early acts of English Courts Christian, are very numerous. The usual contrast to j.c. is *privilegium*: in text books the formal contrast is *jus particulare*. Thus, e.g., any rules special to the *English* church would be *jus particulare*. But the commonest contrast is privilegium, i.e. a papal bull. I have not a doubt that our *jus commune* is the j.c. of the Canonists.[4]

Believe me
Yours very truly
F. W. MAITLAND

96. To Frederick Pollock

Downing Coll. Camb.
1 Novr. 1891

MY DEAR POLLOCK,

Yes, there were two Wulstans. I have never seen the homilies, but I certainly understood York Powell[5] to mean that there was a sermon against slavery by the later and more famous of the two. The story how the later Wulstan preached at Bristol against the export slave trade is told by Will. Malmesb. Vita S. Wulstani, Wharton, Anglia Sacra, ii. 258—unless I am mistaken. Then from the Synod of Westminster 1102 we have 'Ne quis illud nefarium negotium quo

[1] The material on 'A-S immunities', originally intended for *P. and M.*, was later used for *D.B. and Beyond*, Essay II, s. 3. Adams is Henry Adams, a contributor to *Essays in Anglo-Saxon Law* (1876).
[2] Gibbon, *Decline and Fall*, chap. xxvii.
[3] See Letter 87, *supra*.
[4] *P. and M.* i. 176–7.
[5] Frederick York Powell (1850–1904), Lecturer in Law, Christ Church, 1874, and from 1894 Regius Professor of Modern History, Oxford: medieval historian and Icelandic scholar.

hactenus homines in Anglia solebant velut bruta animalia venundari deinceps ullatenus fieri[1] praesumat.'

As to the Vet. Versio of Edgar II—I think it evidence of early 12th century classification, but I don't think it will prove the villanus of D. B. to be the geneat of earlier times. The geneat of the Rectitudines is a horseman, at all events a man with a horse—like Oswald's cnight, minister, etc.[2]

Can you tell me anything of Dove? A month ago I sent him a cheque, happily for a small sum. A week ago I wrote again to him. To neither letter have I had an answer. Is he ill? Does his name still appear at 23 Old Buildings?

At Commemoration time we must take counsel. I have now written in rough five big chapters[3]—Tenure—Status—Jurisdiction—Domesday—Origins of Feudalism. My next task will be the general history from 1066 to 1272. Then the way will be clear for 'private law'.

Yours very truly

F. W. MAITLAND

97. To Paul Vinogradoff

[No original. Printed Fisher, *Memoir*, 51–2: no beginning or ending.]

Downing

15 Nov. 1891

Even the title page has been passed for the press and I am now awaiting your book.[4] I shall be proud when I paste into you the piece of paper that you sent me. I have felt it a great honour to correct your proof sheet and am almost as curious about what the critics will say as if the book were my own. I often think what an extraordinary piece of luck for me it was that you and I met upon a 'Sunday tramp'.[5] That day determined the rest of my life. And now the Council of the University has offered me the honour of doctor 'honoris causa'. I was stunned by the offer for it is an unusual one and of course I must accept it. But for that Sunday tramp this would not have been. As to the reception of your book my own impression is that it will be very well received. Good criticism you can hardly expect, for very few people here will be able to judge of your work. But I think that you will be loudly praised. Perhaps you will become an idol like Maine—who can tell? I hardly wish you this fate, though you might like it for a fortnight.

[1] *Sic*: it should be *facere*. See Wilkins, *Concilia*, i. 383. The 'Two Wulstans' were Wulfstan, Abp. of York (d. 1023), to whom the homilies have been ascribed, and St. Wulfstan, Bp. of Worcester (1012–95), who was the preacher at Bristol. Henry Wharton's *Anglia Sacra* were pub. 1691: see Douglas, *English Scholars*, chap. VII. See also William of Malmesbury, *Vita Wulfstani* (Camden Soc. ed. Darlington), pp. 43, 91.

[2] On this paragraph see *P. and M.* i., chap. II, and *D.B. and Beyond*, Essay II, s. 5. For the *Rectitudines Singularum Personarum* see Stenton, *Anglo-Saxon England*, 465–72.

[3] Of *P. and M.*

[4] *Villainage in England*, pub. Oxford, 1892.

[5] Jan. 20, 1884: see Fisher, *Memoir*, 24, and Vinogradoff, *Coll. Pap.* I. 15, note.

I was ill in September but am better now and have been doing a good many things—preparing myself for some paragraphs about Canon Law.[1]

98. To Selina Maitland (Mrs. Reynell)

The West Lodge
Downing College
Cambridge
22 Nov. 1891

MY DEAREST SELA,

Many thanks for your kind letter[2] and all the trouble that you have taken. The materials for S. R. M.'s life are all now in Jessopp's hands and I do not doubt but that he will make a good thing of them. The ordination by the Bishop of Norwich is still a mystery to me. Ought one not to have some 'title' in the diocese of the ordaining bishop? However Jessopp will be skilled in such questions.[3]

I can well imagine that the grandfather does not receive unbounded admiration from you. But judging him merely as I should judge any other literary man I think him great. It seems to me that he did what was wanted just at the moment when it was wanted and so has a distinct place in the history of history in England. The *Facts and Documents* is the book that I admire most. Of course it is a book for the few, but then those few will be just the next generation of historians. It is a book which 'renders impossible' a whole class of existing books. I don't mean physically impossible—men will go on writing books of that class—but henceforth they will not be mistaken for great historians. One still has to do for legal history something like the work that S. R. M. did for ecclesiastical history—to teach them, e.g., that some statement about the 13th century does not become truer because it has been constantly repeated, that a 'chain of testimony' is never stronger than its first link. It is the 'method' that I admire in S. R. M. more even than the style or the matter—the application to remote events of those canons of evidence which we should all use about affairs of the present day, e.g. of the rule which excludes hearsay. You see how easily I run off into a lecture.

I am just sending off a paper on Becket to the English Historical.[4] It may interest you more than any thing else that I have written.

[1] *P. and M.* i. 112–35.
[2] Not extant.
[3] S. R. M.—Samuel Roffey Maitland (1792–1866), M.'s grandfather. He entered St. John's College, Cambridge, in 1809 but migrated in 1810 to Trinity College. Called to the Bar, 1816, but in 1821 decided to enter the Church. Ordained by Bp. of Norwich and admitted to Priest's Orders by Bp. of Gloucester, 1823. Librarian at Lambeth, 1838–48. He published *Facts and Documents illustrative of the History, Doctrine and Rites of the Ancient Albigenses and Waldenses*, 1832: *The Dark Ages*, 1844: *Essays on Subjects connected with the Reformation in England*, 1849. His life in D.N.B. was by Rev. Augustus Jessopp, D.D.
[4] *Henry II and the Criminous Clerks*, E.H.R., April 1892, and C.P. II. 232.

I hope that the dominus Episcopus will do what is wanted of him.[1]

> Love to you and yours
> Your affectionate brother
>
> F. W. MAITLAND

99. To H. A. L. Fisher

> The West Lodge
> Downing College
> Cambridge
> *29 Novr. 1891*

MY DEAR HERBERT,

Many thanks for your pleasant congratulations. But I do not blossom until Thursday. My colleagues of the Law Club have given me a complete array of doctorial vestments of the most sumptuous kind.[2] The other day I had a little correspondence with R. L. Poole[3]—he said some pretty things about you. What else I hear of you is not so pleasant—but you must make holiday for a while and why not in Cambridge? We shall be delighted to see you.

So you have had to play the Roman father, or rather elder brother. I pity you; but am glad that H.[4] did so very well.

I have it on my mind that I owe you money. The debt has run a long time, I am ashamed to say. Can you tell me its amount? You remember that you bought books for me.[5]

In the English Historical I am plunging into the Becket turmoil,[6] trying to prove that Henry had a very respectable amount of canon law in favour of his way of treating the criminous clerk. I expect to be accursed by both parties.

> Yours affectionately
>
> F. W. MAITLAND

100. To Maxwell Lyte

> The West Lodge
> Downing College
> Cambridge
> *29 Novr. 1891*

DEAR MR. MAXWELL LYTE,

I write to ask you how the work of cataloguing the Parliamentary Petitions stands, for a time is coming when, if I have good luck, I may be able to take up

---

[1] The Rev. Vincent Reynell, who had previously been in deacon's orders, was ordained priest by the Bishop of Gloucester on 20 Dec. 1891.

[2] The degree of L.L.D. *honoris causa* was conferred on M. in Cambridge on 3 Dec. 1891.

[3] No letter of this year to or from R. L. Poole is extant.

[4] Hervey, Fisher's younger brother, who was a life-long invalid: Ogg, *Herbert Fisher*, 19.

[5] See Letter 92, *supra*.

[6] See Letter 98, *supra*.

again the Parliament Roll of Edward I. I made some inquiries in September but understood that I had better wait. I am beginning however to feel that I am somewhat of an impostor when I receive the volumes of the Rolls Series, and I have to work under so many restrictions imposed by doctors that I am unable to make definite promises about what I will do in the future. Still, if I am fortunate, I may be able to do something this Christmas time.

There is another matter about which I should like to say a word. I do not know how far advanced Sir Travers Twiss may be in his edition of Glanvill and I can not well write to him about it, for though I have never published many hard words about his edition of Bracton, still I have of necessity been brought into collision with it.[1] I am sending to an American magazine, the Harvard Law Review, an article on a Cambridge MS. of which I send you a printed copy.[2] That Review has no circulation in England and it is not likely that Sir Travers Twiss will see it. I am not saying that my article contains anything that he ought to notice, but still he might wish to hear of this 'revised Glanvill' if he does not know of it already. Therefore it is that I put a copy of it at your service and, if you think that he would like to see it, at his service. I suppose that it will be published a few months hence. Will you therefore do whatever you think fit in this matter? I shall be happy if any use can be made of my article, but must not thrust it upon the editor.

Believe me
Yours very truly

F. W. MAITLAND

101. To Maxwell Lyte

The West Lodge
Downing College
Cambridge

28 Feb. 1892

DEAR MR. MAXWELL LYTE,

Can you tell me whether the catalogue of the Petitions to Parliament is ready for use? If it is in print I should like to have a copy for I have at last some hope of being able to visit the Record Office and my work there would be the easier if I could previously see the catalogue.

Yours very truly

F. W. MAITLAND

[1] For M. on Sir Travers Twiss's edition of Bracton see *The Materials for English Legal History*, C.P. II. 43, note, and Letter 14, *supra*. On his edition of Glanvill see Letter 186, *infra*.
[2] *Glanville Revised*, Harv. L. Rev., April 1892: reprinted C.P. II. 266.

102. To Maxwell Lyte

The West Lodge
Downing College
Cambridge

6 March 1892

DEAR MR. MAXWELL LYTE,

I am very much obliged to you for sending me the catalogue of Petitions.
I hope to be in London next week and to make a serious start upon the work
of finding those which belong to the Parliament Roll that I have copied. If
the petitions are not yet accessible to the general public, perhaps you will be
able to grant me some privilege in this matter as my visits to London can not
be very numerous. The Calendar of the Petitions looks a very useful one.

When I have made some little progress with my work I should like to have
an interview with you if you can spare me a little of your time.

Yours very truly

F. W. MAITLAND

103. To Maxwell Lyte

The West Lodge
Downing College
Cambridge

20 March 1892

DEAR MR. MAXWELL LYTE,

I thank you for the copy of the Close Roll Calendar and also for the valuable
note about 'council' and 'parliament'.[1]

As to the transcripts of petitions, I think you will find that I long ago returned
to the office the volumes to which you refer, namely, those relating to early
years of Edward I. I have two volumes, but they both deal with later years.
The one is labelled 'Petitions 33 Edw. I', the other 'Petitions Series 2–151'.
Of course I will send you these if you wish for them, but at the moment I am
finding them of use.

Having been much puzzled as to whether the 'Irr' on these petitions stood
for Irrotuletur or for Irrotulatur, I was much pleased to come across one
which had the latter word in full.[2]

Believe me
Yours very truly

F. W. MAITLAND

[1] Note not extant, but see M. *Memoranda de Parliamento*, Intro. lxvi–lxvii.
[2] *Ibid.*, lv.

104. To H. A. L. Fisher

[Letter-card: year from postmark.]

Cambridge

24 March 1892

MY DEAR HERBERT,

The review of Vinogradoff's Villainage in the Oxford Magazine is excellent.[1] I should send it to him. It refreshed me after the chill notice in the Athenaeum— the writer of which is a learned man but has many corns upon which one may not tread.[2] I am extremely glad that you like the book, though I never doubted that you would like it.

I hear of you working too hard. Do not make yourself ill. I write feelingly. I ought to be at the Record Office among the parliamentary petitions—but can only do a day's work now and then. Take warning.

Yours affectionately

F. W. MAITLAND

105. To Maxwell Lyte

The West Lodge

Downing College

Cambridge

4 April 1892

DEAR MR. MAXWELL LYTE,

So far as I can discover from the printed report of the Record Commissioners the modern history of the Ancient Petitions is in brief this. In 1800 the number of petitions known to exist was not very large. Astle reported that at the Tower he had eleven bundles ranging from Edw. I to Hen. VI. Then in 1804–5 'an immense quantity', some 6000 petitions, were discovered by Lysons in the White Tower. 'A particular Report of them was drawn up by Mr. Illingworth by order of H.M. Commissioners on the Public Records and submitted to them in the year 1805.' A few years afterwards another supply was found in the lockers of the chapel in the White Tower. Then from 1806 onwards we have tidings of Lysons and Illingworth engaged in sorting these petitions and arranging them chronologically—they are being 'classed in the reigns to which they relate'.[3]

I think that all this points to the conclusion that, except perhaps in the case of the original bundles, the petitions when they were found bore on their face

[1] *Oxford Magazine*, March, 1892.
[2] Perhaps J. H. Round.
[3] On the whole of this first paragraph see M. *Memoranda de Parliamento*, Intro., ix–xxxiv. Cooper, *Public Records*, I. Chap. XVIII gives an account of Astle (Keeper of Records of the Tower, d. 1803) and of Lysons: see esp. pp. 355 and 385. For Illingworth, see Winfield, *Chief Sources*, 134–5. For the proceedings of the Record Commissioners generally, see Galbraith, *The Public Records*, Chap. V.

no obvious evidence of their date. But if this matter is to be cleared up it seems very important that Illingworth's report of 1805 should be found. I suppose that it was never printed, but if you have any transactions of the Commissioners in your keeping, you may be able to find it.

Believe me
Yours very truly
F. W. MAITLAND

106. To J. H. Round

The West Lodge
Downing College
Cambridge
10 April 1892

DEAR ROUND,

I am glad that the worthy peer King Stephen[1] is off your mind and look forward with great interest to learning all about him; but I am sorry that in other respects your account of yourself is not what your friends would wish it to be. However you are going up against 'Domesday'—that is a good thing. As you say, there is not much encouragement for work upon such a subject, but still, after what has happened in the case of Vol. I of 'Domesday Studies'[2] (vol. 2 is for the most part a thing of naught), I can not help thinking that a book by you would have a very fair sale—not of course the sale of a fourth-rate novel, but still enough to cover expenses. I think that the Clarendon Press— I say it with grief—manages its books better than does our Press, but I have little doubt that, failing Oxford, Cambridge could and would do something for you and of course I would do what I could with the Syndics.

D.B. 'intrigues' me the more one reads it. I lectured on it for a whole term and wrote all that I said; but I have no intention of publishing anything, at any rate for a long time to come. You will probably save me from the necessity of printing anything about it. I shall not be sorry.[3]

At present my head is full of later stuff, for I have an as yet unprinted Parliament Roll of Edward I on my hands. One discovers gradually that the editors of the Parliament Roll never used an original document when they could find a late transcript of it.

You will have heard that Froude is Professor at Oxford. Poor Freeman! I feared that York Powell was not 'in it', but why not Gardiner?[4]

[1] 'King Stephen was a worthy peer': Othello, Act 2, Scene 3. Round had just finished his *Geoffrey de Mandeville*, a study of the anarchy in the time of Stephen.
[2] Round had contributed to Vol. I of *Domesday Studies*, ed. P. E. Dove, an essay on 'Danegeld and the Finance of Domesday'.
[3] When M. published *D.B. and Beyond* in 1897, he explained in the Preface that he had waited for Round's *Feudal England*, pub. 1895.
[4] See Oman, *On the Writing of History*, 235–48. Edward Augustus Freeman (1823–92) had been Regius Professor of History at Oxford from 1884 to 1892. James Anthony Froude (1818–94), who succeeded him, was the man 'of whom Freeman most disapproved' (Oman, p. 239). York Powell succeeded Froude from 1894 to 1902. Samuel Rawson Gardiner (1829–1902), Professor of Modern History, King's College, London, was offered the Regius Professorship at Oxford in 1892 but declined it.

If you are sharing our lovely weather you ought soon to be strong again.

Yours very truly

F. W. MAITLAND

107. To Maxwell Lyte

The West Lodge
Downing College
Cambridge

15 April 1892

DEAR MR. MAXWELL LYTE,

I am very glad to hear that Illingworth's report has been found and is to the point.[1] I should like to see it. I mean to be in the Record Office on Wednesday and the following days in next week and if you can send the report into the round room for me to look at I shall be very much obliged to you.

I am now really getting to the end of my work. I shall be able to give about 100 of the petitions corresponding to the entries out of the 450 on the roll. If you will allow me I should like to give about a score of the corresponding writs issued in consequence of the responses to the petitions—'per petitionem de consilio'—just enough to show how this business was conducted.

The roll ends with a lot of *placita*. I do not propose to print these if upon collation the version of them given in the published Rolls of Parliament (a version which comes through Ryley from the Vetus Codex[2]) turns out to be fairly accurate. In that case a collection of 'variants' would be enough. But in any case my book will not be a very long one, and I hope to put the text of it in your hands before July.

Yours very truly

F. W. MAITLAND

108. To Maxwell Lyte

The West Lodge
Downing College
Cambridge

7 May 1892

DEAR MR. MAXWELL LYTE,

I am now near the end of my work and I have enough ready for the press to keep a printer at work until the whole is printed. Will you therefore allow me to send you the first part of my MS? I think that the time has come when a first sheet might be safely set up. I have written a set of instructions for the printer which I should like to submit along with my MS. for your approval. My own

---

[1] See Letter 105, *supra*.   [2] See Letter 73, *supra*.

opinion is that the difference between the entries on the roll and the original petitions will be best marked if the latter are printed in the ordinary type but solid; but of course about this matter it will be for you to say what should be done.

On the whole I am not dissatisfied with the success that I have had in my hunt for the petitions. About 450 are mentioned on the roll and I shall be able to print more than 100. It is very obvious that an enormous quantity of petitions have perished. At the rate of 400 or 500 petitions per parliament and of two parliaments per year the whole 16,000 that you have would be accumulated in less than 20 years instead of representing two centuries.

I want you to allow me to print about twenty writs issued for the purpose of carrying into effect the answers given to the petitions. One of my chief reasons for this request is that these writs guarantee the date of the roll and, as the roll is not one of the old well-known set of rolls of parliament and does not come from the treasury, its claim to be a roll of parliament and a roll of a particular year requires some support. If you will be good enough to glance at my MS. you will see what I have done.

I ought to say that I have found three of my petitions in Palgrave's transcripts and not been able to trace them further—they are not, so far as I can see, in Mr. Atkins' Index or in Mr. Rodney's. Probably during the great rearrangement they wandered away from their fellows. Shall you mind my printing these three documents from Palgrave's transcripts? I will leave them out if you think this the better course, but after all the convulsions which happened between 1825 and 1873 I do not think it at all strange, or in any way discreditable to your famous predecessors, that I cannot at this moment find three small documents which Palgrave saw some sixty years ago.[1]

I am becoming more and more convinced that the dates on the volumes of transcripts do not in all cases represent ancient labels or endorsements. I feel certain, for example, that the date '33 Edw. I' set upon one of the volumes represents an inference drawn by Illingworth in 1805.

But I must not waste your time and will merely ask once more whether I shall send you some 'copy'.

Yours very truly

F. W. MAITLAND

109. To Paul Vinogradoff

[No original. Transcript by Fisher in Camb. Univ. MSS, but not printed by him in *Memoir*: no beginning or ending.]

Downing
29 May 1892

The University is going to do its duty to Leslie Stephen—at least he is to be Litt.D.[2]

[1] See Letter 70, *supra.* On the 'convulsions between 1825 and 1873' see M. *Memoranda de Parliamento*, Intro. xii–xiii, and Winfield, *Chief Sources*, 105–7.
[2] See M. *Life of L.S.*, 212.

And I did want to talk to you about your volume ii and my volume i.[1] With me the matter stands thus—F. P., who is now in the West Indies and may go to India in the winter, has written an Anglo-Saxon chapter. *Between ourselves* I do not like it very much, partly because it will make it very difficult for me to say anything about A-S law in any later part of the book. My effort now is to shove on with the general sketch of the Norman and Angevin periods so that my collaborator may have little to do before we reach the Year Book period—if we ever reach it. So I am half inclined to throw aside all that I have written—it is a pretty heavy mass—about Domesday and the A-S books. Perhaps when you have got out your folk land papers[2] I may publish in some separate form a few things I want to say about A-S conveyancing—always supposing that you have neither said them nor wished to say them. They would run parallel with your investigations but hardly cut them, for they would be rather about the forms of the instruments than about social and economic history. But this prospect is quite vague at present, and I shall do nothing about it until I have heard from you about the scope and method of your volume ii. Then as to Domesday, I have sweated over it and what I have written reeks of sweat—forgive the phrase—but owing to F. P's agnosticism I am inclined to put it aside and leave D.B. to you and to Round. N.B.— J. H. R. is in the field and you and he will be writing concurrently.[3]

For myself I wish that I could have your advice, for I feel that the History will be an ungodly jumble, a set of fragments. Often I wish that I had set myself to edit Bracton.

I have made Seebohm's acquaintance. He is a good fellow besides being a man of genius.

110. To Maxwell Lyte

The West Lodge
Downing College
Cambridge
5th June 1892

DEAR MR. MAXWELL LYTE,

I am quite satisfied with the form of the specimen.

I wish to ask whether by way of exceptional favour I may be allowed to see at one time the whole of a certain bundle of the Q.R. Anc. Misc. I have some reason for suspecting the existence of another membrane of my Parliament Roll, but owing to the curious way in which the Miscellanea are catalogued

---

[1] 'My volume i' is P. and M. i. 'Your volume ii' is presumably Vinogradoff's expected sequel to *Villainage in England*; but *Growth of the Manor* was published only in 1905 and *English Society in the Eleventh Century* only in 1908.

[2] Vinogradoff's essay on *Folkland* appeared in E.H.R., Jan. 1893: reprinted in his Coll. Papers, I, 91.

[3] See Letter 106, *supra*. In his Preface to *D.B. and Beyond* M. explained the origin of the book and his original intention to include most of it in *P. and M.*

under the initials of defunct clerks I can not be quite certain as to the number
of documents that are in the bundle or as to whether I have seen all of them.

Believe me

Yours very truly

F. W. MAITLAND

111. To J. H. Round

Horsepools
Stroud
Gloucestershire

25 July 1892

MY DEAR ROUND,

I shall be happy and proud to cooperate with you in the matter of early
fines. Where do you propose to fix the hither limit—in 1189 or in 1194 when
the series of 'feet' becomes continuous?[1] You have some good points in Bp.
Nigel.[2] Did you notice among the fines one purporting on its back to be the
first that was made in triplicate? I took a note of it.[3]

Yours very truly

F. W. MAITLAND

112. To Paul Vinogradoff

[No original. Transcript by Fisher in Camb. Univ. MSS, but not printed
by him in *Memoir*. No beginning or ending: omissions as in transcript.]

Downing

4 Sept. 1892

I am putting into the L.Q.R. a protest against Mr. Gomme's 'survivalism'.
I deal with the Malmesbury case and the Aston case. I should like to clear the
field of some of this loose 'pre-Aryanism' and folk-lore.[4] ... I am helping
Whittaker with the Mirror which becomes more and more interesting. The
extreme stupidity of its first editor has concealed from view a statement in the
preface that it was written in gaol by one who had been imprisoned by unjust
judges. I doubt it is older than 1300.[5]

---

[1] M. wrote introductions to the first three of the four volumes of *Feet of Fines, 1182–1199*,
pub. by the Pipe Roll Society (1894–1900).
[2] *Dialogus de Scaccario*, compiled (1177–9) by Richard Fitz Nigel, Bishop of London:
see now the edition by Charles Johnson (1950).
[3] *P. and M.* ii. 97.
[4] See Letter 95, *supra*. Mr. Gomme was the author of *Village Community*, dissected by M.
in L.Q.R. Jan. 1893, reprinted C.P. II. 313.
[5] S.S. Vol. 7, Intro., esp. pp. x–xi, where the first edition of the *Mirror* (1642) is discussed:
no editor is named. W. J. Whittaker, the editor of S.S. Vol. 7, had been Whewell Scholar in
1890 and then became a Pensioner of Trinity College, Cambridge. After some years teaching
in Cambridge he was Assistant Reader to the Inns of Court from 1905 to 1931. He was a
friend and devoted follower of M. and was joint editor of M.'s *Lectures on Equity and on the
Forms of Action at Common Law*, pub. in 1909.

113. To J. H. Round

Horsepools
Stroud
Gloucestershire
6th Sept. 1892

DEAR ROUND,

I am glad to hear that you are in London, for this looks as if you were well—also it gives me some hope of seeing you, for I ought to be at P.R.O. next week.

I need not tell you that your Geoffrey de Mandeville[1] interested me deeply—particularly all of it that concerns London. Your results in that region are of very great importance.

It is a very curious thing that only yesterday I was saying to myself that the stray fines of Henry II's day ought to be collected—and this morning I have your letter.[2] I had just come across a pretty little nest of such fines in a Winchcombe Cartulary[3] published—or at all events printed—by Royce, a parson of these parts. Very likely you know the book—what don't you know?—if not, you may like to see it, for it is creditable. The original MS. belongs to Lord Sherborne. I have now some ten or a dozen fines to add to the list that I printed.[4] One nest I found in a Bury Cartulary at Cambridge. I think that between us we might make a very fair show. I shall be very willing to hand over to you notes or transcripts of those which I have spotted. It would I think be well to print pretty full particulars—date, place, names of justices, names of parties and of lands. I shall be very glad indeed to hear that you have persuaded the Society[5] to adopt this scheme and that you have taken charge of it. To me these fines are of very great interest.

I shall hardly add to the 'great confidence' with which you have explained 'terra ad duplum' by telling you that I have absolutely no doubt about the matter.[6]

Are you likely to write anything about the frequency of eyres temp. Hen. II? I feel pretty certain that the good Madox made a big mistake about this matter and has led even Stubbs astray. I must look into the affair if no one else is likely to do it, but should be only too glad to hear that you claimed the field as your own.[7]

The delay in the publication of Rot. Cur. Regis does not lie at my door. They are awfully bad copy and I do not like to hurry the excellent Vincent.[8]

Yours very truly
F. W. MAITLAND

---

[1] See Letter 106, *supra*.   [2] Not extant.
[3] See *P. and M.* ii. 94–106, esp. pp. 96 and 97.   [4] S.S. Vol. 1, Intro. xxvii–xxviii.
[5] Pipe Roll Society: see Letter 111, *supra*.
[6] See Round's essay, *Terra ad Duplum*, E.H.R. vii. 533.
[7] Neither M. nor Round seem to have written papers on the itinerant justices of Henry II. Stubbs, *Gesta Regis Henrici II (Benedict of Peterborough)*, Vol. II, pp. lxiii, ff. (R. S.) relied—in part at least—on Madox, *History of the Exchequer* (1711 ed. pp. 83, ff.). Perhaps the 'big mistake' was to assume that fresh eyres took place every year after 1166. See H. G. Richardson, 43 E.H.R. 167–71.
[8] M.'s *Memoranda de Parliamento* was published in Nov. 1893. Vincent was presumably the printer.

114. To Henry Sidgwick

[No date, but from contents probably early 1893. Sidgwick was on the Council of the Senate which, late in 1892 and early in 1893, was engaged in controversy with the Town over University privileges and Proctorial powers—provoked especially by the jurisdiction of the Vice-Chancellor in the Spinning House (see Letter 92, *supra*). Legal issues had been raised by Dr. Kenny and R. T. Wright. See Winstanley, *Later Victorian Cambridge*, Chap. IV, esp. pp. 130–5.]

MY DEAR SIDGWICK,

Herewith notes which seem to me better than those formerly sent, and you may do with them whatever seems good. The whole of the case before Mansfield is valuable—it was in the celebrated contest between Lords Sandwich and Hardwicke for the High Stewardship[1] and the judges took a most liberal view of the university constitution. If you think right, leave out the reference to *Kemp v. Neville*; but I have spoken of it in such a way that it will not I think hurt anybody's feelings and have even suppressed its name. I refer to it because of its late date.[2]

As regards the Bible privilege:—the Universities have this privilege under letters patent from the Crown—of old date, but of *what* date I have not discovered; apparently however of date shortly after the making of the A.V.[3] How the Crown came by the power of granting such a privilege seems doubtful. As to the licencing of books in general, the Vice-Chancellor was made *one* of the licensing authorities by the Licensing Act (14 Car. 2, c. 33, sometimes cited as 13 and 14 Car. 2, c. 33). The Judges, the heralds, secretaries of state, archbishops, were also licensing authorities, and (unfortunately) the Vice-Chancellor's authority seems to have extended only to books published within the University.

Yours very truly

F. W. MAITLAND.

P.S. Your letter has just arrived.[4] I send these notes to you believing that this will really save time as I know nothing of the proceedings of the University Press.

F. W. M.

NOTES.

The notion that the University of Cambridge is a corporation created by the Statute 13 Eliz. c. 29 with rights and functions strictly limited by the words of that Statute is certainly opposed to the construction which has been put upon that Act of Parliament by the very highest legal authorities from the time of its passing downwards. The University is a corporation by prescription, existing from time immemorial, with many privileges and rights to which its

---

[1] See Winstanley, *The University of Cambridge in the 18th Century*, 55–139.
[2] *Kemp v. Neville* (1861) 10 C.B.N.S. 523: Winstanley, *Later Victorian Cambridge*, 92–4. The case concerned the Proctorial powers of arrest and the judicial powers of the Vice-Chancellor.
[3] Authorised Version.   [4] Not extant.

only, though sufficient, title is a title by prescription. The object of the Act in question seems to have been (1) to fix once for all the style and title of the ancient universities, (2) to give parliamentary sanction to certain privileges which these prescriptive corporations enjoyed under royal grants the legality of which was questionable. In particular there had been granted to each university the privilege of deciding cases arising in the university courts according to the Civil or Roman Law, and the privilege, being in derogation of the Common Law of the land, had been considered invalid. This privilege the Act confirmed, and thenceforth the Civil Law continued in use in the Chancellor's Court.

Coke explains his view of 'this blessed act', as he calls it, in his Fourth Institute (p. 227). According to him it was passed in order that each of the Universities might be incorporated *by a certain name* 'albeit they were ancient corporations before', and in order that they might enjoy all privileges granted to them by whatsoever name or names they had been designated in the letters patent. Then, with the marginal note 'Nota, (proh dolor) the ancient charters, records, etc. of the university of Cambridge burnt by rebels', he tells of the destruction of the university charters by the townsmen in Richard the Second's reign and the transfer then made to the university corporation of the forfeited privileges of the town of Cambridge. (The proceedings in Parliament relating to these charters will be found in Rot. Parl. 5 Ric. ii, ss. 45–60).

What privilege of the University it was which required confirmation by Act of Parliament Coke explained on more than one occasion.

'Coke, Chief Justice. In 8 H.4. a charter was granted to both the Universities of Oxford and Cambridge to enable them in their proceedings. They by force of this charter did proceed in temporal cases in a civil manner' [i.e. according to the Civil Law], 'their power being first by this charter. Afterwards, by means of the Earl of Leicester, they in 13 Eliz. obtained a confirmation from the Queen by Act of Parliament, by which their charters were confirmed, and that they might proceed by force of their charter as before they had done, their proceedings before by their charter being against the Law of the Land.'

'Popham was very strongly against this, but afterwards when he did see that the Act of Parliament was passed for them, then he wished that they would prove honest men in their proceedings' (3 Bulstrode, p. 212).

So again on another occasion Coke says that the Universities have a special Act of Parliament made 13 Eliz. to confirm the privilege of holding pleas according to the course of the Civil Law (Godbolt, p. 201, also Jenkins, pp. 97, 117).

Hale gives the same account of the matter:—

'And altho' King H. 8. 14 anno regni sui granted to the University' [in this case the University of Oxford] 'a liberal charter to proceed according to the use of the university, viz. by a course much conformed to the Civil Law; yet that Charter had not been sufficient to have warranted such proceedings without the help of an Act of Parliament: and therefore in 13 Eliz. an Act passed whereby that charter was in effect enacted' (Hist. Com. Law. ch. 2).

Blackstone writes to the same effect. After mentioning the Oxford charter of Hen. viii, he says that a similar charter was granted to Cambridge in the 3rd of Elizabeth. But these charters were invalid because the king could not alter the law, and *therefore* in the reign of Elizabeth an act was obtained, 13 Eliz. c. 29, 'confirming *all* the charters of the two universities, and those of 14 Hen. viii and 3 Eliz. by name' (Comment. vol. 3, p. 84).

In a case tried in 4 Geo. ii. Mr. Justice Denton doubts whether a particular form of legal proceeding (replevin) be within the charter of the University of Cambridge, to which Mr. Justice Fortescue answers, 'The reason why the Charter was confirmed by Parliament was because it took away the benefit of the Common Law from the subject, which the King's grant alone could not do; so that the argument drawn from that matter has no weight.' (Fitzgibbon, p. 155).

If then the Act 13 Eliz. c. 29 had any special object more limited than that of confirming the ancient universities in all their existing rights, that object was to sanction the use of the Civil Law in the University Courts. This interpretation is not only that given to the Statute by the highest authority but is in itself reasonable, for of all the many charters belonging to the two universities only two are *specifically* confirmed by the Act, and these are the Oxford charter of Hen. viii. and the Cambridge charter of 3 Eliz.

Again, the claim of the University to be a corporation not by statute but by prescription has been repeatedly made and allowed.

Thus when Bentley obtained a mandamus to compel his restoration to the degree of D.D. the university returned

'that the University of Cambridge is an ancient university and a corporation by prescription, consisting of a chancellor, masters and scholars, who time out of mind have had the government and correction of the members. . . . That time out of mind there has been a court held before the chancellor or vice-chancellor, etc.' (*Rex v. Cambridge*, Strange, p. 557, ff.).

It was on the ground that the University was a corporation by prescription and as such had no visitor that the Queen's[1] Bench interfered on Bentley's behalf. Counsel for the King says 'The defendants have shown themselves to be a corporation by prescription, and as such they are under the control of the Court' (*Ibid*. p. 559). In the same case Mr. Justice Fortescue says that the right to grant degrees is prescriptive, adding that *universitas* is the proper Latin for *corporation* and that degrees were not granted until the university was a corporation, i.e. about the year 1200. He then gives once more the often given explanation of the Statute of Elizabeth, namely, that it was passed to sanction the use of the Civil Law. (8 Modern Reports, p. 163, and Fortescue, p. 205).

Lord Mansfield, giving judgment in a case directly concerning the powers of the University, a case arising out of the election of a high steward,[2] spoke of the Academic Statutes of Elizabeth as follows:—

'When Queen Elizabeth gave these statutes, the University of Cambridge was

----

[1] *Sic:* should be King's Bench.   [2] See p. 106, note 1, *supra*.

of ancient establishment and had many prescriptive rights as well as former charters of very old date. And there was no intention to alter and overturn their ancient constitution. These statutes undoubtedly meant to leave a vast deal upon the ancient constitution of the university, without repealing or abrogating their old established customs, rights and privileges; nor could the university mean to accept them upon any such terms. Therefore I am clear that the statutes of Queen Elizabeth can not be set up to invalidate establishments subsisting long before she was born'. (*Rex v. Cambridge*, Burrow, pp. 1647 ff.).

It is plain then that in the opinion of Lord Mansfield, in whose judgment three other judges concurred, the university is no 'statutory corporation' the limits of whose powers are to be found in an Act of Elizabeth, but an ancient corporation with 'many prescriptive rights' and 'establishments subsisting long before she was born'. Mr. Justice Wilmot added that he could not help rejecting the attempt to overturn one of these ancient usages 'with the utmost indignation'. (*Ibid.*, p. 1661).

To pass to quite modern times—In 1838 the Queen's Bench refused a quo warranto to inquire into the Vice-Chancellor's authority to license alehouses on the ground that the Vice-Chancellor had exercised that privilege 'from a very remote period, from a period, indeed, so remote that the first exercise of it cannot be distinctly traced, nor the origin to which it is referable at all certainly assigned'. Mr. Justice Littledale reasons that a control over alehouses 'was highly expedient, if not necessary; the University was not unlikely to procure from the Crown what might be so reasonably asked for; and, being a learned body, was likely to procure it in such a form and with such sanction as would render the grant valid.' (8 Adolphus and Ellis, pp. 281, ff.).

Not one word is there about the Statute which is now supposed to lay down in strict terms the exact functions of the University. The franchise had long been exercised and was one which might reasonably have been granted. This was sufficient.

In a still later case decided in 1861 in which another privilege of the University was successfully asserted,[1] it was pleaded that the chancellor and scholars of the University of Cambridge, from time whereof the memory of man is not to the contrary until the passing of the Act of Elizabeth, were a body corporate by various names of incorporation; and that the office of proctors 'is, and from time whereof the memory of man is not to the contrary was, an ancient office, and that the persons for the time being holding such office have, and each of them hath, during all the time aforesaid, by custom of and in the said university from time whereof the memory of man is not to the contrary', there used and exercised certain authorities, and that 'the office of vice-chancellor is, and from time whereof the memory of man is not to the contrary was, an ancient office', and so forth. (10 C.B.N.S. 523).

In view of these authorities it seems impossible to regard the University as a statutory corporation comparable, as has been suggested, to a joint-stock

---

[1] See p. 106, note 2, *supra*.

company for the manufacture of railway carriages,[1] or to treat as *ultra vires* every act of the University which can not be brought within a narrow construction of certain words stating the motive for the passing of an Act confirming the University in all its ancient privileges. We must, it seems, hold on the contrary that the University enjoys all those prescriptive rights and privileges which have not been expressly taken away by any Act of Parliament, and that the objects and powers of this ancient corporation are only defined by long continued usage and reasonable custom. 'A vast deal', as Mansfield said, has been left 'upon the ancient constitution of the University', a constitution existing long before Queen Elizabeth was born.

F. W. Maitland.

115. To Maxwell Lyte

The West Lodge
Downing College
Cambridge

14 Jan. 1893

Dear Mr. Maxwell Lyte,

I am leaving along with this letter some 'copy' which, if you think fit, I should like to print by way of appendix to my book.

First, there are thirteen Gascon petitions of my year. Then there are a few writs from the Gascon roll which will be of importance to me in my Introduction. Lastly, there is a short account of the Vetus Codex which I want as a supplement for some remarks that I have to make in my Introduction.[2]

I should very much like to submit to you the first part of my Introduction. I have been compelled to say a little about the modern history of the bundles of Ancient Petitions.[3] I have said as little as I could, but, do what I can, I can not altogether avoid the suggestion that bundles were broken up without enough care being taken to preserve evidence of their contents. I do not say this, but I can not help telling a story which may suggest this conclusion to the minds of readers.

If you see any way out of the difficulty I shall be very glad to adopt it. Such is my admiration for Palgrave that I do not like saying anything that anybody, however perverse, could twist into blame. I have written some pages over and over again without satisfying myself and so shall welcome any advice that you can give me.

Yours very truly

F. W. Maitland

[1] *Ashbury Railway Carriage Co.* v. *Riche* (1875), L.R. 7 H.L. 653.
[2] M. *Memoranda de Parliamento*, Intro. App. I and IV.
[3] *Ibid.*, xii–xiv, xxvi–xxviii, lv–lvi, lxii–lxv.

116. To Charles Gross

The West Lodge
Downing College
Cambridge

16 Jan. 1893

MY DEAR SIR,

I am very grateful to you for a copy of your very learned and interesting essay on the coroner, which had escaped me in the Political Science Quarterly.[1] I am not quite certain that you have convinced me on all points, but conviction may come in time.

I have lately been reading with great interest your Exchequer of the Jews. I hope that the Selden Society will publish some of the Jewish rolls.[2]

If ever you are undertaking an *iter Anglicanum* I hope that you will let me know of this betimes.

Yours very truly

F. W. MAITLAND

117. To Maxwell Lyte

Downing College
Cambridge

5 March 1893

DEAR MR. MAXWELL LYTE,

I am obliged to you for your letter[3] and glad to hear of your discovery. I think that there are many petitions belonging to the September parliament of 33 Edward I. If my last set of slips has passed through your hands you may have seen that I have taken one long extract from a Coram Rege Roll.[4] It disclosed so picturesque a story about Oxford that I could not refrain from copying it, and I think it will show the very close connexion which exists in Edward I's time between the pleas held by the king and council in their parliaments and the pleas that are heard in the king's bench.

Yours very truly

F. W. MAITLAND

---

[1] *The Early History and Influence of the Office of Coroner:* see S.S. Vol. 9, Intro. xiv, note 8.

[2] S.S. Vol. 15. For Gross, *The Exchequer of the Jews of England* (1888), see S.S. Vol. 15, Preface, note 5.

[3] Not extant.

[4] M. *Memoranda de Parliamento,* 44–7.

118. To Charles Gross

The West Lodge
Downing College
Cambridge
21st May 1893

DEAR SIR,

I am glad to think that you are to be in England this summer and hope that we may meet. When you are here I shall probably be in Gloucestershire and I trust that you will pay me a visit.

As regards the Selden volume of Jewish Pleas, I believe that it is still in the air, but that the Secretary has a promise from Mr. Jacobs[1] to the effect that he will do something. I do not know Jacobs but will try to discover what his intentions are. I need not say that were I editing the volume I should jump at your offer of help; but Jacobs, as you know, is a specialist[2] and I must not speak for him. However I will certainly let the secretary know of your proposal, and if (as may hap) Jacobs is not willing to do the work, then with your aid some other arrangement might be made.

Then as to the coroners' rolls. I hope that before you publish them elsewhere you will consider whether you will not offer a volume to the Selden Society. The pay that it can offer its editors is but small—I think that I have had about £40 per volume—but still it pays a little, while my own experience is that publishing records at one's own risk means less. So will you think this over?

The 'English Historical' sent me your 'Coroner' for review and I have been hardy enough to pass some remarks upon it—which I hope will not offend you.[3]

Wherever I may be in the summer, a letter addressed to Downing College will find me.

Yours very truly

F. W. MAITLAND

119. To Maxwell Lyte

The West Lodge
Downing College
Cambridge
30th May 1893

DEAR MR. DEPUTY KEEPER,

I now venture to submit to you the first sheets of my Introduction in the hope that you will be kind enough to look at them and to tell me of anything

---

[1] Joseph Jacobs, author of *The Jews of Angevin England* (1893): see Letters 124 and 158, *infra*.
[2] See S.S. Vol. 15, Preface.
[3] See Letter 116, *supra*. M.'s review is in E.H.R., 1893, pp. 758–60. See also Gross, Intro. to S.S. Vol. 9, p. xvi.

that is amiss in them. I have tried not to say more than enough, but something I had to say about the bundles of petitions and Palgrave's transcripts.[1] I am sorry to put such dull stuff before you, but I could not make it lively. The second part of my introduction will I hope be brighter; it deals with the parliament of 1305.

Believe me
Yours very sincerely
F. W. MAITLAND

120. To Maxwell Lyte

The West Lodge
Downing College
Cambridge
11th June 1893

DEAR MR. MAXWELL LYTE,

I am much obliged to you for reading the beginning of my Introduction and for saying that I have not been indiscreet. I am making a correction which will make the passage that you queried less misleading. On Monday the 19th I hope to be in the Record Office and I shall be grateful to you if you will have the volume that contains Illingworth's MS. Reports[2] sent into the round room for my use, as I should like to have one last look at it. I will carry with me to London the two volumes of Palgrave's transcripts that I have had. I regret to say that their backs have fallen off.

Yours very truly
F. W. MAITLAND

121. To Charles Gross

Horsepools
Stroud
Gloucestershire
5 July 1893

DEAR SIR,

It will give me great pleasure if you will consent to be my guest in Gloucestershire on Saturday and Sunday next. This house is about four miles from the Stroud station on the Great Western line. A good train leaves Paddington at 12. Less than three hours will bring you here, and if you tell me that you are coming I will meet you at Stroud. I can promise you pretty country and we can have a long talk about coroners, etc.

Yours very truly
F. W. MAITLAND

[1] See Letter 115, *supra*. [2] See Letter 105, *supra*.

113

122. To Charles Gross

[No date; but from Letters 121, *supra*, and 123, *infra*, it is probably 7 July 1893.]

Horsepools

DEAR GROSS,

I rejoice. If on arriving at Stroud station you do not find a fly from Horse-pools at one side, try the other.

Yours very truly

F. W. MAITLAND

123. To H. A. L. Fisher

Horsepools

7 July 1893

MY DEAR HERBERT,

I am more grateful than I can say for the trouble that you have taken over my proof sheet[1] and I am relieved of a great weight of anxiety by finding that you have little to reprehend. Jumiéges was very bad, Bellême I adopted deliberately for the same reason that I prefer Marlborough to Marlberge, to say nothing of Marlbridge, which is an idiotism. I have had more qualms about this chapter than about any other except one in which I became sceptical over 'the family' as a legal 'unit'[2]—this will bring on me the wrath of Gross of the Gild Merchant who is to stay with us for Sunday.

Please think from time to time of Gloucestershire as an alternative place. I want to hear about the Lombards.[3]

Yours fraternally

F. W. MAITLAND

124. To Charles Gross

Horsepools

Stroud

14 Augt. 1893

DEAR MR. GROSS,

I think that I must be right in thanking you for a copy of *The Merchant and the Friar* which came here while I was away. It is kind of you to send a book that I shall enjoy and treasure.

I have just received the doctoral dissertation of Frank Zinkeisen.[4] I ought to thank him for it but know not whither to send my thanks. Can you tell me his address? The paper is interesting.

---

[1] *P. and M.* i. Book I, Chap. III. The names cited in the second sentence of this letter will there be found.

[2] *P. and M.* ii. Book II, Chap. VI. s. 1.

[3] Possibly part of Fisher's preparatory work for his *Medieval Empire*, published in 2 vols. in 1898.

[4] See Letter 125, *infra*.

I hope that you are enjoying England and its coroners.

To-morrow I am going to see the Bracton MSS. at Cheltenham.[1]

Believe me
Yours very truly
F. W. MAITLAND.

I understand from Dove that Jacobs would not undertake a Jewish volume. I would much rather see it [in] your hands than in his, for his last book does not fill me with confidence.[2]

125. To Charles Gross

Horsepools,
Stroud
30th Augt. 1893

DEAR MR. GROSS,

I hope that I need hardly tell you how welcome any friend of yours will be, especially if he comes in nomine legis. So tell Mr. Wells[3] that I shall be delighted to see him.

I believe also that I did write to thank you for the Merchant and the Friar. I fear that I misdirected my letter. Once more I thank you heartily. In the unfortunate letter I asked you for the address of Zinkeisen who has sent me his disquisition on the courts; but as I have now promised to review it in the E.H.R., perhaps I need not write to him. So take no trouble about this.[4]

I am right glad that you have found a publisher for your book. It will be most valuable and ought I think to sell well.[5]

Very truly yours
F. W. MAITLAND

126. To R. Lane Poole

[This and the subsequent letters to R. Lane Poole here reprinted were first printed in Cambridge Historical Journal, 1952, pp. 318–51, by Dr. Austin Lane Poole. The originals were presented by him to Camb. Univ. Library. In the present edition notes by Dr. Austin Lane Poole are in square brackets.]

The West Lodge
Downing College
Cambridge
22 Oct. 1893

MY DEAR POOLE,

There is not the slightest hurry for the Wilburton notes.[6] I should be sorry if you allowed them to upset any of your arrangements. The E.H.R. grows more and more interesting. I should like to have one once a month.

---

[1] See S.S. Vol. 8, p. 250.   [2] See Letter 118, *supra.*

[3] See S.S. Vol. 9, Intro. xxxvii, note 1, and xl–xli, note 16.

[4] Zinkeisen, *Die Anfänge der Lehngerichtsbarkeit in England*, reviewed by M. in E.H.R. 1894, p. 600.

[5] Possibly *Bibliography of British Municipal History*, pub. in England by Longmans (1897).

[6] [A.L.P. M., *The History of a Cambridgeshire Manor*, E.H.R. (1894) 417: C.P. II. 366]. See Letters 64 and 69, *supra.*

If you have a spare moment will you be kind enough to give me your opinion about 'churchwardens'—men not pipes? I have been looking for them in cent. xiii but hitherto without success. I daresay however that I have not looked in the right quarter, which I suppose would be the accounts of episcopal or archidiaconal visitations. But are there such accounts for this period? I feel sure that if there are you know about them.

As I understand, one finds similar creatures in France and Germany in recent times; but on the other hand they do not seem to be parts of the catholic organization of the church and they are distressing me a good deal. The English books on ecclesiastical law are useless: they assume the church-warden as aboriginal.[1]

If I am trespassing, tell me so.

Yours very truly

F. W. MAITLAND

127. To J. H. Round

The West Lodge
Downing College
Cambridge

30 Oct. 1893

DEAR ROUND,

I ought to have written before now in answer to your letter[2]; but I have been waiting in vain for a time when I should have leisure to chat in comfort. That time now seems distant—somewhere in December—and even now I am sitting and likely to sit in council.[3]

So far as I can tell you have made good your point about the derivation of Worc. from William of Malmesbury: it is interesting and important. Its bearing on 'current controversy' is obvious. Six centuries hence some Round of the future will have a theory about the relation of E.H.R. and Quart. Rev.—'curious coincidences', 'strong internal evidence', etc. etc.[4]

Pollock is *in partibus infidelium*, to wit in India or thereabouts[5]—but he is a methodical man and I expect he made all provisions necessary for the Mowbray abeyance: he will be back in February I guess.

The reeve and four men temp. Hen. VIII are very nice; many thanks for them. I am fast printing a great deal of stuff—each sheet is a relief though I am trailing my coat through many fairs.[6]

I have my fears, and you obviously have yours, about the New Society.

[1] See *P. and M.* i. 614.   [2] Not extant.
[3] Presumably as a member of the Council of the Senate.
[4] For William of Malmesbury and Florence of Worcester and the question, 'Who borrowed from whom?', see Galbraith, *Historical Research in Medieval England* (1951), 15–24, and Darlington, *Anglo-Norman Historians* (1947).
[5] Delivering the Tagore Lectures, pub. 1894 as *Law of Fraud, Misrepresentation and Mistake in British India*.
[6] The 'sheets' were the proofs of *Memoranda de Parliamento*. See Cam, Intro. to *Select Hist. Essays*, xvi.

Delisle's name will look well.[1] Do you know the lovely type that is used in the new edition of Liber Landavensis?[2] A small dot is put under all the letters that are not in the original; you need not see the dots unless you like, but can find them if you want them; they are pleasanter than italics to the eye.

> Yours sincerely
> F. W. MAITLAND

128. To Charles Gross

> The West Lodge
> Downing College
> Cambridge
> *10th Novr. 1893*

DEAR MR. GROSS,

I have to thank you for several papers and for a visit from Wells.[3] He stayed two nights with me here. I liked him well and was much interested by his thesis. I fear that I was not able to give him many hints for his investigations. I hope that he will come upon something good either at the Record Office or at the Museum.

When may we look for your book on the Quellen of English history?[4] I feel the want of it every day. You will see in English Hist. Rev. that I have dared to differ from you about a small point.[5] In all probability I must be wrong. At any rate I trust that I have not offended you.

Shall we see you 'this side' in the summer? I hope so.

> Believe me
> Yours very truly
> F. W. MAITLAND

129. To James Bradley Thayer

[Post-card. Year from post-mark.]

> Cambridge, England
> *12 Nov.* [*1893*]

Many thanks for the Harvard Law Review.[6] The story is extremely interesting and was little if at all known on this side the ocean.

> Yours very truly
> F. W. MAITLAND

---

1 The 'New Society' may have been a scheme in which Round was at this time interested 'for an Anglo-Norman Record Society, with a view to printing the chartularies of some of the French monasteries that had cells and possessions in England': Page, Preface to Round, *Family Origins and Other Studies* (1930), p. xxvi. The scheme did not materialise.

2 *Liber Landavensis*, the ancient register of the Cathedral Church of Llandaff, reproduced from the Gwysaney manuscript by J. G. Evans; privately printed Oxford, 1893.

3 See Letter 125, *supra*.

4 Probably *Sources and Literature of English History*, pub. 1900; but perhaps *Bibliography of British Municipal History*, pub. 1897: see Letter 125, *supra*.

5 See Letter 118, *supra*.

6 Probably *Origin and Scope of the American Doctrine of Constitutional Law* (1893), 7 Harv. L. Rev. 129.

130. To Charles Gross

The West Lodge
Downing College
Cambridge

26th Novr. 1893

DEAR DR. GROSS,

I fear that I can not help you or Prof. Child[1] to 'horne and lease'. I never saw the phrase before. As to Dillon on Corporations[2] accept my thanks. I have seen the book and it gave me a lift at the difficult place for which I am thankful.

When I tell you that my section on 'Jews' is just through the press and that my section on 'Boroughs' is ready you will know that you have often been in my thoughts of late. I could have made no way without The Gild Merchant. I find that I am in for *three* volumes.[3] I liked Wells very much. Zinkeisen might be bolder.[4]

I hope that you flourish.

Yours very truly

F. W. MAITLAND

131. To Henry Sidgwick

The West Lodge
Downing College
Cambridge

8th March 1894

MY DEAR SIDGWICK,

I shall not be at the Council on Monday. I want to make sure of being able to do all my work next term and therefore am going to the country. As I think it possible that Clark's[5] letter may come before the Council and you evidently take an interest in it, I wish to suggest to you that a good deal would be gained if he could be induced to place himself under the statute and that a little compensation would be well expended in bringing about this result.

[1] Francis James Child (1825–96), philologist: Professor of English at Harvard University, author of *Observations on the Language of Chaucer*, etc. The phrase that follows is almost illegible in the MS, and, if correctly deciphered, its meaning is obscure.

[2] Used and cited by M. in his Introduction to *Gierke*, esp. at p. xii.

[3] M. seems at this time to have been contemplating three volumes for *P. and M.*

[4] See Letters 125 and 128, *supra*.

[5] E. C. Clark, Regius Professor of Civil Law. Two years later the Special Board for Law, of which M. was a member, recommended new qualifications for the degrees of LL.M. and LL.D. Under existing regulations the Regius Professor (a) was paid in part from lecture fees and in part from the fees for these degrees, (b) was the sole judge of theses submitted for the LL.D. The Board was not empowered to recommend a change in the method of payment but it did recommend that the adjudication of theses be transferred to a Committee. In a debate on 7 May 1896 M. spoke gratefully of Prof. Clark's co-operation, and the recommendation was approved by a large majority (see *Cambridge University Reporter* for 10 March 1896 and 12 May 1896).

A good deal remains to be done before the LLM and LLD degrees are creditable to the University: but I have refrained from proposing further changes because the Regius himself took part in recommending the change which was made in the qualification of the LLM degree and this must have decreased his income. He—if I may say so—behaved so well about this that I feel that any further change should include a compensation. The number of LLM's is growing very small indeed and this will soon tell upon the number of LLD's.

Of course it is not a satisfactory plan that the fee for the LLD should go to the one person who pronounces upon the candidate's claim.

I do not think that in the end the University would be a loser by compensating Clark and putting the degree upon a more satisfactory basis. I think that I could name several men who would apply for and do credit to the doctorate if it was more of an honour than it is. Just by way of example I may mention Westlake's[1] case. I have no reason for supposing that he would care to be a doctor, but he could not become one without presenting himself for one part of the Law Tripos.

Thus, though I do not think that Clark's case for a commutation of the lecture fees is, in the present state of finance, a very strong one, I should be glad to make this a part of a more general settlement, and I gathered from Clark's letter that he is not indisposed to open the whole subject.

I thought that nothing would be gained by a reference to the Law Board, for the question is a financial one. Perhaps you will be able to think of some plan which will bring about a desirable result.

> Yours very truly
>
> F. W. MAITLAND

132. To James Bradley Thayer

> The West Lodge
> Downing College
> Cambridge
>
> *22nd April 1894*

DEAR PROFESSOR THAYER,

Very many thanks for your Cases on Constitutional Law.[2] They are most inviting and I long to read them. But this pleasure I must for a while deny myself, for a spell of illness and idleness has left me sadly in arrears of my duties. When leisure comes once more I shall be yet more grateful to you than I am now—and this is saying much.

> Yours very truly
>
> F. W. MAITLAND

[1] The Whewell Professor of International Law. He became LL.D. in 1895.
[2] Thayer's *Cases on Constitutional Law* were published in four parts: Parts I and II in the Spring of 1894, to which this letter clearly refers, Part III in the Autumn of 1894 (see Letter 141, *infra*), Part IV early in 1895.

133. To H. A. L. Fisher

Cambridge

17 May 1894

MY DEAR HERBERT,

I hope that you have decided to 'run for' the chair at Glasgow. If you think that the smallest good could come of anything that I wrote about you, I will most gladly write it.[1]

Invigilans invigilo—it is dreary work—but an honours candidate has just finished a list of kings of England with Geo. I. II. III. IV., Anne, William IV and Mary, Victoria.

You know that Ashley is in for Glasgow—*necnon* O.B.![2]

Yours affectionately

F. W. MAITLAND

134. To J. H. Round

The West Lodge
Downing College
Cambridge

8th June 1894

DEAR ROUND

It is kind of you to write to me. I am now doing fairly well—I wish that you gave a better report of yourself.

No, I don't know that Berkeley settlement[3] and should be happy to make its acquaintance. You always tell me of something good.

I understand that I may thank you for an extremely kind review of my parliament roll in the Athenaeum. I do so very heartily. Your praise is the more welcome because no one else out of Scotland has said one word of the book.[4]

Is *the* battle over yet? It has amused me much and I hope that you are not quite worn out by this terrific conflict.[5]

What of the Anglo-Norman cartularies?[6]

Yours very truly

F. W. MAITLAND

[1] Fisher did 'run for' the Professorship of Modern History at the University of Glasgow, but 'did not ask Maitland for a testimonial on the ground that he was related by marriage': Ogg, *Herbert Fisher*, 41. See Letter 136, *infra*.

[2] O. B. = Oscar Browning. Sir William James Ashley (1860–1927), economic historian, was Professor at Toronto, 1888–92; at Harvard, 1892–1901; at Birmingham, 1901–25.

[3] See M., *D.B. and Beyond*, 318.

[4] Round's review appeared in the *Athenaeum* of 3 March, 1894. For the reference to Scotland, see Cam, Intro. to *Selected Hist. Essays*, xvi.

[5] 'The battle' was the Battle of Hastings (New Style) fought primarily between Round and Freeman and carried on in many contemporary English journals and reviews between 1892 and 1897: see the articles referred to by Round in his *Feudal England*, 333–418.

[6] In a letter to M. of 11 Dec. 1892 (Camb. Univ. MSS) Round had canvassed the possibility of preparing an edition of Anglo-Norman cartularies. In 1899 he did in fact edit for the P.R.O. *A Calendar of Documents preserved in France, illustrative of the History of Great Britain and Ireland, A.D. 918–1206*. See also Letter 127, *supra*.

135. To J. C. Smuts

[Printed in part by Sir Keith Hancock, *Smuts—The Sanguine Years (1870–1919)*, at p. 46. Now printed from the original in the Smuts Archives, Jagger Library, University of Cape Town.]

The West Lodge
Downing College
Cambridge

15 June 1894

DEAR MR. SMUTS,

Will this do? I have seldom written a testimonial with a better will.

I think that I shall not be indiscreet in telling you that your place in Part II was due very largely to your exceptionally good essays.[1]

I hope to hear of you again. At the Cape you have a most interesting state of things and I think that what you have learnt here will enable you to see the interest of it. I am always hoping that some day Cambridge will turn out a great Romanist—a Ihering who knows English law. Germans I fancy can never put themselves quite outside the system. An Englishman might do it— but then our own best lawyers are always immersed in practice. There is a great chance for you.

I am going to ask you to accept a copy of Bracton's Note Book which will come to you from the Press in memory of

Yours very truly

F. W. MAITLAND

136. To H. A. L. Fisher

Horsepools

6th July 1894

MY DEAR HERBERT,

I am disgusted with these Glasgow folk.[2] They had come so near to a real 'good thing' and they have preferred the commonplace. Towards the end I had good hope and therefore I am disappointed.

When you are at Oxford you are very near us. Do come to see us and this place—it really is worth seeing. If you won't then we must compromise by meeting at Cirencester or Stow on the Wold or Moreton in Marsh or some other half-way house.

Yours very truly

F. W. MAITLAND

---

[1] Smuts had been placed first in the first class of each part of the Law Tripos.
[2] See Letter 133, *supra*. Richard Lodge (1855–1936), then Fellow of Brasenose College, Oxford, was elected: Ogg, *Herbert Fisher*, 42.

137. To J. H. Round

> Horsepools
> Stroud
> *15 July 1894*

DEAR ROUND,

It is kind of you to give me these tidings.[1] I am very glad indeed that you are going to tackle D.B. To what you write I shall look forward with delight—perhaps mixed with dread, for I am not quite certain that this news has not come too late to prevent me from exposing myself. I am reconsidering my position which is complicated by the existence in irretrievably printed sheets of a supposed chapter on D.B.[2]

As to the East Anglian essay I, like you, am surprised that it is not in print. This hampers me in my own work, for, as you know, I am 'in a fiduciary position'—which is always a —— uncomfortable position. Does not H. H. know Corbett?[3]

> Yours very truly
> F. W. MAITLAND

138. To Leslie Stephen

[No original. Typewritten transcript without signature or ending in Camb. Univ. Add. MSS, perhaps by Fisher, who has headed it 'omit'—presumably from the *Memoir*.

On 26 July 1894 Leslie Stephen wrote to M. (Camb. Univ. Add. MSS), urging him to ensure that Pollock's share in *P. and M.* was made public. '. . . If the question were simply between you and Pollock I should say no more. Be as generous as you please would be my only remark. But you have in my opinion to consider two other points. . . . [The first is that] the public has some right to say that they shall not be asked to buy a book by a statement as to the authorship which certainly gives an inaccurate impression of the facts. My other point is one of more importance. . . . When the book comes out the intelligent and the experts will see clearly what are the real shares of the work. . . . The impression which will be made upon them will be that Pollock has been claiming a great deal more than he has any right to claim. . . . I am sure that such things will be said in private. There are a good many people who don't like Pollock: he is rather a dab at giving offence, and a chance of making unpleasant remarks about him will not be missed. . . . The whole difficulty may be got over by the simplest possible expedient. Write a preface, just showing the facts as they are in the most business like way. "F. P. wrote chaps. so and so: F. M. wrote chaps. so and

---

[1] Round's letter is not extant, but its tenor appears from M.'s reply.

[2] The 'printed sheets' were suppressed in anticipation of Round's *Feudal England*: Preface to *D.B. and Beyond*. See Letter 109, *supra*.

[3] For the East Anglian essay by W. J. Corbett, see M. *D.B. and Beyond*, 429: it was printed in *Cambridge Medieval History*, V.p. 508. William John Corbett (1866–1925) was a Fellow of King's College, Cambridge.

H. H. = Hubert Hall (1857–1944): entered Public Record Office, 1879, Assistant Keeper, 1912–21, and for some time Director of the Royal Historical Society. He edited volumes for the Pipe Roll Society and for the Rolls Series, including *The Red Book of the Exchequer* (1896), and for the Selden Society Vols. 46 and 49.

M. was perhaps 'in a fiduciary position' because of his association with Pollock in the *History of English Law*.

so: F. M. and F. P. mutually criticized each other's work" (I assume the last statement to be correct). After that no complaint can be made. You will have given fair notice. . . .']

Horsepools

27 July 1894

MY DEAR LESLIE,

I am grateful beyond words for your long and kind letter and at once I will say that I shall take your advice about the preface. You certainly have put before me one aspect of the case that I had overlooked. My difficulty has been that in this matter I have really been having my own way. The original scheme would have divided the work into approximately equal shares—but I soon discovered (as I suppose a 'collaborator' often will) that I wanted one thing while my yoke-fellow wanted another. Our different views I need not explain to you. Perhaps it would have been well if difference had led to discord; but the discrepancy was but slowly borne in upon me and, when it was becoming apparent, I pushed on my work in order that as much as possible might be done in the way which—rightly or wrongly—I like. Therefore I was not displeased when F. P. went first to the West and then to the East Indies. You see therefore that I cannot accuse him of not doing his fair share, for I did not want him to do it. What I have always been fearing was not that he would get any credit that would belong to me but that he would take chapters out of my hand. I must add that only a little time ago he said of his own accord that the preface must notice the unequal division of labour, and of any wish to get praise (if such is to be had) for what is not his own I hold him absolutely innocent.[1]

But as you very truly say—and I had not thought of this before—there is some chance, especially in America where we hope for a little sale, that his name may be attractive—it certainly ought to be so among lawyers—and therefore I will be the more careful that the preface warns readers to expect a lot of me.

[Memorandum to be kept with the will
of
F. W. Maitland.[2]

MEMORANDUM.

The contract for the publication of the History of English Law was made between the Cambridge Press and me. Sir F. Pollock was not a party to the contract. The Press pays to me the whole of that share of the profits of the book which is payable to the author or authors. There has never been any formal agreement between me and Sir F. Pollock about our respective shares in the profits; but hitherto when the Press sent me any money I have, with his approval, sent him a one fifth share of that money. I regard this arrangement

[1] See Pollock-Holmes Letters, I. 60–1.
[2] This Memorandum in M.'s handwriting immediately follows the letter in Camb. Univ. Add. MSS.

as fair and have every reason to believe that he is satisfied. Should any profits arise after my death I think that my representative should treat one fifth of them as belonging to Sir Frederick; but I earnestly desire that no dispute may arise of what has been a pleasant friendship. None is likely to arise, but in the improbable event of a claim being made on behalf of Sir F. to a larger share, I would rather that my representative yielded to it than resisted it.

F. W. MAITLAND
19 Octr. 1898.]

139. To Charles Gross

Downing College
Cambridge
England
20 Oct. 1894

DEAR GROSS,

I am grateful to you for your kind letter and for news of you. I am very anxious to see your coroners' rolls; they ought to be very interesting. In the book that I am now finishing[1] I am treating the coroner shabbily, partly because I regard him as having been manucapted for your book, partly because I am ignorant.

As to your Quellen,[2] I very much hope that it will soon appear. There is great need of it. The new Gardiner and Mullinger[3] sadly neglects records and runs on lines which seem to me old-fashioned.

What of Mrs. Green? To me it is a brilliant and entertaining book, but I can not get any clear theory of town government out of or into it.[4]

In the winter I had a bad time and even now a little work goes a long way with me—still I hope to get two volumes of history out early in next year.

Of course I quite agree with you about the folly of supplying translations of Latin records—but Dove is peremptory and I suppose that he knows his public.

Believe me
Yours very truly
F. W. MAITLAND

140. To Melville M. Bigelow

Downing College
Cambridge
25 Nov. 1894

MY DEAR BIGELOW,

I had assigned to-day for a long letter to you—it is a Sunday—and now there is but one thing that I can write about, the sad disaster. Dove has

---

[1] *P. and M.*   [2] See Letter 128, *supra.*
[3] S. R. Gardiner and J. B. Mullinger, *Introduction to the Study of English History* (1881: 3rd edn., 1894).
[4] Alice Stopford Green (1847–1929), *Town Life in the Fifteenth Century*, 1894.

destroyed himself,[1] and there can I fear be no doubt that the cause of his act is to be found in the affairs of the Selden Society. How bad the matter is I hardly yet know but I dread the very worst, namely that the funds of the Society have totally disappeared. This will involve some of us in heavy liabilities and I fear that the very best that can be hoped for will be the issue of those volumes that are already due to subscribers. The blow is crushing and bewilders me. Please do not say much about this for a few days. The Executive Council meets on Tuesday and will, I hope and believe, do all that can be done to save whatever honour is left.

I fear that one need not say *cherchez* la femme—she is apparent. Poor Dove! I did not like some of his ways but I never suspected this.

I had meant to write about divers pleasant things—North Woodstock[2] and so forth; but all is out of my head.

Happily I wrote my 'Explicit' at the end of Vol. II 'in festo Animarum' and then took up the Mirror. I was deep in the affairs of Andrew Horn when this catastrophe came. However I hope that the committee will publish this and the Bracton-Azo. I can now give them a good bit of time.[3]

My wife who wishes you to remember her has just nursed our babes through the measles. Her menagerie, on the other hand, has suffered severely—the poor cockeyed kitten perished and, so said the vet, of Tim's bite. Also that 'covey' (I know not how he spelled itself[4]) has departed. We may get to Horsepools for Christmas if the babes make rapid recovery.

You can guess that I am down-hearted. I had so many hopes mixed up with the Selden Society.

Yours very truly

F. W. MAITLAND

141. To James Bradley Thayer

Cambridge
England
25th Novr. 1894.

DEAR MR. THAYER,

Very many thanks to you for your kind gift of Cases on Constitutional Law.[5]

At the moment I am struck down by a horrible disaster. Dove has removed himself from this world and (between ourselves) the affairs of the Selden Society are left in far worse than confusion. In a few days time the Executive Committee

---

[1] [AULT. The coroner's inquest was reported in the *Times* of Sat. Nov. 24, 1894. Dove was 'found dead in his chambers, Lincoln's Inn, on Wednesday last with a bullet wound in his head'. The jury's verdict was 'suicide during temporary insanity'.]

[2] Bigelow's summer home in Vermont.

[3] Vol. II of *P. and M.* For the Mirror and Andrew Horn see S.S. Vol. 7, and for Bracton-Azo see S.S. Vol. 8: both pub. 1895.

[4] *Sic.* The menagerie was replenished: see Letters 166 and 173, *infra.*

[5] See Letter 132, *supra.*

will have met and no doubt will issue a circular to subscribers. They will also I trust and hope resolve to make the end of the Society as honourable as it can possibly be, but, as this will I fear involve the provision of a large sum of money out of purses some of which are not very full, I dare hope for no better than an issue of those volumes that are due in respect of subscriptions already received—and then my beloved Society will come to an end. You can guess what I feel. I know what you will feel. Of course much of what I tell you will in a day or two be public property—but please do not say very much about it until the Committee has spoken. That Committee comprises Lindley, Romer, Stirling[1] and others, and I feel sure that they will try to save whatever honour can be saved.

> Believe me
> Yours very truly
> F. W. MAITLAND

142. To H. A. L. Fisher

> Downing College
> Cambridge.
> *26th Nov. 1894*

MY DEAR HERBERT,

Can you put me in the way of finding a good book about Henry the Lion of Saxony which would tell of his first wife Clementia and his divorce? I have come across the extraordinary statement that he was married to and divorced from Isabella (alias Avice) daughter of the Earl of Gloucester and afterwards wife of King John—and though I know that this is a blunder I should like to track it to its source.[2]

You have perhaps seen that Dove, the secretary of the Selden Society, has taken his own life—this means that the Society's affairs are, to say the least, disordered. I do not yet know how bad the mess is, but fear the worst.

The babes are pretty well through the measles and we have hopes of moving to Horsepools for Christmas. I should like to think that we could see you there or elsewhere.

I have finished my book. I hope that you see your way to The Empire—even if you go with Mrs. Chant.[3]

> Yours very affectionately
> F. W. MAITLAND

[1] Nathaniel Lindley (1828–1921), Judge C.P. 1875, Lord Justice 1881, M.R. 1897, Lord of Appeal, as Baron Lindley, 1900–5. Robert Romer (1840–1918), Judge, Ch. Div., 1890, Lord Justice 1899–1906. James Stirling (1836–1916), Judge, Ch. Div., 1886, Lord Justice 1900–6.
[2] M. was probably interested because he was preparing his review of Luckock, *History of Marriage*: see Letter 150, *infra*.
[3] 'My book' is *P. and M.* Fisher was thinking to write *The Medieval Empire*: see Letter 123, *supra*. Mrs. Ormiston Chant was leading a moral crusade in the music halls of London, including The Empire: Holbrook Jackson, *The Eighteen Nineties*, 24.

143. To James Bradley Thayer

Cambridge
England
2nd Dec. 1894

DEAR PROFESSOR THAYER,

I have an uneasy feeling that last Sunday I sent you a letter with an inadequate stamp. If so, I beg your forgiveness.

A general meeting of the Selden Society is to be held and I have good hope that it will resolve to continue the work. But if not, I feel sure that the executive committee will see that the subscribers have all the books that are due to them including the Mirror and Azo. Possibly good may come out of all this evil. I think it was from muddle that our late secretary fell into worse, and the late L. C. J. was an all too easy-going president. If we can pull ourselves together we shall have Romer at the head of affairs. I will write again very soon and what I hope to be able to say is that the world at large need know no more than that we have a new secretary.[1]

Yours very truly
F. W. MAITLAND

144. To R. Lane Poole

Horsepools
Stroud
13 December 1894

MY DEAR POOLE,

May I have another 'pull' of the proof of Henry Clement?[2] I have spoilt that which was sent me in an endeavour to correct it.

You see that I have fled early from Cambridge, in order that I may make an index.[3]

The *Germania* lies like a weight on my soul. Shall I ever have cheek enough to write about it?[4]

Are you coming Winchcombe way? I hope so.

Yours very truly
F. W. MAITLAND

145. To H. A. L. Fisher

Horsepools
13 Decr. 1894

MY DEAR HERBERT,

Already we are here. If you can tear yourself from Oxford do come hither and spend a little while. I hope that your memories of Horsepools are not unpleasant.

---

[1] 'The late L. C. J.' was Lord Coleridge. The new secretary was Benjamin Fossett Lock and the new president Lord Herschell, then Lord Chancellor. Mr. Justice Romer was a Vice-President.

[2] *The Murder of Henry Clement*, E.H.R. (1895), 294: C.P. III. 11.

[3] Presumably to *P. and M.*

[4] [A. L. P. Furneaux's edition of the *Germania* was reviewed by M. in E.H.R. (1895), 779.]

Owing to a series of absurd mistakes I have not yet got my Fortnightly. I am impatient to see it.[1]

Do not say No if you can say Yes. Crump[2] is to the fore and gives a ball!

Yours affectionately

F. W. MAITLAND

146. To H. A. L. Fisher

Horsepools

16th Dec. 1894

MY DEAR HERBERT,

Let me say that—though you ought not to have talked of me—I admire your essay extremely. The point that you make on p. 810 I tried to make in a discussion with Sidgwick in which I endeavoured to convince him that 'inductive political science' is rubbish, and I had far more success than I expected. I don't despair of him. Also I feel something like gratitude for what you say of Madox. He was born out of his due time.[3]

Did you ever hear that Simon de Montfort was divorced from one wife and married another? This is stated by Luckock, Dean of Lichfield, in what he calls a History of Marriage. I think that I have traced his blunder to an absurd prize essay written in 1822; but before I go for him, which I mean to do, I should like to be certain that this fable had no other origin. Did you ever hear it?[4]

We shall be here until term begins. Please remember that and believe that we wish to see you.

Yours affectionately

F. W. MAITLAND

147. To J. H. Round

[No date, but probably December 1894 both from contents and from the fact that M. was then at Horsepools.]

Horsepools

Stroud

DEAR ROUND,

Your letter comes to me just in the nick of time if you are willing to do me a kindness. The enclosed pages will show you that I am now correcting sheets which will endeavour to tell the history of fines.[5] They will not be before the world for another six months and of course I should like them to look 'up to date'. This they will not look if in the meanwhile you publish your newly discovered fine. Therefore, if you are not going to keep it back but are on the

---

1 See Letter 146, *infra*.
2 Crompton Hutton, a County Court judge who lived near M. in Gloucestershire.
3 For Thomas Madox, see Douglas, *English Scholars*, Chap. XI.
4 See Letter 150, *infra*.
5 Round's letter is not extant, but the 'sheets' would seem to be *P. and M.* ii. 94–106.

point of publishing it, perhaps you will of your charity allow me to say something of this sort—

'Mr. J. H. Round has discovered a fully developed fine of 11 ——, of which he will give an account in The ——.'

Of course, if for any reason you are going to retain your discovery for a time, then you will take no heed of my petition: but if you are on the point of publication you may be willing to give me this 'advance note'.[1]

I am meditating a postponement of all my Domesday stuff in order to avoid collision.[2]

As to *the* battle,[3] I think that it is only *per finem duelli* that a *concordia* can be made.

Yours very truly
F. W. MAITLAND

148. To Sidney Lee

Downing College
Cambridge
1st Feb. 1895

DEAR MR. LEE,

know that Mr. Searle is a very laborious and accurate scholar and that he has been devoting a long time to the writings of the so-called Peter of Blois, also that he convinced me that extremely little is known of the real Peter and that there are reasons for suspecting an elaborate imposture. I have not myself gone into the subject but from frequent conversations with Mr. Searle and from the voluminous notes that he has shown me at various times I know for certain that he has worked at this problem hard and long. On the other hand I do not know that he has any great faculty of explaining his opinions briefly and pointedly.[4]

Yours very truly
F. W. MAITLAND

149. To H. A. L. Fisher

Downing College
Cambridge
3 Feb. 1895

MY DEAR HERBERT,

I have a distressing letter from Vinogradoff.[5] For reasons that he does not give he finds that the situation at Moscow is beoming intolerable and asks

---

[1] See *P. and M.* ii. 96–7.   [2] See Letter 137, *supra*.
[3] See Letter 134, *supra*.
[4] Peter of Blois (fl. A.D. 1190), 'archdeacon of Bath and author': D.N.B. XV. The life is by C. L. Kingsford who says at p. 937—'The Rev. W. G. Searle of Cambridge, from a careful study of Peter's works, is inclined to doubt the trustworthiness of many of the statements found in them; but the results of his investigations have not yet been published.' It would seem that Sidney Lee had been asking M.'s opinion of Searle as a contributor to the D.N.B. Mr. Searle published in 1897 *Onomasticon Anglo-Saxonicum* and in 1899 *Anglo-Saxon Bishops, Kings and Nobles:* see Stenton, *Anglo-Saxon England*, 699–700.
[5] Dated Jan. 12/24, 1895, as from the University, Moscow, and in Camb. Univ. MSS.

whether there is any hope of a livelihood in England. This between ourselves, for he does not wish it talked of at present. I was compelled to tell him that the outlook at Cambridge for a teacher of history is very black. We are so very poor that I see no prospect of the foundation of any more readerships or professorships. Can you say anything better of Oxford? I feel sure that in course of time a man of P. V.'s power would come to the front at O. or at C.; but I fear that at C. he would have a long struggle for his first bread and butter. What think you? I wish to heaven that I were prime minister at this moment! I would risk a war to put P. V. in the vacant chair.[1]

I am glad to hear that you are able to do some work and hope that your book will get itself written.[2]

Here we are saying 'O. B. or not O. B., that is the question.'[3]

Yours very truly

F. W. MAITLAND

150. To R. Lane Poole

Downing College
Cambridge
3 March 1895

MY DEAR POOLE,

I return the proof and accept the reproof in the spirit in which etc., but your candour will confess that I refused the book in the first instance.[4] I think that you say no more than is just and am ashamed of myself for falling into feeble laudation—but I felt the cheek of having opinions about the classics and their editors, and after playing the savage with the Dean[5] I was in a melting mood. So forgive. It shall not happen again. That German on the towns[6] is as unreadable as the Catalogue of Ancient Deeds.

About Acton I agree with you.[7] Glad as I am that he should come here, I fancy that Oxford was the place for him.

My two fat volumes are through the press—bar index—and I am now deep in Azo. I hope that before the week is out the Selden Society will be alive once more. Has Marsden's Admiralty volume been sent to E.H.R.?[8] It is good and new.

Yours very truly

F. W. MAITLAND

[1] The Regius Professorship of Modern History at Cambridge was vacant by the death of Sir John Seeley.
[2] See Letter 142, *supra*.
[3] Oscar Browning was thought to have hopes of the Regius Professorship: but see Letter 150, *infra*.
[4] [A. L. P. Tacitus, *Germania*, ed. Furneaux]. See Letter 144, *supra*.
[5] [A.L.P. The reference is to a very unfavourable review by M. (E.H.R., 1895, p. 755) of 'The History of Marriage, Jewish and Christian, in relation to Divorce and certain Forbidden Degrees', by H. M. Luckock, D.D., Dean of Lichfield].
[6] [A.L.P. Keutgen, *Untersuchungen über den Ursprung der deutschen Stadt-Verfassung*, 1895]. See Letter 164, *infra*.
[7] Lord Acton had just been made Regius Professor of Modern History at Cambridge.
[8] S.S. Vol. 6.

151. To B. Fossett Lock

Horsepools
Stroud
Gloucestershire
22nd March 1895

DEAR LOCK,

Let me introduce myself to you. I am exceedingly glad to find that you have consented to pull the Selden Society out of its difficulties. I am not quite sure of being able to attend the meeting on the 29th; for I am but beginning to get rid of the influenza which seized me after the last meeting. So I will explain how matters stand as regards the two partially printed volumes.

(1) Almost the whole of the Mirror is in type. I think that no more than three sheets of the text have yet to be set up. The whole of the 'copy' for the text is in the printer's hands. The introduction is written. Altogether, if the press was set to work hard, the book could be finished in a very few weeks.[1]

(2) The printers have got a great deal of copy for the 'Bracton and Azo'. I am within a few days of finishing the whole text. If the press is active, I can (bar accidents) have the book finished and published in July.[2]

Perhaps the Committee will wish to look forward to a volume for next year. You may know that Dove at one moment of his career obtained a number of promises or half-promises of volumes from various people, and these he advertised.[3] I only know of two cases in which work has been done in pursuance of these promises. As to the first of these two, Munton,[4] at one of the meetings that took place after the crash, read a letter from Leadam who, as I understand, said that he had done some work. I do not know him; perhaps Munton can tell more of him and of what he has done.[5] The other case is that of W. P. Baildon who, as I understand, has got a volume of the earliest Chancery cases pretty ready.[6] Of course he stopped work when the catastrophe happened.

My impression is that we could not do better for next year than take Baildon's volume. He has just issued a very good volume of Star Chamber Cases—privately printed for Mr. Morrison who owns the manuscript and is wealthy.[7] It will be for the committee to say whether any announcement of a volume for next year should be made in the volumes that are to be published this year.

Have you any questions to ask me?

Yours very truly
F. W. MAITLAND

---

[1] The Introduction to Vol. 7 is dated April 18, 1895. It is by M., though the book itself was edited by W. J. Whittaker.

[2] The Introduction to Vol. 8 is dated June 19, 1895.

[3] See the end papers of Vol. 6.

[4] Francis K. Munton, the Hon. Treasurer of the Selden Society.

[5] Isaac Saunders Leadam (1848–1913), editor of S.S. Vols. 12, 16 and 25, and part editor of Vol. 35. He also published *The Domesday of Inclosures of 1517* (1897) and *The History of England, 1702–1760*, Vol. IX of *The Political History of England:* ed. W. Hunt and R. L. Poole (1909).

[6] S.S. Vol. 10.   [7] See S.S. Vol. 16, Intro. cxxxv, note 4.

152. To B. Fossett Lock

Horsepools,
Stroud
25 March 1895

DEAR LOCK,

My letter to you was posted before I received your circular and letter and so was not an answer to them.

Nothing at all has been done towards a Vol. II of Manorial Cases.

I believe that the work done consists of (1) Chancery cases by Baildon (2) something or another, but I know not what, by Leadam, and (3) transcripts of Coroners Rolls made for Charles Gross of Harvard.[1] These last I forgot when I wrote to you. I believe that Gross employed a lady at the Record Office to make transcripts,[2] but that he was waiting for instructions when Dove died. He told me in a letter[3] that he was disappointed with the material which he had received, and I do not think that he would be anxious to finish the book. On the other hand he has probably paid the transcriber.

I do not believe that the Jewish Exchequer Rolls have been touched,[4] and I feel pretty certain that nothing whatever has been done towards the French dictionary. This was a project of Skeat's.[5] It fell flat from the first and I hope that we shall hear no more about it.

I mean to be at the meeting if I possibly can. I think that we might reduce our printer's bill by abandoning the wasteful practice of printing octavo pages on quarto paper—from the first I have hated it.

Also I think that some plan might be devised for disposing of our back volumes. Occasionally I hear of a demand for them. A few weeks ago a Hungarian was inquiring after them. As we are starting afresh, might we not make up some complete sets and offer them at a reduced price? A few libraries might be glad to take them.

Yours very truly
F. W. MAITLAND

153. To Melville M. Bigelow

Horsepools
Stroud
30th March 1895

MY DEAR BIGELOW,

I hope that you have received a copy of the book that Pollock and I have just published. With my share of the gift go pleasant memories of hours spent over the Placita Anglo-Normannica[6] and of pleasant talks with its author. I

---

[1] These became respectively Vols. 10, 12 and 9.
[2] Miss M. T. Martin (Preface to Vol. 9).
[3] Not extant.
[4] S.S. Vol. 15.
[5] See 'Publications' at p. 4 of end papers of S.S. Vol. 9.
[6] Bigelow (1879).

hope that when looking at the book you will remember Downing and Horsepools.

Mine and I flourish.

Yours most truly

F. W. MAITLAND

154. To J. H. Round

Horsepools
Stroud
30 March 1895

DEAR ROUND,

Your letters are much too kind; but they do me good.[1] I hope that I am only
a short head in advance of you, for Hall tells me that you are near your 'finis'.[2]

Yours very truly

F. W. MAITLAND

155. To B. Fossett Lock

Horsepools
Stroud
16th April 1895

DEAR LOCK,

I return the correspondence and the draft circular. I have suggested a small
change in the description of 'Bracton and Azo'; but in other respects the
document seems to be all that it should be. I do not see how to water down the
'Contemplated'.[3]

As to the order of publication—of course I see the objection to our sending
out two successive volumes with my name on the title page; but on the other
hand my Bracton-Azo will be finished, if all goes well, long before Gross can
get his Coroners Rolls done. I have already 96 pages in type and the whole
book will hardly contain more than 250 exclusive of Introduction. I am receiving more than a sheet a week, and so if we do not stop the press the book
can be published in the summer. Also this book will make no pull upon the
finances of the Society. I had a letter from the donor[4] the other day and he says
that he will pay the cost of the book through my hands so soon as it is finished.
Probably you know or guess his name; but at any rate I must not mention it.
Altogether then, unless you see some objection, I think that we had better let
our subscribers have this book as soon as possible.

I think that the order Gross, Baildon, Leadam, Marsden which you suggest

---

[1] In a letter to M. of 28 March 1895 (Camb. Univ. MSS) Round had congratulated him
on the 'opus mirabile'.
[2] Presumably the 'finis' of *Feudal England*.
[3] Prospective volumes: see pages at end of S.S. Vol. 7.
[4] Mr. Justice Stirling: see letter of 4 April 1895 from him to M. in Camb. Univ. MSS.

is good.[1] Could we at the next meeting authorize Gross and Baildon to begin printing?

Looking back at your letter I observe your reason for interpolating another book between 'the two text books'. Of course I will at once give way if you are strongly of opinion that this should be done; but in any case I hope to have the Azo printed and ready for issue in the middle of the summer and the question will be whether we should keep back from subscribers what we have in our hands. 'Bracton-Azo' is a grim bit of Romanism while the Mirror is half political squib and half fairy-tale, so that there is little resemblance between the two. However, be this as you please.

As to the Mirror, both Whittaker (he is staying with me here) and I wish you to know that neither of us will accept any money from the Society in respect of this book—though we will ask for a few copies as we have some debts of courtesy to repay, e.g. to Dr. Liebermann of Berlin who gave us some valuable information.[2] We both feel that the catastrophe could not have been so bad a one if the Mirror had been finished with due speed. Besides, we want, if you do not object, to put the Society to the expense of a rather long Introduction (rather more than two sheets), for the origin of this silly book is a mystery which can not be cleared up by a few words. At any rate we shall not go back from our decision about this matter of reward.

Other financial arrangements I leave to you; but I take it that we ought to have some definite agreement with Gross, Baildon, etc. Under the old régime, when everything was kept as indefinite as possible, there was I believe at starting some notion that 2 guas. per sheet was a fair reward.

When do you think of holding a meeting? When it is held I should like to have authority for sending out a few review copies of Marsden's volume[3] and of the Mirror. I think that our editors should have a little to hope and to fear, and we have before now had good (by 'good' I mean intelligent not laudatory) reviews in the Athenaeum, the English Historical and the Revue Historique.

Sometimes a Cambridge man does not object to spending a Sunday in Cambridge. I should be delighted if you could be persuaded to spend one—any one—in Downing (whither I go on Wednesday) and then we could settle a report in conference.

Yours very truly
F. W. MAITLAND

156. To Charles Gross

Downing College
Cambridge, Eng.
21 April 1895

MY DEAR GROSS,

I expect that Lock will have written to you about your Coroners' Rolls. The poor old Selden Society has I hope taken out a new lease of life. We have

---

[1] Respectively S.S. Vols. 9, 10, 12, 11.
[2] See M. Intro. to S.S. Vol. 7.   [3] S.S. Vol. 6.

got a good council and a good secretary. To decide what volume shall be published next rests with the council; but I have not very much doubt that at its next meeting it will give your book precedence and authorize the printing thereof. If this be done, as I hope it will be done, you will be able to get it through the press very quickly. Could I help you in correcting proofs?

I am correcting the very last sheets of the Mirror and about half of the Azo is in print.

I fear that America is not for me. Pollock will have to carry my love to my friends.[1]

If you criticize Mrs. Green,[2] let me know when and where your criticism appears, for I shall be keen to see it.

Yours very truly

F. W. MAITLAND

157. To Leslie Stephen

[No original. Typewritten transcript in Camb. Univ. Add. MSS: no ending.]

Cambridge

9 May 1895

MY DEAR LESLIE,

I have an irrepressible wish, however foolish and wrong it may be, to touch your hand and tell you in two words that I think of you. And yet you will know that, and will know also how my thoughts go back to what happened in your house nine years ago.[3] To-day you must feel that all men are strangers to you since none can help you to bear your grief; but some day believe that it is (let me say it) with something of filial love that I think of you and write these useless words.

158. To B. Fossett Lock

Downing College

26th May 1895

MY DEAR LOCK,

Many thanks for your newsful letters. Also I feel very grateful to you for your conduct of this meeting which has done so much work.

1. In the matter of Gross. I am sending his MSS to you. My suggestion is that Baildon should be asked to do the work of collation. By way of fee I would suggest 7 guas, or 10 if he will not take 7. I feel pretty sure that we should have to pay more if we employed a professional and I hardly think that we could offer less as this work brings no credit. If Baildon fails, Turner might accept, but he is not as yet nearly so good a reader as Baildon is. Failing both

---

1 See Pollock-Holmes Letters, I. 57.
2 See Letter 139, *supra.*
3 Leslie Stephen's second wife Julia (née Jackson) died on 5 May 1895. M. had proposed to Florence Fisher in Stephen's house: see Letter 472, *infra.*

I must consult Hall.[1] If I had to do the work I should collate the proof (not Gross's script) with the roll; but Baildon will very likely prefer to take the other course so as to finish the task before a summer holiday. I think that the first proof had better go to Gross, also that he will perhaps be content with seeing the first proof, and in that case I will make myself responsible for the concordance of the revised with the corrected proof.

2. In the matter of the Chancery volume.[2] Will you tell Baildon that this volume is for 1896 and that the Bracton is almost finished; and will you make the financial arrangement with him? Of course I will do this if you wish it, but as I can not do it without your authority I suggest the direct communication between you and B. to save circuity of action. He might be told that he could go to press late in July. I can not finish the Appendix to Bracton until I have been to Oxford[3] or go to Oxford until this term is overpast.

3. In the matter of the Jewry.[4] If the necessary meeting can be postponed until after the 18th of June I shall be best pleased. The three next weeks are for me the busiest time of the year. I have many meetings to attend almost daily besides a Tripos. I should like then to have a talk with you before we meet the Hebrews. We might arrange the scheme of a book.

I feel that the only manner in which I could edit the book would be one which would necessitate the employment of a copyist, for a prolonged spell of work in London is just what I never can promise myself. I think that Baildon would be a good editor, provided that you and I had settled a plan for his operation. I take it that our Jewish allies will want an abstract or note of all entries, as they will be in search rather of names and pedigrees than of legal matters. We shall have to consider how we can give them what they want. Always provided that Jacobs is not relying on some pact with Dove, I do not think that he could object to our committing the work to Baildon, who has already done so much for the Society.

The important question for our consideration seems to me to be whether we should take Baildon into our counsels before facing the Hebrews. I think his advice would be valuable, for he has a lot of experience. If you fix some time for the meeting after the 18th of June I will try to spend a day or two in London; but the change in the handwriting that has just taken place signifies that I am spending a morning in bed.

Gross's papers were sent to you yesterday by railway and insured.

Yours very truly

F. W. MAITLAND

---

[1] The collation was done by Turner: see Preface to S.S. Vol. 9. George James Turner (1867–1946), St. John's College, Cambridge, of Lincoln's Inn barrister-at-law, was a devoted member of the Selden Society. M. paid tribute to his scholarly help in the Prefaces to S.S. Vols. 17, 19 and 20, and he was responsible for the posthumous edition of M.'s Vol. 22. He was himself the editor of Vols. 13, 26, 42, 45 (with W. C. Bolland) and 66 (completed by Prof. T. F. T. Plucknett with an appreciation of his work for the Society). See obituary by Sir Cecil Carr in *Proceedings of the British Academy* (1954), 207–18.
[2] S.S. Vol. 10.   [3] S.S. Vol. 8, App. 4: the Digby MS in the Bodleian Library.
[4] On 21 May 1895 Mr. Jacobs had written to Lock suggesting that the Selden Society might join with the Jewish Historical Society of England to publish the Jews' Plea Rolls (S.S. Corr.). See also Letter 118, *supra*.

159. To B. Fossett Lock

Cambridge

6th June 1895

DEAR LOCK,

Many thanks for your correction.[1] Often in trying to trace the names of small places I have had to use very imperfect instruments.

On Sunday who should appear but J. Jacobs. I was extremely cautious; and he was not very communicative. I gathered however that he does not want to edit the book on terms such as those that we offer; also that he does not conceive himself to have had any contract with Dove. Also he spoke as if it was by no means certain that the Hebrews would do anything for us. I told him that you and I were discussing the matter and that he would hear from us. When this term is over I must try to spend a day with the rolls and form some estimate of the number of Jews mentioned in them. My mind is inclining towards something in the nature of an English calendar with a few examples of the Latin entries.

I send this to London as I do not know where circuit may have taken you.

Yours very truly

F. W. MAITLAND

160. To R. Lane Poole

Cambridge

7 June 1895

MY DEAR POOLE,

I have read through that article on the Office of the Constable[2] and can not suggest any corrections. I think it pretty perverse, but the perversity does not consist in any corrigible mis-statements. For my own part, I am glad that someone should try to bolster up the constable, because we ought to see how weak the case for his antiquity is, and yet it does not seem to me that there is in this paper anything that is discreditable to the E.H.R.

Yours very truly

F. W. MAITLAND

161. To B. Fossett Lock

Downing College

16th June 1895

DEAR LOCK,

I am very much annoyed about the Mirror. I wish that I had long ago taken the Index into my own hands. Whittaker now assures me that half the Index shall go to the printer to-day or to-morrow. If this does not happen I will seize it and carry it off to 'Horsepools, Stroud, Gloucestershire', whither I go on Tuesday.

[1] Probably in the MS of Gross's Vol. 9: see Letter 158, *supra.*
[2] [A.L.P. By H. B. Simpson, E.H.R. (1895), 625.]

The other book[1] is waiting for its Appendix IV which I can not finish until I have visited Oxford and (perhaps) Eton. This I hope to do in a few days after a little rest has cleared my head of a long Law Tripos. The Introduction is finished.

Also I shall after the said few days be ready to meet you in London if you think that we ought already to make plans for the Jews.

For my own part I agree with Marsden that to translate the ordinary Latin of plea rolls, etc. is wasteful. Also (as the American's letter shows[2]) it is dangerous—for to make such slips as those of which Marsden is accused is exceedingly easy. But Dove always insisted that everything must be translated and I do not think that we can break through this tradition without the consent of the Council. When it meets in the autumn we can (if you agree) advise it to get as much stuff as possible into the Admiralty volume.

I do not myself think (but then I am a hardened editor) that the mistakes alleged against Marsden are of a very bad kind and I don't think that I should show him the letter. It might make him unnecessarily unhappy.

Has Gross gone to press? I shall tell the printers to send me proofs.

Yours very truly

F. W. MAITLAND

A gem from the examination room—A deed is a document written on two pieces of paper and then torn in half.

162. To Charles Gross

Horsepools
Stroud
Gloucestershire
22nd June 1895

DEAR MR. GROSS,

Sometimes an outsider sees a small misprint or mistake which an author does not see; therefore I send herewith some sheets of your Coroners' Roll which both Lock and I have read and upon which we have scribbled some observations. I have checked all your dates by Giry's Manual.[3] In one or two cases I suggest a reconsideration. I thought that you would not be offended by my doing so. I like these records much.

I have lately found 'entre chien et loup'[4] in novels by Balzac and Anatole France.

You see that I am holiday making.

Yours very truly

F. W. MAITLAND

[1] *Bracton and Azo:* S.S. Vol. 8.
[2] Not extant. The criticism is of R. G. Marsden's *Select Pleas in the Court of Admiralty*, S.S. Vol. 6. Marsden had on 31 May 1895 written to Lock about his second volume—to be published as S.S. Vol. 11 (S.S. Corr.).
[3] Arthur Giry (1848–99), French historian: published *Manuel de Diplomatique* in 1894.
[4] See S.S. Vol. 9, p. 133.

163. To B. Fossett Lock

Horsepools
Stroud
15 July 1895

DEAR LOCK,

As I am not quite certain of being able to attend on Thursday and see that the Jewish Plea Rolls are on the list of Agenda, I will tell you what I think of them. I think that we could make a very interesting volume of Select Pleas. The cases were more varied than I expected them to be and some of them touched matters of which very little is known. On the other hand I do not think that a calendar of these cases which would give all the names that occur would be interesting. Some membranes contain many names of Jews but for the rest give nothing but common form. If then the Jewish Historical Society wants all the facts about individual Jews that are recorded on these rolls I do not think that we could meet their wishes without producing a volume which would be very dull to most of our subscribers. The most, so it seems to me, that we could do would be to give, in addition to our selections, an index of all Jewish names which would give references to rolls and membranes. But I doubt whether the Jews would care to have this.

I gathered from Baildon that he would be willing to undertake the book.[1]

I saw Martin.[2] He is still thinking about the Forest Pleas and says that he will soon write to you or to me.

Yours very truly
F. W. MAITLAND

164. To R. Lane Poole

Horsepools
Stroud
15 July 1895

DEAR POOLE,

I shall be glad of the loan you kindly offer of Pirenne's *first* article.[3] I meant to bring away from the University Library all the numbers of the *Revue* which contained his papers, but failed to bring the first. I do not well know how far Keutgen is saying what is new when he lays stress on the *Burg* element.[4] I believe this to be very important in the early English history.

Pollock went to America and returned in the twinkling of an eye. If he does

---

[1] He did not in fact edit the Jewish Plea Rolls: see Letter 185, *infra*.

[2] Charles Trice Martin, a member of the Selden Society; pub. *The Record Interpreter* (1892) and ed. *Registrum epistolarum Johannis Peckhami archiepiscopi Cantuarensis* (R.S. 3 vols. 1882–95). The Forest Pleas were edited by G. J. Turner: see Letter 204, *infra*.

[3] [A.L.P. The first of the three articles by H. Pirenne on 'L'Origine des Constitutions Urbaines au Moyen Age' appeared in the *Revue Historique* for 1893; the other two in 1895.] On Henri Pirenne see Powicke, *Modern Historians and the Study of History*, Chap. 3.

[4] See Letter 150, *supra*. [A.L.P. The theories of Keutgen and Pirenne are discussed by M. in E.H.R. (1896), 13]: reprinted C.P. III. 31.

not want to speak of Round's Domesday work I will do this.[1] I had been thinking of asking you to let me have a talk about Domesday. I have a great deal of stuff written. Some of it Round has forestalled as I knew he would. At one time it was to have gone into the book that Pollock and I published. Then I did not wish to collide with Round, and now I know that Vinogradoff is again at work and there are many economic and social questions which I would rather leave to him. So I have not and shall not have enough that is new to make a book.[2] On the other hand I have a few legal theories that I should like to put before the public in one form or another. What do you think? Would the E.H.R. bear a little Domesday—two or three articles? However, I will stand out of F. P.'s way if he has anything to say, so, when you have ascertained his intentions, will you tell me whether you would take some papers from me? I could begin with some talk about Round's work, of which I think very highly. I hope that you will say just what you think; in no case shall I be disappointed.

You will soon have from the Selden Society two books in which I have been concerned—the Mirror, and Bracton and Azo. I don't know that you will think them worth reviews, but in case you do I should be rather glad if you could put the latter of the two into the hands of a professed Romanist. It is a work of ultra-trepidation, for I don't know any Roman law and consequently I should like to hear whether I have been guilty of many 'howlers'—in short I want to know the worst.

I shall hope to see you here when you visit Gloucestershire.

Yours very truly

F. W. MAITLAND

165. To James Bradley Thayer

Horsepools
Stroud
Gloucestershire,
England.

29 July 1895

DEAR PROFESSOR THAYER,

Many thanks for your kind letter; I have had none kinder from any one. My book of which you speak so pleasantly is selling well, so well that I am beginning to hope that I may have an opportunity of revising it. If that opportunity comes I hope that I shall have courage and industry enough to make both retreats and advances.[3]

Do not forget that to the best of my ability I have committed you to a speedy publication of 'Trial by Jury'—*Juravi in animam tuam*—you must save me harmless.

---

[1] Round's *Feudal England* was reviewed by Pollock: E.H.R. (1895), 783.
[2] See Letters 109, 137 and 147, *supra*. In fact there was enough material to make *D.B. and Beyond.*
[3] The second edition of *P. and M.* was pub. in 1898.

Also I have to thank you for sending Hale to me, or, if you did not, Mr. Ames did. Hale stayed with me here for a day or two. I liked him very much and think that he will make an excellent Secretary for the Selden.[1] The 'Mirror' is published. I am just writing *imprimatur* on the very last page of 'Bracton and Azo' and I have in slip the whole of Gross's 'Coroners Rolls', also a trial proof of Baildon's 'Equity Cases' which is the book for 1896—so our arrears will soon be cleared off and we shall, I hope, do all the better for the severe shaking that we had.

I should like before I die to see an edition of the Year Books starting—but there are big difficulties to be overcome. One of these will perhaps pass away if the people at the Record Office definitely declare that the Rolls Series is at its end.[2]

Yours very truly

F. W. MAITLAND

166. To Melville M. Bigelow

Horsepools,

Stroud

29 July 1895

MY DEAR BIGELOW,

I am much indebted to you for all the trouble that you have taken in my interest and for your very kind letter.[3] The History is doing better than I expected and a second edition in my lifetime is not beyond the limits of possibility. Since I finished it I have been very busy over the Selden books. The Mirror is published; I am to-day getting an *imprimatur* on the last page of Bracton-Azo, and the whole of Gross's 'Coroners Rolls' are in print. So in a short time all our arrears will be cleared up. The judges and others behaved well in the crisis and I think that we have taken out a new lease of life.

We are, you see, in Gloucestershire, where there are many memories of you. One American visitor we have had, Hale, who is American Secretary of the Selden Society. I took him to Gloucester as I took you and we made a contract by correspondence in 'the whispering gallery'[4]—but the justices of Assize were absent.

Madame's menagerie has been enriched by a merekat from South Africa— an amusing little beast—and a stolid English badger. The whole household salutes you, more especially the babes.

Yours very truly

F. W. MAITLAND.

[1] Richard W. Hale, attorney and counsellor at law of Boston, was Honorary Secretary and Treasurer of the Selden Society in the United States for over forty years.
[2] The last volume of YBB. in the R.S. was published in 1911. See Letter 182, *infra*.
[3] Not extant.
[4] In Gloucester Cathedral.

167. To B. Fossett Lock

[No year, but from contents clearly 1895.]

Horsepools

6th Augt.

DEAR LOCK,

I will see to it that 'capta' is 'taken', also that people shall come to their deaths.

I should be very glad to submit the proofs to Norman Moore. Do you know him? I do not.

As to *greva* I remember satisfying myself years ago that there was such a word and I think that Gross translates it rightly. I found it in some old French dictionary.[1]

As to the lettering on the back of the last finished book, I have a slight preference for the shorter title 'Bracton and Azo'—but it is very slight.

Those infernal verses![2] I should quite agree that in 1300 and long afterwards no one spoke of 'the Bar' as an institution—but we already find the *apprenticii* as a body of men that is being subjected to regulation, and as they are present in court and at the bar of the court it seems to me that to speak of them as apprentices at the bars (or bar) was natural.

The reason why I said nothing of York was because I do not think that York ever had any shorter name in Latin than Ebor*acum*, in French Everwyck, and I do not think that any one would have heard an allusion to York if he did not hear that *k* sound which both in French and English seems to be of the essence of the name. But once more I curse that versifier![3]

Yours very truly

F. W. MAITLAND

168. To R. Lane Poole

Horsepools

Stroud

15 August 1895

MY DEAR POOLE,

The question that you put to me is very difficult. One may look at 'The History of the Law of Real Property' from so many different points of view.[4] Is this title beyond change? If so, and if the fixed period is not to end until the Restoration, I do not well see how you can leave Coke out of the programme.

---

[1] These first three paragraphs are concerned with M.'s reading of the proofs of S.S. Vol. 9. In the preface Gross thanks Dr. Norman Moore 'for suggestions in medical matters'. For *greva* see Vol. 9, p. 133.

[2] At the beginning of *The Mirror of Justices*, S.S. Vol. 7, p. 1: see also Introduction, liv–lv.

[3] The word in the third line of the verse on p. 1 of Vol. 7 is *Ebore*—'with ivory'.

[4] [A.L.P. The reference is to a special subject for the Honour School of Modern History at Oxford under this title which was then under discussion.]

The 'History of the Law of Real Property' has by this time become the history of a large body of legal doctrines, many of which are extremely subtle and are far removed from the world of political and social interests. It seems to me that if you come down to Coke's day you will be obliged to give a large place to The Metaphysics of Law. Now I think that a training in this may be very valuable for a few men; but it seems to me to be as remote from the general current of English history as is the history of theological dogmas. I think that with you I should have voted for stopping at the Statute of Uses.

Has Littleton been considered? I don't mean Coke upon Littleton. It is a short book. I always recommend it strongly to the men whom I have to teach. I don't know any book which puts the outlines of the classical common law in so clear a shape. I think that you might require men to read the first half of it. Even the last half of it, though now-a-days it is quite obsolete, is by no means difficult and gives the clue to many of Coke's mazes. There is, if I remember rightly, a modern reprint of Littleton's text without Coke's commentary. But copies of even the best edition of Co. Lit. are cheap.

Then, at the other end, what of Glanvill? His book also is easily obtained and I do not see why the whole of it should not be recommended. Of course there are some things in it that are not 'Real Property Law', but is there not much to be said for recommending the whole of a book? I think that I should vote for Glanvill rather than for more Bracton. It is so difficult to make good selections.

As to records which show the facts of land tenure, I am inclined to think that Domesday is too disputable. If you do take anything from cent. xi, should it not be Hamilton's Inq. Com. Cantab.?[1] I fully agree with Round, that this is the key of D.B. and is much more intelligible. But I should suppose that some record from cent. xiii would better serve your purpose. A volume from the Rolls Ser. would have the advantage of being cheap. What should you say to the Ramsey cartulary?[2] Or again there is the Oxfordshire Hundred Roll. This would be less accessible but deals with a country which all your men could know.

You see then that as first hand stuff I lean towards Glanvill, Littleton and a cartulary. But I don't well know how much time your men can give to one 'subject'.

Can I make even one line out of the Index of Statutes?[3] I will try.

I ought to have been writing lectures about the history of the Canon Law. Instead of so doing I have been led away into a lengthy discourse on Lyndwood.[4] I have come to a result that seems to be heterodox, but I do not know exactly how heterodox it is and should be exceedingly grateful if you would give me your opinion upon a question that lies rather within your studies than

[1] *Inquisitio Comitatus Cantabrigiensis* ed. N. E. G. A. Hamilton (1876). See M. *D.B. and Beyond*, Essay I, p. 1.
[2] S.S. Vol. 2, pp. 48–51.
[3] [A.L.P. 12th edition, 1893.]
[4] See Cam, Intro. to *Selected Hist. Essays*, xx. William Lyndwood's *Provinciale* (1679) 'is the most authoritative digest of the ancient Canon Law of England' (Winfield, *Chief Sources*, 67).

within mine. It seems to me clear that in Lyndwood's view the law laid down
in the three great papal law books is statute law for the English ecclesiastical
courts and overrides all the provincial constitutions, and further that apart
from the law contained in these books the church of England has hardly any
law—in short, there is next to nothing that can be called *English* canon law.
I must wait until I am again in Cambridge to read what has been written about
this matter in modern times, but any word of counsel that you can give me
will be treasured. From a remark that you once made I inferred that in your
opinion our church historians have been too patriotic. I feel pretty sure of this
after spending two months with Lyndwood, and if I find that my conclusions
about the law of our ecclesiastical courts are at variance with the prevailing
doctrine, may be I shall print what I have been writing, that is to say if either
L.Q.R. or E.H.R. will let me trail my coat through its pages. Do you know of
any one (other than Stubbs) who of recent years has written about the authority
of decretals in England?[1]

I am glad that you enjoyed your holiday and hope that you are refreshed.

Yours very truly

F. W. MAITLAND

169. To Charles Gross

[Post-card. Year from post-mark.]

Horsepools, Stroud,

30th Augt.

[*1895*]

All is going well. The whole is in sheet and I am setting *Imprimatur* on some
second revises. A learned doctor (Norman Moore) advised us to substitute
'the falling sickness' for epilepsy and I have ventured to do this.[2]

Certainly let there be but one Index of Names if you prefer this. Qu. as to
putting some brief indication of the county after the name? e.g.

Prepositus, Ric. (Bed).[3]

I can take this work if you are short of time. I suppose that you will make the
Index of Matters.

I look forward to the Introduction and think that this volume will do us
good.

Yrs.

F. W. MAITLAND

[1] See E.H.R. (1896), 446: reprinted in *Roman Canon Law in the Church of England* (1898).
For Stubbs on the Canon Law see his *Hist. Appendix to the Report of the Commissioners
on the Ecclesiastical Courts* (1883) and his *Lectures on the Study of Medieval and Modern
History* (1887), Lectures 13 and 14. In the third edition of these Lectures (1900) Stubbs
discussed M.'s views in a prefatory note.
[2] S.S. Vol. 9, Preface, and pp. 3, 5, 109.
[3] *Ibid.*, Index of Names.

170. To R. Lane Poole

Horsepools
Stroud
23 September 1895

MY DEAR POOLE,

The Winchcombe Landboc[1] crossed my mind. But, if I remember rightly, it does not give any typical 'extents' of villages. It would be no bad deed if some one were to reprint a little bit of the Oxfordshire Hundred Roll: say, the extents of a dozen villages near Oxford, or of one complete hundred. About Littleton I do not feel very certain. Of course there are many things in the second half of his book which are highly technical. There would I think have to be a general understanding that questions would not be asked about some of these things, but I agree with you that the practice of setting a part of a book is to be avoided, especially when the book is short.

I should indeed be grateful to you if you make me a gift of your Wickliffe editions[2] and should value them very highly—but I feel that the offer is almost too kind.

By and by I will send you what I have written about Lyndwood. It would make a long article and I fear that this must be followed by another[3] as it deals only with one side of the story. My own impression is that the English canonists were very strong papalists, or rather I should say very helpless papalists. When I send you my stuff you and S.R.G.[4] can say whether you will open your pages. I think it not impossible that what I say will irritate some good folk, though I hope to stick close to the legal point.

Yours very truly

F. W. MAITLAND

171. To R. Lane Poole

[No date; but the first two sentences show that this letter follows closely on Letter 170 and may be dated September 1895.]

Horsepools
Stroud

MY DEAR POOLE,

I am very grateful to you for your kind gift. These two books are wonderfully interesting.[5] I have been skimming over Fitz Ralph's discourse, which I had never seen before, and it entertains me. What a labour you must have

---

1 See *P. and M.* ii. 90, 96–7, 236–7. M. is continuing the discussion of the special subject in the Oxford History School begun in Letter 168, *supra*.

2 [A.L.P. *De Civili Dominio* and *De Dominio Divino*, ed. for the Wyclif Society by R. L. Poole, 1885 and 1890.]

3 [A.L.P. *Church, State and Decretals*, E.H.R. (1896), 641: reprinted in *Roman Canon Law in the Church of England*.]

4 S. R. Gardiner, joint editor of E.H.R.

5 See Letter 170, *supra*.

endured when you were editing these tracts—I see such care everywhere. It interests me that Wycliffe should cite 'the archdeacon', as if every one must know who the archdeacon is.

As to the *Mirror* I shall be well content with Leadam or Jenks.[1] A Frenchman would see our weak side, the linguistic, but I should be glad of French criticism. I have seen a letter written by Stubbs to Pollock wherein he said that he should not be surprised if the *Mirror* came from a German forger of his acquaintance who wrote 'de recuperatione terrae sanctae', a work that I must read at the earliest opportunity.

I am in no hurry whatever to begin an assault on the established theory of Anglican canon law, but shall be ready for your April number if you are still willing to shelter me.

Good luck in the Canterbury archives!

Yours very truly

F. W. MAITLAND

172. To B. Fossett Lock

Horsepools
Stroud
5 Octr. 1895

DEAR LOCK,

I know that I ought to be at Cambridge; but I am not there. I go next Friday.

Coroners Rolls. I have passed the whole text for the press. I adopted nearly all of Norman Moore's corrections.[2] I have not thanked him for them, because they came through your hands.

As Gross complained of a press of work I offered to make indexes of persons and places. He accepted the offer and I am now sending these indexes to the press. The list of obscure men is rather long.

Bracton. The course that you suggest is a very good one. In a short time I will send the bill to the anonymous one.[3] I suppose that there is no hurry and that I can wait for a fortnight or thereabouts. The book can be issued as soon as you think fit.

Yours v. truly

F. W. MAITLAND

---

[1] S.S. Vol. 7 was reviewed by I. S. Leadam in E.H.R. (1897), 148. Edward Jenks (1861–1939) was Reader in English Law, Oxford, 1896–1903, Director of Legal Studies, Law Society, 1903–24, Professor of English Law, London, 1924–9.
[2] See Letters 167 and 169, *supra*.
[3] Mr. Justice Stirling: see Letter 155, *supra*. Lock's letter to M. is not extant and his suggestion is therefore unknown.

173. To Melville M. Bigelow

The West Lodge
Downing College
Cambridge
3rd Nov. 1895

MY DEAR BIGELOW,

I am heartily grateful to you for your generous review of the History, also for sending me a copy of the new magazine;[1] it promises well. Truth to tell I was so anxious to see what you had written that I ordered a copy of the Review as soon as I heard of its appearance. Two copies will do me no harm though you do your best to turn my head by talking of Sohm.[2] I admire him enormously; indeed he is an idol of mine.

We are all flourishing. The beasts I include in the 'all'.[3] It is mid-term time and therefore my hands are full of work. When I am not doing more disagreeable things I am making some study of ecclesiastical law which is likely to issue in essays.[4] I wonder how many treatises you have on hand—two or three I will be bound.

My wife desires you to remember her, and the babes or quondam babes send their love.

Yours very truly

F. W. MAITLAND

174. To B. Fossett Lock

Cambridge
8th Feb. 1896

DEAR LOCK,

If other things were equal I think that I should vote for giving precedence to the Court of Requests; but the Admiralty will do very well.[5]

No, I most certainly have concluded no pact with the Anglo-Jews.[6] I liked the look of the Jewish Rolls. They gave some cases about gages of various sorts which were very new to me.

Two Americans[7] have pressed the claims of Glanvill—so has Stirling, J. I feel that a perfect edition would involve a good deal of running about the

---

[1] *American Historical Review*, Oct. 1895, in which Bigelow's review of *P. and M.* appeared.
[2] Bigelow had written in his review: 'We do not hesitate to say that in Mr. Maitland we have . . . what we find in Sohm . . . the gift which men call genius.'
[3] Mrs. Maitland had written to Mrs. Bigelow on 1 Oct. 1895 (Boston Univ. Law Rev., 1957, No. 3, at p. 304): 'Chloe is well. She has a puppy whom we are keeping and who is quite an attractive little dog named the Earl of Gloucester. I have by me now a charming little Harvest mouse—you would adore it. It . . . sits on my hand and eats there and washes its face in the most attractive manner. I hope I shall be able to keep it in spite of our 2 dogs and 3 cats, to say nothing of my sister's Mongoose who is here on a visit.'
[4] Ultimately *Roman Canon Law in the Church of England. Six Essays* (1898).
[5] Respectively S.S. Vols. 12 and 11.
[6] See Letters 158, 159 and 163, *supra*.
[7] Unknown: but possibly one was Professor J. H. Beale who in 1900 reprinted Beames' edition f Glanvill (1812) with an introduction.

country; there are so many MSS and they are widely scattered. Still, if we could not get this big job undertaken, a very creditable text could be made in London and there is a French translation which has never been printed and is a very early specimen of French prose.[1]

I should like to find an early place for Turner's Brevia.[2] I think that he will do them well.

I asked Gross about the destination of his presentation copies. He wishes to have all sent to him.

I shall see you on Tuesday.

Yours very truly

F. W. MAITLAND

175. To Henry Sidgwick

Downing College

28th Feb. 1896

MY DEAR SIDGWICK,

I will write one line to tell you that there does not seem much hope that the History Board will adopt your proposal,[3] though it is still possible that they may add some qualificatory regulation to explain General History in your sense. Oddly enough, when you were gone I found myself attempting to obtain two 'alternative' papers for your 'development'—I mean two papers such as you wish alternative for the old 3 and 4; but I was very badly beaten.

I am awfully weary of the whole affair. I never came upon any Board that had so little cohesion as this History Board has.

Probably I ought to have limited my remark to the medieval time[4]—but as to that I have not any doubt that all the work that has thrown new light on 'polity'—most of it French—has been done by men who were immersed in the study of property law or of ecclesiastical matters. However you will know that as well as I know it.

I had it on the tip of my tongue to to reply your remark about Freeman and Florence that, just because the said Freeman believed that history was past politics, he never succeeded in adding anything to our knowledge of medieval politics but spoilt everything by inept comparisons. But already we were becoming discursive.

I wish that I could resign my place at the Board, but for decency's sake must hold on to the end of the year.

Yours very truly

F. W. MAITLAND

[1] See *P. and M.* i. 166, n. 4, and Plucknett, *Early English Legal Literature*, 38. The French translation is found in four MSS (Lansd. 467, ff. 86–113: C.U.L. Ll. I. 16, ff. 100–48b: C.U.L. Ec. I. 1: Duke of Northumberland's MS. 445).

[2] Ultimately pub. in 1951 as S.S. Vol. 66: see Preface by Professor Plucknett.

[3] It does not seem possible to identify the proposal: *Henry Sidgwick* contains no reference to it.

[4] M.'s 'remark' is irrecoverable; but Sidgwick was frequently discussing with his friends his projected book on *The Development of European Polity*, pub. posthumously in 1903. *Henry Sidgwick*, 500. Florence = Florentine History.

176. To H. A. L. Fisher

Downing College
Cambridge
17th May 1896

MY DEAR HERBERT,

Forgive me for not answering your letter until now. I fear I must say no more even now than that if an opportunity offers I will do all I can, but, as I dare say you would expect, college patronage is usually in the hands of a committee of clerks in orders and yet more clerical laymen, and a recommendation from me might do more harm than good. I saw this in the case of my brother-in-law 'the Rector'. However, if a word can safely be said, I will say it.[1]

That History Board still consumes endless time and after all I do not think that I can sign their proposals. At present Acton = 0. I wish he would bless or curse or do something.[2]

Yours affectionately
F. W. MAITLAND

177. To R. Lane Poole

Downing
20 June 1896

MY DEAR POOLE,

Yours is a very brilliant guess. Pray give it to the world. I do not think that there can be any etymological difficulty in the way, for see Ducange, s.v. *vera* 1. If you compare this with his *veru*, I think you will see that *vera* would do for *arrow* and *veratus* for transfixed by an arrow.[3]

I send off 'Canon Law I'. May I have half-a-dozen copies? In 'Canon Law II' I end by promising a third article. This is written. But the promise can easily be struck out from the second article if you are getting tired. No. III deals with the inedited William of Drogheda. I am not sure that it is not even heavier than its precursors.[4]

I am off to Horsepools in order that I may count 'hides' in Domesday. I wish I could think that your labours were over.

Liebermann's visit was a great success, though he drew no applause from the undergraduates. That was reserved for Duchesne and had, I am told, some

---

[1] Fisher's letter to M. is not extant, but he had presumably asked M. to use his influence as to a College living. M.'s 'brother-in-law, the Rector', had recently been presented by the Bishop of Gloucester to the living of Tidenham.

[2] See Letter 150, *supra.*

[3] The context of this paragraph is unknown.

[4] 'No. III' appeared in E.H.R. (1897), 625, and later in *Roman Canon Law in the Church of England*: see Letters 168 and 170, *supra.*

connexion with the validity of Anglican orders. I could not induce our highly classical orator to say 'Lagam Eadwardi vobis reddo'.[1]

Yours ever

F. W. MAITLAND

178. To James Bradley Thayer

Horsepools

Stroud

26 July 1896

DEAR PROFR. THAYER,

I am delighted to see your book on the Jury[2] and grateful to you for your gift. The second copy I have sent to Pollock: I know that he admires it. To me a copy comes just at the right time, for (thanks to America!) I have just been informed that a second edition of our History will be wanted in a few months. A certain note in it I shall retain but with an addition—for I shall be proud to keep on record my wish that your essays should be generally accessible.[3]

If at any time something that is not in your book or mine occurs to you, will you remember that I am at work on a second edition and that the correction of my blunders is to me a pleasure?

Believe me

Yours very truly

F. W. MAITLAND

179. To J. H. Round

Horsepools

Stroud

7 Sept. 1896

DEAR ROUND,

No, I certainly did not mean to 'scare' you about the Geld Roll—quite the contrary. I am glad that you hold to your opinion and I am building a little edifice upon it. It bears witness to an enormous reduction of geldability between its date and the date of D.B. and so helps to explain the case of Leicestershire where an enormous abatement seems to have been granted between D.B. and the Pipe Rolls. Also it hangs on in a curious way to that list which I am calling The County Hidage (Kemble printed a form of it) and

---

[1] Henry I's Charter of Liberties, Chap. 13. For the *Leges Henrici Primi* see Liebermann, *Gesetze der Angelsachsen*, I. 547–611. Both he and Duchesne (1843–1922) had just received Honorary Degrees at Cambridge. Duchesne, who was for a time Professor of Church History at the *Institut Catholique* in Paris, had in 1894 affirmed the validity of Anglican orders; but they were officially condemned by a Papal Bull of 1896.

[2] In 1896 Thayer published as a book, under the title *Development of Trial by Jury*, a number of essays in the Harv. L. Rev. which were later to form the first four chapters of his *Preliminary Treatise on Evidence at the Common Law*.

[3] A number of notes both to Thayer's essays and to his book appear in *P. and M.* ii. Book II, Chap. IX, s. 4.

which is not so false as it looks. The witan were first rate hands at jerrymandering the geld.[1]

Private

I quite agree that the Q. Reviewer has a weak spot in his love for Swereford— but I think that this is evident enough and will do no harm, certainly not to you nor I think to any one else; and as there are but few people in the world who are of such a right good sort as he is, I am hoping that you will be content with the status quo. I am thoroughly convinced that you can 'afford' to let the matter be. Pray do not think that I am 'tendering advice'—nothing of the kind! I am pleading for a friend.[2]

Yours very truly

F. W. MAITLAND

180. To J. H. Round

Horsepools
Stroud
29 Sept. 1896

DEAR ROUND,

Very many thanks for the Athenaeum. The review is very interesting. I shall find that volume of Fines at Cambridge and after what you say am keen to see it.[3]

I am right sorry to hear that you are again unwell.

Can you tell me how I can acquire a copy of that book by Airy on the D.B. of Bedfordshire to which you refer in your F.E.?[4] I ordered it a while ago, but my booksellers do not send it. I should like to see it before I send to the press my last instalment of copy. I have practically finished the book. I hope to send you a copy—timorously—by Christmas.[5] At a few points I have doubted whether to repeat arguments that you have used or to take them for granted, and I am generally adopting the latter course, saying 'this is proved, see Round, etc.'

Yours very truly

F. W. MAITLAND

---

[1] *D.B. and Beyond*, Essay III, s. 2.
[2] Hubert Hall reviewed Round's *Feudal England* in the Quarterly Review for July 1896. They had been joint editors of the R.S. edition of *The Red Book of the Exchequer*, but had parted company over their opinion of Swereford, its 13th century compiler. Hall published the edition in 1896. Round did not respond to M.'s appeal. See Letters 221, 224, 225 and 238, *infra*: Cam, Intro. *Selected Hist. Essays*, xxiv–v: Winfield, *Chief Sources*, 117–18.
[3] See *P. and M.* ii. 96–7.
[4] *Digest of the Domesday of Bedfordshire*, by Rev. William Airy (1881): see Round, *Feudal England*, 55.
[5] M.'s Preface to *D.B. and Beyond* is dated 20 Jan. 1897.

181. To B. Fossett Lock

Downing College
Cambridge
25th Oct. 1896

My dear Lock,

I am glad that you think hopefully of the Year Book project. I think that we might take it up even if we only published one volume a year, by making every alternate volume a Y.B. If, however, we could put out three volumes in two years, so much the better. My thoughts have turned to Turner, for I know no one who looks more hopeful. He seems to be editing the Brevia Placitata very well.[1] I have been thinking that he and I could work together and supply each other's defects. He is to be with me next Sunday and I propose to have a few words with him about the matter. I do not know anybody who cares more than he does for the old 'forms of action' and this is a great point.

I have found so much work to do on Marsden's sheets that perhaps I have neglected Baildon too much. I have sent him, however, a good many suggestions. I quite agree that his notes are not very wise; but he is doing the main work so well that I do not like to interfere very often. I doubt we should improve matters by subjecting his text to the eye of one of H.M. judges.[2]

As all this is 'private', I may tell you that I have another offer of financial help from a certain J.S.[3] I am telling him that a scheme for the Year Books is in the air.

I am right glad to hear that the C.J.[4] is captured—he has ideas and energy, and may do us good.

Yours very truly

F. W. Maitland

182. To B. Fossett Lock

Downing College
8 Novr. 1896

Dear Lock,

When in the natural course of events will you be calling a meeting of the Selden Council?

The Year Book project grows in my mind and I am nearly ready to make a proposal touching Edward II; but before I laid anything before the Council I should wish to have your advice on my first draft. Therefore I wish to be informed in good time of any imminent meeting.

The matter is, I regret to say, complicated by this, that after a long interval Pike is being allowed to go ahead once more with the Year Books of Edward III.[5] I have some reason to fear that if we announced a series of YBB the

---

[1] See Letter 174, *supra.*
[2] Lord Justice Fry. It was so subjected: see Preface to S.S. Vol. 10.
[3] Mr. Justice Stirling: see Letters 155 and 172, *supra.*
[4] Lord Russell of Killowen, L.C.J., had become a member of the Selden Society.
[5] See Introduction to R.S. Y.B.B. 16 Ed. III. 1, and Letter 165, *supra.*

Treasury would make this an excuse for stopping Pike's work and this I should regard as a grave disaster, for he is doing it very well. I should like to frame some treaty with the Deputy Keeper,[1] but he could not bind the Treasury and (between ourselves) I fear that there is friction between him and Pike. I do not think that if we started with Edward II we ought to be prejudicing Pike's work, for it would be long before we could touch Edward III— but people become unreasonable when they don't like each other. So I feel that we have rather a difficult course to steer.

My project would involve the appointment of a small committee to settle rules for editors and a model sheet. There must be several members of the Council who would be willing to take a little trouble about this matter.

As to Turner, I like him more and more and I think that I could work with him.

MSS of the Edw. II are crowding in; we have four here; there are two in Lincoln's Inn and others elsewhere.

Yours very truly

F. W. MAITLAND

183. To B. Fossett Lock

Downing College

6 Decr. 1896

MY DEAR LOCK,

I am glad that you have this assurance from the D.K.[2] that our project— if ours it is to be—would not affect his plans. This opens the question whether we could secure Pike. I think that it will be a great pity if his knowledge and acquired skill are wasted. On the other hand, he has been receiving a wage the like of which we could not pay. This distresses me, for I have a high opinion of him.

As to that transcript at the Temple I will make inquiry. We have several good MSS at the Univ. Lib.[3]

I will attend the meeting on the 15th. I shall come to it from Gloucestershire, whither I go on Friday.

Yours very truly

F. W. MAITLAND

184. To J. H. Round

Horsepools

Stroud

17 Decr. 1896

DEAR ROUND,

Many thanks for your kind hints about scutage. Of course I shall carefully study *Feudal England* before I touch the subject. But I am beginning reprinting

---

[1] Of the Public Records: H. C. Maxwell Lyte. He was a member of the Council of the Selden Society.

[2] See Letter 182, *supra*, and Letters 185 and 208, *infra*.

[3] See S.S. Vol. 17, Intro. lxxxix–xcii.

with vol. 2, for it needs less change. I want to simplify scutage if I can, for I don't understand it and am trying to make room for a new chapter.[1]

I trust that you are better.

Yours very truly

F. W. MAITLAND

185. To B. Fossett Lock

Downing

24 Jan. 1897

MY DEAR LOCK,

I meant to have a word about Baildon's book,[2] but Lyte had engaged me to talk of something else. All I had to say is that so far as I am concerned the book can issue at once. The order to issue would, I take it, proceed from you.

I think it a pity that Pike's remote and precarious interest in the matter should postpone our Year Book scheme. One more effort a year hence, and, if that fails, I shall see whether an edition can be 'made in Germany'. *Ecce convertimur ad gentes.*

I am sorry also that Gross will not take up the Jew rolls. I must think of some one else. Do you know any intelligent young Hebrew?[3]

Since I saw you I have been abed, for the cold took me by the inside—but to-morrow I hope to be about again, and really there are worse places than bed these days.

Yours very truly

F. W. MAITLAND

186. To Maxwell Lyte

Downing College

Cambridge

15th Feb. 1897

DEAR MR. MAXWELL LYTE,

I am returning the Glanvill to you with some observations.[4] I wish that they were of a more decisive kind: but you will see that, owing to the goodness of the translation, I think the case a difficult one.

Believe me

Yours very truly

F. W. MAITLAND

[1] See *P. and M.* i. 266–77.
[2] S.S. Vol. 10.
[3] They were edited by J. M. Rigg: S.S. Vol. 15.
[4] Sir Travers Twiss had prepared for the R.S. an edition of Glanvill, actually printed in 1896. His previous edition of Bracton had been severely criticised: see Letter 14, *supra.* Maxwell Lyte seems to have been nervous about the reception of the Glanvill and to have submitted it to M. for his opinion. The 'observations' follow the short letter and were included with it.

PRIVATE. *To the Deputy Keeper of the Public Records*
Glanvill

I have looked through the whole of this book and have studied some pieces of it.

The Translation seems to me creditable. It is almost infinitely better than the translation of Bracton. I have noticed but few positive errors, and of these few some are not of a kind that would shock the generality of readers.

> See e.g. p. 282: *a sacramento levare* does not mean *to relieve him from the oath*, but to prevent him from swearing by making a charge of attempted perjury against him. The phrase is technical but odd and uncommon, and not to know its meaning is not shameful.

There is a worse mistake on p. 235. But I think, as already said, that the translation is creditable.

Some of the Notes are very bad. There is a very ugly misprint on p. 225, where Henry II's coronation is placed in 1145. This might be passed by. But see the note on p. 209 about the legitimation of bastards.

> 'Cf. Decretal Greg. IX anno 1172. Concil. Lateran Decreta anno 1179.'

There seems to me to be some blunder here the nature of which I can not fathom. The date of course is far too early for Greg. IX; on the other hand it is too late for the decisive decretal which came from Alex. III.

And see p. 287: 'Hovard[1] in his Anglo-Norman (!) text of Glanvill.'

Happily the notes, other than variants, are few.

The Text is based on very few out of many MSS. I do not think that the editor has consistently used more than three. However, I am not prepared to say that many important variants would have been discovered. So far as my small experience goes, the MSS of Glanvill are very harmonious and the traditional text is a good text. In this respect there is a great difference between Glanvill and Bracton. I only know about half-a-dozen passages in which I have any reason to suppose that there is a real difficulty. At these points the editor does little to settle the open question.

> See e.g. p. 140. It is an important question (discussed by Gross)[2] whether Glanvill wrote *in eorum communem gildam* or *in eorum communam scilicet gildam*. At such a point the editor ought to have consulted all MSS. As it is, he leaves us doubting whether a single MS bears out his text.

> So p. 306. There is an important and well known variant of *quartum* for *quotum*. Here we have references to one MS and the printed Regiam Maiestatem.[3]

This is bad; but, as already said, I do not know and do not even think that a collation of MSS would reveal many variants of substantial importance.

This leads me to what is said in the Preface about the MSS and their collation. I find it difficult to speak about this matter, because I seem to see a state-

---

[1] See S.S. Vol. 7, Intro. xi: M. *The Materials for English Legal History*, C.P. II. 29.
[2] *The Gild Merchant*, I. 102–3. See also Tait, *The Medieval English Borough*, 222–4.
[3] See H. G. Richardson, *Juridical Review*, LXVII, 155; and Letter 83, *supra*.

ment that the Cambridge MSS were 'collated', and yet not only can I perceive no trace of their use but I can barely believe that the editor had ever seen them. One of them is in French. One begins in Latin but soon falls into French. One contains what I have called the 'Revised Glanville'[1] which swerves at innumerable points from the received text. Now the editor says nothing of the French Glanvill nor of the Revised Glanvill. I think that he ought to have printed the one (for it is very important) and described the other. But at any rate he ought not to say that he has collated them. I can only suppose that he gave to the word 'collated' a sense that it does not generally bear. My belief is that he, or Westlake for him, glanced at one passage in the preface and that this was all the collation that these MSS received.

Of the Introduction I think badly. The editor had seen much too little of the MSS to justify him in saying a word about the development of the text. Even his list of MSS is far from perfect. As regards the 'Leges' that are in Hoveden[2] he ignores all Liebermann's work. The paragraphs about Ricardus Anglicus, which are dragged in, ignore Blakiston's article in Dict. Nat. Biog. (Poor, Richard le) which shows the baselessness of the identification of Ricardus Anglicus and Bishop Richard. The reasoning about the date of the book seems to me of the feeblest. We are introduced to an Eleventh (!) Lateran Council. Coke is made an authority for Glanvill's life. The well-known facts of his life are incorrectly stated and the best authorities are not used.

At the same time I feel it difficult to counsel the suppression of the book. If it had come to my hands as executor of a friend of whose reputation I was careful, I should suppress it. But I feel that it might be difficult for a public department to take this course after the expense had been incurred. I mean that in the improbable, but not I suppose unimaginable, event of a question being raised about the suppression, I feel that the suppressor might not be able easily to justify his action in the eyes of men who are not scholars. The case is not like that of the Bracton for there blunders in translation had been committed about which even a jury would have given the right verdict. Here the sins are mostly of omission. The ordinary man might ask whether much real knowledge would have been gained by a collection of variants, and I am not sure that a confidently affirmative answer could be given. Again, it would be hard to prove that the editor did not 'collate' MSS from which he has taken no variants. As to the introduction, people would talk of 'matters of taste'. Moreover, I understand that the department is in no way responsible for the contents of the books contained in the Rolls Series and that in England this is sufficiently well known. And so it might be urged that it should publish what has been paid for except in some grossly scandalous case. Now I am not prepared to say that in the present state of affairs this book is grossly scandalous. I do decidedly think that among scholars it will add to the causes of regret that in the past the Rolls Series was not subjected to central and official

---

[1] See Letter 100, *supra*.
[2] See *P. and M.* i. 163, n. 1: Stubbs, *Roger de Hovedene Chronica*, Intro. lxxv, ff.: Letter 187, *infra*.

supervision, and I do decidedly think that critics who know their business will speak evil of the book. But I can not say that there is likely to be any general outcry, and I can not say that I should like the task of endeavouring to convince (e.g.) a parliamentary committee that, after all expense incurred, suppression was advisable.

As to possible improvement, the sins being for the most part sins of omission, I think that very little could be done. The collation of MSS would result in a large collection of variants at the foot of the page and the book would have to be reprinted. The cancellation of a few pages, e.g., that which has the false date for Henry II, might be advisable. So too the Eleventh Lateran Council might disappear from the Introduction. But I do not see how, except in this way, the Introduction could be improved by a second hand without being re-written. Suppose (e.g.) that a good list of the Glanvill MSS were inserted, this would only emphasize the fact that the editor had not used them. I do not even see how the statement about collation could be omitted. On the whole I fear that little improvement is possible.[1]

F.W.M.

15th Feb. 1897

187. To Maxwell Lyte

Downing College

Cambridge

20 Feb. 1897

DEAR MR. MAXWELL LYTE,

I have to thank you for your letter.[2] It seems to me quite possible that Mr. Leadam or some one else could, by cancelling a few pages, supplying a short table of the really important variants and *rewriting* the Introduction, produce a valuable book. I should not myself shrink from the work, though I should not like it; but I have just engaged to do something which will cost me my leisure for a year.[3]

You are quite at liberty to show Leadam what I wrote.[4] I enclose an article by Liebermann which, since it appeared in a philological journal, Leadam may not have seen. It gives a useful hint about the connexion between Glanvill and the 'Leges'.[5]

---

[1] The book was suppressed, though a further exchange of views preceded the decision (Letter 187, *infra*). See Winfield, *Chief Sources*, 258, n. 2: 'The only copy we have seen is in the Harvard Law Library, and we learn from a MS note in it that the Deputy Keeper of the Rolls, acting on the advice of the author of this note, destroyed all except a few copies of the book because it fell below the standard of the Rolls Series. This has given the surviving copies a value to the book collector which they never had for the reader. A remarkable consolation for literary damnation!' Six copies in fact escaped destruction, three of which are now in the Public Record Office, two went to Leadam (see Letter 187, *infra*), and one was kept by Maxwell Lyte. (*Per* Mr. G. D. G. Hall, M.A., Fellow of Exeter College, Oxford.)
[2] Not extant, but presumably upon the fate of Sir Travers Twiss's Glanvill, with which M.'s present letter is concerned.
[3] See Letter 188, *infra*.   [4] Letter 186, *supra*.
[5] *Eine Anglonormannische Uebersetzung des 12 Jahrhunderts von Articuli Willelmi, Leges Eadwardi und Genealogia Normannorum* (Gröber's Zeitschrift für romanische Philologie, xix. 79).

If I can give the editor any help at the Univ. Libr. or Caius or Corpus, I am at his service.

What I thought the best part of T.'s Introduction consists of the tidings from a Balliol MS of marginal notes ascribing certain opinions to various ancient justices. Of these I should like to hear more.

Believe me

Yours very truly

F. W. MAITLAND

188. To H. A. L. Fisher

Downing

21 Feb. 1897

MY DEAR HERBERT,

I am bowed down by this honour[1]—by far the greatest that has fallen this way. I felt that I ought to decline it, but could not. What on earth to talk about I don't know. I suppose that there is no great haste for an announcement. At present my mind is turning towards a favourite theme of which we have talked before now—the haziness of medieval ideas about 'property', 'communities' and so forth, and the consequent disputes. But I hope that come Easter I may have the benefit of your advice. Elizabeth I must leave alone.[2]

Meanwhile there are these women—drat them. I have some hope that in another week I may have done my share of the work and may be able to think of other things.[3]

Yours very truly

F. W. MAITLAND

189. To J. H. Round

[No year; but clearly from contents and context 1897.]

Downing College

Cambridge

23rd Feb. [1897]

DEAR ROUND,

This is exceedingly kind of you. Certainly the electors[4] might have done better—as they will find out by and by.

[1] The Ford Lectureship at Oxford, of which the first series had been delivered in 1896 by S. R. Gardiner.

[2] M. had been persuaded by Lord Acton to write for the Camb. Mod. Hist. a chapter upon the 'Anglican Settlement and the Scottish Reformation' and had to reserve 'Elizabeth' for this work.

[3] In June 1896 M. had reluctantly agreed to serve on a Syndicate appointed to discuss the position of women in the University. Their proposals were debated on 13 March 1897, when M. described the Syndicate as 'a Syndicate of peaceful men, not all logical men, but peaceful men, dull men, perhaps the thirteen dullest men in the University': Hollond, *Frederic William Maitland*, 18–20. See also *Henry Sidgwick*, 544–52.

[4] To the Ford Lectureship.

Owing to some bad luck I have only just been able to get hold of the Nineteenth Century and read your article on the Elizabethan Religion.[1] It is admirable and will do a deal of good. I have long wished that some one would write what you have written, or rather would write to that effect, for though I guessed that the case was strong I did not know how strong. You have, I feel sure, put it most effectively and I congratulate you.

I am looking forward to Early Fines and hope that they will come with April—I want them soon.[2]

With more thanks
Yours very truly
F. W. MAITLAND

190. To R. Lane Poole

Downing
23 Feb. 1897

Did'st ever feel like a bubble that was going to be pricked?[3]

Yrs.
F. W. MAITLAND

191. To Henry Sidgwick

Downing
23rd Feb. 1897

MY DEAR SIDGWICK,

The Syndicate[4] sat for near five hours yesterday. We finished our Report, but there is a little printing to be done. I doubt it will be distributed before Saturday.

My object in writing is to warn you that there may be some severe skirmishing at the Council on Monday. At the end of the meeting the minority claimed a right to submit a 'minority Report'. The V.C.[5] ruled that our constitution knows nothing of such a procedure. I think him right, and Jackson whom I saw last night says that there is no precedent. I think that on Monday Robinson[6] may urge the Council to put to the Senate resolutions alternative to those proposed by the Syndicate. This would I believe be an unheard of novelty, but considering the present composition of the Council I can not say that there is no danger. Hence this warning.

[1] 'From 1897 to 1899 Round was fanning the flames of [theological] controversy with articles in the *Nineteenth Century* and the *Contemporary Review* on "The Idolatrous Mass" and kindred sixteenth-century subjects': Cam, Intro. to *Selected Hist. Essays*, xxi.
[2] See Round's article in E.H.R. (1897) 293–302. M. wanted it for the second edition of *P. and M.*: see ii. 97.
[3] Dr. A. Lane Poole in his note on p. 324 of the *C. Hist. J.* suggested that M. wrote these words in expectation of an attack by Round on *D.B. and Beyond.* But Professor Cam (Intro. to *Selected Hist. Essays*, xvii) refers them to the forthcoming Ford Lectures. The latter reference seems preferable: see Letters 188 and 189, *supra*.
[4] See Letter 188, *supra*.
[5] Vice-Chancellor.
[6] Armitage Robinson, afterwards Dean of Westminster.

Our proposal, signed by 9 out of 14, is (in brief) to give the titles of the degrees of B.A., M.A., D.Sc. and D.Lit.—to do this and no more. The minority would wish alternative resolutions in favour of fancy titles.

If you are to be away when the Report appears I can tell you more—but this is the substance. We make no change in preliminary examination.

A certain Appendix will amuse you. Satan's invisible world is displayed. We can put the scheme for 'a new University'[1] in black and white before the Senate—with the names of its founders.

Yours very truly

F. W. MAITLAND

To-day in the gladness of my heart I proclaimed a holiday and took my children to the Zoological Gardens—but it is only a brief interval of peace between one storm and a bigger.

Private. Whitehead was a real Godsend. He of John's[2] jibbed at the last moment.

192. To B. Fossett Lock

Downing College

28th Feb. 1897

DEAR LOCK,

Leach's offer[3] seems to me to be extremely helpful. Where does he dwell? May I write to him?

I will send some specimen blunders from Y.B. Edw. II.

I have been reading Marsden's Introduction again.[4] It is full of valuable matters. He ought to turn out a book for the laity. Certainly he has worked hard for the Society.

Yours very truly

F. W. MAITLAND

193. To B. Fossett Lock

Downing

14 March 1897

MY DEAR LOCK,

What Leach says in the accompanying letter[5] dashes some of my hopes. I fear that the Provost's Book is a book of 'privileges'. Books of that kind kept

---

[1] To be called 'The Queen's University of the British Empire'. In his speech in the Senate House on 13 March 1897 M. proposed as an alternative 'The Bletchley Junction Academy' where 'you change for Oxford or Cambridge': see Hollond, *Frederic William Maitland*, 19–20.

[2] Probably William Bateson (1861–1926), biologist, Fellow of St. John's College: see *Henry Sidgwick*, 545. Alfred North Whitehead (1861–1947) was Fellow of Trinity College, Cambridge, 1884–1947, Professor of Applied Mathematics, Imperial College of Science, 1914–24, Professor at Harvard University, 1924–37.

[3] On 22 Feb. 1897 A. F. Leach had proposed to Lock to edit 'a book of the Provost of Beverley made in 1416, with extracts from Manor Rolls from the time of Stephen' (S.S. Corr.). See Letter 193, *infra*.

[4] To S.S. Vol. 11.   [5] Not extant.

by prelates are not very uncommon. I think them a little dreary because they heap up evidence about a few points, viz. the occasions on which 'liberties' were granted and allowed. They are something like prolonged 'briefs' for the church's advocates. However, Beverley was an exceptionally favoured spot and I am not at all prepared to say that a good editor who tackled the whole history of Beverley might not make a good book.[1]

What of Leach himself? To me he is a name. Turner was a little scornful, but I should not accept his judgment of men very quickly.

> Yours very truly
>
> F. W. MAITLAND

On Wednesday to Horsepools—much weary of women's degrees.[2] On the 24th I will be with you.

194. To Henry Sidgwick

> Horsepools
> Stroud
> *24th March 1897*

MY DEAR SIDGWICK,

Many thanks for your news. I will see that all the points which you mention are before the Syndicate.[3]

I have been turning over what I may call the Clarkian proviso and meet with a small difficulty. If we append it only to the first resolution, this (we should be told) would found the inference that the other resolutions implied membership. I have thought of putting the proviso into the statute.

I don't want to say that our tariff of fees is too high. I only want to show in some way or another that we set little store by our opinion about this matter.

I feel that in this case the non-resident is an unknown quantity of almost infinite size, but whether positive or negative I do not know. What I fear most is an attempt to raise the undergraduates, i.e. to get from them some emphatic declaration. I am pretty sure that the attempt will be made.[4]

All this is on my mind, but I am enjoying myself thoroughly over a terrier of the Cambridge common field. I think of making it the basis of my lectures at Oxford.[5]

No, I hardly hope to find our A-S ancestor calling the same piece of land

---

[1] S.S. Vol. 14 became *Beverley Town Documents*, ed. by Arthur F. Leach, of the Middle Temple, Barrister-at-law, Assistant Charity Commissioner. See Letter 212, *infra*.

[2] See Letters 188 and 191, *supra*.

[3] This and the next three paragraphs concern the further proceedings of the Syndicate on the position of women in the University. Their proposal to confer titular degrees on women who had passed a Tripos examination, though debated in March, was not voted upon until 21 May 1897, when it was defeated by 1707 to 661: *Henry Sidgwick*, 550–2.

[4] After the vote on 21 May 'a considerable number of undergraduates, losing their heads and their manners, came up to Newnham College with the intention of burning on the lawn an effigy of a woman graduate. They were met with closed gates and after a little time induced to disperse': *Henry Sidgwick*, 551, note.

[5] *Township and Borough*, Lecture I.

book-land and folk-land. I only suspect him of doing it.[1] We are always speaking of 'leasehold land'. I let you a house in High St. for 21 years—it will pass under your will as your leasehold house and under my will as my free-hold house.

> Yours very truly
> F. W. MAITLAND

I guess that this struggle will cost a good deal in the way of stationery, etc. I will gladly bear a share.

195. To Alfred Marshall

> Horsepools
> Stroud
> *17th April 1897*

DEAR MARSHALL,

I am very grateful to you for letting me see Dr. Pierson's interesting letter. I will write to him[2] and am proud to have an introduction from you. But in the presence of Merovingians I always feel painfully shy.

The story about Java is most instructive.[3] I am just learning that from one century to another there simmered a quarrel between the University and the Town as to what King John meant or did when he granted 'the town of Cambridge' to its burgesses at a rent.[4] The University asserted that this did not convey 'the ownership of the soil' in the waste places. The quarrel was hot about 1600, and as late as 1803 it broke out once more when 'the Cambridge Field' (your house stands in it) was enclosed. At a critical moment Trinity, in order to acquire its now paddocks, admitted the Town's title. You Johnians were properly furious at this betrayal. Scott, your bursar, has printed some entertaining correspondence about this episode.[5]

> With more thanks
> Yours very truly
> F. W. MAITLAND

196. To B. Fossett Lock

> Downing
> *5 May 1897*

DEAR LOCK,

1. Are you a member of the Senate and as such coming here to vote about the women on the 21st?[6] I stand lunch to the evil and to the good. I have some hope that you may be among the good who say *placet*, but even if you

[1] See *D.B. and Beyond*, Essay II. s. 2, esp. pp. 257–8.
[2] No letters between M. and Dr. Pierson seem to be extant.
[3] This allusion remains obscure.
[4] *Township and Borough*, Lectures I and VI.
[5] Sir Robert Forsyth Scott (1849–1933), Senior Bursar of St. John's College, Cambridge, 1883–1908, Master, 1908–33. In *Township and Borough*, at p. 93, M. cites R. F. Scott, *Enclosure of Trinity College Walks* (Camb. Antiq. Soc. Proc. VIII 261).
[6] See Letter 194, *supra*.

are among the evil and like to be victorious, we might talk over other things, e.g. YBB.

2. I have no afternoon engagements that could not be cut.

3. As to the editorship of YBB, I don't know where to look. I don't want to thrust myself upon the Society, but, sooner than that the plan should fall through, I would do my best on a volume or so if Turner or some one else would give me his assistance. Between us, I think that Turner is as yet a little flighty—but I have more hope of him than of Baildon, who, though he is a very good copyist, has not I think a real interest in law. If the arrangement succeeded I might after a while leave Turner to himself. I do not want the job for there are other things that I would rather do, but, failing others, I would take it. What think you? I should much like to hear your thoughts and, unless you are coming to Cambridge, I will visit you in Lincoln's Inn if so be that you have anything to say.

4. I should think that Leadam[1] might go to press.

5. When do you issue Marsden?[2]

Yours very truly
F. W. Maitland

197. To Henry Sidgwick

Downing College
3rd June 1897

My dear Sidgwick,

(1) I think that you are right about mere passive concealment of a crime, and that it is only itself a crime when the concealed crime is treason.

(2) But to assist any criminal after his crime with the intent of shielding him from justice is a crime. The case of homicide is not in any way peculiar. The old law was that there could be 'accessories after the fact' to *any felony*, while to 'receive and comfort' one guilty of treason or misdemeanour was to share his guilt. Nowadays this distinction has disappeared, but I believe that I am right in what I have just said, namely that to assist a criminal with the object of shielding him from justice is always a crime.

I do not think that hard cases under this rule are at all common. As to the case of husband and wife, the rule which excludes the one from giving evidence when the other is on trial does, I believe, a good deal of harm and seems to be disappearing bit by bit along with the rule which prevents the prisoner himself from giving evidence.[3] I do not know that I would make any exception in favour of near relatives.

To prevent misunderstanding of some words which dropped from me when we met at Lyttleton's[4] house, may I say that my objection to the Law

---

[1] S.S. Vol. 12. [2] S.S. Vol. 11.
[3] See now the Criminal Evidence Act, 1898.
[4] Possibly Hon. A. T. Lyttleton, the first Master of Selwyn College, Cambridge, and later Bishop of Southampton, a former pupil and constant friend of Henry Sidgwick.

Special is merely my objection to allowing the poll man[1] to spend fully one half of his time on so professional a subject as law—or, for the matter of that, divinity; as one among several subjects which he had to study law might well stand, and now that we have got rid of the Roman rubbish and have Anson's Contract as a text book[2] I think that we may get some decent results.

Yours very truly

F. W. MAITLAND

198. To Melville M. Bigelow

[Post-card. Date from post-mark.]

Downing

[6 June 1897]

DEAR BIGELOW,

It is good news that you are on this side, and I am glad to think that you are coming to Horsepools. But if you wish to see Cambridge friends come here for a night this week. My wife will have told you how things stand in the domestic way, but I think that I could make a night tolerable to you. So come.

Of course I will forward letters.

Yours very truly

F. W. MAITLAND

199. To B. Fossett Lock

Horsepools

9th July 1897

MY DEAR LOCK,

I went to Cambridge yesterday to see the Year Books and to have some talk with Rogers, an assistant in the Library, of whose powers as copyist I think highly. He made what I think a modest offer, that is, to transcribe at the rate of $1s/3d$ for a page with the long lines that we have been lately using: that is 20/- per sheet. Supposing that I think one of the Cambridge MSS sufficiently good to serve as a basis,[3] do you think that I should be justified in setting Rogers to work? I doubt I could get a competent copyist in London at so low a figure. My impression is that even if it turned out that one of the

---

[1] An undergraduate who read only for a Pass and not for an Honours Degree. At this time such men had to take (a) a General Examination, comprising some Latin, Greek, Mathematics, History and Divinity, and (b) a Special Examination in one of the subjects in which candidates for an Honours Degree were required to take a Tripos Examination, e.g. Law.

[2] Sir William Anson's *Principles of the English Law of Contract* was first published in 1879.

[3] The text of the Y.B. 1 & 2 Edward II chosen by M. was one of the Cambridge MSS: S.S. Vol. 17, Intro. xc.

London MSS was a little better, I should save money by having so cheap a transcript which I could use as raw material.

Rogers writes a lovely hand taught to him by Bradshaw.[1]

Yours very truly

F. W. MAITLAND

200. To James Tait

[This letter is printed by Sir Maurice Powicke in *Modern Historians and the Study of History*, 55–6.]

Downing College

Cambridge

20th Oct. 1897

DEAR SIR,

Will you allow me to take an unusual step and to offer you my warm thanks for the review of a book of mine which you have contributed to the *English Historical Review*?[2] If the step is unusual (and I have never done anything of the kind before) the occasion also is unusual and in my experience unprecedented, for I have never seen a review of anything that I have written which has taught me so much or gone so straight to the points that are worth discussing. I cannot refrain from telling you of my gratitude. If ever I have to make a second edition of that book I shall have to alter many things in it in the light of your criticisms. Certainly this would be the case in the matter of the boroughs, and I must confess that you have somewhat shaken one [of] my few beliefs in the matter of the *manerium*, namely that this term had *some* technical meaning. I can't give up that belief all at once, but may have to do so by and by.

So repeating my thanks

I remain

Yours very truly

F. W. MAITLAND

201. To H. A. L. Fisher

Downing College

Cambridge

3rd Decr. 1897

MY DEAR HERBERT,

I want you to do for me a really brotherly act and to tell me from the bottom of your heart whether those lectures to which you were kind enough to listen are worth print. I have got stuff for a book about the Cambridge Field and this I am minded to publish in any case. My thought had been to make the

---

[1] Henry Bradshaw (1831–86), Librarian, University of Cambridge, 1867–86.
[2] *D.B. and Beyond*, reviewed by James Tait in E.H.R. (1897), 768–77.

stuff an appendix to my lectures; but now I am hesitating. Every one at Oxford was enormously kind, but just for this reason I feel sadly in need of a little objective criticism. I do not want to emphasize a failure. There is no one I can appeal to or should think of appealing to but you. So do tell me how it strikes you. I shall be grateful beyond words. I don't want you to say much or to put you in an awkward place. 'No' will be quite enough. And 'Rewrite in a more serious vein' will be quite enough. And my gratitude for these or any other brief remarks of the kind will be very true.[1]

Treat me as a brother on this occasion and I will be

Yours more than ever

F. W. MAITLAND

Florence is better and I am glad to say so far consoled that she is thinking of another Maltese.

By the way, did I see in your room a copy of Clark's edition of Wood's City of Oxford?[2] If so, will you lend it me for a short while? The copy that should be, is not, in Univ. Library.

I feel a beast for troubling you with that question about the lectures—but am unhappy and in need of advice. So forgive.

202. To Henry Sidgwick

[No year, and the problem of supplying it is hard. The letter was certainly written before 1898: M. was in the Canaries in December 1898 and 1899 and Sidgwick died on 28 August 1900. Possibly Sidgwick had raised the significance of Ihering's 'large phrase' for the purposes of his book on *The Development of European Polity* (see Letter 175, *supra*); but as he began work on it in 1888 and had not—to his own satisfaction—prepared it for publication by the time of his death, this possibility does not help to supply the year of the letter (*Henry Sidgwick*, 487, 500, 509, 584, 587). Perhaps the most plausible guess is 1897.]

Downing College

8th Decr.

MY DEAR SIDGWICK,

I think Ihering might say that his large phrase[3] covered the whole of the long process, beginning in cent. xi or xii and not yet ended, which has been romanizing the law of all European countries. I say 'not yet ended' because I am told that in the Russia of this century there has been an important romanistic movement.

But when a German historian speaks of 'the Reception' he is, I believe, usually referring to what happened in Germany from circ. 1450 onwards. He distinguishes a 'theoretic Reception' which begins far back under the

---

[1] The Ford Lectures were published under the title *Township and Borough* in 1898.

[2] *Survey of the Antiquities of the City of Oxford* by Anthony à Wood (1632–95), 'composed in 1661–6'. The edition by Andrew Clark was pub. by the Oxford Historical Society in 3 vols. 1889–99.

[3] The opening words of Ihering, *Geist des römischen Rechts*.

Ottos from the 'practical Reception' which belongs to cent. xv and xvi. The former consists in the adoption of the dogma that, as Otto, etc., are the successors of the old Emperors, so the Corpus Juris (the old Kaiser-recht), in so far as it has not been repealed, is or ought to be in force. But I understand that this dogma has little practical importance inside Germany. It is chiefly useful in the struggle with Italian princes and communities and enables the emperor to take up high ground in his quarrel with the pope. Inside Germany law remains very German and very rude—much more barbarous than English or French law—until in the second half of cent. xv there comes a catastrophe and the Roman law of the Italian commentators is swallowed whole. I think that a good book in which to look for an account of this movement is Schröder, *Lehrbuch der Deutschen Rechtsgeschichte*[1]: see *Rezeption* in index. If you wish to read of the earlier movement, the theoretical reception, I will ask my brother-in-law, Fisher of New, about the latest books; he is studying the Empire. I should think that Giesebrecht[2] must talk a good deal of this matter.

I have said so much because in Germany 'Rezeption' has become almost a technical term; and it generally stands for the movement that takes place in Germany at the end of the middle age. As I understand, German legal history is much more catastrophic than French—to say nothing of English. I do not find French legal historians speaking of the 'reception' of Roman law. What they tell us is that from (say) 1250 onwards the parlements are romanizing and that this process goes on without interruption until the Revolution and Code Nap. But all along they are professedly administering the Coutume of Paris or Orleans or the like. (Of course I am not speaking of the south of France where Roman law of a kind has *survived*.) In Germany on the other hand there is an open 'reception' of R.L., not as mere 'written reason' but as imperial law. This is due in some measure to the imperial theory, but in the main to the wretched chaos of particularism which is the end of Germanic law in its own home, where there have been no such kings as our Henry II or Philip Augustus. I do not think that Ihering, for whom I have a great admiration, knew much of medieval legal history, and I think it very possible that he supposed that Roman law had been 'received' in other countries, e.g. France, in the same definite way in which it was 'rezipiert' in Germany. Old German law has in this century been disinterred by historians after it had long been forgotten. Frenchmen—let alone Englishmen—have never had to perform a similar feat.

I hope that Schröder[3] will put you in the way of getting what you want. I assume that you don't want books about the *survival* of a Römisches Vulgar-recht between 500 and 1100.

Yours very truly

F. W. MAITLAND

---

[1] Cited by M. *English Law and the Renaissance*, notes 12 and 48.
[2] Giesebrecht, *Geschichte der deutschen Kaiserzeit:* included in Gierke's list of authorities, IV, *Political Theories of the Middle Age.*
[3] See note 1, *supra*. On the whole of this letter see M. Intro. to *Gierke*, I.

203. To J. H. Round

Horsepools
Stroud
27th Dec. 1897

MY DEAR ROUND,

Thank you. Your hint about Lee shall not be forgotten. I have been so far outside all these combats that I hardly know who the trustworthy persons are and therefore am I grateful to you.[1] I do not wonder that your articles should have won praise in more than one camp. I have lately re-read them and admired.[2] My suspicion is that the Anglican legend of the Reformation has seen its best day and that its popularizers have done it a mischief by their recklessness.

Yes! How short fifty pages may be when one is full of matter. I have lately been struggling with the unnecessary adjective and can sympathize. We must have as many substantives and verbs as possible in that introduction.[3]

Yours very truly
F. W. MAITLAND

204. To B. Fossett Lock

[M. wrote the year as 1897; but the contents and the following four letters show that 1898 is the correct year.]

Horsepools
Stroud
3 Jan [1898]

MY DEAR LOCK,

I have heard some important news about the Year Books which I must communicate to you. Thayer of Harvard has just paid me a visit after visiting Markby at Oxford, and Markby had given him to understand that the Clarendon Press would still be willing, as it was willing some years ago, to undertake the printing of the YBB and to bear the charge thereof wholly or at least in part. Now this of course may be very important news. I had thought that Markby's scheme had broken down a good many years ago owing to the backwardness of the Inns of Court and that no help was to be looked for in this direction. I should like to know what you think of this matter. I should dearly like to get this help towards payment of the printer's bill, because if we could find relief in this quarter we might be able to make an offer to Pike: if we had money he would be the man for it.[4]

---

[1] See H. R. T. Brandreth, *Dr. Lee of Lambeth: A Chapter in parenthesis in the history of the Oxford Movement* (London, 1951), esp. pp. 160–1, where a letter from Round is quoted expressing admiration for Lee's work on the Elizabethan Church and stating that he will bring it to the notice of 'one of the greatest living scholars'—perhaps M.

[2] See Letter 189, *supra*.

[3] 'That introduction' remains obscure; possibly one of the three introductions written by M. to the *Feet of Fines*, pub. by the Pipe Roll Society (1894–1900): see Letter 111, *supra*. M. had lately been pruning his adjectives in writing three articles for the *Encycl. of Laws of England*, Vol. ii. 302–3, 354–9, and Vol. iv. 3–7.

[4] See Letters 182 and 183, *supra*.

I write to you before I say a word to any one else. I have a slight, very slight, acquaintance with Markby. Of course I shall be willing to open correspondence with him, though I am not a good negotiator. But before doing anything I wish that you would turn the matter over in your mind. There will be various points to be considered if anything is to be done. Thus, e.g., I should suppose that Oxford would wish that its generosity should be distinctly recognized and perhaps that the YBB series should be a more or less distinct affair from our ordinary publications. But you will, I think, agree that something ought to be done. I understand that Markby is a very important man at the Clarendon Press and generally one of the chief men of business at Oxford. I don't think that he is likely to have spoken without warrant or that Thayer misunderstood him. (By the way, Thayer is worthy to be met.)

I foresee that, if anything comes of this, we may have to put out another non-Year Book volume after Turner's Forest Rolls.[1] I don't think that there would be much difficulty in filling the gap.

When you have thought over my news, let me know whether you see the outlines of a working project.

Markby showed to Thayer a large heap of letters which belonged to the old negotiation with the Inns of Court, and T. gathered that M. had been keen for the project and would like to see it renewed.

Yours very truly

F. W. MAITLAND

205. To B. Fossett Lock

Horsepools

8 Jan. 1898

MY DEAR LOCK,

Together with your letter, for which many thanks, there came this from Markby. You will see that he has big ideas: much too big I fear to do much good in this day of small things. I am answering him in such a way as just to keep a correspondence alive, telling him of the humility of our finances and so forth.[2] The practical question for us will be whether there is sufficient hope in this quarter to induce us to postpone our own little project. I feel that a failure or 'qualified success' on our part at the present moment might possibly damage the chances of a greater enterprise. So will you turn this over and in course of time give counsel?

It is fortunate that you are in touch with one who knows his Oxford.[3]

Yours very truly

F. W. MAITLAND

I send this to Linc. Inn, not knowing whether 'Dorchester' would find you.

[1] S.S. Vol. 13.

[2] M.'s letter to Markby seems not to have survived; nor have Lock's or Markby's letters to M. But Markby would appear to have suggested a possible edition of Year Books by the Clarendon Press: see Letters 206 and 207, *infra*.

[3] Allusion unknown.

206. To B. Fossett Lock

Downing College
Cambridge
16th Jan. 1898

MY DEAR LOCK,

I agree that we have as yet nothing to lay before a Council meeting. Nor am I very hopeful. But at the same time I don't want to quench any smoking flax. So I am going to tell Pollock how the matter stands and ask him to open the subject when he meets Sir W.[1] at Oxford.

The Benchers of Lincoln's Inn have asked me to dine on Tuesday. I have accepted chiefly in the hope that I may edge in a word of Year Books in some good quarter. Possibly on Wednesday I may seek you out and try to obtain your ear for two minutes.

Yours very truly

F. W. MAITLAND

207. To B. Fossett Lock

Downing
19 Jan. 1898

MY DEAR LOCK,

There are those who believe that all Colleges are in Oxford. Hence it falls out that I only received your letter on my return to Cambridge the day after the orgy.[2] Had it been otherwise I should have made a point of visiting you. As it was I thought that I had no sufficient cause for calling you from your work this morning.

Until I had your note I did not know that the matter was as pressing as it is. I now see that there is no time for vague pourparlers. I had a few words with Stirling, Romer and Renshaw[3] about the matter. None of them was hopeful. Stirling remembered Markby's original effort. Renshaw, with whom I had a long walk, is, as you know, very doubtful about the policy of attacking the Year Books.

I think that the question whether anything more should be done is now in your hands. I can not myself see the outline of any scheme that would be at all likely to suit both us and the Clarendon Press, our finances being what they are. Do you think otherwise? If you do, perhaps the best course will be that I should come to see you between two trains and settle a statement to be laid before Markby. I misdoubt my own power of dealing with the negotiation, and on the other hand do not want to burden you with letter writing; so I might write under your eye.

[1] Sir William Markby. Pollock wrote to Lock on 7 Feb. 1898 that Markby 'was off for a tour round the world' and would not be back until October; meanwhile it was 'useless' to open the matter with the Clarendon Press (S.S. Corr.).
[2] See Letter 206, *supra.*
[3] W. C. Renshaw, Q.C. Like Stirling and Romer, L.J.J., he was a member of the Council of the Selden Society.

I am quite willing to go on with the original scheme and have already been incurring debts (not as agent) for 'copy';[1] but, as you know, I should be extremely sorry to hinder a big project, especially if it involved the employment of Pike.

Yours very truly

F. W. MAITLAND

208. To B. Fossett Lock

Downing

29th Jan. 1898

MY DEAR LOCK,

It is good of you to take all this trouble. I fully approve your suggested course, and it now being clear that Pike is not to be had,[2] I shall be quite willing to do all I can for the YBB according to any scheme that may be contrived by your wisdom. So soon as I am in harness I shall like the work.

A day or two after our pleasant walk I received an unexpected invitation from Shadwell[3] to a feast at Oriel which I could not accept. I was sorry to decline it, for it might have led to useful talk.

Hitherto my opinion about the Year Books has fluctuated owing to Pike's strong claims. I have been unwilling to take, or even to seem to take, work away from him. But if he is once out of the question, the course will be much smoother.

I hope that you did not regret your visit to Cambridge. Our walk cheered me amazingly.

Yours very truly

F. W. MAITLAND

209. To J. H. Round

Downing College

Cambridge

20 Feb. 1898

MY DEAR ROUND,

I have several hints given in your last letter[4] for which I ought to thank you and do 'hereby' thank you.

No, I don't know the Strongbow charter, nor have I studied Marshal's jurisdiction, nor again have I seen that paper on scutage.[5] All this I should like to look into. I have two courses of lectures to run and few free moments.

[1] See Letter 199, *supra*.

[2] The Treasury had sanctioned the continuation of the Rolls Series of YBB down to the 20th year of Edw. III, and Pike was to be fully occupied with this work (letter from Pike to Lock of 23 April 1898 confirming this decision: S.S. Corr.). See Letters 182, 183 and 185, *supra*.

[3] Charles Lancelot Shadwell (1840–1919), Provost of Oriel College, Oxford, 1905–14.

[4] Not extant.

[5] See Round, *Commune of London*, esp. the essays on 'The Marshalship of England' and 'The Conquest of Ireland'. Strongbow—Richard, earl of Pembroke—was hereditary Marshal of England and the Anglo-Norman leader in the conquest of Ireland, 1170. On scutage see a review by Round in E.H.R. (1898), 569.

Some of these I give to the Athenaeum wherein I read an article on Jenks, also a reply to the Arcadian Augustus: he can say funny things at times, and you do right to correct him.[1]

I have been making at odd times a few preliminary studies for the first years of Elizth. Your friend Lee has some good things but can make wonderful blunders of the kind called 'howler'. However, he is better than some of the continuators. Meanwhile I am among Calvin's letters. I think that he and Elizth. understood each other.[2]

When are we to look for the Charters?[3]

Yours very truly

F. W. MAITLAND

210. To J. H. Round

Downing
4 March 1898

DEAR ROUND,

I thank you many times. These papers are most interesting, and I am glad to have had the advantage of reading your letters.[4]

I wonder what these people would have to say about John Knox. Apparently they would have to say that he was sound.

I know Pocock's paper: it is very good. I fancy, however, that before 1558 a more mystical view of 'the supper' than true Zwinglianism had got the upper hand among the Swiss reformers. I believe that you would find it easy to pick out from the Scotch divines and Beza and Calvin passages that are quite as 'catholic' about this matter as any that are to be found in Guest and the Articles.[5]

I grieve to think that you are in pain.

Yours gratefully

F. W. MAITLAND

211. To J. H. Round

Horsepools
22nd March 1898

MY DEAR ROUND,

I have more than one letter for which to thank you. Sir James Ramsay's[6] letter I restore. I feel sorry for any one who has to read Domesday and Beyond

---

[1] Edward Jenks, *Law and Politics in the Middle Ages* (1898). The 'Arcadian Augustus' was Edward Augustus Freeman.

[2] M. was already preparing for the essay on the Anglican Settlement and the Scottish Reformation, to appear in 1903 as Chap. XVI of Vol. II of the Camb. Mod. Hist: see Cam, Intro. to *Selected Hist. Essays*, xxi–ii. For 'your friend Lee' see Letter 203, *supra*.

[3] See Letter 134, *supra*.

[4] The papers and letters would seem to be ammunition for the controversy provoked by Round: see Letter 189, *supra*.

[5] This paragraph concerns men and matters discussed by M. in his chapter in the Camb. Mod. Hist. See Letter 209, *supra*. Edmund Guest (1518–77), Bishop of Rochester, assisted Archbishop Parker in the revision of the English articles of religion.

[6] (1832–1925), medieval historian. Published *Lancaster and York* (1892), *The Foundations of England* (1898), *The Angevin Empire* (1903), *The Dawn of the Constitution* (1908), etc.

unless he is of the small number of the Elect, who were predestined to fall under the Conqueror's spell.

Oh yes! I know your Colchester papers and give a reference to one of them ('tis mighty good) in this last book of mine. I forget whether you sent me a list of them—but I remember searching the Antiquary a while ago to be sure that I missed nothing.[1]

I have lately been through all the titles of inclosure acts and am coming to a suspicion that there is some big difference between the boroughs that lie south and those that lie north of the Thames line. So if you know of any first class town south of that line which had wide unenclosed fields I should be very glad of its name. I see acts for very important towns to the north of that line, e.g. Lincoln, Leicester, Nottingham, etc.

I am afraid that your new book which I pine to see can only supply me with 'addenda et corrigenda'—but I shall be glad of early intelligence if anything about fee farms and bailiffs is on the point of appearing, for a much renovated chapter on the boroughs will be the last part of my 'history' that will go to press.[2]

As to the idolatrous mass: I feel surer every day that you are right. After grinding through many books, some of which are here, I shall probably have but half a page to give to this subject—but I want to say what is true. If you plunge into any more controversies I beg you to let me know.[3]

To-morrow I dine in London with the resuscitated[4] Pollock.

Yours with many thanks

F. W. MAITLAND

212. To B. Fossett Lock

Downing Coll.

23rd April 1898

MY DEAR LOCK,

I yesterday saw Leach and the Provost's Book.[5] I can not say that I think well of the latter for our purpose. It is a collection of extracts from manorial court rolls. The entries seemed to be of the ordinary dreary kind—and I do not think that the publication of them would to any appreciable degree advance our knowledge of legal history.

On the other hand, Leach had in his house what seemed to me far more hopeful, namely a lot of records of the *town* of Beverley—town by-laws, ordinances of the gild merchant, ordinances of the craft gilds, etc.—15th and 16th century work. I am inclined to think that a good volume might be made

---

[1] M. cited the 'Colchester papers' in *D.B. and Beyond*, Essay I. s. 9, and in *Township and Borough*, Lecture I.

[2] Second edition of *P. and M.* Round's new book was probably *The Commune of London*: see Letter 209, *supra*.

[3] See Letter 189, *supra*, and Camb. Mod. Hist. Vol. II, p. 565.

[4] Presumably 'resuscitated' by his re-election to the Corpus Chair at Oxford for a further five years: see *Pollock–Holmes Letters*, I. 81.

[5] See Letters 192 and 193, *supra*.

of them. We have not done much for our boroughs, and Hudson's Norwich book[1] does not touch all sides of the legal life of towns. Leach also told me that he could get at a good book of Lincoln ordinances. He further said that he was not unwilling to make a volume out of Beverley or out of Beverley and Lincoln.[2] What think you? Will you have a word with Leach? I told him very plainly that the decision did not rest with me.

Are you opposed to female labour? I ask this because Miss Bateson[3] occurred to me as a possible editor of Jew rolls. She has been editing the records of Leicester for the corporation, and is careful and instructed. I have said no word to her. Baildon was immovable; his hands are full of Lincoln's Inn.

Yours very truly

F. W. MAITLAND

213. To F. J. H. Jenkinson

Horsepools

Stroud

6 July 1898

MY DEAR JENKINSON,

Allow me to introduce to you Profr. C. H. Haskins of the University of Wisconsin[4] who is desirous of consulting some of the MSS in the University Library.

Yours very truly

F. W. MAITLAND

214. To E. J. Watson

[Year from post-mark on envelope.]

The Horsepools

Stroud

July 26th [1898]

DEAR SIR,

You are quite at liberty to take from my Gloucester book[5] whatever you think fit. I ought to tell you, however, that I was by no means an expert copyist

---

[1] S.S. Vol. 5.

[2] Leach's volume, S.S. Vol. 14, was confined to Beverley: see Letter 246, *infra*.

[3] Mary Bateson (1865–1906) was the daughter of William Henry Bateson, Master of St. John's College, Cambridge. She taught and lectured at Newnham College of which she had been a student. She spent her life in the study of history, especially local history, and edited the Records of the Borough of Leicester, and (with M.) the Charters of the Borough of Cambridge (1901). She did not edit the Jewish Rolls, but did edit two volumes of Borough Customs (S.S. Vols. 18 and 21). See D.N.B. (1901–11) and the moving obituary by M. (C.P. III. 540–3).

[4] Charles Homer Haskins (1870–1937), medieval historian. Between 1902 and 1931, when his health broke down, he held various chairs in succession at Harvard University. Among his books are *The Normans in European History* (1915), *Norman Institutions* (1918), *Studies in the History of Medieval Science* (1924). See a memoir by Powicke, *Modern Historians and the study of History*, Chap. IV, reprinted from E.H.R. (1937), 649.

[5] *Pleas of the Crown for the county of Gloucester before the Abbot of Reading, A.D. 1221* (pub. 1884).

when I published that book and may have made mistakes. I do not know of any book on the government of boroughs that I could recommend to you. What I wrote on that subject in the History of English Law is not satisfactory add I am trying to improve it for a second edition. Do you know Dr. Charles Gross's Bibliography of Municipal History? It is a very useful book.

Yours very truly

F. W. MAITLAND

215. To Charles Gross

[No date; but from the contents and the four following letters early August 1898.]

Horsepools,
Stroud.

MY DEAR GROSS,

I have been hoping and hoping to say that we could meet, and as there is not much hope of my travelling yet a while I have been waiting to ask you whether you would come here. How much longer will you be in London? I put off inviting you, for I am still a poor creature and have to spend much time in bed *vel quasi*—but I do want to see you and every day brings a little improvement.

Yours very truly

F. W. MAITLAND

216. To Charles Gross

Horsepools
Stroud

7 Augt. 1898

DEAR GROSS,

If in your charity you can bring yourself to devote next Sunday to an invalid (for so I must still call myself) I shall be grateful and shall hope to see you on Saturday the 13th. Our station is Stroud and the 3.15 is a good train.

Yours very truly

F. W. MAITLAND

217. To F. J. H. Jenkinson

Horsepools
Stroud

15 Aug. 1898

MY DEAR JENKINSON,

I have written to Major Barnard, who seems to be a neighbour of mine.[1]
I have been spending my time unprofitably and in bed: the cold of an English

---

[1] Allusion unknown.

June attacked me in the shape of pleurisy. Whenever I am ill I always tell myself that you are worse and are only working all the harder instead of giving way: but I give way all the same, and now I have almost forgotten how to write.

If you could stretch a point in my favour I shall be extremely grateful for a read of Harland's 'Mamecestre', a Chetham book,[1] which I believe can not go out without your order. Could this be negotiated?

I am glad to hear that Codex Bezae[2] is so far advanced. Of Beza's self I am learning something. A learned man tells me that, if our library has not, it ought to have

> Chevin, L'Abbé, Dictionnaire
> Latin-Français—Paris, 1897,

it being good for identification of place names.

Yes, I confess it warm; but I am swathed.

Yours very truly

F. W. MAITLAND

218. To Charles Gross

Horsepools
Stroud

17 Augt. 1898

MY DEAR GROSS,

Ever since you left I have been enjoying myself partly with the dream of Harvard which I can not yet dismiss, partly with attempts to remember some of the things that I learnt from you in our delightful (at least to me) conversation.

And now I have to thank you for these charity notes: they are much to the purpose.[3]

I do not like to ask for more: but if at any time you are in the MS room and have the minutes to spare, will you set my mind at rest about that 'Revocation' by Henry II of his anti-ecclesiastical claims?[4] It is in MS. Add. 34, 807. f. 95. All depends on this—In the first lines after 'legatis', should we read 'full stop.

[1] The Chetham Society was founded in 1843 for the publication 'of remains historical and literary connected with the palatine counties of Lancaster and Chester'. J. Harland's *Mamecestre* was printed in Vols. 53, 56 and 58 of the Chetham Soc., 1st Series, (1861–2).

[2] Theodore Beza (1519–1605), French theologian and follower of Calvin, presented to the University of Cambridge in 1581 The Codex of the Four Gospels and Acts, known as Codex D or Codex Bezae (present classmark M.S. Nu. 2. 41). A facsimile was in course of preparation for an edition to be published at Cambridge in 1899.

[3] Reference obscure: possibly for the chapter on the Boroughs which M. was revising for the 2nd ed. of *P. and M*. See Letter 222, *infra*.

[4] See Letters 219, 220 and 244, *infra*.

Priori et conventui' or 'comma, Priore et conventu' [governed by coram]? It is a shame to trouble you but this document intrigues me.

Yours very truly

F. W. MAITLAND

More in a few days.

219. To R. Lane Poole

Horsepools

Stroud

19 Aug. 1898

MY DEAR POOLE,

Herewith divers reviews. Forgive untidiness. I scribbled in a state of convalescence. Des Marez's book I read in bed with great pleasure.[1]

I hope that you are far away from historical cares but will take this opportunity of asking what you think of Mr. Herbert's 'Revocatio', E.H.R. xiii, 507. It seems to me that one very small emendation would convert this document from an almost impossible to a highly correct form. It is this: in line 4 reduce the full-stop to a comma and turn *Priori et conventui* from dative to ablative: then in line 6 reduce the full-stop to a comma. This done, the document is formally unexceptionable. It is not a *letter* but an *act*, recording what Henry did in Canterbury cathedral before the two legates, the prior and convent and divers other persons there congregated. I don't carry the Becket story in my head; but if this change brings this document into collision with known facts, we may none the less be right in making the change, and then we may choose between forgery and exercise in composition. You see how ignorant I am without books; but I thought that the diplomatic point might interest you. As the document stands, I can not make head or tail of its form. I have ascertained through a friend[2] that Mr. Herbert is blameless: the thought crossed my mind that he had made a small mistake over *Priori et conventui*.

To leap over some centuries. Did I not see that the Clarendon Press was to publish a book by Gee (?) on the Elizabethan clergy?[3] Do you know anything as to the probability of this book's appearance within a reasonable time? It might save me a long hunt after deprived papists.

As you may suppose, we here are joyful over the news that Herbert Fisher is to be married.[4]

Do not notice my queries unless to do so is very easy.

Yours very truly

F. W. MAITLAND

---

[1] [A.L.P. 'Étude sur la Propriété Foncière dans les Villes du Moyen Age et spécialement en Flandre', reviewed by M., E.H.R. (1899) 137.] The 'divers reviews' were probably of *Yorkshire Inquisitions*, Vol. ii, ed. W. Brown, and Fournier, *Les collections canoniques attribuées à Yves de Chartres*, in E.H.R. (1898), at pp. 775 and 815 respectively.

[2] Charles Gross: see Letter 218, *supra*.

[3] [A.L.P. Henry Gee, *The Elizabethan clergy and the settlement of religion* (Oxford, 1898).]

[4] To Lettice, daughter of Sir Courtney Ilbert, Parliamentary Counsel to the Treasury and author of *Legislative Methods and Forms* (1901) and *Mechanics of Law Making* (1913).

220. To R. Lane Poole

Horsepools
Stroud
29 Aug. 1898

MY DEAR POOLE,

I should like that book very much and am grateful for the offer[1]: also for your letter. It may be expedient that a word should be said of that Canterbury document. I am right glad to hear that the emendation had occurred to you— but who is Herbert? (I fear that I argue myself unknown.) If he is a young man he might like the opportunity of having a second word about his document, and I should be unwilling to hurt his feelings.[2]

The point about dedication did not occur to me. I had a vague notion, founded on something that I once saw in a book—belike a bad book—that dedications to Christ and to S.S. Trinity were treated as equivalents—perhaps some generalization from the case of Canterbury—when I think of it, it seems improbable, but I am fairly sure that I did not invent this theory.[3] Is there a good book on dedications? I never attended to them and have felt the lack of knowledge when dealing with town parishes.

Believe me
Yours very truly
F. W. MAITLAND

221. To J. H. Round

[No year: but from contents and context clearly 1898.]

Horsepools
31 Augt.

MY DEAR ROUND,

I thank you for your letter and your book.[4] I see that the latter will instruct me if it also pains me, and I am keen to read it. At the moment I am suffering from a small relapse which is of no great consequence, but I am knowing a little of what your headaches must be and feel that scutage is a little too hard.[5] I have acquired Baldwin's book[6] at your recommendation but have not mastered it.

Your *Church Historians* would admirably suit me and I must hasten to get a copy of the Contemporary.[7] I have been making my own estimate of certain people who have dealt with Elizabeth and am most anxious to see yours.

[1] Gee, *The Elizabethan Clergy:* see Letter 219, *supra*.
[2] See Letters 218 and 219, *supra*, and 244, *infra*.
[3] [A.L.P. Cf. E.H.R. (1900) 86.]
[4] *Studies on the Red Book of the Exchequer*, a pamphlet attacking Hubert Hall's edition of the *Red Book* for the R.S. See Letter 179, *supra*, and Winfield, *Chief Sources*, 118.
[5] See Letter 209, *supra*. A paper on scutage was also included in Round's *Studies on the Red Book of the Exchequer*.
[6] J. F. Baldwin, *Scutage and Knight Service in England* (Chicago, 1897); reviewed by Round in E.H.R. (1898) 560.
[7] See Cam, Intro. to *Selected Hist. Essays*, xxi.

The charter book I badly want as you may well suppose.[1]

My first lucid interval shall be given to the Red Book. I shall learn much, though I expect to feel in my proper person some of the blows that you inflict upon H. H.[2] I fear that what I shall read will be all too true, and yet of the said H. H. I am fond.

Forgive this scrawl,

With more thanks,

Yours very truly

F. W. MAITLAND

222. To Charles Gross

Horsepools

2 Septr. 1898

MY DEAR GROSS,

I fear that the time has come when I must write to you and 'make the grand refuse'. I hate doing it: the prospect has been so honourable and so pleasant. You know how I regard the Harvard Law School: I feel as if I lived in the 12th century and was rejecting a 'call' to Bologna. But really I am hopeless and must not allow you to hope that you have found a substitute for your sabbatical. This vacation has been to me a sore disappointment. Not only have I left undone many things that I meant to do, but I am none the better for my idleness. If I do a couple of hours work I become useless, and already I am dreading next term—all the more because Whittaker will I fear be disabled by a bad accident which has happened to him.[3] All I can expect at the best is just to keep up with the little work that Cambridge requires of its professors, and I can not believe that I shall be in a position to ask leave of absence—H. Sidgwick would be the first to refuse it unless it had been earned by a strict attention to business.[4] But this is not all. I should hate to go to Harvard with nothing to say that was worth saying and, as I told you, I *can not* improvise: so, though the occasion may seem far off, the question to me is whether I could write many lectures, and the answer is No.

There! Forgive this Jeremiad! I ought not to inflict it on you; but I wished you to know exactly how things stood, so that I might not seem ungrateful to you for your kindness when really I am full of gratitude.

I send you a sheet which begins my rewritten chapter on Boroughs. I wish that with your book[5] at my elbow I could devote a life to the study. My main object this time will be to *state* the legal questions. Answers will come in due course I hope. A little volume of choice charters would be so useful!

This comes de profundis.

Yours very truly

F. W. MAITLAND

---

[1] See Letters 134 and 209, *supra*.   [2] Hubert Hall.

[3] See Letters 223 and 224, *infra*.

[4] Sidgwick was from 1882–99 a member of the General Board of Studies and for several years acted as its Secretary: *Henry Sidgwick*, 371–5. See also Letters 229 and 230, *infra*.

[5] Presumably *Bibliography of British Municipal History*.

223. To F. J. H. Jenkinson

Horsepools
Stroud
6 Septr. 1898

MY DEAR JENKINSON,

I am returning to you Harland's 'Mamecestre'[1]—very gratefully, for it has helped me. Also I have to thank you for a letter. As term draws nigh I am recovering my spirits; moreover the weather is delightful. Whittaker's fall on to that massive head has made me anxious, but I got some good news of him to-day. I am hoping for a day at Cheltenham if only Fitzroy F.[2] will attend to business. Could I do anything for you there and save an additional gua?

Yours very truly
F. W. MAITLAND

No, not gua, only £1. On one occasion the elder F. returned the shilling to me, but pocketed the sovereign. Bless him!

224. To R. Lane Poole

Horsepools
Stroud
7 Sept. 1898

MY DEAR POOLE,

Your request torments me greatly.[3] 'I have prayed that this cup', etc.—but can't finish the text. I have been asking myself whether it is want of proper courage that deters me, and feel this point the more because, as H. H. was good enough to let me see his proofs, I was in a position in which I might have helped him out of messes, but must confess to have read with but a selfish purpose, looking for something new of scutage.

What I saw showed me that my good friend—and he has been my very good friend—was incapable of conducting an argument—but I did not suspect the blunders. This however is not all. I think that in bare justice to Hall the reviewer of Round's pamphlet ought to satisfy himself that a considerable number of the charges are just. I fear that they are—but Hall is so poor a hand at saying what he means that the reviewer ought to distinguish between the gross mistake and the muddled statement. Now it is out of the question that for many weeks to come I should seriously work at the Red Book. Illness has thrown me behind hand, and now the dear Whittaker who usually stands between me and 'elementary real property' has been ejected from a trap and has concussed his massive brain—so I am writing lectures for dear life. Therefore I beg of you to look elsewhere. Someone might really like to sit in justice and would not feel that his inside was being torn by every word that he wrote. Would not the good bishop intervene?[4]—really this is an occasion worthy of his intervention and

---

1 See Letter 217, *supra*.
2 T. Fitzroy Fenwick of Cheltenham, who was concerned with antiquarian publications.
3 To review Round's *Studies on the Red Book of the Exchequer*: see Letter 221, *supra*.
4 [A.L.P. William Stubbs, Bishop of Oxford.]

he could appear at his very best. What you say of your own lack of *financial* lore is true of me also. I feel e.g. that, if I shut myself up for year and day, I could get that scutage-story straight—but I should have to think neither of elementary real property nor of Anglican settlements nor of anything else. Therefore mercy! if this is possible.[1]

Yours very truly

F. W. MAITLAND

If all that R. says is true, I still think he is using language which should be reserved for cases of a very different sort—some of which have occurred in the Rolls Series. Poor Hall has a curious fluffy mind but never scamps work, besides being (but this alas is irrelevant) the most unselfish man I have ever known.

If you do hear aught of Gee[2]—let me know and I shall be grateful.

225. To R. Lane Poole

Horsepools

12 Sept. 1898

MY DEAR POOLE,

In the matters of Marcellus and Miete I am grateful. I once found myself puzzling over Germanen*t*um which I took for a Latin noun with gen. in i. So in a footnote of mixed Latin and German Verrall once struggled with 'verbumst' and discovered the verb 'verbummen'. So I thank you for helping me with Rat and Tat.[3]

As to the Round-Hall controversy. I see that you have one qualification which I lack, to wit 'objectivity', and I am quite sure that your knowledge of the financial detail is sufficient, and equal to mine at the very least. Therefore if it lies between me and you (and perhaps R. thinks so, for he is highly civil to you and flatters me absurdly) then Thou art the man. You see from my parenthesis that I am not 'objective', and I am not. The E.H.R. (=you) has been very kind to me in printing my stuff, and I don't like refusing to serve it—but I have heard a good deal (and can hope that you have not) from both sides about a very painful quarrel between two co-editors,[4] and the more I think over the matter the less able am I to separate the merits and demerits of this published book from disputed questions of fact and disputable questions of morals. I can believe that you are in a happier position and can criticize Hall's work as it stands without considering its genesis. And of course I fully agree with you that he has made bad blunders and has hardly the faintest idea of the way in which a story should be told or an argument conducted: so I don't in the least think that you will be too severe.

I hope and trust that you were not very serious when you said that the

1 [A.L.P. Round's *Studies* was ultimately reviewed by R. L. Poole, E.H.R. (1899) 148.]
2 See Letter 219, *supra.*
3 The allusions in this paragraph remain obscure.
4 See Letter 179, *supra.*

bishop was 'sore'. I feel for him a respect so deep that if you told me that the republication of my essays[1] would make him more unhappy than a sane man is whenever people dissent from him, I should be in great doubt what to do. It is not too late to destroy all or some of the sheets. I hate to bark at the heels of a great man whom I admire, but tried hard to seem, as well as to be, respectful.

Yours very truly

F. W. MAITLAND

226. To Charles Gross

Horsepools

Stroud

4 Octr. 1898

MY DEAR GROSS,

I hardly know how to thank you for this list of twelve-penny burgages.[2] It is most interesting to me.

Since we parted things have not gone well with me. I am condemned to spend the whole of this winter in idleness and warmth; also I must beg leave of absence from the University. I am told that all should be well by Easter; but this robs me of my last hope of seeing Harvard—if only Harvard were in Algiers! So I grieve to say that the offer of which you spoke would do no good, and I do not wish to have the pain—for pain it would be—of refusing. I do hope to be at work again at Easter, and I am still hoping that I may not be sent beyond seas, but I shall have exhausted the patience of Cambridge.

I think that you will like Miss Bateson's Leicester Records.[3]

Yours full of regrets

F. W. MAITLAND

227. To Henry Sidgwick

Horsepools

Stroud

7th Oct. 1898

MY DEAR SIDGWICK,

You will probably have heard in the course of business that I am hindered from coming to Cambridge, but I fancy that Cunningham is away and so write to inform you expressly that to my great grief I shall not be able to entertain the Eranus,[4] and I believe that my turn is the next.

[1] *Roman Canon Law in the Church of England*, in which M. dissented from Stubbs: see Letter 168, *supra*.

[2] See Hemmeon, *Burgage Tenure in Medieval England*, 26 L.Q.R. 331.

[3] The first of 3 vols., to be published in 1899. See Letter 212, *supra*.

[4] A Cambridge society founded in 1872 and limited to twelve members representing different aspects of academic study. It met five or six times a year at the house or rooms of a member. The host of the evening read a paper which was then discussed: *Henry Sidgwick*, 223–4.

I have made my application to the General Board through its Secretary. There is just one word that I should like to say to you in private. If there is to be a resident as deputy, I think that, failing Kenny, Wright should not be forgotten, and that there may be some chance of his being forgotten, for he is so modest.

I am hoping against hope that I may not be sent out of England. Any way the time is coming when I would gladly attend the meetings of the G.B. of S.[1]

Yours very truly

F. W. MAITLAND

228. To F. J. H. Jenkinson

Horsepools
Stroud
17 Oct. 1898

DEAR JENKINSON,

I hope that the books that I returned 'as per' my last letter[2] arrived safely. I shall go abroad with an easier conscience if I have paid my fines before I go.

Could I have *one* library book for a short time?—I will send it home before Christmas. Say No if duty prompts. It is Hinschius, Kirchenrecht, 3.[3] For the most part I am debarred from work but there is one small job that I should like to complete. My wife is going to Cambridge to-morrow and will call at the Library on Wednesday morning in the hope of being able to discharge my fines and (perhaps) to obtain the said Hinschius.

I know that if all men had their deserts you would be sharing my sentence of transportation.[4]

Yours very truly

F. W. MAITLAND

229. To Henry Sidgwick

Horsepools
Stroud
18 Octr. 1898

MY DEAR SIDGWICK,

I am driven by stress of steamers into a hurried departure for the Canaries. I feel sure that the General Board will do what is right. Outside Cambridge there is no one whom I could prefer as deputy to Cyprian Williams[5]: I mean among men likely to accept. He has been my friend these thirty years, and so I

---

[1] General Board of Studies.
[2] See Letter 223, *supra.*
[3] Paul Hinschius, *Das Kirchenrecht der Katholiken und Protestanten in Deutschland,* 6 vols. (1869–97).
[4] See Letter 217, *supra.*
[5] (1854–1932), of Lincoln's Inn, Barrister-at-law, Conveyancing Counsel to the Court and the son of Joshua Williams whose books on *Real Property, Personal Property* and *The Law of Vendors and Purchasers of Land* he edited.

feel a little shy about recommending him—still, friendship apart, I think highly
of his work.

> Good-bye,
> Yours very truly
> F. W. MAITLAND

230. To Henry Sidgwick

> Las Palmas
> *31 Oct. 1898*

DEAR SIDGWICK,

I shall, no doubt, hear in an official way what the General Board has done
in my case, but if you think that there is anything that I ought to know but will
not be officially communicated, I will ask you to take notice of my where-
abouts and, if you ever have time to spare, to tell me of what has passed.
This will be a charity; but I must not forget that while I am idle you are not.

I am idle in such idleness as is impossible in Europe. For the first time in my
life I am feeling that mere existence is pleasant. In spite of all that I had heard,
I did not believe in the demoralizing effect of the sun. I can hardly bring myself
to ask whether England and France are at war.[1] Still, if there is anything that
I ought to be told about the situation at Cambridge, will you tell it?

> Yours very truly
> F. W. MAITLAND

231. To Leslie Stephen

[No original. Printed by Fisher, *Memoir*, 113–14: no beginning or ending.]

> Hotel Santa Catalina
> Las Palmas
> Gran Canaria
> *5 Nov. 1898*

I am beginning Guy Fawkes's day by sitting in the verandah before breakfast to write letters for a homeward-bound mail. Certainly it is enjoyable here
and I mean to get good out of a delightful climate. Also I mean to convert your
half promise of a visit into a whole, and without going beyond the truth I can
say that there is a good deal here that should please you. At first sight I was
repelled by the arid desolation of the island. I suppose that I ought to have
been prepared for grasslessness, but somehow or another I was not. But then
the wilderness is broken by patches of wonderful green—the green of banana
fields. Wherever a little water can be induced to flow in artificial channels
there are all manner of beautiful things to be seen. I have picked a date and

[1] Over the 'Fashoda incident': after a French expedition had occupied Fashoda in the
Sudan in July 1898 Lord Kitchener arrived there in September with a British force.

mustered enough Spanish to buy me a pair of shoes in the 'city' of Las Palmas —a dirty city it is with strange smells; but we are well outside of it. Between Las Palmas and its port there is a little English colony. This hotel is so English that they give me my bill in £.s.d. and my change in British hapence which have seen better days. Indeed now I know where our coppers go to when they have become too bad for use at home. Also the 'library' of this hotel seems a sort of Hades to which the bad three-voller is sent after its decease. But the proposition that all the worst books collect there is (as you must be aware) not convertible into the proposition that only bad books come there, and I see a copy of a certain *Life of Henry Fawcett*[1] which you may have read. I laze away my time under verandahs and in gardens—but am not wholly inactive. Sometimes when it is cool I walk some miles and explore country that is well worth exploration. By the time you come I shall be ready for an ascent of our central range with you—it touches 6000 ft. I think—and by that time we shall be having cooler weather. Yesterday we were breathless: to-day is cloudy but would be September in England.

It is breakfast time and the porridge is good.

232. To H. A. L. Fisher

> Hotel Santa Brigida
> Monte
> Gr. Canaria
> *22nd Dec. 1898*

MY DEAR HERBERT,

Your book[2] comes with your letter. I will send my thanks—and they are warm—at once, for if I begin looking at your book there will be no more writing for me until the last word has been read. Surrounded by libraries, you will not be able to imagine the lust that is in me for a book of history, and my joy will be greatly increased by hearing, as I shall, your voice when I read your words. I feel that a very great treat is in store for me.

I had a treat of another kind yesterday. The weather was so glorious that I could not refrain from an ascent of our central range at what I thought would be its lowest point. I succeeded in tramping for six or seven hours and was amply rewarded, for at the top I had a most glorious vision of Tenerife soaring out of the sea. Really it was some 50 miles away, but the foreground was so arranged that it all looked part of one island, and the Peak is so big that I could hardly persuade myself that it was not close at hand. I was grilling in what for an Englishman was a July day, yet in shady places I found a little ice. From this you will gather that I am no longer the very feeble creature that left England: indeed I am at last persuaded that I am a humbug.

Before you receive this you will, I suppose, have decided between Oxford

---

[1] By Leslie Stephen (1888). [2] *The Medieval Empire.*

and Edinburgh,[1] and in any case I should feel that advice was superfluous since all the elements in the case are well known to you. For my own part I shall not be sorry if you make for the north since I imagine that in the long run leisure lies that way, though no doubt there would be an initial 'grind' to be accomplished. Of course you and Miss Ilbert know that the east wind of Edinburgh is somewhat terrible, but I believe that Mrs. Prothero[2] flourished there—I shall be curious to know your decision. With us the east or south-east wind is a real delight. It comes off the desert and sweeps away the clouds from the mountains.

Florence sends her love.

Yours very affectionately

F. W. MAITLAND

233. To J. H. Round

Hotel Sta. Brigida
Monte
Gr. Canary
29 Dec. 1898

DEAR ROUND,

The news that you give me of your book is by no means what I should like to hear. I hoped that you would find a publisher without much difficulty, and shall indeed be sorry if any of your work goes lost. And in the matter of indexing I can sympathize, though I never had on my hands so heavy a task as yours must be.[3]

I write however chiefly to answer your kind offer concerning a volume of essays; or rather to say that, if you must have an answer at once, it must be that I can not at present join your team.[4] When I get back to England I shall have a great deal of routine work to do, for I really must write some new lectures. Also I can not make any arrangements touching the Reformation until I have had an interview with Lord Acton. It is just possible that hereafter I may be compelled in self-defence to justify with 'authorities' some sentences which I have written and which may (or may not) appear in the Cambridge History,[5] but I shall do this, if I do it at all, with reluctance; and of course I can not ask you to wait until I have made up my mind. Are you well-advised

[1] Fisher applied for the chair at Edinburgh University, but Richard Lodge, who had been elected at Glasgow University in 1894, was again preferred to him: see Ogg, *Herbert Fisher*, 42, and Letter 136, *supra*.

[2] Afterwards Lady Prothero. Her husband, Sir George Prothero (1848–1922), was Professor at Edinburgh from 1894 to 1899 and co-editor of Camb. Mod. Hist. from 1901 to 1912.

[3] The 'book' was probably *The Commune of London*: the indexes perhaps those to Round's volumes in the series *Great roll of the pipe* in the reign of Henry II issued by the Pipe Roll Society.

[4] This seems to refer to a projected volume of essays on the Reformation which did not materialise: see Page, Intro. to Round, *Family Origins*, xxxii.

[5] 'The Cambridge Modern History repudiated footnotes': Professor Cam, note at p. 210 of *Selected Hist. Essays*.

in seeking to form a team? Would not your own papers look better by themselves? You will be your best adviser. If Acton suppresses, as he very probably will, certain parts of my chapter, I don't know that I shall want to say anything more of cent. XVI. I like most centuries better.[1] Perhaps when after Easter I am once more in England, you will let me know how your plan stands.

I would that you were enjoying this blessed sunshine.

Yours very truly

F. W. MAITLAND

---

[1] The four *Elizabethan Gleanings* which appeared in E.H.R. for 1900 and the fifth which followed in 1903 may be regarded as by-products of M.'s work for the Camb. Mod. Hist.

1899-1906

The alternation of English summers and of winters in the sun diverted the stream of Maitland's correspondence. A new note of intimacy is evident in the letters that passed between England and the Canaries or Madeira. Vivid pictures of island scenes and manners were exchanged for the news and gossip that would normally have drifted in fugitive talk at High Table or in Combination Room. Henry Sidgwick died in August 1900, and, though his place in Maitland's heart was left empty, his rôle as correspondent had to be taken by others. Buckland, who spent a winter in the Canaries, was a link with the Law School and recorded its progress and its problems. But it was Henry Jackson, deep in University and College business, a repository of Cambridge tales and recollections, who above all kept Maitland in touch with a life that must often have seemed as distant in time as in space.

The new routine inevitably conditioned the work that Maitland could do. Where he had leisure he had no books: where he had books he had no leisure. In the crowded months of summer and autumn he must meet the demands of a year—demands from which, in despondent moods, he felt he could escape only by resigning his chair. How he came to terms with life may be shown by two examples in 1899 and in 1900. He had been persuaded by Lord Acton to write for the Cambridge Modern History a chapter on the Anglican Settlement and the Scottish Reformation; at first sight an unlikely and uncongenial choice. But he had already probed with relish the mysteries of the Canon Law in the Church of England, and the charm and humour of these essays echoed in the graver environment of the History. In the summer of 1899 he was at work upon this chapter and before he left for the Canaries it was in Acton's hands, though the volume itself did not appear until 1903. He took with him in its place Gierke's *Political Theories of the Middle Age*. In January 1900 he wrote that the work of translation had been completed 'after a sort' and that he now 'shivered on the brink of an Introduction'.[1] By the middle of June he was busy with the proofs, and the book was published before the end of the year —only too late to meet the eyes of Henry Sidgwick at whose suggestion it had been begun.

Throughout these years he was unremitting in his care for the Selden Society. His tact and patience were ever at hand to guide its editors. He must restrain the exuberance or correct the grammar of an enthusiastic amateur.[2] He must, with infinite tenderness, coax the best out of Turner, a born scholar as quick to take offence as he was slow to complete a task which at last justified the care lavished on it with such exasperating solicitude. He felt the urgent need to find and train young men or women who would ensure a succession of editors for work rewarding in all but money. One exceptional disciple he

---

[1] Letter 259. [2] Letter 268.

found—Mary Bateson—whose untimely death by only three weeks preceded his own. Above all he sought to realise the ambition he had confided to Thayer in 1895 to see before he died the start of an edition of the Year Books. Now that he had to spend half of his years beyond the reach of libraries the deciphering or translation of manuscripts which could be photographed was not only what he could do but what he longed to do. For his own peace of mind, he wrote in 1904, he should like to edit Year Books to the end of his days.[1]

Three years saw the publication of three successive volumes of the Year Books, the first of them with the excursion into philology which revealed yet another facet of his rich variety. But across his chosen path a shadow fell that clouded the rest of his working life. In February 1904 Leslie Stephen died. Maitland had at first thought to write nothing about him. 'He is too big for one sort of writing and too dear for another.' But Stephen's expressed wish was too strong for him, and little by little the task became ever more formidable. 'A brief memoir to be prefixed to some last papers' grew into a full biography.[2] His instinct warned him that by training and temperament he was unfitted for it, but he acknowledged a debt that must be paid and one whose burden was always with him. In his letters to English and American contemporaries of Stephen he sought the evidence which, as historian and as lawyer, he felt he had not only to trace but to sift. He must deserve the confidence that Stephen had placed in him. 'The ghost of the work visits me in the night-watches', he wrote to Fisher, 'I am perplexed as I never was before.' He tried to relieve the tension of the book by copying from his beloved manuscripts, but with only partial success. Chief Justice Bereford and Leslie Stephen could not be sandwiched.[3]

At last in September 1906 he could write, 'My weary experiment in biography is near its end. . . . Never no more biography for me.'[4] He turned with relief and renewed hope to the Year Books and in the next two months completed the text and translation of a fourth volume. In December he left Cambridge on the first stage of his voyage to the Canaries whither his wife and elder daughter had preceded him. He was in good heart and, for him, in good health. But in London he seems to have caught influenza which developed on board ship into pneumonia. He reached Las Palmas desperately ill and, despite his wife's devotion, he died just before one o'clock on the morning of December 20th.

[1] Letters 165 and 397.   [2] Letters 381 and 398.
[3] Letters 418 and 465.   [4] Letter 481.

234. To H. A. L. Fisher

Hotel Santa Brigida
Monte
Grand Canary
8 Jan. 1899

MY DEAR HERBERT,

I told you in my last that your book had come and that I was eagerly wishing to read it. I have read few books so greedily and am now re-reading it. I feel that I am your debtor for some hours of unalloyed enjoyment and for much information that was entirely new to me. My one and only doubt is whether you have not a little underrated English ignorance of German affairs—but there! you were not writing a schoolbook, and it is a good thing to bring home to people like me their lamentable lack of elementary knowledge. You will find your critics very kind—you will probably think them too kind—such at least has often been my feeling; but I make no doubt that this book will place you very high in the estimate of those who know, while its liveliness will certainly secure you a large audience. I go about repeating vol. i, p. 191[1]: I would dearly like to have written it, for it gives excellent expression to a thought which has lurked in the dim back chambers of my mind—and now it is out in the best of prose and I should like to preach many sermons upon your text.

What you say of Edinburgh interests me. I hope that you will be successful and think that you ought to be now that the Medieval Empire is in print.[2] My one doubt is whether Scottish feeling will not make a great effort to exclude another southron if there be any passable Scot in the field. All that you tell me of dinners with distinguished people makes me jealous: I should like to hear some good talk—but on the whole I am well content with my bath of sunshine. Certainly I am wonderfully well here and have hopes of doing a little more work. My thoughts play at times around the future, and the subject that attracts me most is the English Borough. Sometimes I think I will give to it whatever time is left me. I shall ask your advice before I take any big step. Meanwhile I will draw a smaller draft upon your kindness. I have a special reason for being interested in the village or 'bourg' of Breteuil.[3] Would one of your French friends tell me whether there is any monograph or local history on or about that place? Do not take any serious trouble, for you must be engaged on all hands.

Once more you have my warm congratulations touching the Empire. All happiness comes to you at once—'Parnass und Paradies'.[4] Make the best of it.

Florence sends love. The children are now doing well.

Yours very affectionately

F. W. MAITLAND

[1] *The Medieval Empire:* see Letter 232, *supra.*
[2] See Letter 232, *supra.*
[3] Miss Bateson, in whose work M. took the liveliest interest, was working on the 'Laws of Breteuil' and published her researches in E.H.R., vols. xv and xvi (1900–1).
[4] Fisher was engaged to be married: see Letter 219, *supra.*

235. To Leslie Stephen

[No original. Printed Fisher, *Memoir*, 114–15: no beginning or ending.]

Sta. Brigida
Monte,
G. Canary
9 Jan. 1899.

I won't pretend but that I am disappointed by your decision, the more so because my hopes of your advent stood higher than Florence's and I had endeavoured to argue that your half-promise was a valuable security.[1] However, I know that we are far from England and that you are unwilling to leave your household for any long time. Also the two last boats that have come here suffered much in the Bay of Biscay and were very late. So I forgive, though I badly want someone to walk with. The time has come when I feel that walks are pleasant and do me good, but that I am very tired of the contents of my own head. But even a solitary tramp is better than a day in bed, and I am really grateful to this magnificent climate and to those who sent me here. To those who cannot speak Spanish, and I cannot and never shall, the remoter parts of this island are not very accessible. I sometimes find myself beset by a troop of boys who take a fiendish pleasure in dogging the steps of an Englishman who obviously is deaf, dumb and mad. Attempts to reason with them only lead to shouts of Penny! or Tilling!—I cannot even persuade them that Tilling is not an English word. Still at times they leave me in peace and then I can be happy until the next crowd assembles.

236. To Melville M. Bigelow

Hotel Santa Brigida
Monte
Grand Canary
22 Jan. 1899

MY DEAR BIGELOW,

First let me offer you from my heart all good wishes[2] and then let me explain as best I may the tardiness of this salutation. In England I was but going from bad to worse and a chorus of doctors bade me go abroad for the winter. Very unwillingly I obeyed, having obtained from the University leave of absence for two terms. After a long discussion of Palermo, Algiers, Morocco and so forth, we took ship for the Canaries and landed at Las Palmas. 'We' I say, for my wife and children accompanied me. After staying for a time on the sea coast we have come up about 1400 feet into the hills and have settled down in what certainly is a very beautiful spot. Of winter I have therefore known nothing: Christmas day we celebrated by a picnic in the open. I hope that this

---

[1] See Letter 231, *supra*.   [2] On Bigelow's marriage (to his third wife).

holiday in a bath of sunshine will do me some permanent good and that when I return to England in April I may be strong enough to work without wanting any more winters abroad: and certainly since I have been here I have been well and happy. Meanwhile you, I feel sure, have found happiness, and if due to any one it was due to you. I think that this sun bakes morality out of me and I have now a considerable sympathy for those Spaniards who by their lazy inefficiency get into trouble with decent peoples such as that of which you are a member. At any rate as regards letter writing I have fallen into the habit of using the one Spanish word which every one here is bound to understand: I mean *Manana*—yes, to-morrow and to-morrow and to-morrow. It is sad but it is true. Think of me then as a Spaniard with whom you have no longer any cause of war, and be merciful. By the way I am glad that the United States did not exact these lands from Spain[1]: there should be some spot where broken-down professors will not be stimulated into premature activity by the sight of energy in any shape or form. But once more I will collect my dissipated forces in order to tell you, what is very true, that from the inmost part of me I wish you and your wife all the best that life can give.

Yours very truly if also illegibly

F. W. MAITLAND

237. To Leslie Stephen

[No original. Printed by Fisher, *Memoir*, 115–16: no beginning or ending.]

Hotel Sta. Brigida
Monte,
Grand Canary
23 Jan. 1899

I fear from your last letter that you may take too seriously what I said in play. No, there was no promise, only a certain hope that you might come here, and Reason (with a capital) tells me that your decision is wise and that you must not give up to Canarios what was meant for your home and the *Utilitarians*.[2] I am really glad to think that you are booking them, and at times I envy you. However I cannot say that I am unhappy in my idleness. When I despaired of you for a companion, I took to myself the soundest looking man in a hotel full of invalids, and gat me up into the hills to accomplish the expedition that I had reserved for you, and we succeeded in mastering not indeed the highest but the most prominent mountain of the island, if a mountain may be no more than 6000 feet high. This raised me in my own conceit and certainly I had a very enjoyable time. I doubt whether in any of your good ascents you can have seen so gorgeously coloured a view as that which I beheld. A great part of the island lay below me; many of the rocks are bright orange and

---

[1] [AULT. In the treaty between the United States and Spain, Dec. 10, 1898, the latter ceded Puerto Rico, the Philippines and Guam. Cuba became independent.]
[2] *The English Utilitarians*, 3 vols., pub. 1900.

crimson and these are diversified by patches of brilliant green; the whole was framed in the blue of sky and sea. It was like a raised map that had been over-coloured.

238. To R. Lane Poole

> Hotel Sta. Brigida
> Monte
> Grand Canary
> *29 Jan. 1899*

MY DEAR POOLE,

I thank you for sending an E.H.R. You can hardly guess how pleasant its cover was in my eyes. The inside I shall take by small doses, trying to spread my enjoyment over a week. But already I have read your Round-Hall review and, since I was coward enough to evade the task that was offered me, let me tell you that I admire your performance of it.[1] I hope that this is not an insult added to an injury: it is not meant as such. I am hoping to recover here a little moral as well as physical strength and to be less unwilling to face the disagreeable than I was when we were in correspondence last summer.

It is good to be here in the sunshine and among the flowers and I wish that you and other hard-driven souls were sharing my rest.

Should you see Stevenson, be good enough to tell him that if, when I return in April, I do not find the Anglo-Saxon Chancery in print I will swear in Spanish.[2]

I have been enjoying Herbert Fisher's Empire. I hope that it is well spoken of by those who know. With best wishes but a minus quantity of news, I remain

> Yours very truly
> F. W. MAITLAND

239. To Henry Sidgwick

> Hotel Santa Brigida
> Monte
> Grand Canary
> *25 Feb. 1899*

MY DEAR SIDGWICK,

I am grateful for your letter though it tells me some bad news of yourself. It seems to me that the 'fine old English disease' has just of late been resuscitated from a well-merited obscurity: at least more than one friend of mine has

---

[1] See Letter 224, *supra*.

[2] [A.L.P. In 1898 W. H. Stevenson was appointed Sandars Reader in the University of Cambridge and gave to a small but select audience, including M. and Mary Bateson, a course of lectures on the Anglo-Saxon Chancery. Though these lectures were fully written out, they were never published.] William Henry Stevenson (1858–1924), historian and philologist. Between 1892 and 1908 he edited 11 vols of *Calendars of Close Rolls* for the P.R.O. In 1895 he edited, with A. S. Napier, *The Crawford Collection of Early Charters and Documents now in the Bodleian Library*, and in 1904 Asser's *Life of King Alfred*.

suffered from quinsy. I hope that the wretch has turned his back upon you for good and all, for I am told that he has a trick of making a feigned departure. I could not wish you exiled from Cambridge even to the Canaries, though I have every reason to speak well of this island. For three months I have enjoyed such a relief from all fleshly woes as I have not known for a good many years, and I shall be everlastingly thankful to the University which has allowed me this bath of blessed sunshine. When another month has gone by, I shall take ship for England, strong enough, I hope, to face the asperities of an English summer.

Yes, the 'crisis in the church',[1] or what of it may be heard in the Hesperides, interests me in various ways. It may even bring me a few shillings that I had no right to expect, and it may also drive me into controversy in defence of my essays.[2] But this also I do not expect. I see that the Right Reverend Father in God whom we used to know as G. F. B.[3] has passed the word that the Canon Law is a pathless wilderness. My lord of London[4] said to me something of the same kind. I think that these highly prudent prelates will discourage their young men from excursions over ground which, whether I am right or wrong, is certainly full of ugly holes for Anglicans. To express a tolerant contempt for lawyers will be the popular and the safe course. Lawyers have written a great deal of nonsense in all ages: the middle not excepted. Besides, the medieval Canon Law is not a subject about which strictly orthodox Romanists can write with freedom, or, if they are at all learned, with pleasure. Were it otherwise, all that I have said would have been said by their English champions long ago. So I think it possible that I may be left in peace. Unfortunately, however, Acton (whose blandishments you know) has obtained from me a promise of a chapter for his big history—and a chapter on the Anglican settlement. Before I left England I was very unhappy about this, and the outbreak of this ecclesiastical storm will make me much unhappier so soon as I allow my thoughts to turn towards work; for I shall have to say something about many controversial points, and (as footnotes are not allowable) I may afterwards be compelled to defend what I have said with chapter and verse. This prospect is not pleasant, for I was hoping to pass the evening of my days in the medieval towns which are fairly peaceful places: at least they are undisturbed by the *odium theologicum*.

These personal matters apart, I am extremely curious to see what is going to happen. As you say, the world is a very odd world. Will some future edition of your *Principles of Politics* make the journey to Canossa? I have long had my eye upon these ritualists, viewing them from the standpoint of Formal Jurisprudence. You once proposed to put the Austinian doctrine on the back of a postcard; and now will you not have to put that postcard behind

---

[1] Especially over ritual: see *Life and Letters of Mandell Creighton*, vol. ii. chap. xi.
[2] On the Canon Law.
[3] Dr. G. F. Browne, Bishop of Bristol. He had been a Fellow of St. Catherine's College, Cambridge, and an active University administrator: Secretary to the Examination Syndicate and on the Council of the Senate.
[4] Mandell Creighton (1843–1901), Bishop of London 1896–1901.

the fire? And you will have to begin your theory of the State in medieval
fashion, explaining that the Church is an organism co-ordinate with the State.
You will have observed that certain acres of parchment 'do not bind the con-
sciences of the clergy', not because they are bad laws but because they proceed
from an incompetent body. Well, I suppose that nowadays the journey to
Canossa can be made with reasonable comfort—perhaps in a sleeping carriage.
I have been reading Old Mortality to my children, and of course an intelligent
babe asked, 'What is Erastianism?' I ought to have said, 'a played-out game,
my dear'.

I have also been wondering whether, after all, Comte was not right about
Protestantism:—not a stage on the main-line but a siding out of which you
must back. Altogether the days seem very distant when I sat at your feet—they
must, I think, have occurred 'somewhere about the beginning of these renovated Middle Ages'. I should much like to hear your forecast, and the time is
coming when we shall meet.

This is good news about the finances of the University. It seems to me that
Hill[1] has made a great success of his Vice chancellorship.

Will you kindly tell Mrs. Sidgwick that I wrote to the young lady who desires
to explore municipal history and hope to meet her in the Easter term.

Believe me,
Yours very truly
F. W. MAITLAND

240. To H. A. L. Fisher

Hotel Santa Brigida
Monte
Grand Canary
16th March 1899

MY DEAR HERBERT,

My sister, who should be starting for England to-morrow in the Tintagel
Castle, will carry this note to Plymouth. We follow in the Braemar Castle on the
31st. It is with many regrets that I shall leave this island where I have passed a
blessed and painless time; but if I am not strong enough for England now I
never shall be and I am anxious to see books once more. Yesterday I had a
long tramp into our hills and got fairly through the clouds into the superior
sun-light, and the sun-light here is a highly superior article. If I am well enough
to tramp for six or seven hours, it may fairly be said that I am well enough to
lecture. That Anglican Settlement awaits me. I gather from the public prints
that during my absence the subject has risen from red to white heat.[2] I do not
relish my task and fear that it may lead to some controversy of a futile kind:

[1] Dr. Alex Hill (1856–1929), Master of Downing College, Cambridge, 1888–1907, Vice-
Chancellor 1897–9, Principal of University College, Southampton, 1912–19.
[2] See Letter 239, *supra*.

but I must keep my promise to Lord A. As you say, Why does not his omniscient lordship write the whole of the book? He could do it and come up smiling.

All you say of your *Empire* interests me very much. I think that I have seen the most important reviews of it, and some very trivial performances also. I am glad that Keutgen[1] has spoken warmly and hope that other Germans will follow suit. I often give your book a turn and always find something instructive in it that I am glad to know.

I am delighted by the news of Joe's engagement. But do not let him steal a march on you. Primogeniture has its rights and duties, and you were first in the field.[2]

I shall dearly like to read of Napoleon[3]—I never knew him.

Yours very affectionately

F. W. MAITLAND

There is little here to mark the lapse of time. Yesterday at 3 p.m. a muleteer opined that it was 6. I am told that the names of the months are rarely known.

241. To J. H. Round

Downing

6 Apr. 1899

DEAR ROUND,

I am safe and sound. I thank you for your welcome and the copy of Tomlinson's article. You may suppose that I am knee-deep in accumulated papers, but I must rapidly answer your question as best I may.[4]

I have not directly faced Stubbs's assertion about appeals.[5] All that his evidence proves is that *de facto* the Lollard heretics did not appeal. I strongly suspect, but cannot at this moment prove, that this was because a criminal prosecution for heresy had been placed *by the decretals* outside all the ordinary rules of justice (and decency also). The procedure was of the most summary and 'extraordinary' kind, and I doubt there was any appeal allowed to metropolitan or pope or anybody else. Then, if criminal proceedings for heresy be left out of account, there was I believe little if any litigation about doctrine and (if possible) less about ritual. You will put your adversaries in a hole if you ask them to produce records of cases touching doctrine or ritual judicially decided by English bishops and not being summary criminal proceedings against heretics.

As to the Lollards, we have also to remember that, even if an appeal were

---

1 See Letters 150 and 164, *supra*.
2 'Joe' was Herbert Fisher's younger brother, Edmund. Herbert Fisher himself was married on 6 July 1899.
3 Fisher 'now decided to devote himself in particular to Napoleonic Studies' (Ogg, *Herbert Fisher*, 44). The chief outcome was *Napoleonic Statesmanship, Germany* (1903).
4 Round's letter is not extant and his question may be inferred only from M.'s reply.
5 See Letter 168, *supra*.

lawful, an appeal to Rome from one of Wyclif's followers would have been ridiculous besides being absolutely futile.

When I have a bit more time, I will look about me to see whether there is not a text expressly depriving convicted heretics of the right to appeal. Meanwhile I wish you joy in your combat.

Yours very truly

F. W. MAITLAND

242. To James Bradley Thayer

Downing College

Cambridge

England

9 April 1899

MY DEAR THAYER,

You may have heard that I was driven by stress of medicine-men to winter in the Canaries. It was a pleasant remedy and thus far successful that I now feel well and strong. On my return I was welcomed by your book on Evidence.[1] How good it looks! I shall enjoy it by and by. I see that it wears the dark-blue buckram which is the livery of the Selden Society. Many hearty thanks.

In a short time I hope to write to you of Year Books.[2] At the moment I can hardly guide a pen, so unfamiliar an instrument has it become to me—besides in Gran Canaria some 80% of the people can neither read nor write. O fortunati nimium!

I hope that you and yours are well.

Yours very truly

F. W. MAITLAND

243. To J. H. Round

Downing College

Cambridge

7 July 1899

MY DEAR ROUND,

This is exceedingly kind of you. But I am not quite sure whether I am to be congratulated.[3] This comes to me rather early and rather easily and the consequence will be that I shall be exposed while I am yet alive. Next Sunday I shall read your article: just at present I keep Elizabeth for Sundays.[4]

I can fully share your doubts about radchenistres in Essex: I remember some qualms that I had. So I am glad that you are exploring the subject.[5] About the

---

[1] *A Preliminary Treatise on Evidence at the Common Law* (Boston, 1898).
[2] No such letter, if written, seems to have survived.
[3] M. was made an Hon. D.C.L. by the University of Oxford.
[4] Presumably one of Round's articles on the ecclesiastical controversy: see Cam, Intro. to *Selected Hist. Essays*, xxi–ii, and Letter 189, *supra*.
[5] M., *D.B. and Beyond* (see Index for various references): *P. and M.* i. 286, 289, 323.

way in which the word was made only phonologists can speak: but you will remember the Frenchman's difficulty with *th*, illustrated by *grist* for *grith*, etc.

I am glad that you are to feast at Oxford, even if this does not lead to a meeting.

Yours with renewed thanks

F. W. MAITLAND

244. To R. Lane Poole

The Grove
Shelford
3 Augt. 1899

MY DEAR POOLE,

Herewith two reviews—one long overdue. Also I send a note on Herbert's 'Revocatio' which you may or may not print.[1] I don't like to see that document lying about unqueried, but would not make an unnecessary fuss.

Last year we had some converse about the 'church of S. Trinity at Canterbury'—do you still think this a blunder? I see in Dugdale[2] a deed which seems to give this name to the cathedral and believe that I read somewhere how 'Christ' and 'S. Trinity' might be interchanged.

I hope that you are well 'as this leaves me'. Indeed I have flourished in this vill.

Yours very truly

F. W. MAITLAND

245. To Charles Gross

The Grove
Stapleford, Cambs.
25 Augt. 1899

MY DEAR GROSS,

I am exceedingly glad to hear that you are here and to stay. We are spending all summer five miles from Cambridge in a cottage, and this glorious weather has kept me abnormally well. I hope soon to spend a week in London and to see you there. Lots of things must be talked of when we meet.

Yours very truly

F. W. MAITLAND

[1] E.H.R. (1899) 735: C.P. III. 114. See letters 219 and 220, *supra*. The 'two reviews' were probably of the 1st vol. of Fagniez, *Documents relatifs à l'histoire de l'industrie et du commerce en France*, E.H.R. (1900) 142, and of *The Records of the Honourable Society of Lincoln's Inn, The Black Books*, vol. ii, E.H.R. (1900) 170.
[2] *Monasticon Anglicanum* (1655–73): see Letter 220, *supra*.

246. To B. Fossett Lock

Stapleford, Cambs.

28 Sept. 1899

MY DEAR LOCK,

Your telegram prevented your letters. I am exceedingly sorry to hear of Turner's escapade. Certainly you have no cause for self-reproach: indeed I feel that you have carried patience and T. laziness as far as they should go. However, sometimes a little storm does good, and I hope that T. will get to work after it. I have just been straining a point to get him an examining job.[1]

Then, in the matter of Leach, who is as rapid as t'other is slack, will you kindly tell me what is the *maximum* number of sheets that he may fill with *text*. It is becoming a question whether there will be any room for Lincoln.[2] I have not liked to check the flow of Beverley documents, because they seem to me to be illustrating a really important point, B. being one of the few English towns outside London where the trade companies were part of the town's constitution. I hope that you don't disapprove.

I have sent L. some queried sheets. He is a little rough in translation, but the roughness is not of a bad kind.

I hope to be in London next week and will look in upon you at the Inn. Would you be there on Wednesday at lunch time?

I am coming round after a bad time. A cold wind can make me miserable for days and sometimes I think that I shall want an astral body before I tackle Year Books. But of this we can talk if we meet.

Yours very truly

F. W. MAITLAND

247. To Charles Gross

Stapleford, Cambs.

1 Octr. 1899

MY DEAR GROSS,

I feel that I am an inhospitable beast; but I have had some of my old troubles and I hope the time is soon at hand when you and Mrs. Gross will visit us at Cambridge. Meanwhile I mean to pass some of Wednesday in Mus. Brit. (MS room) and Thurs. and Frid. at P.R.O., and to shake your hand and hear your plans would be pleasant.

Yours very truly

F. W. MAITLAND

---

[1] On 25 Sept. 1899 (S.S. Corr.) Lock wrote to Turner, complaining of his delay in completing the proofs of S.S. Vol. 13 and asking for an explanation. On 26 Sept. Turner replied refusing any explanation and saying that he would 'return all the proofs in my possession and leave the Society to find another editor'. M. mediated with success. Turner continued the work, writing to Lock on 30 Nov. 1899, 'I regret the delay' and adding 'I have already devoted two thousand hours to the book and, if I had spent less time over it, many serious errors which I have avoided would have appeared in it'. In his Preface to Vol. 13 he confesses that the book is two years late and writes of Lock that he 'has devoted more time and attention to this volume than the Society or its editor could have hoped to secure'.

[2] S.S. Vol. 14: see Letter 212, *supra*.

248. To R. Lane Poole

Stapleford

8th Oct. 1899

MY DEAR POOLE,

I am profoundly grateful to you for your kindness and am vexed at having put you to trouble.

At the moment I am in the blues—for I hear talk of warm places. If I have to sing a Nunc dimittis, it will run 'quid oculi mei viderunt originalem Actum de Uniformitate primi anni Reg. Eliz.' Few can say as much. It was hardly so well worth seeing as I hoped it would be: but 'twas a Lords' Amendment that spared the feelings of the detestably enormous Bp. of Rome.[1]

Yours obligedly

F. W. MAITLAND

249. To R. Lane Poole

Stapleford
Cambs.

10 Oct. 1899

MY DEAR POOLE,

Yesterday it became but too clear that I must leave England. I had just finished the enclosed which I meant to be the first of a set of Elizabethan Gleanings.[2] It is now more than likely that the residue will never get written, but perhaps the E.H.R. will take this trifle. We move to Downing on Friday, but I am forbidden to lecture. I think of a voyage to S. America, as S. Africa looks too warm for a man of peace.[3] Wherever I go I shall expect my E.H.R. 'reglar'.

Yours very truly

F. W. MAITLAND

P.S. I had it from a Switzer—is not his name Bonard?—that Erastus wrote his own name as Lüber not Lieber. This because I may not be here to correct a proof.[4]

---

[1] M. discussed the Act of Uniformity (1 Eliz. c. 2) in the fifth of his *Elizabethan Gleanings*, pub. E.H.R. (1903) 517: reprinted C.P. III. 185 and *Selected Hist. Essays*, 229.
[2] *Defender of the Faith, and so forth*, E.H.R. (1900) 120: C.P. III. 157: *Selected Hist. Essays*, 211.
[3] The South African War began on 11 Oct. 1899.
[4] E.H.R. (1900) 121: C.P. III. 158: *Selected Hist. Essays*, 212.

250. To Charles Gross

Downing College
13 Oct. 1899

DEAR GROSS,

When I was having my pleasant talk with you I did not think that I was doing my last bit of work. Next day I was bad and now I am told to scuttle out of the country as fast as possible. Those who profess wisdom in these matters tell me that I cannot resist any cold and shall be but a living skeleton if I stay here much longer. As you may suppose I am very sad and I can tell you with strict truth that the loss of some more talks with you stands near the top of my catalogue of losses. You always teach me and always inspire me.

Now I have a many things to do, for in about ten days time we shall take ship for Grand Canary. *Do think of the Selden Society as a medium for Select Docts. illustrating Municipal History.*[1] B. F. Lock would be mighty glad to hear from you. He warmly admires your method of editing. Pay poor—as you know: but you also know the outside market.

My telegram stopped that unlucky review of Fagniez.[2] 'Twas better luck than I deserved.

Yours pitifully
F. W. MAITLAND

251. To Henry Jackson

[Date noted on letter—probably by Jackson—as 25 Oct. 1899.]

Downing College
Wednesday

MY DEAR JACKSON

I was very sorry to learn what you told me last night before dinner; but (between ourselves, for I don't talk of it) I have this much experience to put at your service. It is more than ten years ago since a doctor pronounced over me the word diabetes, and undoubtedly I was then voiding sugar in considerable quantities. They now tell me that he ought to have said intermittent glyko—something or another. Slowly it is doing for me; but quite slowly, and it may cheer you to know that I have had ten happy and busy years under the ban. I hope that you have many before you.[3]

When, as sometimes happens, I try a new doctor, he always begins by scoffing at my tale of diabetes—but after a while I succeed in showing him sugar and then he falls back on his Greek, a language that I never understood. So I write myself

Yours in pari delicto
F. W. MAITLAND

---

[1] No such volume was prepared by Gross for the Selden Society. His next contribution to it was Vol. 23 for 1908, *Select Cases concerning the Law Merchant*, Vol. I.

[2] See Letters 244, *supra*, and 283, *infra*.

[3] See Parry, *Henry Jackson*, p. 31. The penultimate sentence of this paragraph was quoted by Fisher, *Memoir*, 111–12.

252. To R. Lane Poole

Hotel Quiney
Las Palmas

26 Nov. 1899

MY DEAR POOLE,

I am very grateful to you for the trouble you have taken over 'etc.' I am returning the sheets: but the Spanish Post Office is an absent-minded beggar.[1] It is for this reason that I keep an address at Las Palmas—really I am some miles away in a very pleasant villa, and my last sentence was broken by an altercation with the milkman.

Your discovery of the Revocatio in Giles may put my charitable hope out of court. I am glad that you will mention the matter in E.H.R.[2]

I am sorry that Round has taken offence. I tried to do him full justice and thought that by this time he would have lost the taste for unmitigated praise such as is rightly bestowed upon promising young persons.[3]

Pressure was being put on me when I left Cambridge to join in some kind of joint protest over that infernal palisade.[4] I thought the project a sad mistake and said so. I hope that no more will be heard of it.

To Round's remark about my blunders[5] I wrote a reply for the Athenaeum. I happen to think that I am right and he is wrong. But as the Orotava dropped down the Thames my heart softened and the pilot took off at Gravesend a 'revocatio' addressed to MacColl.[6] If R. is too triumphant I can speak later on.

It is right pleasant here; but I am still a feeble creature. However I have books with me this time—the whole of Creighton, S. R. G., 'and so forth'. If I return, it will be as a well informed person.

If you see W. H. S., remind him of me.[7]

With all good wishes
Yours very truly

F. W. MAITLAND

---

[1] The 'etc.' was the first *Elizabethan Gleaning:* see Letter 249, *supra.* The 'absent-minded beggar' alludes to Rudyard Kipling's verses, pub. 31 Oct. 1899: Carrington, *Rudyard Kipling*, 303–4.

[2] E.H.R. (1900) 86. See Letters 219, 220 and 244, *supra.*

[3] See Cam, Intro. to *Selected Hist. Essays*, xxv–vi. M. had criticised Round's *Commune of London* in the *Athenaeum*, 21 Oct. 1899, reprinted in *Selected Hist. Essays*, 259–65. Round wrote 'a peevish rejoinder' in the *Athenaeum*, 28 Oct. 1899.

[4] [A.L.P. For Round's attack on Freeman and 'the Palisade' at the battle of Hastings see *Feudal England*, 340, and the memoir of Round in *Family Origins*, xxvii.]

[5] See note 3, *supra.*

[6] *Canon MacColl's New Convocation*, Fortnightly Review, Dec. 1899: C.P. III. 119: *Selected Hist. Essays*, 247.

[7] S. R. Gardiner: W. H. Stevenson. 'The whole of Creighton'—*History of the Papacy from the Great Schism to the Sack of Rome*, 6 vols. (2nd edn. 1897).

253. To Frederick Pollock

[No original. Printed Fisher, *Memoir*, 116–18: no address or date, but both supplied in body of letter: no beginning or ending.]

[*Dec. 4, 1899*]

Dated in Timelessness, but with you it may be some such day as Dec. 4, and I fancy that cent. xix may still be persisting.

Dated also nominally at Hotel Quiney in Las Palmas where I preserve address for service, but de facto in the garden of a messuage or finca called or known by the name of Bateria in the pueblo of Sta. Brigida—a fortlike structure which I hold as a monthly tenant—windows on four sides all with fine views—on ground floor lives major domo, a hard-worked peasant savouring of the soil—first and only other floor inhabited by me and mine, including our one servant, a Germano-Swiss treasure acquired as we left England— furniture a minimum and no more would be useful—small boy coatless comes to clean boots, run errands and the like, Pepé to wit—much bargaining at house door with women who bring victuals round and would rather have a chat than money. Madame's mastery of their jargon surprises me daily—I can rarely catch a word. One might fall into vegetarianism here, such is the choice of vegetables.

Lies in the garden on a long chair mostly—has there written for Encyclop. Brit. article on Hist. Eng. Law,[1] space assigned 8 only of their big pages: consequently tight packing of centuries: work of a bookless imagination, but dates were brought from England. Qu. whether editor will suffer the few lines given to J. Austin: they amount to J. A. = 0. Now turning to translate Gierke's chapter on 'Publicistic Doctrine of M.A.'[2] O. G. has given consent—will make lectures (if I return) and possibly book—but what to do with 'Publicistic'? Am reading Creighton's Papacy and Gardiner's History—may be well informed man some day. Harv. L. Rev. and King's Peace came pleasantly[3] —Alphabet not yet presented to babes but reserved for approaching birthday when it will delight. Meanwhile parents profit by it and are very grateful.

Influence of climate on epistolary style—a certain disjointedness. Can live here or rather can be content to vegetate. A tolerable course for the Lea Francis[4]—some 5 miles long—lies not far away, but must shoulder her and climb a rocky path to reach it. No puncture yet. The alarums and excursions of horrid war are but little heard here. Interesting talk last night at hotel with German Consul in Liberia much travelled in Africa—very unboerish but thinks we are in for a large affair—all good (says he) for (German) trade. Much that we buy here made in Germany—they spread apace.

[1] Encycl. Brit. (10th edn.), Vol. XXVIII, 246–53 (pub. 1902): *Selected Hist. Essays*, 97–121.
[2] M. was translating the section *Die publicistischen Lehren des Mittelalters* from the third volume of Otto Gierke's *Das Deutsche Genossenschaftsrecht:* pub. with M.'s Introduction in 1900.
[3] Pollock, *The King's Peace in the Middle Ages*, Harv. L. Rev. XIII, 177: reprinted A.A.L.H. II. 403.
[4] Bicycle.

254. To Henry Sidgwick

[Post-card. Year from contents of letter and from Sidgwick's reply, printed in *Henry Sidgwick*, 578–9.]

Hotel Quiney
Las Palmas
Gran Canaria

Dec. 4 [1899]

I have Otto G.'s permission to go ahead and ahead I am slowly going.[1] The choice between Jargon and Verbosity is ever present. I wish that I could consult you in detail. To which extreme would you lean? I suppose that I must not say (e.g.) Organic Idea when I mean that society is organic: but, fleeing Slang, I wander in a maze of *whiches* and *thats*.[2]

I am not in Las Palmas but in a farm some miles away where life is very pleasant. But it is well to keep a postal address in the ciudad. I would the University would migrate hither in the old Italian fashion.

Yours

F. W. MAITLAND

255. To F. J. H. Jenkinson

12 Decr. 1899

MY DEAR JENKINSON,

Your letter[3] came pleasantly to the exile. But, to tell truth, I am well off and indeed began to live so soon as the blessed sunshine was roasting me once more. For postal purposes I am still at Quiney's Hotel in the odorous ciudad of Las Palmas: for all other purposes I am about eight miles off in a villa or farmhouse, the ground floor whereof is occupied by the proprietor's bailiff while we inhabit the only other floor. It is a delightful place and I am leading a most peaceful and enjoyable life. I feel it a crumpled rose-leaf that to-morrow I must visit the town. About once a month I must go there. My wife has rapidly mastered the Canario dialect and can now bargain with the peasant folk who bring provisions to our door. The tradesman hardly exists. Our larder is never far from bankruptcy but is always saved at the last moment.

I have a good many books with me. Only one from the Library.[4] I am idly translating part of it and will duly pay my fines when it is done with. I propose to return to England a well-informed person, that is, if I do return; but all manner of reasons for not returning, except as a visitor, occur to me as I bask. As a visitor I should like to see that there MS. Your tidings of it excite

---

[1] In the last note to his Introduction to *Gierke*, completed just after Sidgwick's death on 28 August 1900, M. wrote: 'Last year, being sent from England, I was encouraged to undertake this translation by Professor Henry Sidgwick. What encouragement was like when it came from him his pupils are now sorrowfully remembering.'
[2] See Letter 259, *infra*.
[3] Not extant.
[4] A note in Camb. Univ. Add. MSS shows that this was Vol. 3 of Gierke, *Das Deutsche Genossenschaftsrecht*.

me. Is it not the same that had attracted the lynx-eye of Liebermann when he wrote the bit of post-card which I enclose?[1] It (to wit, the post-card) came to Cambridge just after my departure.

I think that somehow or another you must have come upon a copy of an unsuccessful dissertation composed by one who would have accepted a fellowship had it been pressed upon him. If so, it is not published and should have been 'wiped up' like the products of the infant Grotius—it was Grotius, I think.[2]

It was kind of you to give me a little of your time.

Yours very truly

F. W. MAITLAND

256. To B. Fossett Lock

Hotel Quiney
Las Palmas

5 Jan. 1900

DEAR LOCK,

I am in my old quarters about seven miles from the ciudad and about 1400 feet above it, and ever since I have been here the weather has been at its very best. On the other hand I have been compelled to spend more time than I liked in bed. However that is, I hope, a concluded event. Had it not been for this drawback I should already have copied a great deal of Year Book. As it is I have read a good deal: enough to show that there is a big job before us. I have a great deal that is not in the printed book—including a long report of a Kentish Eyre. It is just about this that I want to ask a question. Perhaps if you have already retained Baildon you will pass that question on to him. I would write to him directly only I do not know what has as yet passed between you and him. The said question is this: Is there at P.R.O. any roll of a Kentish Eyre of 6 Edw. II?

I ask this because a Y.B. for an Eyre is so very rare that I do not feel sure that we might not make a separate volume of it if there is a 'record' with which it can be compared. Any way I shall copy this report—we shall want it sooner or later, at least I hope so.[3]

---

[1] '10 Bendlerstr. Berlin, 26 Oct. 99. I beg to call your attention to a MS, possibly no use, possibly of importance, viz. No. 47, Assisarum Liber et Placitorum Coronae; catal. of books and MSS of Constable, originally Aston, to be sold by Sotheby, Wilkinson and Hodge, 6 Nov. 1899. Truly yours, F. Liebermann.'

[2] Presumably M.'s own unsuccessful dissertation, *A Historical Sketch of Liberty and Equality as Ideals of English Political Philosophy from the time of Hobbes to the time of Coleridge*; printed C.P. I. 1. See Hollond, *Frederic William Maitland*, 8–9: Fisher, *Memoir*, 10–11. If not previously 'published', it was printed in 1875 by Macmillan & Co., Cambridge, and stated to be by F. W. Maitland, B.A., Scholar of Trinity College, Cambridge. 'The infant Grotius' had written, but not published, *De jure praedae* in 1604: in 1868 it was found and edited.

[3] See Letter 280, *infra*.

I still feel very uncertain about the shape that our books should take. If all goes well I shall be able after Easter to take your opinion about some alternative projects, and perhaps a reference to the Council will be expedient. Something will depend on the number of instances in which I find two substantially different reports of the same case.

I wish that you and all good men could enjoy this sunshine and, like the Almighty, I would include the evil also.

Yours very truly

F. W. MAITLAND

257. To Frederick Pollock

[No original. Transcribed by Fisher in Camb. Univ. MSS and printed by him in *Memoir*, 118–19: omissions as left by Fisher: no ending. Now printed from transcript.]

Hotel Quiney
Las Palmas

5 Jan. 1900

MY DEAR POLLOCK,

I have been wasting too many of my hours in bed—and such hours too—and have consequently written few letters. Somehow or another I was chilled in the course of my voyage: I think it was on board the little Spanish steamer that brought me here from Teneriffe: and after a few days, during which I improvidently cycled to Las Palmas and found that I had to trudge back, I collapsed. However that episode is over, and certainly we are in luck this year. For three weeks the weather has been magnificent: no drop of rain has fallen and day after day the sun has shone. It is like the best English June, and there is nothing that tells of midwinter except some leafless poplars and chestnuts. I brought out a minimum thermometer which has refused to register anything less than 54°.

I have been devouring too rapidly my small store of books since I have been cut off from the writing which I projected. What I have seen of my two MSS of the Year Books of Edward II tells me that there is a solid piece of work to be done. One of these MSS is much fuller than the printed book. I cannot understand what demand there can have been for that printed book: it is so very unintelligible—mere nonsense much of it.

The B.G.B. will have to wait—at least so I think at present—as I shall give all my working time to the Y.B.B. But the volumes of *Materialen* are very interesting—especially so much as consists of the debates in the Reichstag.[1] By far the keenest debate was about damage done by hares and pheasants: the sportsmen of the Right were very keen about this matter.

. . . You will gather from this scrawl that I am recumbent in a garden—the fact is so and I won't deny it.

[1] The debates recorded in Mugdan, *Die Gesammten Materialen zum Bürgerlichen Gesetzbuch* (B.G.B.). See Fisher, *Memoir*, 119.

258. To Leslie Stephen

[No original. Printed by Fisher, *Memoir*, 119–21: omissions as left by Fisher: no address heading, beginning or ending.]

22 Jan. 1900

I can well believe that England is a gloomy place just now. Even here, where I see few papers and few English folk except the family, this ghastly affair sits heavily upon me and is always coming between me and my book—at the moment Gardiner's *History*: from which my thoughts flit off to England and the Transvaal. It don't make things better to doubt profoundly whether we have any business to be at war at all. I remember telling you at Warboys[1] (what a good day that was!) that I deeply mistrusted Chamberlain. Since then I have been thinking worse and worse of him: I hope that I am in the wrong, but only hope.

. . . Then I feel a beast for lazing here in the sunshine among the Spaniards who heartily enjoy all our misfortunes. And the worst of it is that lazing is obviously and visibly doing me good. Really and truly the temptation comes to me, when the sky is at its bluest, to resign my professorship, realise my small fortune and become a Canario for the days that remain. On the other hand three or four projects occasionally twitch my sleeve—connected with the Selden Society, which has behaved more than handsomely by me. But both sets of motives conspire to keep me lying in the sun and saying with the Apostles 'Lord! it is good for us to be here'.

Well, you don't laze. I congratulate you heartily on coming out at the other end of the *Utilitarians*.[2] You would not give me the pleasure of proof sheets— I regret it but shall have the whole book soon and enjoyable it will be. Especially I want to see what you say of Austin. Since I was here I wrote an article 'Hist. Engl. Law' for the *Encyclop. Britan.*[3] and risked about Austin a couple of sentences which are not in accordance with common repute—and now I feel a little frightened. I don't want to be unjust, but I cannot see exactly where the greatness comes in. So I am curious to know your judgment about this— and many other things. I should like a long talk with you in these prehistoric surroundings.

259. To Henry Sidgwick

Hotel Quiney
Las Palmas
22 Jan. 1900

MY DEAR SIDGWICK,

I am grateful for your letter.[4] It told me more than I had learned from any newspapers about the gloom of England, though I had read something between

---

[1] In Huntingdonshire, where Leslie Stephen had in the autumn of 1899 rented a country parsonage for a holiday: see *Life of L. S.*, 453–4. 'The Stephen cousins, the daughters of James Fitzjames, with a Stephen sense of humour called it Peacegirls' (Letter from Leonard Woolf to Ermengard Maitland, 13 March 1963).
[2] See Letter 237, *supra*.   [3] See Letter 253, *supra*.
[4] Of 5 Jan. 1900: printed in *Henry Sidgwick*, 578–9.

lines which seemed to me Tapleyan. One of the few intelligent beings that I have had converse with was the German consul at Liberia who knew many parts of Africa, thoroughly disliked the Boers and wished us well in the interests of German trade. Before the bad news came[1] he told me that in his opinion we were making too light of a very big affair which might well end in conscription. I begin to think that he knew what he was talking about.

For the purpose of a complete hedonistic calculus some value—I don't say much, but some—should be set upon the keen joy of many Spaniards occasioned by our misfortunes: I hear of candles offered to the B.V.M. I wish that I felt more strongly than I do that we had not deserved any of this hatred. Some of my American friends are only trying to think well of us.

Hamilton's 'evacuation passage' (instance of jargon) came to me like an old friend: it is duly scored in a copy which may, or may not, be still in existence. Encouraged by you, I shall 'opt' for J. I want 'nature-rightly' very badly, and perhaps 'private-rightly' too. F. Pollock is shocked by 'publicistic', which however implies more than 'political'. What is one to do? I can't make Otto G. into an Englishman. He resents the attempt.[2]

After a sort the 'publicistic' chapter of the *Genossenschaftsrecht* has been translated. But I shiver on the brink of an Introduction. Indeed madness seems to lie that way. So far as I remember, T. H. Green and his disciples have not properly prepared the British Public for a vast number of 'general wills' or, as I should like to say, 'group-wills'; but if they stop short at giving the State (or more vaguely 'the Community') a 'real' will, surely they make philosophic shipwreck. Every community, though it be a 'one-man company', must have its group-will.[3]

All this means that, were I in Cambridge, I should plague you with questions. There are a whole set of very interesting 'juristic' theories going around— in America the conflict has practical consequences—and, so it seems to me, the choice must lie with the philosopher who will tell us what is real—in that nine-penny (or ten-penny) manual that you promised.

The crumpled rose-leaf is that if and so long as I am very lazy I am very well. I did not think that this would be so, but it is.

When we last met, I misjudged Creighton's Papacy. It cannot be tasted in sips. Reading it straight through I became deeply interested. I would that I could say as much of Gardiner.

Yours very truly
F. W. MAITLAND

---

[1] The three British defeats in South Africa in the week Dec. 9 to 16, 1899. The situation was soon retrieved by the skill of Lord Roberts.

[2] In answer to M.'s request for advice on the relative merits of Jargon and Verbosity in translation (Letter 254, *supra*), Sidgwick had replied: 'There are writers who prefer the two in combination, and they are by no means irreconcilable. Have you still any remembrance of Sir William Hamilton who, I think, was still living an *examinational* life—if no other—in your day? I seem to remember that, in a polemic against Brown, he accuses that philosopher of "evacuating the phenomenon of everything in it that desiderates explanation". Don't you call that J. and V.?' M. discusses the problems of translating Gierke in his Introduction to *Political Theories of the Middle Age*, III.

[3] M. develops this and the next paragraph at the beginning of his Introduction.

260. To Frederick Pollock

[No original. Transcribed by Fisher in Camb. Univ. MSS. and printed by him (with omissions) in *Memoir*, 121–2: no ending. Now printed from transcript.]

Hotel Quiney
Las Palmas

5 Feb. 1900

MY DEAR POLLOCK,

My opinions about the origin of this wretched war are not worth stating and are extremely distressing to one who holds them. It will be enough to tell you that this summer John Morley[1] seemed to me the one English statesman who was keeping his head cool, and I have not read anything that has changed my mind. I fear that the whole affair will look bad in history and that for Joe himself[2] a very low place is reserved. And the worst of it is that the cold fit will come with a vengeance.

We have no good news yet. I hope for some this afternoon. Your letter came by Marseilles—to my surprise, for we rarely get a mail that way. Our last tidings are of speeches made by generals and these do not cheer me. Last night I had talk with a man who knew the Transvaal and who fears that our volunteer marksmen will not hit much until they have had two months of South African atmosphere: the unaccustomed eye makes wildly incorrect estimates of distance.

You speak of dragoons. 'My period',[3] a very short one 1558–63, is full of the 'swart-rutter'. The English government's one idea of carrying on a big war, if war there was to be, was that of hiring German 'swart-rutters'. They did much pistolling, and I suppose that you know, I don't, how big a machine was the pistol of those days. Well, the War Office temp. Mary (only there was not one) was open to criticism. Every ounce of powder that England had was imported from the Netherlands. This had to go on for a while under Elizabeth—there are amusing letters from English agents wherein 'bales of cloth', and so on, have an esoteric meaning.

A starved Canarian hound has attached itself to us, of the greyhound type, and sundry small additions are made to the menagerie as occasion serves. A parrot died yesterday—had drunk too much water, so an expert says—was called José—his fellow Juan still screams. In the neighbouring hotel is another with atrocious German habits acquired from the head waiter—will drink himself drunk with beer and swear terribly. I hear rumours of an additional monkey whose name is to be Loango.

I play schoolmaster[4]—How they have turned the Latin grammar inside

---

[1] John Morley (1838–1923), created Viscount Morley of Blackburn 1908: author and politician. Chief Secretary for Ireland 1886 and 1892–5: Secretary of State for India 1905–10: Lord President of the Council 1910–14. He opposed the South African War.

[2] Joseph Chamberlain (1836–1914) was Secretary of State for the Colonies from 1895 to 1903.

[3] For the Camb. Mod. History.

[4] To his daughters: see Ermengard Maitland, *F. W. Maitland—A Child's-Eye View*, 8–9.

out!—and I miss my Rule of Three. In a Spanish Census paper I for once made myself 'doctor iuris': Glasgow allows me to say 'utriusque'.[1] I added to the population capable of reading and writing no less than five names—for our trilingual Switzer[2] was to be included—and this will seriously affect Canarian statistics.

But I like this illiterate folk.

261. To Henry Jackson

[Printed, with many omissions, by Fisher, *Memoir*, 123–5. Now printed from the original in Camb. Univ. MSS.]

> Quiney's Hotel
> Las Palmas
> *18 Feb. 1900*

MY DEAR JACKSON,

It will not have escaped your observation that only the people who have many other things to do write letters. However, that perhaps is no reason why the other people should not be grateful, and grateful I am to you for giving me so much of your time and telling me all the Cambridge news.[3]

It is downright wickedly pleasant here. By here I do not mean in Las Palmas —which stinketh—but some seven miles out of it and some 1300 feet above it, in a 'finca' that we were lucky enough to hire: that is something between a farm house and a villa. The Spaniard of the middle class is a town-loving animal. He likes to have up country a house to which he can go for six weeks or so in the year and where he keeps a major domo (= bailiff) who supplies the town house with country produce. Such a finca we hired for £1 a week and there we live very comfortably and very cheaply among vines and oranges and so forth. Life here would have been impossible if my wife had not acquired the Spanish, or rather the Canario, tongue with wonderful rapidity. I fancy that some of her language is strong; but if you want anything here you must shout.

I am right glad to hear that it is no worse with you. But just you be careful about cold. I know it is the worst enemy that I have, and I suspect that you will find the same. I have often wondered how you contrived to live in 'a thorough draught'. The time comes when one cannot do it, and that time came to me early. In the sunshine I begin to make some flesh, the wind no longer whistles through my ribs and I have not had ache or pain these two months. (Interval during which the writer gets himself out of the aforesaid sunshine which to-day has an African quality.) I wish you could be here, but wonder whether you could be demoralized: some demoralization would do you good but I cannot imagine you as lazy as I am. Still you might try. And really, though I am lazy, I have managed to do some things that I should not have

---

[1] M. had been made an honorary LL.D. of Glasgow University.
[2] See Letter 253, *supra*.
[3] Jackson had written a long letter to M. on 29 Jan. 1900 (in Camb. Univ. MSS.).

done at home and hope to have something to offer the Press when I return. The subject of my meditations is the damnability of corporations. I rather think that they must be damned: the Chartered[1] for example.

News as you suppose comes here fitfully. Sometimes a telegram reaches Las Palmas, and occasionally it is not contradicted. But in the main we depend upon newspapers. I feel somewhat of a beast for being outside all this war trouble, more especially as I went abroad with a very low opinion of the Government's South African policy. That opinion I should like to change but I cannot. Your amateur strategist must be pretty intolerable. I have met a few people here who know something of the Transvaal and they have none of them been cheerful. The puzzle to me 'after the event' is why more was not known in Downing Street. I can't help fearing that when all comes out the whole affair will look very bad and that history will put our Joe into a hot corner.

What you say of Ward[2] is a surprise to me. I thought that he was dull, but did not guess that he would be unruly. I never met him. It will be a very strange book, that History of ours. I am extremely curious to see whether Acton will be able to maintain a decent amount of harmony among the chapters. Some chapters that I saw did not look much like parts of one and the same book. Before I went off I put my chapter into his lordship's hands. I never was more relieved than when I got rid of it. His lordship's lordship was considerate to an invalid and only excepted to a few new words that I had made, but I daresay he swore—if he ever swears—in private. I have been reading a good many of the Prothero series. Quality very various. The Spain seems to me an unfortunate instance of co-operation, and I don't like Hume's part of it.[3] For the rest I have been reading a good deal of historical stodge that I had put away for rainy weather and read here in the sun. If only Gardiner had a little skill in story telling how good he would be.

No, not Kipling—thank you. I have had enough and more than enough. I am inclined to think that he ought to have died young.[4]

I shall find Cambridge changed. The loss of Dale is serious. It is well that you are on the Council once more. I am heartily glad to hear of it, and wholly agree with what you say about the representation of the Left.[5]

I never knew time run as it runs here. Soon I shall have to be thinking of my return with the mixedest feelings. I am going to give Cambridge a last chance. If it cannot keep me at about 9 stone I shall 'realize' such patrimony

[1] The British South African Company, promoted and directed by Cecil Rhodes on the model of the East India Company.
[2] Sir Adolphus William Ward (1837–1924), Fellow of Peterhouse, Cambridge, 1861; Principal of Owens College, Manchester, 1889–97: Vice-Chancellor of the Victoria University of Manchester 1887–91 and 1895–7; Master of Peterhouse 1900–24.
[3] Martin Andrew Sharp Hume (1843–1910), historian. Pub. *Spain: its greatness and decay* (1898) and *Modern Spain* (1899, as Vol. 53 of the series *The Story of the Nations*); editor of Calendar of Letters and State Papers relating to English affairs preserved in the archives of Simancas 1558–1603 (4 vols. 1892–9).
[4] Jackson had asked M. if he had read Kipling's *Stalky & Co.* (pub. Oct. 1899).
[5] Jackson had written that 'Dale [A. W. W., Fellow of Trinity Hall, Cambridge] succeeds Glazebrook at Liverpool' [as Principal of University College], and that he himself had filled the resultant vacancy on the Council of the Senate. He criticised the recent practice of 'taking men mostly from the Liberal Right' which 'plays into the hands of the Tories'.

as I have and buy a finca. Then for the great treatise De Damnabilitate Universitatis.

I shall hope to find you keeping that there fiend at arm's length and eating bread and drinking whisky (in Spanish one asks for 'icky' and gets it cheap and good) like a Christian and an ordinary man.

> Yours very truly
>
> F. W. MAITLAND

262. To B. Fossett Lock

[Post-card.]

> Quiney's Hotel
> Las Palmas
> *11.3.00*

What a swell you are! as we used to say. You tell of nothing but boundless prosperity. To me it seems clear that the Seld. Soc. only prospers if and so long as the Lit. Dir.[1] remains *in partibus et sine cura*. I am indeed happy about the Jews and various other things and persons of whom you write. A strict avoidance of all exertion physical or mental has done wonders for me and I feel more like Year Books than I have felt for a long time past. About Easter week I must take ship: I confess that the thought of Cambridge makes me shiver: still it must be faced. I am very glad to hear of negotiations with L.O.P.[2] of P.R.O. Before Pentecost we must meet.

> Y.v.t.
>
> F. W. M.

263. To Henry Jackson

> Downing College
> *28 April 1900*

DEAR JACKSON,

Is it not the fact that the Eranus meets on Tuesday the 8th and that I am bound to read to it?[3] I think so, but cannot lay my hand on the card. And, if so it be, may I ask whether you would object to a transfer to that day of your very kind invitation to dinner? Forgive this cool request, but it is convenient to many grave persons that they should not walk to Downing after dinner.

> Yours very truly
>
> F. W. MAITLAND

---

[1] Literary Director (M.). J. M. Rigg had told Lock (S.S. Corr.) that he was making good progress 'with the Jews': S.S. Vol. 15.
[2] L. O. Pike. See Letter 208, *supra*.
[3] Probably the paper on *The Body Politic*, reprinted C.P. III. 285.

264. To R. Lane Poole

Downing College

6 May 1900

MY DEAR POOLE,

I have to thank you for a kind letter and to hope that you have profited by the holiday that you announced.

I can send you a small garb from the Elizabethan field.[1] I believe that the document is 'inedited', but, as you know, my life has of late been broken, so I shall be extremely glad of any suggestion or criticism. I have some earlier documents to mention hereafter: but there will I think be no great harm done if my 'gleanings' are not arranged chronologically.

I foresee that I shall now have J.H.R. as an assailant until the end of our joint lives. At least for a while I must be passive, and indeed I doubt whether I shall ever be able to turn back to Domesday. I now regret that I did not take occasion of Tait's review[2] to explain my guesses about the manerium—for in substance R. is saying what T. said very well. Perhaps I may get in a word hereafter: but at any rate I don't want to be hurried. Have you any advice to give? You know that I value your counsel.

No, I don't like England! I regret to say it.

Yours very truly

F. W. MAITLAND

265. To R. Lane Poole

Downing College

20 May 1900

MY DEAR POOLE,

I hope that Froude did not forge this. I think that I will with your leave publish it and see what happens.[3]

Yours very truly

F. W. MAITLAND

266. To Charles Gross

Brookthorpe

nr. Gloucester

25 June 1900

MY DEAR GROSS,

The sight of a letter from you makes me feel very penitent, for since I returned from the Canaries I have been hoping that I might see you—and putting off the hope for a few days at least until lectures were over (and I had at short notice to make a new course) and then until I should be free enough

---

[1] E.H.R. (1900) 757: C.P. III. 180: *Selected Hist. Essays*, 226.
[2] See Letter 200, *supra*. J.H.R. or R. = Round: see Letter 252, *supra*.
[3] *Pius IV and the English Church Service*, E.H.R. (1900) 531, esp. note 3: C.P. III. 177–80, esp. at p. 179: *Selected Hist. Essays*, 224–6, esp. p. 225, note 1.

from pain to thoroughly enjoy a long talk with you. Now against my will I
have been carried off into the wilds to recover from a bad assault of the neural-
gic fiend; but in a day or two I shall be back in Cambridge and will then suggest
a meeting. There are whole heaps of things that I want to talk about and masses
of questions that I want to put to you. That inability to do any worth-while
research which I fear is coming upon me only makes me the keener to know
what the real workers are doing. I am sorry that we can not catch you for the
Selden[1] and have told this to Lock—but can well believe that you are better
employed. I begin to get some proof-sheets of translated Gierke—my one
completed job this twelve month.

> Believe me
> Yours very truly
> F. W. MAITLAND

267. To B. Fossett Lock

> Downing
> *1 July 1900*

DEAR LOCK,

I will attend on 12 July at 4.15. At the moment I feel quite robust and
hopeful.

As to the volume for 1903 I see no reason why Baildon and I should not
undertake the Year Book, for even if I am sent abroad next winter I could
there do a good deal of work in the way of making a rough translation: that
is the sort of occupation that does me good. I don't want to abandon the project and do not think that I need do so if I have so competent a helper as
Baildon.[2]

I note what you say of Leach. I will help in any way that I can; but no sheets
of Introduction[3] have come to me.

If by any chance I cannot attend on the 12th I will write at length: but I
mean to be there.

> Yours very truly
> F. W. MAITLAND

268. To B. Fossett Lock

> Downing
> *4 July 1900*

MY DEAR LOCK,

Have you seen the beginning of Leach's Introduction? I don't like it at all.
It is all higgledy-piggledy: even the grammar is hardly respectable. I should

---

[1] See Letter 250, *supra*.
[2] It was not in fact Baildon but Turner who helped M. with the first Year Book in the S.S.
series: see M.'s Preface to S.S. Vol. 17.
[3] To S.S. Vol. 14. Lock's letter is not extant, but he must have expressed misgivings over
Leach's Introduction: see the three Letters next following.

much like to tell him that this won't do for the Selden. But it seems necessary
to press on the publication of the volume. So what to do? Do you think this
stuff too bad?

I don't like suffragan or other bishops, but Leach's gird at them can hardly
stand.

Yours in perplexity

F. W. MAITLAND

269. To B. Fossett Lock

Downing
Wednesday

18 July 1900

DEAR LOCK,

Eugh!

Three more slips of this stuff to-day. I should like to get the book out but
really some of it is bad.

I suppose that I may transmit your slips—I mean the slips that you anno-
tated—to Leach: it will do him good. If you do not wish this done, please wire.
I will not send them until to-morrow, Thursday, night.

Am trying a new kind of pen. At present it seems no great success.

Yrs.

F. W. MAITLAND

P.S. After reading new slips, I incline to tell Leach that he must leave all
this out. He gives the rashest judgment about the most disputable matters.

270. To B. Fossett Lock

Downing

25 July, '00

DEAR LOCK,

I return Leach's letter.[1] I am failing to persuade him not to plunge into
speculations about the craft gilds of cent. xii. He is perfectly civil, nay jovial,
but sweet on his own stuff and has not read enough to know how thin it is.
So I suppose that I must tinker it in detail.

Yours v. truly

F. W. MAITLAND

[1] Leach had written to Lock: 'Please sir, I have been a very naughty boy, and I will try
to be good next time' (S.S. Corr.). In his Intro. to S.S. Vol. 14, at p. lxii, Leach pays a generous
tribute to M.

271. To R. Lane Poole

Downing College

26 Aug. 1900

MY DEAR POOLE,

I think that it was in the December *Fortnightly* that I spoke of Malcolm MacColl.[1] I do not seem to have a copy. I learn that he is answering and I tremble, for there are three or four ghastly misprints in it which will give him an opening.

It grieves me that you should brood over my Domesday. Of all that I have written that makes me most uncomfortable. I try to cheer myself by saying that I have given others a lot to contradict. What I am most inclined to stick to is the king's 'alienable superiority'.[2]

I am to be at Brighton during September. Before I go I will try to finish a 'gleaning'.[3]

We are hearing very bad news of Henry Sidgwick.[4]

Yours very truly

F. W. MAITLAND

272. To Mrs. Sidgwick

Downing College

11 Octr. 1900

DEAR MRS. SIDGWICK,

I have been and still am extremely unwilling to intrude upon your sorrow, but no day has passed and for a long time to come none will pass without my thinking of one whom I loved and honoured with my whole heart and to whom I owe whatever there is of good in me. I should not now write were it not that I learnt from Frederick Pollock that you were collecting your husband's letters and think that you may like to see the only one that I have. It was written to me last winter when I was abroad in answer to the question whether in the translation of a German book on which I was engaged 'jargon' or 'verbiage' would be the worse offence.[5]

I beg you not to think it necessary to make any reply and to believe me

Yours very sincerely

F. W. MAITLAND

[1] See Letter 252, *supra*, and Letter 274, *infra*.
[2] M., *D.B. and Beyond*, Essay II, s. 2.
[3] The fourth *Elizabethan Gleaning* appeared in E.H.R. October 1900, p. 757, and the fifth not until July 1903, p. 517.
[4] He died on 28 August 1900.
[5] See Letter 259, *supra*.

273. To B. Fossett Lock

Downing College
Cambridge
14 Octr. 1900

MY DEAR LOCK,

(i) A week ago I wrote to Turner a letter[1] that, as I thought, would draw tears from a stone. No reply.

(ii) I had the enclosed from Leach, together with a portfolio of prospectuses, advertisements, etc.—you know what it is like. I tell him that 'I will mention the matter' to you, but that I don't think that the Society will take up another town for some time to come.[2]

My plan of carrying YBB to the Canaries still holds good.

Yours v. truly

F. W. MAITLAND

274. To R. Lane Poole

Downing
17 Octr. 1900

MY DEAR POOLE,

I fully agree that there should not be in one number of your *Review* two articles dealing with the difference between MacColl and me. Therefore let Pollard go ahead: and I see no reason for confining him to one portion of the dispute. Very likely he will say of Nich. Hereford all that need be said. If not, I can say it. I think that I will write it out, so that if it is going into your March number I may (if you please) see it in print while I am still among books.[3] I have always liked what I have seen of Pollard's work: but I must not take his book for review.[4] I don't know Edwd. VI at all well and my hands are pretty full. Yesterday my lecture room overflowed, but, as I told the boys, I never knew the room I could not empty. Still I shall have a pretty hard time of it while term lasts and I could not touch P.'s book unless a library were near.

Very many thanks for your offer of borrowed books.

Yours very truly

F. W. MAITLAND

[1] Not extant, but presumably about S.S. Vol. 13: see Letter 246, *supra*.
[2] Neither Leach's letter nor M.'s reply is extant. Leach would seem to have suggested a volume on Lincoln: see Letters 212, *supra*, and 275, *infra*.
[3] [A.L.P. M.'s reply to MacColl was printed E.H.R. (1901) 35; A. F. Pollard reviewed MacColl's *The Reformation Settlement examined in the light of History and Law*, ibid. (1901), 378.] See Letters 271, *supra*, and 276, *infra*.
[4] [A.L.P. *England under Protector Somerset* was reviewed by James Gairdner, E.H.R. (1901) 151.] Albert Frederick Pollard (1869–1948) was specially interested in the Tudor period. From 1903 to 1931 he was Professor of Constitutional History at University College, London, and took a large part in founding the Institute of Historical Research, University of London.

I grieve to think that you or any other human being should have to lecture about Domesday.

Forgive the blots overleaf which I have just discovered.

275. To B. Fossett Lock

Downing

28 Oct. 1900

DEAR LOCK,

I think that Leach will construe as a 'declension' of his offer the letter that I wrote to him, though in it I said that I would mention the matter to you. If he writes again I shall say that Lincoln is not wanted. I quite understand the situation.[1]

I also am beginning to fear about Turner. He does not answer me though I wrote what I thought to be a sympathetic letter:—i.e. I asked him to come here and to let me do all I could upon the book. If you decide to employ an assistant, I will gladly help to pay. I should like to see Turner and would run up to London if I had any security for finding him.

The medicine men advise me to go once more to Canary when term is over, though they are well satisfied by my present behaviour. I am making arrangements for the transport thither of two MS Year Books and shall come back at Easter with much 'copy' in a rough state.

Can you remember the number of vols. into which Edward II was to extend?

It may be that I shall thus miss a meeting of the Council—but I hope to be seriously copying all the time.

Yours very truly

F. W. MAITLAND

276. To R. Lane Poole

Downing College

30 Octr. 1900

DEAR POOLE,

I send you what I have written in reply to MacColl[2] and will ask your advice about two or three points. I will only ask you to speak in your capacity of editor, for I should not think it fair to request a judgment from you about the merits of the case. What I should like to know from you is whether as editor you would rather have in the E.H.R. the whole of my screed or only the part of it that relates to Nic. Hereford. I am divided in mind and your verdict would be decisive. On the one hand I dislike controversies even when I am not engaged in them: they seem to me dull reading because the question of misrepresentation is apt to arise and that is deadly dull. On the other hand, to take one instance, this is I think the third (certainly the second) time on which MacColl has challenged me to speak about the Greek church, and he can

1 On this and the succeeding paragraph see Letter 273, *supra.*
2 On the whole of this letter see Letter 274, *supra.*

address an audience much larger than any that I can command: can sell eight editions while I fail to sell one. So I am in doubt and shall be very glad if you, desiring only to make a good number of the E.H.R., will decide how much had better appear. You will see that I take 5 points—no. 3 being Hereford's case.

I have added notes because I like showing my evidence and I fancy that about this you are likely to agree. Also I feel that in this instance I have to deal with an experienced controversialist and, though I don't say or think any real harm of him, he seems to me a clever tactician, especially when in retreat. Whatever your decision is I shall not complain and I shall look forward to next Sunday.

Yours very truly
F. W. MAITLAND

277. To Edwin Ashworth

Downing College,
Cambridge
12 Nov. 1900

MY DEAR SIR,

I am glad to hear of any one who is interested in the growth of English Towns and Villages. I think that you will find Gross, *Bibliography of British Municipal History* (Longmans) a useful book though it is only a book about books. Do you know Toulmin Smith, *The Parish*?[1] There is good stuff in it, though as regards early times he too easily identifies parish and township. There are some books by Mr. C. L. Gomme[2] that are worth looking at. What I know about the matter I tried to say in Pollock and Maitland, *History of English Law*, ed. 2, and in *Township and Borough*. As regards agrarian matters Seebohm, *English Village Community*, made an epoch.

If it is in my power to answer any more specific question I will gladly do so.

Yours very faithfully
F. W. MAITLAND

EDWIN ASHWORTH, ESQ.

278. To Henry Jackson

[Printed, with omissions, by Fisher, *Memoir*, 125–6: now printed from the original in Camb. Univ. MSS.]

Hotel Quiney
Las Palmas
12 Jan. 1901

DEAR JACKSON,

It was very good of you to give me a piece of your New Year's Eve and to tell me much that I wanted to know.[3] I sincerely hope that the vein you mention gave no more trouble and that you are in good trim for the Lent Term. For my

---

[1] See note by M. to *The Survival of Archaic Communities*, L.Q.R. (1893) 224: C.P. II. 363–4; and Intro. to *Gierke*, xxxv.
[2] Discussed by M. in *The Survival of Archaic Communities*.
[3] M. is replying to Jackson's letter of 31 Dec. 1900, in Camb. Univ. MSS.

part I am practising the art of writing while lying flat on my back and am flattering myself that I make some progress, though the management of a pipe complicates the matter. The result of lying abed is that I am getting through much too quickly the small store of books that I brought with me and am falling back on the resources of the one book shop that the island contains. If this sort of thing goes on I shall be driven to Spanish translations of Zola. I have just finished Feuillet's *La Muerta*—but then I knew the French original. After what you say I must see whether Erckman-Chatrian has been done into Spanish. In a list that I have before me I see Dickens down for 'Dias penosos' and some Wilkie Collins—but apparently the novel-reading Spaniard lives for the most part on Frenchmen, especially Zola. I shall never talk Spanish. I believe that what is or used to be called a classical education makes many cowards: the dread of 'howlers' keeps me silent when I ought to plunge regardless of consequences.

I fancy that the comparison that you instituted between the life of the Roman and the life of the Spaniard as seen by me in these islands might be extended to a good many particulars. When, as happens for about eleven months in the year, you are not living at your finca, you occasionally pay it visits with a party of friends—male friends only—whom you entertain there. You eat a great deal and you drink until you are merry: then late in the evening you drive back to town twanging a guitar and, if you can, you sing inane verses made impromptu. Our landlord had one of these carouses the day before he handed over the house to us, and my wife's account of the state in which the house was when she entered and got some servants to scrub it is not for publication. Apparently, as host and guests fill up with meat and drink, they become cheerfully careless of the manner in which they make room for more. Isn't this rather classical?

All your suggestions for filling Ewbank's place are good[1]: I should like to meet Jenkinson or Acton or Cunningham. I was sorry to miss A. J. B., for he is always a cheerful sight. I can't imagine Webster making a speech that was not dull.[2] If any paper is printed in the matter of the Sidgwick memorial, slip a copy into an envelope for me.[3] I am curious to know who will follow Ryle at Queens'. Any talk of Rev. Finch?[4]

It is bad that you should have no better news to give of Mrs. Jackson. I hope that your allowance of bread increases—one gets to think well of bread when it is forbidden.

Yours very truly
F. W. MAITLAND

[1] Jackson had written: 'Ewbank is leaving Cambridge, so we shall have a vacancy in the Society'—a Cambridge dining club. See Letter 402, *infra*. Lucas Ewbank (1835–1916), Fellow of Clare College, Cambridge.

[2] Jackson had written about 'our Commemoration'. A. J. B.=A. J. Butler. Sir Richard Webster had already (1900) become Lord Chief Justice with the title of Lord Alverstone.

[3] The *Cambridge University Reporter* printed on 7 Dec. 1900 a 'Report of the proceedings at a meeting for promoting a Memorial of the late Henry Sidgwick', held on 26 Nov. 1900. M.'s speech at the meeting was reported: see also Fisher, *Memoir*, 7–9.

[4] Dr. Ryle, President of Queens' College, Cambridge, had just been made Bishop of Exeter. G. B. Finch (see Letter 74, *supra*) had been ordained.

279. To Frederick Pollock

[Printed, with omissions and different heading, by Fisher, *Memoir*, 127–8.
Now printed from the original in Camb. Univ. MSS.]

Quineys

21 Jan. 1901

MY DEAR POLLOCK,

I wonder whether their Highnesses John and George think that their gods
are *todopoderosos*.[1] That is a good word, is it not? I get a good deal of comfort
out of it in these bad days.

Also I wonder what has gone wrong with the mails—we might be at the
other end of the earth, so slow is news to reach us. A rumour came up yesterday
from the ciudad which makes me reflect that I don't know for certain whether
you have a queen in England or a king.[2] And I can't go and see how all this is,
for if I leave my bed I am soon sent back there again by this blameworthy
neuralgia which threatens to become what Glanvill calls morbus reseantisae.[3]
Et sic jaceo discinctus discalciatus et sine braccis ut patuit militibus comitatus
qui missi fuerunt ad me videndum et qui mihi dederunt diem apud Turrem
Lundoniae in quindena Pasche.

So I make some progress through Spanish novels—or rather novels that
have been translated into Spanish. At present I am in *Resurreccion* by the
Conde Leon Tolstoy—which is easy. I find Perez Galdos[4] a little too hard for
my recumbent position, and dictionaries are bad bed-fellows. I have been
indolently making for subsequent use a sort of Year Book grammar. I have
got a pretty complete *être* and *avoir*—and really I think that the lawyers had a
fair command of all the tenses. I have seen some well sustained subjunctives.[5]

You spoke of Maine. Well, I always talk of him with reluctance, for on the
few occasions on which I sought to verify his statements of fact I came to the
conclusion that he trusted much to a memory that played him tricks and
rarely looked back at a book that he had once read: e.g. his story about the
position of the half-blood in the Law of Normandy seems to me a mere dream
that is contradicted by every version of the custumal.[6]

By the way, when you discoursed of the term 'comparative Jurisprudence',
had you noticed that Austin used it? I was surprised by seeing it in his book
the other day.[7]

Burgenses de Cantebrige dederunt mihi libertatem burgi sui honoris causa
quia edidi cartas suas.[8] Gratificatus sum.

---

1 'Almighty'. 'John and George' are unknown.
2 Queen Victoria died on 22 Jan. 1901.
3 Ground for an essoin.
4 Spanish novelist: see Letter 281, *infra*.
5 See S.S. Vol. 17, Intro. liii–lxxvii.
6 See Maine, *Ancient Law*, chap. V, and the note upon it in *P. and M.* ii. 305.
7 Austin, *Lectures on Jurisprudence*, 5th edn., p. 1072.
8 M., with Mary Bateson, edited *The Charters of the Borough of Cambridge* (1901).

280. To B. Fossett Lock

Quiney's Hotel
Las Palmas
11 Feb. 1901

DEAR LOCK,

Dios Todopoderosismo! What a record! Well, I now see that I shall bring back from Canary a transcript of the Y.B. of that Kentish eyre and precious little else—for I have had bad luck. We must confer when I am in England again. Something will depend upon the other MSS of that eyre, for that which I have been using is by no means good and I suspect its scribe of omissions and other blunders. I am not sure, however, that a volume given to this eyre with its voluminous record might not be good.[1]

I was puzzling the other day over the 'provenience' of a certain Mestre Apolitan who appeared some four or five times in a case relating to a church in the diocese of Durham. After all he was only the Metropolitan. That is the sort of thing a medieval scribe could do.

Many thanks for your winter card. But why not de Wet?[2]

Yours very truly

F. W. MAITLAND

281. To H. A. L. Fisher

Quiney's Hotel
Las Palmas
23rd Feb. 1901

MY DEAR HERBERT,

Many thanks for your letter which contained much information that I was glad to have. First, as to Hervey—the one really definite piece of news that we have had came through you. Your good mother has one failing and no more—she never tells Florence what are the maladies which fall upon members of your family, but merely says that so and so is a little better. It is very kindly meant, but it is a mistake none the less. Florence guesses the worst and this time has been very anxious. Your sister Adeline[3] pursues the same policy. It would be a true charity if, when Florence is out of England and ill befalls, you would tell her in a few lines what has happened. Even now we are only conjecturing. I hope that the worst is over and that all goes well.

I am inclined to envy you your task over Napoleon and am right glad to

---

[1] See Letter 256, *supra*. The Eyre of Kent, 6 and 7 Edw. II, ultimately made 3 vols. of the Selden Society—24, 27 and 29—all published after M.'s death. M.'s transcript was found among his papers, noted as having been finished on 27 Jan. 1901. M.'s suspicion of his MS. was justified, but 15 other MSS. were found. See Preface to S.S. Vol. 24.

[2] A Boer general; but the allusion is obscure. Lock's card is not extant.

[3] She married Ralph Vaughan Williams, the composer. For Hervey, see Letter 99, *supra*.

hear of the projected 'three-voller'. It must be a fascinating subject.[1] I grieve to hear that S. R. G.[2] must give up the E.H.R.—he was an excellent figurehead—but R. L. P. will do very well without him.

Many thanks for what you say of Gierke. Somebody has been very kind to me in 'Literature'. I shall bring back nothing this year but some Year Book copy. I am making up my mind to give what is left of me to starting the Selden Society's edition of the Year Books. I am to have Baildon to help me[3] and I do not know that I could turn my hand to anything more useful.

This year I have not been lucky. My troubles became so constant and acute that I fell into the hands of the English doctor of Las Palmas, who (as I am now thinking) has made a clever job of me—at least I have had a good fortnight. Idleness drove me to reading Spanish novels. Perez Galdos, who aspires to be a sort of Spanish Balzac, is interesting. A play of his now running at Madrid (Electra) is causing great excitement by its anti-clerical or anti-monastic theme. The papers talk of him as the Beaumarchais of the coming revolution.

I shall never learn to speak Spanish and envy Florence her fluency—but I can read novels with some ease.

The weather has been too good for words until yesterday—which day the family had chosen for an expedition to Las Palmas. I never knew the English June that was comparable to our January, and I deeply regret that much of this beauty was lost by me.

When Carnival came, our cook took herself off to spend her wages in *vino tinto* and 'never came back no more'. I think that Florence after struggles has obtained a successor.

And now we must begin to think of moving—I wish that the University would come to its Professor. May we meet soon.

> Yours affectionately
>
> F. W. MAITLAND

282. To John Chipman Gray

[No original: only as printed by Fisher, *Memoir*, 128, where it is headed—
'To John C. Gray, Professor of Law in the University of Harvard.']

> Downing College,
> Cambridge.
> *21 April, 1901.*

My best thanks for *Future Interests in Personal Property*, which has just come to my hands on my return from the Canaries. For a few days my interest in it must be future, but will be vested, indefeasible, real and not impersonal.

> Yours in perpetuity,
>
> F. W. MAITLAND

[1] See Letter 240, *supra*. Fisher had thought to write more than one book upon Napoleon as a statesman; but, after publishing *Napoleonic Statesmanship, Germany*, in 1903, he abandoned the project of a similar volume on Italy: Ogg, *Herbert Fisher*, 144.
[2] S. R. Gardiner.
[3] But see Letter 267, *supra*.

283. To R. Lane Poole

Downing
29 April 1901

MY DEAR POOLE,

Your request for some words about Stubbs is distressing me.[1] I cannot (I am glad to say it) plead ill-health. Nor will I plead other engagements, though I have been idiot enough to take in hand the Rede lecture and know not what on earth to say.[2] I feel that I owe so much to the good bishop and I so deeply admire him that I should not like to put in any such pleas as the above if the editor of the E.H.R., conscious of his responsibility, asked me to write. On the other hand I would have you remember that Stubbs was to me simply and solely the writer of certain books. I never spoke to him. I never saw him but once, and that in church. Therefore I could give none of those 'reminiscences' which people expect, and naturally expect, on these occasions. Not a word could I say of the man as distinguished from the writer—no word of his kindness and geniality or the like—and yet I should suppose from vague report that many words of this sort could be written and are in some sort due to him. Also—and this I think important—I suppose there is a good deal to be said of him in connexion with the Oxford History school and of this I could say absolutely nothing. Do you not think that it would seem strange to friends and pupils if you put this article into the hands of one who will speak of Stubbs merely as he would speak of Hallam or of some other writer of books? I should (so I think) speak warmly—but obviously what I said would come from the merest stranger, and indeed I should be compelled to say in the openest manner that of the man and the bishop I knew naught. Are there not Deans of Durham and Masters of University quite competent to supply the requisite laudation and competent at the same time to put in those touches which come of familiarity and are rightly valued by readers. (I may be showing my ignorance by the names that I suggest[3]—so let us say 'Deans of X and Masters of Y, and the younger men who are teaching at Oxford'.)

You can guess that your request makes me unhappy, for you I feel pretty sure can guess (if others can't) that I should feel myself a humbug when I sat me down to appraise the merits of this very big man. Someone will say (and not without truth) that it is like my impudence.

However I won't say No, if after consideration you still think that I had better take this task upon me. What determines me to say as much as this is the fact that I had the boldness to dissent from Stubbs about the Canon Law and that by so doing I made a little noise and even (which is much harder) a little money. But I still think *very strongly* that you ought only to fall back upon me if for one reason or another you cannot get an article from a friend.

(Is not this a case in which the editor himself might write? I should have thought so.)

[1] Stubbs died on 22 April 1901.
[2] See Letter 287, *infra*.
[3] [A.L.P. G. W. Kitchin, Dean of Durham, and J. F. Bright, Master of University College, Oxford.]

N.B. I am not standing out for greater pressure: I know how valuable your time is: only I would have you look at the question from all points after hearing what I say of my complete and utter ignorance of the man.

I very gravely fear that our woes are not at an end. I hear very bad news of Acton.*

I meant to write to you of Fagniez[1] and some other matters, but good-bye for the present.

Yours very truly

F. W. MAITLAND

* It was said to-day that he was 'no worse', but then I am told that yesterday a doctor said that worse he could hardly be.

P.S. (After the interval of a night.) I still think that what I should write would look distant and ignorant and very short—a sort of *ex officio* commendation.

284. To R. Lane Poole

Downing College

6 May 1901

DEAR POOLE,

So be it. I will try to make 4 or 5 or 6 pages of Wm. St.[2] You must let me be rather late in sending them for I cannot turn to other things until I have concocted a Rede lecture.

I should dearly like to hear you on Dial. de Scac. I think highly of Turner. His introduction to the Forest Rolls[3] is a really good piece of work in the style of Madox. Unfortunately he is the most dilatory of men and has tried the patience of the Selden Society to breaking point. The American subscriber is in full revolt and threatens a Decln̄. of Independcē.

The Regius of Physic gave me on Friday a better account than I dreaded of the Regius of History.[4] It is paralysis: one arm and one leg useless but mind unaffected.

I have read and liked Pollard's Somerset.[5] I remember what you told me of Pollard and meant to speak to Acton about him, but of course the Universal History cannot be talked of at present.[6]

Can you out of diplomatic wisdom suggest an explanation for a bit of legal dialogue temp. Edw. II which runs as follows?—:

You say that the right is not in A: but it is not in B. 'Donque pend le droit auxi cum la cite de Naples by agothey.'

[1] [A.L.P. His reviews of the two volumes of G. Fagniez's *Documents relatifs à l'histoire de l'industrie . . . en France* appeared in E.H.R. (1900) 142 and (1901) 819.] See Letters 244 and 250, *supra*.

[2] William Stubbs.   [3] S.S. Vol. 13.

[4] Lord Acton.   [5] See Letter 274, *supra*.

[6] [A.L.P. In October 1896 Acton wrote to R. L. Poole: 'This University meditates a Universal History of modern times on a large scale.' The 1st vol. of the Camb. Mod. Hist. appeared in 1902.]

If you know anything about the 'pendency' of the City of Naples I shall be glad of a post card: but do not puzzle over the matter for I have no immediate use for the passage.[1]

I hope to see H. Fisher next Saturday and to hear of Oxford.

Yours very truly

F. W. MAITLAND

285. To R. Lane Poole

[No year; but from contents and context clearly 1901.]

Downing

19 May [1901]

Will you kindly tell me what is positively the last day on which you could receive my promised article without great inconvenience?[2]

I will keep my pact: but there is a good deal to do.

That new Pref. to Sel. Chart. is most puzzling. The earlier part looks as if it were aimed at Fustel—but then he was a continuationer with a witness. So is Brunner if you allow him to carry continuation from Normandy and Frankland. So is Seebohm a continuationer. Are not all men continuationers? It is very puzzling. My best guess is that dn̄s ēps meant F. de C.[3]

Yours

F. W. M.

286. To R. Lane Poole

Downing College

2 June 1901

MY DEAR POOLE,

This[4] is detestable—but I don't see how to better it (partly because my familiar fiend is beginning to know [sic] my vitals) and so I send it off at once in order that you may have a good chance of giving me advice that will be taken. I shall be truly grateful if you say that this part or that is bad and I will do my very best to make amendments. Please take me at my word.

I am rather sorry that I saw the passage about folk-land. I have not mentioned it: but the Bp. ought to have named Vinogradoff[5] and seems to me to leave the matter in a mess.

I hope that your headache is in the past.

Yours very truly

F. W. MAITLAND

---

[1] The passage should presumably occur in the MS. of the Eyre of Kent which M. had transcribed in the Canaries: see Letter 280, *supra*. But it does not appear in the three volumes—24, 27 and 29—subsequently published by the Selden Society.

[2] M.'s obituary of Stubbs appeared in E.H.R. (July 1901) 417: reprinted C.P. III. 495, and *Selected Hist. Essays*, 266.

[3] [A.L.P. The Preface to the eighth edition of the *Select Charters* is dated 14 March 1895 and discusses 'the theory of continuous history'.] F. de C. = Fustel de Coulanges: see M.'s obituary of Stubbs.

[4] M.'s obituary of Stubbs.

[5] [A.L.P. His article on 'Folkland' was printed in E.H.R. (1893) 1.] See also Vinogradoff, *Coll. Papers*, I. 91.

287. To R. Lane Poole

Downing College

9 June 1901

MY DEAR POOLE,

I am glad that my words about Stubbs do not displease you as a whole. It will be a really charitable act if on a 'proof' you will mark with pencil any phrase that you would like to see altered. It will not be necessary for you to state the grounds of your objection. I shall understand and be thankful. On such occasions one sometimes with the best intentions uses an adjective— or something of the sort—that jars, and of course I do not know Oxford as Oxford men know it.

I spoke warmly of W. S. in the Rede Lecture and was rewarded by what French reporters call a movement of adhesion. I heard a purr from the Mr. of Trinity.[1]

As to the books—let us split the difference. I will take Viollet but have hardly the time for Keutgen. Miss Bateson already knows his book.[2]

Would Pollard let me ask him a question? It is whether in the time of Qn. Mary he has come upon Antonio Agustin in England. He was commissioned to come here to the Regd. Poole of those days. I think that Pollard is more likely than anyone else to have noticed his presence. I am told that A. A. was 'the Cujas of the canon law'.[3]

Yours very truly

F. W. MAITLAND

288. To B. Fossett Lock

Downing

16 June 1901

MY DEAR LOCK,

Explicit foresta! *Deo gracias*! I am suggesting to Turner that a qualified apology for delay would look better in the Preface than a discourse about *U* and *V*.[4]

For a fortnight my address will be 'Taynton—Burford—Oxfordshire'.[5] I shall be within reach of London.

Of Bateson I heard that, despairing of work, he had thoughts of the colonies. This was told me in strict confidence but with the intention that I should do

---

[1] H.M. Butler. The Rede Lecture, *English Law and the Renaissance*, was delivered on 5 June, 1901.

[2] Viollet, *Communes*, cited S.S. Vol. 21, Intro. xxxv, lxx, cxxviii: Keutgen, *Urkunden zur städtischen Verfassungsgeschichte* (1901), cited by Mary Bateson, S.S. Vol. 18, Intro. x.

[3] See *English Law and the Renaissance*, p. 12 and note 21. Jacques Cujas (1520–90), the French jurist and humanist.

[4] A note on the medieval use of these two letters is given in the Preface to S.S. Vol. 13. See also Letter 246, *supra*.

[5] The home of M.'s friend, Cyprian Williams.

anything that lay in my power to keep him in England. I pass it on to you as it may perhaps form an element in the case that you are considering.[1]

Yours very truly

F. W. MAITLAND

289. To B. Fossett Lock

Taynton

nr̄. Burford

1 July 1901

MY DEAR LOCK,

I felt very much ashamed of myself for not being at the Council meeting but your very kind letter turned the scale: and I think that I did well, for I am out of pain now though absurdly sleepy.

I saw Cyprian Williams who told me what happened. Some day—there is no hurry—you will let me know whether anything is to be said to Miss Bateson. I guess that you are right in thinking that her brother has made the wise choice—though I am sorry that we lose the prospect of having him for your successor when the bad hour comes.

As to Company Charters—I should like to find someone who, while willing to search rolls and copy Latin, would take a modern interest in the beginnings of Company Law—the transferable share, the call, etc. I feel fairly sure that about these matters there is a lot to be known that is not known. What should you say to Rigg as a possible editor? He is versatile, I think, and not too medieval. We want someone who would study the history of commerce, but a pure economist might not see legal points. We have time to spare.[2]

Yours very truly

F. W. MAITLAND

290. To R. Lane Poole

Downing

30 July 1901

No, my dear Poole, I mustn't and I can't. I am setting forth in a letter to Hunt some of the reasons that deter me.[3] I am telling him one thing 'in confidence'. There is no cause however that need prevent me from telling you what I have told him. It is I fear becoming evident that Lord Acton will not be able to do what he was to have done for the *Cambridge History* and I

---

[1] 'Bateson' was a brother of Mary Bateson. She had asked M. if she might prepare for the Selden Society a volume on Borough Customs, and this was perhaps 'the case' that Lock was considering.

[2] See Letters 292, 449 and 471, *infra*; and S.S. Vol. 28.

[3] M.'s letters to Hunt is not extant. On 29 July 1901 Poole had written to M. to persuade him to write a volume on 'the period between William the Conqueror and John' for a projected *Political History of England* to be edited by Poole and William Hunt (C. Hist. J., 334).

have reason to fear that some share (I hope small) of editorial or sub-editorial work may be cast upon me, and you will easily understand that, however unfit for the task, I might be compelled to yield. Even if the fraction of responsibility that fell to me was small, it would be more than enough. I will ask you not to reveal this, for we hope against hope.

Then there are the Year Books, and I have talked so much about the need for a new edition that I am bound to give them the best of my time now that the Selden has taken the matter up.

Also I am premonished whenever a cold day comes in winter that I must either flee or go to bed.

I think extremely well of your project and am really sorry to say No.

Make the best of your holiday!

Yours very truly

F. W. MAITLAND

I don't feel certain that you could not drive J. H. R.[1] in harness, and (if you could) so much the better for history.

291. To Melville M. Bigelow

Downing College
Cambridge

18 Augt. 1901

MY DEAR BIGELOW,

Time flies, torts multiply (as witness your new volume[2]) and I am a bad correspondent. It is a letter of April that I am answering now in August. However I think you find that my better half is a better writer of letters, and a combination of imputed righteousness and the unity of husband and wife might serve my turn.[3]

I am looking back with regret to the days of the Horsepools when you visited us. The house has been sold and I am compelled to spend the summer in Cambridge in order that I may spend the winter in the Canaries. I fear that it will come to another spell of exile this year, for whenever cold strikes me I become miserable and useless. The consequence is that I can't do half what I wanted to do. This summer a few light jobs have been turned off—one of them, a lecture, you shall see anon[4]—and I am getting on with the Year Books of Edwd. II. How bad the printed edition is no words can tell. I envy you your power of turning out book after book and edition after edition. It is so clear

---

[1] In his letter Poole had written that the volume he had in mind needed 'the criticism of Round joined to the constructive gift which he has not'.

[2] [AULT. The reference is perhaps to the seventh American edition of the *Law of Torts*.]

[3] Professor Ault has printed in Boston Univ. Law Rev. a series of letters by Mrs. Maitland from 1889 onwards.

[4] *English Law and the Renaissance*. 'The house'—Horsepools—had been owned by Selina Maitland (Mrs. Reynell).

to me that I shall never see the States that I hope you will bring Mrs. Bigelow to England next summer: the Horsepools are gone, but West Lodge remains and will always be open to you and yours. Don't you want to see a coronation?[1] But there are better things than coronations here. So come!

Yours always

F. W. MAITLAND

292. To B. Fossett Lock

Downing

6 Oct. 1901

MY DEAR LOCK,

I suppose that you are returning to Lincoln's Inn about this time.

My heart rejoiced at the sight of Turner's book. It looks very good. I am not sure that it is not the best book that we have issued.

Rigg progresses rapidly.[2] I have been carefully reading his sheets and like them. I don't altogether agree with his Introduction; but it is ably written and he is entitled to his opinion.

I have not been able to do this summer all that I meant to do for the Year Books, and (between ourselves) I have not found Baildon quite so greedy of work as I hoped that he would be: I fear that some forensic success is spoiling him. I shall take to Canary MSS. YBB. and no other work. If I have reasonable luck I shall come home with a good lot of text and translation. Then next summer I will collate if I possibly can: if I can't, then I will get help and pay my helper. (I am not sure that I could not use Turner if he were willing to assist.[3] Baildon I must keep at work on the rolls—if I can.)

Shall you be holding a Council in this term? There are those who want me to run away at once—but my own plan is to lecture daily throughout the first half of the term and so put a full tale of lectures to my credit. I think of vanishing about the middle of November. Before that time I could attend a meeting; but I have nothing to say, so do not alter arrangements on my account unless you specially desire my presence.

I am not sure that Baildon's increasing weight (physical and moral) might not make him your best successor if you must demise the secretaryship.[4]

Goffin will call upon you in the matter of Charters of Trading Companies.[5] I think that you will like him.

I hope that you have enjoyed the vacation.

Yours very truly

F. W. MAITLAND

[1] Of Edward VII.
[2] S.S. Vol. 15.
[3] In the Preface to S.S. Vol. 17 M. warmly acknowledges Turner's help.
[4] Lock remained Hon. Secretary to the Selden Society until 1913 when he resigned on his appointment to be a County Court Judge.
[5] R. J. Goffin, Fellow of Jesus College, Cambridge, was at this time a possible editor of this projected volume: see Letters 289, *supra*, and 449 and 471, *infra*; and S.S. Vol. 28.

293. To Henry Jackson

Downing
20 Octr. 1901

DEAR JACKSON,

I am afraid that I must not accept your invitation. I want very much indeed to hear your paper and if I can manage to get to your rooms at 9 I will do so; but lumbago has been adding itself to some other ills and I shall not get through my lectures unless I am careful.

I am reading the first volume of the Cambridge history.[1] It is much more coherent than I thought it would be, and I begin to think that the first chapter which Acton was to have contributed, though it would have been a luxury, was not a necessary.

I have a cheerful line from Acton on a postcard.

Yours very truly
F. W. MAITLAND

294. To Henry Jackson

Downing
22nd Octr. 1901

MY DEAR JACKSON,

I fear that this infernal fog will keep me from your rooms to-night. I am downright sorry, for I wanted to hear you. If your paper is on paper I shall make an effort to get it from you.

Yours very truly
F. W. MAITLAND

295. To Henry Jackson

Downing
25 Octr. 1901

MY DEAR JACKSON,

W. J. Whittaker, after inquiring about your health, bids me tell you that he has been trying to think of you as a hunting man for ten days and can't. He adds—'He will understand'. I hope this message is not improper: to me it is not intelligible.

I was well rewarded for breaking bounds the other night. The Byron story was most interesting.[2]

I hope that the news you get of Mrs. Jackson is good.

Yours very truly
F. W. MAITLAND

W. J. W.[3] ought not to have left Cambridge. I mourn the loss.

---

[1] Before publication.
[2] Possibly at a meeting of the Eranus: see Parry, *Henry Jackson*, 135–7.
[3] See Letter 296, *infra*.

296. To B. Fossett Lock

Downing College
Cambridge
10 Nov. 1901

MY DEAR LOCK,

I owe you a great many thanks for excusing me from the meeting. The M.R.[1] was in duty bound to subscribe: I am glad that you have captured him; also that Turner is to be paid at the higher rate. I think that Rigg's book will now go to the end without hitch: I have seen the whole text in first proof. I will write to Leadam to inquire where he stands and to Goffin. The time for inquiry after original charters of the trading companies will come by and by.[2]

My fear is that Baildon will not turn out to be the yoke fellow for whom I hoped. See his letter sent herewith.[3] I am telling him that I hope that by the end of the Christmas vacation he will make up his mind to go on with the work or, if not, to throw it up. I feel that we shall not get through with a man who grudges the time that he gives us, and am not sure that we should not do better with Rigg or even with Turner. It may be that Turner will come out to the Canaries at Christmas.[4] If so, I shall make him useful there. I have three MSS in this room and they are about to be packed.

As regards the cheque: my bankers are Barclays (Gosling's Branch). I believe that all will go well if the cheque is drawn to the account of F. W. M. I have just tried this experiment: a few days ago I paid a cheque to the account of my wife at Mortlocks.[5] I asked 'Do you want her signature?' The answer was, 'No, we endorse it.' So I suppose that this is the course of business.

I go by a Forwood boat on the 20th and potter along the Morocco coast which I have not yet seen.

I wish you joy in your new house. Whittaker, who is now a pupil in J. B. Dyne's[6] chambers, told me last night that he was about to join the Society.

Yours very truly

F. W. MAITLAND.

297. To B. Fossett Lock

Downing
12 Novr. 1901

MY DEAR LOCK,

If you think that Baildon wishes to be out of the bargain then I should desire Rigg as companion. He will know something about requirements as he was present at and took part in a long discussion that I had with Baildon this

---

1 Sir R. Henn Collins was Master of the Rolls.
2 See Letter 292, *supra.*
3 Not extant, but see Letter 292, *supra.*
4 See Letter 308, *infra.*
5 A Cambridge bank which in 1896 had been incorporated in Barclay & Co. Ltd.
6 M. had been for a time in his chambers: Fisher, *Memoir*, 17.

summer in my garden. If he seems inclined to take the work, I will write at length to him.

My arrangement with Baildon in the matter of money was 'share and share alike', but it was said between us that rearrangement might be necessary if one of us was obviously carrying the heavy end of the stick. I should be quite willing to give Rigg half-profits—it being his business to find in the record as many as possible of the reported cases and to make notes of what he finds. I am sorry that this crisis arises just now, especially as it throws work on you—but better now than later.

Turner, whom I may have to employ by and by at Brit. Mus., told me that he could work with Rigg better than with W. P. B.[1]

Yours hastily

F. W. MAITLAND

298. To R. Lane Poole

Downing

14 Nov. 1901

MY DEAR POOLE,

I am sorry that I still have but poor news of you. May it soon be better! A post card to Hotel Quiney, Las Palmas, telling of yourself will be a charity, and I should like to have there the January No. of E.H.R.

I am trying my hardest to persuade Stevenson to leave England with me next Thursday.

I have that Gray's Inn book from the Benchers. I will try to write a few words of it.[2] By the way, I much fear that in the course of my travels that work of Viollet's on the French towns has lost itself. I am penitent but cannot find it.[3]

Don't trouble about finding a reviewer for that lecture.[4] The identification of the Lanfranc of Liber Papiensis with the abp. is not absolutely certain, but seems highly probable; and if the two are one, the abp. was an expert Lombardist. By the way, Böhmer, who was lately here, told me that he had an ugly case of forgery against abp. Lanfranc.[5]

I believe that the Actonian history is on the point of moving forwards—but a definite announcement would be premature. At any rate I am told that there is to be a speedy payment of contributors.

May I soon have good news of you.

Yours very truly

F. W. MAITLAND

[1] Neither Baildon nor Rigg is mentioned by M. in his Preface to S.S. Vol. 17.
[2] [A.L.P. *The Pension Book of Gray's Inn*, 1569–1669, ed. R. J. Fletcher, reviewed by M. in E.H.R. (1902) 613.]
[3] See Letter 287, *supra.*
[4] [A.L.P. *English Law and the Renaissance* was reviewed by H. Goudy in E.H.R. (1902) 358.]
[5] [A.L.P. See *Die Fälschungen Erzbischof Lanfranks von Canterbury*, by H. Boehmer (Leipzig, 1902).]

299. To Mr. Justice Holmes

Downing College
Cambridge, Engd.
18 Nov. 1901

Dear Mr. Justice Holmes,

I am very grateful to you for your little volume of speeches. I have not read it but have packed it up and shall soon be enjoying it in the sunshine of the Canaries. I know from past experience that my enjoyment will be keen.

Believe me
Yours very truly
F. W. Maitland

300. To Henry Jackson

[First half of this letter printed, with omissions, by Fisher, *Memoir*, 129. Now printed from original in Camb. Univ. MSS.]

5 Leon y Castillo
Telde
Gran Canaria
30 Decr. 1901

My dear Jackson,

Here I am lying in the sun which shines as if it were June and not December. This year our 'finca' is in the midst of a 'pueblo'. The front of our house faces a high street which is none too clean; but then you keep the front of your house so shut up that you see nothing of the street, and at the back all is orange and coffee and banana and so forth. Telde is the centre of an important trade in tomatos—the whole village is employed in the work of packing them for the English market and sending them off to the ships in Las Palmas. Really it has become a very big industry in these last years and if English people gave up eating tomatos, hundreds of Canarios would be in a bad way. But there! You don't want to hear of foreign parts, and if we could meet our talk would be of Cambridge. I left on the eve of the division in the matter of the Library. From advices received from England I gather that the Non Placets won the day, also that my vote would have made no difference, also that the Librarian's wrath exploded in a fly-sheet. I am sorry that we are not to have our reading room and still more sorry that the Syndicate and Librarian suffered a defeat. Had I stayed in Cambridge I should not have allowed the grace about the Squire bequest[1] to go through without a protest, though I was not prepared to divide the Senate. I could not stomach the word 'gratefully' when applied to an obstinate ass who had done all that in him lay to spoil another's gift. I

[1] Miss Rebecca Flower Squire, who died 26 Nov. 1898, left her estate in trust (1) for the building and endowment of a law library, (2) for the endowment of scholarships. On 7 June 1900 the Senate formally accepted the first bequest. On 12 Dec. 1901 the Senate approved the following Grace: 'That the offer of the Trustees of the Will of the late Rebecca Flower Squire to found and endow Law Scholarships in the University of Cambridge be gratefully accepted' (J. W. Clark, *Endowments of the University of Cambridge*, 1904).

am told that I have been put back on to the Press Syndicate. I do not refuse and shall be very glad if in any way I can further the interests of the big history. I am very curious to know whether the editorial triumvirate[1] will take what I think the right and courageous course in the matter of two bad chapters. The first volume is with me and I enjoy it.

You I hope are away from Cambridge and I sincerely trust that Mrs. Jackson is better than she was when last we met. I feared from what you then said that you were very anxious, but there was another man in the room and I could not say what I wanted. Also I hope that the allowable quantum of bread increases and that even sugar is within sight. There is a sugar mill at the top of this village—we grow some cane here and complain of bounty-fed beetroot: but personally I don't consume. On the other hand I pay a good deal less than a penny for my cigar. Many things are prohibited, but not that. My voyage was unlucky and unpleasant—somehow it did me harm from which I am only now recovering—but as I may not walk or ride I am getting on pretty fast with a long spell of copying[2] which had to be done.

Here is a poor exchange for a letter that I hope you may be writing and which may come here in course of time—but the mail service seems to be very bad this year. My address at Quiney's Hotel in Las Palmas still holds good, but this house is in a street and even has a number.

Yours with best wishes
F. W. Maitland

Or will you have a Spanish ending?

S. S. S.
Q. B. S. M.[3]

301. To Leslie Stephen

[No original. Printed by Fisher, *Memoir*, 131–2: no beginning or ending. Fisher prints date as 30 Jan. 1902. This, though doubtless so written by M., must be wrong. M. wishes Stephen 'a happy new year' and asks 'for a line in return'. On 12 Jan. 1902 (Camb. Univ. MSS.) Stephen answers M.'s letter and quotes from it. The real date, it is suggested, is 30 Dec. 1901.

5, Leon y Castillo
Telde
Gran Canaria
[30 Dec. 1901]

Let me wish you a happy new year and then ask for a line in return. It doesn't follow in law or in fact that, because I have nothing to say that you care to hear, therefore you have nothing to say that I care to hear. Q.E.D.

Why did you make my life miserable by suggesting that grammar does not allow me to wish you a happy new year and does not allow you to send me a letter? I consulted a professed grammarian who told me that 'me' and 'you' are good datives and 'to' in such cases an unnecessary and historically unjustifiable

[1] In succession to Lord Acton, A. W. Ward, G. W. Prothero and Stanley Leathes (Fellow of Trinity College, Cambridge) had been made co-editors of the Cambridge Modern History.
[2] Of the Year Books.
[3] See Letter 304, *infra*.

preposition. Go on like this and you will end where the Spaniard is, and he loves 'to' his parents, etc. When we still have to contend with relics of a subjunctive you need not be making more difficulties.[1] I am led into these exceedingly uninteresting remarks by the nature of my only pursuit. I had a bad time on the voyage. Something went wrong with my works, and since I have been here I have not had much choice between lying almost flat and suffering a good deal of pain. So I have been copying Year Books from the manuscripts that I brought from Cambridge, and since the scribes did not finish their words and I have to supply the endings I have been compelled to take a serious interest in old French Grammar.

However, things are improving. I had ten minutes on the cycle yesterday and hope soon to see a little of the country. We are in a village this year. It is the centre of the trade in tomatos. Boxes of tomatos with the Telde mark have been seen even in the Cambridge market place. As I lie here, I am surrounded by oranges, coffee, bananas, etc., and we have even a true dragon tree. It is wonderfully beautiful. Florence and the children are exceedingly happy and I am beginning to doubt whether I shall get them back to Cambridge when the spring comes. You would think that Florence had never talked anything but Spanish. Not that I would warrant its Castilian quality, but at any rate it is rapid and highly effectual.

302. To B. Fossett Lock
[Post-card.]

> Quiney's Hotel
> Las Palmas
> *5 Jan. 1902*

This may find you *in crastino S. Hillarii*. It is to report that, though I had a bad time after my voyage, I am now getting ahead with my translation of the YBB. and giving it all my time. If only I could get a month at P.R.O., I believe that I could do Vol. I without any great amount of assistance. Anyhow I hope to have a great deal of stuff copied and translated by April.

My best Midwinter wishes

> Yrs.
> F. W. MAITLAND

303. To Leslie Stephen
[No original. Printed by Fisher, *Memoir*, 130–1: no beginning or ending.]

> 5, Leon y Castillo,
> Telde,
> Las Palmas,
> Gran Canaria.
> *20 Jan. 1902.*

I was glad of your letter. I had been in a poor way and it cheered me. Now I am doing well and ride a bit on my cycle along one of the three roads of the

---

1 In his reply on 12 Jan. 1902 Stephen denies that he 'ever laid down the thesis which you oppugn or, indeed, that I ever had any views about it'.

island. I thought that you would like *Joh. Althusius* if you could penetrate the shell. I like all that man's[1] books, and his history of things in general as seen from the point of view of a student of corporations is full of good stuff, besides being to all appearance appallingly learned. I rather fancy that Hobbes's political feat consisted in giving a new twist to some well worn theories of the juristic order and then inventing a psychology which would justify that twist. I shall be very much interested to hear what you have to say about the old gentleman. A many years ago I saw in the Museum a copy of the *Leviathan* with a note telling how the wretched old atheist was buried head downwards or face downwards or something of the sort in a garden—a nice little legend in the making!

Have you read *De Mirabilibus Pecci*?[2] Stevenson the Anglo-Saxon scholar, who travelled outwards with me,[3] told me that the first recorded appearance of the name of the Peak (something like Pecesus) shows that the great cavern was called after the Devil's hinder parts. Did Hobbes know that? What a thing it is to be a philologer!

304. To Henry Jackson

[Printed by Fisher, *Memoir*, 132–3, with omissions. Now printed from the original in Camb. Univ. MSS.]

5 Leon y Castillo
Telde
Gran Canaria

1 Feb. 1902

MY DEAR JACKSON,

I am sorry indeed that the part of your letter to which I looked anxiously contained such bad news—and having said that I think that I won't say more—it is so useless.

The Spaniard ends his letter with S. S. S. Q. B. S. M.,[4] and I understand this to mean su seguro servidor que besa sus manos—but he puts it in even when he writes to the papers and there is no thought of any real kissing in the case. I send you two little bits of English (!) for decipherment.[5] They appear day by day and month by month in the *Diario de Las Palmas* and I hope that they are intelligible to its non-English readers. The said newspaper is one of some half dozen daily rags published in our 'ciudad'—I am surprised by their number. They seem largely to live upon ancient English papers—I mean papers which have taken a week to get here and have then been lying about in the hotels for another week or more. Hence queer snips from *Tit Bits*, etc.

---

[1] Gierke, whose book on Johannes Althusius M. had recommended to Stephen, esp. in view of Stephen's projected life of Hobbes: see M., *Life of L. S.*, 466.
[2] A Latin poem written by Hobbes between 1626 and 1628, describing a tour in the Peak District made in company with the second Earl of Devonshire: see Leslie Stephen, *Hobbes*, 14–15.
[3] See Letter 298, *supra*.
[4] See Letter 300, *supra*.   [5] Not extant.

Which makes me think of Acton. (His professed admiration of *Tit Bits* has some basis in fact: at least I once entered a railway carriage and found him deep in said paper.) What a prodigious catechism he addressed to you! I should like to have seen your reply.[1] As I write this, my stock of English papers is brought in. Someone has sent a copy of the Cambridge Chronicle and drawn my attention to a strange advertisement proceeding 'ex parte' the Hon. Richard[2]: I hope that this means much less than it might mean.

Many thanks for news of the History. I hope that all will go well now: I think that the team looks strong. I hear that I am to serve on the Press Syndicate: I doubt I shall do much good there—still I am quite willing to hear others talk and shall be interested in all that concerns the big book. I don't much like what you tell me of library affairs: I fancy that J. W.[3] must have been indiscreet, and who is to preside if you go?

These last weeks I have been doing splendidly and have got through a spell of copying which would never have been done had I stayed in England—as you say, life in Cambridge is an interruption. Buckland is a good companion and I think that we have taken our cycles where cycles have not been before: a crowd of ragged boys pursues—'chiquillos' convinced of our insanity.

If you have good news to give, give it.

Yours very truly

F. W. MAITLAND

'Dr. Rowland'[4] must have given you something to talk of.

305. To George Burton Adams

[Post-card.]

5 Leon y Castillo

Telde

Gran Canaria

23rd Feb. 1902

MY DEAR SIR,

Allow me to thank you cordially for your kindness in sending to me your paper on Anglo-Saxon Feudalism.[5] I have read it with great and admiring interest. How far we differ I am not quite certain: about that I shall have to make up my mind. But if I do differ it will be with reluctance and after much hesitation.

Renewing my thanks

I remain

Yours truly

F. W. MAITLAND

[1] Allusion obscure.
[2] Lord Acton's son and heir: the allusion is obscure.
[3] Perhaps John Westlake, Whewell Professor of International Law.
[4] Perhaps Sir R. Blennerhassett: see Letter 335, *infra.*
[5] *Anglo-Saxon Feudalism*, Amer. Hist. Rev. Vol. 7, pp. 1–35.

306. To F. J. H. Jenkinson

5 Leon y Castillo
Telde
Gran Canaria
2 March 1902

MY DEAR JENKINSON,

Before now I have offered premature congratulations—a painful experience —so I have delayed writing to you until I heard from more than one quarter of your felicity.[1] And now I think that I can certainly offer you my best wishes and admire your wisdom and good fortune. I hope that a great deal of happiness is in store for you. Do not make reply. I shall be in Cambridge by the middle of April and can then say more than I say now.

Of late I have been having a good time and have copied more of those MSS. than would have been copied had I not left England. I hope to restore them in good condition.[2]

With all my best wishes
Yours very truly

F. W. MAITLAND

307. To Melville M. Bigelow

5 Leon y Castillo
Telde
Gran Canaria
17 March 1902

MY DEAR BIGELOW,

I am truly grieved to hear this very bad news! From Thayer's books and papers I had formed a very high opinion of his powers and his views and during the too short visit that he paid to be [*sic*] in Gloucestershire[3] I felt that he must be a man to be admired and loved. I cannot but think him happy in the manner of his death,[4] though such blows fall very heavily on those who survive. It is some small satisfaction to me at this moment that this summer I with his permission dedicated a lecture to him.[5] I wanted him to know that his work was valued on our side of the sea. At Harvard the loss must be severely felt.

I regret to hear that the grip has had you for a victim. That it has long ago relaxed its hold I earnestly hope. We have all been doing well among the bananas and I have made good progress with Year Books. Now I must be packing up and facing Cambridge.

[1] On Jenkinson's marriage.
[2] See Intro. to S.S. Vol. 17, p. xc.
[3] See Letter 204, *supra*.
[4] [AULT. Thayer died at his home after an illness of a single day.]
[5] *English Law and the Renaissance.*

If you only lived where winters are mild, would not I accept your very kind invitation! As it is, I seem to want perpetual sunshine to keep me going.

My wife joins me in good wishes for you and Mrs. Bigelow.

Believe me

Yours very truly

F. W. MAITLAND

308. To B. Fossett Lock

Downing

17 April 1902

DEAR LOCK,

This is to say that I am back. I had Turner with me in the Canaries. I think that the outing did him a great deal of good. He has not yet returned and I fear may have fallen in love with the land of 'mañana'. He has sworn to work for me during the next months and I have some hopes of keeping him to the task by a system of payment by results. He is very flighty, but on the other hand he knows a lot and at the moment professes a great desire to help me. So I have a little hope.

I see a good deal of accumulated Leadam[1] that I must at once read.

If you could give me and Cambridge a week-end I should be delighted. For about a month I am in bachelorhood, for the family lingers behind.

Yours very truly

F. W. MAITLAND

309. To George Burton Adams

Downing College

Cambridge

17 April 1902

MY DEAR SIR,

Yesterday I landed in England and found awaiting me your kind letter of 24 March and a second (or rather the first) copy of your very interesting article.[2] I feel that I must at once thank you, but at the same time I fear that some weeks or even months must pass before I can say anything that will even look like an answer to your observations. However I can at once add that with the main theme of your letter I am in cordial agreement.[3] It is a pity that we are bound to speculate about these 'might have beens'; but this seems our only way of stating what we think to be the chain of cause and effect.

Perhaps some day I may have the pleasure of welcoming you to Cambridge.

Believe me

Yours very truly

F. W. MAITLAND

---

[1] S.S. Vol. 16. [2] See Letter 305, *supra.*

[3] Adams' letter is not extant; but from a rough draft preserved in Yale University Library it would seem to have contained some qualifications of his article.

310. To John Chipman Gray

[No original. Printed by Fisher, *Memoir*, 134: no beginning or ending. The date seems doubtful: cf. Letters 308 and 309, *supra*. Perhaps M. wrote 19 April for 17 April.]

Downing College,
Cambridge.

19 April, 1902.

I returned yesterday from a winter spent in the Canaries where I am compelled to take refuge. Already I have read your article[1] about gifts for non-charitable purposes and have been delighted by it. It puts an accent on what I think a matter of great historical importance—namely the extreme liberality of our law about charitable trusts. It seems to me that our people slid unconsciously from the enforcement of the rights of a c.q.t.[2] to the establishment of trusts without a c.q.t.—the so-called charitable trusts: and I think that continental law shows that this was a step that would not and could not be taken by men whose heads were full of Roman Law. *Practically* the private man who creates a charitable trust does something that is very like the creation of an artificial person, and does it without asking leave of the State.

I only saw Thayer for a few hours, but I feel his death as the death of a friend. The loss must be deeply felt at Harvard.

311. To R. Lane Poole

Downing

22 April 1902

MY DEAR ~~Pol~~ POOLE (I was nigh to omitting an o),

I am sorry that I added 1 to 63.[3] I also have been and am suffering under accumulated circulars, presentation copies, proofs, etc.

When (if ever) you have a little time to spare you will earn warm thanks from me if you could tell me of any young man who would be willing to help me over Year Books. I fear it is necessary that he should be moderately well to do, for the pay that is to be had at present is very modest. But I think that there is an opening which might lead in course of time to a 'competence', a little good repute and possibly a professorship. Some persons of importance including law lords and the like are moving at the Inns, and I think that if we began well money would come—and about 200 fair-sized volumes ought to be produced sooner or later. I think that there is a prospect for a young man who could afford to wait. I shall not stand in his way very long, and while he was my co-adjutor *cum spe successionis* I would teach him what I know and give him a liberal share of what money comes my way. Good health, industry and a little enthusiasm are main desiderata.

Baildon finds more profitable work: Rigg's eyesight is I fear failing, and I cannot rely on Turner except for brief spurts. Have you a diplomatic pupil

---

[1] *Gifts for Non-Charitable Purposes* (1903), Harv. L. Rev. XV. 509.
[2] Cestui que trust.
[3] Allusion obscure.

whom you could recommend? Do not answer until you have leisure. If hereafter a name occurs to you I shall be glad to know it. We may be at the beginning of a very big affair—but the project will fail if I have to tackle it single handed.

As I read Savine's admirable article[1] I said to myself—What splendid English these Russians write.

I fear that I must not go a-gleaning in the Elizabethan field while the YBB. sit so heavy upon my soul. But by the way may I ask you whether James Gairdner has not during my last absence published something about Amy Robsart? You if any one will know. I have a half written note about her.[2] Do not be in a hurry to answer.

I will try to make time for Tait. I hope that you like Rigg's Jews. Proofs of Leadam's Star Chamber are pouring in.[3]

Yours very truly

F. W. MAITLAND

312. To Harold D. Hazeltine

Downing College
Cambridge.

24 April 1902.

MY DEAR SIR,

I should like to meet you.[4] On Saturday I may have to go to London. But can you come on Monday, e.g. by a train that leaves King's Cross at 11.10? This would bring you to my house in College just before I finished lecturing, but at 1.0 we would lunch.

Yours very truly

F. W. MAITLAND

313. To Henry Jackson

Downing

5 May 1902

MY DEAR JACKSON,

I fear that I can't get to the Eranus to-morrow. After the walk from Newnham the other night I had a bad bout with the fiend that persecutes me and I

---

[1] [A.L.P. Alexander Savine, *Copyhold Cases in the early Chancery Proceedings*, E.H.R. (1902) 296.]

[2] M. refers to her story in his Chap. XVI of the Camb. Mod. Hist., vol. II. James Gairdner (1828–1912) was at the Public Record Office from 1846 to 1893. He published, *inter alia*, *Lollardy and the Reformation of England*, 4 vols., 1908–12, and edited the *Paston Letters* and volumes in R.S. and Camden Society.

[3] S.S. Vols. 15 and 16 respectively. The allusion to Tait (presumably James) is obscure.

[4] Hazeltine had come to London to pursue legal research in the British Museum and the Inner Temple and had written to ask M. if he might call upon him in Cambridge. M. was then giving a course of lectures on Equity, posthumously pub. 1909 as edited by A. J. Chaytor and W. J. Whittaker (see Notes by H. D. Hazeltine now in the Harv. Law School Library). See also Hollond, *Harold Dexter Hazeltine*, Proceedings of the British Academy (1961), at p. 314.

am compelled to argue *post hoc ergo propter hoc*. Just for a bit I must forswear going out of nights—otherwise I may be useless. So forgive me for not accepting.

N.B. The Society[1] dines with me next Monday, May 12th. I think that we shall dine in the Combination Room and at 7.45. I have just read that my family will be returning on or about that day and my house may be topsy turvy. I will send you another note betimes.

Yours very truly

F. W. MAITLAND

Have you heard bad news of Leslie Stephen? I fear that his case is but too like Sidgwick's. This is not being said openly, but I have little doubt. I went up to see him a few days ago: he was cheerful but, as you may suppose, without illusions.[2]

314. To H. A. L. Fisher

Downing

6 May 1902

MY DEAR HERBERT,

Many thanks for your invitation. Were I to stay in Oxford you do not doubt where I should wish to be. But I am not going to the Ambarum.[3] (1) I think that Florence is at sea and may arrive any day. She tells me by wire that her boat is the Nigeria—I cannot discover any such boat and consequently am perplexed—but I hope to see her on Sat. Sun. or Mon. (2) That cold wind went and undid a lot of the good done by three glorious months and last week I had some real bad days. I went up to town to see the philosopher.[4] I deeply fear that he has heard a sentence from which there is no appeal and that any reprieve will be but for a short time. (I don't know what is thought or said in his home circle—so you will, I know, be careful at this point: but I gather it is Sidgwick's case over again.) It is very sad: he, as you would expect, is courageous and is writing the little book on Hobbes and some Ford lectures.[5] We had a pleasant talk.

You must certainly come here on May 15 and I badly want a talk with you. F. also will wish to see you. We will do what we can for your comfort.

Yours affectly

F. W. MAITLAND

[1] See Letter 278, *supra*.
[2] In April 1902 Stephen had been told that he had cancer.
[3] An Oxford and Cambridge dining club.
[4] Leslie Stephen. In a letter to M. of 16 Feb. 1901 (Camb. Univ. MSS.) Stephen had said that he was writing a number of articles, 'not very exalted work but good enough for a decayed "philosopher"—as Florence gave me that name I accept it'.
[5] *English Literature and Society in the Eighteenth Century.*

315. To B. Fossett Lock

Downing College
Cambridge
18 May 1902

MY DEAR LOCK,

I think you will be glad to know that little Turner is doing well. In a fortnight he has found a very respectable number of my cases and if he keeps going for another fortnight the bulk of the work to be done at P.R.O. will be safe in note books. When he works he is worth ever so many B.'s.[1]

My lectures are almost done. One of my first visits will be to Linc. Inn. Will you in the meantime consider the question—to whom among the Benchers should I address myself if I want to borrow a MS? Horwood in a preface tells how he had a Linc. Inn. MS lent to him.[2]

I am thinking of getting photographs from a Bodleian MS.

I hope that you are getting a Pentecostal holiday.

Yours very truly
F. W. MAITLAND

316. To B. Fossett Lock

Downing College
Cambridge
25 May 1902

MY DEAR LOCK,

The enclosed letter from Chas. C. Soule crossed one from me which was in the nature of a feeler. I regret to hear of this movement because I don't think that it will come to any really good result.[3] It does not quite please me to learn that C. C. S. had 'a satisfactory talk with Mr. Pike', for I should have thought that Pike would have told him that a 'scholarly translation' of the existing text was out of the question. Will you give a thought to the question whether we could in any way turn to our advantage the wind that the enterprising man is raising? The nature of my reply to him would be influenced by your opinion. I don't want to water any spark of grace.

I hope to be in Lincoln's Inn on Thursday next and to get a look at the YBB. Photographs are coming from Oxford.

Yours very truly
F. W. MAITLAND

[1] Baildon.

[2] See A. J. Horwood's preface to R.S. Y.B. 30 and 31 Edw. I, p. liii. M. used a Lincoln's Inn MS. in S.S. Vol. 17: see Intro. lxxxix–xc.

[3] M.'s letter to Soule is not extant. In his letter to M. (Boston, 13 May 1902) Soule wrote that he was planning a reprint of the printed Year Books with 'a scholarly translation' and that the 'professors of the Harvard Law School are very eager in the matter' (Camb. Univ. MSS.).

317. To R. Lane Poole

Downing

22 June 1902

MY DEAR POOLE,

Have I been too free with my pen? The 'five rolls' were puzzling, for I thought of the Pentateuch. I was afraid that J. M. Rigg would get himself into a little trouble by finding a grain of truth in the crucifixion stories. The good F. Liebermann is more crabbed than usual.[1]

And so you must have yet another 'éloge' in the E.H.R. I shall never forget a few talks that I had with Acton. He seemed to know all the letters that ever were written, especially the most private. In a short time he did an enormous deal to improve the position of history here and I think the loss irreparable.[2]

I am troubled by a man who went to some place 'in the sea of Greece' which my MSS. call 'Ypeta, Ypota, Spota, Spoca'. Can you give me any help? If not, can you and will you give me a note of introduction to Bury[3] whom I suppose you know well? He, if any one, might deliver me.

I am labouring with Year Books—not very hopefully.

I hope that you have seen the end of Oxford drudgery for a while.

Yours very truly

F. W. MAITLAND

318. To Henry Jackson

Downing College,
Cambridge

26 June 1902

MY DEAR JACKSON,

I don't suppose that you often happen to want news from Cambridge and I don't know that I have any to give. But when the news came of Acton's death I wanted to have a talk about him with you and should have gone to see you had you not been away. There was a requiem yesterday at the R.C. church. The V.C. announced it to residents. I went. A good many folk were there— the V.C., Stokes, Foster, Butler—who was about the only Anglican parson in the assembly—Forsyth, H. M. Taylor, perhaps as many as could be expected at this time of year.[4] I am inclined to think that on such an occasion a language not understood by the vulgar and not really heard by any one is the best. I

---

1 See Rigg's Intro. to S.S. Vol. 15 and Liebermann's review in E.H.R. (1902) 551.
2 [A.L.P. Lord Acton died at Tegernsee on 19 June 1902.]
3 John Bagnell Bury (1861–1927), Professor of Modern History, Trinity College, Dublin, 1893–1902, Regius Professor of Modern History, Cambridge, 1902–27: pub. *History of the Later Roman Empire* (1889), *History of Greece to death of Alexander the Great* (1900), etc. See also Letters 320 and 322, *infra*.
4 Sir George Stokes (1819–1903), Lucasian Professor of Mathematics 1849–1903, Master of Pembroke College, Cambridge, 1902–3: Sir Michael Foster (1836–1907), Professor of Physiology, Cambridge: A. R. Forsyth, Sedleian Professor of Pure Mathematics 1895–1910: H. M. Taylor, mathematician and Fellow of Trinity College, Cambridge (see Hollond, *Frederic William Maitland*, 6).

just caught the mention of the Sibyl[1] in the Dies Irae—not much more. I know that you will agree with me in thinking that the loss to Cambridge is very severe. It seems to me that Acton did an enormous deal of good in the history school in a wonderfully short time.

I want to tell you how very much I was interested by your allocution from the apostolic chair.[2] I would not have lost a word—nobody else could have done it and this was agreed by all. It was exactly what we wanted from you and glad am I that I did not stay away. You are now I suppose at Bournemouth[3]: you know what my wishes are.

The news has just come that Leslie Stephen is to be K.C.B. I am glad. I think that at this time it will cheer him. Of the rest of what is in the papers there is no need to speak.[4]

Shall you come to the Press Syndicate? It meets I think in the Long.[5]

Yours very truly

F. W. MAITLAND

319. To Leslie Stephen

[No original. Typed transcript in Camb. Univ. MSS.]

Downing

26 June 1902

MY DEAR LESLIE,

My congratulations are not from the teeth outwards. I really was overjoyed this morning by what I saw about you in the Times and have been thinking of it ever since. I am right glad that on this occasion the King has spoken the meaning of the wise and good and I hope that this comes pleasantly to you. As to H. M., I the more heartily wish him well—and you too, may you long reign over us. For the rest[6] I feel that I am living in melodrama or a bad sort of novel. Nature does not generally admit these climaxes.

I hardly know how to address you. Do you want dubbing—like a pair of boots? I think that you must be content with 'Esq.', though perhaps for the last time.

I went to a requiem for Acton yesterday. Perhaps there is much to be said for the obscurity of a dead language on such an occasion. We were spared that chapter of St. Paul on which you commented in an essay read by me for the 20th time last week.[7] 'Teste David cum Sibylla' sounds very queer if you

---

1 Dies irae, dies illa
  Solvet saeclum in favilla
  Teste David cum Sibylla (*Dies Irae*, verse 1).
2 The Apostles.
3 From 1895 onwards Mrs. Jackson's health had compelled her to live in Bournemouth.
4 The K.C.B. was awarded to Leslie Stephen as one of the Coronation Honours. Edward VII was to have been crowned on 26 June 1902, but his illness necessitated a postponement.
5 Vacation.
6 Presumably the postponed Coronation, its cause and effects: see Letter 318, *supra*.
7 *Dreams and Realities*, in *An Agnostic's Apology* (1893), pp. 86–126: see M. *Life of L. S.*, 281.

catch it—for you ask what the Sybil had to do with it.[1] And then they sprinkled and censed an empty coffin, and so on. Well, the loss here at Cambridge is I think irreparable.

But to return once more. I wish you all the joy that is to be had and the conviction—a very true conviction—that countless people are glad to see you honoured.

Yours very affectionately

F. W. MAITLAND

Acton once spoke to me very warmly of a certain Hist. of Engl. Thought.[2]

320. To R. Lane Poole

Downing College

27 June 1902

MY DEAR POOLE,

It will not I hope be impertinent in me to urge you to write yourself what should be said of Lord Acton. I can't think that either of your reasons for hesitation is really valid. Any one, if such there be, who really knows the inside of the infallibility episode would be likely to make a deal too much of it and could hardly tell his story without vouching chapter and verse, for I take it that many people would be eager to controvert any statement of such of the facts as are not generally known. And then I don't see that you are called upon to swear to Mr. G.'s first ministry. On the other hand it is for you to represent just the sort of learning that Acton had.[3]

As to my Ypota or Spoca I am downright grateful to you for what seems a very valuable suggestion. In 1308 a lady demanded dower. The reply was—'Your husband is still alive'. She answered 'He is dead'.—'Where did he die?'—'At Spoca in the sea of Greece'. It has just occurred to me, however, that when the Univ. Library opens I may find help—for the plea roll shows that the husband in question was a Sir John Mandeville of Marshwood, and I feel sure that the adventures of every bearer of that name must have been closely scrutinized by Yule and Warner.[4]

Yours very truly

F. W. MAITLAND

[1] See Letter 318, *supra*.

[2] Leslie Stephen, *History of English Thought in the Eighteenth Century* (1876).

[3] Poole wrote Acton's obituary in E.H.R. (1902) 692. Acton opposed the dogma of Papal infallibility. He was a close friend of Gladstone and influenced him in such matters as Irish Home Rule and Disestablishment.

[4] See S.S. Vol. 17, pp. 22–3. [A.L.P. Sir Henry Yule, editor of Marco Polo and many works for the Hakluyt Society: Sir George Warner, editor of the travels of Sir John Mandeville (Roxburghe Club, 1889).] See also Letters 317, *supra*, and 322, *infra*.

321. To R. Lane Poole

[No date, but from contents and context early July 1902: no address heading.]

[July 1902]

DEAR POOLE,

Enormous thanks for the Paston Letters.[1] I am really grateful.

Your apology was absolutely unnecessary—but still my sister thanks you.

The inevitable movement for a memorial has begun. I had just time to say to the mover that you were one of the very first persons to be consulted. Said mover is Whitehead of Trinity. I believe that he is near the top of our mathematical tree. You may hear from him or from A. W. W. I have been rushing round all day talking of this to Selden people.[2]

With renewed thanks,

Yours very truly

F. W. MAITLAND

322. To Henry Jackson

[Printed in part by Fisher, *Memoir*, 134–5. Now printed from the original in Camb. Univ. MSS.]

Downing

6 July 1902

DEAR JACKSON,

You repay me my letter with usurious interest. However you are *sui juris*—or ought I to say *tui*?—and I doubt a court of equity would extend to you the protection which it bestows on improvident young gentlemen.

No, I had nothing to write of Acton. A few memorable talks on Sunday afternoons were all I had. To my great regret I did not hear the first of the Eranus papers—nor the outburst about the murder of a prostitute. Some day I must get you to tell that story for I have heard more than one version and I know that I can trust your memory.

What the literary Nachlass is like I cannot tell and am not likely to know. I saw the notes for an introductory chapter confided to Figgis.[3] They seemed to me to be quite useless in the hands of anyone save him who made them. They struck me as very sad: the notes of a man who could not bring to the birth the multitude of thoughts that were crowding in his mind. I very much fear that the introductory chapter was among the causes of the collapse. (By the way I gather from Allbutt[4] that the immediate cause of death was, as A. put it, 'in the water works'). I hope that the English Historical will get a good memoir. The Editor is taking trouble about it.

[1] Ed. by James Gairdner (1900).

[2] The memorial was presumably to Lord Acton. A. W. W.=A. W. Ward.

[3] In his life of Acton in D.N.B. the Rev. J. N. Figgis (1866–1919) wrote: 'The notes prepared for what should have been the first chapter [in the Camb. Mod. Hist.] on "The Legacy of the Middle Ages" were not sufficiently advanced for publication.' J. N. Figgis was Lecturer of St. Catherine's College, Cambridge, from 1896 to 1902 and afterwards a member of the Community of the Resurrection at Mirfield: he pub. *The Divine Right of Kings* (1896) and *From Gerson to Grotius* (1907), etc.

[4] Sir T. C. Allbutt (1836–1925), Regius Professor of Physic, Cambridge.

Whom shall we have here as Regius? I am speculating as to what Ward would do if an offer came his way—as I suppose that it very well might. I hear nothing from Trinity Hall.[1] But I have been hearing nothing at all this fortnight. Cambridge has been beatifically empty. I have been happy in the warmth and have been putting on steam to get some editing done. To-morrow I must begin lecturing: it is an unpleasant interruption—but I shall soon be hearing a little talk.

Have you seen Sidgwick's small book on philosophy?[2] I think it is in some respects the most Sidgwickian thing that is in print. I can hear most of it—some of it from the hearth-rug or at the Eranus.

I think that the K.C.B. came to Stephen just at the right moment and that he is really pleased by it. About his condition I don't know the exact truth. The good thing is that there is little discomfort. He is writing Ford Lectures for Oxford, but says that he will not be able to deliver them. Have you seen in his *George Eliot* the remark about Edmund Gurney? 'I have always fancied —though without any evidence—that some touches in Deronda were drawn from one of her friends, Edmund Gurney, a man of remarkable charm of character and as good-looking as Deronda' (p. 191). What think you?[3]

Can you give me any help in finding a place that ought to be in Greece or thereabouts? In 1308 a lady says that her husband died 'at the town of Ypota (var. Ypeta, Spoca) in the sea of Greece'. I should not take much trouble over her only unfortunately it happens that her husband was by name 'Sir John Maundeville', and anything showing that a man of that name ever was as far east as 'the sea of Greece' will be used in discussions with which I have no concern. I am thinking of Hippola. R. L. Poole suggested Sibota, a small island (which I can't find) between Corfu and the mainland. Does anything occur to you? The learned, I gather, say that there never was no Sir J. M., or rather that no Sir J. M. wrote the famous book.[4]

Yours very truly

F. W. MAITLAND

323. To Henry Jackson

[M. wrote the year as 1903: but contents and context show that this was a mistake for 1902.]

Downing College
Cambridge
13 July [1902]

MY DEAR JACKSON,

Thanks for divers favours and in particular for Hypata.[5] It looks very nice. The name seems to exist in modern times in the form Hypati and so may have

---

[1] The Mastership was vacant by the death of the Rev. Henry Latham.
[2] *Philosophy, Its Scope and Relations: An Introductory Course of Lectures* (pub. posth, 1902).
[3] Leslie Stephen's *George Eliot*, pub. 1902 in the *English Men of Letters* series.
[4] On this paragraph see Letters 317 and 320, *supra*.
[5] On the whole of this paragraph see Letter 322, *supra*.

traversed the middle ages; but I read that the town was then known as Neo-patra and was the capital of a Wallachian prince. I have had a vain hunt in what seemed the best place, namely indexes to books published by the (French) 'Latin Orient Society'—itineraries to Jerusalem, chronicles of crusades, etc. In the last resort I shall appeal to Bury. My Hippola is a little north of Matapan on the Messenian Gulf side—but your place looks better despite its distance from the sea.

Thanks also in the matter of what was said by Kennedy, J. I have talked to Bond and the hint will not be lost. It is a sign of grace—or of a fear that will do as well as grace—but I wish that it had been seen in some one more influential than Kennedy, e.g. in Macnaghten. It is curious that the worst enemies of legal education have been highly educated men—on the other hand we lost much when Charles Russell died. E. C. Clark is very reasonable about this affair—very willing to make concessions to the Inns and so on. Kenny's book on Criminal Law is very good reading and I think that it will do us a lot of good in the country.[1]

No, I don't think that I would give up law for history if I had the chance.[2] But though I can believe a good deal of H.M.'s present advisers I can't be-lieve that they would go far out of their way into a scandal—for no less it would be. But without explaining why other grapes are sour, I can say that what grapes I have are sweet. We are a peaceful lot at the Law Board and my colleagues are exceedingly kind to me. I have not to contend with a Gw–tk–n, a M–rs–ll, an O. B. and a couple of archaeologists.[3] All that could weigh on the other side would be a wish to see Kenny in my present shoes 'and which' ought to be his. But I don't know that he would wish me to leave Downing at this moment. Common fame has probably told you that we are not altogether at peace in this little college. As to the main matter I hear no names but those of Ward and Prothero. The figure of Lecky[4] has crossed my view. Of the people at Oxford Firth is the most distinguished.

I spoke to Wright[5] about Acton's papers, lectures, etc. He said that he was writing to you and seemed to think that Ward had done what was possible.

By the way it was said to me that Carnegie, having Acton's books on hand,

[1] Jackson's letter is not extant, but this paragraph seems concerned with the relations between the University and the Council of Legal Education. Sir W. R. Kennedy (1849–1915), Judge, Q.B.D., 1892–1907, Lord Justice 1907–15: Lord Macnaghten (1830–1913), Lord of Appeal 1887–1913, Chairman of the Council of Legal Education 1895–1913: Lord Russell of Killowen (1832–1900), Lord Chief Justice of England 1894–1900: Henry Bond (1853–1938), Fellow of Trinity Hall, Cambridge, 1887–1912, Master 1912–29.

[2] M. here refers to a suggestion that he might succeed Lord Acton as Regius Professor of Modern History. See Letter 343, *infra*.

[3] H. M. Gwatkin (1844–1916), Professor of Ecclesiastical History 1891–1916: Alfred Marshall: Oscar Browning. The archaeologists were presumably Sir William Ridgway (1832–1926), Professor of Archaeology, and Sir Charles Waldstein (afterwards Walston), 1856–1927, Professor of Fine Art.

[4] William Edward Hartpole Lecky (1838–1903), author of *History of Rationalism*, 1865, *History of European Morals*, 1869, *History of England in the Eighteenth Century*, 8 vols., 1878–90.

[5] William Aldis Wright (1836–1914), Fellow of Trinity College, Cambridge; editor of the Cambridge Shakespeare and literary executor of Edward Fitzgerald, whose works and letters he edited.

might be on the look-out for a donee: also that he was approachable through John Morley. Do you think that you could put in a word for the University Library? I think that you know J. M. very well. What the link is between him and the rich man I don't know, but I am told that it exists.[1]

Your French idioms beat me. The 'Anglo-French' that I am writing would astonish you. It is still quite pure of English words temp. Edw. II, but as regards spelling each clerk seems to have his own private usage and an *e* is shoved in or left out in a most puzzling fashion.

Yours very truly

F. W. MAITLAND

I walked with E. Gurney in the Tyrol. What moods he had! On a good day it was a joy to hear him laugh. I think your criticism of Stephen's remark is probably right.[2] The K.C.B. never wants for a word. Do you remember how he writes of persons who have 'thrown Noah's flood overboard'?

324. To B. Fossett Lock

Downing College

Cambridge

13 July 1902

DEAR LOCK,

Some day when you have leisure give me your thoughts about the specimen of a Year Book which I suppose that you have received from Spottiswoode.[3]

I. As to matter—am I making too much of the record? The result of course will be that we shall make very slow progress. Here are 10 of our pages corresponding to less than a page of the old folio. At that rate it will take us or our heirs 20 volumes and 40 years to see the end of this 'agonizing king'.[4] But I think that a few cases thoroughly done may be worth many cases unexplained.

II. As to form—please speak your mind. Some of the pages will I fear look sprawly—like page 4: but, given as unalterable the shape of the page, I have only minor improvements to suggest. The chief are:—

(a) Names of cases must be bolder; e.g. try small pica caps.

(b) Begin a numeration of foot-notes on each page—see p. 2.

(c) Leave less space between the variants at the foot of the Latin page. Will you look at the way in which variants are printed in the 'Court Baron'[5] and tell me which mode you like best?

(d) In such a case as that shown by p. 2 (English) would you bring over the beginning of the note from p. 3 (English)? I think that I would.

---

[1] Andrew Carnegie acquired Acton's library of over 59,000 vols. and gave it to John Morley, who in 1903 gave it to Cambridge University.
[2] See Letter 322, *supra*. Jackson's criticism is lost with his letter.
[3] The printer.
[4] Edward II.
[5] S.S. Vol. 4.

(e) I should like to balance on the Latin side the head-note on the English side and don't see how to do it. Shall I get rid of head-notes? Your advice at this point will be highly valued.

(f) The numeration of cases to be bolder and carried into margin.

I am sorry to trouble you with so many details—but we may be setting a precedent. Would you rather talk than write? If so, I will run to London.

Soule is coming here[1] to collogue with Green about reprint and translation. I am writing to tell him that a reprint without correction from at least one MS will be a scandal. I fear that I may not see him until he has seen Green in Edinburgh.

> Believe me
> Yours very truly
>
> F. W. Maitland

325. To Henry Jackson

> Downing College
> Cambridge
>
> *1 Augt. 1902*

Dear Jackson,

I was on the point of asking you whether you held the key to the Morley cum Carnegie riddle. It beats me: and I have not met anybody who even professes to understand it. I pray that J. M. may be convinced that this loyal body still wants learning.[2] If so, let him be Lit.D.

May be that on the 10th I may have a glimpse of you at Trinity.

R. V. Lawrence is to edit the Lectures.[3]

By the way, in the Athenaeum article[4] 'the philosopher' was, so I should guess, Hegel: but the guess may be bad. One of the younger people here must have written it.

> Yours very truly
>
> F. W. Maitland

[1] I.e. to the United Kingdom. Green was the Edinburgh publisher of *The English Reports* (series begun in 1900). See Letter 316, *supra*. M.'s letter to Soule is not extant, but see Letter 330, *infra*.

[2] 'Our royal master saw, with heedful eyes,
The wants of his two universities:
Troops he to Oxford sent, as knowing why
That learned body wanted loyalty:
But books to Cambridge gave, as well discerning
That that right loyal body wanted learning.'
(Anecdotes of the late Samuel Johnson, LL.D., by Mrs. Piozzi: Camb. ed. 1925, p. 28.)
On the first paragraph of this letter, see Letter 323, *supra*.

[3] Acton's *Lectures on Modern History* were edited by J. N. Figgis and R. V. Lawrence (1906).

[4] On Acton.

326. To B. Fossett Lock

Downing College
Cambridge
3 Augt. 1902

My dear Lock,

Many thanks for your letter. I will take the course that you suggest. I think that we have now done all that we can to make the book look pretty.[1] You suggested that I should write a memorandum about the matter. I have done so and here it is.[2] I leave it for you to decide whether use should be made of it. Also I authorize you to improve it as you think best.

I have got into shape my discourse on language which I mean to be the larger part of my Introduction.[3] I have a mind to send it to the press so as to save time hereafter and I should like it to pass under the eyes of one or two learned friends. Will you authorize this step? I don't press if there are objections.

Yours very truly
F. W. Maitland

TO THE MEMBERS OF THE COUNCIL OF THE SELDEN SOCIETY

Herewith are sent specimen pages of the projected edition of the Year Books of Edward II. The editor is desirous of knowing whether the plan which he is adopting meets with the approval of members of the Council, and he will be very grateful for criticisms and suggestions.

The most important question is how to utilize the information which is being obtained from the record (plea-rolls). Some practical difficulties would be avoided if all of this were printed at the end of the book in an appendix. On the other hand it seems desirable that the record or an English abstract of the record should be brought into close proximity with the report: this was the course taken by Plowden and Saunders when they published their own reports.

But as the editor is to give on opposite pages the French text of the report and an English translation of it, a place for the matter that is taken from the record cannot very easily be found. If it were all put on the left-hand or all on the right-hand pages, the result would be a great deal of blank paper: so an attempt has been made to divide it between the two pages. Where the Latin record contains pleas or other matter of sufficient importance to demand verbatim reproduction, the Latin extract is placed on the left-hand page and an English note on the right-hand page. Where no extract from the record seems to require verbatim reproduction, the English note of the record will be begun on the left-hand page and continued on the right-hand page. The

[1] S.S. Vol. 17: see Letter 324, *supra*.
[2] It is here printed immediately after this letter.
[3] S.S. Vol. 17, Intro. xxxiii–lxxxi.

result is not altogether satisfactory; but on the whole it seems to the editor that all other courses are open to more serious objections.

In the manuscripts the report of a case generally has a short marginal note set against it. The origin of these notes, which vary from copy to copy, cannot be determined. They are often very rough and sometimes become a mere string of catch words. While printing one of these at the head of the case, the editor has endeavoured to utilize the corresponding space on the opposite page by inserting an English head-note of his own which should draw attention to what seems to be the point of the case.

327. To B. Fossett Lock

Downing College,
Cambridge

11 Augt. 1902

My dear Lock,

I am sorry to trouble you again and so soon, but there seems no help for it.

This morning came the enclosed from Soule.[1] I have replied to it briefly explaining my view, namely that there can be nothing that is worth doing done for the Year Books without the formation of a good French text with sufficient notes from the records. I said that if this is meant I am friendly—but that if a 'reprint' is meant I am hostile. I sent him our specimen page to show the sort of thing that wanted doing—and about a republication of the old text I used strong words.

Now will you turn over in your mind the question how this affects our own scheme? As regards the Society, I merely said that if Green's project really covered the ground I thought it possible that the Society would not wish to do one little piece of what was being done by others on a large scale—but that on the other hand anything in the way of a reprint would afford the best of reasons why we should press on with the task. I further gave him to understand that the volume for 1903 is going to appear.

And now what to do? Address ourselves to Green and inquire what is really being done—saying that our own arrangements may depend on the answer? If so, shall I draft a letter and send it to you for approval?

My own feeling is that perhaps Green might be induced to allow money and time enough for the production of something not discreditable—he seems to have secured Pike's adhesion and Pike would not allow what was very bad to

---

[1] Soule had written from Oxford on 10 Aug. 1902 (S.S. Corr.) to say that he had spoken to Green in Edinburgh, to Pike in London and to Markby in Oxford, and that all were 'hopeful' of the project for a new edition of the YBB. 'We have all come to the conclusion that an Editorial corps of ten or a dozen . . . could get out a good preliminary translation in three or four years.' Pike would compare MSS in London if the printed text was obscure. In America Ames and others 'were eager to do what they can'. Soule regretted that he had not time to visit M., 'the most scholarly of all', but hoped for his collaboration. M.'s reply to Soule is not extant, but its tenor is clear from the present letter. See also Letters 324, *supra*, and 329, 330 and 339, *infra*.

appear over or under his name. Perhaps this may be the real solution of the Year Book problem, so far as this generation can solve it—and if the Society saw something tolerable appearing or likely to appear, the Society might well devote its money to other tasks.

Meanwhile I think there is nothing to impede our publishing a volume in 1903. I think that in any case this may do good. I think that the projectors will see that their Vol. I will come under the eyes of someone who knows a little about the MSS of Edward II, and this may screw up their standard a bit.

However the point about which your counsel is needful at the moment is the ascertainment of the character of the project. Do you approve of a letter to Green? If so, shall I sketch it? Or do you think that you could get the information elsewhere, e.g. from Pike? (I don't think Markby would be useful.)

'And to advise generally upon the case'—I wish that I could add blank gūas.

Yours perplexedly

F. W. MAITLAND

328. To Mrs. Jenkinson

Downing College,
Cambridge

12 Aug. 1902

DEAR MRS. JENKINSON,

The Russian Vinogradoff, who is known to your husband, is to be here with his wife at the beginning of next week. Would you consent to dine here on Monday the 18th at 7.45? I know that Vinogradoff would like to meet Jenkinson. I cannot say for certain whether my wife will be here or no: at the moment she is in Gloucestershire: but I shall be delighted if you can come.

Yours very truly

F. W. MAITLAND

329. To B. Fossett Lock

Downing College
Cambridge

13 Augt. 1902

MY DEAR LOCK,

I think that I can write a letter to you that will not require an answer. Not but that I am grateful indeed to you for all that you have written,[1] but now that vacation comes I do not mean to burden you.

---

[1] Lock had written on 12 Aug. 1902 (S.S. Corr.) suggesting (a) that M. 'warn Green off Edward II as occupied ground: let him do the rest, *if he can*'; (b) that 'we get our first volume out in good time and they will soon have to come to you for help'. He added that the Society will not draw back from the work 'if you are willing to go on with it', save in the one possible case that to do so would be greatly to M.'s financial advantage. He was sorry that M. had given Soule the specimen page: see Letter 327, *supra*.

I feel quite at ease now about Soule. You have I think a little misunderstood the trouble that his letter caused me. The thought of bargaining with him for a place in his scheme together with some shekels never crossed my mind—and a desertion of the Selden Society, so long as the Society can get any good out of me, I should regard as very base. What I did fear, perhaps unnecessarily, was that the Selden might within a few years consider that enough was being done for the Year Books by other hands. And I still think that hereafter this may be a reasonable or at any rate a pardonable opinion. I can't think that people like Ames and Pike will like to be mixed up with anything that is really discreditable, and it seems to me possible that they may screw up the scheme of translation to a decent pitch—so that people will be able to say, 'Well, we have in English the legal grit of these books and that is all we want'. (If they are wise they will begin with some late books—they are much easier, partly because they were soon printed, partly because the French has become a grammarless professional jargon with limited vocabulary). However all this lies in the future; and if even while I live the Society says, 'We have had Year Books enough', I shall not be discontented.

As to the present you have quite reassured me. I may regard it as certain that if I live vol. 1 will appear—and if I have to run away this winter I shall go on with the copying for vol. 2 and perhaps vol. 3, hoping that I or someone else will make something of my transcript. On the whole my tenure of life and strength (and certain other affairs with which I need not trouble yr. l'dship) being what they are, I do not see any other work for me that is so likely to be of use. So the Society can reckon on my copying so long as copy is wanted and I can make it. And after what you say I don't think it is my duty or yours (if you agree with me) to bring the Green affair before the Council. If any member wishes to stay my hand it is for him to move.

Nor do I see any need at present for communicating with Green or Pike. This time next year when I am giving a last touch to the last sheet of introduction some knowledge of the lie of the land may be valuable. At present what I have written is very friendly to Pike—and I mildly controvert the opinion 'perhaps held by some' that the books could be translated without the making of a new French text.[1] Meanwhile I think it is for the other people to move. Of course, if a 'reprint' is hurried out in the interval, the string of my tongue will be loosened. Soule well knows this—I promised him 'uncompromising hostility' and a 'protest'. I spoke so strongly and ended with so solemn a 'liberavi animam' that after all I did not write again to withdraw the specimen page— though I had better not have sent it. I don't think that it can do much harm and I did not want to suggest to him that we dreaded any use that he could make of it.

I should now be quite happy about the whole affair if only I saw my successor. Perhaps a published volume may help us to find him. Meanwhile Turner is all that I can wish. Do you remember that obscure third case on the specimen page? Little T. has found the record—I doubt any one else would

---

[1] S.S. Vol. 17, Intro. xxiii.

have done it: and, by the way, it does not reflect credit on the reporter. I wish Turner would allow me to put his name on the title page—I must say something very handsome of him in the Preface.

In ten days time I shall have resided enough[1] and then I hope for London. I think of a lodging in Bloomsbury (your offer is most kind, but it is now or never), and if the fiend spares me I can do a mighty lot in a fortnight.

Et sic ad patriam—Go to the country and the sea with my profound gratitude.

Yours very truly

F. W. MAITLAND

F. Pollock is here. His only criticism on the specimen is that I am giving too many variants.

Since I finished, a screed has come from Soule. I won't trouble you with it, as it does not change my view of the situation. I gather that Green will write by and by. If he does I will tell you before I answer.

Yrs.

F. W. M.

330. To B. Fossett Lock

Downing College
Cambridge

15 Augt. 1902

MY DEAR LOCK,

I hoped that I had bored you for the last time. But events will move. I had a letter from Soule stating that he had only just received the note that I wrote weeks ago[2] inviting him to Cambridge: it had, he says, been pursuing him and he apologized for discourtesy, etc. He added that he had sent my other letter about Year Books[3] to Markby, Green and Pike. A little cool perhaps! But I had not marked it as private. So now this comes from Markby. I promise to answer in a few days.[4] Meanwhile may I plague you with a rough pencil draft of a reply in order that you may see that I do nothing prejudicial to the Society? A scribbled word or two in the margin I should understand. You see that with the translating project, if confined to the later books, I have a good deal of sympathy, and I would even help it on if I could. I think that there is no harm in repeating this.

Yours ever

F. W. MAITLAND

[1] i.e. kept his statutory period of University residence.
[2] Not extant: see Letter 324, *supra*.
[3] See Letter 327, *supra*.
[4] See Letter 331, *infra*.

331. To Sir William Markby

[No date or heading, but from contents and context Mid-August 1902.
It is in M.'s handwriting in Camb. Univ. MSS., and is clearly a copy kept
by him of his letter to Markby: see Letter 330, *supra*.]

[*Mid-Aug. 1902*]

DEAR SIR WILLIAM,

I have to thank you for your letter and I will endeavour to answer your
questions to the best of my ability.[1] It is a great pleasure to me to talk of Year
Books, more especially to some one who thinks that something ought to be
done and can be done to redeem them from the kingdom of darkness.

I should at the outset draw two distinctions, namely (1) between early and
late YBB and (2) between the publication of a translation and a publication
of anything that purported to be the French text.

I have at one time and another read a good bit of the later YBB, but have
never read them in the sort of way in which one reads a text of which one is
going to publish a translation. Still I am disposed to think that a very interesting and in no way discreditable book might be produced by translating the
printed books as they stand with occasional references to the MSS when
difficulties arise. I feel pretty sure that some blunders would be the result—in
particular the proper names would often be wrong—still I think that if the
translators were wary men, kept their eyes on Coke and the Abridgement, and
were supervised by Pike or some one (if such there be) who is equally competent, their work would be of great value. And, the state of things being what
it is, they could make a good defence of their procedure—on the ground that
life is short and that the establishment of a really good French text would be a
vast undertaking.

As to the earliest YBB it is otherwise, and I can speak with some certainty
of the Edward II. I have been copying at intervals for two years—and now for
some nine months I have done little but work at the first two years of the reign—
and of this I am quite sure, that no one can turn out a moderately correct
translation (such a translation as will correctly state the legal point of the cases)
unless he has first made a text out of four or five MSS as a minimum. I am quite
ready to wager that in two cases out of every five no one will extract even the
legal gist of the discussion unless he uses both a good many MSS and the
record. Take the first case in the book[2] (it happens to be in Latin and so should
be easy) and see whether you can construe it. There is a blunder in it that
obscures the whole story and that blunder stands already in some of what for
other purposes are the best MSS. I believe that if I were in rude health and

---

[1] Markby understood M.'s view to be that 'the existing printed books must be discarded
and a new text constructed from the MSS' and asked for an estimate of cost. 'Mr. Soule is a
man of great energy and I should not be surprised if he got a large sum of money in America:
there is no hope of getting any in England . . . He thinks that, if this question of text be got
over, he sees his way to pay for translation, printing and publication. This is nearer than has
yet been got, and I don't like to give up the attempt until it is shown to be quite hopeless'
(Camb. Univ. MSS.). See Letter 339, *infra*.
[2] S.S. Vol. 17, p. 1.

could give all my time to the business I might perhaps get through the twenty years of Edward II in ten years. And please do not think that I am speaking of an ideal edition which would serve the turn of a student of the Anglo-French dialect. I am merely speaking of an edition which would warrant its readers in saying with some certainty, 'These are the points of law that are discussed and decided'.

The reasons for distinguishing between late and early YBB are these. (1) The late books went into print pretty rapidly and therefore had not a long manuscript life; and I need not say that a text deteriorates at every transcription. (2) The later reports are fuller and this gives a translator a much better chance of amending a blunder by reference to the context. (3) In the late books 'personal' actions are coming to the front, and, being more intelligible to us than real actions, we can make better guesses about them. (4) The French of the earliest books is a living language: the French of the latest books is a grammarless jargon which borrows largely from English. The French of the oldest books is apt to go wrong in transcription and become mere nonsense just because to start with it was better French than the later transcribers could understand. I have been much struck in the course of my work by the numerous instances in which some common—but utterly wrong—word was substituted for a good French word that was not in the lawyer's technical vocabulary.

I can't say positively that any book is as bad as the printed Edward II— worse it could not be—but I should much doubt whether Edward III was good enough to be translated. What I should be inclined to advise if I had any voice in this matter would be that a beginning should be made with Henry IV— with a new dynasty, a new century and the end of the great hiatus (Richard II, you will remember, is not in print). Then, if that succeeds, the earlier time could be attacked some years hence, and meanwhile the Selden Society would, so I hope, have made progress with Edward II. I am now working at nothing else and mean to go as far as I can. You will not forget in your estimate of success (1) that modern lawyers will understand a great deal more of the later cases than they will of the earlier and (2) that your translators will in all probability be none the worse for some training in a relatively modern age.

Then as to the publication of anything French, I do not quite understand what the project is. I cannot think that a 'reprint' of even the latest books as they stand would be a credit to those who produced it, while I am quite sure that a reproduction of the oldest books would be sheer lunacy. If you ever had an hour to spare I believe that I could easily convince you that the 1678 edition of Edward II is a sort of Nonsense Year Book made by a man who did not mind printing the merest rubbish, who knew no French and very little law. Believe me that it is not rivalry that prompts me to say this. The reappearance of that text would be a reason why the Selden Society should put all other schemes aside and press on with the Year Books. But I don't want to see the names of reasonable beings connected with such an enterprise. However I hope and trust that I am disquieting myself in vain and that no one intends to begin an edition of the English law reports with such a travesty as a 'reprint' of this book would be. If there really is such a project in the air then I think that those who meditate a translation had better bide their time than become in any way connected with a laughing stock.

To end a long letter—A scheme for translating the late books (in itself a pretty big task) would have my sympathy and at odd times I might be able to aid it, though Edward II will always have the first claim upon my time. But to putting out a French text that had not been laboriously made from a good supply of MSS compared with the record I will be neither party nor privy.

Yrs.

F. W. M.

332. To R. Lane Poole

Downing College
Cambridge

30 Aug. 1902

MY DEAR POOLE,

The devil has me and I am compelled to be abed—but I must write at once to urge you to go on with your Acton. Justice has not been done to him and I am sure that you could do it.

As to the Cambridge career I think that you could excuse yourself well enough for saying nothing—for what has to be said (and it is a good deal) could only come from one who had been watching Cambridge pretty closely. My own very strong opinion is that within a few years A. did more than any one else could have done to elevate the study of history here towards the position that it has at Oxford. If we had had him here ten years earlier we might by this time be within a measurable distance of you. That is my opinion, and if I had the good fortune to be talking with you I could explain it. The work was being done among the older men and can not easily be described on paper —described in print it could not be without a good many comparisons expressed or implied. For myself I learnt to admire A. enormously—and on his merits, for I was not by any means prejudiced in his favour.

The upshot of this is that if you do say anything about Cambridge it might I think show that to your knowledge there are some people here who regard his professorship as an immense benefit to the University—I know that I am not alone.

As to the lectures I can not speak. They were fully written and will be published. A great deal of his best work here was done among grey-headed people —classical scholars and such, prone to regard history as an elegant form of trifling.

I deeply fear that I shall not get to Oxford, and indeed the duty of resigning my place here stares me in the face—for whenever I have to do anything the messenger of Satan lays me flat. But I will not say that I will forgo your festival[1] until I am compelled to do so.

I am curious to know whom Balfour will send us.[2]

> Yours very truly
>
> F. W. MAITLAND

333. To B. Fossett Lock

[Post-card. M. writes from his father-in-law's house.]

> 19, Second Avenue
> Hove
> *15 Sept. 1902*

Green asks for an interview saying that he descends to South Britain at the end of this or the beginning of next month. If you are then in town I should be very glad of your countenance. So I ask whether you have fixed a day for returning.

I have had execrable luck and have been enforcedly idle: am sent here to recruit. Think I shall have to indulge in photographs of one MS at Museum. French grammar is in type.[3]

> Yrs.
>
> F. W. MAITLAND

334. To R. Lane Poole

> 19 Second Avenue
> Hove
> *24 Sept. 1902*

MY DEAR POOLE,

Quite sincerely I think this capital.[4] It is (1) true, (2) judicious. Will you forgive one small verbal criticism? 'But he strengthened it'—is 'it' the chair or the tendency? I am not perfectly sure that Acton 'strengthened', in the ordinary sense of the word, any tendency exhibited in his predecessor's work. That he strengthened the chair I do not doubt. Am I pedantic or unintelligent —which?

In a moment of lunacy I promised to write two or three words about Acton for the Cambridge Review—since when I have enjoyed no peace.

By the way, in a fifteenth century precedent—summons to Canons of Barnwell to attend meeting for election of Prior—I come upon 'NN' in the

---

[1] The commemoration of the tercentenary of the Bodleian Library, to be held in October 1902.

[2] Balfour had succeeded Lord Salisbury as Prime Minister and as such had to recommend the appointment of a new Regius Professor of History.

[3] S.S. Vol. 17, Introduction.

[4] Poole had sent to M. the proof of his paper on Acton (E.H.R., 1902, p. 692).

place of the name of the man who is to be summoned; also in place of the name of the late Prior.[1]

I am much better but do not feel sure of getting to Oxford. It is of great importance to me to get through a course of lectures without a break-down.

Yours very truly

F. W. MAITLAND

On Sat. to Cambridge.

335. To Henry Jackson

[Post-card.]

Downing

27 Sept. 1902

Am just back in Cambridge and find yours of 24th. On looking at statutes I seem to see that what I reported to you about a restriction on eligibility was untrue. Apparently choice is unrestrained.

Of him whom you speak I really know O. I should not have gone for testimony on such a matter to the witness you name.[2]

More hereafter.

Y.v.t.

F. W. M.

336. To R. Lane Poole

Downing College

Cambridge

28 Sept. 1902

MY DEAR POOLE,

In writing the few words that I have to write about Acton for the *Cambridge Review*[3] I must be careful not to say anything that seems to be pointed at a successor who may just have been appointed or whose appointment must soon be made. I find that people here believe for some reason unknown to me that the minister's choice will fall upon Sir R. Blennerhassett.[4] I will argue myself

[1] On 5 Sept. 1902 Poole had written: 'As for N. or M. I have always understood that they meant, not indeed Nicholas or Mary as some do vainly talk, but, as you say, Nomen or Nomina. The latter I did not interpret in the sense of a multiple name—as the Princess of Wales is believed to have been christened Victoria Mary Augusta Louise Olga Pauline Claudius Agnes—but thought simply that the Catechism might be addressed to more than one child . . . I do not remember anything like N. or M. in the medieval "polite letter writers".' (C. Hist. J. (1952) 339.)

[2] On 24 Sept. 1902 (Camb. Univ. MSS.) Jackson had written to M. that Sir Rowland Blennerhassett was suggested as Lord Acton's successor by Arthur Strong, Librarian to the House of Lords. Jackson was 'astonished' and had understood that, as Sir Rowland had no Cambridge degree, he was ineligible. Sir Rowland Blennerhassett (1839–1909) had studied at Munich with Döllinger and had been intimate with Acton. He was a contributor to the Fortnightly and National Reviews, had been M.P. for Kerry from 1874 to 1885 and was President of Queen's College, Cork, 1897–1904.

[3] *Cambridge Review*, 16 Oct. 1902: reprinted C.P. III. 512.

[4] See Letter 335, *supra*.

unknown by asking you whether he represents anything in particular. As I
have nothing to do with the history school here I am anxious not to say in a
paper read by undergraduates anything that could be tortured into praise or
blame of an actual or potential appointee. You must know all the historians
in England—and a line from you might keep me out of a mess.

Believe me

Yours very truly

F. W. MAITLAND

337. To B. Fossett Lock

Downing College

Cambridge

28 Sept. 1902

DEAR LOCK,

I am once more in Cambridge. I put off answering your letter as I expected
from day to day to hear from Green. However he has not written. Do not take
any trouble about the interview—only if it takes place in London and you
happen to be about I shall be glad of your support.[1]

I have heard from Pike and send you his letter (but must ask for its return).
In some ways it is satisfactory. If I can get an assurance from Green that *he*
does not mean to touch Edward II, then I think that our project is sufficiently
safeguarded and we can afford to be benign to other people. I think of telling
Pike that I cannot promise co-operation as my working hours have to be
few.[2]

I spent a day in London on my way here making arrangements with one
Dossetter for photographs of the most important of the Museum MSS. I am
glad to find that a fiver will go a long way in plates sufficiently large to be read
with a glass. So I think I can say that, unless my luck is very bad indeed, a
tolerable Vol. I will be produced in due course. I fear that my best chance of
finishing involves a winter in the sun, but I shan't be idle there and hope to
put about 100 of our double pages into the printer's hands in a few days so
that proofs may go with me. Your kind words about the grammar were encouraging.

I have just found my friend Bereford, C. J. lapsing into an English phrase.
Can you explain? Counsel says, 'We put forward this plea merely to the form
of the count'. Bereford says, 'Though you want it to go merely to the form, the
Court must take it for what it is worth', and 'si nous aloms a jugement ele
trench for wynd and candle'. He means—if you persist in asking for a judgment,
that judgment will settle the whole matter for good and all. But do you know
any proverb about 'wind and candle'.[3]

Yours very truly

F. W. MAITLAND

[1] See Letter 333, *supra*.
[2] Neither Pike's letter to M. nor M.'s letter to Pike is extant.
[3] The phrase is '*wine* and candle': see S.S. Vol. 20, p. 190, and Intro. lxix–xx.

338. To Henry Jackson

Downing College
Cambridge
30 Sept. 1902

DEAR JACKSON,

I asked R. L. Poole (editor of Eng. Hist. Rev.) about Sir R. B. Answer: 'I never heard that he engaged in history except vicariously through his German wife; and her contributions are a trifle dull'. I think that you may like to see this sentence, though obviously it is not meant for repetition.[1]

I want you to do me a service. In some sort you owe it to me for it was you who set the young man Harrison[2] upon me. Will you look at what I have written about Acton for the Review? I have disliked the job. The wretched thing must be so very short and I feel that it must be either flat or tawdry. Also the present condition of the Cambridge Modern History and the emptiness of the chair make it impossible for me to say all that is in my mind—and I have some fear that the historians proper may resent my intervention.

I think that for Acton's sake you may be willing to help me. There is still time for another attempt on different lines if you think that what I have written is too damnably bad.

Yours very truly
F. W. MAITLAND

339. To B. Fossett Lock

Downing College
Cambridge
5 Oct. 1902

MY DEAR LOCK,

Green has not appeared. On the other hand I have had a very satisfactory interview with Markby. He distinctly told me that his patronage of the new scheme would be conditional on the exclusion of Edward II and showed me a paper in Pike's handwriting which definitely excluded it. In conversation I was able to tell him just what my fear has been, namely that G. has desired to brag of having published *all* the Reports.[3] A Harvard professor, Wambaugh,[4] who was here, warned me that alleged completeness of an edition would be a valuable asset in America. He gave me an amusing scene illustrating Soule's power of forcing people to buy even the old Year Books:—an imaginary C.J. of West Virginia finally capitulates before the argument that the Court of Vermont has a copy. Several people tell me that Soule, though he has a shrewd nose for business, is also a high-toned enthusiast.

---

1 See Letters 335 and 336, *supra*. Poole's letter is printed in C. Hist. J. (1952) 340–1.
2 Presumably the editor of the *Cambridge Review*.
3 See Letters 324, 331, 333 and 337, *supra*.
4 Eugene Wambaugh (1856–1940), Professor of Law, State Univ. of Iowa, 1889–92, and at Harvard 1892–1925; author of *Study of Cases* (1892) and editor of *Littleton's Tenures in English* (1903).

On the whole I am inclined to think that the danger is overpast. Pike himself seems to be concerned in asserting that the books of 11–20 Ed. III must not be touched[1]: so the new edition cannot be 'complete'.

Yr. ldship will observe that for once I require no answer.

Yours very truly

F. W. MAITLAND

To visit Cambridge and not me would be grossly immoral.

340. To Henry Jackson

Downing College

Cambridge

6 Octr. 1902

DEAR JACKSON,

I am afraid that I must ask you to let me 'cry off' from the kind and half-accepted invitation. I am very anxious indeed to get to the end of term in working order and am advised that I have nothing to spare for a chill—and I want to get to the Society on Monday. Forgive me.

That   [2] in the Daily News has wrung a few words from me.

I have poked into certain R.C. pamphlets in Univ. Library—have seen the episcopal letter against Home and Foreign, etc. Certain persons did fear Acton—they don't conceal it.[3]

Yours very truly

F. W. MAITLAND

The recipient of the 'mountainous jackass' which I shall mention in the Review was no other than Ewald whom I supposed to be a most reputable person.[4]

341. To R. Lane Poole

Downing College

Cambridge

14 Oct. 1902

MY DEAR POOLE,

Many thanks—very many. Bale does look beautiful.[5] I am proposing to myself some pleasant hours with him and you.

[1] Pike edited for the Rolls Series the Y.B.B. 11–20 Edward III.

[2] Left blank in the original. In a letter to M. of 3 Oct. 1902, presumably answering one from M. that has not survived, R. L. Poole wrote, 'No: I did not see the scurrilous article you mention. The *Daily News* does not often come my way. It will at least have served a good turn if it makes you more emphatic' (C. Hist. J. (1952) 341). The article was directed against Acton whose obituary M. was preparing for the *Cambridge Review:* see Paul, Intro. to *Letters of Lord Acton to Mary Gladstone*, p. lxxiv.

[3] From 1862 to 1864 Acton edited *The Home and Foreign Review* as an organ of the liberal catholic movement. It aroused orthodox hostility and drew a rebuke from Cardinal Wiseman (D.N.B. by J. N. Figgis).

[4] In his obituary of Acton (reprinted C.P. III. 512), M. wrote: 'Once it happened that a solemn filler of many volumes, a German too and a historian, was dismissed with "mountainous jackass".'

[5] [A.L.P. *Index Britanniae Scriptorum*, ed. R. L. Poole with the help of Mary Bateson.]

I trust that you are recovering from the fatigue of Celebration.[1] All our Cambridge people tell me of a great success.

Rumours of Sir R. B. persist.[2] I gather that he has rushed into print to tell a story of Bismarck and Spain which I once heard Acton tell in his wonderful way.

Yours very gratefully

F. W. MAITLAND

342. To R. Lane Poole

Downing College
Cambridge

19 Oct. 1902

MY DEAR POOLE,

And I yours with pleasure.[3] I don't think that we differ much—but we had to speak to very different audiences. I should like to tell you that as regards Acton's interest in 'the philosophy of history' I did not finally settle my words until I had seen yours in the proof that you sent me, but before that the substance of the remarks was fixed. I don't say this to ward off a charge of plagiarism which you are not going to bring, but that you may know that what struck you struck me also (though I knew so much less of the man): so far as I can see no one else has written of this but you and me. I wrote of it somewhat noisily because there was an impression here that A. was a sort of Dictionary of Dates with a leaning towards scandal.

Do you know a bit in Schulte's Gesch. d. Altkatholics. p. 339, which brings the names of Lord A. and Sir R. B. into contact?

Thank you for the sentences from Purcell. I had seen them, but one cannot see them too often. Some day when we meet I should like to have your explanation—I am sure that you have one—of that curious book: it puzzles me.[4]

W. H. S. seems to have done for Guest. I have long had my doubts.[5]

Yours very truly

F. W. MAITLAND

I like what you say of A.'s style—it is just what I wanted to see said.

---

1 See Letter 332, *supra*.

2 See Letters 335, 336 and 338, *supra*.

3 On 18 Oct. 1902 Poole had written to M., 'Many thanks for the *Cambridge Review*. I have read your article with very great pleasure' (C. Hist J. (1952) 342).

4 In his letter of 18 Oct. 1902 Poole had quoted Cardinal Manning's account of Acton, as noted in Purcell, *Life of Manning*, II. 488.

5 [A.L.P. W. H. Stevenson, in an article in E.H.R. (1902), p. 625, demolished the theories of Dr. E. Guest on the English conquest of South Britain contained in *Origines Celticae* (1883).]

343. To A. J. Balfour

[On 25 October 1902 Mr. Balfour, as Prime Minister, wrote to M.: 'Will you permit me to submit your name to the King for the post of Regius Professor of History? Your eminent qualifications for the post are beyond dispute; and I should be glad to do anything in my power to compel you to display them on a somewhat wider stage than that provided by the professorship of Law! Do think favourably of the suggestion' (Camb. Univ. MSS.). The letter following is M.'s copy of his reply in his own hand (Camb. Univ. MSS.). Though it is dated by him 26 Oct. 1903, the year is clearly a mistake for 1902.]

Downing Coll: Cambridge
26 Oct. [1902]

MY DEAR BALFOUR,

I must not trifle with the temptation that you have very kindly placed in my way. There are many reasons, all of them sufficient, which would deter me from endeavouring to fill the vacant chair of history: but I will trouble you with only one. For some time past I have been compelled to do very little work and to absent myself from England for some months every winter. Twice I have offered to resign the professorship that I hold and I have only been able to retain it because the University has gone great lengths in the way of exceptional indulgence. I must not even think of burdening our rising school of history with an invalid professor, and the very little that I can do to further its interests can best be done from without.

I will ask you to regard this letter as final and at the same time to accept my hearty thanks for the great honour that you have done me and my yet heartier thanks for encouraging words that I shall not forget.

Believe me
Yours very gratefully
F. W. MAITLAND

344. To F. J. H. Jenkinson

Downing Coll: Camb.
25 Nov. 1902

MY DEAR JENKINSON,

I did not thank you for your very kind letter[1] because I made sure of seeing you at the Society's dinner. I was indeed shocked to see nor you nor Jackson nor Forsyth.[2] I very much hope that you are rapidly recovering: the weather also has been very exasperating.

I don't suppose that anybody at Trinity guessed how much the honorary fellowship would mean to me. I have been happy ever since.

With many wishes for your recovery
Yours very truly
F. W. MAITLAND

[1] Jenkinson had written on 19 Nov. 1902 (Camb. Univ. MSS.) to congratulate M. on his election as Honorary Fellow of Trinity College.
[2] A. R. Forsyth (1858–1942), Fellow of Trinity College, Cambridge, Sedleian Professor of Pure Mathematics, 1895–1910.

345. To Henry Jackson

[Printed, with many omissions, by Fisher, *Memoir*, 136–7. Now printed from the original in Camb. Univ. MSS.]

20 Decr. 1902

MUY SEÑOR MIO

Deseo que pase Vd. bien las Pascuas y que tenga feliz año nuevo
Quedo de Vd. atento y seguro servidor que besa su mano

F. W. MAITLAND

From an exercise on the use of the subjunctive. Beyond this point my Spanish will not carry me. Compulsory Greek, acting on a fine natural stupidity, deprived me early of all power of learning languages. I envy my children who chatter to the servants in what is good enough Canario, though I doubt it being Castilian.

My voyage was abominable. I am driven into the second class. I like second class *men* (not women): they are often very interesting people who have seen odd things and been in strange places—but a cabin close to the screw is bad and sleep was out of the question. Two lines of F. Myers[1] (have I got them rightly?) got into my head and set themselves to the accompanying noises:—'doubting if any recompense hereafter waits to atone the intolerable wrong'. But this was faithlessness—it is all atoned by a few hours of this glorious sunshine. Already I am regenerate and a new man. One miserable day was alleviated by your friend the 'stinker'. Do you know Paul Bourget's *L'Étape*? It is not great but it served to kill some bad hours. And do you know Huysmans? He looks to me like a debauchee who has turned himself into a ritualistic curate and is very sweet upon his highly artificial style. I am now tackling Gil Blas in the classical Spanish translation which some say is better than the original.

As I was departing I saw L. Stephen who told me that the operation was to take place a week after I left. Since then I have had no news and am anxious. From F. Pollock I learn that J. Morley was good at Commemoration. I wish that I had been able to exercise my new rights[2] on that occasion: as it was I was blaspheming while crockery smashed. I have never before been reduced to holding my soup plate in hand just under my mouth, but the table was like unto the troubled sea. I hope that at Bournemouth you discharge all aches and pains as I discharge them here and that the shawl is not necessary any longer.

I am hoping that there will be no great rumpus at Downing while I am away. If only A. H.[3] would keep his fingers from the ink pot! But mind you that man is a saint and will go straight to heaven without questions asked.

My house of call is Quiney's, but I am up country at a spot called Tafira.

---

[1] See Letter 11, *supra*. For the story of his prize poem on St. Paul, as told by Henry Jackson, see Coulton, *Fourscore Years*, 106–8.
[2] As Honorary Fellow of Trinity College.
[3] Alex Hill, Master of Downing College.

Bennett of Emmanuel[1] lunches with us to-day. Heaven send that in his de-moniacal cycling he kills no child—for homicide when committed by an 'inglese' is sometimes seriously treated.

Yrs. once more,

F. W. M.

346. To Frederick Pollock

[No original: printed by Fisher, *Memoir*, 137–8: no beginning or ending. Now printed from transcript in Camb. Univ. MSS.]

Quiney's
Las Palmas
17 Jan. 1903

Your letter about Paris is to hand. Well, I envy you. Yours are the joys that I should have liked if I had my choice—but I must not complain for I am having a superlatively good time. I don't exactly know why it is, but the sun makes all the difference to me—I live here and don't live in England. I am even beginning to boast of my powers as a hill rider: but if ever I come here again I shall bring a machine with a very low gear and a free wheel. That is what you want if you live half way up a road that rises pretty steadily for 21 kilometres to 2600 feet. My friend Bennett,[2] who has vast experience, recommends a gear of 50 for such work.

Meanwhile I push on with the Year Books. My first volume is done in the rough and a good piece is in print. Being away from books I become intrigued in small verbal problems. Am now observing the liberal use of the verb *lier*.[3] In French you (the advocate) are said to *lier* the seisin or the esplees or the like in this person or that. When translating I naturally write 'lay', and I have a suspicion that the 'to lay' of our legal vocabulary (e.g. to lay the damages) really descends from *lier*—que piensa Vd.? This is the sort of triviality that occupies my mind:—however I am meditating a final say about the personality of states and corporations.[4]

Why not bring over Salmond to succeed you at Oxford?[5] He is a good man.

Local politics are interesting. I think that when Gladstone was in power he never was subjected to such continuous assaults as are directed against the Alcalde of Las Palmas by the organ of opinion that I patronise. Drought and flood, mud and dust, small-pox and measles are all from him, he fills the butchers' shops with large blue flies. But I should like to hear the lectures that you make for los Yanquis[6] (N.B. in a Spanish mouth Americano is apt to mean a Spanish speaking man and Yanqui is not uncivilly meant).

[1] George Thomas Bennett (1868–1943); Fellow of Emmanuel College, Cambridge, 1893–1943, College Lecturer in Mathematics 1893–1918.
[2] See Letter 345, *supra*.
[3] S.S. Vol. 17, Intro. lxxix.
[4] Probably *Moral Personality and Legal Personality*, the Sidgwick Lecture for 1903, delivered at Newnham College, Cambridge: reprinted C.P. III. 304.
[5] As Corpus Profession of Jurisprudence. John William Salmond (1862–1924), Professor of Law, University of Adelaide, 1897–1906, and of Victoria University College, Wellington, N.Z., 1906–7: Judge of the Supreme Court of New Zealand 1920–4. He published *Essays in Jurisprudence and Legal History*, 1891: *Jurisprudence*, 1902: *The Law of Torts*, 1907.
[6] The lectures were subsequently published as *The Expansion of the Common Law*, 1904.

Much rain has fallen—but a road recovers from the most appalling mud in a very few hours.

347. To Leslie Stephen

[No original. Printed by Fisher, *Memoir*, 138–9: no beginning.]

Casa Verda,

Tafira.

17 Jan. 1903.

The news that we get of you out here is satisfactory rather than satisfying—I mean that we have heard little, but it was all to the good. The last intelligence takes you back to your home and I feel good reason for hoping that long before now you have become reasonably comfortable. What I wish you know.[1]

All here goes well. I am having a supremely good time—the only pains are those given by my conscience or by the voice that exists where my conscience should be—but the remedies for moral twinges are not difficult to come by in this world of sin—which also is (locally) a world of corrupting sunshine.

I brought with me this time all the three supplementary volumes of *Dict. Nat. Biog.* I stare at them and wonder how anybody can have the energy to make such things.[2] Even novels strike me as laborious productions when the sun is at its best.

We have been having rain: and when it rains here you find that the roof of your house has been surprised by the performance. I am now engaged in drying a boxful of copied Year Book which unfortunately was left beneath a weak point in the ceiling. Is it 'ceiling' by the way? I don't know, and while I am in the garden the dictionary is in the house and I don't care a perrita (primarily little bitch but also a five centimo piece) how this or any other word spells itself; and all this I ascribe to the sun.

It will be a good day when I get a postcard signed L. S.—but don't be in a hurry to send one before the spirit moves you.

Back at Hobbes again?[3] I hope so. Florence joins me in hopes—as you can well suppose.

Yours very affectionately,

F. W. MAITLAND

348. To A. W. Verrall

[No original. Printed by Fisher, *Memoir*, 141–2: no beginning or ending.]

Quiney's Hotel,

Las Palmas.

14 Feb. 1903.

Until just this week I have been doing wonderfully well. Now the messenger of Satan has returned to buffet me and abate my pride. So the cycle has to rest:

[1] Leslie Stephen had been operated on, 12 Dec. 1902.
[2] As the first editor of the D.N.B. Stephen had himself written 378 biographies.
[3] A life of Hobbes for the series *English Men of Letters*.

but I am hopeful that the visitation may be short—it ought to be if the climate has anything to do with the matter, for after some rainy weeks we are in the sun again. El Señor Cura 'clapped on the prayer for rain' so very effectually that he had to protest before all saints that he had not meant quite so much as all that. Rainmaking is still one of the duties of the priesthood in such a country as this.

The proposal made by 'the minister' and mentioned by you was rejected by return of post.[1] There were seven or eight good causes for the refusal—all of which will at once occur to your l'dship except perhaps one which I will tell you. My present place has been made extremely easy to me by the very great kindness of such colleagues as it has happened to few to have. Even if I had been a historian and an able-bodied man I should have thought many times before I changed my estate. And what you say of the crowd at Bury's first lecture—I thought the appointment very good—confirms my view.[2] The Regius Professor of Modern History is expected to speak to the world at large and even if I had anything to say to the W. at L. I don't think that I should like full houses and the limelight. So I go back to the Year Books. Really they are astonishing. I copy and translate for some hours every day and shall only have scratched the surface if I live to the age of Methusalem—but if I last a year or two longer I shall be a 'dab' at real actions. It was a wonderful game as intricate as chess and not like chess cosmopolitan. Unravelling it is an amusement not unlike that of turning the insides out of ancient comedies I guess.

349. To W. W. Buckland

[Printed, with some omissions, by Fisher, *Memoir*, 142–3. Now printed from the original in Camb. Univ. MSS.]

Tafira

14 Feb. 1903.

MUY ESTIMADO COLEGA Y QUERIDO AMIGO MIO

Espero que Vd. no ha olvidado lo que ha aprendido de la lengua castillana cuando estaba en Gran Canaria el año próximo pasado. Por tanto me esforzaré escribir una corta en aquel lenguaje aunque no puedo expresar mis pensamientos sin muchas disporates ridicolosas que quizas Vd. perdonará.

Mientras las primeras semanas de mia estancia en Tafira hacia buen tiempo y D. Benito del colegio de Manuel[3] y yo dabamos algunos largos paseos en nuestras bicicletas. Despues de su partida en Enero llovia muchas veces y se ha visto nieve en las cumbres. Los barrancos fueron llenos de agua y la agua se introdujó por el tejado de nuestra casa. El fango me recordaba el viaje que hicimos en Marzo de Galdor a Telde. No mé gustaba el frio y no estoy tan

[1] See Letter 343, *supra*.
[2] Bury had been appointed Regius Professor of Modern History. In his letter to M. of 31 Jan. 1903 (Camb. Univ. MSS.) Verrall had written that Bury's inaugural lecture had 'gone off well, except that the public of curious ladies, etc. were allowed as usual to fill up the room, and actually indeed some of the most important people in the University were turned away from the door'.
[3] See Letter 345, *supra*.

bién que estaba hace poco tiempo. Mi antiquo enemigo me amenaza pero espero que le venceré. De consiguiente no he ido a Telde; pero espero ir luego, y si fuere buscaré a Santiago su criado de Vd. y le daré el duro que me dió para él. La viruela todavia se enfurece en Telde y en Las Palmas también.

Todos sus amigos de Vd. estan muy bien pero un señor cuyo nombre no mencionaré y que vive en la ciudad estaba fuertemente ébrio cuando le vi la ultima vez. Temo que este un borrachón.

Quiero leer el libro de Sen. Dr. Roby[1] aunque no sé si le podré entender. Es un hombre docto, doctísimo pero stogioso—esta ultima no puedo deletrear.

Estas pocas palabras son una recompensa muy ligera por su carta de Vd. que me interesó mucho y por que estoy muy agradecido pero he tomado un largo tiempo escribiendolas. Si pudiere* escribir mas facilmente le contraria a Vd. todos los sucesos que han acontecido en Gran Canaria. Pero es preciso acabar.

Con muchas memorias
Quedo su afectuoso amigo

F. W. MAITLAND

Al my excellente
    Sen. D. G. G. Buckland

 * Mire Vd.! No verá cada dia el condicional de subjunctivo.

350. To Henry Jackson

[Fisher printed a fragment of this letter, *Memoir*, 140. Now printed from the original in Camb. Univ. MSS.]

Quiney's Hotel
Las Palmas

14 Feb. 1903

MY DEAR JACKSON,

It was good of you to remember me at the beginning of the year.[2] I did not altogether like the account which you gave of yourself but hope that some rest sent you back to Cambridge in good case. Sugar production is a d—d unprofitable business as all say who have tried it. Here the canes are disappearing and the mills are falling to ruin. I have no wish to compete with the bounty fed.

We have been having bad news of sorts from home and this has spoilt what would otherwise have been a pleasant time, for though we have had heavy rain—even snow on the hill tops—we keep a really working sun that is up to a sun's business and converts the most appalling mud into dust in the space of a few hours. Until just lately I have been wondrous well. My amusement I have taken in the shape of lessons in Spanish from the hostess of the village

---

[1] Henry John Roby (1830–1915), Fellow of St. John's College, Cambridge, 1854–61; Professor of Jurisprudence, University College, London, 1866–8. Published *Roman Private Law*, 2 vols., 1902.

[2] Jackson's letter to M., dated 31 Dec. 1902 from Bournemouth, is in Camb. Univ. MSS.

inn. She prides herself on not talking like the other folk of Tafira—but asked me whether Perez Galdos wrote *Gil Blas*. P. G. is by birth a Canario and mighty proud they are of him here. Every little town has a street named after him. To my mind he is a most unequal story teller—sometimes very good, at others dull.

One way and another I have heard a good deal of news from Cambridge. No, it was not a poll man from *Trinity* that was to be bursar of Downing. The result is public property now.[1] Some day you must let me talk to you about what lay behind. I am wondering whether in Spanish one can say 'Busca la mujer'—I must ask my instructress.

I hear of an immense mob at Bury's inaugural lecture.[2] I dare say it was very good—by 'it' I mean the lecture not the mob. The expectation that the R.P. of M.H. must have something to say to the 'muchedumbre' seems to me a misfortune. I am hoping to hear that somehow or another a place will be found for Bury among the editors of the History, and I also hope to hear that the first volume is selling. There are some blots in it. I think that Acton in a few instances gave a little too much weight to established reputations—possibly this was the right thing to do in a first volume—but people who are travelling on the up grade, young men, will I think be the people to do the best part of the work.

Just now I hear that Stokes is no more and the Master of Caius is very bad.[3] I don't know that the lugubrious news that thus comes in is all that Cambridge has to give. A draft report from the Economics Syndicate is comparatively lively.

Once more, I hope to hear that you are getting well through the term.

Yours very truly

F. W. MAITLAND

351. To C. C. Soule[4]

Hotel Quiney,
Las Palmas
1 March 1903

DEAR MR. SOULE,

I am once more in the Canaries and your letter of 30 Jan. 1903 has only just come to my hands.

I thank you for sending me your Plan for a Translation of the Year Books and will make a few remarks upon it so far as it concerns the Seld. Soc. and so far as it concerns me.

It is not for me to say what the Council of the Society might do, but for my

---

[1] From letters to M. from Dr. Hill, Master of Downing College, of 26 Dec. 1902 and 1 Feb. 1903 (Camb. Univ. MSS.) it is clear that the election of the Bursar had provoked internecine controversy. See also Letter 353, *infra*.

[2] See Letter 348, *supra*.

[3] For Sir George Stokes see Letter 318, *supra*. Dr. Norman Macleod Ferrers (1829–1903) was Master of Gonville and Caius College from 1880 to 1903.

[4] Apparently a copy made by M. of his letter to Soule.

own part I do not think it likely that a proposal to alter the shape of the Society's books would be accepted. It so happens that I have never liked our page, but the arguments against change are weighty and would, so I think, prevail. If you wish it, the matter can be laid before the Council.

Then I do not think that the Council would desire to be pledged even by implication to a completion of the YBB of Edw. II, or at any rate to a completion of them within a given time. Our first volume will only cover two years. I am doubting whether our second vol. will cover more than one.[1] We are only to publish a vol. of YBB in alternate years. At this rate progress will be slow and I myself can only hope to see just the beginning of it.

I think it far better that we should go our several ways: that is to say the Seld. Soc. on the one side and you and your associates on the other. And of course you will understand that the Society, even if it had the will, has not the power to prevent you from including the books of Edw. II in your scheme.

Thus I fear that I must ask you to withdraw my name, etc.

F. W. M.

352. To Frederick Pollock

[Fragment only: no original: printed by Fisher, *Memoir*, 140. Now printed from transcript in Camb. Univ. MSS.]

Las Palmas

14 March 1903

. . . Did I tell you that a while ago I was informed that I had been elected a bencher of Lincoln's Inn (with the 'usual fees' forgiven)? The news made my hair stand on end—one of the vacant bishoprics would have been less of a surprise . . .

353. To Henry Jackson

Tafira

Gran Canaria

5 April 1903

MY DEAR JACKSON,

I am glad of your letter[2] but sorry indeed that your home news is no better. You supply me with some new facts from Cambridge and many comments which interest me. I feel that the place has changed with unusual rapidity this winter. I must try hard not to leave it again for otherwise I shall soon be a stranger. Only in the most casual way have I heard of Dew's[3] death: I was not expecting that bad news. The Pembrokian proceedings[4] surprised me

---

[1] See S.S. Vols. 17 and 19.

[2] Of 26 March 1903, in Camb. Univ. MSS.

[3] Albert Dew-Smith, M.A., Trinity College, Cambridge. 'His official work was the grinding and polishing of lenses at the Cambridge Observatory, at which he was reputed to be unrivalled': Sir John Pollock, *Time's Chariot*, 146–7. See also Gwen Raverat, *Period Piece*, 203.

[4] The election of Rev. A. J. Mason (1851–1928), Lady Margaret Professor of Divinity, to succeed Sir George Stokes as Master: see Letter 350, *supra*.

much. Granted that they wanted a divine, surely they might have done much better. If I wrote what you say that I did (and I have no reason to doubt it) I must have broken a very elementary rule: 'a la mujer' it would have to be, if anything.[1] Having asked why it was that a man without any love of learning entered the University at an unusually late age and made a dogged and successful attempt to obtain a degree (to be followed ultimately by a fellowship) I was told that the answer was 'Cherchez la femme'. I can give you the tale some day—it is not in any way discreditable to the lady or any one else, but curious.

I am beginning to pack up my traps and next Saturday I take boat—about a week will take me to the port of London. I want two or three days in the Museum before term begins. For some time past I have been reduced to Perez Galdos, for a fortnight in bed rapidly consumed my books. He is not bad though he writes too much. I have lived in the society of fighting priests and so forth, very queer beings but well-drawn I should suppose.

I am very glad to see that you have joined the tribe of Israel.[2] I want to see all my friends 'estopped' from jeering and, as it were, circumcised.

What least attracts my returning feet is the prospect of a rumpus about Economics. In a second edition I signed the report.[3]

Until a Sunday afternoon I am
Yours v. truly
F. W. MAITLAND

354. To Leslie Stephen

[No original. Typed transcript in Camb. Univ. MSS: no ending.]

Downing
1 May 1903

MY DEAR LESLIE,

I didn't say on Saturday a lot that I meant to say or at any rate a lot that I felt. And I'm not going to say it now. I am taking the cheerfulest view of your case and am hoping that I may see and hear you for a long time to come. Still I feel that it is a horrible thing to have the surgeon impending—more especially if he says that he is not going to begin just yet. My thoughts will often be with you and I shall be thinking how brave you are.

Do you know that you were a great 'admiration' of mine before you were my guide (on Sunday tramps), philosopher and friend. I often think of that fortunate first tramp and bless the good F. P.[4] who brought us together. As you know, the central thread of my life seems to begin just about that point: there were certain visits to Hyde Park Gate—or Gardens, wasn't it?—not to be forgotten by me, and I cannot, and would not if I could, dissociate you from

[1] See Letter 350, *supra*.
[2] M.'s nickname for the British Academy, of which Sir Israel Gollancz (1863–1930) was an original Fellow and Secretary from its foundation in 1902 until his death. He was Professor of English Language and Literature at King's College, London, 1903–30.
[3] See Letter 350, *supra*.
[4] Frederick Pollock.

others whom I met in your house.[1] And apart from that, my admiration for you has just gone on increasing, and I am going to admire to the end. As to those zigzags of which you write,[2] I am not at all sure that I cannot race you down hill and beat you even if you have recourse to the help of a surgeon. In any case we shall not be far apart and in any case the sight of your courage will cheer me.

355. To B. Fossett Lock

Downing College
Cambridge
12 June 1903

MY DEAR LOCK,

Two or three questions.

(1) How many sheets may I have of Y.B. exclusive of introduction? I am getting a little frightened that I may not be able to cram in the whole of the Second Year. I am struggling to get rid of the fat: but this does not shorten the amount of copy.

(2) Would you like a volume from Miss Bateson next year? She says that she could do it if required. Is there *any* chance of a Glanvill from Leadam?[3]

(3) Might Miss B. have two volumes for her borough customs?[4] She is proposing a scheme that I like very much, namely to cut the stuff up and arrange it under legal titles: e.g. take 'Descent', then put under this title all the rules about descent that you get in the various custumals. She has made out what I think a very good scheme of titles and sub-titles. But this plan cannot be adopted unless she may have a second volume within a reasonable time. I am inclined to back this proposal. I doubt we shall get more interesting matter or a better editor. But what think you?

Yours very truly
F. W. MAITLAND

356. To B. Fossett Lock

Downing College
Cambridge
14 June 1903

MY DEAR LOCK,

Many thanks. I return Leadam's letter and I tell Miss Bateson what you tell me.[5] Her proposed scheme was not alphabetical but systematic. One

[1] It was there that M. met Florence Fisher: see Fisher, *Memoir*, 28, and M. *Life of L. S.*, 359.
[2] In a letter to M. of 23 April 1903 (Camb. Univ. MSS.) Leslie Stephen had written: 'What I think, my dear Fred, is that I am come to the last zigzags. Every step will be down hill; but the doctors apparently cannot tell me how many zigs and zags there may be.'
[3] This appears as 'contemplated' in the list of publications in S.S. Vol. 17 at p. 226, but it never materialised.
[4] She did: vols. 18 and 21.
[5] On 13 June 1903 Lock had replied to Letter 355, *supra*, and enclosed a letter from Leadam apologising for delay over Vol. 16 (S.S. Corr.).

volume would be criminal and tortious in tone: the other would have a good deal of real property.

As to my volume. If I am pinched for room, as I think that I may be, shall I sacrifice the end of Year II or the French grammar?[1] The latter is in slip—I think you have seen it—but I can hold it back for another occasion. In any case there will I suppose be no harm in my getting the whole of Year II into print (slip), for what is not used now can be used hereafter.

A word of indexes. I propose to reduce the indexing of men and places to a minimum:—to give only the true names obtained from the record and to neglect the many corrupt forms of the reports: also to give only family names, e.g. 'Devereux' not 'Devereux, Eva', 'Devereux, John', etc. I think that in this way I can get the index of persons and places into a small space. What should you say to a tricolumnar arrangement? Our page is wide.

Then as to matters. I thought of such an index as is put to modern law reports —an index of legal propositions. For example, I have a heading Fine: under this comes 'Fine 1' and a brief statement of a case on page 100. Then under 'Advowson', 'Seisin', 'Quare Impedit', I give references to 'Fine 1'. This will take some space. What I want to ask of you is whether you would think such space well occupied by this sort of thing. The alternative is a mere list of words with figures referring to pages on which those words occur. This question you can answer briefly by 'Digest' or 'Mere Index'. Of course I am not at all sure that I get the right legal proposition in all cases—that is a point to be considered.

I hope that this letter will not waste much of your time.

Yours very truly
F. W. MAITLAND

357. To R. Lane Poole

Downing College
Cambridge
20 June 1903

MY DEAR POOLE,

I return proof.[2] Forgive me for having added yet another sentence. I thought that my recognition of Pollen's priority looked grudging—and this was not my intention. I called him 'Mr.' because I do to others—but if this looks (1) rude or (2) pedantic or (3) protestant, let him be fathered by all means.[3]

I am arguing against Maurice Prou[4] that in Anglo-French the sign ꝰ does not necessarily mean —us, but may stand for —es or —ms or simple —s.

[1] The end of Year II was sacrificed: see Vol. 17, Intro., esp. p. lxxxix.
[2] Of *Elizabethan Gleanings*, V: E.H.R. (1903) 517: C.P. III. 185: Selected Hist. Essays, 229.
[3] In E.H.R. (1903) 527, note 25, M. refers to 'the article in the *Dublin Review* (January 1903) in which Father J. H. Pollen has forestalled me'. Father J. H. Pollen (1858–1925), historian, esp. of English Catholic history.
[4] See S.S. Vol. 17, Intro. xli, note.

Thus I read no⁹ trovam⁹ as nous trovames not as nous trovamus. If you have a decided opinion about this I shall be glad to hear it.

Yours very truly
F. W. MAITLAND

358. To R. Lane Poole

Downing College
Cambridge
2 July 1903

MY DEAR POOLE,

Why did I trouble you at such a moment?[1] I have my punishment in that I must look for Trenholme.[2] I had forgotten him altogether.

But many thanks for your conclusive answer to my question.[3] I now see that *my* Bond (Selby's edition of 1887) gives

Johannis, decollatio Aug. 28,

but   Decollatio, Johannis Aug. 29,

which is absurd.[4]

Your suggestion that not the year but the day was the seat of the blunder is very welcome.

I shall not cease to trouble—I am not wicked enough for that. But for the future I will be good enough not to trouble when the E.H.R. is expecting her confinement.

Yours very truly
F. W. MAITLAND

359. To R. Lane Poole

Downing College
Cambridge
7 July 1903

MY DEAR POOLE,

I know nothing at first hand of the history of Coke's Reports. I have been in the habit of trusting Macdonell's article in Dict. Nat. Biog.—a laborious piece of work by a good man. Qu, whether Mr. Usher has not been using the same without acknowledgment.[5] Compare his list of MSS (p. 3) with D.N.B. vol. XI, p. 242. The agreement *may* be due however to a Report on Public Records (1837) which Macdonell cites.

I cannot square what your contributor says with some words which Macdonell cites from Roger Coke: see p. 240. Roger says that Windebank, when he came to seize papers, took (inter alia) 'his 11th and 12th (qu. 12 and 13)

---

1 See last sentence of this letter.
2 See Letter 394, *infra.*   3 Not extant.
4 [A.L.P. In the fourth edition of Bond's *Handy-Book for Verifying Dates* (1889) both entries have the correct date—29 August.]
5 [A.L.P. See Roland G. Usher, *James I and Sir Edward Coke*, E.H.R. (1903) 664.]

in manuscript'. This seems to imply that Part 12 (if not Part 13) was in existence as a whole. It seems to me that this passage in Roger's Detection should have been noticed.

For the rest, it is orthodox legal tradition that Parts 12 and 13 are not books of high authority.

As you say, the performance is youthful but as far as I know the comparison of the divers accounts of the famous scene and the doubts thus cast on Coke's tale are new and will be useful. What a pity S. R. G. is no longer here.[1]

I fear that I can say no more.

To change the subject. Have any examination papers been set at Oxford on Palaeography and Diplomatic? If so, could a man obtain copies for money or for love? In October I shall try to start a little scriptorium.

Yours very truly

F. W. MAITLAND

360. To B. Fossett Lock

Downing College

Cambridge

12 July 1903

DEAR LOCK,

If the first part of the Introduction to the YBB has come to your hands I shall be extremely grateful for criticism. Even if you only mark with red lead any passages that you dislike I shall understand.

In particular, what about my mention of Pike in the first foot note?[2] Our relations are quite amicable, but he is a touchy man and I am not quite sure whether that note will do good or harm.

Say if you think me too noisy—I can easily tone down. You know that some sober French grammar is to follow.

I have nearly done indexes, tables, etc. We meet on Thursday.

Yours very truly

F. W. MAITLAND

361. To B. Fossett Lock

Cambridge

19 July 1903

MY DEAR LOCK,

Many thanks for your words about the Introduction. I am a bit of an enthusiast about the YBB. and therefore feared that my tone might seem strident. Thanks also for your approval of the double columned Table. I can't bring myself to think that this vol. will sell better than the others. If my introduction

---

[1] [A.L.P. S. R. Gardiner died 23 February 1902.] On Coke's Reports in general and on the inferior and doubtful character of Parts 12 and 13 see Wallace, *The Reporters* (Coke) and Holdsworth, H.E.L. V. 461–6.

[2] There is no footnote to Pike in S.S. Vol. 17, Intro. I; but see Intro. II. xxi.

DOWNING COLLEGE,

CAMBRIDGE.

12 July 1903.

Dear Lock

If the first part of the Introduction to the
YBB. has come to your hands, I shall be extremely
grateful for criticism. Even if you only mark with
red lead any passages that you dislike I shall
understand.

In particular what about my mention of Pike in
the first foot note? Our relations are quite amicable
but he is a touchy man and I am not quite
sure whether that note will do good or harm.

Say if you think me too noisy — I can
easily tone down. You know that some sober French
grammar is to follow.

I have nearly done indexes, tables etc.

We meet on Thursday

Yours very truly

F. W. Maitland

LETTER 360

DOWNING COLLEGE,

CAMBRIDGE.

27 April 1904

My dear Jackson,

The little Greek that I ever had was of the compulsory kind and has long since flown.

Therefore tell me whether the accents on the Greek words in the enclosed snip (from a proof of Stephen's Hobbes) are correct

et ceo pur dieu et en oevre de charité (as the old bills in Chancery say)

Yours very truly

F. W. Maitland.

attracts a few, the fact that we give comparatively little material for pedigree-makers, etc. will repel others.

As to binding, I send a suggestion. I don't think that anything *very* distinctive would be prudent.[1] I hope that you also will make suggestions, so that we may compare specimens.

I wrote to Miss Bateson telling her in a general way that the Council was with her.[2] She will however expect a business letter from you.

I think it possible that by a few copies of my vol. sent with the Council's compliments to a few Frenchmen—e.g. Paul Meyer[3]—we might do good.

The MSS. for Ann. 3 are but too numerous.[4] I am going to give an order for £15 worth of photographs.

Yours very truly

F. W. MAITLAND

362. To Melville M. Bigelow

Downing College
Cambridge
9 Augt. 1903

MY DEAR BIGELOW,

I think you can guess what a thrill of pleasure it gave me to see my name along with Wright's at the beginning of your new Torts. You could not have given me a pleasanter proof of our friendship. And what a good book it is! I have been reading it with satisfaction and hope soon to be teaching out of it.

I am truly sorry to be sending to your friend and pupil Mr. Simpson an answer to his letter that he will not like.[5] We exact six terms of residence even from graduates of other Universities if they want a degree. I shall be truly sorry if this keeps Mr. Simpson away: such a visitor would do us good—but you know enough of the organization of our universities to tell him that I have absolutely no power to procure dispensation from a rule of this kind.

You will soon have before you a volume of Year Books—I am just finishing it. Often have I thought that it would never be done—but thanks to the Canarian sun I am through. I never work upon Year Books without thinking of Thayer: I should have liked to satisfy him. Shall I satisfy you?

This year I have done wondrous well. They tell me that the sunshine has a cumulative effect. Really I have little excuse for dreading a winter in England; still I am laying in a large store of photographs of MSS, to be deciphered among the bananas.

---

[1] To mark that Vol. 17 was the first Y.B. volume in the S.S. series.
[2] See Letter 355, *supra*.
[3] (1840–1917), French philologist, Director of École des Chartes: cited *passim*, Vol. 17, Intro. III.
[4] See Intro. to S.S. Vol. 20.
[5] [AULT. Frank L. Simpson, later Professor of Law in Boston University.] M.'s letter to him is not extant, but its purport appears from the paragraph.

Yesterday I had a long and pleasant talk with Woodrow Wilson. I wonder how vol. 2 of the History is being received on your side.[1]

Would that we could talk!

Yours as of old

F. W. MAITLAND

363. To B. Fossett Lock

Downing College
Cambridge
13 Sept. 1903

DEAR LOCK,

Forgive my delay. I was away from Cambridge and the porter did not forward the parcel containing the specimens of binding.

I am very much pleased by the green-grey. I think it very pretty and should vote for it only, as I said before, I am afraid that it may look foolish hereafter, for I do not feel that the continuance of the Year Book Series is as yet well assured. However, if that objection does not come home to your prudent mind, I will waive it. My own decision would be in favour of dark blue but I shall be glad to be over-ruled.[2]

I fear that I see no reason for any increase in the number of copies.

I note all you say of Miss B's book.[3] She lately told me that she will be glad of marching orders. Let it weigh with you a little that she would prefer the new style.

I am soon going forward with vol. 2 of YBB—but fear that I must spend a few days in bed for the damp has been sinking in to me.

Photographs are coming in rapidly.

Yours very truly

F. W. MAITLAND

364. To John Chipman Gray

[No original. Printed Fisher, *Memoir*, 144–6: no beginning or ending and *semble* with omissions, as M. clearly writes in reply to Gray's letter of 23 Sept. 1903 (Harv. Law School Lib.) and, as printed, M. does not answer Gray's question, there put, as to the history of probate jurisdiction in England.]

Downing College,
Cambridge.
4 Oct. 1903.

I should like to take this opportunity of asking you a question which you will be able to answer very easily. In 1862 our Parliament[4] made it possible for

---

[1] Woodrow Wilson was then President of Princeton. Professor Ault suggests that 'vol. 2 of the History' refers to Wilson's *History of the American People* (1902); but it is also possible that it refers to Vol. 2 of the Camb. Mod. Hist. (1903) and esp. to M.'s chapter 16 therein.
[2] Dark blue it was.   [3] Mary Bateson: S.S. Vol. 18.
[4] Companies Act, 1862.

any seven or more persons associated for any lawful purpose to form themselves into a corporation. But this provision was accompanied by a prohibition. For the future the formation of large partnerships (of more than 20 persons) was forbidden. In effect the legislature said that every big association having for its object the acquisition of gain must be a corporation. Thereby the formation of 'unincorporated joint stock companies' was stopped. I may say in passing that nowadays few Englishmen are aware of the existence of this prohibitory law because the corporate form has proved itself to be very much more convenient than the unincorporate. Now what I should like to know is whether, when in your States the time came for general corporation laws, there was any parallel legislation against unincorporated companies. I have some of your American books on Corporations and I gather from them that the repressive or prohibitory side of our Companies Act is not represented among you. But am I right in drawing this inference, and (if so) should I also be right in supposing that you would see constitutional objections to such a rule as that of which I am speaking: i.e. a rule prohibiting the formation of large partnerships or unincorporated joint-stock companies? A friend in New York supplied me with some very interesting trust deeds which in effect seemed to create companies of this sort. Should I then be right in supposing that in the U.S.A. the unincorporate company lived on beside the new trading corporation?

I am endeavouring to explain in a German journal[1] how our law (or equity) of trusts enabled us to keep alive 'unincorporate bodies' which elsewhere must have perished. Of course I must not speak of America. Still I should like to know in a general way whether the development of the 'unincorporated company' which we repressed in 1862 was similarly repressed in the States, and a word or two from you about this matter would be most thankfully received.[2]

By the way—and here I enter your own particular close—I observed that those New York deeds were careful to confine the trust within the limits of the perpetuity rule.[3] Is it settled American law that this is necessary? We explain our *clubs* by saying that as the whole equitable ownership is vested in the original members there can be no talk of perpetuity, and I believe that there are some extremely important unincorporated companies with transferable shares (formed before 1862—in particular the London Stock Exchange) which are built up on this theory: the theory is that the original shareholders were in equity absolute masters of the land, buildings, etc. Does that commend itself to you?

[1] *Trust und Korporation* (Vienna, 1904): reprinted in English C.P. III. 321.
[2] On 4 Nov. 1903 Gray replied: 'I do not know of any legislation in this country prohibiting joint stock companies. . . . They have lived on alongside the corporations. In Massachusetts they are not common; in New York they are more common' (Camb. Univ. MSS.).
[3] Gray replied: 'Clauses putting lives into trust instruments are common. . . . In *Howe v. Morse*, 174 Mass. 491, the Court of this state had a great fight over the question. I was not counsel but I was trustee of a real estate trust which had no lives in it, and we submitted a brief to the court on the question. They would not receive our brief, but a new judge, who had been brought up in my office on sound principles, turned the scale, and, after holding the case a year, they decided that lives were unnecessary.'

There! you see what comes of writing to me! A whole catechism! Please think no more of it unless a very few words would set my feet in the straight road.

Most of my time is being given to the Year Books. The first volume is with the binder.

I often look back with great pleasure to the few hours that you and Mrs. Gray spent with us in Gloucestershire. Would that I could see you again, but all my journeys have to be to the Canaries.

365. To H. A. L. Fisher

Downing College
Cambridge
17 Oct. 1903

MY DEAR HERBERT,

It was very pleasant to have a letter from you: this was the next best thing to seeing you. Of your visit I hope we are not to be deprived by a change in the date of the Ambarum dinner. (Is the election of a Chancellor a serious affair? I should have supposed that it would be 'settled out of court' by those who pull the wires).[1] But whether you come upon the original or the substituted date you and Mrs. H. will be very welcome.

I have just been reading A. W. Ward's review of your Napoleonic book.[2] I could have wished that he had said more about you; still I hope that you are satisfied. Yesterday he told me that he had been reading your book on a day on which he dined with us and had then no notion that you were his hostess's brother. 'As a man' I like him very much—but his pen seems full of German.

These last days I have often wished that you were at my side, for at Leathes' request I have been reading a chapter on Revolutionary Legislation stiffly translated from the French of Paul Viollet—and I have not always known what the good man was driving at. A duller man would have written a more useful chapter. It is possible that we may have to appeal to you to explain to us the sentence concerning Boney and the Jews.[3]

I am sorry to hear that even you find Henry VII dull, for if you cannot put life into him his case must be hopeless and dull he will have to be for ever. However I shall not easily believe that you have not infused a little new blood into his pale person.[4]

Leslie is wonderful. I have never had pleasanter talks with him than this year. Still I can't help seeing that in the matter of mere strength the ebb is rapid. His reminiscences are delightful and I have no doubt that the Hobbes will be worthy of him.

[1] Lord Goschen was elected to succeed Lord Salisbury as Chancellor of Oxford University.
[2] *Napoleonic Statesmanship, Germany* (1903).
[3] See Fisher's Chap. VI in Camb. Mod. Hist. Vol. IX.
[4] Fisher was preparing a volume on the period 1485–1547 for Longman's series *The Political History of England*.

You know that I have not been lucky. One unfortunate ride in the rain squelched numerous projects—and I fear that in December I must get into the sun or run the chance of passing much time in bed. I don't like going—exile in the Hesperides is exile still, and I deeply fear that if and when I return there will be a big gap in the small circle of my friends.

I am making an attempt to start a class in palaeography and am teaching three hours every other day—thus I apologize for the retention of a professorship—but I feel that the apology is pretty thin.

> Until we meet,
> Yours v. affectionately
> F. W. MAITLAND

366. To John Chipman Gray

[No original. Printed by Fisher, *Memoir*, 146–7: no beginning or ending.]

> Downing College,
> Cambridge.
> *15 Nov. 1903*

Your very kind letter of the 4th is exactly what I wanted.[1] But surely there is nothing 'odd' in my asking you questions which you of living men can answer best. It would be odd if I went elsewhere.

The brief in *Howe v. Morse* is extremely interesting. I think that an English Court would take your view in such a case, but when it comes to questions about legacies our judges sometimes *say* things which stray from the path of rectitude as drawn by Prof. Gray.

I have been trying all this summer to finish an essay designed to explain to Germans the nature of a trust, and especially the manner in which the trust enabled us to keep alive all sorts of 'bodies' which were not technically corporate. I am obliged now to flee to the Canaries leaving this unfinished, for a particularly fraudulent summer has made me very useless. Some one ought to explain our trust to the world at large, for I am inclined to think that the construction thereof is the greatest feat that men of our race have performed in the field of jurisprudence. Whether I shall be able to do this remains to be seen—but it ought to be done.

367. To H. A. L. Fisher

> Downing College
> Cambridge
> *16 Nov. 1903*

MY DEAR HERBERT,

I am truly grateful for Vandal[2]: it looks as if it would carry me far towards Canary.

---

[1] For Gray's letter of 4 Nov. 1903, on which M. here comments, see Letter 364, *supra*.
[2] Vandal, *L'Avènement de Bonaparte* (1903).

The Hobbes is, as you would expect, very good indeed—but the MS was very bad in places and the typist had a difficult task, not always well performed. I fear that I cannot bring the typed copy into shape before I go. You can guess the sort of little problem that arises on page after page, and I am not well able to run about and solve them rapidly. So it may be that later on I may have to ask you some questions not answerable in the Canaries.[1]

I have, I can assure you, been carrying altruism to its limits when I have not pestered you with commendations of Cambridge. I fear it is not to be—but how you would have made that Camb. Mod. History hum![2]

I have done pretty well these last days and have a good account by wire of the voyage to Tenerife.[3]

May you soon polish off the two Tudors and return to your beloved Boney![4]

Yours very affectionately

F. W. MAITLAND

368. To Leslie Stephen

[No original. Printed by Fisher, *Memoir*, 147–8: no beginning or ending.]

Leon y Castillo 5,
Telde,
Gran Canaria.
6 Dec. 1903.

I fear that I must not carry my good wishes beyond the point of hoping that the improvement that I saw last time I visited you has gone further and that at any rate you are easy and free from pain. I have just had a week in this island. Part of it I spent foolishly in bed, but now I am in a delightful atmosphere and have been thoroughly enjoying your Hobbes. It is worthy of you, and you know what I mean when I say that. I have been all through it once and have corrected most of the typist's errors. A few little points must stand over until I can command the whole of the 'Works' (I only brought two volumes with me), but they are not of such a kind as would prevent the copy going to the printers, and I propose to send it to them very soon, for they will let me keep the stuff in type until I am again in England. The difficulties to which I refer are words occurring in your quotations from Hobbes—just here and there your writing beats me, but a few minutes with Molesworth[5] will settle the matter . . .

I think I told you that in my estimate you have written, more rather than less, your due tale of words. I shall add nothing save some tag which will serve as a substitute for the missing end of the final paragraph (said tag I may

---

[1] 'The *Hobbes*, the work of a man who was dying by inches, was finished. A friend carried off the manuscript and proof-sheets to a remote land after receiving some lucid instructions and saying or trying to say farewell' (M. *Life of L. S.* 486).
[2] Reference obscure.
[3] Whither Mrs. Maitland had preceded him.
[4] See Letter 365, *supra*.
[5] *The Works of Hobbes*, ed. by Sir W. Molesworth, 1839–46.

be able to submit to you) and I shall omit nothing save trifles unless the publishers insist.

I have been speculating as to what T. H. would have said had he lived until 1688. If it becomes clear that your 'sovereign' is going to acknowledge the pope's claims, this of course is no breach of any contract between ruler and ruled (for there is no such contract), but is there not an abdication? Putting theory out of the question, which would the old gentleman have disliked most, Revolution against Leviathan or a Leviathan with the Roman fisherman's hook in his nose?

Well, he was a delightful old person and deserved the expositor whom he has found.

369. To W. W. Buckland

> 5 Leon y Castillo
> Telde
> *13 Dec. 1903*

MY DEAR BUCKLAND,

This place is full of memories of you[1] and I cannot cross the bridge without seeing your beloved daughter balancing herself on the parapet. I had a warm and calm voyage, strange to tell, and the Bay was really delightful. Then what we call Canary fever took me and I had some days in bed, during which the rain descended in very serious earnest, having been moved thereto by a procession bearing the milagroso Cristo de Telde flanked by a brass band. The mud after that was appalling and cycling was out of the question. Now the sun has shone for some days and yesterday I pedalled and pushed almost as far as Jinamar—but, apart from mud, the road is in much worse plight than it was two years ago. Never in my life here have I been so jolted as I was in my ride in a tatana from Las Palmas hither. The climate has begun to do its blessed work and already I am making good progress with my photographs[2]; but would that you were here!

Are you Christmassing at Caius or at the (forgive me!) Pseudo-Telde on Dartmoor? I fancy from telegrams in the Diario—that marvellous Diario!— that it has been cold and stormy up north.

Just before I left 'the Squire' came to see me and he told me that he thought your book on Slavery was pretty well finished.[3] I hope that this is so. I very much desire to know that you are fully committed to publication. Unquestionably the Press would be glad of the work—but perhaps another publisher would give you better terms. I am quite sure—as sure as I can be of anything— that you have a lot to teach the world, yea, even the German part thereof, and I hope that you will not wait too long. For many reasons—not all selfish—I

---

[1] Buckland had spent a previous winter in the Canaries with M. See Buckland, *F. W. Maitland*, C.L.J. Vol. I (1923), 279.

[2] Of Y.B. manuscripts.

[3] From Buckland's reply to this letter (24 Dec. 1903, in Camb. Univ. MSS.), 'the Squire' would seem to be W. J. Whittaker. Buckland's *The Roman Law of Slavery* was published by Camb. Univ. Press in 1908.

want to see Cambridge and you producing a great book on Roman Law. Take the admonition in good part and be not modest, muy señor mio. Let your light so shine before men that they may see your good works.

Don Luis kisses your hand. I have not yet seen the limping Santiago.[1] Your house is empty—I wish it were not.

Yours very truly

F. W. MAITLAND

The drought had been serious. Vegetables were costly, but a few hours of rain bring out the green.

370. To Henry Jackson

[Printed, with omissions, by Fisher, *Memoir*, 148–50. Now printed from the original in Camb. Univ. MSS.]

Leon y Castillo 5
Telde
Gran Canaria
13 Dec. 1903

MY DEAR JACKSON,

This may—I cannot be sure that it will—be in time to salute you on Christmas day. Posts are irregular and nine miles of bad road separate us from Las Palmas. So, not being able as yet to cycle to our ciudad, I shall just drop this into the village letter-box and trust that it may reach you some day.

I had the good luck to find the Bay of Biscay reflecting a really warm sun, and very soon I could hardly believe that so grey a place as Cambridge existed. I arrived here at the end of a prolonged drought and the good folk of Telde 'clapped on the prayer for rain'—or rather they did much more; they carried round the town a milagroso Cristo whom they keep for great occasions. I am not sure that the priest let him go his rounds until he, the priest, saw that the clouds were collecting thick over the mountains. Anyhow the rain came at once to the great edification of the faithful. Since then we have celebrated the Immaculate Conception. It is very queer how events get turned into persons. The Conception becomes a person for the people. I think that the historian of myths would learn a good deal here. Just lately I discovered—it was no great discovery—that the pet name 'Concha' is the short for Concepcion, as Lola is the short for Dolores. My protestant mind has been a little shocked by a female form of Jesus, namely 'Jesusa'.

I am living in hope that Pollock's successor at Oxford may be Vinogradoff. My own belief is that he will make a better professor than either Sir F. P. or Sir H. M. I wish much that we had him at Cambridge—but I felt last year that it was useless to say anything about him to Balfour as the Crown could hardly

---

[1] Don Luis was the local shopkeeper, a man of dignity save when he unbent, riding 'in a tatana with his chosen companions—standing up singing an improvised song to the tune of a guitar' (*Fredegond and Gerald Shove*, priv. printed 1952, p. 23). The 'limping Santiago' was perhaps one of the 'chosen companions'.

appoint a man to whom the Russian Government was (in effect) giving the sack. A board of electors has freer hands.[1]

I am curious to hear any news that there may be concerning the deliberations of the great Syndicate.[2] I suppose that something will be known before I return to Cambridge—if ever I return. I say 'if ever' for I am always thinking of resignation. Out here I can do a great deal with photographed manuscripts and so on, whereas in England I get nothing done.

You, I suppose, are deep in 'Josephism'—by the way has anybody endeavoured to transfer that term from a manner of treating the church to Mr. C.'s fiscal policy? My latest newspaper gives the Duke's oration—how very good our Chancellor can be!—but no doubt that is with you a very ancient history. My own impression when I left England was that the crusade was failing.[3]

I forget the name of your house in Eastbourne,[4] so this must go to Trinity. I hope that all goes well with you.

Yours very truly

F. W. MAITLAND

371. To B. Fossett Lock

Leon y Castillo
Telde
Gran Canaria
20 Dec. 1903

DEAR LOCK,

Your good letter[5] came to my hands yesterday and I am very grateful to you for the trouble that you are taking in the matter of the Year Books. I was indeed thinking of laying before you some statement of my doings, for during the last fortnight I have got through a good deal of work and this blessed sun converts despondency into hopefulness.

Allowing space for 'Notes from the Record' I have pretty well finished as much as the volume for 1905[6] will hold. The photographs are excellent material and collation becomes easy when you have everything on one small table. I believe that another fortnight will see all done that can be done without the plea rolls. I was thinking whether to go on or not. The year 1907 seems far off and I do not feel sure that anyone would without difficulty be able to pick

---

[1] Vinogradoff was elected: see Letters 372 and 374, *infra*.
[2] Buckland, in a letter to M. of 4 Dec. 1903 (Camb. Univ. MSS.), had written: 'You will have seen that a Syndicate has been appointed to see what we must do, academically speaking, to be saved. It is expected to report that we must sell all we have and give it to the Professors of Science.' See Letter 377, *infra*.
[3] Joseph Chamberlain and the Duke of Devonshire (Chancellor of Cambridge University) had both resigned from Balfour's cabinet in the autumn of 1903, the former to 'crusade' for Protection, the latter to oppose it.
[4] A mistake for Bournemouth.
[5] Of 11 Dec. 1903 (S.S. Corr.). Lock urged M. to 'proceed at your own pace with Edw. II. YBB, leaving us to publish as fast as we can'.
[6] S.S. Vol. 20.

up the threads if they fell from my hands. But of course it would make a great difference in my estimate of the situation if I knew that the Society would allow me to go on printing. In that case even if I left behind me a considerable mass of unpublished stuff, someone could be found to make it into volumes. As I do not see any hope of employing my time more profitably than in copying, collating and translating, I am much inclined to catch at your kind suggestion.

There is one point, however, to which I would ask your attention. I will put it in the form of a question. Do you think that it would be a very expensive plan to print *in slip* my text and translation of the reports before the records are searched? The amount of change necessary in the printed stuff if and when a record was found would never, I think, be large. It would consist chiefly of the substitution of the proper 'proper names' for contorted versions of them. I suppose that the mere introduction of 'Notes from the Record' at appropriate places would not be costly. But I will ask you to give this a thought. The reason why I raise this question you will easily guess, for you know the strong and weak points of little T.[1] But I must also add that if I were employing anyone less familiar than he is with the forms of action, I should think it a great gain to be able to put into his hands a printed version of the reports in order that he might find the corresponding records.

I think that in the meanwhile I will go ahead with vol. III.[2] I do not like to throw up the projected Edward I, for the Univ. Press has already paid for photographs,[3] but, as I do not expect to find more than one manuscript, this would be 'a little holiday' for me (I have about ten MSS of 3 Edw. II!), and I could leave this behind with a fair hope that some one else would see it printed.

I do not think myself that the Society would be wise in dropping all other work—I am admiring the Borough Customs[4]—but if an additional volume is within our budget it might well be a volume of YBB. You know that I have copied, though only from one faulty MS, the unprinted Kentish Eyre.[5]

As to Academy and Treasury, I gathered from some papers that came just before your letter that there was a move in the direction that you name—the mover seemed to be Ilbert.[6] I rather hope that I may not be officially asked for an opinion about the size of the task. I am now in doubt whether, taking an average, we can get more than one year into one of our volumes—there is so much that never has been printed. Pike can't make a volume hold a whole year. Very simple arithmetic tells us that $200 \div 1 = 200$: but of course if 'fat' were 'expelled' and there were heavy folios, there could be a great saving in the matter of indexes. A grant from the Treasury does not seem to me very

[1] G. J. Turner.
[2] To become, posthumously, Vol. 22: see Intro. by Turner, xlii–iii.
[3] This project remains obscure.
[4] S.S. Vol. 18.
[5] Later published as S.S. Vols 24, 27, 29: see esp. Preface to Vol. 24.
[6] Sir Courtenay Ilbert, Parliamentary Counsel to the Treasury and a Fellow of the British Academy. Lock had written: 'To-day I got a private letter from [Lord] Lindley that he is hoping to get the British Academy to move to get money from Government in support of the Y.B. work.'

likely. And at any rate I am not disposed to minimise in order to obtain it: I mean that in my opinion it will in the end be better that I should give two or even three versions of a case when two or three are to be found than that I should constantly feel that at all hazard I must be short. On the whole it seems to me that people will take more interest in the reports if there are a few volumes which show how the work was done. However, about this, as about all such matters, I shall highly value your opinion.

What you tell me of the reception of the volume by the Society is cheering and will keep me going through the winter.[1]

Really this place is too divine for words. I came here a very poor creature and now can both walk and copy.

It remains to wish you very many happy new years.

Yours very truly
F. W. Maitland

372. To H. A. L. Fisher

5 Leon y Castillo
Telde
10 Jan. 1904

My dear Herbert,

Many thanks for your letter. It was full of news. I greatly rejoice over Vinogradoff's appointment,[2] but cannot claim any share in bringing it about unless indeed I may have removed some dread of political agitation. That was the point to which I directed the remarks that I sent to the President of Corpus. I envy Oxford—getting him and keeping you! But you must admit that in the latter case we did our little best.[3]

I have been having a really good time, so good that I am beginning to think that, even if I vanish from the scene, not only vol. 2 but also vol. 3 of the Year Books will be published, though it is not due until 1906. It is not exciting work —not half so grand as writing of Tudors and Boney—but it seems the best that I can do nowadays and will bring a little money to my exs., ads. or assns, even when photographs are paid for. The only drawback or crumpled rose-leaf is that it makes the time pass with terrible rapidity—and life is so good here and (I regret to say it) so bad at home.

I am very glad that you are a Ford elector. Really you ought to begin by electing yourself—but I should be very glad to hear that Round's merits were recognized: they are very real and I should be sorry if he gave himself wholly to pedigrees.

In a paper concerning the children of Israel I thought that I saw the hand of your excellent father-in-law.[4] I am not quite sure that I should like to see

---

1 Lock had written: 'Your Vol. I has taken the Society by storm, and not only the Society.'
2 See Letters 370, *supra*, and 374, *infra*.
3 Reference obscure: see Letter 367, *supra*.
4 Sir Courtenay Ilbert: see Letter 371, *supra*.

any great scheme for Year Books formulated yet, for I am making experiments and 'greater freedom and less responsibility' is a phrase that often occurs to me.

Our mail is very late this week. I am writing under a sense of impending loss—but I suppose that I ought not to hope that the philosopher will linger among us. It is a grand end, I think—worthy of him. I hope that the world will like the Hobbes. You can guess what it is like—a beautiful sunset.

I long to talk of all manner of things, but at present must content me with silence and sun worship.

Yours affectionately

F. W. MAITLAND

I have put too much water into my ink to suit this thin paper. The mixture is meant for 'blue draft'.

Florence, who loves Telde, greets you.

373. To Henry Jackson

Leon y Castillo 5
Telde
Gran Canaria
10 Jan. 1904

MY DEAR JACKSON,

Your good letter[1] told me many things that I was glad to know. Vinogradoff's appointment at Oxford pleases me greatly and I think that he will make a first rate professor. Yes, he had to quit Moscow, though whether it came to an actual 'sack' I don't know. He told me years ago that this event must happen sooner or later. He was expected to teach an official version of history and there were always spies of the Minister of Education among his audience. When last year—or rather I mean in 1902—he lectured to extension students in the theatre at Cambridge I knew that he was finally cutting the painter, though all that he said was studiously moderate, as you may see from the printed book.[2] I think that Mrs. V. (a Swede)[3] and I were the only people in the theatre who knew what was happening—I mean that boats were being burnt and bridges destroyed. I don't precisely know why F. P. made room at Oxford, but he is very well paid as editor of the Law Reports and I think that he had difficulty in obtaining hearers—or rather that he would not make any effort to obtain them. He has no notion of adapting supply to

---

[1] Of 24 Dec. 1903 (Camb. Univ. MSS.).
[2] *The Reforming Work of the Tsar Alexander II and the Meaning of the Present Development in Russia*, printed in *Lectures on the History of the XIXth Cent., given at the Cambridge University Extension Summer Meeting, 1902*.
[3] A Norwegian.

demand: you must take what he thinks good for you or leave it alone, and the young gents with examinations before them left it alone.

Many thanks for the jest about Verrall.[1] It is so very good that some one ought to have made it twenty years ago—but at any rate it is new to me. I have often thought that with another voice Verrall would have been one of the greatest of advocates,[2] would have won hopeless cases and have saved all sorts of rogues from their due punishment. It is good news that he takes a term 'off': I wish that he had done this before now, for I believe and have reason to believe in the sun—God bless him!

Yes, before your letter came I saw the Athenaeum and said to myself 'But what will the other J. say to this?' It was a very nasty little screed. The author I can't guess. I don't know your classical men well enough. Our mail is late this week—and most weeks—but before I close this another Athenaeum with a reply from the true and only J. may come to hand and be enjoyed.[3]

With what you say of 'the children of Israel' and the Treasury I agree. I saw signs of Ilbert's hand in the circular, especially in what was said of Year Books. I don't think for certain that I should like any national treasure at present. I am enjoying great freedom and little responsibility and for the time being I think it will be better that I should go on making experiments than that a grand scheme for a couple of hundred volumes should be formulated. I fear to hear it said that this or that device would be too expensive. As it is, I order photographs whenever I please and am not out of pocket. By the way, can you give me some Latin 'tag' beginning with the word 'Discas'? My friend Bereford, Chief Justice, makes this remark—'Vous estes en le cas de discas, etc.'[4] What he means is (so I think) 'Be wise another time' or 'Learn from this failure'; and all will go well if I can get an appropriately moral verse likely to be known to an Englishman in 1310. I think it very possible that the right 'tag' will at once occur to you, though I can't agree when you call yourself a 'damned scholiast'. A post card would enlighten me. I won't ask for more for term must be beginning.

Can you read this? I find that I have put more water into my ink than suits this thin paper. I made the mixture for 'blue draft'.

I dread the approaching mail though I can hardly wish that Leslie Stephen should linger.

Yours very truly

F. W. Maitland

---

[1] Jackson had written: 'Have you heard that Verrall gave a lecture in which he maintained that the *Birds* is a satire on that Palestinian religion now best represented in England and that what is satirised appears in the chapels of Jesus, John's and Trinity?... The lecture was set up for publication in the *Cambridge Review* when Verrall, the evening before the *Review* appeared, withdrew it. The Editor revenged himself by publishing the facts and commenting upon the lecture—"si non è vero, è Verrall".'

[2] In 1877 Verrall was a pupil, with M., in the chambers of B. B. Rogers (Hollond, *Frederic William Maitland*, 9).

[3] Jackson had written: 'Last Saturday a new "Cambridge Correspondent" of the *Athenaeum* had a letter about compulsory Greek which abounded in insinuations and misrepresentations. He signs himself J. as I did . . . J. will answer him.'

[4] S.S. Vol. 20, pp. 25 and 68.

374. To Paul Vinogradoff

[No original: a fragment printed by Fisher in his memoir of Vinogradoff in Vinogradoff, *Coll. Pap.* I. at p. 31. No date, but from contents and context clearly Jan. 1904.]

. . . Well, it is pleasant. We did not think of this when in an Oxford garden[1] you told me that I ought to go the Record Office. Now I shall look to you to fire some one else. I badly need a coadjutor *cum spe successionis* in my Year Book work. You must find me one, Señor Catedratico.

375. To B. Fossett Lock

Leon y Castillo 5
Telde
Gran Canaria
20 Jan. 1904

MY DEAR LOCK,

Your hero worship is of the best kind. Many thanks for the portraits: also for your letter. No, I won't trouble myself about that array of 0000's.[2] I think that 0 will come of it—and indeed I should be rather sorry if anything came of it at present. I don't want to have the Chancellor of the Exchequer pulling at my coat-tails just when I have got the pace on. If Providence allows me to work in the Lincoln's Inn Library for a few days I think that I shall be able before the summer is out to put not merely a volume but two volumes into the printer's hands—vols., that is, of text and translation. I like the project of working in the notes from the record into an already printed text. Turner also *ought* to like it: but one never can predict his dislikes.

You will I think like to know (and will not think me vain for telling you) that I have a very pleasant note about Vol. I, from the great Paul Meyer.[3] I did not know him and he was the man whose judgment I most feared, so when he says that the task was difficult and could not have been better done I feel warm and comfortable. He can do us a good turn in France.

Can you as a classical scholar supply me with a Latin tag beginning with the word *discas*—and meaning something like 'Be wise another time' or 'Learn from this failure'? I get it thus:—

Ber. Vous estes en le cas de discas.

On another occasion a serjeant's speech is made to end (corruptly) with 'addistas al'.[4] There was, I think, some moral tag so well known that you had

---

[1] According to Fisher, *Memoir*, 24–5, the talk between M. and Vinogradoff took place in the Parks at Oxford: but see Plucknett, *Early English Legal Literature*, 8–9. See also Letter 370, *supra*.
[2] In his letter of 2 Jan. 1904 (S.S. Corr.) Lock wrote that he had been trying, for the possible use of the Treasury (see Letter 371, *supra*), to estimate the cost of producing 200 volumes of Y.B.B. and thought that 'it ought to be £100,000'. There is nothing in his letter about 'the portraits'.
[3] See Letter 361, *supra*.   [4] See Letter 373, *supra*.

no need to finish it. Very likely you will be able to put it on a postcard.

I hope that you are as well 'as this leaves me'.

Yours very truly

F. W. MAITLAND

I believe that the Kentish eyre would fill a respectable volume when notes were added;[1] but I have not got it with me here and it is long since I looked at it. I could not send that to the Press until after another winter with photographs—before when I shall have had speech with you.

376. To Charles Sweet

[No original. In 26 L.Q.R. (1910), pp. 196–8, C. S. (Charles Sweet) transcribed three passages from a letter written to him by M. and 'dated Gran Canaria, 23 Jan. 1904', in reply to three suggestions made by Sweet in a letter not extant and prompted by M.'s Intro. to S.S. Vol. 17, pp. xlvii–iii. Sweet's suggestions are here repeated in square brackets in Sweet's words].

Gran Canaria

23 Jan. 1904

['In answer to a letter suggesting that *cestui que trust* was a justifiable phrase made up by analogy to *cestui que use* and *cestui que vie*': C. S.]

. . . The remark that *cestui que trust* is worse than 'prescription in a *que estate*' was perhaps unfortunate.[2] I suspect, however, that *cestui que trust* was not made until people were regarding as verbs the *use* and the *vie* in the two older terms that you cite. I feel pretty sure that the clerks of 'my time'—let us say circ. 1350—would not have written either *cestui que vie* or *cestui que use*. They would have written *cestui a qui oes le feffement fut fait, cestui pour qui vie le dit x tient*, and the like. I have here on my table photographs from seven MSS. additional to those that I previously examined, and I can repeat now with greater certainty that circ. 1350 the 'indirect object case' is usually *qui*. One may find *que heir il est*, as one may find almost anything, but it is not usual.

By the time that 'uses' are becoming prominent the language has fallen to a considerably lower level than that represented by my introduction. I suspect a gradual descent from *cestui a qui oes* (*la terre est tenue* or the like) to *cestui que use*, but I fancy that by the time that men have fashioned the latter phrase they are beginning to think of *que* as the subject of a verb. The gradual substitution of *use* for *oes* (*opus*) shows that the language is already in a bad way. Is it not also to be remembered that the early feoffments to uses are generally feoffments to the use of the feoffor? I think one might say that in the first stage of the development the *cestui que trust* is a trustor who has placed trust in a feoffee; he is author of the trust as well as sole beneficiary. This makes further confusion possible. . . .

---

[1] It filled three: S.S. Vols. 24, 27, 29.
[2] In S.S. Vol. 17, Intro. p. xlviii, M. had in fact written: 'Our phrase "to prescribe in a *que* estate" is less justifiable than our *cestui que trust*.' Naturally he would not have had the volume with him in the Canaries.

['In answer to the suggestion that *que* in the sense of "because" might possibly be derived from the Latin *quia*': C. S.]

... I thought much about the *que* which means 'for' being derived from *quia* and nearly made this suggestion; but I could not find the slightest support for this in French grammars and dictionaries. All seemed to agree that *quia* did not live and that *que* is *quod* even when it means 'because'. In Spanish one can use *que* in this way as an equivalent for *por que*, and I understand that in Latin this could be *quod* instead of *per quod* (*Ande V., que es tarde*—says a grammar— Come along, for it is late) . . .

['In answer to the suggestion that the —ee, in which many old French words terminate, resembles the —é in masculine words in modern French, such as *musée* (from *museum*) and the e in *foie* (from *ficatum*) and that the second or final e represents the Latin —*um*': C. S.]

... As to —ee for mod. Fr. —e. I think that if we said that in *Le bref fut portee* the last e really descended from the —*um* of *portatum*, we should be flying in the face of a rule that is based on a very wide induction, and I suspect that we should be told that even in Anglo-French the doubled e does not appear until long after the Conquest. Are your examples to the point? *Musée* is a word of 'learned formation'. I think we should be told that if *museum* had had a continuous life in the mouths of the people it would have come out as *musé*; just as *senatum* would have become *séné* and not the 'learned' *sénat*. As to *foie*, I have not my books with me and I forget how the *foi*— is explained; but I fancy that the final e is the *a* of —*atum*, not the —*um*.

377. To Henry Jackson

[Printed, with many omissions, by Fisher, *Memoir*, 150–2. Now printed from the original in Camb. Univ. MSS.]

Leon y Castillo 5
Telde
Gran Canaria

14 Feb. 1904

MY DEAR JACKSON,

It was much too good of you to write me a long letter when you were laid up. Very seriously I wish that you had not done it. I sincerely hope that said vein gives no more trouble—but have a care and don't waste precious energy in sending me news, even though you know that your letters make a lot of difference to the exile.[1]

No, you draw a wrong inference from my silence. When I am hurt I cry. When I am not crying I am happy. In this instance I have been very happy

[1] In his letter of 27 Jan. 1904 (Camb. Univ. MSS.) Jackson wrote that a vein in his leg had been 'playing the giddy goat' and feared that M., in not writing of *his* health, was concealing illness.

indeed and so busy that I have taken six weeks over a novel and am once more developing a corn on my little finger by copying. One of my few sorrows is that somehow or another I contrived to miss just that Athenaeum in which you spoke your mind about the Pseudo-J, or I suppose that I might now say the Faux Jackson.[1] Also I should have liked to see the answer to the Spectator's Appanage—the article itself I have seen—not very well informed.[2] All that you tell me of the Studies Syndicate[3] is extremely interesting—you may rely upon my discretion for, as you remark, there is nobody to whom I could babble: even La Mañana which is often hard up for news would I fear give me nothing for secret intelligence concerning the S.S.

Writing those initials made me think of your Eranus.[4] I wish that I had heard you. I think that I might have been able to add an ancient story or two. I think that I once told you how 'to wit' placed after the name of a county at the beginning of a legal record (e.g. Cambridgeshire, to wit, A. B. complains that C. D. etc.) represents a mere flourish ʃ dividing the name of the county from the beginning of the story. This was mistaken for a long S which was supposed to be the abbreviation of *scilicet*. The Spaniards are fond of using mere initials: after a dead person's name you can put q.d.h.e.g. = que Dios haya en gloria. The case that amuses me most is that you can speak of the Host as S. D. M. (his divine majesty—just like H. R. H.). One day in Las Palmas I had to spring from my bicycle and kneel in the road because S. D. M. was coming along. But I have just had my revenge. I have been mistaken for S. D. M. They ring a little bell in front of him. I rarely ring my bicycle bell because I don't think it a civil thing to do in a land where cycles are very rare. However the other day I was almost upon the backs of two men, so I rang. They started round and at the same time instinctively raised their hats—and instead of S. D. M. there was only an *hereje*.

To be sure those letters of Acton's are thrilling. I saw them out here last year. Mrs. Drew wanted me to edit them.[5] I guess that I saw a good deal more than you have seen. I declined the task, after talking to Leslie Stephen. Obviously I was not the right man. I am boundlessly ignorant of contemporary history and could not in the least tell what would give undeserved and unnecessary pain. On the other hand I should think that H. Paul was the right man for the job. I gather from you that he suppresses the end of the correspondence. That was one of the points about which I felt a good deal of doubt. In some respects it 'tailed off'. Also so far as I could estimate it was likely to strengthen the impression that Lord A. was 'Mr. G.'s evil genius'. There were things about South Africa and Egypt that made in this direction, and yet I felt

[1] See Letter 373, *supra*.

[2] Jackson had written: 'The *Spectator* of last Saturday had an unkind article on *The Appanage of Audley End*'. It attacked Lord Braybrooke who had the right to appoint the Master of Magdalene College, Cambridge. The previous Master had just died.

[3] Jackson had written: 'I hear it whispered that the Studies Syndicate is going vigorously to work and that the dread word "Greek" has been mentioned.' See Letters 370, *supra*, and 383, *infra*.

[4] Jackson had read to the Eranus a paper on *Scribes' Errors*.

[5] Mrs. Drew was Gladstone's daughter. The letters were edited by Herbert Paul (1853–1935) and published in 1904 as *Letters of Lord Acton to Mary Gladstone*.

that they were too allusive and too meagre to stand as representations of A.'s opinions, especially where those opinions were not of the kind that is popular.

I also gather from you that you have not seen all that was written about George Eliot. I remember that when writing to Mrs. Drew I took as an example of passages which in my opinion ought not to go out to the world a bit of a letter in which A. said in effect that he knew (and thought that Gladstone ought to know) something that was very much to G. E.'s discredit. What that something was did not appear—but I could not suppose that it was just what we all know about Mr. and Mrs. Lewes. I told Mrs. Drew that just because the nature of the charge did not appear (and consequently defence would be impossible) it ought not, in my opinion, to be repeated. There were, too, some casual expressions about divers people of no public importance (O. B.[1] for one) which I should have left out, and I dare say that H. Paul has thought the same. As to Newman and Manning all that is splendid.

I am very glad indeed to hear that you are supplying Cambridge reminiscences.[2] No one else could do it so well. Mrs. Drew wanted me to review the book for the Quarterly: if I could have done that anywhere I could not have done it here.

Send me a post card—not more—about yourself. I hope that Vol. II[3] is doing well, though I foresee that I shall be slated in all quarters. Acton was an adroit flatterer and induced me to put my hand far into a very nest of hornets.

Yours very truly

F. W. MAITLAND

378. To Henry Jackson

[Post-card.]

Leon y Castillo 5

Telde

Gran Canaria

25 Feb. 1904

Please do not give yourself more trouble over *discas*. I have found a chap lapsing from French into Latin in order to say 'discas alias ut cautius negocieris [sic]'.[4] This is prosaic enough. I suspect that it must come from a fable: it seems the sort of thing that Brer Fox might say if he talked Latin.

I am simply amazed at the onesidedness of the fiscal debate.

George E. was not quite 'goddess'—or was 'goddess' with a flaw.

I devoutly hope that su pierna de Vd.[5] gives no further trouble.

Y.v.t.

F. W. M.

[1] Oscar Browning.

[2] Jackson had given Herbert Paul information about Acton at Cambridge: see Paul, Intro. to *Letters of Lord Acton to Mary Gladstone*, pp. lxix–lxxiii.

[3] Of the Camb. Mod. Hist., containing M.'s chapter on *The Anglican Settlement and the Scottish Reformation*.

[4] S.S. Vol. 20, p. 25, n. 1. See Letters 373 and 375, *supra*.

[5] The leg that Jackson had written was troubling him. On this and the two preceding sentences, see Letter 377, *supra*.

379. To Henry Jackson

5 Leon y Castillo
Telde
5 March 1904

MY DEAR JACKSON,

Thanks for yet another note. I hope it means that the said vein has ceased its goatings.[1]

I did not expect to see Leslie Stephen again and I ought to be glad that he is out of pain.[2] But it is very true what Greenwood[3] says in the Pilot about him—at least in his later life—if you got as far as friendship you went much further. I don't know that it had always been so and perhaps you knew him too soon, but it was so when I began to tramp on the Sundays in his company: on this followed events important to me, e.g. marriage. I am now correcting the proof sheets of his 'Hobbes' for the 'Men of Letters'.

I have nothing to send you unless there is enough of the 'damned scholiast' about you[4] to care for a puzzle in Anglo-French circ. 1285 (n.b. the occurrence of an English word is very rare).

Il pert ke il ne poet tenyr si

yl ne les tynt de acun seynur. e

pur coe dyt um mon avez mon ẏenne

avez louerd to.

But the 'y' of ẏenne, though dotted, is not the writer's ordinary 'y.' I now see that he tried to copy a 'thorn' (þ)[5]—that gives the clue though the second 'mon' is redundant.

'It seems that he cannot hold unless he holds of some lord. And so me says (dyt um = on dit) when you have a man, then you have a lord too.'

You must well know the joy of making sense of unpromising script.

Yours very truly but (as regards the vein) anxiously

F. W. MAITLAND

380. To H. A. L. Fisher

Telde
5 March 1904

MY DEAR HERBERT,

I am in debt to you for a letter and had been meaning to pay it as best I could. And now I feel that I have something to write of and can't well write it. I suppose that we ought to be glad that Leslie has gone to his rest—and certainly to be glad that he suffered so little. Still when the event happens, though

---

1 See Letter 377, *supra*.
2 He had died on 22 February 1904.
3 Frederick Greenwood (1830–1909), journalist and editor of the *Pall Mall Gazette*, to which Leslie Stephen contributed many papers. M. cites his notice of Stephen in the *Pilot* in *Life of L. S.* 161–2.
4 See Letter 373, *supra*.
5 See Letter 383, *infra*.

one has been expecting it, there is a bad time for those who remain behind. I am sure that you feel it, and I feel it too. I cannot tell you how much I admired him—and F. Greenwood has said what is very true: it was impossible to stop at friendship.[1]

We are getting divers newspapers and cuttings. If anything *very* good appears, do preserve it for me. A bit of Greenwood, not quite the whole, was very good indeed. A letter from your mother tells us of the funeral. I would I had been there—though it would have been painful, especially as the children were present. He will, I think, stand out very big in course of time—but never as quite what he was to some of us.

Proofs of the Hobbes are coming in. When I have done all that I can I will ask you to look through them. A second eye will be useful in this case, for when I take them up I hear his voice and that may make me inattentive to commas and the like. I think that people ought to say that the book is quite as good as its predecessors—there could be no question as to authorship if it were an anonymous work: only one man could have done it.

Let us meet and talk of him. I must be thinking of moving. The thought is not quite so pleasant as I should wish it to be, but I have had so good a time that perhaps I may be able to keep out the cold of an English summer.

In the matter of the Tudors[2]—has it struck you that a glance at a few original acts of parliament might give you a little new material? I mean you might be able to say that parliament did or did not amend government bills—and this seems to me a rather interesting question.

I shall be curious to learn what Paul the son of Gabriel says of Sir Henry[3]—I have just had a letter from him (Paul).

Take an Easter holiday if you can.

Yours affectionately

F. W. MAITLAND

381. To H. A. L. Fisher

Telde

18 March 1904

MY DEAR HERBERT,

It was very kind of you to forestall my wishes—you knew what they would be. In the matter of newspaper notices I like Greenwood and I like the Times on the new book, which book attracts me to England for I have not yet seen it.[4] I have some fear that the critics will say foolish things of the Hobbes:

[1] See Letter 379, *supra*.
[2] See Letter 365, *supra*.
[3] Maine. Vinogradoff's Christian names were Paul Gavrilovitch. In his letter to M. of 24 Feb. 1904 (Camb. Univ. MSS.) Vinogradoff wrote: 'I am going [to Oxford] on the 1st of March, when my Inaugural will have to be delivered after an "exciting" theological debate in Congregation. My lecture ought to give a mild relaxation to the impassioned minds of the dons that will attend both events. It will treat of Maine, quite a cool subject nowadays.' The inaugural lecture, *The Teaching of Sir Henry Maine*, is reprinted in Vinogradoff, *Coll. Papers*, II. 205.
[4] *English Literature and Society in the Eighteenth Century*, the Ford Lectures for 1903, which had been read at Oxford on Stephen's behalf by Fisher and published in 1904.

about failing power and so on. I don't think that they will be true; but, after despatching in one chapter what is known of Hobbes' life, Leslie set himself to an exposition (with running comment) of the philosophy. It is a bit like the *Utilitarians*—and I fancy that the gentlemen who write for the newspapers will think it heavy, though really it is full of excellent thinking.

Perhaps John Morley[1] will allow me a short note about the manner in which the book was written. I think readers ought to know that finishing touches were not given: also that they ought not to suspect (only foolish people would do that, but there are fools) that they were not getting the real Leslie.

I don't think that I shall write anything else of him, though if I had been on the spot I might have been tempted to try. He is too big for me for one sort of writing and too dear for another.

Cast your eye over the Greek in the enclosed slip, 'there's a good chap'. My own Greek is of the most compulsory order. Are all the accents right? Just before I left England I looked up Στιγμή and Στίγμα,[2] but I was ill at the time and may have blundered. A false accent is so grave a crime that I trouble you with this small matter. Also will you, if you are within reach of a Wordsworth, verify Leslie's version of a famous verse. If his prepositions are right, most people misquote it.[3]

When I get to England I will ask you to go through the whole mass of proofs —it is no great mass, and I know that you will enjoy reading what he wrote even if you are attending to p's and q's.

I was an idiot to promise Prothero something about Liebermann. I cannot get into shape anything fit for the Quarterly and would give up the task only I think that 'Stubbs's Jew', as Freeman called him, would have just cause for complaint if no Englishman sang his praises.[4]

I hope that you are making holiday and that we shall meet soon. That dreary week at sea begins to sit heavy on my soul.

Florence sends her love.

Yours affectly

F. W. MAITLAND

382. To R. Lane Poole

Leon y Castillo 5
Telde
Gran Canaria
18 March 1904

The Reader in Diplomatic may be amused at hearing that the village postman

[1] He was responsible for the series *English Men of Letters* in which the *Hobbes* appeared. See Letters 385 and 388, *infra*.
[2] Leslie Stephen, *Hobbes*, 54.
[3] *Ibid.*, 185.
[4] G. W. Prothero was at this time editor of the *Quarterly Review*. M.'s review of Liebermann, *Die Gesetze der Angelsachsen*, Vol. I, appeared in the *Quarterly Review* for July 1904 and was reprinted in C.P. III. 447.

insists that a receipt given by me for a registered letter is invalid unless I put a flourish under my name: thus

Federigo Maitland

Apparently 'from the cross to the date' is a quite common phrase in colloquial Spanish—e.g. 'I know that book from cruz to fecha'.

383. To Henry Jackson

Telde

28 March 1904

MY DEAR JACKSON,

I am just now hesitating between two boats: the one leaves on the 8th, the other on the 9th. In any case I hope to be in Cambridge by the 16th and soon after that I shall present myself at your door, though I hope for the leg's sake you will make your vacation as long as it can be. This being so I should not have troubled you with news from an island which has no news if you had not been so very kind as to write two long letters full of all sorts of interesting things. Really I am very grateful indeed, for were it not for you and two or three other friends (Kenny is a first-rate chronicler) I should grow mouldy here, though lusty. I at once sent you a card to say that in the Free Trade matter I am all with you[1] and I am finding it very pleasant to be in line once more in the liberal ranks—the war it was that extruded me from the other side, but protection is a bit too strong. I have not heard whether Sir R. C. has 'elected' his side of the fence—if he chooses the wrong will there be opposition? I hope so. I go a long way with you about Harcourt and wish C. B. at the bottom of the sea.[2] Once at Trinity (at one of your old boys dinners) I was set next him and from that moment onwards I thought him a poor creature—about as 'ornary' as creatures are made.

It was very pleasant to read all that you wrote of Leslie Stephen. Every now and then he would tell of the Jesus set and of John Perkins whom he knew as Boots.[3] My acquaintance began when F. P. took me for 'a Sunday tramp'— Pollock now says that I appeared in a high hat, but that I had forgotten—and

---

[1] In a letter of 11 March 1904 (Camb. Univ. MSS.) Jackson had written that a 'University Free Trade Association' had been formed. M.'s card is not extant.

[2] Sir R. C. Jebb was Conservative M.P. for Cambridge University. Sir William Harcourt represented the Liberals who had opposed the South African War and Sir Henry Campbell-Bannerman as Liberal leader sought to preserve party unity.

[3] In a letter of 15 March 1904 Jackson had recalled Leslie Stephen as a Fellow of Trinity Hall, 'the life of the place . . . You may be surprised to hear that in the late sixties I knew well the roistering crew which assembled at Jesus: Stephen was quite at home there' (Parry, *Henry Jackson*, 236–7). See M., *Life of L. S.*, Chap. V.

as acquaintance ripened he took me home to supper and I found a wife, and (between ourselves) I think that 'the philosopher' as we used to call him, did a little match making, for which I am grateful. There were sides of him which few saw. He was for one thing a most tender hearted man and would suffer torments—almost amusing to the onlooker—if he thought that he had given pain by what he wrote to some well meaning creature—and all this would come out in strong language about himself and his victim. I don't think that people who stood outside would guess this.

What you wrote of Bateson and Clark was very good reading. I also admire Bateson and I am very anxious indeed to know what he is doing on that Syndicate.[1] I feel that much depends on his action—also (to tell truth) when he says that littlego Greek does the science man good, he—well he doesn't convince me, but he makes me a little less confident than I was.

I received the Shipleyan manifesto[2] with a request for my signature. I am much too far from Cambridge to sign such things and am wondering what is the inner meaning of it all, for of course there is some inner meaning. As to the Classical Assocñ, I had not so much as heard, etc.

Many thanks for your emendation of my Anglo-French.[3] I must ask W. H. Stevenson whether 'have he' could possibly come out as 'avez'. I rather think that you want all the letters of þenne to make the equivalent for modern 'then'. By the way I have very sad news of Stevenson—I think that I introduced you to him, the man who was given a fellowship at Exeter without ever having faced a competitive examination—self taught in an attorney's office. The fellowship has expired and now the poor beggar is almost starving, and yet I am told by a German luminary that something that Stevenson published along with Napier (the Crawford Charters) is out and away the best bit of 'diplomatic' that has ever come from England. It will be a pity and a scandal if he goes to the wall, and he is damnably modest and will not strive nor cry. When I get home I must see whether anything can be done. A. W. Ward was writing to me about the need of a palaeographer in the History School. I must tell him how Oxford has been foolish enough to let Stevenson go.[4]

But to come back to our French—that coe[5] is modern ce—the usual English form is ceo, like jeo, but some clerks are fond of coe and joe. I fancy from what I see in books that this is only a case of perverted spelling and does not point to a difference in pronunciation. I have been watching a clerk who writes *tiel* and *teil* alternately for the modern *tel*, and believe that he always means *tiel*.

I look forward to the first dinner of the Society and shall hope to see you in full vigour and to have as good report from Bournemouth as may be.

---

[1] See Letter 377, *supra*.

[2] On 15 March 1904 Jackson had written: 'Shipley is running a private association which aims at taking over all the College teaching and controlling the payments.' Arthur Everett Shipley was Fellow of Christ's College, Cambridge, 1887–1910, and Master 1910–27.

[3] See Letter 379, *supra*.

[4] For the happy turn in Stevenson's fortunes see Letter 386, *infra. The Crawford collection of early charters and documents*, ed. (1895) by A. S. Napier and W. H. Stevenson, had been reviewed by M. in E.H.R. (1896) 557–8.

[5] See Letter 379, *supra*.

I am laying in novels for the voyage. Pérez Galdós has to serve—his last play has made a great sensation at Madrid and as he comes from Las Palmas we are all very proud of 'our illustrious compatriot'.

> Yours very truly
> F. W. MAITLAND

I suppose that in the Spanish decadence love of rhetoric is rather symptom than disease, but all these people are orators. You should hear our cook— especially on religious matters—and as noise it is magnificent.

384. To Henry Jackson

> Downing College
> Cambridge
> *27 April 1904*

MY DEAR JACKSON,

The little Greek that I ever had was of the compulsory kind and has long since flown.

Therefore tell me whether the accents on the Greek words in the enclosed slip (from a proof of Stephen's Hobbes) are correct.[1]

et ceo pur dieu et en oevre de charité (as the old bills in Chancery say).

> Yours very truly
> F. W. MAITLAND

385. To H. A. L. Fisher

[The end and signature of this letter have been cut out—presumably by Fisher.]

> Downing College
> Cambridge
> *1 May 1904*

MY DEAR HERBERT,

I am very grateful to you for reading and annotating the Hobbes: your corrections are most useful. I am now sending the sheets to Macmillan for a revise in pages. I had not much doubt that you would admire. At first my pleasure was spoilt by the necessity of attending to p's and q's—for of course the script was pretty bad—but afterwards I enjoyed the book thoroughly. Now I think it excellent.

Yes, the end is abrupt. I am glad to have your opinion about that point, for it in effect tells me that the true story ought to be told in a short prefatory note. The facts are that Leslie thought of writing two or three paragraphs about Hobbes's posthumous fate and asked me to write them if I thought fit in

---

[1] See Letter 381, *supra*,

accordance with some notes that he gave me. When however I saw how complete the book was I sent him word that I should add nothing. Do you agree with me that this explanation must be given? I don't want in any way to thrust myself between author and readers—but I am inclining to think that Leslie's fame requires me to say that he did not regard this book as quite finished. I am consulting Macmillan's upon this point, and will ask your advice more fully hereafter when I have their reply.[1]

When you see York Powell, tell him that I am among the many who are earnestly wishing for better news.[2]

Daily lectures sit heavy upon me. So soon as they are over I *must* see you here or at Oxford.

386. To R. Lane Poole

Downing College
Cambridge
19 May 1904

MY DEAR POOLE,

I think that in your place I should accept Mr. Clark's offer. The only lists of that kind which I know in print are the Norwich lists printed by Hudson and they come from a borough. We still want a little more light on the tithing system. If notes tending to show whether these tithings coincided with geography were added, the lists would be the more valuable. So I should say Yes.[3]

York Powell was one of those men whom it did one good to meet. I grieve that he is gone. I take it that a good deal of him lives in other people's books. You may get a more professorial professor very easily but not another York Powell. My guess is that if A. J. B.[4] is left to himself he will do the unexpected.

Ballard looks nice in type. I am glad the Delegates accepted him.[5]

It was a real joy to me to hear that Stevenson is once more with you at Oxford.[6] I was beginning to fear desperation. Surely the Times treated him very ill.

I have been trying to make up for lost time by assiduous lectures and am looking forward to the beginning of the Tripos which will set me free.

You do not tell me how over-worked you are at this season: but I can guess.

I have an unusually bad pen.

Yours very truly

F. W. MAITLAND

---

1 See Letter 388, *infra.*
2 York Powell died on 8 May 1904.
3 [A.L.P. Andrew Clark's *Tithing Lists from Essex, 1329–1343*, was printed in E.H.R. (1904) 715.] See Hudson, Intro. to S.S. Vol. 5.
4 A. J. Balfour. See Letter 389, *infra.*
5 [A.L.P. Adolphus Ballard's *The Domesday Boroughs* was published by the Clarendon Press in 1904.]
6 [A.L.P. In 1904 W. H. Stevenson was elected to a research fellowship at St. John's College, Oxford.]

387. To R. Lane Poole

Downing College
Cambridge
22 May 1904

MY DEAR POOLE,

I must certainly see the Oxford Magazine. Also I must certainly read Ker's book.[1] You speak so very highly of it and I trust your judgment so much that I am thinking of applying the supreme test—viz. the Bay of Biscay.

You mention Boehmer-Romundt and by so doing prompt me to ask two questions—answerable upon a post card. Am I right in thinking that the indictment against Lanfranc is to be taken very seriously? I do not want you prematurely to reveal what I hope you will publish, namely your verdict: but if you told me that B-R. had merely been mares-nesting I should delete something that I have written.

Secondly, I cannot quite understand this man's use of his name or names. I thought that Boehmer had become Boehmer-Romundt, but within the last few days have received a book about St. Francis written by Lic. Dr. H. Boehmer, Professor de Theologie [sic] in Bonn. I take it that there is only one man in question—a pleasant unassuming young man who dined with me a while ago and talked of Lanfranc—but the 'Romundt' seems to come and go in a puzzling manner.

I should not trouble you were it not that I have mentioned the book about Lanfranc in an article that Prothero has extracted from me by diabolical arts. I have had the impudence to write about Liebermann's Gesetze.[2] It has been hateful work, the attempt to talk to a Quarterly audience—but I did not want the little man to go unpraised.

Observe that I have not asked for more than will go upon a post card. If others will not spare you I must.

Yours very truly
F. W. MAITLAND

388. To H. A. L. Fisher

Downing College
Cambridge
22 May 1904

MY DEAR HERBERT,

Many thanks for letting me see the *Author*. I have enjoyed it. G. M. is very good.[3]

[1] [A.L.P. W. P. Ker, *The Dark Ages* (1904).] The Oxford Magazine of 18 May 1904 contained an obituary of York Powell.
[2] See Letter 381, *supra*. M.'s reference to Boehmer, *Die Fälschungen Erzbischof Lanfranks*, will be found in M. C.P. III, at p. 462.
[3] *The Author* of 1 April 1904 contained a paper on Leslie Stephen by George Meredith: see Letter 408, *infra*.

I send you a print of a projected note to the Hobbes. Will you tell me frankly what you think of it? I should have preferred signing it with initials only—but this seems to involve the assumption that the world ought to know who F. W. M. is. What think you?[1]

Florence thoroughly enjoyed her visit to Oxford. I wish that I had been with her.

Would it trouble you very much to tell some Oxford bookseller to send me a copy of the Magazine that contained a notice of F. Y. P.[2]—together with a bill? I hear that it, the notice, is good.

You well know what I hope about the vacancy.[3]

Yours affectly.

F. W. MAITLAND

389. To H. A. L. Fisher

Downing College

Cambridge

14 June 1904

MY DEAR HERBERT,

This is not at all what I hoped and I feel as if I myself had lost something. Still age tells in such cases—it would tell with me if I were P.M.—and the man is worthy.[4] What I regret is the drudgery of tutorship as practised at Oxford.

Don't reply.

Yours affectly

F. W. MAITLAND

390. To B. Fossett Lock

Downing College

Cambridge

26 June 1904

MY DEAR LOCK,

I have not the least wish to hurry out a Year Book, but will tell you how the case stands.[5] In addition to the stuff that is in page I have 25 slips. Another 2 or 3 slips would take me to a natural stopping place. Then I have already written out corresponding notes from the Record. On the whole I have been lucky and Turner has served me well. If I can find about half a dozen more cases I shall have got all that could be hoped for and a good deal more than I expected.

---

1 The note was signed 'F. W. Maitland': Stephen, *Hobbes*, 237.
2 Frederick York Powell: see Letter 387, *supra*.
3 In the Regius Professorship of Modern History at Oxford, caused by York Powell's death.
4 C. H. Firth, appointed Regius Professor of Modern History at Oxford: see Letters 386 and 388, *supra*.
5 This letter refers to S.S. Vol. 19: see esp. Prefatory Note by Lock and M.'s short Introduction.

The (say) 28 slips of text would make (say) 112 pages (56 double pages). Add to 112 a fifth part for notes from the record or (say) 20 pages: sum 132 pages. Add 144 pages already made—or say 150 (for there is a little more to come at the junction). That makes 282. An appendix of (translated) cases found in one MS would bring us to (say) 290.

Result that all heavy work for a book of 290 pages (exclusive of indexes, etc) is done, though I have much to do in the way of reading and correcting proofs. With luck I ought to be able to finish all this in October. What I could not do would be to write an elaborate introduction.

I merely put the facts before yr. l'dship without suggestion.

Yours very truly
F. W. MAITLAND

391. To Sidney Lee

Downing College
Cambridge
26 June 1904

DEAR MR. LEE,

As regards the Memorial to Leslie Stephen, I feel that the Clark Lecture-ship at Trinity[1] would be a very good model. On the one hand I should like to see the memorial closely connected with Trinity Hall, for as you well know Stephen was fond and proud of his college. And on the other hand I cannot help thinking that even in the largest college a college prize does little to preserve a memory. Every one here and many elsewhere would know who was the Stephen lecturer at Trinity Hall and we should all be well content that the choice of the lecturer rested with the College: but very few of us here and hardly anyone elsewhere would know who had obtained a college prize.

As literature has many more votaries than philosophy, I should like to express my hope that in any scheme that is made Stephen's philosophic side will be adequately represented.[2]

Believe me
Yours very truly
F. W. MAITLAND

392. To Sidney Lee

Downing College
Cambridge
3 July 1904

DEAR MR. LEE,

I am sorry, but it so happens that on Tuesday just at the time that you mention I have to attend the Council of the Selden Society. The engagement is of old standing and some busy people are coming.

[1] See M., *Life of L. S.*, 373, 380–3.
[2] The Leslie Stephen lectureship at Cambridge was founded in 1905 for the biennial de-livery of a public lecture 'on some literary subject, including therein criticism, biography and ethics'.

There is just one point that I should like to mention, though only as a rock ahead. I think that there may be some little difficulty about founding an university lectureship unless the appointment of the lecturer is given to the University or to some such body as the Council of the Senate which represents the University. I am not sure that there is a precedent for anything of the kind, and I am not sure that there are not people who would represent the difficulty as a legal objection. If the Master of Trinity Hall is with you he will be able to speak with greater weight, for it is long since I have taken much part in University affairs. Meanwhile I will try to get speech with Henry Jackson who is a store of precedents.

You see the point. Is the University to include among its officers (and the Rede lecturer appears as an officer) a lecturer chosen for it but not by it?

One other little matter. Do not make the use of the Senate House compulsory. We are getting many better rooms and a lecture in the Senate House is always funereal.

Yours very truly

F. W. MAITLAND

P.S. Perhaps I have not made my point quite clear, so I add that the objection which I have mentioned could not be brought against a scheme which placed the appointment of the lecturer in the hands of the Vice Chancellor and/or the Master of Trinity Hall. The appointment by a committee external to the University is what, so I think, might rouse some opposition. Jackson, to whom I have been speaking, does not fear this, but the only precedent that he had at hand, the Cobden Prize, is not very close, and he has not wholly convinced me that there is no danger of that sort of friction which all of us would wish to avoid.

393. To Sidney Lee

Downing College
Cambridge

6 July 1904

DEAR MR. LEE,

I will put your question[1] to the Vice Chancellor. You will of course understand that all that could be had from him would be an expression of his own opinion that the proposed scheme would be acceptable to the University. Whether he will give this without first mentioning the matter to the Council of the Senate I do not know. The Council does not hold weekly meetings in the Vacation, but will I believe meet before the end of the month. There would, I conceive, be no difficulty about making the Master of Trinity Hall an elector ex officio.

There is another matter of which I should like to speak to you. Stephen desired that I should see some papers of a very private kind that were intended

---

1 Lee's letter stating the question is not extant.

for his children's eyes and that I should make some use of this matter in a memoir. Well, I must do my best, and the value of the book will be very greatly enhanced if I can get from a few of his most intimate associates some pages, paragraphs, passages about special points in his career—not criticism of his work (that will not be attempted) but reminiscences. Of course I thought of you in the very first line, for there is nobody in the world who could say of the Dictionary what you could say. I have been a little shy of speaking to you however, because I thought it possible that you might have in view a real 'Life' of L. S., with a critical estimate of work done. Should that be the case our books would not compete, but you would naturally desire to keep for your own use your own reminiscences. But, whatever may be your plans, I will venture to say to you that you will earn my profound gratitude if you will give me a little. The whole book will be small and there are papers of Stephen's own to be included, but some paragraphs coming from you about—not the Dictionary— but Stephen as editor would be to me, and others, of the highest value.[1]

In any case I hope that you will forgive my importunity. I had some encouragement from Gerald Duckworth.[2]

Yours very truly

F. W. MAITLAND

394. To R. Lane Poole

Downing

6 July 1904

Having first said of my eyes anything that occurs to you, can you tell me by card how the Sanctuary paper is procurable?[3] I cannot find the review copy—maybe I took it to the Canaries. I will gladly purchase another if one can be had for money.

Forgive, if you can,

Yrs.

F. W. MAITLAND

395. To R. Lane Poole

Downing

8 July 1904

At a GREAT pinch and if Paul fitz G.[4] fails I would take the *Gesetze*. It is not so much time that fails as matter—for I have shot it all into G. W. P.'s receptacle.[5] Besides F. L. has a right to more than one reviewer. Could not you get a philologian, for really (I suppose) the interest of vol. 1 lies quite as much

---

[1] In March 1890 Sidney Lee's name appeared upon the title page of D.N.B. as joint editor with Leslie Stephen, but 'for two or three years previously his services had been indispensable' (M. *Life of L. S.*, 365).

[2] The publisher of *Life and Letters of Leslie Stephen* and the son, by a previous marriage, of Stephen's second wife.

[3] [A.L.P. Perhaps a reference to N. M. Trenholme's *The Right of Sanctuary in England* (Columbia, Missouri, 1903).] See Letter 358, *supra*.

[4] Vinogradoff.

[5] See Letter 381, *supra*. Liebermann's *Gesetze* was not reviewed by M. in E.H.R.

within the linguistic as within the legal department. Why not Napier? Why not Stevenson?

Yes, I could find 3 or 4 sentences for Paul on Maine.[1]

Yrs.

F. W. MAITLAND

396. To B. Fossett Lock

Downing College
Cambridge
11 July 1904

DEAR LOCK,

It struck me that his Lordship was rather hasty than speedy.[2]

I will peg away and see what can be done and then when *cras Animarum* comes we shall see where we stand.

I ought to tell you that I am not quite so free as I hoped to be. I am practically compelled, I fear, to take up a task for which I am not at all suited, namely some sort of memoir of Leslie Stephen. I believe that with reasonable luck this ought not to prevent me from getting two volumes out before 31 Dec. 1904; still, as you know, luck is not always reasonable, and the other piece of work is to me of so new a sort that I shall not be able to do it rapidly.

Meanwhile, however, I will simply go ahead. It may be that I must soon go to London for a day about another piece of business. If so, I will tell you and then, if you wish to see me, I will attend you in chambers.

Yours very truly

F. W. MAITLAND

397. To B. Fossett Lock

Downing College
Cambridge
17 July 1904

DEAR LOCK,

If I did not answer your very kind letter[3] at once, it was because I waited for a Sunday morning when I should have neither proofs nor lectures upon my mind. I feel that I ought to tell why I may not be able to accept your excellent advice. For my own peace of mind I should like to edit Year Books to the end of my days, and if I departed from that straight road it would not be to attempt biography. But in a sort of way L. S. left it on record that what (if anything) was to be said about his private life should be said by me (you know that I was a sort of quasi nephew and even quasi-quasi godson) and such was

---

[1] Vinogradoff, *The Teaching of Sir Henry Maine*, L.Q.R. (1904) 119: Vinogradoff, Coll. Pap. II. 173. It was not reviewed by M. in E.H.R.

[2] Allusion obscure.

[3] Not extant; but from M.'s letter Lock would seem to have urged M. to get some 'literary gent' to 'polish off' Stephen.

my admiration for him that his wish must be a command unless his children prefer to do what has to be done. Whether you would class this necessity as objective or subjective I do not know—that depends on your system of philosophy—but there it is. It is not very much that should be done in this case *ex parte familiae*, and literary criticism is out of the question. I feel that some of the literary gents whom you mention would polish off a memoir in a month. I can't do that, but at the same time I am necessarily a little less keen than I was to promise *x* year books in a given time.

Let us then see how things are going in October. I am now occupying the press with some last notes from the Record. An appendix goes off to-morrow—also sheets B–K for a last revise, and I hope that in September I shall send in the text of a large part of Vol. 3.[1] It is in the making of Introductions that there may be delay, but I am not sure that if we give 'bonus' volumes they need have substantial Introductions.[2]

Have you anything of a general nature to say of Miss B.'s[3] Introduction? I tell her that her last section will not do, as it states the disadvantages but not the advantages of our 'digest' plan. For the rest I think it good. (I tell her that, if she thanks me, it must be in a simpler style). If you have any criticism, now is your time.

With many thanks for advice that was not only 'well-meant' but very sound as well as very kind,

I remain

Yours very truly

F. W. MAITLAND

I hope that you love 80 in the shade as I do.

398. To James Bryce

Downing College

Cambridge

17 July 1904

DEAR BRYCE,

I hoped that the other day I might have had a word with you, but that was not to be. So many other people must at this time be hoping the like hope that I have many scruples about writing to you[4]; still there is something that I should like to say before you begin such holiday, 'if any', as you allow yourself.

I will begin by bluntly putting the request that I have to make. Would you of your charity and piety contribute—say within the next six months—a few

---

[1] S.S. Vol. 20.
[2] See Prefatory Note and Intro. to S.S. Vol. 19.
[3] Mary Bateson: S.S. Vol. 18.
[4] Bryce was one of the leaders of the Liberal party, and the internal conflicts of the Conservatives were offering lively prospects of a Liberal return to power.

personal reminiscences of Leslie Stephen to a brief memoir to be prefixed to some Last Papers? I have from him a mandate (vel quasi) to see to this matter. I should not attempt any literary criticism—*that* he certainly would not have entrusted to me—only a sketch of his life as revealed in certain family papers and as seen by close friends. Of course you at once occur to me. I fancy—I don't ask questions—that you have already done all that friendship required; but still am not without hope that you may consent to do a little more. What I should especially like to have from you would be a few pages about the Stephen that you knew when you travelled and walked together. A little of what I have to draw from papers will, I fear, suggest too strongly a certain gloom and despondency, and I should like someone who knew him in his full vigour to say how delightful a companion he was.

It is all too likely that I have chosen the wrong moment, but if I wait until you are disengaged I shall wait for doomsday, and indeed I feel that I had better get my promise while you are still in opposition. May I have it?—or a half-promise?—or at any rate an assurance that you will think about my request—for his sake?

Among last papers put away for my eye was the speech proposing you as President of the Alpine Club.[1] It is of the old days when Leslie and Freeman fought for your soul that I should like some words.

At any rate forgive me and believe me

Yours very truly

F. W. MAITLAND

399. To James Bryce

Downing College
Cambridge

19 July 1904

MY DEAR BRYCE,

This is extremely good of you, and yet I will own that I am not surprised by your prompt and kind reply.

Take your time. If I get my materials together before the winter, that will be soon enough: but I seemed to foresee that you might be busier some months hence than you are now.

It must be pleasant indeed to turn back to the *Holy Roman* and see how few repairs are necessary.[2]

Yours very truly

F. W. MAITLAND

Once more, the more the better.

[1] See M., *Life of L. S.*, 449.
[2] Bryce was preparing the fourth edition of the *Holy Roman Empire*.

400. To Henry Jackson

Downing College
Cambridge

7 Augt. 1904

MY DEAR JACKSON,

It may possibly interest you for a moment if I tell you a little of the progress that, thanks to your kind suggestions, I am making in collecting material for the projected memoir of Leslie Stephen.[1] I hold a handsome promise from Morgan[2] and the like from C. B. Clarke, who says that his anecdotes will require editorial discretion. Then Romer promises something and so does Fitzgerald, to whom I was sent as to a representative boating man. Venn is extremely useful. He has a wonderful memory and, though he did not know Stephen well, has suggested many hopeful lines of inquiry. Vernon Lushington I drew blank. So also Robert Campbell. So also Elphinstone, who however volunteered the information that he never thought of L. S. as a *possible* apostle. I hear from Thoby[3] that a certain (Rev.) F. F. Kelly has anecdotes. Do you know anything of the man? He was at the Hall but I cannot find his degree. I have an excellent maternal journal which will keep me straight in the matter of dates. A young Alpinist at Christ's, one Valentine Richards, has been very useful in the matter of mountaineering literature, and Cartmell put me on the track of the famous walking match.

I want to ask you whether you think that I should get anything out of H. M. Butler. He and Stephen talked in the same debates at the Union—but I don't want to make an application if it would bring me nothing or the wrong sort of thing.

And what of Sedley Taylor?[4] If he told a good story, would it be true? I don't know him well enough to answer this question. I have not yet made up my mind how to deal with Morley. My experience of him is that he does not answer letters or else makes promises that he does not perform. Bryce is all that I could wish.

Forgive me for bothering you with any questions in vacation time. If I do not take care I shall make you dread your return to Cambridge.

The committee of the Free Trade Association had a plaguey long 'comma' hunt one afternoon at H. Darwin's.[5] I hope that you were tolerably satisfied by the final result.

I hardly like to ask you what news you can give from your home.

Yours very truly

F. W. MAITLAND

---

[1] On the persons and incidents mentioned in this paragraph see in general M., *Life of L. S.*, Chaps. IV and V, and p. 104.

[2] H. A. Morgan (1830–1912), Master of Jesus College, Cambridge, 1885–1912.

[3] Leslie Stephen's son by his second marriage.

[4] (1834–1920), Fellow of Trinity College, Cambridge.

[5] See Letter 383, *supra*. On Horace Darwin see Gwen Raverat, *Period Piece*, 203–8.

401. To H. A. L. Fisher

[Post-card in pencil. The address is that of M.'s sister Kate.]

21 Palace Gardens Terrace
Kensington, W.

28 Sept. 1904

MY DEAR HERBERT,

I am very grateful to you for getting me those letters from Smith. Two or three of them are useful. One of them throws a little light on an episode that I don't understand—a certain antagonism between Leslie and 'Ben' Latham.[1]

Shall I ever finish or even begin the book? Sometimes I am very despondent. I am up here partly after Year Books, partly after a long series of articles written by Leslie for the New York *Nation*[2] and visible, I hope, at Brit. Mus., but I can't yet sit long at a table and so I try your eyes with this scrawl.

I can't tell you how I enjoyed your visit to Cambridge. It now stands in relief against a bad time—but I have read a lot of L. S. in the interval and admire more and more.

Good luck to your Dutch! Pray relieve the Cam. Mod. Hist. with an anecdote or two.[3]

Yours affectly

F. W. M.

402. To Henry Jackson

Downing College
Cambridge

9 Octr. 1904

MY DEAR JACKSON,

I hope that we may meet soon but just at this moment I am housebound, and in order that I may not forget a question that I have to ask I will put it on paper. You will, I think, be able to answer it by a word when we meet.

C. B. Clarke tells me of something that occurred when he and Stephen were at a 'Junior Apostles' dinner. E. Dicey, speaking of an earlier time, speaks of an essay or discussion society 'something like the Apostles' of which he and Stephen were members as undergraduates. What is this? Is it 'The (dining)

[1] Horace Smith had been a pupil of Leslie Stephen at Trinity Hall: see M., *Life of L. S.*, 65–7, 399, 413–14. Rev. Henry (Ben) Latham (1821–1902), Fellow of Trinity Hall 1847, Senior Tutor 1855, Master 1888: see *Life of L. S.*, 55–6, and Coulton, *Fourscore Years*, 86–8.
[2] *Life of L. S.*, 164.
[3] Fisher was to write Chap. XXII in Vol. VIII of Camb. Mod. Hist. and Chap. VI in Vol. IX.

Society' of which you and I are members—or is it something that has utterly perished?[1]

Yours very truly

F. W. MAITLAND

I have a tale which ends with 'Damn your soul, Sir! Don't you know that I'm a parson?'[2]

403. To Sidney Lee

Downing College
Cambridge
27 Octr. 1904

DEAR LEE,

I am grateful to you for your account of the committee meeting.[3] I feel that in the matter of subscription Cambridge hardly had a fair chance, as the appeal appeared at the worst moment in the year. Still I do not know that more than a few pounds would be gained by distributing the circular among resident members.

I shall be in England until (at least) the first week in December and would always try to get to a meeting. Give me as much notice as you can, for there are some meetings here that I am compelled to attend.

As regards your kind promise of some matter for a memoir I should like to think that you would give me from (say) six to ten pages of print about the D.N.B. If you could do that I should be inclined to say no more myself. I need not tell you that what you, with your intimate knowledge, can say of Stephen as editor would be very valuable to me and others. If you find a few very good letters perhaps you will let me see them; but in the matter of letters I am pretty well off, for I have 30 years of close correspondence with C. E. Norton.[4]

Yours very truly

F. W. MAITLAND

If a few pounds are still wanted, let me know.

404. To Charles Eliot Norton

Downing College
Cambridge
England
30 Oct. 1904

DEAR MR. NORTON,

Gerald Duckworth will have explained to you who I am and how it comes about that I have undertaken to put together some sort of memoir of your dear

---

[1] Edward Dicey was a cousin of Leslie Stephen and the brother of Professor A. V. Dicey. Jackson, replying on 10 Oct. 1904 (Camb. Univ. MSS.), wrote: 'I know nothing about the "Junior Apostles" and . . . can only suppose that they were one of the many societies which had no more than an ephemeral existence.'

[2] It appears expurgated in *Life of L. S.*, 106–7,

[3] On the proposed Leslie Stephen memorial: see Letter 391, *supra*.

[4] See Letter 404, *infra*.

friend Leslie Stephen. I now want to thank you in person for your great kindness in sending me the great mass of letters that you received from him: also for the permission to use them. I may tell you at once that they are by far the best materials that have come to my hands, and indeed are so good that they are revolutionizing such idea as I had formed of the book that has to be made. I feel that you are placing great confidence in me, and in return I can only tell you that I am very grateful and that, though I am not an expert biographer, I hope that I shall in no way show myself unworthy of your trust. Stephen used to say that affection is not sufficient equipment for a biographer. I have little else to boast of, but this perhaps will keep me straight.

And now there is one question that I should like to ask you. When did you first meet Stephen? I have copies of a long series of letters written by him to his mother during his first visit to America in 1863. He landed at Boston in July, stayed a few days there, saw Lowell, Holmes and others, went out west, worked his way round to Washington, visited Meade's army in Virginia and was in New York at the end of October. Here the letters cease, but he was intending to return by way of Boston and hoped to see once more the friends whom he had visited there and at Cambridge. I should like to know from you whether your friendship goes back to this time, and I need hardly tell you that if you could bring yourself to write for the public a few sentences about the beginning of that long friendship they would delight me and others also.[1]

I am hoping that of the second visit to America (1868) there are some notes in shorthand which Miss C. E. Stephen can decipher.[2]

As to the third visit (1890) it was, as you will remember, very short; but I think that Stephen received some honours (LL.D. Harv.?) and made some speeches.[3] I should be very sorry indeed to give you any trouble, but perhaps you may be able to put me on the track of newspaper reports that I ought to see.

Already however I feel that I cannot thank you too warmly and that if the public sees in print a tolerable likeness of our friend this will be in a large measure due to you.

> Believe me
> Yours very truly
> F. W. MAITLAND

405. To Mr. Justice Holmes

> Downing College,
> Cambridge.
> *30 Octr. 1904.*

DEAR JUDGE HOLMES,

I have undertaken to put together some sort of memoir of Leslie Stephen. He had in effect told his children that if they wanted anything of the kind they

---

[1] On this paragraph see *Life of L. S.*, Chap. VII. It would seem from p. 118 of the *Life* that Stephen first met Norton in Oct. 1863: see also Letter 419, *infra*.
[2] *Life of L. S.*, 203–10. Caroline Emelia Stephen was Leslie's sister: see Annan, *Leslie Stephen*, 296.
[3] *Life of L. S.*, 401–2.

were to ask me to try my hand at it. I do not feel that I am the right man for the task; but I loved and admired Stephen and must do my best.

After this recital I will come to the operative part of these presents and at once ask you whether you have any letters written by Leslie to yourself or your father which would in your opinion help me in my book-making and, if so, whether I may see them or copies of them.

C. E. Norton has been good enough to place at my disposal a long correspondence, and up to the present date this is the best material that I have. I have also some good letters written by L. S. during his first visit to the States in 1863 in which you appear as riddled with wounds; and I have also a good deal about the long friendship with Lowell.[1] Altogether I think that a skilled biographer might make something which would interest a good many people on your side.

I need hardly tell you that if you can recall the Stephen who visited America in the war time[2] and would put your recollections on paper this would please me and any readers whom I may have. But if I may not hope for so much as this, you still may have some letters that you would let me see.

> Believe me
> Yours very truly
> F. W. MAITLAND

406. To Alfred Marshall

> Downing
> *6 Novr. 1904*

MY DEAR MARSHALL,

As regards law in the Economics Tripos, I do not want to revive over-ruled objections and I wish to suggest what will satisfy you. I should like to know therefore what you think of some such formula as the following, to which Westlake and I tended yesterday afternoon. 'Candidates are required to study the principles of English, French and German law relating to contract in general and also to study more particularly the English, French and German law relating to (1), the sale of goods, (2) partnership, (3) bills of exchange.'

Our (1) (2) (3) are chosen *partly* because at these three points English law has been recently codified.

As you know, I foresee great difficulties. I think that the inclusion of foreign law to be read in foreign books, though highly desirable, will deter almost all candidates, and that if now and again one wishes to take up this subject, it will be worth no one's while to learn enough to teach him or even to examine him.

I believe that you would have done better to accept, at least *pro tem.*, what some of our law lecturers could have provided: viz, English contract and English tort. But I am not going to raise that point again, and I now only want

---

[1] *Life of L. S.*, esp. pp. 114–15, 203–12, 407–12.
[2] *Ibid.*, pp. 111 and 116.

to know whether the formula stated above would in a general way meet your wishes—for Westlake and I are proposing to make some inquiry in France and elsewhere about the best books.

Believe me

Yours very truly

F. W. MAITLAND

407. To Alfred Marshall

Downing

7 Nov. 1904

MY DEAR MARSHALL,

Many thanks. I see that we must modify our suggestion which was merely a first draft; and I write to Westlake accordingly.

As to companies I have my doubts.

(1) What I call 'company law' is necessarily a pretty far advanced subject—bearing to partnership law somewhat the same relation that the differential bears to algebra.

(2) *Our* 'company law' is (formally) a pretty bad mess—an odd act ('62) and a heap of amending acts.

(3) I doubt whether many of the questions about companies which you would like young economists to study really fall within the range of what we call 'company law'—e.g. (this is only an example) the Mogul case[1] had no company law in it.

However I will think what could be done. Perhaps you hardly realize how bad for students are some of the books that practitioners use.

Yours v. truly

F. W. MAITLAND

408. To H. A. L. Fisher

Downing College

Cambridge

20 Nov. 1904

MY DEAR HERBERT,

I want to ask you whether you still possess that number of 'The Author' (was it not?) which contained articles about Leslie by Freshfield and Meredith, and, if so, whether you will lend it to me once more.[2] I have succeeded pretty well in collecting material, for I have a great body of letters written to Lowell and Norton. On the other hand it is quite curious to discover how hard it may be to get the exact truth about facts that are not yet sixty years old. I

---

[1] *Mogul S.S. Co. v. McGregor, Gow & Co.* [1892] A.C. 25.
[2] See Letter 388, *supra.* For Douglas Freshfield (1845–1934), who succeeded Leslie Stephen as editor of the *Alpine Journal*, see *Life of L. S.*, Chap. VI and p. 359. For George Meredith's article see *Ibid.*, 265, 357, 432–3.

319

have by this time a large correspondence concerning the resignation of the tutorship and yet it is obvious to me that none of my correspondents really remember just what happened; and then I am told that a college minute book is mislaid!

Florence leaves England on next Saturday for Madeira. I follow on 10 Dec. You know our troubles: Florence is wonderfully brave and I am always hoping for better days.

I must now lunch with Bury, where I am to meet Poole—afterwards I must pay my Sunday visit to 'Milly'[1] who helps me much.

I like our report about Greek,[2] but fear that it has no chance of being carried.

Yours affectly

F. W. MAITLAND

409. To B. Fossett Lock

Downing College

23 Nov. 1904

MY DEAR LOCK,

Year Books vol. 2.

I have passed Introduction, title pages, etc. for the Press, and now all that remains is to answer any queries that the 'reader' may send. He has passed almost all the sheets and I have still a fortnight.

I like the Borough book's[3] looks. It came to-day and I think will do us credit.

Yours v. truly

F. W. MAITLAND

410. To Mr. Justice Holmes

Downing College,

Cambridge.

27 Nov. 1904.

DEAR MR. JUSTICE HOLMES,

I have safely received the packet of Leslie Stephen's letters that you very kindly sent me. They will be most useful to me for I have little else yet that illustrates Stephen in the sixties and early seventies. I will take care that they are returned to you, and if by any chance I should vanish before I send them back, Stephen's son Thoby will know where they are. Also I will promise to be discreet and in any case of doubt I will refer to you. I think that I may desire to publish a few characteristic outbursts and even a few swear-words,

---

[1] Stephen's sister, Caroline Emelia, who lived in Cambridge.
[2] On the possible abolition of Greek as a compulsory subject for the Cambridge University entrance examination or 'Little-Go' as it is commonly called.
[3] S.S. Vol. 18.

for I don't want to destephenize Stephen—but this can I think be done without my doing anything to which you would object.

I really am deep in your debt for your confidence and it is no mere figure of speech if I subscribe as

Yours very gratefully

F. W. MAITLAND

411. To W. W. Buckland

[Post-card. Postmark Funchal, Madeira.]

18 Decr. 1904

Natal alegre! This much I venture—but as yet the lingo of the natives seems chiefly to consist of 'shish'. Those big Castles are really good. I had an excellent deck cabin with 'practicable' window, etc. all to myself. One day we ran 402 miles and, having left Southampton at 6 p.m. on Sat., I awoke on Wed. at anchor. Hitherto I like the climate. Certainly it has not erred on the side of mugginess and to-day a smart gale is blowing. We have a house on *the* road to the west of the town, and, being outside the postal radius, our address for service will be

c/o Leacock and Co., Funchal.

I believe that I have already cycled all that is cyclable. My poverty of language compels me to repeat 'Natal alegre'.

Yr.

F. W. MAITLAND

412. To Henry Jackson

18 Decr. 1904

c/o Leacock & Co.

Funchal, Madeira

MY DEAR JACKSON,

As you encouraged me to hope that by and by I might have a letter from you, I now inform you that the above will be my permanent 'address for service', as the lawyers say. We have got a house a little way out of the town—so far out that letters are not delivered to us, and Don João Leacock, whom we knew as Don Juan in Grand Canary, is a friendly wine-merchant. We are in luck and I think that we shall be happy here. My wife is rapidly picking up the Portuguese language from our cook who, like other Portuguese cooks, is a man:—at present I hear nothing but 'shish' and 'shing'. By the way, when Jebb was talking that stuff about 'Boots' and 'Andromatch', Cartmell, who was next to me, said that he had heard a Fellow of St. John's give 'Geethey' (pronounce this Englishwise) as the name of a certain German poet, and I wondered whether even our cultured Allbutt can prescribe 'Cascara' without a blunder as bad as any that shocked Sir Richard,[1] for I am very proud of knowing that one ought to write Cáscara and throw a heavy stress on the ante-

---

[1] Jebb. For Austen Cartmell, Barrister and Junior Counsel to the Treasury, see Sir John Pollock, *Time's Chariot*, 21, 196.

penultimate. How it comes about that you can use 'Cáscaras' as a substitute for a swear-word I don't know, but I fancy that you begin something worse and check yourself: cf. Crikey! Somehow or another I have got round to the debates on the Greek question. Keep me posted up—this means postcarded up—in our prospects: I say 'our' though I have basely fled. Who described you as 'truculent' in the Review? Yourself? I wish I had heard you, but was electing Whewell scholars.[1]

That trivial little question that I put to you about Stephen's resignation of the tutorship intrigues me. The result of many letters that I have written and received is making me more sceptical than I was before concerning all history sacred and profane. I could make a paper for the Eranus about it. Another queer little point that may interest you for a moment is this, that when Stephen became a fellow it was recorded that he was (not 'electus' but) 'nominatus jure Custodi devoluto'—which means I take it that the Master nominated him as upon a 'lapse': 'devolutio' had been technical among canonists in this sense. Then it appeared that other fellows about the same time (e.g. Latham) were also 'nominated'. I asked Malden, the historian of Trinity Hall, about this, and his conjecture was that a fellow could only be elected at a College meeting and that, as almost all of the fellows lived in London, the matter was settled by them 'out of court', so to speak, and then the Master (when the right had technically 'devolved' to him) would nominate the man who had been informally elected. That strikes me as plausible. Have you any parallel passage?[2]

Well, I wish you all that can be wished at this or any other time of year, and you know all that I mean. I will risk 'Natal alegre'—why Spaniards should use 'Pascua' for Xmas as well as Easter is a mystery.[3]

Yours very truly
F. W. Maitland

Confound this paper. I can't make the ink bite.

413. To W. W. Buckland

[Post-card.]

c/o Leacock & Co.
Funchal,
Madeira
2/1/05

Thanks for good letter. It contains one very important piece of news. I am congratulating hypothetically. I fear that you and I are not to be congratulated.

[1] Whewell Scholarships in International Law had been established in 1867 by a bequest of William Whewell, Master of Trinity College, Cambridge. A member of another College, if elected to a Whewell Scholarship, could, but need not, become a member of Trinity. On 'the Greek question' see Letters 408, *supra*, and 426, *infra*. Jackson replied to M. on 25 Dec. 1904 (Camb. Univ. MSS.): 'It is supposed that the man in the *Review* who signed himself *Placet* is Glover, who wants to see Greek made optional but wants also to keep the set book.'
[2] On this paragraph see *Life of L. S.*, 53–4, 139–41, and Annan, *Leslie Stephen*, 28, n. Henry Elliott Malden (1849–1931), scholar of Trinity Hall, of which he wrote the history in the *College Histories* series (1902): he was for nearly 30 years Hon. Sec. of the Royal Historical Society.
[3] See Letter 345, *supra*.

Life is rather a sad story in that respect, and Dios Todopoderoso[1] only made one squire. But I suppose that he told it to increase and multiply.

Kept New Year's day by ascending into the hills aided by railway. Returning, missed train and had in all a descent of 3300 ft. (vertical) on well polished cobbles. Don't understand the art yet; but clearly English boots are misplaced. At the end of our day in the 'cumbres' such a descent would have tried the resources of our language.[2] Fireworks all night long and then all *day* long. It is a funny folk.

Once more Boăs festas! Telde would now look like a bleached bone: but my heart is there. No oranges here—only ants which have destroyed oranges. They walk over this card.

Y.v.t.
F. W. M.

414. To Henry Jackson

[M. wrote the year as 1904, but this has been crossed out in the letter by an unknown hand and 1905 substituted. From contents and context 1905 is clearly right.]

c/o Leacock & Co.
Funchal
Madeira
9 Jan. [1905]

MY DEAR JACKSON,

Thanks for your annual[3]: I am glad that I can by this time think of it as a hardy annual. Since 'Placet' was not you, I can say that I also thought him very unfair. I had some kind of notion that he was the product of your disposition to be absurdly (forgive me!) fair to adversaries, and the mention of your 'truculence' seemed to point that way. I have now seen the Report of the Debate. Bateson is not a good listener. I did not go within a hundred yards of calling him an impostor—but there!

---

¹ See Letter 279, *supra*. Buckland's letter is not extant, but the news would seem to be of the marriage of W. J. Whittaker, the 'Squire' (Letter 369, *supra*), and his withdrawal from teaching at Cambridge. In *F. W. Maitland*, C.L.J. I. 296, Buckland quotes from a 'later letter' written by M., apparently not extant: 'If what you said of the Squire be true, he is a deep 'un—a secretive Squire. The wretch sent me a beery though pretty postcard from the Koenigliches Hofbrauhaus zu Muenchen and alluded not to the domestic event. Talked of a journey on business to tackle a German lawyer. Honeymoon, I believe. Or Meadmoon, if mead be beer and honey.'

² On M. and Buckland's 'day in the Cumbres' see *F. W. Maitland*, C.L.J. I. 283–4. Buckland there quotes from a letter written by M. 'a week or two later' than the present Letter 413 (perhaps the same letter as in note 1, *supra*): 'Was up in the hills yesterday as high as 5,300. Not comparable to Cumbres. Feet much knocked about by cobblestones. Fair thirst. Language occasionally. My thoughts went back to Valsequillo.' See Letter 427, *infra*.

³ Jackson's letter to M. is dated 25 Dec. 1904 (Camb. Univ. MSS.). On this paragraph see Letter 412, *supra*.

Thanks for what you say of the elections at Trinity Hall. I had not time to look into their statutes before leaving. It is a difficult job to do all one's writing in one place and keep one's books in another. I fancy that even if the old statutes had nothing directly to the point, there would be a 'devolution' to the master after six months. There was a great deal of old canon law about collegiate bodies which came into play if statutes were silent.[1]

Atkinson[2] I have sounded about some points unsuccessfully and I don't think that I shall trouble him any more: he is not inclined to help.

Do you remember some contest at Cambridge in 1866 over the offer by one Thompson to found some sort of 'international lectureship'? I have a spirited account of the affair given by Stephen to Lowell. I remember reading about this elsewhere but cannot remember what I read. Some day I may have to ask you who the Thompson he was (Yates?) and what the Thompson he wanted to do. A shorter question demanding only a post card is whether one M. M. U. Wilkinson is still living. I see a good many allusions to him as a member of Stephen's 'set'.[3]

Some of Stephen's pupils are enthusiastic. If I repeated all that they say I should have to suggest that in the resuscitation of the Hall Stephen laboured and Ben entered into, etc.—but I must not raise controversy over the unprovable. N.B. Already in the sixties Stephen was a university reformer in a sense in which Fawcett was a mere tory—this appears from an article in Fraser —already he was advocating all that was done by the Second Commission and more.[4] I am getting to admire him so much that I am in danger of becoming a hagiographer—and (to you) a bore.

I may hereafter ask you for a loan of that saying of yours about beards, volunteering and swearing, if you don't want it for a thesis on the Kulturgeschichte etc. etc. Englands—loan to be duly acknowledged.[5]

Yes, I remember MacColl and liked him. He went Sunday tramps in kid gloves and seemed to me a model editor—all ears for literary gossip and very few words.[6]

Good luck in the Greek matter and all others.

Yours very truly

F. W. MAITLAND

[1] See Letter 412, *supra*.

[2] Jackson had suggested that M. should consult G. B. Atkinson, a Fellow of Trinity Hall until 1862 and a relative of Leslie Stephen.

[3] On the abortive attempt by Henry Yates Thompson to found in Cambridge a lectureship to be filled by appointments from Harvard see *Life of L. S.*, 175–8. In a letter to M. of 16 Jan. 1905 (Camb. Univ. MSS.) Jackson wrote: 'I think that M. M. U. Wilkinson (M^{2}U^3 or "the squared cube" as he was called) may have been a member of the set; but, if so, he must have been the butt. He played badly on the piano and had a face like a sun rising in a fog.'

[4] On Stephen as a university reformer and on his relations with Fawcett see Annan, *Leslie Stephen*, 27–60. Henry Fawcett (1833–84), Fellow of Trinity Hall and Professor of Political Economy 1863; later M.P. for Brighton and Postmaster-General.

[5] In his letter of 16 Jan. 1905 Jackson replied: 'It is not my story but Bacon's or Shakespeare's or Shakon's—"Then a soldier, full of strange oaths and bearded like the pard".' See *Life of L. S.*, 64.

[6] Norman MacColl (1843–1904), editor of the *Athenaeum* and Spanish scholar.

415. To A. W. Verrall

[No original. Printed by Fisher, *Memoir*, 152–3: no beginning or ending.]

c/o Leacock & Co.
Funchal
Madeira
15 Jan. 1905

It is good to see your hand and kind of you to write to me, especially as I fear that writing is not so easy to you as it once was. I do very earnestly hope that things go fairly well with you and that you have not much pain. Yesterday I was thinking a lot of your courage and my cowardice for I took an off day—off from the biography I mean—and attained an altitude of (say) 5250 feet (a cog-wheel railway saving me 2000 thereof however) and I was bounding about up there like a kid of the goats—and very base I thought myself not be to lecturing. There is not much left of me avoirdupoisly speaking, but that little bounds along when it has had a good sunning; and to-day I have a rubbed heel and a permanent thirst as in the good old days. Missing a train on said railway, I made the last part of the descent in the special Madeira fashion on a sledge glissading down over polished cobble stone pavement—a youth running behind to hold the thing back by a rope: it gives the unaccustomed a pretty little squirm at starting. Up in the hills it is a pleasant world—you pass through many different zones of vegetation very rapidly—at one moment all is laurel and heath—you cross a well-marked line and all is tilling—then you are out among dead bracken on an open hill-top that might be English. Get on a sledge and wiss (or is it wiz?) you go down to the sugar and bananas through bignonia and bougainvillia which blind you by their ferocity.

416. To H. A. L. Fisher

c/o Leacock & Co.
Funchal
15 Jan. 1905

MY DEAR HERBERT,

It is exceedingly good of you to send me that admirable book of cartoons. It has been giving all of us much joy, though it is a poor substitute for yourself which is what I wanted. I hope that you did not think me ungrateful last week for not mentioning your gift and thanking for it. It arrived on Wednesday and my letter went out on Tuesday. This trick of the mails makes Madeira a bad place for correspondence.

I have not much to tell you. Yesterday I had my first long walk. Our little cog-wheel railway took me up to about 2000 feet and I then got as far as 5300. It's good up there; but not quite as good as the 'cumbres' of Grand Canary as there is no peak of Tenerife soaring out of the sea into the clouds.

I press on with the philosopher[1] about six hours a day. How I wish that I had the benefit of your criticism! My loneliness makes for rapid work but not for balance. However you must help me by and by.

Yours affectly.

F. W. MAITLAND

417. To Henry Jackson

c/o Leacock & Co.

Funchal

24 Jan. 1905

MY DEAR JACKSON,

I have to thank you for some very useful information[2] and will try to do it in an orderly way (can I remember the few first letters of the Greek alphabet? I wonder—here goes).

(α) What you tell me of the Thompson lectureship is much to my point. I have a good letter from Stephen to Lowell about the defeat.[3] He mentions Kingsley's eagerness. Says that opposition began with the cry that the Americans were Socinians and the Church was in danger. Lowell in reply is amusing. By the way Lowell says that a letter of his to Stephen is the first that he has written to England since the war began: he was very sore indeed about the sympathy with the South. I may ask you to reminisce a bit more concerning the lectureship when we meet.

(β) No, I didn't think that you were Shakon—but you did tell me (or how could it be in my notes?) that among the Cambridge dons oaths became fashionable along with beards and volunteering; and this profound observation I intend to use by way of apology for some of my hero's language while as yet he wore a white tie.[4] He must be deemed to have damned in his military capacity.

(γ) Latham's dictum about G. B. A.[5] and the *w*avens I find in a letter written in 1867. I shan't trouble him any more.

(δ) Your account of M.²U.[3] is not such as to incite me to further investigation. I *do* see a good deal of Hammond's name[6]. Apparently he was one of the party that went down to Brighton to back Fawcett when Stephen ran a newspaper—'the rummiest lot that ever came to Brighton' said an election

---

[1] Leslie Stephen: see Letter 314, *supra.*
[2] Jackson's letter of 16 Jan. 1905. For this and much of M.'s present letter, see Letter 414, *supra.*
[3] *Life of L. S.*, 176–8.
[4] I.e. was still a clergyman. See also Letter 402, *supra.*
[5] G. B. Atkinson: see Letter 414, *supra.* In his letter of 16 Jan. 1905 Jackson recalled 'Ben' Latham's dictum that 'G.B.A. expected to be fed by "*w*avens in the morning and *w*avens at night", but that he would be very particular about the bread and flesh which the "*w*avens" brought and that he would certainly not be contented with the water of the brook.'
[6] For M.²U.[3] see Letter 414, *supra.* On James Lempriere Hammond see *Life of L. S.*, 479–80; and for Fawcett and the Brighton election, *Ibid.*, 105–7.

agent. What you say of Fawcett does not at all surprize me. In his latest years L. S. could hardly understand his friendship for F. The truth is that he was exceedingly shy and got on best with people who were the reverse—up to a certain point that is. In the presence of a 'damned intellectual', or of anyone who seemed to be such, he shut up tight.

Dare I report that Matthew Arnold 'is a humbug and a prig' and that *Ecce Homo* is 'sickening'? I fancy that you would agree with a good deal of what I am reading—especially with some sentences about Farrar which must certainly remain in manuscript.[1]

I had nearly forgotten to thank for those bits of Trinity Hall Statutes—but am very glad to have them and really am grateful for so much of your time. Some of my problems must stand over: indeed I am beginning to see that I shall want another winter for this job, for my Year Books are calling me and I have just been defrauded of a week by that cursed influenza. It lies in wait for mankind even in this paradise. One of my girls has been really bad with it and I have had enough to make me both idle and stupid.

Well, I am wondering how the Greek question moves—I suppose the Syndicate is reconsidering its report. I am inclined to hope that there will be no change of front—but you on the field of action may see things differently.

The more I think of a Cambridge Ancient History the more impossible I think it. We should have a shuffling compromise between real history and myth—unless we could get for editor a man who doesn't exist. 'Classical Antiquity' would be a different matter—but we aren't ready by a long way for a Cambridge History of the Jews,[2] let alone 'the second part of the Jewish religion' as Dizzy called it. That's my opinion. I wonder whether it is yours.

Somehow I don't take kindly to the ink pot to-day. I will put that down to the 'flu' and remain

Yours very truly

F. W. MAITLAND

I think that you are a master of the slang of all schools. After reporting how Balston at Eton recommended the removal of Leslie Stephen because he could not write good longs and shorts, I want to say something pleasant of Balston. Shall I say that he goes down in my estimation? When, upon the complaint of O. B., I was told by Balston to 'go down', two little 'tugs' raised my shirt tails. I suppose that a biographer ought to be more solemn and less obscure.[3]

---

[1] Neither the description of Matthew Arnold nor that of Sir John Seeley's *Ecce Homo* (1865) appear in *Life of L. S.*; but the sentences on Dean Farrar's *Life of Christ* (1894) appear —in part at least—at p. 245.

[2] Possibly a covert allusion to Professor Waldstein: see Letter 323, *supra*, and Sir John Pollock, *Time's Chariot*, 142-4.

[3] On Dr. Balston, Stephen's tutor at Eton, and Stephen's 'removal', see *Life of L. S.*, 34. On the relations between Dr. Balston as Headmaster and Oscar Browning as master see Wortham, *Victorian Eton and Cambridge*, chaps. III and IV. A 'tug'—togatus—is a Colleger (King's Scholar) at Eton.

418. To H. A. L. Fisher

c/o Leacock & Co.
Funchal
6 Feb. 1905

MY DEAR HERBERT,

Many thanks for a long and interesting letter. How splendid all that south of France must be: but I guess that this part of the family would turn up a haughty nose at the climate. Save one wet week we have had perfect weather: one lovely day after another. I feel a little less disposed for exercise here than I did in the Canaries. Perhaps that is just as well for I have much to do. Oh! that we could talk of that biography or collection of letters or whatever it is to be! I can't make up my mind about plan or scale or anything else, but go on cop-cop-copying six or seven hours a day—and the ghost of the work visits me in the night-watches. The letters to Lowell, Norton and ('young') Holmes are so good—or seem to me so good while I am about them; and then comes the cold fit and I say that, though they interest you and me and a dozen others, the world will see no point in them; and then I hear the dear old philosopher himself damning my eyes for exposing all this 'trash' or 'twaddle' to the public gaze. What to do? I am perplexed as I never was before.

On two points you could advise me. Are you decidedly against two volumes? It is so easy to be long but I feel strongly that Leslie's vote, even if given quite impartially, would have been for one; and I feel also that if I were he I could do it in one. But then I am not he. I can no more draw a character than I can ascend the Schreckhorn[1]; all I can do is to let the character draw itself. A word of counsel would not be wasted.

Then I don't want to 'bowdlerize' Leslie and yet I don't want to give the Gnostics occasion for turning up their blessed eyes. I think that I must give a few of his condemnatory judgments *totidem verbis*—e.g. that Farrar's Life of Christ turns his stomach, that Maurice is 'muddleheaded', etc. etc. What think you? Leslie, when he was writing to people who knew his humour, said a good bit that he would never have printed. Is it fair to print it? To take an example, shall I say that Sidgwick's Ethics seems (when first read) a very weak book?[2]

What a selfish beast I am! I fill up this sheet with my own woes. But I will urge in excuse that you also loved L. S. and would not gladly see a mess of a memoir.

I thought your review of Freeman admirable—though I have not seen the book that you reviewed.[3] You do these things very well. Also what you said of my Canon Law pleased me, for I got more fun out of that than out of any other job I ever did. And in a way the fun continues. The other day came a letter about it from one Walsh who, so I gather, is (R. C.) Abp. of Dublin[4]—

[1] *Life of L. S.*, 83–5.
[2] *Ibid.*, at pp. 245, 243 and 250, respectively.
[3] The reference is unknown.
[4] Most. Rev. William Walsh (1841–1921), Archbishop of Dublin.

it had a cardinal's hat upon it, but I did not know whether the man was a cardinal or not and there is no 'Who's Who' here. So I did not risk 'Eminence' and said 'My Lord'. Florence advised 'Holy Sir'.

My kind regards to your good lady.

Yours affectly.

F. W. MAITLAND

419. To Charles Eliot Norton

c/o Leacock & Co.

Funchal

Madeira

6 Feb. 1905

DEAR MR. NORTON,

The address that I give above will tell you why I have not before now thanked you for those two last letters of Leslie's that you have kindly sent me. I thank you now. They are a worthy end to a very beautiful series.[1] As I go further, I see more and more plainly how valuable your friendship was to him. I very much wish that I could talk to you, for I am very unhappy about the biography. It is a new job to me and I cannot make up my mind about the plan or the scale of the work. I can hear his voice begging me to be short, and yet his letters are so good, especially those to you and Lowell, that I go on copying one after another. In a sort of way I have rough-hewn the material as far as 1875 and already the pile of MS. is weighty. I should be much tempted to sail for America and plague you with my troubles were it not that in the winter I must keep in the warm and in the summer I must make up the due tale of 'residence' at Cambridge. As it is, I will venture to put one question to you. Would you vote for two volumes or for one? I think you can guess the nature of the material. It consists chiefly (when youth is past) of letters to you, Lowell, O. W. Holmes the younger, some to Morley, Sidgwick, Croom Robertson.[2] And then I must tell you that I am absolutely unpractised in the art of painting a character and find it much easier to allow the character to paint itself by letters. I will add that I am very solitary: that is to say there is no one whose opinion I could thoroughly trust in these matters—no one I mean on this side, for the people whose judgment I should value in literary affairs don't know enough about my material. Any advice that you could give me would be highly valued. I need hardly say that Gerald Duckworth (qua publisher) is for one volume, or that Miss Stephen—Miss Caroline I mean—and Virginia[3] would like a great deal more.

Notes of the first journey to America, decyphered by Miss Stephen, show that Leslie *did* see you in 1863,[4] also that you did discuss the future of religion

---

[1] *Life of L. S.*, 437–8.

[2] George Croom Robertson (1842–92), Professor of Mental Philosophy and Logic, University College, London; first editor of *Mind* (1876).

[3] Leslie Stephen's daughter, afterwards Virginia Woolf.

[4] See Letter 404, *supra*.

in America. I have a pretty full account of the second journey (1868) in which
you do not appear—you had already started for Europe. Then so soon as he
is back in London he begins to tell Lowell how he enjoys meeting you.

Another question that I should like to ask is whether I may make some
(sparing) use of Lowell's (unprinted) letters to Leslie? There are just two or
three that I should like to cite in order that I might illustrate the encouragement
given by Lowell when Stephen was taking his first steps in literature: more than
this I do not want. I fancy that you are in a position to give me the requisite
permission. Am I wrong?

Forgive me for troubling you. Really I am very much troubled myself and
often wish myself safe back in the middle ages. Any advice, any hints, will not
be thrown away upon

Yours very truly but perplexedly

F. W. Maitland

420. To W. W. Buckland

c/o Leacock & Co.
Funchal
Madeira
13 Feb. 1905

My dear Buckland,

You are a good soul to write me such letters. Only those who, like you and
me, have been in exile know how pleasant letters from Cambridge can be.
Encourage your talent for letter writing—it is not for the napkin.

All news from Cambridge is not good, however. I am truly sorry for the
loss of Leigh.[1] When he was Vice-Chancellor and I was on the Council (how
long ago that seems!) I learnt to admire him greatly. As you say, he was very
straight—straightness personified, and I always felt a great respect for him.
What will the King's men do? I haven't a notion.

The selection of Rawlinson as the Chamberlainite candidate—I suppose that
I must call him that—came as a little surprise to me. I should not have thought
that he was (as seen from the party point of view) quite distinguished enough,
and that some votes would go to Gorst for this reason.[2] However, I suppose
that the caucus knows its own business and feels that it could secure the return
of any X. Y. whom it selected.

Of the unfinished 'battle of the books'[3] I have reports from Clark and
Kenny, besides that which you were good enough to send me. On the whole
I gather that all went well. But the older I grow, the less I can predict the motions
of the Senate. I feel that it might even abolish compulsory Greek one of these

[1] Augustus Austen-Leigh (1840–1905), Provost of King's College, Cambridge, since 1889.
His father was the nephew of Jane Austen and wrote her *Memoir* in 1870.
[2] For Sir John Gorst see Letter 95, *supra*. J. F. P. Rawlinson, K.C. (1860–1926) was member for the University from 1906 to 1926.
[3] M. and other members of the Cambridge Law Faculty were seeking 'to stock the Squire
Library from the University Library' (Jackson to M. on 10 March 1905: Camb. Univ. MSS.).
Jackson opposed the proposal.

fine days—my stars! but they are fine days here! Sometimes I take a little advantage thereof; but on the whole I have kept my nose very close to the grindstone and have even redeveloped a corn on my little finger of which I began to get rid when I took to idling some seven years ago. If I apologized to you for the deterioration of my admirable hand writing, would you or would you not accuse me of irony? Anyway I must not attack the hand that feeds me with letters from Cambridge—so I will change the subject, stating simply that I have read your letter. What I think I was going to say when I slipped into personalities was that L. Stephen takes and will take a devil of a lot of biographing. I am not at all hopeful of the result: but he was a fine fellow and I wish that I could do for him what he did for some inferior persons—I include Fawcett and Fitzjames.[1] But what with him and what with Year Books I have been hard pressed and I don't see much prospect of a holiday. But I am most blessedly free from pain.

Yes, it does look ignorant to spell Corporation with a K. I think too that in one or two passages Redlich has translated me 'out of honesty' into German.[2] Learned Deutschers continue to send me cards. By the way, are the Twelve Tables going the way that the Pentateuch went? Tell me whether that gent. in the English Historical is good and a little of your own opinion—just a little quite dogmatically.[3]

With inter-familiar salutations
Yrs. v.t.

F. W. MAITLAND

421. To Henry Jackson

c/o Leacock & Co.
Funchal
20 Feb. 1905

MY DEAR JACKSON,

The 'flu' that made *you* 'whine' must have been a pretty good 'flu' of its kind. The specimen that came my way turned out to be a mild sort of fellow and soon disappeared. This seems a good climate for convalescing in.

As to Hammond I only see allusions.[4] You know that Stephen said a few words about him, very pleasant words, in the Life of Fawcett. I see that a couple of years ago you must have asked Stephen to write a little more about old Cambridge. I have copied his reply which was among the letters that you gave me: it contains a sentence or two that may be useful.[5] But he was past 'reminiscing' then. As to your being in your anecdotage, I very much fear that you will never get there: to any good purpose I mean. I fear that Plato etc. will always be too interesting and that the history of Cambridge which

[1] Leslie Stephen wrote the life of Henry Fawcett in 1885 and of Sir FitzJames Stephen in 1895.
[2] *Trust und Korporation* written in English by M. and translated into German by Dr. Josef Redlich of Vienna, for *Grünhuts Zeitschrift*, Vol. xxxii (1904).
[3] A. H. J. Greenidge, *The Authenticity of the Twelve Tables*, 20 E.H.R. (1903), p. 1.
[4] For these and other allusions in the present letter see Letter 417, *supra*.
[5] *Life of L. S.*, 479–80.

is in your head will remain there. Could you not get a Boswell? However, I shall come some day for the humours of the international lectureship. Does the name Dod or Dodd bring back anything?[1] I ought not to ask questions. Don't consider them as questions: they are but jogs to a memory that I will set going hereafter, for you must have enough to do without writing letters—except to the 'Times', which the weekly edition does not give. It would be a joke if that report went through after all. I hear of some very old—very, very old—Madeira which is sold at 3/6 the glass, and, if compulsory Greek goes, I will get hold of some of that stuff and see the inside of a Portuguese lock-up. All the people on our side who write to me seem to think that we shall make a right good show—but that I suppose will be all. Meanwhile more power to your elbow when you lay on to Ridgways and such.[2]

What you say about Fawcett is a bit strange to me. Stephen was so very sure that, whatever else he might be, he was *not* a humbug. I find this in letters which show that he had become painfully aware that F. was narrow-minded and at times a bore; but 'there is not an ounce of humbug in him'.[3] I can't judge: I came too late. I should like to hear your version some day.

Do you—but this is not a question—in a desert isle every remark takes the form of interrogation—well—Do you know C. E. Norton? There must have been something curiously attractive about the man—so many people wrote him such very intimate letters. He was a sort of father confessor to English literary gents.

On looking back to your letter I see that it was not Fawcett that you charged with humbugery, but Farrar—which shows, I fear, that I am a stupid reader: there was a transition that I had not noticed, and Farrar, no doubt, was as little to your taste as to Stephen's. But I can't expect you to read this.[4] Some greasy devil has got at the ink and pens and papers: they may do for compositors, at least I hope so, but you must have had enough of them. I will try another shop.

Yours very truly
F. W. MAITLAND

I see that the Medieval History has moved one stage forward.

422. To W. W. Buckland

c/o Leacock & Co.
Funchal
Madeira

25 Feb. 1905

MY DEAR BUCKLAND,
  URBANE SIR,

I am glad indeed to hear that your urbanity was victorious. I think that you must have managed this little job uncommonly well and I am sure that all we

---

[1] 'Dod or Dodd' does not appear in *Life of L. S.*   [2] See Letter 323, *supra.*
[3] *Life of L. S.*, 386.   [4] The writing here becomes faint.

of the house of the law ought to feel grateful to you for your exertions. Kenny has been good enough to send me the fly sheets.[1] It seemed to me that you and Wright were much on the spot. H. J.[2] is a dangerous opponent and I think that on this occasion he had a plausible sort of case.

No more to-day. I vanquished the 'flu', so I thought—but his tail has come swishing round and I have had a little more bed. A *sequela* I suppose! See Magna Carta, c. 50: Nos penitus amovebimus ... cum tota sequela ...: which I construe 'with all their litter'.

Portuguese are a lot *nastier* than Spaniards—not perhaps so rude but nastier to ladies.

But I seem to drivel.

Yrs.

F. W. MAITLAND

423. To W. W. Buckland

c/o Leacock & Co.
Funchal
Madeira

5 March 1905

Reduced to Portuguese stationery
which (though you might not think it)
is very expensive. Am I legible?

MY DEAR BUCKLAND,

Thank you for your remarks about the Twelve Tables.[3] You tell me just the sort of thing that I wanted to know. Of course I can't say a word about the matter: still in a vague way I have felt that Roman legal history is very long (in the ordinary representations thereof) and I should rather like to see it telescoped, as you say.

What you tell me of Rawlinson is very interesting. The choice surprised me a good deal. It will not be without a qualm that I shall vote for Gorst—perhaps Providence and Mr. B.[4] will so arrange the date of the Election that I shall not vote at all—and it would not be without regret that I should vote against S. H. Butcher. I should have to say to myself that the question was Chamberlain or No Chamberlain, and that, I take it, would be about true.

I am right glad the Christians have bestowed a fellowship on Mitchell.[5] I like him and think that he ought to do something good.

---

[1] Leaflets printed for widespread distribution—a favourite instrument of controversy in Cambridge at this time.

[2] Henry Jackson. The motion in favour of the Squire Library (see Letter 420, *supra*) had been successful.

[3] See Letter 420, *supra*. Buckland's letter is missing.

[4] Balfour. On this paragraph see Letter 420, *supra*. Samuel Henry Butcher (1850–1910), Fellow of Trinity College, Cambridge, 1874–6, Professor of Greek, Edinburgh University, 1882–1903, M.P. for Cambridge University 1906–1910.

[5] William Mitchell, Fellow of Christ's College, Cambridge, 1905–8: d. 1912. He published, as the Yorke Prize Essay for 1903, *An essay on the early history of the Law Merchant*.

As to Dr. Henry Jackson I will feel my way once more. I say 'once more', for I made an attempt and found that his manner underwent a sudden change as I approached the subject.[1] Something or another—or perhaps I ought to say someone or another—has riled him. However I think that he is a man who takes defeat pretty well, and I have some hope that he won't carry on a guerilla after the vote.

How has the Greek question gone? Decided yesterday—and I shall know nothing until the middle of *next* week. Such is the perversity of mails. But I am hopeless.

Yours very truly

F. W. MAITLAND

424. To H. A. L. Fisher

c/o Leacock & Co.
Funchal
5 March 1905

MY DEAR HERBERT,

Thank you for your letter[2] and the advice and encouragement that it contains. In the matter of the philosopher I shall trust to your opinion rather than to that of anyone else and I much hope that you will allow me to show you my rough-hewn material and then give me your honest opinion about it. For the present I have put the thing aside in order that I may write an Introduction to vol. 3 of the Year Books—a long and dull affair about the manuscripts. When I have had this interval I will turn back to the memoir. My first inclination I know will be to put the whole thing behind the fire and begin again—but life is so short and these Year Books run away with a devil of a lot of time.

It seems odd to think that the Greek vote was taken at Cambridge yesterday and that ten days will pass before I know the final result. However that is so, for the mail leaves England on the Saturdays. I have no hope; but my friends say that we shall make a good show. As to that speech, I was ashamed of it afterwards, but I had some fun out of it at the time.[3]

I am sorry to think that P. V.'s book is lying at Downing. May be I can procure a copy from another quarter. I am curious to see what he has said. A little book by one Chadwick on Anglo-Saxon history has just come to me. It looks very good and Stevenson commends it.[4]

When Lettice goes to Madrid ought not you to go to Simanças? Or could

[1] The Squire Library: see Letters 420 and 422, *supra.* In his letter to M. of 10 March 1905 (Camb. Univ. MSS.), Jackson admitted defeat for the time being, but intended 'to fight your board three years hence.' See Letter 426, *infra.*
[2] Not extant.
[3] For M.'s speech in the debate on the question of compulsory Greek see *Camb. Univ. Reporter,* 17 Dec. 1904, and Buckland, C.L.J. I, at pp. 290–1.
[4] The two books were Vinogradoff, *Growth of the Manor,* and H. M. Chadwick, *Studies on Anglo-Saxon Institutions.*

not you come here and pick up a little local colour for a chapter on voyages of discovery?[1] You would be just in time to take me home.

Tell me if money is being subscribed for York Powell's daughter. I have a guinea or two—or at least some reis—lying about, and would testify, for he was a good soul.

Florence sends her love. If Lettice is off to Spain, may I be permitted to say that I kiss her feet? The Portuguese does not seem nearly as courtly as the Spaniard, and physically he is a very poor creature.

How I should like to talk and listen.

Yours affectionately
F. W. MAITLAND

425. To Charles Eliot Norton

c/o Leacock & Co.
Funchal
Madeira
12 March 1905

DEAR MR. NORTON,

Allow me to thank you very warmly for your kind letter.[2] It encourages me greatly. I have put my memoir on one side for a time in order that I might do some other work. What it will look like when I take it up again I hardly dare to think.

As regards length I am just now recoiling from the idea of two volumes. I feel so very strongly that *he* would have counselled brevity.

I ought to tell you that the letters to you, Lowell and Holmes (the younger) are nearly the only letters that are good when seen from the bookmaker's point of view. This leads me to ask a question which you may be able to answer. I read a great deal of Mr. Field. Do you think it likely that Leslie wrote to him letters of the publishable kind, and, if so, can you tell me in whose possession they are likely to be? I am sorry to say that to me Mr. Field is hardly more than a name and I have no one here to tell me anything about him.[3]

Once more thanking you for words which do me good, I remain

Yours very truly
F. W. MAITLAND

426. To Henry Jackson

c/o Leacock & Co.
Funchal
25 March 1905

DEAR JACKSON,

I can't thank you enough for your long letter,[4] but I am very grateful indeed. I wanted to hear some 'reflections' on the Greek question and yours are much to the point. I was disagreeably surprised by the size of the majority. I made a

---

[1] For Fisher's book on the early Tudors: see Letter 365, *supra*. The national archives of Spain were deposited at Simanças near Valladolid by order of Philip II in 1563.
[2] Of 20 Feb. 1905 (Camb. Univ. MSS.).
[3] *Life of L. S.*, 112, 209–10.   [4] Of 10 March 1905 (Camb. Univ. MSS.).

last guess as I opened my newspaper and said 'Beaten by 200', and lo! it was worse. Of course I had not been able to follow the manoeuvering—the weekly edition of the Times does not give correspondence—so I knew nothing except by very dim report of G. F. B.'s[1] intervention. Damn him!—if bishops are damnable—he is a dangerous man. One thing that you say interests me especially. For a little while past I also have been coming to the conclusion that at bottom this is a social question.[2] Having learnt—or what is precisely the same thing—pretended to learn Greek has become a class distinction which is not to be obliterated. From what you and others tell me I am inclined to suppose that we shall in the end have some new degrees. I heard that William Bateson is much dissatisfied by the turn that things took: a B.Sc. implying no Greek is just what he wouldn't like. I can well imagine that *A Greekless clergy!* was a good cry, but wonder how Greekful our clergy really is. Your 'leaders' I should like to have read.[3] But the people I wonder at are those who can write leaders when they have nothing to say.

As to the Squire Library I heard a good deal from Kenny and others and I have read your 'flies'. Clark[4] asked me for a letter but, so I gather, read only a small part of it in the Senate House—wisely I think. A while ago I hesitated, partly because I feared that the Squire Library would be made a dumping ground for rubbish, partly because I would rather not remove books from the old building if there were any chance of their being useful while they are there. What brought me to ground was the economic argument. I guess you hardly know how exceedingly bad the Univ. Libr. is as a law library—in the matter of foreign law books and periodicals it is shamefully poor. I don't like taking an American into it: the land is so naked. Now we shall have a little Squire money and I hope that in course of time we may be able to get together a creditable collection of foreign—remember that this includes American and colonial—books. Any way this will be a long job, but even the first beginning of it will have to be postponed for many years if at the outset we have to acquire the first necessaries of life, namely the English reports: and gifts of them we are not likely to get if there are already copies in the place. Then as to the Copyright Act, I don't say that there is no danger, but I do think that the danger is trifling when compared with that which we are incurring all day and every day by allowing books to be taken out of the Library. That, so it seems to me, is our weak point and a very weak point indeed. I feel that it would not be difficult to write a good slashing leader about it on the side of the publishers. On the other hand books are not to go out of the Squire building.

[1] Dr. G. F. Browne, Bishop of Bristol: see Letter 239, *supra.*
[2] Jackson had written: 'People are beginning to be alarmed about the new Universities and they want to distinguish the two old Universities and to keep them "socially select"'.
[3] Jackson had been writing 'leaders' about the Greek question for the *Morning News.*
[4] The Regius Professor of Civil Law. Jackson justified his own opposition on the ground that 'if we give out our books to departmental libraries, our defence of the University privilege [to claim a copy of every book published in England] against the publishers—that we hold the books as a great collection for the use of the nation—is gone'. The privilege was granted by the Licensing Act, 1662, which expired in 1693, and re-granted by the Copyright Act, 1709. M. discussed it in his address to the members of the Conference on the Local Lectures of the University, 9 July 1890. See also Letters 420, 422 and 423, *supra.*

For an obvious reason I don't want to talk about these dangers in public. I don't want to suggest arguments to the common enemy—and perhaps I got too near to doing this in my letter to Clark—but to you I can say that 'books preserved in separate buildings' seems to me a less attackable position than 'books not (continuously) preserved in any building'.

But I am always sorry not to follow you—even to defeat.

I guess you used the right word about Norton.[1] Clearly he had some strange power of making other people effusive—people too who were not generally effusive but very reticent. He writes a very beautiful hand—the best sort of ladylike script.

On investigation Bond[2] tells me that fully half the fellows of Trinity Hall under the old dispensation are not 'elected' but are 'nominated by the Custos *jure devoluto*':—so there was nothing strange in the case I am concerned with. I think that this must point to a desire to avoid college meetings and to a consequent practice of making informal elections 'out of court' so to speak.

No, the scandal about F. L. H. was not *my* scandal.[3] By the way, F. L. H. has been more useful to me than other people who might have known more. He seems to have a good memory. My scandal is an older tale. An application of the exhaustive method brought me to the conclusion that the hero's name was Roupell. But I have hopes of Morgan, at whose feet I hope to sit when I return, for he has promised to 'reminisce'.

I must be returning soon and look forward to Newton's dinner[4] as the occasion of our meeting. You I hope are at Bournemouth and not unhappy: I wish that I could say more.

Yours very truly

F. W. MAITLAND

Nossa Senhora of Lourdes (!) is going round the town this afternoon. I am ashamed of the Portugee. The Spaniard has virgins enough of his own without importing French ladies.

427. To W. W. Buckland

c/o Leacock & Co.

Funchal

26 March 1905

MY DEAR BUCKLAND,

Once more I am in your debt—and insolvent, producing only 3d in the pound or thereabouts. What have I to tell you? Did I tell you that I had one

[1] Replying to M.'s question in Letter 421, *supra*, Jackson wrote: 'Norton must be very attractive to draw such confidences. Is he perhaps somewhat feminine?'

[2] See Letter 323, *supra*.

[3] Jackson had written: 'Do you remember asking me about a scandal affecting a tutor at Trinity Hall?'; and had suggested that this might have concerned a baseless charge against the Rev. F. L. Hopkins. Nothing of any 'scandal' appears in *Life of L. S.*; but see p. 140 for Rev. F. L. Hopkins.

[4] Alfred Newton (1829–1907), Professor of Zoology and Comparative Anatomy 1866–1907, Fellow of Magdalene College, Cambridge.

real walk? It was to a show place—the Gran Curral—a big crater, not so perfect as the Caldera de Vandama known to your lordship but savage. I fell in with a Portuguee who attached himself to me as guide. In the end I was glad of him for he brought me home by a way that I should not have discovered—along a 'levada', i.e. a water-course of the Canarian pattern. Altogether I was on the tramp for some nine hours and glad to find that I could do so much. On this followed my annual debauch, to wit, a glass of beer. But I think that I did tell you this.

When we meet—it will be ere long—I want to ask you something about civil death[1]: but that will keep. Also I find in Sir T. Smith's Commonwealth of England[2] a queer statement about your friend the *libripens*. In all editions this has become a proper name in the form of Lipripeus. But indeed I badly want a talk.

The squire has behaved nobly by me despite his billing and cooing.[3] He has sent me a delightful 'baboo' letter and Anatole's[4] last, which I am keeping for the voyage. I look to land on Easter Eve, when you I hope will still be in the (Pseudo) Telde.

This afternoon I go to see a procession from the house of the Conde da Torre Bella, who is the head of the great wine firm Cosart and Gordon—and a cousin of Gordon Campbell, to whom I believe that I owe this entry into the aristocratic cask—not caste.

With salutations by all to all

Yrs. ever

F. W. MAITLAND

428. To H. A. L. Fisher

Funchal

10 April 1905

MY DEAR HERBERT,

It is good of you to send me those two books. The novel I keep for the worst moment of the voyage, knowing that it will cheer me. I have not had continence enough to leave Vinogradoff unread.[5] I think it a perfectly splendid book and am quite enthusiastic about it. My only fear is that people who have not read certain other books will find it difficult to understand at places. Of course I see that he has knocked many holes in my armour; but most of them I had expected for a little time past. Just now and then I should like to break a lance in self-defence; but this I shall probably never do. Domesday seems very distant from me now and I don't suppose that I shall get back to it. Anyway I thank you for your very great kindness.

I leave next week and, if all goes well, shall be in Cambridge once more on

---

[1] See *P. and M.* i. 433-8.
[2] *De Republica Anglorum*, Sir Thomas Smith (1513-77), was published posthumously in 1583. In 1906 M. wrote a Preface to an edition by L. Alston.
[3] See Letter 413, *supra*.
[4] Anatole France. On the '(Pseudo) Telde' see Letter 369, *supra*.
[5] *Growth of the Manor:* see Letter 424, *supra*.

Easter Eve. Florence and the family will stay a fortnight longer. I am glad not to be starting at this moment, for there is a raging tearing storm at work and the sea runs high.

I am carrying home an enormous pile of manuscript. I doubt I have ever written more in a given time. What I hope will (in a certain sense) interest you is a great chunk of memoir—I don't hope that you will like it as it stands, but I do hope that, for the love that you bore to L. S., you will read it and give me as much advice as you can about it. I mean to get a typewritten copy made which I can submit to the children and Miss Caroline and you—if you let me. What to say about the *Science of Ethics*[1] is one of my puzzles. I somehow feel that it was not nearly so successful as it ought to have been and I don't quite know why. If you, in the interstices (if any) of Boney and the Tudors, could think about this point—think what you would say—I shall be exceedingly grateful and would ever pray.[2] I approached our Cambridge philosopher McTaggart,[3] and he told me that he had never read the book, which chilled me.

I am not happy about the memoir and think that I should have destroyed all that I have written were it not that Florence encourages me.

We *must* meet. I hope for two or three days at my sister's in Easter week. Then lectures will tie me tight. But meet we *must*—at least those are my sentiments.

Yours affectionately

F. W. MAITLAND

429. To Charles Eliot Norton

Downing College

Cambridge

30 April 1905

DEAR MR. NORTON,

I have once more to thank you for a very kind letter. I did not know of the tragedy of which you tell me. Pursuit of letters to Mr. Field would I fear be hopeless.[4] Having just read what Mr. C. F. Adams said at a meeting of the Mass. Hist. Soc.,[5] I am asking him for any letters he may have and I am venturing to tell him that, if need be, you will say that I am a respectable person.

I need not tell you how much I admired your little speech.

I am just back from Madeira and find that I have many things to do, so I will ask you to forgive me for writing so curtly.

Believe me

Yours very truly

F. W. MAITLAND

[1] *Life of L. S.*, 326–7, 351–2: Annan, *Leslie Stephen*, chap. VII.
[2] 'And your petitioner will ever pray'; the stock conclusion to a petition.
[3] J. M. E. McTaggart (1866–1925), Fellow of Trinity College, Cambridge.
[4] See Letter 425, *supra*. A note pencilled on the present letter reads: 'Death of Mrs. Field—by burning of house'.
[5] *Life of L. S.*, 126, 129, 417.

430. To James Bryce

Downing College
Cambridge
30 April 1905

DEAR BRYCE,

During the winter I have been making some progress with the memoir of Leslie Stephen and you may be sure that I have not forgotten your very kind promise of help. I now want to ask you whether you have any memoranda of your expedition to Austria and thence to Transylvania in 1866. I gather from various letters that you and Stephen meant to see something of the war but were too late. A date or two, if you have them, would be useful at this point. That summer Stephen was climbing in Switzerland with 'young' Holmes. Then by appointment he met Mrs. Huth and the Miss Thackerays at Zermatt and (to use his own words) began to know that his fate was fixed, but 'somewhat perversely' went off to keep his engagement with you.[1]

I need not say that if you can write anything that would come in at this point—or for the matter of that any other point—I shall be deep in your debt. But even any bare facts—e.g. about the meeting with George Meredith—would be useful. The essay on 'The Eastern Carpathians' I know.[2]

I mean to 'lift' a great part of your speech at the Alpine Club unless you forbid me to do so.

May I offer my congratulations on the last *Holy Roman*? It is an evergreen.

Believe me
Yours very truly
F. W. MAITLAND

431. To Henry Jackson

Downing College
Cambridge
29 May 1905

DEAR JACKSON,

Thanks for those letters. You did show them to me once before; but I am glad to see them again. I will put them with the other letters that you sent me and you shall soon have them again.

I am a bit puzzled as to what I ought to say about the Apostles. In my view Stephen's disappointment was rather serious—he was in a way driven into the society of men who were not his peers. He was very shy and belonged to a very small college.[3] What I have written is now being typed. When that is done I shall ask you to let me show the Cambridge part of it to you. Shall I be asking too much?

[1] On this paragraph see *Life of L. S.*, chap. X.
[2] *Ibid.*, p. 181.
[3] *Ibid.*, pp. 47–9.

Morgan[1] is not so helpful as I hoped that he would be. His anecdotes would lose all point but for the mimicry of voices, and I cannot attach a phonograph to my book. He had never heard of R–p–l or the Trinity Hall scandal![2]

> Lives of great men all remind us
> As we o'er their pages turn
> That we often leave behind us
> Letters we had better burn.

Who wrote this?[3] I don't know; but it runs in my head.

Yours very truly

F. W. MAITLAND

432. To Henry Jackson

Downing

6 June 1905

MY DEAR JACKSON,

Many thanks for Smith's address.[4]

I am going to take you at your kind word and to send round to your rooms a box containing five typed chapters about Stephen. Don't shudder at the sight of the box, for there is little in it. If you can find time to glance at the contents and to give me any hints or criticisms in the shape of pencil marginal notes or any other shape I shall be exceedingly grateful to you. I have still a chance of making big changes, so please tell me that 'this sort of thing won't do' if you think it won't. I yet hope to get a little from Morgan for the last of those chapters. I am keeping back the religious affair until I have disposed of mountaineering and the journey to the seat of war.

I am sure that you will tell me to begin again on a different plan if you think this bad and I need not tell you that I shall attend to all that you say.

Yours very truly

F. W. MAITLAND

433. To A. T. Carter

Downing Coll. Camb.

9 June 1905

DEAR MR. CARTER,

I must put in a dilatory plea to your writ or rather cast an essoin de malo lecti. A plague of sore throat has been ravaging this borough and has laid me by the heels. I hope to be about in a few days and then will look into your interesting question.

---

1 See Letter 400, *supra.*
2 See Letter 426, *supra.*
3 The author of this parody of Longfellow's *A Psalm of Life* is unknown.
4 Presumably Horace Smith: see Letter 401, *supra.*

Meanwhile I can only say that I should expect to find cases before 1285 in which writs were quashed on the ground that they showed no recognized form of action. It seems to me that the statute[1] almost tells us that this had been done with pedantic severity.

A little while afterwards despite the statute this was being done. I have just got two cases of 1310 in which, after quashing a writ, the C.J. of C.B. has to go into the Chancery to explain why he did it and there takes part in the formulation of a better writ. These two cases have the effect of putting the writ of entry 'in consimili casu' beside the writ 'in casu proviso' given by Stat. Glouc.[2]

Thanks for your invitation. I am afraid that when I can get out of Cambridge I must go straight to the Record Office, for I am behind hand.

I wish that I could talk to you or indeed to anyone.

Yrs. v. truly

F. W. MAITLAND

434. To Henry Jackson

Downing College
Cambridge

10 June 1905

MY DEAR JACKSON,

Alas! I shan't see you to-morrow. I have picked up a sore throat and am kept in bed. The worst of it is that the said throat is of the kind that is supposed to be infectious and I am to be secluded for a while. We are advised that so long as I am kept under lock and key there is no reason why our friends should not come; so the Vinogradoffs are coming and I hope that you will dine here. Still it is a —— nuisance.

Your post card cheered me. I should like to hear your criticisms. As regards special points (which you might forget) possibly you could find time to set a query or a few words over against places where I go wrong. Then as regards plan, style, etc., you can tell me what you think by and by, for there is no hurry.

It will have struck you that I have not got the testimony of any one who was just of Stephen's own age *and* who knew him well. I had hopes of H. A. M.,[3] but it begins to strike me that he did not see very far.

Yours v. truly

F. W. MAITLAND

[1] Statute of Westminster II. cap. 24.
[2] S.S. Vol. 20, pp. 16–19 and 106–9. 'The C.J. of C.B.' was Bereford.
[3] H. A. Morgan: see Letters 400 and 431, *supra*.

435. To Henry Jackson

[M. dated this letter 12 June 1904; but from contents and surrounding letters, esp. Jackson's letter of 11 June 1905 to which this is a reply, the year must be 1905.]

Downing College
Cambridge

12 June [1905]

MY DEAR JACKSON,

Thanks for your note, but please come to-morrow.[1] It is not certain that I cannot appear, and, if I don't, your presence will be all the more indispensable—there are to be a few people at dinner. In my absence our Master would play host. I don't know that there is any great reason why I shouldn't appear but the doctor was dubious yesterday.

Anyway, however, I can't get to Trinity on Wednesday, and I shall be very grateful to you if you can keep a corner of your eye on Vinogradoff. All is so well managed at Trinity on these occasions that I have no real fear of his going wrong, and my wife and his wife will be at the stand up[2]: still, if you have no one else in tow, perhaps you may be able to give him a tip or two—he is hardly a foreigner now. I feel sure that you will like him.

After what you told me at our last interview it is clear that 'not dissolute' must go. Many thanks for the correction.[3]

The essay society I had from C. B. C.; but he was not precise. I don't feel sure that this was not Liveing's Society—the acta whereof seem to be mislaid. I drew H. M. B. blank—quite blank about the Union: Fitzy as orator he remembered well. (Elphinstone is no good. I haven't tried Hawkins: I fancy that he is queer and not likely to be useful—do you ever see him?) The 'rowing rough' and 'sanctimonious prig' are from Venn—his first cousin. So also the longer passage with the phrase about the Moral. Sci. Trip.[4]

Clearly the Omar Kayyám anecdote should come later. I had some doubt. What you say is decisive. I see too that I must alter what I said of the reform of the college statutes so as to show that I know the dates. Also I can add a word about the poll-men and professors' lectures.[5]

I shall soon have to consult you about a sermon which John Mayor preached at Leslie four or five years ago. I don't know whether to give Mayor's name or

---

[1] On 11 June 1905 (Camb. Univ. MSS.) Jackson had expressed sorrow at M.'s 'sore throat' and suggested that it might be better if he did not dine with M. but rather took Vinogradoff to dine at Trinity: see Letter 434, *supra*.

[2] Presumably after the dinner at Trinity there was to be a 'conversazione' to which ladies were invited.

[3] Jackson had written: 'You speak of the Hall as "not dissolute". It was very dissolute in 1860.'

[4] On this paragraph see *Life of L. S.*, chaps. IV and V. C. B. C. was C. B. Clarke; H. M. B. was H. Montague Butler; Fitzy was Sir FitzJames Stephen. Howard Elphinstone became a distinguished conveyancer (see Letter 86, *supra*), and F. Vaughan Hawkins was the author of the paper on the Interpretation of Wills given by Thayer as App. C to his *Preliminary Treatise on Evidence*.

[5] *Life of L. S.*, pp. 66, 77–8, 139–41.

to call him the Revd. A. B. The chapter that raises this question is being copied.[1]

Once more many thanks. If I don't see you on Tuesday I hope at least to hear your voice in the distance.

Yrs. v. t.

F. W. MAITLAND

436. To H. D. Hazeltine

[Post-card.]

Cambridge

22 June 1905

I have read with great interest and delight the papers that you sent me and hope soon to see the book.[2]

I have to lie on my back, so forgive pencil: essonium de malo lecti.

Yrs.

F. W. MAITLAND

437. To Henry Jackson

Downing

DEAR JACKSON,
26 June 1905

I am taking you at your word and sending another chunk of memoir. Yesterday Lapsley[3] told me that you were still in Cambridge. I had supposed that you would have fled. As to me, I am without a voice and am trying to recover it by lying abed. Next week I must lecture.

This here chapter[4] is rather important to me and I shall like to have your opinion on two or three points.

(1) As I have not material enough to tell accurately the story of the resigned tutorship and retained fellowship, have I said too much about it?

(2) Shall I name John Mayor or make him 'the Rev. A. B.'? For more than one reason I don't want to hurt the old gentleman or his friends: but I think that Stephen's letter to Duff is so much to the point that I must print it.

(3) Shall I keep the passage about French novels (from a letter to O. W. Holmes the younger)?

(4) Generally, does what I say of Xtianity strike you as (a) cowardly, (b) unnecessarily offensive? I want people to understand that I am in the same

---

[1] Chap. VIII, esp. pp. 148–53. See also Annan, *Leslie Stephen*, 33–40.

[2] The papers were essays written by Hazeltine while studying at the University of Berlin, and the book was his History of the English Law of Mortgage, *Die Geschichte des englischen Pfandrechts*, pub. Breslau, 1907. See Hollond, *Harold Dexter Hazeltine*, Proc. of the Brit. Acad. (1961), pp. 313 and 328–9.

[3] Gaillard T. Lapsley (1871–1949), born in New York and educated at Harvard, was Tutor of Trinity College, Cambridge (1904), and University Reader in Constitutional History—'for many years the outstanding exponent of medieval English history in Cambridge' (Powicke, *Modern Historians and the Study of History*, 130).

[4] Chap. VIII.

boat with L. S., while at the same time I have no call to teach mankind about this matter.

You will do me a great service by criticism.[1]

Yours very truly

F. W. MAITLAND

You are supposed to have read a chapter on Mountaineering (which is not written) and one on the Visit to America (which is in other hands).

438. To Henry Jackson

Downing

27 June 1905

DEAR JACKSON,

I am downright grateful to you for your criticisms[2]—the more so because you have been at pains to read my pencil scrawl. In the Etonian dialect I am still 'staying out': it may also be called 'staying in'.

I think that I shall accept all your suggestions: certainly most of them. I am now inclining towards a total omission of Mayor's name. For your remark about Duff's position many thanks. I had not thought of that. I think now of leaving the 'friend' anonymous, though I must somehow show that I am not he. Of course I shall tell Duff what I am going to do when I have made up my mind.

Thanks also for the remark about the French novels. Also about 'the grosser forms of superstition'. I put that in as an afterthought, because I fancied that I might fairly be accused of a cowardly sort of reticence. N.B. I do most seriously believe that the increasing desire for a 'real and objective' theophagy is a very remarkable instance of retrogression, and that the bulk of the clergy is becoming more superstitious. But then I've had to read all the ritualist cases—and the offensive sentence shall go.

I am glad that you don't think my talk about the tutorship and fellowship too long. Some day some of those 'mislaid' records may turn up,[3] and it may be proved that I have gone astray; and I can't protect myself by saying that records *are* mislaid. However, I must say what I think is true and take the risk. (I have nothing definitely to complain of: still it would have been better for me if one of the sons had gone to T.H. I see that L. S.'s dislike for 'B'. L. never quite vanished—it was a sort of distrust).[4] In the letter to Duff stood 'I believe that Thompson and other distinguished men would have been half on my side'. For 'Thompson and other' I substituted '[certain]', not wishing to give

1 Replying on the same day as this letter was written, Jackson approved M.'s treatment of (1) and, with some softening of language, e.g. 'delete *the grosser forms of superstition*', of (4) of these questions; on (2) he recommended anonymity but publication; on (3) doubted its relevance to the chapter. See Letters 435, *supra*, and 438, *infra*.
2 See Letter 437, *supra*.
3 See Letters 408, *supra*, and 447, *infra*.
4 'The sons' were Thoby and Adrian Stephen: 'B'. L. = 'Ben' Latham. M. clearly sensed some lack of co-operation from Trinity Hall (T.H.). See Letter 447, *infra*.

rise to any dispute about T.'s creed. Shall I say 'X and other'? You could tell me this on a post card.[1]

I am very glad that you have in a sort of way 'passed' this chapter. I don't feel at all sure of getting to the end of the book, but the daughter (Virginia) can do the last part very well, and I think that I have now done just what it would have been hardest for her to do.

All your 'stylistic' notes are to the point. I am now hopelessly bewildered by conflicting theories of 'commation' and should like a talk about them. Meanwhile I obey.

I could not overstate my gratitude to you for seeing me so far.

Yrs. v. truly

F. W. MAITLAND

439. To A. T. Carter

[Post-card.]

Downing, *13 July 1905*

You will find Bracton's doctrine about new writs on f. 414b. I certainly think that he would have held it his duty to quash a writ that was 'contra jus', though at least in the case of a personal action he concedes a power of making new writs which are 'praeter jus'.

I suspect that it is in the case of writs professedly founded on statute but not dealing with precisely the case expressly mentioned by the statute that the Court chiefly manifests its power of quashing writs as unwarrantable. This I think was being done pretty freely temp. Edw. II.[2]

Forgive this hurried note.

Yrs. v. t.

F. W. MAITLAND

440. To Henry Jackson

Downing

16 July 1905

DEAR JACKSON,

Since you told me that you would look at another chapter, even though written in Madeira ink,[3] I have been busy with proof sheets[4] and have not had time to tinker this screed. As I cannot yet get free, I send the thing off to you now, though a good deal of it (especially the first page) is obviously bad.

What I want specially to submit to you is the part consisting of bits out of letters from Cambridge. Do you think these bits good enough when names are suppressed? They amuse me and may amuse you; but we are, so to speak, insiders. What of outsiders? I want to give *some* specimens of letters written in high spirits, for there are many of another sort to come hereafter.

---

[1] The original words were kept: *Life of L. S.*, 152. William Hepworth Thompson was Master of Trinity College, Cambridge, from 1866 to 1886.
[2] See S.S. Vol. 20, pp. 91–2, 106–9, and Letter 433, *supra*.
[3] See Letter 421, *supra*. The chapter was Chap. X, *The First Marriage*.
[4] Of S.S. Vol. 20.

Then I do also want very much to ask your opinion about the general scheme of the chapter. I hesitate between saying all this and saying that on a given day Mr. L. S. married Harriet Marion, second daughter of the late W. M. Thackeray, Esq. I don't think there is any harm in what I say; but at times it seems to me profane. I so rarely read biographies that I don't trust my own judgment. Your word will be very weighty.

Then will you kindly consider whether even American idiots could say that I am damaging the character of a Judge of the Supreme Court? The said judge[1] has trusted me so thoroughly that I feel specially bound to think of what may be said of him.

The backs of my pages are very much at the service of your pencil. But it is as to the general effect that at present I ask for your advice.

I croaked a lecture yesterday.

Yours very truly

F. W. MAITLAND

441. To Henry Jackson

Downing College
Cambridge
23 July 1905

DEAR JACKSON,

You shan't have to say that I ask for advice and yet don't take it. I have run my pen through the scene in chapel and the electoral proceedings—with some little regret because I wanted to suggest a certain 'levity' (that is about the right word—at any rate the word that would be used by unfriends) and also a certain enthusiastic and not precisely scrupulous partisanship in a friend's cause. However, all this can be done where there is no chance of hurting other folk—so I don't bow to but agree with your judgment.

Why yes! it seems to me that the election must have been a pretty plain breach of statute.[2]

I have now no less than four solid articles on University Reform by Stephen in *Fraser*—all as Anti-Fawcettian as they can possibly be.[3]

To come to what is in my eyes a much more serious matter, I am very greatly relieved by your non-condemnation of the general plan of the chapter. I have no one else to advise me but his near relations—and they like these (very innocent) revelations of a love affair. Also if I don't tell this sort of thing I have precious little to tell, for I am not going to turn the critical mill. Still the cold fit comes upon me at times, so I am honestly glad that you don't disapprove.

---

[1] Holmes: see Letter 441, *infra*.
[2] The election was that of Henry Fawcett to a Fellowship at Trinity Hall (the 'friend's cause'), when Stephen 'persuaded the Fellows to break the Statute': Letter of Jackson of 24 July 1905, commending M.'s decision to omit the passage (Camb. Univ. MSS.).
[3] *Fraser's Magazine*, Vols. 77, 82, 84 and 89. See Letter 414, *supra*.

It was a splendid bit of luck for me that I fell in with you at a meeting of the B. Academy when I had been persuaded that I must take up this job. I bubbled over upon you—and have no cause to regret it.

I took a shot at Thomas Hardy and to my great surprise have got from him some excellent reminiscences of the old *Cornhill* time,[1] ending with a sonnet(!) *in piam memoriam*. I shall want your advice about that sonnet by and by. I don't know exactly how good it is: in other words, whether I must keep it for the end of the book. At the moment the young Stephens have got it.

As to *Ecce Homo*—I fear that, if I copied what was said of that, you would strike it out. The fate ordained for those who are 'neither hot nor cold' is described in the words of our matchless English bible. Any way I can't let this stand in a letter to O. W.[2] I will see what can be done hereafter. I must give a few typical explosions.

I am now collecting Alpine matter. Can you tell me whether G. D. Liveing's brother, the Doctor, is living and active? I don't want to write to G. D. without knowing this. L. S. did some of his very first climbs with the Doctor, who may have memoranda. Stephen kept none, and only 'first ascents' get into books.[3]

You will have plenty more letters from me unless you tell me that I must mind my own business. You, I know, have your own.

Yours very truly

F. W. MAITLAND

442. To R. Lane Poole

Downing College

23 July 1905

DEAR POOLE,

Do you know a Latin proverb or tag beginning with the words 'Discas alias' and meaning 'Learn to be more careful another time'? I see allusions to it pretty frequently in my Year Books—such as 'Vous estes en le cas de discas, etc.' It looks like something that might have fallen from a medieval Brer Fox.

Possibly if you cannot give me an answer, you can tell me of some one learned in fables. I have another tag that I should like to submit to an expert. 'If we give judgment on this point, ceo sera pur vin et chandeille'—meaning 'That will be final—it will end the whole case—you won't have another chance'.[4]

I hope that this will not find you at Oxford—but wherever you be you may be able to write a card which will put me in the right track.

[1] Stephen edited the *Cornhill* magazine from 1871 to 1882.
[2] Holmes. See *Life of L. S.*, 195, and Letters 417 and 440, *supra*.
[3] *Life of L. S.*, Chap. VI, *The Playground of Europe*, esp. at pp. 83, 90–1.
[4] On these two paragraphs see Letters 337 and 373, *supra*, and S.S. Vol. 20, pp. 25, 68, 190, and Intro. lxix–lxx.

I am getting buried alive under these Year Books, but hope to put out a third volume this autumn.

Yours very truly

F. W. MAITLAND

Clarke's paper interested me. Mr. Davis seems amazingly learned.[1]

443. To Mrs. Sidgwick

Downing College

Cambridge

30 July 1905

DEAR MRS. SIDGWICK,

Here is the letter[2] of which I spoke. It tells nothing that you did not know; but you may like to see it.

Yours very truly

F. W. MAITLAND

444. To Henry Jackson

Downing College

30 July 1905

MY DEAR JACKSON,

Don't you remember a day on which Jebb, O. M. [= Optimus Maximus— by the way someone will be suggesting that Deus received the Order of Merit, when the origin of titles has to be explored] read a paper to the B. Acad.? That was the occasion of my bubbling over.[3] I am glad indeed that it was so little remembered by you. We walked to the Athenaeum in the rain. I told you what I was in for and you proposed an evening in your rooms, which in due course I had to my profit. Since when I have tried your patience and as yet am impenitent.

Well, this time I send you Hardy's contribution. What to do? Natural place for it is end of a chapter on 'Cornhill' in very middle of book. But is the sonnet to be put there or to be kept for last words? I like it—but then I hardly know a sonnet when I see one. 'To advise generally on the case'—this is what solicitors say when they don't know what question to ask.[4]

Gosse has given me a nice little tale of L. S. and R. L. S.—none the worse because E. W. G.[5] figures in the tale. Altogether I am seeing my way to more about the 'Cornhill' than I hoped to get.

---

[1] [A.L.P. 'Clarke's paper' was *Serfdom on an Essex Manor*, E.H.R. (1905), 579.] Henry William Carless Davis (1874–1928), Fellow of All Souls, Oxford, 1895, Professor of Modern History, Manchester, 1921–5, Regius Professor of Modern History, Oxford, 1925–8.

[2] From Leslie Stephen to M. on the death of Henry Sidgwick, dated 2 Sept. 1900: *Life o, L. S.*, 458–9.

[3] See Letter 441, *supra*.

[4] *Ibid.*, and *Life of L. S.*, 263–4, 270–8.

[5] Sir Edmund William Gosse (1849–1928), author, man of letters, Librarian to the House of Lords. R. L. S. = Robert Louis Stevenson. See *Life of L. S.*, 267–9.

Bryce has done handsomely—half an article in Quarterly (residue by H. Paul) and éloge in Alpine Journal. He lets me use these and I can't press for more. Morley is curiously costive—yet for some years he and L. S. walked in the house of 'god' as friends.

I am very glad that you like the 'rigmarole' to Holmes.[1] I am thinking of restoring some bits that I omitted merely because the letter was very long.

A large batch of letters to George Smith[2] has come in. If they were not selected to glorify G. S., he must have been a model for publishers and for friends.

Tell me something of Sir G. Y.[3] I had a hint from one of the children that 'relations were strained'.

My voice is back again though not always under control. Now that I am fit for London, I have to keep residence and to lecture. I hope for a September in the Record Office.

I sympathise with you in the matter of A. Leigh.[4] How to describe anybody! I can only shovel evidence into heaps and chuck it at the public.

When you meet H. Fisher[5] I should like to make a third.

Yours very truly

F. W. MAITLAND

445. To Henry Jackson

[In pencil and undated: but from contents and Letter 446, *infra*, written at end of August, 1905.]

Downing College
Cambridge

[*Aug. 1905*]

DEAR JACKSON,

Are you still in Cambridge? If so, I will ask you to read a letter by L. S. to Sir R. U. P. Fitzgerald,[6] in which something is said about the resignation of the tutorship. I should like to know how it strikes you—but I won't trouble you with it if you are making holiday.

I still have to spend most of my time in an armchair—so forgive this scrawl. Damn it!

R. U. P. has sent me a nice little batch of letters. Perhaps you might like to see the lot—they give some glimpses of the Hall that might amuse you.

Yrs. v. truly

F. W. MAITLAND

[1] *Life of L. S.*, 182–5, 186–9.
[2] (1834–1901), publisher; founder and proprietor of D.N.B.
[3] Sir George Young (1837–1930), Fellow of Trinity College, Cambridge, 1862; Chief Charity Commissioner, 1903–6.
[4] See Letter 420, *supra*. Jackson had undertaken to write his obituary.
[5] At Winchester, where Jackson and Fisher were on the Governing Body of the College.
[6] Conservative M.P. for Cambridge Borough. See *Life of L. S.*, 58, and Winstanley, *Later Victorian Cambridge*, 98–9.

446. To Henry Jackson

Downing College
Cambridge
1 Sept. 1905

DEAR JACKSON,

I send the letters to Fitzgerald under another cover. It is very good of you to say that you will look at them.

One of them—that of 16.6.62—threatens to give me some trouble. I may have to 'hedge' about the retention of the fellowship even more carefully than I have already 'hedged'. You will see that Stephen just does not say that the retention of the fellowship was due to a vote of the fellows—though it was by their vote that he became bursar, etc. Altogether I am rather more in the dark than I was before. You will notice that Stephen thought that he would have to leave Cambridge. I don't feel quite sure whether this means that he thought that he would lose the fellowship. I suppose that the bursarship brought some money.[1]

You will see that *most* of the fellows had been very kind. That would exclude our friend Roupell, I take it, and possibly Latham. If Latham wanted to get rid of Stephen, I confess that I don't much wonder at it, for I think it clear from these letters and from what Morgan has told me that Stephen encouraged Fitzgerald and others in their noisy ways.

The 'Old 'Un' is the Hughes of whom Stephen wrote long afterwards in the 'Forgotten Benefactors'.[2]

I have got to the ink but am not managing it with much success.

Yes, I pumped Horace Smith. He was affable and useful.[3]

I am afraid that you could not give me any very good home news.

Yours very truly

F. W. MAITLAND

447. To Henry Jackson

Downing College
Cambridge
4 Sept. 1905

DEAR JACKSON,

The parcel of letters is safe to hand and I thank you for the commentary.

The hero of the tumble on the Col de Miage was Birkbeck. Hudson told the story in 'Peaks, Passes, etc.'[4] Stephen was of the party and did some enormous feat of walking in search of a doctor. He used to tell how he fell asleep while he

---

[1] *Life of L. S.*, 139–44.
[2] *Ibid.*, 61, 70. Henry Salisbury Hughes was the younger brother of Thomas Hughes of *Tom Brown's Schooldays*.
[3] See Letters 401 and 432, *supra*.
[4] *Peaks, Passes and Glaciers*, ser. 2, p. 108: see *Life of L. S.*, 84.

walked and how 'dream objects' got mixed up with real objects: e.g. he saw Cambridge friends who suddenly vanished.

I suspect the 'judy call' to be a small instrument in the mouth of the proprietor of a Punch and Judy show, whereby the sound conventionally represented as 'Roo-y-too' is produced. I had one in my youth. It may have been an effective engine in the pastime that was known (*teste* Morgan) as 'drawing Ben'.[1]

As to the 'resignation'—my difficulty lies in the fact that I am told that the minute book is not to be found. I cannot, I think, reveal this to the public, and if I try to tell the story with any minuteness my version of it will be open to contradiction if ever this missing book is found. So it seems to me that I shall have to give the tale in a very vague shape.

Stephen, I feel pretty sure, was under the ancient statutes. In other words, he had not put himself under the new statutes—and the ancient statutes have, I need not tell you, nothing to say about tutorships or qualifying offices. What (apart from heresy) could be said against Stephen's retention of his fellowship was, I think, that it had been given to him upon the understanding that he would serve as tutor and therefore that he must not keep it after the tutorship had been resigned.[2] This, it seems to me, would be quite enough to make him feel that he could not keep the fellowship unless that was the wish of the College.

I much wish that I could ransack certain cupboards in the Library at Trin. H. As it is, I must take the answer that is (very civilly) given to me and 'hedge' as well as I can. After all, I don't know that the details are of much importance, though they 'intrigue' me.[3]

Yes, it is amusing to learn that Sir R. was a liberal—to say the least. I think that what you say about Stephen's letters to him is very true. I must bag a few sentences.[4]

What surprises me most about the Stephen of this time is the willingness— or more than willingness—to hear Fawcett talk for 6 hours a day.

Yours very truly
F. W. MAITLAND

448. To Mrs. Sidgwick

The Cot
Heacham
Norfolk
26 Sept. 1905

DEAR MRS. SIDGWICK,

I shall be very glad if you include in your book the letter to me.[5] It gave me great pleasure when I received it in exile.

---

[1] This paragraph presumably concerns one of Fitzgerald's letters (see Letters 445 and 446, *supra*), but its contents do not appear in *Life of L. S.*
[2] Stephen resigned his tutorship because he felt that he could no longer accept the historical evidence of Christianity or take part in the chapel services.
[3] See Letter 438, *supra*.   [4] *Life of L. S.*, 68–9.
[5] *Henry Sidgwick* (1906), 578. See Letter 259, *supra*.

I hope that your work makes rapid progress.

I use your envelope a second time, for I don't think that this village would produce one of the right size.

Yours very truly

F. W. MAITLAND

449. To B. Fossett Lock

Downing College
Cambridge
22 Oct. 1905

DEAR LOCK,

Many thanks for your letters.[1] I can now say that vol. 20 is done. Yesterday I turned to Miss Bateson's (manuscript) Introduction for vol. 21. It is very learned and instructive but very formless. I will do what I can to induce her to give it a little more shape.

If a great deal is paid to the printers this year you will remember that the whole text of vol. 21 is already in page and that even a piece of vol. 22 (Year Books) is in slip.

I should not have thought that there was a volume to be made out of the Sewers[2]—but I will think of them. Surely I have somewhere seen an exposition of the customs of Romney Marsh; but I can't say where.[3] Certainly we must not allow 'the Crown' to use us.[4] My sentiments about that bauble I will not put upon paper.

Have you said a word to Marsden about Charters of Trading Companies? I still think it a good subject and R. G. M. might be attracted by it, for it has about it a slight savour of sea salt.[5] Also I still think that Fines would be a very good subject if we could find a man with the right sort of mind: someone who would be keen about contingent remainders and so on. I think that a young man might make some reputation by a good book on this subject.[6]

I have often wondered where the Americans found their eminent domain[7]— or rather how they came to borrow just this from continental sources. Has it ever struck you that what protected us against this was the completeness of our feudalism? Unquestionably we all hold of the King, but the lord has no right to 'expropriate' the tenant. Just because there is supreme landlordship there is no eminent domain in the foreign sense.

As sometimes happens with me, I have suffered a common recovery on the first day of term—*vel quarto die post*. I am teaching six hours per week and

---

1 Not extant.
2 Perhaps suggested by W. P. Baildon: see S.S. Vol. 32, Intro. xiii, and Index, 335–6.
3 See Mary Bateson's Intro. to S.S. Vol. 18, xlvii–ix.
4 Allusion obscure, but see Letter 375, *supra*.
5 R. G. Marsden had edited S.S. Vols. 6 and 11, *Select Pleas in the Court of Admiralty*. See Letters 471 and 475, *infra*, and S.S. Vol. 28.
6 No such volume has been published by the Selden Society.
7 *P. and M.* ii. 3. 'Eminent domain' is the legal concept whereby government can take land for public purposes compulsorily in return for compensation: see Kent's *Commentaries on American Law*, 12th ed. (1873) by Holmes, Vol. II. 438–40.

hopeful of staying here through November—whereat I rejoice. But I don't go out after dusk and live like a hermit. I hope to begin A.R.4[1] among the bananas.

Yours very truly

F. W. MAITLAND

450. To Henry Jackson

[Post-card. No year, but clearly 1905: see Letter 452, *infra*.]

25 Oct. Downing

I shall be very sorry indeed to miss the pronunciamento, but a change in the weather might yet bring me, and I think that it would be a great pity if the place of meeting were changed.

Perhaps if this song in the time of revolution is committed to writing I may be allowed to see it hereafter.[2]

F. W. MAITLAND

451. To C. H. Firth

Downing College
Cambridge
1 Novr. 1905

DEAR FIRTH,

I am endeavouring to put together some sort of memoir of Leslie Stephen. Among the very few letters that he preserved was one from you in which you spoke of the service that he had done in the cause of history as editor of the D.N.B. I venture to ask whether you would write about this matter a few words—a couple of paragraphs—that I could print. I am not by way of collecting 'testimonials' for Stephen, and as regards the dictionary I am not making a similar application to anyone else. But some sentences from you, if you could bring yourself to write them, I should value very highly, and so, I am sure, would all who read my book. I think there is some little danger that this part of Stephen's work will be insufficiently remembered, and a word from you would make a great difference.

And I will make another request. Herbert Fisher thinks that you may have preserved a few of Stephen's letters. If that is so, may I be allowed to see them? I am making no general request for letters for Stephen wrote so many, but his letters to you may have been interesting.

I feel that I am taking a great liberty; but the letter of yours that Stephen

[1] 4 Edward II: for S.S. Vol. 22.
[2] The reference is to a paper by Jackson to be read to the Eranus Society: see Letter 452, *infra*.

kept makes me think that you may not be offended by this request. Anyway I hope that you will forgive me.[1]

Yours very truly
F. W. MAITLAND

452. To Henry Jackson

Downing College
Cambridge
8 Nov. 1905

DEAR JACKSON,

Many thanks for allowing me to look at your Eranus paper. I found no difficulty in reading it and was much interested. I am not quite sure, however, that what interested me most was not a few words concerning the foundation of the republican club.[2] Also I have been greatly pleased—also surprised—by your letter to the Times. If ever there was a 'moral victory' it was our defeat by the parsons.[3] This makes me think that a good bit of 'tinkering' may yet be done before the Triposes go 'and which' they will see us out. Meanwhile I note that humanism means one of the four Gospels in the original Greek.

Cambridge Modern Hist. vol. i[4] is a sort of palimpsest. I don't want to see the last traces of Acton's scheme effaced, though perhaps his conception of what had to be done was not the best.

Yours very truly
F. W. MAITLAND

453. To Henry Jackson

Downing College
Cambridge
9 Nov. 1905

DEAR JACKSON,

I return some letters that you lent me and thank you for the loan. I believe that I did return another letter which you sent separately and in which Stephen look leave of the Ad Eundem. It seemed to me so good that I copied it.[5]

Morgan told me a little about 'Ben' and Leslie of which I can tell you something when we meet.[6]

Yours v. truly
F. W. MAITLAND

---

[1] No letter from Stephen to Firth is quoted in *Life of L. S.*, but Firth's appreciation of Stephen as editor of D.N.B. appears on p. 370.
[2] See Letters 450, *supra*, and 459, *infra*.
[3] On the Greek question: see Letter 426, *supra*.
[4] See Letter 293, *supra*.
[5] *Life of L. S.*, 479.
[6] See Letters 438, 446 and 447, *supra*.

454. To R. Lane Poole

Downing College
Cambridge
10 Nov. 1905

My dear Poole,

I am with great regret declining a very pleasant invitation to Oxford, because before Dec. 15 I must once more be beyond the four seas. I am sorry for many reasons that it must be so, but so it must be, and, as I shall not have the pleasure of joining in the chorus of cheers that awaits you, I will put a few words on paper.[1] I have long hoped that your services would be recognized in some public and festive manner by the people who are most interested in history. There are hundreds of people more competent than I am to set a value on your learning, but I would not be behind any of them in admiration of the great qualities of heart and head which have made you the best of editors. I have very pleasant memories of the time when I used to send you papers and of the great kindness with which you received them, and I have no doubt that what you did for me you have done for many others. Also I think that you have set us all a good example in the matter of equity and charity and self-effacement. I shan't be here to read vol. 50 or vol. 40, but I can wish nothing better for English historians than that you may edit it.

I think that I ought to sign myself as 'your decayed contributor'. I had ill luck this summer, and finishing another volume of Year Books (which will soon be sent you) was all that I could do. But I always look forward to and always enjoy my E.H.R.

So, my dear Poole, I shake your hand and wish you a pleasant jubilee—or whatever it is—and all possible happiness.

Yours very truly
F. W. Maitland

455. To H. A. L. Fisher

Downing College
Cambridge
17 Novr. 1905

My dear Herbert,

Esmein[2] has arrived safely. Many thanks for returning it. It is an amusing work, isn't it?

Florence is recovering, not quite so quickly as I wish; but I still have some hope that it may be possible for her to travel next week. I think that the sea voyage will do her good, and I am sure that the Canarian sun will work wonders. Adeline[3] is here to-day and I am very grateful to her for coming.

---

[1] [A.L.P. The twentieth anniversary of E.H.R. was celebrated on 15 December 1905 by a dinner at Balliol College.]

[2] *Histoire du droit francais.* Fisher presumably wanted it for the chapter on *The Codes* that he was writing for Camb. Mod. Hist. Vol. IX.

[3] Mrs. Maitland's sister.

I fear that you have found your work for the Cambridge history rather depressing, so I shall like to tell you that Prothero, who was here the other other day, spoke in very warm terms not only of the excellence of what you have written but also of your readiness to submit to the very unpleasant process of being edited. I don't know, however, that you will find much consolation in this quarter.

I am filling a big box with material for my memoir and hope to get to work when I am beyond the seas. So long as I am here my time is so broken that I cannot settle to the task.

I wrote to Smith[1] about the records of ecclesiastical courts. As he did not answer I suppose that I told him nothing new. I should like to be at Poole's fête and have sent him my felicitations.

Would that there were a chance of meeting you this winter! I fear it may not be. G. C., though distant, is the safest place for us.

Please give my kind regards to Lettice.

Yours very affectly

F. W. MAITLAND

I have been reading Merovingian documents with my one pupil and they seem to have spoilt my hand.

456. To R. Lane Poole

Downing College
Cambridge
19 Nov. 1905

DEAR POOLE,

My house of call during the winter will be Quiney's Hotel, Las Palmas, Grand Canary. This I say because you were good enough to ask for my address.

In your diplomatic studies have you ever seen a paragraph-mark mistaken for a word? I believe that this occurred when English took the place of Latin as the language of judicial records. Every entry begins with the name of a county ('marginal venue') followed by 'to wit', and the words 'to wit' seem to me to have no meaning whatever. The truth, I believe, is that Oxoñ SS is read as Oxoñ scilicet, and then 'scilicet' is translated into 'to wit'.[2] In the latest version of 'court hand' the paragraph-mark exactly resembles a double (minuscule) S of the kind used in the middle of words, and I see that in old printed law books it is represented by 'ss'. Does my conjecture strike you as absurd, or can you make any sense of 'to wit' in this context?

---

1 Arthur Lionel Smith (1850–1924), Fellow of Balliol College, Oxford, 1882–1916, Master, 1916–24. In 1905 he published *Notes on Stubbs's Charters* and in 1913 *Church and State in the Middle Ages*. In 1908 he published *Frederic William Maitland, two lectures and a bibliography*.
2 See Letter 377, *supra*.

Don't answer if you are busy. It is a trifle, but it has amused me.

I shall carry off Adams and Tout[1] into winter quarters, whither I go about the 5th of December.

Yours very truly

F. W. MAITLAND

457. To Mr. Justice Holmes

Downing College,
Cambridge.

30 Nov. 1905

DEAR MR. JUSTICE HOLMES,

You may have wondered at my not having returned to you the letters of Leslie Stephen which you very kindly lent me. My excuse is that divers causes have prevented me from making as rapid progress with my memoir as I had hoped to make. I am now on the point of leaving England for the Canaries and think that when I am in the sunshine I shall be able to write. I want, however, to ask your opinion about one matter. I have been trying to tell the story of Stephen's engagement and marriage to Miss Thackeray chiefly by means of the letters that he wrote to you, which in my view are about the best letters that he wrote at that time in his life. Will you therefore be kind enough to look at a rough-hewn chapter of which I am sending you a typed copy?[2] Stephen's sister and children have seen it and do not disapprove of the way in which I am telling the tale; but I do not like to publish it until it has been under your eye. As regards later letters, I do not think that I am at all likely to abuse the confidence that you have placed in me, but just at this point I can't feel absolutely certain that you might not object to the use that I am making of letters written to you.

You need not be at pains to return the typed copy, for I have another; and a few words upon a post-card will be answer enough. I know that you are very busy. My address I give below.

Believe me
Yours very truly

F. W. MAITLAND.

Hotel Quiney
Las Palmas
Gran Canaria.

---

[1] [A.L.P. Volumes II and III of the *Political History of England*, ed. W. Hunt and R. L. Poole.]
[2] *Life of L. S.*, chap. X.

458. To Sidney Lee

Downing Coll. Camb.
1 Dec. 1905

DEAR LEE,

I write to tell you that for some months to come my house of call will be

Hotel Quiney
Las Palmas
Grand Canary.

I am still hoping that you may be able and willing to send me some small contribution towards my memoir of Stephen. I say 'small' merely because I have no doubt that you are very busy and because a very little from you will be a great deal better than nothing—even a few words about the amount and kind of work that Stephen did in the first days of the D.N.B. I have his letters to George Smith and can obtain a good many facts from printed sources. What I should like is a little 'appreciation' by his lieutenant and successor: a couple of pages if you have no time for more.

I wrote to you a few weeks ago in this sense[1] and fear that you will think me importunate, but as I do not know that you received the letter and wish you to have my winter address I write again. Forgive me if I am troublesome.

I leave Cambridge next Wednesday.

Yours very truly
F. W. MAITLAND

459. To Henry Jackson

Downing Coll. Camb.
2 Dec. 1905

DEAR JACKSON,

I return the True History of the Republican Club[2] as you may like to deposit it among your records. I need not say that it has interested me deeply. No one could have guessed the true tale. F. Pollock believes that he has a copy of the rules.

May be I shall visit you to-morrow with a few questions. But any way I mean to dine with the Society on Monday, as the devil himself cannot now prevent me from keeping this term.

Yours very truly
F. W. MAITLAND

---

[1] M. had asked Lee for such a contribution on 27 Oct. 1904 (Letter 403, *supra*), but no later letter to this effect is extant.

[2] See Letter 452, *supra*. With a letter of 13 Nov. 1905 (Camb. Univ. MSS.) Jackson had enclosed the 'True History' and added some notes of its origin. He and Fawcett were its chief founders in 1868. By Rule 2, 'Republicanism shall be taken to mean hostility to the hereditary principle as exemplified in monarchical and aristocratic institutions': by Rule 3, 'The profession of Republican opinions shall be the only qualification for membership'. The members were to dine together six or seven times a year and then discuss 'conversationally' some social or political subject. A few dinners were held, 'most of them good; the discussions were so so.' The club seems to have disintegrated after 1871.

460. To B. Fossett Lock

Downing College
Cambridge
2 Dec. 1905

MY DEAR LOCK,

Semble that I shall not see Y.B. vol. III[1] before I leave England next Saturday. So I will ask you to look at the enclosed order to Spottiswoode and, if I am entitled to give it, to corroborate and confirm it by your initials. You can add, for I suppose that this will be right, that the cost of postage must be charged to me. I rather want to have a copy with me in Canary, for it may help me when making vol. IV.[2]

I don't know what is done in America about review copies of our books. Perhaps Hale looks after this; but it strikes me that the *Nation* (N.Y.) might do us a good turn.

I see that a set of our 19 vols. is advertised for 19 gūas and am glad to see that so much is asked.

I mean to spend Friday in London, having a bit of business there, and have some hope of intruding upon you about the hour of lunch so that we might exchange a few words.

My wife has reached Las Palmas after a long and rough voyage.

Yours very truly

F. W. MAITLAND

461. To F. J. H. Jenkinson

Downing
5 Dec. 1905

DEAR JENKINSON,

The book that I saw to-day in room Theta[3] was very much newer than what I expected to see. So please forget what I said about Pseudo-Isidore.[4]

This is the genuine Collectio Hispana[5] of canons and decretals made in Spain early in the 7th century, into which the forgeries were afterwards foisted. This Madrid edition is, I believe, the only edition of the original Coll. Hisp., though there is a reprint in Migne.[6] Tardif, *Hist. des sources du droit canonique*, p. 117, calls it 'très médiocre'. There is a great deal about the Hispana in

---

[1] S.S. Vol. 20.
[2] S.S. Vol. 22.
[3] The forerunner in the Old Library of the Reading Room now called the Anderson Room.
[4] 'About the year 1850 [the] Spanish Collection [of canons and decretals] became the foundation for a superstructure of forgery. Someone who calls himself Isidore Mercator, and who seems to have tried to personate St. Isidore, foisted into the old book a large number of decretals which purported to come from the earliest popes': M. *Canon Law*, C.P. III, at p. 67, reprinted from Encyc. of Laws of England (1897).
[5] *Collectio Canonum Ecclesiae Hispanae . . . nunc primum in lucem edita* (Madrid, 1808–21).
[6] Jacques Paul Migne, ed. *Patrologiae cursus completus: Series Latina*, Paris 1844–1902; *Series Graeca*, Paris 1857–1903. The reprint is in Vol. 84.

Maassen,[1] but I have not his book at hand. I imagine that your book is well known and that every good library should have it. It is handsome.

Good bye, once more.

Yrs. v. t.

F. W. MAITLAND

462. To Henry Jackson

Leon y Castillo, 5

```
 * But 'Quiney's Hotel,                    Telde
        Las Palmas'                  Gran Canaria*
 is almost equally good.                25 Dec. 1905
```

DEAR JACKSON,

In the hopes that you will not be unmindful of an ancient and laudable custom, I sit down to wish you *felices Pascuas*—'and which' may they be many and of the best. Technically I am not correct when I speak of 'custom', for really I mean that I am now in a position to 'prescribe for' a new-year's letter, and I am now dropping a hint about my rights. I can't put it so high as 'do ut des', for what have I to give—I who have just now learnt the names of the new Ministry (a ministry 'of all the Tramps'—so it seems to me—though I am not sure that Morley, Bryce, Haldane, were formally enrolled)?[2] This ? seems belated, but, if I remember rightly, I was asking a more or less rhetorical question, the import of which was that I have no news to give you in anticipation of any crumbs that you may throw my way. I have not even been able to do much towards the memoir in which you are good enough to profess an interest, for soon after landing I had to betake myself to bed and my friend Pérez Galdos (by the way I am sorry that our press chose so poor an example as 'Trafalgar'),[3] but that stage is, I hope, in the past, and I am itching to get on.

When I left Jebb was still living, but I feared that I should hear what I have now heard.[4] I never knew anyone with whom I found it more difficult to talk—my own fault I suppose; but so it was.

I am wondering who is to be sent to Parliament. Butcher?[5] Are you too radical? I doubt it; and many people would sink some differences to see you representing the University. But there! I haven't the slightest notion whether the founder of the R–p–b–c–n C–b[6] would care to go to Westminster. I suppose that he might consent to take the oath of allegiance.

---

[1] Friedrich Maassen, *Geschichte der Quellen und der Literatur des Canonischen Rechts im Abendlande bis zum Ausgange des Mittelalters* (1870).

[2] Of these three only Haldane appears in the list of Sunday Tramps compiled by Stephen (*Life of L. S.*, 500); but Sir John Pollock in *Time's Chariot*, 56, adds Morley and Bryce.

[3] Benito Pérez Galdos, *Trafalgar*, ed. with notes and introduction by F. A. Kirkpatrick (Camb. Univ. Press, May 1905).

[4] Sir Richard Jebb died on 9 Dec. 1905, leaving a vacancy both as Regius Professor of Greek and as M.P. for Cambridge University.

[5] See Letter 423, *supra*.

[6] See Letter 459, *supra*.

Some Agenda of the Brit. Acad. make me thankful that I have a good excuse for absence. Divers cranks seem to be on the loose.

Stephen's latest essays require as much conjectural emendation as any classic. Can you suggest something 'palmary' for the following sentence: 'or drive over with Pope himself in a chariot to sit with Bolingbroke under a haystack and talk bad metaphysic in a pasture *painted* with spades and rakes'? I would ask Verrall: only he would say that *none* of the words are right.[1]

I have only advertised my existence and, repeating my *felices Pascuas*, remain

> Yours ever
>
> F. W. MAITLAND

463. To Henry Jackson

[Year written 1902, but from contents and context clearly 1906. Printed in part by Fisher, *Memoir*, 153–4. Now printed from the original—the first four paragraphs in Camb. Univ. MSS., the last four and subscription in Trinity College, Cambridge. There seems little doubt that all belong to the same letter. Throughout M. answers questions and takes up references from Jackson's letter to M. of 3 Jan. 1906. Jackson may have sent the first part, esp. on the 'canaries', to his wife in Bournemouth, and kept the second, esp. on the 'Clark Lectureship', in Cambridge.]

> Leon y Castillo 5
> Telde
> Gran Canaria
>
> *15 Jan.* [*1906*]

DEAR JACKSON,

I have your second letter, not your first.[2] The first may be lying in the hotel at Las Palmas and I must attempt to get it. This year it is difficult to communicate with the 'ciudad' for there has been a prolonged drought and the roads—but did you ever try cycling across a ploughed field? Moreover people here are lazy and casual and the semi-hispanised English people who keep the English hotels are perhaps more casual than the true Jack Spaniards. Well, I must get that letter, for which I thank you in advance, even if it costs me a day's labour and some strong language.

Meanwhile I will talk of canary birds.[3] The birds are named after our islands. What our islands are named after nobody, so I am told, knows for certain. Whether the birds are found wild in all the seven islands I don't know. Certainly

---

[1] Replying on 3 Jan. 1906 (Camb. Univ. MSS.), Jackson wrote: 'I suspect that the text is right and that Stephen is quoting from some letter of Pope's or Swift's, the meaning being that the plots of the pasture are some of them dug out, others just reaped. In short, I take the phrase to mean "mapped out", picked out, not with pencils or brushes but with spades and rakes.'

[2] Jackson's letters of 31 Dec. 1905 and 3 Jan. 1906 are in Camb. Univ. MSS.

[3] In his letter of 3 Jan. 1906 Jackson had written: 'My wife tells me to ask you for information about canaries. One of my girls has just now got a pair.'

there are many in Gran Canaria. Also there are many in Madeira. The wild canary is, I believe, always a dusky little chap, brown and green. The sulphur-coloured or canary-coloured canary is, I am told, a work of art, and I have heard say that he was made at Norwich: by 'made' of course I mean bred by human selection. The most highly priced canaries are, I believe, made in Germany. I have known two guineas asked for a 'Hartz Mountain canary': it sang *pp.* like a very sweet musical box. On the other hand, wild canaries are cheap here, especially if you go up country and buy of the boys who catch them. My wife quotes as a fair range of price half a peseta to a peseta and a half. The peseta ought to be equivalent to the franc, but is much depreciated. So let us say that a bird can be had for a shilling. My wife adds that she would be very happy to import birds for your daughter—and this is not a civil phrase but gospel truth: she is never happier than when she is acquiring pets as principal or agent:—so it is, and I can't help it. I like the song of these dusky birds: it is not nearly so piercing as that of the Norwich variety. I dare say that I have told you some untruths in this ornithological excursus—but at any rate I make no mistake about the price of wild birds or about my wife's willingness— I might say eagerness—to transact business.

I fear from what you say that vengeance may be taken upon you for your leadership of the holy war against compulsory Greek.[1] I hope that this will not be so—but somehow or other I feel that, if it is so, you would not like 'condolence', so-called. The Council of the Senate is a queer body to be electing a professor of Greek—would the specialists do better?

Of the ministry I must say nothing; I am so blankly ignorant. You say 'mediocrities'—but are they not the best men of your side—my side too? Of course I suppose that there is personified mediocrity in the highest place of all.[2]

I biograph away cheerfully. It will be a straggling sort of book and I could be very unhappy about it if I stopped to think; but I must go ahead now and afterwards tinker.

I don't like to ask questions; you have so much to think of—still it is very pleasant to get letters or cards in this solitude. So I will set a little trap into which you need not fall. The snare is spread in sight of the bird. How, then, should one speak in one line of print about the Clark lectureship? 'A lectureship [in English Literature?] had recently been founded by [at?] Trin. Coll. Camb. out of money bequeathed by W. G. Clark [?]. The office was tenable for three [?] years.' It isn't a very good trap, is it? You may well say 'Damn the fellow; he can get this up at Cambridge.' I think, however, that you once told me that the lectureship was often inaccurately described. I must say a word of this matter in order to introduce an explosion of Stephen's over ornamental lectures, which I think would please you.[3]

By the way I guess that you are right about 'painted'. What a thing it is to be

---

1 Jackson was a candidate for the Regius Professorship of Greek.
2 Sir H. Campbell-Bannerman: and see Letter 462, *supra.*
3 *Life of L. S.*, 373, 380–3.

a scholar! I am really grateful.[1] Here at any rate is a good misprint: Johnson said that Homer (!) was milking the bull.[2]

I wish I were a member of the Council these days[3]—though I should sleep pretty soundly at intervals.

Yours very truly

F. W. MAITLAND

464. To H. A. L. Fisher

[The references to the 'Englishman' in the first paragraph of this letter and in the last paragraph of Letter 465, *infra*, suggest that the date of the present letter is 17 Jan. 1906. The foot of the letter, including signature, has been cut out.]

Leon y Castillo 5

Telde

Gran Canaria

[*17 Jan. 1906*]

MY DEAR HERBERT,

I am very grateful to you for your letter. Letters are especially pleasant this year for I am especially solitary this year. For five weeks I had no word with an English*man* until yesterday when our landlord called. Owing to the appalling state of the roads, which are mere heaps of white dust, I cannot as of old cycle into the 'ciudad'—also I suppose that annus domini has got into my legs. Your account of the poolificatio[4] and the list of guests interested me greatly—but it all seemed very distant and it made me a bit melancholy. But I gulp that down. I can well believe that Paul, son of Gabriel, made the best speech.

Tell me someday *how* S. Lee sinned. I am puzzled as to what to do with him. He gave me a kind of promise that he would write me some pages about L. S. and the dictionary,[5] but he has not shown any eagerness to keep the promise and now I have many doubts about exacting specific performance. I fear some indirect self-laudation which I could not omit. What say you? (By the way tu padre politico—Sir Courtenay[6]—has given me just what I wanted in the matter of the London Library. Would that all were like him!). Oh, I could curse and swear to you a good lot if you were here! I find that I must go on and on as hard as I can, for if I looked back I should burn everything. A sickening time will come by and by. Meanwhile I forge ahead and have got as far as 1892, so that the end is in sight. Never, never no more! Once and for

---

[1] See Letter 462, *supra*.

[2] Speaking of Hume, Dr. Johnson said that he 'and other sceptical innovators are vain men and will gratify themselves at any expense. Truth will not afford sufficient food for their vanity; so they have betaken themselves to error. Truth, Sir, is a cow which will yield such people no more milk, and so they are gone to milk the bull' (Boswell, *Life of Johnson*, 21 July 1763).

[3] To take part in the election of the Regius Professor of Greek.

[4] See Letter 454, *supra*.

[5] See Letter 458, *supra*, and *Life of L. S.*, 375, 402, 457.

[6] Ilbert: see *Life of L. S.*, 427.

one only! (Or rather—you know what I mean—for two only). Then Year Books for the rest of my natural life. But all this is abominably egotistical. If I could talk to you of (a) Boney and (b) Tudors, I should not be so selfish and should do my own work better.

Here is a little puzzle. Do you know Herbert Paul—I mean sufficiently well to say how humourous a dog he is? He writes a pleasant essay about L. S., appreciative and even affectionate. Therein he says that L. S. made only one Latin quotation, 'which consists of two words and contains, perhaps intentionally, a blunder'. The two words are *emollunt mores*. Is 'perhaps intentionally' a jest or had H. P. forgotten the source of the quotation? I can't make up my mind. If this is a jest, Paul can keep his countenance very gravely. I hope for the best.[1]

If you happen to be talking to Firth and can slip in a word to the effect that you know that I am hoping for ten lines about the dictionary as a training ground for historians, you will do me a real service. Firth gave me three-quarters of a promise, and I hate to play the dun, partly because I find that *exacted* debts are sometimes paid in coin that I can't use.[2]

Florence sends her love to you and Lettice. I wish F. looked stronger. We get first-rate news from Bex[3]—a great blessing.

465. To B. Fossett Lock

Leon y Castillo 5
Telde
Gran Canaria
17 Jan. 1906

MY DEAR LOCK,

Your winter greeting was as pleasant as heretofore: more I can't say, for you always send something good to look upon. Them there verses be main good to read.[4]

I send you a note that I had from Paul Meyer.[5] I am inclined to send him Year Books vol. II. Do you think that a 'review copy' could be sent to him? I don't press this request in the least—do not give it a second thought if it does not seem grantable at first sight. But in that case may I ask you to tell the printers to send a copy at my cost? I have not seen the review of vol. I in 'Romania'—and, for anything that I positively know, it may be damnatory. But Meyer's 'précieux' does not point in that direction, and even a moderately good word from him might do us a good turn in linguistic circles. Also he could teach me and subsequent editors some things worth knowing.

---

[1] *Life of L. S.*, 280, 422.
[2] See Letter 451, *supra.*
[3] In Switzerland, whither Fredegond had been sent for her health.
[4] Lock's letter is not extant.
[5] The note is missing; but see Letters 361 and 375, *supra,* and *In Memoriam, Frederic William Maitland*, L.Q.R., April 1907, p. 142.

I have been forgetting YBB. and biographing at a great rate. I found that I could not sandwich Bereford, C.J. and Leslie Stephen—so on I go with my work of piety—or mixed piety and impiety. I am beginning to see the end of the continuous writing. There will be a deal to do afterwards, and I shall be deadly sick when I read what is written. But with good luck I hope to copy a good chunk of YBB. before my return.

This place does suit me. Sometimes I wish it did not, for I am becoming a hermit. I had not spoken to a male English for about five weeks when yesterday our landlord called. However, you are busy: at least I hope so.

Yours very truly

F. W. MAITLAND

466. To Henry Jackson

[Post-card, addressed to The Regius Professor of Greek, Trinity College, Cambridge.]

Leon y Castillo 5,
Telde
12 Feb. 1906

Wal it du seem a curious thing,
But then Hooraw, etc.

I don't mean that it seems a curious thing, but this is the only poetry[1] that occurs to me at the moment. The news came from H. Fisher. Once more

⊥ ¡ ¡ ¡ Hooraw for J—n ¡ ¡ ¡

⊥ This, you know, is a Spanish device.

F. W. M.

467. To John Chipman Gray

5 Leon y Castillo
Telde
Gran Canaria
18 Feb. 1906

DEAR PROFESSOR GRAY,

Your kind note has found me here in my winter quarters—far from both Cambridges—and has given me a great deal of pleasure, for I hardly believed that anyone would wade through that awful preface.[2] In a way it is disappointing to find that a new edition of the Year Books cannot be 'rushed': but such is the fact, and all the industry of the medieval apprentices has for me a sort of interest.

Your tale of Epaminondas P. Stokes comes in pat and I have a mind to exploit it discreetly.[3] Also I shall look forward to the new 'Perpetuities'.[4] It is a fascinating subject and you handle it lovingly.

[1] Lowell, *The Biglow Papers*, 1st Series, No. II.
[2] Intro. to S.S. Vol. 20. Gray's 'note' is not extant.
[3] Allusion obscure. [4] See Letter 484, *infra*.

I have had to turn from my usual occupations to a very different job, namely, a memoir of Leslie Stephen which I have been concocting. It would be long to tell you why this job falls to me. I mention it because I think that you knew L. S. and am going to ask you whether you have any printable letters from him. The best part of my material consists of letters to Americans: Lowell, C. E. Norton, O. W. Holmes the younger, C. F. Adams.[1] The three last have been very good to me. I have a notion that you accompanied Stephen to England when he had been paying his last visit to Lowell. If that was so, may I ask you a question or two?

I shall be here until the middle of April and if you sent a postcard to the above address it would find me. I think that it would be better to send the card via Liverpool, for boats from the States to Grand Canary are not frequent.

Forgive my question. I was thinking of writing to you and your kind note brought my thoughts to a head.

With all good wishes
Yours very truly
F. W. MAITLAND

468. To Henry Jackson

Leon y Castillo 5
Telde
Gran Canaria
25 Feb 1906

MY DEAR JACKSON,

I put my congratulations on to a profane sort of post-card, but you know that they are from the heart. After I had sent the card came the Weekly Times with your election just below Moulton's appointment.[2] That took me back to the occasion on which I first heard the lines from the Biglow papers applied to you. The applier (could I say applicant?) was T. O. Harding. The occasion was a scene in which you, he, Moulton and I played our several parts—when the Union was opened on Sunday. I guess that you are the one of the four who has no cause to be ashamed—*secus* (as the law reports say) our new Lord Justice. Well, some of us were very nervous and when we had got our majority T. O. said to me, 'Wal, it du seem a curious thing, etc.'[3]

Now that I have put this down it looks silly and pointless. You will forgive in memory of a good time—at least I thought it so; and, to get back to time

---

[1] Only one letter from Stephen to C. F. Adams is printed in *Life of L. S.*, at pp. 417–18, and none to Gray. For letters to Lowell, Norton and Holmes see Index to *Life of L. S.*

[2] John Fletcher Moulton (1844–1921), Lord Justice 1906–12, Lord of Appeal 1912–21.

[3] See Letter 466, *supra*. Thomas Oliver Harding (1850–96), Fellow of Trinity College, Cambridge, 1873–83, was President of the Cambridge Union Society in Michaelmas Term, 1872, and was succeeded in Lent Term, 1873, by M. In the debate referred to in the present letter Moulton had proposed a motion opposed to the views of Harding, Jackson and M. The motion was defeated (Minutes of the Society, 1872–3, by courtesy of the Chief Clerk of the Society). Replying to the present letter on 11 March 1906 (Camb. Univ. MSS.), Jackson wrote: 'Of course I remember all about the Committee of the Whole House and your speech, which I can still repeat, and the smoking party at Moulton's afterwards.'

present, I want to say in all sobriety that your election gave a great deal of joy in León y Castillo, 5. I hope this means that you will have time to write whatever you would like to write.

In a kind of way I have finished my biographical job. At the moment I loathe the whole thing—but I am told that such a feeling comes upon most people who attempt biography. I have been reading Herbert Paul's Froude.[1] I wish I were Paul but am exceeding glad that Stephen wasn't Froude.

What is the true inwardness of this movement for a Matriculation Examination? I must ask you that when we meet.[2]

Yours very truly

F. W. MAITLAND

469. To H. A. L. Fisher

Telde
11 March 1906

MY DEAR HERBERT,

Thanks for a real good letter which cheered me.[3] I don't think that I ought to want cheering but sometimes I do, and any way it is very pleasant when it comes from you.

I brought out with me some—nearly all—the proof sheets of the Napoleon volume of the Cambridge Modern History, but I did not bring the list of the authors. So I have had the pleasure of trying to 'spot' you from internal evidence. I am not often in doubt. Some people can be dull even when Boney is on the stage, can't they. By the way the Mr. of Peterhouse[4] was writing to me the other day and said something pretty about the excellence of your contribution. Of course he ought to do so, but people don't always do what they ought, so I record this fact to his credit.

I have read a queer screed by your friend Belloc, M.P.[5] He had better stick to his novels I think—but I don't suppose that Davis[6] or 'the Oxford School' generally will feel much pained by his remarks. How the devil can Belloc know the income of an average English Jew of the 13th century? Oman I must read by and by.[7] Also I am looking forward to the memoir of H. Sidgwick which ought to be interesting, for H. S. could write very good letters. So soon as I get back to England I shall be sending my own memoir to the press—whether I shall ever smile again I don't know, but certainly I shall have some bad

---

[1] Published 1905.

[2] It appears from Jackson's letter of 11 March 1906 (Camb. Univ. MSS.) to have been another incident in the controversy over Compulsory Greek: see Letters 408, 412 and 426, *supra*.

[3] Not extant.

[4] A. W. Ward. For Fisher's 'contribution' see Letters 401 and 455, *supra*.

[5] Hilaire Belloc (1870–1953), author and man of letters: Liberal M.P. from 1906 to 1910. The particular 'screed' has not been identified.

[6] H. W. C.: see Letter 442, *supra*.

[7] Sir Charles William Chadwick Oman (1860–1946), Fellow of All Souls College, Oxford, Chichele Professor of Modern History, 1905–46. In 1906 he published *The Great Revolt of 1381* and *The History of England from 1377 to 1485* (Vol. IV in the *Political History of England*, ed. W. Hunt and R. L. Poole).

moments when the thing appears. Meanwhile by way of sedative I have copied large chunks of Year Book and feel that this is the work that suits me.

Is there to be a University Commission? If so I shall scuttle before it and purchase the fee simple of one of the Guanche caves in these parts. Florence professes a liking for the prospect—caves are said to be warm in winter and cool in summer and the beasts share them with the humans.

May we meet soon.

Yours affectly

F. W. MAITLAND

470. To Henry Jackson

[Reproduced in facsimile in Hollond, *F.W.M.*, opp. p. 12.]

León y Castillo 5

Telde

Gran Canaria

26 March 1906

MY DEAR JACKSON,

Two letters from you by one post! I am in luck, and they tell me much that I wanted to know about the Syndicate and other things.[1] In other respects I am out of luck just now, for some damned germs are working their wicked will in my inside and I fear that I shall not come to the scratch at the beginning of the next round or term and in that case our 'professoriates' will only just overlap, for I must not try the patience of the university and of my legal colleagues any longer. This being so, I feel that I am in a position to write to you an interesting letter full of good advice from an old to a young professor. I could tell you that you have illusions and beg you to retain them as long as possible for your own sake. Lord! what a lot I meant to do when I was elected! But I will keep these reflections and the moral for a time when (if ever) this diarrhoea—for that is the trouble—can take the form of words.

Meanwhile many thanks for a copy of the problem.[2] The 'undergraduate' was Percy Thornton—now, I see, a Unionist Free Trader. I construe E.C.U.-C.B. as 'English Church Union Cambridge Branch'. Do you agree?

My wife is delighted by the commission for the purchase of birds.

I am eager to see the Life of Sidgwick. Who reviewed in Times? Sir George Trevelyan? I admired.

I hope soon to write more at my ease.

Yrs. v. truly

F. W. MAITLAND

[1] See Letter 468, *supra.*
[2] After a walking-match in 1864 between Leslie Stephen (then a don) and P. M. Thornton (then an undergraduate), during which 'some say that before the end [Stephen] had no clothes upon him except a shirt collar ... a jocose mathematician invented an elaborate problem about the "successive denudations of a certain graduate whose regard for appearances varies inversely as his velocity"': see *Life of L. S.*, 61–2.

471. To B. Fossett Lock

[No address, but clearly from the Canaries.]

10 Apr. 1906

DEAR LOCK,

Here am I on my back once more just when I ought to be starting for England with D. Jorge Tornero![1] Malady this time only diarrhoea—but of a persistent sort that returns whenever it has been vanquished; but I won't trouble you with diagnosis. Prognosis that I can't be in England before first week of May at earliest. This I tell you because of your letter about Gross. I have not yet got any that he has written to me and shall not get it before I am in England. Of course I should very much like to get a volume out of him, but I don't quite understand from his letter to you that he can give us anything like a definite promise—poor fellow! it is a sad tale. If you think that anything must be done at this very moment, perhaps you will tell him that you know that I am delighted by the notion that there is any chance of his being able to give us a piepowder volume and that I will write so soon as I see his letter to me.[2]

His man for Trading Companies is I believe a very good man, but before negotiating with him I should like to consider Carr carefully, for there seemed to be a chance that he would turn out to be just the sort of recruit that we want. We do want young men, don't we, with a little enthusiasm.[3]

I hope that the General Meeting went well. Up to date I have only two lines from F. Pollock on a post-card.

I am rather tired of stopping the leaks of this crazy boat and now at last I am *definitely* in default as professor. How I am to go on I don't well see. However, I have got a good sized piece of Vol. IV copied.[4] I wish that I were in D. Jorge's shoes, for I would soon have a chat with you.

Yrs. v. truly

F. W. MAITLAND

472. To Melville M. Bigelow

Telde

Gran Canaria

19 April 1906

MY DEAR BIGELOW,

It is a long, a shamefully long, time since I wrote you a letter. I never was a good correspondent and during these last six or seven years I have been an execrably bad correspondent. A really adequate excuse I have not got, still I will ask you to believe that I have often been on the point of writing to you.

[1] G. J. Turner.
[2] Mrs. Gross had for some years been a confirmed invalid. *The Court of Piepowder* was pub. Boston, 1906; but Gross edited for the Selden Society *Select Cases concerning the Law Merchant*, Vol. 23 for 1908.
[3] See Letter 475, *infra*, and S.S. Vol. 28.
[4] S.S. Vol. 22.

For a long time now I have, as the phrase goes, been 'enjoying bad health'. It has not been so bad that I could not write to my friends, but it has compelled me to give up one by one a good many projects that I have had in my head and also to discharge, or fail to discharge, my academic duties in the most perfunctory way. Consequently when I see a lucid interval before me I make a rush at some piece of work and try to send to sleep a conscience that tells me that I do not earn my salary. Then my crazy carcase springs another leak which has to be stopped and I am packed off to 'a warm place', and packings and voyages plus the lyings in bed take up much of my time. Altogether I fear that I lead a somewhat distracted and useless life.

As I have got into this plaintive tone I will add that said life is in many ways very happy. Those two little girls that you used to know are young women now and all that I could wish. As to my wife—I will only say that she sends her love to you.

I have been doing one job of which you may like to hear a word, for it has an American flavour and anyway I have nothing better to talk of. 'Tis a memoir of Leslie Stephen and in one sense a work of piety. My wife was a niece of his second wife and it was in his drawing-room that I asked a (to me) important question twenty years ago. Well, in one way and another it became plain that if there was to be any memoir of L. S. I must make it; that was his own wish, and his children are still young for the task. In a sort of a kind of a fashion the book is now written and the dreadful moment of publication may come before the end of the year. Dreadful it is. I have been writing books for a long while now, but only for a very small circle. If I blunder about the writ of entry in the quibus only you and two or three other learned fellows will find me out; but now I shall have the whole pack of reviewers in full cry after me. However I don't want to talk of that. What may interest you is that about half, and the better half, of my material consists of letters to Americans—Lowell, C. E. Norton and Judge Holmes. Norton and Holmes have both been very good to me. Also I have letters from Stephen written from America during your great war. He was a strenuous champion of the North and paid his first visit to U.S. in order to collect ammunition for controversial warfare in England. I have letters also to C. F. Adams and Judge Gray.[1] Stephen also had words with Lincoln, Seward, Sumner, Chase, Meade, Grant, Johnson and also Emerson, O. W. H. Senior,—and some of his thumb-nail sketches are, I fancy, rather good.[2] Altogether I am hoping that people on your side of the sea will find some interest in the book and will say a good word—not of me—but of my hero. He was a bit of a hero of mine but I am not at all sure that I shall do him justice and this distresses me. Some folk will be on the outlook for blemishes in a very plain-spoken agnostic and Stephen had a fault or two, which I shan't try to conceal. Shall I make them too prominent? But there! I can leave you to imagine the sort of interminable debate which goes on in my mind. Often I sigh for *cui in vita* and the growth of the medieval borough.

1 Judge Horace Gray: *Life of L. S.*, 206.
2 *Life of L. S.*, Chaps. VII and XI.

Serious legal history got stopped by constant transportations. These 'Islas Afortunadas' are, as you may suppose, bookless and I can't afford to buy heavily. So I have had to concentrate all my rather fitful strength on Year Books. Photography is a blessed art. I have had with me this winter the relevant pages of some seven or eight medieval MSS. This makes a hole in my cash-box, but I think that this editing is now the best work I can do for the advancement of our good old friend, the Hist. of Eng. Law. As to jurisprudence I sit at your feet whenever—to my knowledge—you write anything.

Do you ever regret the whole equitable development? I sometimes do, but of course I have to convert into facts a good many 'might have beens'—and when one gets among 'might have beens' one's hands are very free. Still at times I hate Equity and think of her as a short sighted busybody. Yet I was bred in equity chambers and used to despise the common lawyer as an inferior person.

Charles Gross holds out a hope that he may be able to take in hand a volume concerning Piepowder Courts for the Selden Society. I am glad to hear it. Poor man! I fear that he has a very sad life.[1] I hear of him at times from G. T. Lapsley who's winning everybody's good word at Trinity.

In two or three days I shall be on the sea journeying homeward and then I shall be immersed in neglected duties. If only Massachusetts were warm in winter how gladly would I go there! Things haven't quite turned out as I hoped they would turn in the good old days when you visited me at Downing and at my beloved Horsepools. In particular I have not seen you. But you often come back to me and your coming cheers me—and I wish you all that can be wished. Keep a corner of your heart for me and my wife.

Yours as of old

F. W. MAITLAND

473. To Mrs. Sidgwick

[Year written as 1905; but from contents and from Letter 469, *supra*, clearly 1906.]

Downing College

Cambridge

1 May [1906]

DEAR MRS. SIDGWICK,

I am just back from the Canaries, having been detained there longer than I could have wished, and I find a copy of your memoir awaiting me.[2] I am glad indeed to find it and must ask you to accept my warm thanks. To get a copy of the book from you is very pleasant. Still I could not wait. I had another copy sent to me in my winter quarters, read it eagerly and re-read it and went on re-re-reading.

I suppose that every one is telling you that you have succeeded. I think that you have succeeded admirably. You know that at this moment I have on hand

[1] See Letter 471, *supra*.
[2] *Henry Sidgwick: a Memoir by A. S. and E. M. S.* (1906).

a similar piece of work and I can tell you very honestly that you fill me with envy and jealousy. I wish that I could do for Leslie Stephen just what you have done and I am trying now to take a leaf out of your book—in a metaphorical sense.

However I should think that by this time you must be tired of praise, and my own efforts as a biographer are teaching me the painful truth that of the biographer's art I know nothing, so that praise from me is far from being 'praise indeed', though I mean well.

I want to say something else. Can I say it? Your book has brought back to me some old days, and the more I think over them the more I adore the memory of your husband. I feel that I owe to him far more than I could put into words. I am cursed with shyness. I never could tell him what he had been to me and I can't tell you. I can only hope that he guessed what I felt and also that you have not thought me an ungrateful brute. Even now—as you see—I am tongue-tied. I must ask you of your charity to put a favourable construction on my silence and to believe (for this is the truth) that, if I worship silently, I do worship. To me your book is holy writ. I can't say more.

Yours very truly

F. W. MAITLAND

474. To Henry Jackson

Downing

6 May 1906

DEAR JACKSON,

Early this afternoon I sought you in your rooms but found you not. Part of my purpose was to tell you an apologetic tale about Canary birds.[1] It is this. My wife delayed negotiations because it was the breeding season and prices ran high. Shortly before her departure she began to haggle and she was in treaty for a pair with a boy up country. Then her boat arrived unexpectedly and she had to go on board without an opportunity of closing the bargain. She did not think that your daughters would care for a high-priced yellow bird such as can be had in the port—but quite as cheaply in England. Then she started believing that she would have time to buy birds in Madeira, but the boat, being full, did not call at Madeira. Altogether she is remorseful and asks for forgiveness from your daughters. For once a laudable desire to beat down prices has ended in disaster.

I hoped to see you at Newton's, but I have not yet seen the back of 'the snivelling intruder', as you call him, and am counselled not to break bread outside my own house.[2]

I hope that we may meet soon for I want to hear the news.

Yours very truly

F. W. MAITLAND

[1] See Letter 463, *supra*.
[2] For 'Newton's' see Letter 426, *supra*. On 4 April 1906, replying to Letter 470, *supra*, Jackson had written: 'I shall hope to hear soon from you that you have got the better of what old Adam Sedgwick [1785–1873, Professor of Geology at Cambridge] once called "the snivelling intruder"' (Camb. Univ. MSS.).

475. To Cecil Carr

Downing College
Cambridge
13 May 1906

DEAR MR. CARR,

I hear from Mr. B. F. Lock and am glad to hear that there is some chance of your being willing to undertake a volume of Charters of Trading Companies for the Selden Society.[1] If this is so, I should very much like to have a talk with you, and, as I am at present tied to Cambridge by daily lectures, I am going to ask you whether there is any chance of your being in these parts during the next few weeks. At this time of year Cambridge is not unattractive to some 'old' Cambridge men.

Believe me
Yours very truly
F. W. MAITLAND

476. To Cecil Carr

[Post-card.]

Downing, *1 June 1906*

Many thanks. I will not at present trouble you to send Cawston and Keane, but will await its return to the Library.

I am sorry that anyone has been before us, still from what you say I gather that there is room.

The Royal Society might deserve a word.[2]

Yrs.
F. W. MAITLAND

477. To Selina Maitland (Mrs. Reynell)

Downing College
Cambridge
3 June 1906

MY DEAREST SELA,

Many hearty thanks for your kind birthday wishes. I should have written before now but have not been having a very good week. When I am 'down' I feel that I can't write and during the 'ups' I try to do a little bit of professional duty. I sent off some Reviews yesterday to Vincent.[3] I will certainly send the next and will try to send them regularly. That horrid lecture looms in the near foreground. I wish that I had never promised it. A sight of Kate will be my

[1] S.S. Vol. 28, ed. Cecil T. Carr.

[2] Sir Cecil Carr had visited Cambridge in response to M.'s invitation. M. 'took me round the book-stacks of the old University Library buildings. I mentioned to him Cawston and Keane's not very impressive book on Chartered Companies: we didn't find it on the shelves. Writing to him afterwards, I must have offered to send him my copy of it' (Letter by Sir Cecil Carr, 31 Aug. 1961). The Royal Society is noted in S.S. Vol. 28, Intro. cxxxv.

[3] Dr. Reynell: presumably numbers of *The Cambridge Review*.

one consolation.[1] I do hope that she and your young lady have had a really happy time. Fredegond is full of the glories of Bex[2]: she is making us very happy indeed. The girls are enjoying some of the May Term festivities: their papa wishes that he could, but he can't. They are to have one grand dance[3]— the garden parties are endless.

Goodbye my dearest.

Your affectionate brother
F. W. MAITLAND

478. To Henry Jackson

[Month written as July, but clearly June. The letter was answered by Jackson on 5 July 1906 (Camb. Univ. MSS.).]

Downing
30 [June] 1906

DEAR JACKSON,

I had meant to see you many times during the summer term for the purpose of picking your brains, but nowadays a single wetting is enough to knock me out of time, and just when I had done my tale of lectures I caved in. Now I am at a spot called Heacham near Hunstanton and in two or three days I mean to come up for the next round at Cambridge. When I last saw you, you also had been in the wars. I hope that the swollen face and all that it implied are in a distant past—also I hope that you are not unusually anxious[4]—more than that I dare not hope.

F. Pollock, who was at the Society's dinner, tells me that the wise and good had taken offence at part of the Sidgwick memoir.[5] Perhaps the offence is to be understood in an apostolic sense. If not, I am a little surprised—also a little alarmed. So I put a case to your l'dship. You saw what I had written of the Society. Briefly this—'of a certain small society called the Apostles,— diligent readers of memoirs will know something about its history—Stephen was never a member. He regretted it both then and afterwards'. I then go on to quote a few words from 'a letter written' [to you] 'late in life which I have been allowed to see', to the effect that this was a disappointment, but a lesson in humility. Do you think that there is any harm in this? I can't think so but

[1] The 'horrid lecture' was the Presidential Address delivered to the Social and Political Education League, printed in the *Independent Review*, Aug. 1906, and reprinted in C.P. III. 474 as *The Making of the German Civil Code*.

[2] See Letter 464, *supra*.

[3] In a letter to her sister Fredegond wrote: 'I remember his dancing round and round first with you and then with me when we were ready for the King's College ball and that Mamma said, "Oh, Fred, you will crumple them and make their hair come down"': Hollond, *F. W. M.*, 22.

[4] About Mrs. Jackson.

[5] *Henry Sidgwick*, 29–32; an account of the Apostles' Society. Writing to M. on 21 June 1906 (Camb. Univ. MSS.) Pollock said that at its dinner in Richmond 'the Society read with disapproval certain 3 or 4 pages of the H. Sidgwick memoir'—a disapproval which his letter shows was shared by Pollock.

am not perhaps a fair judge, as I think that these few words will tell something of my man that is worth telling—something about his position at Cambridge that Cambridge men and readers of memoirs will understand. Really by this time any outsider who looked about him could collect a good deal of apostolic lore. If I were not a member of the Society I should have no scruple in publishing what I have written, and I don't show that either the recipient of the letter [=you] or I have any greater knowledge than all may have. But what think you? A word on a post-card will tell me.[1]

Bless its mealy mouth!—as Carlyle said. I am now sacrificing a paragraph meant to illustrate Stephen's honesty as a biographer. In a very long letter he insisted that Fawcett was rude [to Latham] at a college meeting and Stephen would not mitigate the adjective. I tried to tell this tale very delicately—but it must go. I can't ask in the proper quarter whether it would give offence. As you once said to me, it is always best to cut out what one likes.

I thank my stars that I have no widow looking over my shoulder. Widows spoil books. The Quaker sister[2] is as good as gold and makes me think that Quakerism is the best form of Christianity.

By the way I want you to tell me someday whether in or about 1869 other Cambridge men besides H. Sidgwick resigned fellowships, etc. because of religious scruples. W. G. Clark gave up orders. What of Sedley Taylor? I am not going to name names, but I wanted to have my 'atmosphere' right. I think that Stephen's resignation of the tutorship in 1862 was a very early case of anything of that sort at Cambridge.[3]

However I must not forget that L. S. is more interesting to me than he is to you. So I shut up but remain

Yours v. truly

F. W. MAITLAND

479. To B. Fossett Lock

Downing College
Cambridge
15 July 1906

DEAR LOCK,

May I transfer to the Selden Society the burden of this debt of 1 gua. incurred in printing a list of cases which Turner is now using? On a former occasion you told me to do this.

---

[1] Replying on 5 July 1906, Jackson wrote: 'If people seriously took offence at what is said in the life of H. S. they were very unreasonable . . . I think that F. P.'s summary statements sometimes give false impressions . . . But whatever the Society may think about the memoir of H. S., it seems to me clear that they can make no objection whatever to what you have written about the Society in respect of L. S.'
[2] Caroline Emelia Stephen.
[3] *Life of L. S.*, 139–54, 173.

I want to make a gift to our Squire Law Library of the past and future vols. of the Selden Society. Is the right sum

$$
\begin{array}{r}
10. \quad 10 \\
21. \quad 0^1 \\
\hline
£31. \quad 10.
\end{array}
$$

Since I came from Heacham I have been doing well. Leslie Stephen takes a lot of time: I have many feelings to consult. But with good luck I shall get back to YBB. pretty soon. Tw....ms[2] is sending in stuff.

Yrs. always

F. W. MAITLAND

480. To H. A. L. Fisher

Downing College

Cambridge

9 Sept. 1906

MY DEAR HERBERT,

I am sorry not to be with you to-day either at Oxford or in the pleasant county of Gloucester, but I have been working (for me) very hard to finish the philosopher—indexing and so on. Happily this place is as silent as the grave, the weather is charming and I have been unusually vigorous. I go to London to-morrow to copy at the P.R.O., but I fear that I must spend the week-end here with my bibliography, index, etc. I send you my last sheets. You need not read them and I feel rather a brute for sending them to you when Henry[3] is heavy on your hands. But if you do read them, kindly tell me of anything that you dislike.

How I should like a talk about the Statute of Uses![4]

I went for one day to Heacham. I think that the sea will do good to my three—but I can't give you the best of news—I wish I could.

I hope to see your mother when I am in London. My address, if you return the sheets, is 21 Palace Gardens Terrace, Kensington.

Yours affectly

F. W. MAITLAND

481. To Frederick Pollock

Downing College

Cambridge

21 Sept. 1906

MY DEAR POLLOCK,

I have to thank you for an exquisitely written post-card and also for a letter which makes me envious. It must be pleasant to travel about and see men and cities and monks and pictures and bedevilled cats. When you get to where the

---

[1] The life subscription.   [2] Twidlums or Little T.: G. J. Turner.
[3] Henry VIII. Fisher was finishing his volume on the period 1485–1547 for *The Political History of England.*
[4] See Letter 483, *infra.*

Rolls series is you must look at Thomas of Eccleston's 'De adventu fratrum minorum'. What you have seen was possibly a copy of it. If I remember rightly (but I don't possess the book and the University[1] is closed for a while) it tells of the settlement at Canterbury. A benefactor wished to give them a dwelling place, but as they might not hold any property he conveyed it to the civic community for their use, *ut patet in quadam historia legum Anglie*.[2] I forget whether there is any talk of Benedictine rudeness.

You know the friar's reply when before meat the monk said 'Benedictus benedicat', viz. 'Et Franciscus franciscat'.

I have been sitting here all alone. The family is at Heacham, but I have been tied to the study table by divers bonds. My weary experiment in biography is near its end and I am indexing. Never no more biographies for me! I have also been grinding at Year Books and am deep in *quod ei deforciat* and other delights of the same sort.[3] I have to work while the sun shines, and as it has shone I have worked pretty hard. Now I must make up some lectures on Perpetuities. Blessed be John C. Gray! By the way, when you come back I must draw your attention to a pretty blunder made by the Court of Appeal—a vested remainder, vested from the very first moment of its existence, was held to be too remote; but I am pledged not to say anything openly until the time for an appeal is past.[4] Out in Italy I daresay the contents of the Law Reports seem too remote even to their editor.

An occasional American drops into my solitude, and yesterday Delbruck of Berlin paid me a visit on his way to the ceremony at Aberdeen.[5]

Yours ever

F. W. MAITLAND

482. To H. A. L. Fisher

Downing College
Cambridge
21 Sept. 1906

MY DEAR HERBERT,

I want to thank you very heartily for your kind letter. It did me good and gives me courage whenever I think of it. So I am leaving the last part of my book substantially as you saw it. I fear that other people's eyes will not be so friendly as yours, but it is a pleasure to please you.

I suppose that I tried to put too much into my London days; so I had to

[1] Library.
[2] Pollock had written on 18 Sept. 1906 from Perugia, not only of 'wicked-looking cats possessed by the devil', but of his finding an account of the first Franciscans who went to Canterbury and were flouted by the Benedictines. He asked M. 'if he knows the story' (Camb. Univ. MSS.). M. replies by referring to *P. and M.*, where it appears in Book II, Chap. V, *Note on the early history of the Use.*
[3] S.S. Vol. 22, p. 104.
[4] *In re Mortimer, Gray v. Gray* [1905] 2 Ch. 502.
[5] Hans Gottleib Leopold Delbrück (1848–1929), historian and politician; esp. *Geschichte der Kriegskunst* (1900–2). He was a representative of the University of Berlin at the Quartercentenary celebrations of the University of Aberdeen held on 26 and 27 Sept. 1906,

pay the penalty in bed. I am right again now, indexing the 'Life' as the pages come in and getting on with another volume of Year Books, which I wish to get into type before I abjure the realm for the winter. Florence and the girls seem to be doing well at Heacham, but I think that this is for a time the best place for me.

Can I read proofs for you? I should be delighted to do so.

My kind regards to Mrs. Herbert.

Yours affectly

F. W. MAITLAND

483. To H. A. L. Fisher

Downing

22 Sept. 1906

MY DEAR HERBERT,

Our letters crossed, it seems. As to Stat. Uses, what I think I must have mentioned is an article by Ames in 'The Green Bag'. I cannot find my copy and suppose that I must have lent it with the usual results.[1]

I doubt whether it would interest you, but I can put the point quite briefly. The old story ran thus. Soon after the Statute the Courts of Common Law decided that there could not be 'a use upon a use'. So if land were conveyed 'unto *and to the use* of A to the use of B', then B would get nothing. The Chancellor, however, held that he could and would enforce the secondary use; so that A would be legal owner under an equitable duty of holding for B. And so 'this ambitious Statute added three words to a conveyance'.[2] What Ames did was to show that there is no sign that the Chancellor had begun to enforce these secondary uses until about a century after the statute. You will see the new doctrine well stated in the *last two* editions of Williams on Real Property.

Thus the Statute was not so futile as it used to look in our text books. For about a century it was a very serious impediment to anything like trusteeship of freehold land. I don't know that this concerns you greatly. It may warn you against some too contemptuous phrases that have been current. That is all.

As to Henry's object I have no doubt that it was fiscal—the extinction of the quasi-testamentary power of the landowners (or rather of the men for whom land was held in use) which had been depriving him of reliefs, wardships, marriages and escheats: in a word, as you say, of death duties. Then, after the Catholic Rebellion, he was driven to the compromise expressed in the Statute of Wills. Even after that he had, I expect, scored heavily. A great deal of land had to descend from ancestor to heir—and putting it out in feoffees would not prevent this.

Can I say more? Tell me if I can.

Yours affectly.

F. W. MAITLAND

[1] Ames, *The Origin of Trusts*, first pub. *The Green Bag*, IV. 81, and reprinted in *Lectures on Legal History*, 243.

[2] *Hopkins v. Hopkins*, 1 Atk. 591, *per* Lord Hardwicke.

484. To John Chipman Gray

Downing College
Cambridge
14 Oct. 1906

DEAR PROFESSOR GRAY,

I have been revelling in your 'Perpetuities'. It is a beautiful book. But I want you to explain on a post-card a point that puzzles one benighted Englishman.

Who was Mr. Pooley?
Why was he great?
Why is his shade invoked on p. 565?[1]

Yours very truly
F. W. MAITLAND

I have just finished 'Leslie Stephen' and am returning to Year Books with appetite.

485. To Charles Eliot Norton

Downing College
Cambridge
14 October 1906

DEAR MR. NORTON,

My memoir of Leslie Stephen is finished and in print. It will I believe be published in about three weeks. The only reason for delay is that under an agreement for simultaneous publication some copies must reach Putnam on your side before the book can appear in England. At this moment I feel that I could say a great deal of its demerits; but they will be patent to you. Indeed that is one of the things that distress me most. Other people may guess, but you will *know* that I have not made a profitable use of some excellent material, and if I could prevent you from seeing the book I think that I should do so. That being impossible, I shall order a copy to be sent to you and trust that you

[1] Of the 2nd edition, just published. M.'s questions, to which no answer from Gray is extant, have puzzled many readers. Mr. Pooley appears in a dialogue between Gray and a 'student' upon future interests in personalty, first printed in 14 Harv. L. Rev. (1901), 397–8. Provoked by a bizarre aspect of the subject, the student exclaims 'By the shade of that great man, Mr. Pooley, that is strange!' Gray: 'It is indeed strange.' The fruits of research have now been recorded by Professor Leach in a note to his *Cases and Materials on Future Interests*, 2nd ed., p. 213.

'Mr. John Gorham Palfrey of the Boston bar, the 'student' of the dialogue, was consulted. He had wondered about Mr. Pooley for years; had heard Gray mention him several times; had concluded *faute de mieux* that this was Gray's substitute for profanity; when pressed, conceded that Gray needed no substitute. . . . However, Mr. Roland Gray, son of the author, had the object of search efficiently catalogued among his Grisiana. The man was Henry Pooley, Barrister-at-Law of the Middle Temple, reputed author of *Precedents in Chancery* (1733) and 1 *Equity Cases Abridged* (1734): Wallace, *The Reporters* (3rd ed.), 305, 310. Viner refers to him in a footnote (Vol. 5, p. 408) as 'that great man'. . . . But why he should receive Viner's accolade . . . or why Gray should take oath by his shade or what he had to do with John Gorham Palfrey and future interests in personalty still remain matters for scholarly research.'

will look at it with charitable eyes. Biography is the last sort of work that I should have chosen for myself.

One point will I hope be clear to every reader. If it is not clear then indeed I have failed. I mean that your friendship and encouragement were of extremely great importance to Stephen. It will also be plain that without having the run of your letter boxes Stephen's biographer could never have told more than half that there was to tell. That prolonged and noble friendship deserved a better chronicler: but even I cannot spoil all the letters.

I am on the point of packing up the letters, both those to you and those to Lowell, and I will send them off as soon as I can ascertain the best means of transmission. In travels to and from the Canaries one of your neat boxes suffered damage; I have had it repaired but cannot, I fear, describe it as being as good as new. I must also apologize for a few marks made with blue pencil on some of the letters. They proceed from a member of Stephen's household who was selecting passages and did not realize that marks made with blue pencil are permanent. I hope you will forgive this offence, for which I am to blame.

Once more I must offer you my heartiest thanks. You at all events have done all that could be done for the memory of your friend.

> Believe me, my dear Mr. Norton,
> Yours very truly and gratefully
> F. W. MAITLAND

486. To Mr. Justice Holmes

> Downing College,
> Cambridge.
> *14 Oct. 1906.*

DEAR JUDGE HOLMES,

I am returning the letters written to you by Leslie Stephen which you very kindly lent me. I am exceedingly grateful to you for the loan and I feel that if 'my damned book', as Stephen would have said, is not a dismal failure, it will be largely due to these letters. I am on the eve of publication, and Putnam will be instructed to send you a copy which I hope you will accept as a token of my gratitude.

> Believe me
> Yours very truly
> F. W. MAITLAND

487. To R. Lane Poole

> Downing College
> Cambridge
> *26 Oct. 1906*

MY DEAR POOLE,

I am not sure that I could find anything to say about the De Legatis—but if you like to give me the book in exchange for O, I will not refuse to transact business.

You don't happen to want anything about Webbs' 'English Local Government', do you? I have been reading it with admiration—S. W. and B. W. are strangers to me, but they seem to me to have written a marvellously good book.[1]

The contest between Mr. B. and Miss B. is amusing.[2]

Yours very truly

F. W. MAITLAND

488. To F. J. H. Jenkinson

Downing College
Cambridge
9 Nov. 1906

MY DEAR JENKINSON,

I am afraid that I must not dine with you on Monday. I want to get to the end of term without cutting lectures, and until the end is in sight I must stay at home of nights—so it seems; but really I am very sorry for I enjoy my few dinner parties.

Yours very truly

F. W. MAITLAND

489. To H. A. L. Fisher

Downing College
Cambridge
12 Nov. 1906

MY DEAR HERBERT,

It was very pleasant to read your kind letter. As to the book I think from what Gerald[3] tells me that in a temporal sense it is doing surprisingly well. Also all the criticisms that I have seen have been friendly except one in the Academy which pooh-poohed L. S. as a mere journalist. I was really grateful to Gosse for introducing me to the millions of the 'Dilely Mile'.[4] I have had some curious peeps into the religion of the daily press of which I will tell you something when term is over and I am at Malaga or Grand Canary—which it is to be I don't know yet.

I fear that I shall not be able to carry off your book.[5] If it is out in time I shall read it on board ship—a test I keep for very good books. If it is not ready,

[1] Sidney (1859–1947) and Beatrice Webb (1858–1943), *English Local Government*, pub. 1906.
[2] [A.L.P. Adolphus Ballard and Mary Bateson: the one a strong upholder of the garrison theory, the other of the market theory, of the origin of boroughs. Cf. E.H.R. (1905) 143: (1906) 99, 699, 709.]
[3] Duckworth.
[4] In 1906 the *Daily Mail*, in imitation of the *Times*, published a weekly literary supplement of which Edmund Gosse was editor. 'It was believed that among readers of the journal there might be found persons sufficiently interested in literary topics. . . . The belief proved to be without solid foundation': Charteris, *Life of Sir Edmund Gosse*, 300.
[5] See Letter 480, *supra*.

then it must follow me. Despite Poole's efforts you have, no doubt, stiffened your back. That it will be a most interesting book I am very sure. Oman writes well but his is not the sort of history that I care for.[1]

After a bad interval I am well and lively again—so much so that I felt that I ought to be at Oxford—but a chance shower of rain is enough to lay me low.

Yes, Gerald Balfour[2] is charming.

To-day I hear, alas! that Thoby[3] has added typhoid to pneumonia. It makes me almost glad that Leslie is not here.

Yours affectly
F. W. MAITLAND

490. To B. Fossett Lock

Downing College
Cambridge
13 Nov. 1906

MY DEAR LOCK,

I am going pretty strong once more and could attend a meeting if wanted. I shall be quite glad to see those two books[4] if you care to send them.

After long hesitation between Canary and Malaga we have decided to return to our old love. My wife goes at once. I think that Dec. 8 will see me starting.

All things considered, I have been extremely lucky this year. I did not hope to see the whole text of Vol. IV in type before starting for winter quarters. Some introduction is in my head. I want to have a talk about the rolls this time.[5]

I hope that trade flourishes.

Yours v. truly
F. W. MAITLAND

491. To Florence Maitland

[Envelope addressed 'Mrs. Maitland, Midland Hotel, St. Pancras, W.C.]

Downing College
Cambridge
16 Nov. 1906

BELOVED,

I hope that you have not had quite so much rain as we have had. The court is a lake. It has been very cold and cheerless. So I stopped at home all this

[1] See Letter 469, *supra*.
[2] (1853–1945), brother of Arthur Balfour; Chief Secretary for Ireland, 1895–1900, President of the Board of Trade, 1900–5. He was M.'s friend from Eton days: Fisher, *Memoir*, 6.
[3] Julius Thoby Stephen (1880–1906); Leslie Stephen's elder son by his second wife.
[4] Allusion unknown.
[5] See Preface by Lock to S.S. Vol. 22, pub. 1907. The Introduction was written by G. J. Turner.

afternoon working at proof-sheets. Corbett[1] looked in after tea and we had a long talk.

Well, you are on your way to the sun, and very soon you will be cheered by a sight of it. I am dreadfully sorry about our poor Goose.[2] You must certainly take a first class if the second looks very bad—don't scruple to do so—we can live cheaply when once we are out in Canary.

Now good-bye and a happy voyage to you. I shall soon be with you. Give my love to the Isleta as soon as you see it. I do hope and trust that you are going to be happy.

So with many kisses good-bye.

Your own

F.

492. To W. W. Buckland

Downing College
Cambridge
25 Nov. 1906

DEAR BUCKLAND,

I congratulate you on having got that MS. finished.[3] I promise myself a good time someday.

I learn by telegram that wife and daughter are once more in the Triana.[4] On the 8th I shall follow them—O Susanna![5]

Yours v. truly

F. W. MAITLAND

493. To James Bryce

Downing College
Cambridge
27 Nov. 1906

MY DEAR BRYCE,

I must thank you for your very kind words. After what has happened they come to me the more pleasantly. I have been cursing myself for not having

---

[1] Probably William John Corbett: see Letter 137, *supra*.
[2] Ermengard.
[3] *The Roman Law of Slavery* (pub. 1908).
[4] The Calle de la Triana was the principal street in Las Palmas.
[5] 'O Susanna, don't you cry for me,
   I've come from Alabama with my banjo on my knee'.
American song by Stephen Foster, which first became popular with miners and prospectors during the California Gold Rush of 1849. Stephen Foster's songs, including *Old Folks at Home*, were collected under the title 'Foster's Plantation Melodies as sung by Christy's Minstrels'.

dunned you; but when I thought of your governing that distressful country I held my hand.[1]

Yours very gratefully

F. W. MAITLAND

You will have heard that Thoby died the other day of typhoid picked up at Athens. I am really glad that Leslie went first.[2]

494. To Florence Maitland

Downing

27 Nov. 1906

MY BEST BELOVED,

I don't know in what order you will get your letters or in what order you will open them. First let me tell you that I get very good reports of our dear child at Bex[3] both directly and indirectly. Nothing could be better. I have given her careful instructions as to sending me letters for you. Next I can tell you that I am well; no aches or pains.

When I wrote to you last I was very sad indeed. Thoby's death was heart-rending and I could think of nothing else. Now I am not so sad but I am per-plexed. Perhaps you will know from your mother what is coming. However I will tell you. Yesterday I had a short note from 'Ginia saying that Nessa is engaged to marry Mr. Clive Bell, Thoby's great friend.[4] Apparently they exchanged promises before the funeral. Well, it isn't conventional but it seems to me all natural and right and beautiful. My only fear is that Nessa may have caught rather hastily at the first support that offered itself. Your mother from whom I had a note to-day says that she rejoices, but adds that she doesn't know Mr. Bell. I have great faith in Nessa and guess that all will go well. But there will be some exclamations, won't there? My next sentence was going to be 'What will Milly say?' At the moment that I was beginning it the enclosed note came. I send it to you—for I would not conceal anything from my wife, and it may amuse you; it has amused me. Milly has a soft heart for lovers.

---

[1] Bryce was at this time Chief Secretary for Ireland in the Liberal Government. In his letter of 26 Nov. 1906 (Camb. Univ. MSS.), congratulating M. on the *Life of L. S.*, he had written: 'I felt vexed not to have told you of certain incidents that might, though small, have been illustrative, but when I read further I saw this would have been superfluous.'

[2] See Letter 489, *supra.*

[3] Fredegond: see Letter 464, *supra.*

[4] 'Ginia' and 'Nessa' = Virginia and Vanessa Stephen. Thoby Stephen and Clive Bell had met at Trinity College, Cambridge, where, with others (including Leonard Woolf, later married to Virginia), they had founded in 1899 'the Midnight Society which met on Satur-days to read plays and poetry at that hour': Annan, *Leslie Stephen*, 123, n.

What will Lady Stephen say?[1] That does not matter much, does it? I can't help thinking of poor 'Ginia. If her head stands all this anxiety and sorrow and joy, it is a good steady head.

Have I expatiated too much on this affair? I have precious little else to tell you. I was really glad to get your telegram—it seems to have been delayed; as it is I fear that your voyage was long and rough. I like to think of you and the dear duchess[2] sallying forth into Triana. My fate will be the Durham. I am sorry to spend so much money, for I am quite well enough to face a second class, but I don't want to wait another week. The Durham calls, as I hoped, at both islands: so I may hope to be with you late on the Friday and happy shall I be when I see you once more.

I have had some kind letters about the book—Hardy is very laudatory, so is Bryce.[3] Last night I ate a Society dinner and am no worse for it. We have had some really warm days—almost muggy.

I look forward to a letter, then to a meeting.

Your own

F.

495. To W. W. Buckland

Downing College
Cambridge
28 Nov. 1906

MY DEAR BUCKLAND,

I guess that you are one of those people who suffer from nausea during parturition.[4] I have been at that business a long time and my vanity keeps me pretty happy until the very last moment. But really you have nothing to fear. Of course there is some truth in what you say—observe the compliment. You aren't addressing and won't get a large audience. But I am quite sure that the book will be very good and that the few will see that it is so. Therefore pluck up courage and go through with the job. If any one can give us a good book on this matter, you can. I am sure of it—and what I tell you three times is true.

Many thanks for your other remarks. Your correspondent is quite right in thinking that there should have been more letters of the non-intimate kind. I might have got them had I not done the main part of the book in Madeira and Canary. As it was, I could not make a real hunt for materials.

[1] Mary, Lady Stephen, widow of Sir FitzJames Stephen and Leslie's sister-in-law.
'The enclosed note from Milly':

The Porch, Cambridge.
27 Nov. 1906.
Oh indeed I *do* agree with you, dear F. W. M. (but I am longing badly to know more!). Yes, we may be quite sure of Nessa—even of her choosing wisely—and that is the one thing that matters.

Yr. affect.
C. E. S.

[2] Another name for Ermengard.
[3] See Letter 493, *supra*. The letter from Thomas Hardy, dated 24 Nov. 1906, is in Camb. Univ. MSS.
[4] See Letter 492, *supra*.

The whole thing has been saddened for me by the death of Stephen's eldest son—a very fine young fellow he was.

Yours very truly

F. W. MAITLAND

496. To Mrs. Sidgwick

Downing College
Cambridge
28 Nov. 1906

DEAR MRS. SIDGWICK,

I am returning the letters[1] that you very kindly lent me and once more thank you for the loan.

Yours very truly

F. W. MAITLAND

It is sad work reading old letters—but I need not say that to you.

497. To Henry Jackson

Downing College
Cambridge
2 Dec. 1906

DEAR JACKSON,

I think that you know Morshead[2] who used to climb Alps. Can you give me *on a card* his address, and is he a Revd. Also if I write to him may I say that I am a friend of yours and so use you as an introducer?

The object of my letter to him would be to ask one small question of fact. The whole matter is hardly worth explaining to you. But Coolidge,[3] who I am told is very learned in the history of mountaineering, has challenged a statement quoted by me from C. E Matthews (lately dead) to the effect that Mathews was with Stephen on the Bietschhorn.[4] I have good reason to believe that what Mathews said was quite true and that Morshead was with them. It is a trivial point, but apparently Coolidge who, according to Butler,[5] is 'eaten up with vanity', takes offence at my having consulted Whymper,

---

[1] See *Life of L. S.*, 301, 351.

[2] Frederick Morshead (1836–1914), housemaster at Winchester from 1868 to 1905; mountaineer and elected to the Alpine Club in 1861. He was not in orders (*Alpine Journal*, May 1914, pp. 186–93).

[3] Rev. William Augustus Brevoort Coolidge (1850–1926), Fellow of Magdalen College, Oxford; elected to the Alpine Club 1870; prolific writer on mountaineering (*Alpine Journal*, Nov. 1926, pp. 278–89).

[4] *Life of L. S.*, 90. See also Stephen, *Round Mount Blanc*, a paper read to the Alpine Club, 12 Dec. 1871, reprinted in *Men, Books and Mountains* (1956), 190.

[5] Presumably A. J. Butler, an ardent mountaineer: see Letter 11, *supra*. On the whole paragraph see *Life of L. S.*, Chap. VI.

Freshfield, etc., and not having gone to the one really great authority. In truth I had been told that if I consulted him I must consult no one else.

I think you told me that Morshead might not write of Stephen in a very friendly way. But I suppose that he would give me a civil answer to a civil question about a pure matter of fact, especially if I said that I was a friend of yours.

I hardly think that Coolidge will explode in public. Still I should like to be forearmed. He has written in a friendly way to me, but evidently detests some of my warrantors.

I hear from Pollock that Mrs. Brookfield's book is out.[1] He says that really she has nothing to tell that is not common knowledge. This is, I think, what you expected.

Where's our Medieval History now? We may find another editor, but not another Miss Bateson.[2] I can hardly believe that she has gone.

Yours very truly

F. W. MAITLAND

498. To F. J. H. Jenkinson

Downing College
Cambridge
3 Dec. 1906

MY DEAR JENKINSON,

Pray forgive me. I fear that I cannot be with you at lunch to-day. I dare not face the chance of a wetting—more especially as I greatly desire to be at St. John's to-morrow.[3]

Ask Bridges[4] kindly to remember a fellow 'tramp'.

Yours very truly

F. W. MAITLAND

I have just been asked to write a few lines for the Athenaeum and they must be written at once—also for the Review.[5] You will I hope understand and forgive.

499. To Henry Jackson

Downing College
Cambridge
3 Dec. 1906

DEAR JACKSON,

Many thanks.[6] I fully meant to come round and have a long talk with you: but troubles of sorts have come upon me rather thickly in these last days. However I must try just to put in a 'good bye'.

[1] Frances M. Brookfield, *The Cambridge Apostles* (1906).
[2] She died on 30 Nov. 1906 after a short illness. In 1905 she had been appointed a co-editor of the projected *Cambridge Medieval History*.
[3] At the funeral service for Mary Bateson.
[4] Robert Bridges (1844–1930), the poet: see *Life of L. S.*, 500.
[5] M.'s notices of Mary Bateson appeared in *The Cambridge Review* of 6 Dec. 1906 and in the *Athenaeum* of 8 Dec. 1906 (the latter reprinted in C.P. III. 540 and *Selected Hist. Essays* 277).
[6] Presumably for Morshead's address, asked for in Letter 497, *supra*.

New Year's Eve will come and my house of call will be the old one.

Quiney's Hotel
Las Palmas.

Yours v. truly

F. W. MAITLAND

500. To R. Lane Poole

Downing College
Cambridge

5 Dec. 1906

MY DEAR POOLE,

I had not much time to think or capacity for thoughts yesterday, otherwise I should have said more emphatically than I did that you are quite clearly the man to write a couple of pages in the E.H.R. about our friend. I am quite sure that they will be admirable.[1]

I don't feel at all sure that the editor of the Athenaeum will not suppress what I wrote in a hurry and call it hysterical—and may be he will be right. I was not very cool.

Our good Turner said without invitation that he would greatly like to help in making a volume of Miss Bateson's papers: and I much hope that a place may be found for him—but he knows and I know and you had better know that his name cannot be mentioned at the Press Syndicate.[2] At the last moment his name might be put in its proper place, but he will not be treated as a responsible person. As I say, he knows this and is not the least offended. When I tell him of it, he only laughs. That is the worst of it—but I need not say more to you for I saw that you love the little man. I love him very much.

Some of the most determined men that I know, including Romer and Ingle Joyce,[3] have failed to hurry 'little T.' However, what I had to say was that he would like to have part in anything that is done in memory of Miss Bateson.

No doubt William Bateson will consult you by and by. I shall be glad to hear what is doing. I think I told you that A. W. Ward presides at the Press Syndicate, so all is right in that quarter.

It was a joy to see you at this moment.

Yours very truly

F. W. MAITLAND

[1] R. Lane Poole's notice of Mary Bateson appeared in E.H.R. (1907), 64.
[2] Because of his dilatoriness. See Preface to S.S. Vol. 66.
[3] Sir Matthew Ingle Joyce (1839–1930), Judge of the High Court, 1900–15, was, like Lord Justice Romer, on the Council of the Selden Society.

INDEX

References are to letters, not to pages. Those in heavy type are to biographical notes. Biographical notes of correspondents will be found in the List of Correspondents and not in this Index.

Act of Uniformity, 248

Acton, Lord, as Regius Professor, 150, 176, 317, 318, 332, 334; *Cambridge Modern History*, 188, 233, 239, 240, 261; *Lectures on Modern History*, 325, 332; *Letters to Mary Gladstone*, 377: library, 323, 325; illness, 283, 284, 290, death and requiem, 317–19.

Ad Eundem Club, 453.

Adams, C. F., 429, 467.

Adams, G. B., 305, 309, 456.

Adams, H., 95

Airy, Rev. W., 180.

Allbutt, Sir T. C., **322**, 412.

Alpine Club, 398, 430.

Althusius, Johannes, 303.

Ambarum Club, 314, 365.

American Historical Review, 173.

American Law Review, 74, 78

Ames, James Barr, 24; on Assumpsit, 39; on disseisin of chattels, 39, 52, 67, 82; on origin of trusts, 483; on seisin, 39.

Andreae, Johannes, **87**.

Anglo-French language, 279, 301, 323, 326, 346, 357, 376, 379, 383.

Anglo-Norman cartularies, 134.

Anglo-Saxon law, 87, 95, 109.

Anson on Contract, 197.

Apostles, The Cambridge, 10, 318, 402, 431, 478, 497.

Appeal of Felony, 35, 83.

Arnold, Matthew, 417.

Ashley, Sir W. J. **133**.

Astle, T., 105.

Athenaeum (magazine), 134, 209, 325, 373, 377, 498, 500.

Atkins, J. R., 73, 108.

Atkinson, G. B., 414, 417.

Austen-Leigh, A., **420**, 444.

Austin, John, 38, 239, 253, 258, 279.

Author, The, 388, 408.

Azo, 94; and see Maitland, Frederic William, and Selden Society.

Baildon, W. P., 65, 71, 84, 94, 151, 152, 158, 163, 181, 196, 256, 267, 281, 292, 296, 297, 311.

Bain, Joseph, 73.

Baldwin, J. F., 221.

Bale, John, 341.

Balfour, A. J., 332, 343, 370, 386, 423.

Balfour, Gerald, **489**.

Ballard, A., 386, 487.

Balston, Dr. E., 417.

Bateson, Mary, *Borough Customs*, 355, 356, 361, 363, 371, 397, 449; edits Leicester Records, **212**, 226; on Keutgen, 287; *Laws of Breteuil*, 234; origin of boroughs, 487; death, 497, 498, 500.

Bateson, William, **191**, 383, 414, 426, 500.

Becket, Thomas, 98, 99, 219.

Bell, Clive, 494.

Bellinzona, revolt at, 85.

Belloc, Hilaire, 469.

Bennett, G. T., **345**, 346.

Bereford, Chief Justice, 337, 373, 375, 433, 465.

Beza, Theodore, 210, **217**.

Bigelow, Melville M., *Law of Estoppel*, 80; *Law of Fraud*, 74, 78; *Placita Anglo-Normannica*, 27, 153; reviews *P. and M.*, 173; on Torts, 14, 21, 27, 28, 32, 34, 44, 56, 80, 291, 362; visits M., 65, 198.

Blennerhassett, Sir R., 304, **335**, 336, 338, 341, 342.

Bodleian Library, 23, 85, 332, 341.

Boehmer, H., 298, 387.

Bona adirata, action for, 67.

Bond, Henry, **323**, 426

Book-land and Folk-land, 194.

Bourget, Paul, 345.

Bracton, 14, 67, 83, 94, 100; and see Maitland, Frederic William, and Selden Society.

Bradshaw, Henry, **199**.

Bridges, Robert, 498.

British Academy, 353, 371–3, 441, 444, 462.

Brookfield, Mrs. F. M., 497.

Browne, Dr. G. F., 239, 426.

Browning, Oscar, **2**, 133, 149, 323, 377.

Brunner, Heinrich, 65, 285.

Bryce, Lord, contributions to *Life of L.S.*, 398–400, 430, 444, 493; on *Life of L.S.*, 494; in Ministry, 462, 493.

Buckland, W. W., *Roman Law of Slavery*, 369, 492, 495; Squire Law Library, 420, 422, 423; visits Canaries, 304, 369, 413.

Burgage tenure, 226.

Bürgerlichen Gesetzbuch, 257.

Bury, J. B., **317**, 348, 350.

Butcher, S. H., **423**, 462.

Butler, A. J., **11**, 30, 278, 497.

Butler, H. M., 287, 318, 400, 435.

Cambridge Ancient History, 417.

Cambridge common field, 194, 195, 201.

Cambridge Medieval History, 497.

Cambridge Modern History, 233, 239, 261, 284, 290, 293, 298, 300, 304, 338, 350, 365, 367, 401, 452, 469.
Cambridge Review, 334, 336, 338, 340, 498.
Cambridge Society (dining club), 278, 313, 340, 344, 383, 402, 494.
Cambridge University, 'compulsory Greek', 408, 412, 414, 421, 423, 424, 426, 452; as corporation, 114; Economics Tripos, 406, 407; History Board, 175, 323; jurisdiction and privileges, 92, 114; Law degrees, 131; Law School, 27, 32, 41, 58, 323; Law Special Examination, 197; Library, 32, 213, 217, 255, 300, 426, 461; Press, 32, 34, 114, 300, 304, 500; Studies Syndicate, 370, 377, 383; Women's Degrees, 188, 191, 193, 194, 196.
Campbell-Bannerman, Sir H., 383, 463.
Canary birds, 463, 474.
Canon Law, 95, 97, 168, 170, 239, 241, 414, 461; and see Maitland, Frederic William.
Carnegie, Andrew, 323, 325.
Carr, Sir Cecil, 471, 475, 476; and see Selden Society, vol. 28.
Cartmell, Austen, 400, 410.
Cestui que trust, 376.
Chadwick, H. M., 424.
Challis, H. W., **86**.
Chamberlain, Joseph, 258, 260, 261, 370, 423.
Chant, Mrs. Ormiston, 142.
Charitable trusts, 310.
Chetham Society, 217.
Child, Professor F. J., **130**.
Churchwardens, 126.
Clark, Andrew, 386.
Clark, Professor E. C., **78**, 131, 323, 420, 426.
Clark, W. G., 478.
Clark Lectureship, 391, 463.
Clarke, C. B., 400, 402, 435.
Coke, Chief Justice, 3, 15, 24, 114, 168, 359.
Collectio Hispana, 461.
Common, rights of, 47.
Company Law, 289, 364, 407.
Comte, Auguste, 239.
Constable, office of, 160.
Contract, history of, 47, 82, 83, 93.
Coolidge, Rev. W. A. B., **497**.
Copyright, 426.
Corbett, W. J., **137**, 491.
Cornhill Magazine, 441, 444.
Corporations, 87, 89, 93, 259, 261, 346, 364.
County Hidage, 179.
Covenant, action of, 83.
Crawford Charters, The, 383
Creighton, Mandell, **239**, 252, 253, 259.
Criminal Law, 5, 6, 197.
Cunningham, William, **66**, 227, 278.

Daily Mail, 489.
Daily News, 340.
Dale, A. W. W., 261.
Daniell, Charlotte Louisa, 1, 2, 18.
Darwin, Horace, 400.
Davis, H. W. C., **442**, 469.
Defamation, 60, 74, 78.
Delbrück, H. G. L., **481**.

Delisle, Leopold, **79**, 81, 127.
Des Marez, G., 219.
Devonshire, Duke of, 370.
Dew-Smith, A., 353.
Dicey, Edward, 402.
Dictionary of National Biography, 347, 393, 403, 451, 458, 464.
Disseisin of chattels, 39, 52, 67, 82, 83.
Domesday Book, 93, 106, 168, 177, 264, 428; and see Maitland, Frederic William.
Dove, P. E., 54, 140–3, 151.
Downing College, 48, 345, 350.
Drew, Mrs. (Mary Gladstone), 377.
Du Cange, C. D., 66, 177.
Duchesne, L., 177.
Duckworth, Gerald, 393, 419, 489.
Dugdale, William, 88, 244.
Dyne, J. B., 296.

Edward VII, 291, 318, 319.
Ejectment, 39.
Eliot, George, 322, 377, 378.
Elphinstone, Sir H. W., **86**, 435.
Eminent Domain, 449.
English Historical Review, 81, 87, 98, 99, 118, 125, 126, 128, 160, 200, 238, 252, 274, 276, 322, 358, 420, 454, 455, 464.
Eranus Society, 227, 263, 313, 322, 377, 450, 452.
Erastus and Erastianism, 239, 249.
Esmein, A., 455.
Ewald, H. von, 340.
Ewbank, L., 278.
Eyre, General, 113.
Eyre of Kent, 256, 280, 371; and see Selden Society, vol. 24.

Fagniez, G., 250, 283.
Farrar, Dean, 417, 418, 421.
Fawcett, Henry, **414**, 417, 420, 421, 441, 447, 478.
Fenwick, T. Fitzroy, 223.
Figgis, J. N., **322**.
Finch, G. B., 74, 78, 278.
Fines, 111, 113, 449.
Firma burgi, 89.
Firth, Sir C. H., 323, 389, 464.
Fisher, Adeline, 281, 455.
Fisher, H. A. L., and Cambridge Modern History, 365, 367, 401, 455, 469; Edinburgh Professorship, 232, 234; engagement and marriage, 219, 240; Glasgow Professorship, 133, 136; *History of England from 1485 to 1547*, 365, 367, 380, 480, 483, 489; on *Life of L.S.*, 424, 428, 482; *Medieval Empire*, 142, 232, 234, 238, 240; Napoleonic studies, 240, 281, 365; studies in Paris, 79, 81.
Fitzgerald, Sir. R. U. P., 400, 445, 446, 447.
Fleta, 94.
Ford Lectures; see Maitland, Frederic William, and Stephen, Leslie.
Forms of Action, 27, 58, 60.
Forsyth, A. R., 318, **344**.
Forty days, Service for, 79, 81.

Foster, Sir M., **318**.
France, Anatole, 162, 417.
Fraser's Magazine, 441.
Freeman, E. A., **106**, 175, 209, 381.
Froude, J. A., **106**, 265, 468.
Fry, Lord Justice, 49, 181.
Furti, actio, 83.
Fustel de Coulanges, 79, 95, 285.

Gairdner, James, **311**.
Galdos, Perez, 279, 281, 350, 353, 383, 462.
Gardiner, S. R., **106**, 170, 252, 253, 258, 259, 261, 359.
Gee, Henry, 219, 220.
Geld Roll, 179.
Geneat, 96.
German law, 53, 202.
Gierke, Otto von, 87, 253, 254, 259; and see Maitland, Frederic William.
Giry, Arthur, 162.
Gladstone, W. E., 377.
Glanvill, 67, 83, 100, 168, 174, 186, 187, 355.
Goffin, R. J., 292, 296.
Gollancz, Sir I., **353**.
Gomme, C. L., 95, 112, 277.
Gorst, Sir J. E., **95**, 420, 423.
Gosse, Sir Edmund, **444**, 489.
Grass, Hans, **85**.
Gray, John Chipman, *Future Interests in Personal Property*, 282; *Gifts for Non-Charitable Purposes*, 310; on joint stock companies, 364; on perpetuities, 364, 366; *The Rule against Perpetuities*, 467, 484; visits M., 364.
Gray's Inn Pension Book, 298.
Green, Mrs Alice Stopford, 139, 156.
Green, T. H., 259.
Green, W., 324, 327, 329, 330, 333, 337, 339.
Green Bag, The, 74, 75, 78, 483.
Greenwood, Frederick, **379**, 380.
Gross, Charles, *Bibliography of Municipal History*, 125, 214, 222, 277; on the Coroner, 116, 118, 139, 152, 156, 158, 162; *Court of Piepowder*, 471, 472; *Exchequer of the Jews*, 116; *The Gild Merchant*, 93, 130; meetings with M., 121–3, 215, 216, 218, 247, 250; *The Merchant and the Friar*, 124, 125; *Sources and Literature of English History*, 128, 139; and see Selden Society, vol. 9.
Guest, Edmund, 210, 342.
Gurney, Edmund, **11**, 322, 323.
Gwatkin, H. M., **323**.

Haldane, Lord, 462.
Hale, Richard W., 165, 166, 460.
Hall, Hubert, **137**, 158, 179, 221, 224.
Hamilton, N. E. G. A., 168.
Hamilton, Sir W., 259.
Hammond, J. L., 417, 421.
Harcourt, Sir W., 383.
Harding, T. O., **468**.
Hardy, Thomas, 441, 444, 494.
Harland, J., 217, 223.

Harvard Law Review, 52, 63, 82, 93, 100, 129, 253.
Harvard Law School, 222.
Haskins, C. H., **213**.
Hawkins, F. Vaughan, 435.
Hazeltine, H. D., *History of English Law of Mortgage*, 436; visits M., 312.
Henry II, 'revocatio' of, 218–20, 244, 252.
Hill, Dr. Alex, **239**, 345.
Hinschius, Paul, 228.
Hobbes, Thomas, 303, 368; and see Maitland, Frederic William, and Stephen, Leslie.
Holmes, Mr Justice, 74, 430, 437, 440, 444, 467, 472.
Horsepools, 121–2, 136, 145–6, 153, 166, 291, 472.
Horwood, A. J., 315.
Howe v. *Morse*, 364, 366.
Hudson, Rev. W., 386.
Hughes, H. S., 446.
Hume, M. A. S., **261**
Hunt, William, **87**.
Huysmans, J. K., 345.

Ihering, R. von, 202.
Ilbert, Sir C., 371, 372, 373.
Illingworth, W., 105, 107, 108, 120.
International Law, 24, 53.
Irminon, Guérard's edition of, 81.

Jackson, Henry, 'Compulsory Greek', 412, 414, 426, 452, 463; Council of the Senate, 261; on Leslie Stephen, 383, 417, 421, 435, 437, 438, 441, 444, 447; on Lord Acton, 377; politics, 383, 463; Regius Professorship of Greek, 463, 466, 468; Squire Law Library, 422, 423, 426; on University procedure, 191.
Jacobs, Joseph, 118, 124, 158, 159.
Jargon and Verbosity, 254, 259.
Jebb, Sir R. C., 95, 383, 412, 444, 462.
Jenkinson, F. J. H., 306.
Jenks, Edward, **171**, 209.
Jessopp, Rev. A., 98.
Jewish Historical Society, 158, 163.
Johnson, Dr., 463.
Johnson, William (Cory), **1**.
Joyce, Mr Justice, 500.
Jus Commune, 95.

Keilway's Reports, 48.
Kemble, J. H., 36, 88, 179.
Kennedy, Mr Justice, 323.
Kenny, C. S., **78**, 227, 323, 383, 420, 422, 426.
Ker, W. P., 387.
Keutgen, Friedrich, 150, 164, 240, 287.
Kipling, Rudyard, 252, 261.

Lanfranc, Archbishop, 298, 387.
Lapsley, G. T., **437**, 472.
Latham, Rev. H., **401**, 417, 438, 446, 447, 453, 478.

Law Quarterly Review, 36, 54, 81, 112.
Lawrence, Rev. T. J., 24.
Leach, A. F., 193, 212, 246, 267–70, 273, 275.
Leadam, I. S., **151**, 152, 171, 187, 308, 355, 356.
Leathes, Sir S. M., 300, 365.
Lecky, W. E. H., **323**.
Lee, Dr., on the Elizabethan Church, 203, 209.
Lee, Sir Sidney, *Dictionary of National Biography*, 393, 403, 458, 464; memorial to Leslie Stephen, 391–3, 403.
Lex Mercatoria, 48, 49, 52.
Liber Landavensis, 127.
Licensing Act, 114.
Liebermann, Felix, 155, 177, 186, 187, 255, 317, 381, 387, 395.
Lindley, Lord, 141.
Littleport, rolls of, 64, 66, 69, 94.
Littleton, *Tenures*, 168, 170
Liveing, G. D., 435, 441.
Lock, B. Fossett, becomes Secretary of Selden Society, 151; on Gross, 250; on Turner, 246; Year Book series, 329, 371, 375.
Lowell, J. R., 408, 414, 417, 419, 467.
Luchaire, Denis, **81**.
Luckock, Dr. H. M., 146, 150.
Lyndwood, William, 168, 170.
Lyte, Sir H. C. Maxwell, and Selden Society, 182, 183, 185.
Lyttleton, Hon. A. T., 197.

Maassen, F., 461.
MacColl, Canon M., 252, 271, 274, 276.
MacColl, Norman, **414**.
Macnaghten, Lord, **323**.
Madox, Thomas, 62, 113, 146, 284.
Maine, Sir Henry, **59**, 62, 87, 97, 279, 370, 380.
Maitland, Emma Katherine, 2, 10, 11, 16, 18, 19, 477.
Maitland, Ermengard, 477, 491, 494.
Maitland, Florence Henrietta (Fisher), engagement and marriage, 16, 18, 19; fluency in Spanish, 261, 281, 301; *Life of L.S.*, 428; 'menagerie', 140, 166, 173, 260; music, 16.
Maitland, Fredegond, 62, 464, 477, 494
Maitland, Frederic William:
I—on Bracton, 12, 12A, 14, 100 109; at Brookside, Cambridge, 19, 21; 'compulsory Greek', 408, 412, 414, 421, 423, 424, 426, 452; Council of the Senate, 127, 131; Downing Professorship, 42, 45, 46, 48; Economics Syndicate, 350, 353; engagement and marriage, 16, 18, 19; first illness, 32; Ford Lectureship, 188–90, 194–5, 201; Freeman of the Borough of Cambridge, 279; on Glanvill, 100, 168, 174, 186, 187; History of Boroughs contemplated, 222, 234, 239; *Hobbes* (Leslie Stephen) prepared for press, 367, 368, 379–81, 384, 385, 388; honorary Bencher of Lincoln's Inn, 352; honorary doctor of Cambridge, 97, 99; of Glasgow,

260; of Oxford, 243; honorary Fellow of Trinity College, 344, 345; History Board, 175, 176; Inaugural Lecture, 51; on Law Reform, 4; lectures at Liverpool, 10; lectures on Constitutional Law, 33; on Equity, 312, on Legal History, 98; on Perpetuities, 481; on Real Property, 224; Library Syndicate, 300; musical interests, 10, 16, 23; offered Regius Professorship of History, 343, 348; ordered abroad, 226–9; Palaeography, classes in, 359, 365, 455; politics and political events, 95, 383, 400, 423; Press Syndicate, 300, 304; Reader in English Law, Cambridge, 14, 17; Rede Lecturer, 283, 287; Selden Society, first plans, 26; on Henry Sidgwick, 272, 473; Squire Law Library, 420, 422, 423, 426; on theological controversy, 239; Women's Degrees at Cambridge, 188, 191, 193, 194, 196; Year Books 17, 39, 311, 331, 348, 371, 373, 472, and see Selden Society and Year Books.
II—*His Books and Articles:* Anglican Settlement and the Scottish Reformation, 188, 209, 210, 221, 233, 239, 240, 243, 260; Body Politic, The, 263; Bracton and Azo (S.S. vol. 8), 94, 140, 150, 151, 155, 156, 158, 161, 164–6, 172; Bracton's Note-Book, 14, 17, 20, 21, 26–8, 31, 32, 34, 35, 42; Canon MacColl's New Convocation, 252, 271, 274; Charters of the Borough of Cambridge, 279; Conveyance in the Thirteenth Century, A, 86; Court Baron, The (S.S. vol. 4), 63, 64, 86, 93; Domesday Book and Beyond, 109, 137, 147, 164, 179, 180, 200, 264, 271; Elizabethan Gleanings, 233, 248, 249, 264, 265, 271, 311, 357; English Law and the Renaissance, 283, 287, 291, 298, 307; Gierke, Political Theories, 253, 254, 259, 266, 281; Glanvill Revised, 100, 186; Henry II and the Criminous Clerks, 98, 99; Historical Appendix to Pollock on Torts, 27; Historical Sketch of Liberty and Equality, 255; History of a Cambridgeshire Manor, 64, 126; History of English Law (Encycl. Brit.), 253, 258; History of English Law (Pollock and Maitland), 78, 83, 87, 96, 97, 109, 123, 130, 138, 140, 147, 150, 153, 154, 164–6, 173, 178, 211, 214, 222, 277, 481; History of the Register of Original Writs, 63, 67, 94; Introductions to Feet of Fines, 111, 203; Justice and Police, 12A, 15; Life and Letters of Leslie Stephen, 393, 396–8, 400–5, 408, 410, 412, 414, 416–21, 425, 428, 430–2, 434, 435, 437, 438, 440, 441, 444–7, 451, 453, 455, 457, 463–9, 472, 480–2, 484–6, 489, 494, 495; Lord Acton, 334, 336, 338, 340, 342; Making of the German Civil Code, 477; Mary Bateson, 498, 500; Materials for English Legal History, 61, 76; Memoranda de Parliamento, 55, 73, 77, 100–3, 105–8, 110, 113, 115, 117, 119, 120, 134; Mirror of Justices, Introduction (S.S. vol. 7), 112, 140, 151, 155, 156, 161, 164–7, 171; Moral Personality and Legal Personality, 346;

Murder of Henry Clement, 144; Northumbrian Tenures, 87; Pleas of the Crown for the County of Gloucester, 12A, 214; Possession for Year and Day, 39; Roman Canon Law in the Church of England, 168, 170, 171, 173, 177, 225, 239; Round's 'Commune of London', 252; Seisin of Chattels, 12, 39; Select Pleas in Manorial Courts (S.S. vol. 2), 35, 37, 39, 41, 44, 48, 49, 51, 52, 54, 58, 60; Select Pleas of the Crown (S.S. vol. 1) 26, 35, 57; Slander in the Middle Ages, 78; Survival of Archaic Communities, 95, 112, Township and Borough, 194, 195, 201, 277; Trust und Korporation, 364, 366, 420; Unpublished 'revocatio' of Henry II, An, 218–20, 244, 252; Why the history of English law is not written, 51; William Stubbs, 283–7; Year Books 1 and 2 Edward II (S.S. vol. 17), 256, 257, 267, 275, 279, 281, 291, 292, 301, 302, 317, 320, 322–4, 329, 337, 346, 356, 357, 360–2, 371, 375; Year Books 2 and 3 Edward II (S.S. vol. 19), 363, 372, 375, 390, 397, 409; Year Books 3 Edward II (S.S. vol. 20), 361, 371, 372, 375, 397, 424, 449, 460; Year Books 3 and 4 Edward II (S.S. vol. 22), 371, 449, 460, 471, 481, 482, 490.

Maitland, Samuel Roffey, **98**.

Maitland, Selina Caroline (Mrs Reynell), marriage, 10; living in Cambridge, 16, 18, 19.

Malden, H. E., **412**.

Malmesbury, William of, 96, 127.

Manorial history, 35, 36, 60, 64.

Mansfield, Lord, 114.

Markby, Sir W., 20, 204–7, 330, 331, 339.

Marsden, R. G., 150, 155, 161, 181, 449.

Martin, C. T., **163**.

Mayor, Rev. J., 435, 437.

McTaggart, J. M. E., **429**.

Meredith, George, 388, 408, 430.

Meyer, Paul, 361, 375, 465.

Migne, J. P., 461.

Mirror of Justices, The, 39, 58, 171; and see Maitland, Frederic William, and Selden Society.

Mitchell, W., **423**.

Modus tenendi Curiam Baronis, 63, 86.

Mogul Case, The, 407.

Moore, Dr. Norman, 167, 169, 172.

Moots at Cambridge, 58, 60, 78, 80.

Morgan, H. A., **400**, 426, 431, 432, 434, 446, 447, 453.

Morley, John, **260**, 323, 325, 345, 381, 400, 462.

Morshead, F., **497**.

Moulton, Lord, **468**.

Munton, F. K., 151.

Myers, F. W. H., **11**, 345.

Napier, A. S., 383, 395.

Nation, The, 401, 460.

Newton, Alfred, **426**, 474.

Norton, C. E., 403, 405, 408, 426, 429, 467, 472.

Nottingham Borough Records, 83.

Novel Disseisin, 39.

Oman, Sir Charles, **469**, 489.

Outlawry, 35.

Oxford Magazine, 104, 387, 388.

Oxford University, History syllabus, 168, 170.

Palgrave, Sir F., **70**, 71, 73, 108, 115, 119, 120.

Parliamentary Petitions, 55, 57, 70–3, 77, 100–3, 105, 107, 110, 115, 117; and see Maitland, Frederic William, *Memoranda de Parliamento.*

Paul, Herbert, 377, 464, 468.

Peter of Blois, 148.

Pike, L. O., 39, **54**, 182, 183, 185, 204, 207, 208, 262, 316, 327, 329–31, 337, 339, 360.

Pilot, The, 379.

Pipe Roll Society, 47, 111, 113.

Pirenne, Henri, 164.

Placitorum Abbreviatio, 35.

Pleas of the Crown, 26.

Political Science Quarterly, 61, 76, 116.

Pollard, A. F., **274**, 284, 287.

Pollen, J. H., **357**.

Pollock, Sir Frederick, and Apostles, 478, 497; Corpus Professor, 9, 211, 370, 373; on Domesday, 164; editor of Law Reports, 373, 481; on Franciscans, 481; on Fustel de Coulanges, 79; introduces M. to Leslie Stephen, 354, 383; *King's Peace in the Middle Ages, The,* 253; *Pollock and Maitland,* 78, 83, 87, 95, 96, 109, 138; *Possession in the Common Law,* 36; Tagore Lectures, 127; *Torts, Law of,* 27, 33, 44; Year Books, 87, 206.

Poole, R. Lane, as editor, M.'s Tribute, 454; obituary of Acton, 320, 322, 334, 342; of Mary Bateson, 500; *Political History of England,* 290; 'Round-Hall controversy', 224, 225, 238; on Wycliffe, 170, 171.

Pooley, Henry, 484.

Powell, Frederick York, 106, 385, 386, 388.

Prothero, Sir George, **232**, 261, 323, 381, 387, 455.

Pseudo-Isidore, 461.

Prou, Maurice, 357.

Purcell, E. S., 342.

Quarterly Review, 381, 387, 395.

Rabelais Club, 10.

Radchenistres, 243.

Ramsay, Sir James, **211**.

Rawlinson, J. F. P., 420, 423.

Real actions, 25, 26, 27.

Real Property, history of, 168.

Reception of Roman Law, 202.

Record type, 17, 26.

Rectitudines Singularum Personarum, 96.

Red Book of the Exchequer, 179.

Red Book of Thorney, 88.
Redlich, Josef, 420.
Reformation in England, 203.
Register of Writs, 63, 67, 94.
Renshaw, W. C., 207.
Republican Club, 452, 459, 462.
Res adirata, 67.
Reynell, Rev. V. C. R., 10, 18, 98, 176, 477.
Ridgway, Sir W., **323**.
Rigg, J. M., 262, 289, 292, 296, 297, 311, 317.
Right, meaning of, 38.
Robertson, George Groom, **419**
Robinson, Armitage, 191.
Robsart, Amy, 311.
Roby, H. J., **349**.
Rogers, Thorold, **69**.
Rogers, William, **2**.
Rolls Series, 17, 57, 186; and see Year Books.
Roman Law in Anglo-Saxon England, 87.
Romer, Lord Justice, **141**, 143, 207, 400, 500.
Round, John Horace, 37; 'battle of Hastings,' 134, 147, 252; *Commune of London*, 209, 211, 233, 252; controversy with Hubert Hall, 179, 221, 224, 225, 238; on Domesday, 106, 109, 137, 164; on Elizabethan Church, 189, 203, 211, 221; *Feudal England*, 137, 154, 164, 179, 184; on Fines, 111, 113, 147, 180, 189; *Geoffrey de Mandeville*, 106, 113; offended with M., 252, 264; *Studies on the Red Book of the Exchequer*, 221, 224, 225.
Russell of Killowen, Lord, 181, **323**.
Ryley, William, 73, 107.

Salmond, J. W., **346**.
Savigny, F. C. von, 87.
Savine, A., 311.
Schröder, R., 202.
Scotch law, 53.
Scott, Sir R. F., **195**.
Scutage, 184, 209, 221, 224.
Searle, Rev. W. G., 148.
Secta, the, 22, 24, 63.
Seebohm, Frederick, **59**, 62, 109, 277, 285.
Seisin, 12, 39, 52.
Selden Society, crisis at Dove's death, 140–3; prospectus and projects, 25, 26, 54, 94, 151, 152, 155, 158; *Vol. 1*: 26, 35, 37; *Vol. 2*: 35, 37, 39, 44, 48, 49, 51, 52, 54, 58, 60; *Vol.. 3*: 58, 65, 84; *Vol. 4*: 63, 64, 86, 93, 94; *Vol. 5*: 212, 386; *Vol. 6*: 150, 155, 161; *Vol. 7*: 58, 84, 112, 140, 151, 155, 156, 161, 164–7, 171; *Vol. 8*: 94, 140, 151, 158, 161, 164–6, 172; *Vol. 9*: 152, 155, 158, 162, 165, 167, 169, 172; *Vol. 10*: 94, 151, 152, 155, 158, 165, 185; *Vol. 11*: 155, 161, 174, 196; *Vol. 12*: 152, 174, 196; *Vol. 13*: 163, 204, 246, 273, 275, 284, 288, 292; *Vol. 14*: 193, 212, 246, 267–70; *Vol. 15*: 116, 118, 152, 158, 185, 262, 292, 296, 311; *Vol. 16*: 308, 311, 356; *Vol. 17*: 256, 257, 267, 275, 291, 292, 301, 302, 317, 320, 322–4, 329, 337, 346, 355, 356, 360–2, 371, 375; *Vol. 18*: 355, 356, 363, 371, 397, 409; *Vol. 19*: 363, 372, 375, 390, 397, 409; *Vol. 20*: 361, 371, 372, 375, 424, 449, 460; *Vol. 21*: 355, 356,
449; *Vol. 22*: 371, 449, 460, 471, 482; *Vol. 24*: 256, 280, 371, 375; *Vol. 28*: 289, 292, 449, 471, 475, 476; *Vol. 66*: 94, 174, 181.
Shadwell, C. L., **208**.
Shipley, Sir A. E., **383**.
Sidgwick, Eleanor M., *Life of Henry Sidgwick*, 272, 448, 469, 470, 473, 478.
Sidgwick, Henry, on Austin, 38, 239; *Elements of Politics*, 53; encourages M. to translate Gierke, 254; and M.'s absence from Cambridge, 222, 227, 229, 230; *Philosophy, Its Scope and Relations*, 322, political science, 146; *Principles of Political Economy*, 4, 5, 8; illness and death, 239, 271, 272; memorial, 278.
Simpson, F. L., 362.
Skeat, Professor W. W., **54**, 64, 152.
Smith, A. L., **455**.
Smith, George, **444**, 458.
Smith, Horace, 401, 432, 446.
Smith, Sir Thomas, 427.
Smith, Toulmin, 277.
Smuts, J. C., M.'s testimonial, 135.
Sohm, R., 92, 173.
Soule, C. C., 31, 316, 324, 327, 329, 330, 339.
South African War, 249, 253, 258–61.
Spinning House Case, 92, 114.
Squire Bequest, 300.
Squire Law Library, 420, 422, 423, 426, 479.
Star Chamber, 61.
Statute of Uses, 480, 483.
Statute of Wales, 35.
Statute of Westminster II, cap. 24: 433, 439.
Stephen, Caroline Emelia, 404, 408, 419, 478, 494.
Stephen, Sir Fitz James, 420, 435.
Stephen, Leslie, advice on *Pollock and Maitland*, 138; death of wife, 157; Dictionary of National Biography, 347, 393; *English Utilitarians*, 237, 258; *George Eliot*, 322; Ford Lectures, 314, 322; *History of English Thought in the Eighteenth Century*, 319; *Hobbes*, 303, 314, 347, 367, 368, 372, 379–81, 384, 385, 388; honorary Doctor of Cambridge, 109; knighted, 318, 319, 322; *Life of Henry Fawcett*, 231, 420, 421; *Science of Ethics*, 428; illness, 313, 345, 347, 353; death, 379, 380; memorial lectureship, 391–3.
Stephen, Thoby, 400, 410, **489**, 493–5.
Stephen, Vanessa, 494.
Stephen, Virginia, 419, 438, 494.
Stephen's Commentaries, 33.
Stevenson, R. L., 444.
Stevenson, W. H., **238**, 252, 298, 303, 342, 383, 386.
Stirling, Lord Justice, **141**, 155, 172, 174, 181, 207.
Stokes, Sir G., **318**, 350.
Stubbs, William, **59**, 62, 83, 87, 113, 168, 171, 224, 225, 283–7.
Sunday Closing, 53.
Sunday Tramps, 7, 40, 97, 354, 383, 414, 462, 498.
Swart-rutters, 260.
Swereford, Alexander de, 179.

Tacitus, *Germania*, 144, 150.
Tait, James, reviews *D.B. and Beyond*, 200, 264.
Tardif, A., 461.
Taylor, H. M., 318.
Taylor, Sedley, **400**.
Thayer, James Bradley, *Cases on Constitutional Law*, 132, 141; *Development of Trial by Jury*, 178; old methods of trial, 22, 24; *Preliminary Treatise on Evidence*, 242; visits M., 204, 307; Year Book project, interested in, 204, 362; death, 307, 310.
Thompson, H. Y., 414, 417.
Thompson, W. H., 438.
Thornton, P. M., 470.
Tit Bits, 304.
Tithing, 386.
Tolstoy, Leo, 279.
Tout, T. F., 456.
'To wit', 377, 456.
Township, 89, 93.
Trenholme, N. M., 358, 394.
Trespass, writ of, 35, 67.
Trial by Jury, 22, 24, 26, 35, 57.
Trial by witnesses, 22, 24.
Trinity Hall, 391–3, 412, 414, 417, 426, 431, 438, 445–7.
Trusts, 364, 366.
Turner, G. J., **158**; *Brevia Placitata*, 174, 181; Canaries, in, 296, 308, 471; dilatoriness, 246, 273, 275, 500; praised by M., 182, 284, 292, 315, 329; *Select Pleas of the Forest*, 204, 246, 273, 275, 284, 288, 292; Year Books, 196, 296, 297, 311, 315, 329, 375, 479.
Twelve Tables, 420, 423.
Twiss, Sir Travers, 14, 100, 186, 187.

Uses, 35, 376.
Usher, R. G., 359.

Vandal, A., 367.
Verba curiae, 54, 58, 76, 86.
Verrall, A. W., 36, 373, 462.
Vetus Codex, 73, 107, 115.
Villa, 36.
Villeinage, 26, 35.
Vinogradoff, Paul, on Bracton, 12, 12A, 14; in Cambridge, 328, 434, 435; Corpus

Professor of Jurisprudence, 370, 372–4; difficulties at Moscow, 149, 373; Domesday, work on, 164; *Folkland*, 286; *Growth of the Manor*, 424, 428; meeting with M., 97; *Teaching of Sir Henry Maine*, 380, 395; *Villainage in England*, 28, 43, 49–51, 59, 62, 97, 104, 109.
Viollet, Paul, 81, 91, 287, 298, 365.
Voucher to warranty, 67, 83.

Wager of Law, 63.
Waitz, Georg, **87**.
Waldstein, Sir C., **323**.
Walsh, Archbishop, 418.
Wambaugh, E., **339**.
Wara, 64, 66.
Ward, Sir A. W., **261**, 321–3, 365, 383, 469, 500
Wells, C. L., 125, 128, 130.
Welsh law, 87.
Westlake, Professor, **24**, 131, 186, 406, 407.
Whewell Scholarships, 412.
Whitehead, A. N., **191**, 321.
Whittaker, W. J., **112**, 155, 161, 222–4, 295, 296, 369, 413.
Wilburton, manor of, 64, 66, 69, **126**.
Wilkinson, M. M. U., 414, 417.
Williams, Cyprian, **229**, 288, 289.
Wilson, Woodrow, 362.
Winchcombe Cartulary, 113, 170.
Wood, Anthony á, *City of Oxford*, 201.
Worcester, Florence of, 127.
Wright, R. T., **27**, 29, 32, 34, 44, 78, 95, 227, 362, 422.
Wright, W. Aldis, **323**.
Writs of Entry, 83.
Wulstans, the two, 96.

Year Books, Clarendon Press project, 204–7; projected edition by Green and Soule, 316, 324, 327, 329–31, 333, 337, 339, 351; Rolls Series, 17, 39, 54, 165, 182, 208, 339; Selden Society Series, 165, 181–3, 185, 196, 199, 204–8, 256, 257, 282, 290, 326, 327, 329, 331, 351, 363, 371, 373; and see Selden Society.
Young, Sir G., **444**.

Zinkeisen, Frank, 124, 125, 130.
Zola, Émile, 278.